T0182057

Lecture Notes in Computer Science 12221

More information about this series at http://www.springer.com/series/7412

Nadia Magnenat-Thalmann ·
Constantine Stephanidis ·
Enhua Wu · Daniel Thalmann ·
Bin Sheng · Jinman Kim ·
George Papagiannakis · Marina Gavrilova (Eds.)

Advances in Computer Graphics

37th Computer Graphics International Conference, CGI 2020
Geneva, Switzerland, October 20–23, 2020
Proceedings

 Springer

Editors
Nadia Magnenat-Thalmann
University of Geneva
Geneva, Switzerland

Constantine Stephanidis
University of Crete
Heraklion, Greece

Enhua Wu
University of Macau
Macau, China

Daniel Thalmann
Swiss Federal Institute of Technology
Lausanne, Switzerland

Bin Sheng
Shanghai Jiao Tong University
Shanghai, China

Jinman Kim
University of Sydney
Sydney, Australia

George Papagiannakis
University of Crete
Heraklion, Greece

Marina Gavrilova
University of Calgary
Calgary, AB, Canada

ISSN 0302-9743   ISSN 1611-3349   (electronic)
Lecture Notes in Computer Science
ISBN 978-3-030-61863-6   ISBN 978-3-030-61864-3   (eBook)
https://doi.org/10.1007/978-3-030-61864-3

LNCS Sublibrary: SL6 – Image Processing, Computer Vision, Pattern Recognition, and Graphics

This Springer imprint is published by the registered company Springer Nature Switzerland AG
The registered company address is: Gewerbestrasse 11, 6330 Cham, Switzerland

Preface

Welcome to the lecture notes in computer science (LNCS) proceedings of the 37th Computer Graphics International conference (CGI 2020). CGI is one of the oldest international conferences in computer graphics in the world. It is the official conference of the Computer Graphics Society (CGS), a long-standing international computer graphics organization. The CGI conference has been held annually in many different countries across the world and gained a reputation as one of the key conferences for researchers and practitioners to share their achievements and discover the latest advances in computer graphics. This year, CGI 2020 was a very special edition of the conference series as it was held virtual due to the pandemic that, at the time of writing this preface, still plagues society. It was organized online by MIRALab at the University of Geneva, Switzerland. The official date of the conference was postponed to October 20–23, 2020, in the hope of a mixed conference outcome, in situ and online. Finally, all presentations from the CGI 2020 accepted papers are available on YouTube.

This CGI 2020 LNCS proceedings is composed of 47 papers. We accepted 16 papers that were thoroughly reviewed at the CGI TVC track from over 100 submissions and we received for the LNCS track 51 papers, accepting an additional 27 full papers and 4 short papers. To ensure the high quality of this publication, each paper was reviewed by at least three experts in the field and the authors of the accepted papers were asked to revise their papers according to the review comments prior to publication.

The accepted papers also feature papers from the ENGAGE 2020 workshop (10 full and 2 short papers), focused specifically on important aspects of geometric algebra including surface construction, robotics, encryption, qubits, and expression optimization. The workshop has been part of the CGI conference series since 2016.

We would like to express our deepest gratitude to all the Program Committee members and external reviewers who provided high-quality, timely reviews. We would also like to thank all the authors for contributing to the conference by submitting their work.

September 2020

Nadia Magnenat-Thalmann
Constantine Stephanidis
Enhua Wu
Daniel Thalmann
Bin Sheng
Jinman Kim
George Papagiannakis
Marina Gavrilova

Organization

Conference Chairs

Nadia Magnenat Thalmann   University of Geneva, Switzerland
Constantine Stephanidis   University of Crete, FORTH, Greece

LNCS Program Chairs

Bin Sheng   Shanghai Jia Tong University, China
Jinman Kim   The University of Sydney, Australia
George Papagiannakis   University of Crete, Greece

Publicity Chair

Ma Lizhuang   Jiao Tong University, China

Publication LNCS Chair

Marina Gavrilova   University of Calgary, Canada

Contents

CGI'20 Full Papers

Comparing Physical and Immersive VR Prototypes for Evaluation
of an Industrial System User Interface 3
  Jean F. P. Cheiran, Laura A. Torres, Antonio A. S. da Silva,
  Gabrielle A. de Souza, Luciana P. Nedel, Anderson Maciel,
  and Dante A. C. Barone

Gaze-Contingent Rendering in Virtual Reality 16
  Fang Zhu, Ping Lu, Pin Li, Bin Sheng, and Lijuan Mao

Hierarchical Rendering System Based on Viewpoint Prediction
in Virtual Reality 24
  Ping Lu, Fang Zhu, Pin Li, Jinman Kim, Bin Sheng, and Lijuan Mao

Reinforcement Learning-Based Redirection Controller for Efficient
Redirected Walking in Virtual Maze Environment. 33
  Wataru Shibayama and Shinichi Shirakawa

Locality-Aware Skinning Decomposition Using Model-Dependent
Mesh Clustering 46
  Fumiya Narita and Tomohiko Mukai

A New Volume-Based Convexity Measure for 3D Shapes 59
  Xiayan Shi, Rui Li, and Yun Sheng

Deep Inverse Rendering for Practical Object Appearance Scan
with Uncalibrated Illumination 71
  Jianzhao Zhang, Guojun Chen, Yue Dong, Jian Shi, Bob Zhang,
  and Enhua Wu

Application of the Transfer Matrix Method to Anti-reflective
Coating Rendering 83
  Alexis Benamira and Sumanta Pattanaik

Dynamic Shadow Rendering with Shadow Volume Optimization 96
  Zhibo Fu, Han Zhang, Ran Wang, Zhen Li, Po Yang, Bin Sheng,
  and Lijuan Mao

Adaptive Illumination Sampling for Direct Volume Rendering 107
  Valentin Kraft, Florian Link, Andrea Schenk, and Christian Schumann

Musical Brush: Exploring Creativity Through an AR-Based Tool
for Sketching Music and Drawings   119
   Rafael Valer, Rodrigo Schramm, and Luciana Nedel

MR Environments Constructed for a Large Indoor Physical Space   132
   Huan Xing, Chenglei Yang, Xiyu Bao, Sheng Li, Wei Gai, Meng Qi,
   Juan Liu, Yuliang Shi, Gerard De Melo, Fan Zhang, and Xiangxu Meng

FIOU Tracker: An Improved Algorithm of IOU Tracker in Video with a Lot
of Background Inferences.   145
   Zhihua Chen, Guhao Qiu, Han Zhang, Bin Sheng, and Ping Li

An Approach of Short Advertising Video Generation Using Mobile Phone
Assisted by Robotic Arm.   157
   Jiefeng Li, Yingying She, Lin Lin, Yalan Luo, Hao He, Weiyue Lin,
   and Shengjing Hou

"Forget" the Forget Gate: Estimating Anomalies in Videos Using
Self-contained Long Short-Term Memory Networks   169
   Habtamu Fanta, Zhiwen Shao, and Lizhuang Ma

An Improved Image Stitching Method Based on Seed Region Growth
and Poisson Fusion   182
   Yewen Pang, Aimin Li, and Jianwen Wang

Illumination Harmonization with Gray Mean Scale   193
   Shuangbing Song, Fan Zhong, Xueying Qin, and Changhe Tu

An Unsupervised Approach for 3D Face Reconstruction from a Single
Depth Image.   206
   Peixin Li, Yuru Pei, Yicheng Zhong, Yuke Guo, Gengyu Ma, Meng Liu,
   Wei Bai, Wenhai Wu, and Hongbin Zha

Fusing IMU Data into SfM for Image-Based 3D Reconstruction.   220
   Hua Yuan, Yifan Ma, and Yun Sheng

Physics-Guided Sound Synthesis for Rotating Blades   233
   Siqi Xu and Shiguang Liu

Elimination of Incorrect Depth Points for Depth Completion   245
   Chuhua Xian, Kun Qian, Guoliang Luo, Guiqing Li, and Jianming Lv

Pose Transfer of 2D Human Cartoon Characters   256
   Tiezeng Mao, Wenbo Dong, Aihua Mao, Guiqing Li, and Jie Luo

Broad-Classifier for Remote Sensing Scene Classification with Spatial
and Channel-Wise Attention.   267
  *Zhihua Chen, Yunna Liu, Han Zhang, Bin Sheng, Ping Li,
  and Guangtao Xue*

GARNet: Graph Attention Residual Networks Based on Adversarial
Learning for 3D Human Pose Estimation.   276
  Zhihua Chen, Xiaoli Liu, Bing Sheng, and Ping Li

GPU-based Grass Simulation with Accurate Blade Reconstruction.   288
  *Sheng Wang, Saba Ghazanfar Ali, Ping Lu, Zhen Li, Po Yang,
  Bin Sheng, and Lijuan Mao*

Flow Visualization with Density Control   301
  Shiguang Liu and Hange Song

DbNet: Double-Ball Model for Processing Point Clouds   313
  Meisheng Shen, Yan Gao, and Jingjun Qiu

Evolving L-Systems in a Competitive Environment.   326
  Job Talle and Jiří Kosinka

ParaGlyder: Probe-driven Interactive Visual Analysis for Multiparametric
Medical Imaging Data.   351
  Eric Mörth, Ingfrid S. Haldorsen, Stefan Bruckner, and Noeska N. Smit

3D Geology Scene Exploring Base on Hand-Track Somatic Interaction   364
  Wei Zhang, Fang Zhu, Ping Lu, Pin Li, Bin Sheng, and Lijuan Mao

GHand: A Graph Convolution Network for 3D Hand Pose Estimation.   374
  *Pengsheng Wang, Guangtao Xue, Pin Li, Jinman Kim, Bin Sheng,
  and Lijuan Mao*

Bézier Curve as a Generalization of the Easing Function in Computer
Animation   382
  Łukasz Izdebski, Ryszard Kopiecki, and Dariusz Sawicki

Generating Orthogonal Voronoi Treemap for Visualization of Hierarchical
Data   394
  Yan-Chao Wang, Jigang Liu, Feng Lin, and Hock-Soon Seah

CGI'20 Short Papers

Preserving Temporal Consistency in Videos Through Adaptive SLIC   405
  Han Zhang, Riaz Ali, Bin Sheng, Ping Li, Jinman Kim, and Jihong Wang

Efficient Non-fused Winograd on GPUs.   411
  Hui Wei, Enjie Liu, Youbing Zhao, and Hongqing Yu

ENGAGE Full Papers

Surface Fitting Using Dual Quaternion Control Points with Applications
in Human Respiratory Modelling 421
  Alex Grafton and Joan Lasenby

Deform, Cut and Tear a Skinned Model Using Conformal Geometric
Algebra 434
  Manos Kamarianakis and George Papagiannakis

The Forward and Inverse Kinematics of a Delta Robot 447
  Hugo Hadfield, Lai Wei, and Joan Lasenby

Constrained Dynamics in Conformal and Projective Geometric Algebra 459
  Hugo Hadfield and Joan Lasenby

Application of 2D PGA as an Subalgebra of CRA in Robotics 472
  Radek Tichý

Outline of Tube Elbow Detection Based on GAC 482
  Roman Byrtus, Anna Derevianko, and Petr Vašík

Optimal Parenthesizing of Geometric Algebra Products 492
  Stéphane Breuils, Vincent Nozick, and Akihiro Sugimoto

Geometric Algebra-Based Multilevel Declassification Method
for Geographical Field Data 501
  *Wen Luo, Dongshuang Li, Zhaoyuan Yu, Yun Wang, Zhengjun Yan,
  and Linwang Yuan*

Homomorphic Data Concealment Powered by Clifford Geometric Algebra ... 513
  *David W. H. A. da Silva, Marcelo A. Xavier, Philip N. Brown,
  Edward Chow, and Carlos Paz de Araujo*

An Online Calculator for Qubits Based on Geometric Algebra 526
  D. Hildenbrand, C. Steinmetz, R. Alves, J. Hrdina, and C. Lavor

ENGAGE Short Papers

On Basis-Free Solution to Sylvester Equation in Geometric Algebra 541
  Dmitry Shirokov

Hyperwedge 549
  Steven De Keninck and Leo Dorst

Author Index 555

CGI'20 Full Papers

Comparing Physical and Immersive VR Prototypes for Evaluation of an Industrial System User Interface

Jean F. P. Cheiran[1]([✉]), Laura A. Torres[2], Antonio A. S. da Silva[2],
Gabrielle A. de Souza[2], Luciana P. Nedel[2], Anderson Maciel[2],
and Dante A. C. Barone[2]

[1] Federal University of Pampa, Alegrete, RS, Brazil
`jeancheiran@unipampa.edu.br`
[2] Federal University of Rio Grande do Sul, Porto Alegre, RS, Brazil
`{latorres,aasilva,gasouza,nedel,amaciel,barone}@inf.ufrgs.br`

Abstract. Since immersive VR devices have become commodities, immersive environments appear as a new tool in the development of high-fidelity prototypes of systems in which the user interaction relies on expensive or unusual hardware, e.g., industrial systems. However, there is not enough evidence that the interface of a complex system and its VR counterpart have equal usability and user experience qualities. Our main objective is to assess the feasibility of carrying out studies on user-based evaluation in industrial interactive systems through immersive VR simulation. To achieve this, we compared user assessment with a conventional prototype of an industrial system with its immersive VR simulation. We performed within-subjects user testing in both the physical and the VR setups, and collected (i) experimenters' observations on usability issues and (ii) subjective and objective measures of 16 participants. Subjective measures were taken using standardized questionnaires and objective measures by logging the elapsed time to fulfill task scenarios. Our results indicate that the perceived quality of the immersive VR system is indistinguishable from the physical counterpart regarding User Experience, usability, and cybersickness. On the other hand, the users' performance on VR simulation was significantly slower in immersive VR. Finally, the same usability issues could be detected with either of the conditions.

Keywords: Virtual reality simulation · User interfaces · Industrial systems · User-based evaluation

1 Introduction

Technologies and principles of Virtual Reality (VR) have evolved over the last 50 years [19]. For instance, flight simulation in VR has been successfully applied

This study was financed in part by the Coordenação de Aperfeiçoamento de Pessoal de Nível Superior - Brasil (CAPES) - Finance Code 001, and by Petrobras under the project INF/LAMECC/PETROBRAS 0050.0098154.15.9.

N. Magnenat-Thalmann et al. (Eds.): CGI 2020, LNCS 12221, pp. 3–15, 2020.
https://doi.org/10.1007/978-3-030-61864-3_1

for decades for developing pilots' skills [19]. This simulation, besides being safer and cheaper, might be placed in an immersive environment by head-mounted displays (HMD) and completely fill the pilot surroundings.

Besides that, VR seems to be a more appropriate display model when trying to recreate physiological responses in environmental studies [5]. Notably, for industrial settings, VR and Mixed Reality (MR) have been aroused interest as tools [2,15,21]. Considering that, it's crucial to guarantee that those simulations are suitable for training and safe for experiencing by measuring their quality.

According to Barbosa and Silva [1], quality in Human-Computer Interaction (HCI) is related to some aspects of interaction and interface that makes them suitable for a specific context of use. The evaluation in HCI is fundamental for collecting information about users' experiences when interacting with the system [17]. User Experience (UX) is a wide concept defined as "user's perceptions and responses that result from the use and/or anticipated use of a system, product or service" [8], covering usability [18] and other more personal components [1].

Common user-based approaches to assess UX and usability include user testing (collecting data from performance) followed by the application of questionnaires or interviews (collecting data from opinion) [17]. In this scenario, standardized questionnaires are more effective to collect reliable data from users [16]. This data collection practices have also been extended to the area of VR to obtain specific measurements that are inherent to the VR simulations, e.g., cybersickness that is associated with discomfort symptoms as headache, eye strain, disorientation, sweating, nausea, vomiting, among others [13]. It is caused by no exact source, but it is strictly induced by visual stimulation in VR environments through VR devices (as HMDs and Caves) [13]. So, assessing cybersickness in VR simulation is essential as it can detriment the user experience [4].

Few studies evaluate the use of immersive VR simulation as an alternative for user testing in expensive and complex systems in an industrial context [2,9,15]. Even though usability and UX are measured in these studies, we noticed that some questions remained unanswered: (i) Is it the same to undergo user test in a desktop system or in a simulated system in VR? (ii) How does it affect the user performance? (iii) How does it affect the usability assessment and usability issues' finding? (iv) How does it affect the User Experience (UX)? (v) Should the experimenter mind about cybersickness?

In this context, the main objective of this research is to evaluate the feasibility of carrying out studies for user-based evaluation of industrial system interfaces using immersive VR simulation. Thus, we compare aspects of a conventional prototype (physical hardware, plus software) with its simulation in VR (virtual hardware, plus software). In order to perform this comparison, we: (1) ran the software system for a remotely operated machine that is going to be used in an offshore platform in a physical prototype and in a immersive VR prototype; (2) performed user tests with 16 participants using two task scenarios; (3) identified and recorded usability issues on both versions of the system through observation; (4) collected participants' opinions on both versions of the system by standardized questionnaires and participants' performance data; and (5) analyzed the results to answer the aforementioned questions.

2 Related Work

In recent years, studies to demonstrate the proximity of a VR environment to a physical environment in different applications have made considerable progress.

Wolfartsberger [21] investigated the potential of VR for engineering projects. For this, the study was divided into two parts to analyze (1) how quickly beginners learn to interact with the system and (2) the effectiveness of VR-supported design review with conventional approaches with CAD software support. The results indicated that the VR-supported design review approach allows users to see more flaws in a 3D model than in a traditional software-based CAD approach.

Higuera-Trujillo, Maldon, and Millán [5] demonstrated by means of comparative validation that 360° Panorama and VR are closer to the physical environment, both in terms of psychological and physiological responses, compared to photograph. In addition, this study also shows that in 360° Panorama and VR environments, there was an increase in the user's sense of presence.

Werrlich et al. [20] conducted a study to measure user satisfaction and workload in training transfer using the HMD and sheets of paper for assembling an engine. The authors concluded that participants made fewer mistakes during training using HMD-based instructions when compared to paper-based ones.

Satter and Butler [15] conducted a usability study on CAD to measure the performance and the user preference for (i) immersive Virtual Environments (VEs) with multimodal gesture-based interface or (ii) traditional non-stereoscopic interface with keyboard and mouse. The study centered on the use of eye-tracking as a mechanism for monitoring the human-computer interface (HCI). It was demonstrated that there is a user predilection for immersive VEs, and "error localization and fix" times are 26% faster using VEs.

Kamide et al. [9] evaluated the feasibility of assessing usability of robots by their virtual representation. The study used the PERNOD scale, and the results showed that the VR robot could be used instead of the real robot, taking specific characteristics of each project into account.

Bolder, Grünvogel, and Angelescu [2] compared the usability of an infortainment system in a car prototype using MR to the same system in a real car. The results indicated by SUS questionnaire analysis that there is no significant differences between them. In addition, 46.67% of the participants made suggestions to improve the system while using the MR environment.

Based on the state-of-the-art analysis, there is still a gap regarding the application of VR for in the assessment of user interfaces of complex systems.

3 Methodology

To verify the suitability of an immersive VR simulation as an environment to assess user interface design, we proposed to perform an experiment with participants. In these usability essays, the participants experienced the same interface in both the physical and the virtual world. We gathered qualitative data about the system usability by observing the users and writing interaction issues down, and quantitative data by standardized questionnaires and task performance logs.

3.1 Annelida System Overview

Our case study focuses on a system developed to drive and supervise a tethered robot designed to move inside oil pipes. The user operation interface includes three touchscreens and a physical control panel. It is installed on board of a Floating Production Storage and Offloading (FPSO) vessel that uses kilometric pipes to extract oil from deep-water wells. Oftentimes, these pipes become clogged with chemicals, preventing the crude oil to flow. The robot is designed to go down these pipes, find out where the obstructions are, and carry out an unclogging process. The vermiform robot has two main components to be controlled by an operator: a locomotion system and an unclogging system. The robot moves slowly, so the operation can take several hours and even days, and the system is continuously supervised by an operator on board of the vessel.

The control panel (Fig. 1) has four modules: locomotion, Graphical User Interface (GUI) control, unclogging tool, and general operation. The first controls direction and speed. The second module has the input system used to control elements on screen. The third allows the operator to control the unclogging process. The last module has general operation commands.

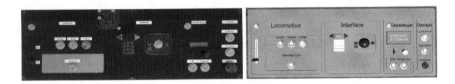

Fig. 1. Physical prototype (left) and virtual prototype (right) of the control panel.

In addition to sending commands to the robot, the operator can visualize the current status of all its sensors in the monitoring interface. It is composed of three screens, that we will refer from now on as "monitoring graphics", "mission reconstruction" and "control and monitoring" screens (Fig. 2). The monitoring chart screen shows a collection of 2D line graphs to represent the temporal behavior of sensors. Since this part of the system is under development, it was not included in our experiment and the respective screen was left blank (the leftmost screen in left and right images in Fig. 2).

The mission reconstruction screen has a 3D model of the robot that moves replicating the path that the real robot is making (left image in Fig. 3). The control and monitoring screen contains widgets to display the individual sensor values sent by the robot. It also has a control module that serves as a replica of the physical control panel (right image in Fig. 3) for fault tolerance.

Fig. 2. Conventional desktop system with physical setup of the experiment (left), participant during a testing session using VR devices (center), VR system simulation with setting close to the real operating environment (right).

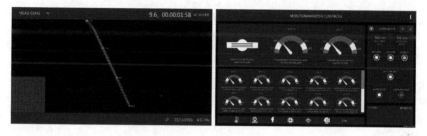

Fig. 3. Mission reconstruction screen from the system Graphical User Interface (GUI) depicting the robot and the pipe where it slides (left image). Control and monitoring screen from the system GUI with sensor gauges and other widgets (right image).

3.2 Methods and Apparatus

The method of user interaction with the system was the same in both control versions. The physical control panel (Fig. 1, leftmost image) was fixed on the table, and the commands were performed through direct actions of the user in control. The virtual control (Fig. 1, rightmost image) was mapped in the virtual environment so that user interaction with it matched the physical control (providing passive haptics feedback [7]). Both console versions were almost identical except for the presence of a tracking plate in the physical panel, the backlit buttons in the virtual console, the size of labels, the overall colors, and a LCD above the numpad at the center of the console that remained with a fake fixed value in the VR version. When performing the VR experiment, the participant used markers on three of they fingers and the virtual representation of their fingers was in a capsule shape. Ultimately, the user was able to control the system through the control console (Fig. 1) or the GUI widgets (Fig. 3).

We developed a user study protocol [14] that is detailed in Subsect. 3.3. To apply that protocol, we implemented two hardware and software setups. One is a completely physical setup, with a table with the control panel and three video monitors plugged to a PC that runs the whole system. The other one is a virtual environment where the same physical elements are depicted in a scene that is experienced by the user through HMD and finger tracking.

The setup counted with an HTC Vive Headset (resolution of 1080 × 1200 pixels per eye). To enable the interaction, our setup included five Vicon Vero v1.3 X cameras (Fig. 2), the Vicon Tracker 3.6 software and three 3D-printed finger markers. The finger markers have three rods each at different angles with reflective tiny points on top, because Vicon cameras capture these points within their field of view and send their position to be recreated as a 3D object. One very important feature of our immersive VR setup was that the physical objects remained in place and were registered to the positions of their virtual counterparts, which provided passive haptic feedback [7] and allowed us to read the interactions with the same equipment in both the real and virtual setups.

To gather user data on usability issues from the two setups, we adopted the direct systematic observation method [11]. The experimenters also took notes of usability noises and barriers on both systems during observations in order to compare them at the end.

We collected users' perceived usability, opinions towards User Experience, and cybersickness symptoms applying three different standardized questionnaires after each test scenario: System Usability Scale (SUS) [3], User Experience Questionnaire (UEQ) [12] and Simulator Sickness Questionnaire (SSQ) [10]. Validated versions of these questionnaires in the subjects native language (Brazilian Portuguese) were used instead of their original English versions. Additionally, two documents were created on Google Forms to keep all the questionnaires in the proper sequence in each of the two conditions. Users handled a 9.7" Apple iPad and used Safari web browser to fill out the forms. Both versions of the target system were developed using Unity platform version 2018.2.15f, and the control panel was prototyped using Arduino kits and 3D-printed pieces. Finally, IBM PASW Statistics 18 was used for statistical analyses.

3.3 Experiment Design

The overall structure of the experiment involved each participant to perform two different sets of tasks with the system (Subsect. 3.1). We call each set of tasks a scenario. Each participant performed one of the scenarios in the immersive VR setup and the other using the physical prototype. In such way, we have two independent variables (scenario and setup) with two treatments each. In each scenario, the operator (participant) needed to move the robot and to unclog pipes in different locations. We followed a latin square schedule to shuffle the order of scenarios. We also randomized the order of the prototype (VR and physical). The resulting latin square configuration is presented in Table 1.

The chosen metrics include (i) usability problems that users had to deal with, (ii) elapsed time to complete a set of tasks in each scenario, (iii) usability score, (iv) User Experience score, and (v) relative cybersickness levels. The questionnaires and support devices are those presented in Subsect. 3.2. Cybersickness was measured before and after each condition, and the resulting value corresponded to the difference between pre- and post-condition measures. The testing protocol included a Profile Form (PF), an Informed Consent Form (ICF) and a Confidentiality Agreement (CA). Additionally, since VR experiences are contraindicated for people with some conditions, a Screening Form (SF) was applied to prevent sensitive participants from joining in.

Table 1. Latin square for session configuration.

Participants	1st Config.	2nd Config.
1, 5, 9, 13	Scen. 1 + physical	Scenario 2 + VR
2, 6, 10, 14	Scenario 1 + VR	Scen. 2 + physical
3, 7, 11, 15	Scen. 2 + physical	Scenario 1 + VR
4, 8, 12, 16	Scenario 2 + VR	Scen. 1 + physical

The complete flow of activities during a testing session was:

1. **Greetings:** the researchers introduce themselves and the experiment.
2. **Documents and Screening:** the participant fills out ICF, CA, PF and SF (they may be prevented to carry on with the experiment).
3. **System Presentation:** the participant is introduced to Annelida system and its functionalities. After that, they answer only the SSQ.
4. **1st Configuration:** the participant receives instructions and performs tasks on the system. After, they answer SSQ, UEQ and SUS.
5. **2nd Configuration:** the participant receives new instructions and performs new tasks on the system. They answer again SSQ, UEQ and SUS.

4 Results

Sixteen participants were recruited and went through the experiment. This population was composed of 13 (81%) males and 3 (19%) females, from 22 to 32 years old ($\bar{x} = 26.13$). Ten participants have a graduate degree (62.5%), four have a post-graduate degree (25%), and two are high school graduated (12.5%). All participants reported some previous experience in VR: eight participants use VR less than once a month (50%), four use it at least once a month (25%), one uses it sometimes a month (6%), and three use it once a week or more (19%).

Most of the participants did not have any vision impairment (75%), and the remaining participants reported myopia, hypermetropia or astigmatism and used correction lens or did not feel affected by the condition during experiments.

According to the protocol described in Subsect. 3.3, each participant completed two task scenarios, each one with a different prototype (physical or immersive VR). Table 2 presents sample size (N), sample mean ($\bar{x}$) and standard deviation (σ) for the differences between SSQ measures taken in different moments of the session. The pre-exposure measure was taken after the system presentation and before the first configuration. The VR measure was taken after the completion of tasks in the immersive VR configuration, and the physical measure was taken after finishing the tasks in the physical configuration.

Table 3 presents the sample size (N), the sample mean ($\bar{x}$) and the standard deviation (σ) for other measures in each prototype.

We applied Shapiro-Wilk's test of normality and a Levene's test of homogeneity of variance on our samples in order to identify the fairest statistical approach

Table 2. Descriptive data analysis for cybersickness.

SSQ differential[a]	N	$\bar{x}$	σ
pre-exposure → VR	7	12.29	20.45
VR → physical	7	−16.03	13.78
pre-exposure → physical	8	−0.47	9.04
physical → VR	8	1.40	12.31

[a]The element on the left side of the arrow indicates the baseline for SSQ differential measure. For example, "VR → physical" means the variation of cybersickness symptoms from an immersive VR scenario to a non-immersive scenario, i.e., the SSQ score in the second scenario with physical prototype subtracted from the SSQ score in the first scenario with immersive VR prototype.

Table 3. Descriptive data analysis for usability, UX and performance.

Measure	Prototype	N	$\bar{x}$	σ
SUS	VR	15	51.1	9.87
	physical	16	55.03	9.57
UEQ - attractiveness	VR	15	1.52	0.91
	physical	16	1.87	0.71
UEQ - pragmatic	VR	15	1.38	0.7
	physical	16	1.8	0.59
UEQ - hedonic	VR	15	1.71	0.66
	physical	16	1.68	0.79
time (in seconds)	VR	15	1118	223
	physical	16	923	111

to compare scores and times. All samples presented normal distribution (p-values higher than .05). Time samples pair presented heterogeneous variance (p-value = **.004**) while other pairs presented homogeneous variances (p-values higher than .05).

For differences in SSQ scores, we applied parametric Student's t-tests. The p-value of **.133** fails to reject the null hypothesis (at significance level of .05) when comparing "pre-exposure → VR" and "pre-exposure → physical", i.e., it's not possible to declare that cybersickness symptoms were worse in either case.

In contrast, the p-value of **.022** allows us to reject the null hypothesis (α = .05) when comparing differences in SSQ scores for "physical → VR" and "VR → physical". So, we can state that moving from an immersive VR scenario to a physical prototype scenario caused a significant decrease of sickness symptoms while the inverse scheme (from physical to VR) probably did not.

Pearson's correlation coefficients (ρ) were also computed for analyzing the overall behavior of cybersickness symptoms during a test session. In sessions that started with a scenario in immersive VR and followed with a scenario in physical prototype, the $\rho = -.930$ indicates a very strong inverse correlation [6]. This is expected as result of the recovery from immersive VR sickness during the tests using the physical prototype. However, in the sessions that started with a scenario in physical prototype and followed with a scenario in immersive VR, the $\rho = -.514$ reveals a moderate negative correlation [6] despite our predictions that no correlation should be found. The expected outcome was that the "physical $\rightarrow$ VR" cybersickness measure would present differential values similar to the "pre-exposure $\rightarrow$ VR" case, but performing tasks in the physical prototype softened cybersickness symptoms somehow in the subsequent VR test.

For SUS, we also applied a Student's t-test. The p-value of $.269$ fails to reject null hypothesis ($\alpha = .05$) which states that there is no significant difference in samples means. Since we identified no bias in usability analysis (participants have never used the target system), the most likely explanation for this result is the perceived usability being the same in immersive VR and physical prototypes.

For UEQ, we again applied a Student's t-test. All p-values for distinct UX dimensions fail to reject null hypotheses ($\alpha = .05$): $.236$ (attractiveness), $.072$ (pragmatic), and $.913$ (hedonic). Again, we noticed no bias in UX analysis (participants have already used VR and are unlikely to feel amazed or baffled).

Finally, for time to go through the scenarios, we applied a parametric Welch t-test. The p-value of $.006$ allows us to reject the null hypothesis (at significance level of .01) and to assert that participants took significantly more time to complete scenarios in immersive VR than in physical prototypes. It sounds reasonable that immersive VR interaction (even with passive haptics and finger tracking) is slower than desktop interaction. We also reinforce that the users' fingers in VR occasionally flickered due to missing tracking references which had to remain in the cameras reach. Similar problems were already reported [2].

Through systematic observation, we were capable of writing down usability issues found on both version of the system. It is worth mentioning that all usability problems were noticed or experienced by users in both immersive VR and physical versions.

5   Research Questions

Ultimately, it is necessary to answer the questions introduced in Sect. 1:

i. **Is it the same to undergo user test in a desktop system or in a simulated system in VR?** Our case study suggests that the answer is "yes, to some extent". We collected evidence that the summative evaluation of interaction aspects is similar in results for immersive VR and desktop system prototypes, except for performance.

ii. **How does it affect the user performance?** The overall performance of the users was significantly worse in immersive VR (users complete desktop scenarios 17.4% faster than immersive VR scenarios). However, this result is heavily bound to our experimental setup. For instance, tracking system inaccuracies, HMD limitations (e.g. resolution and field of view) and small gaps in aligning the physical console to its virtual representation might be responsible for lower efficiency. Werrlich et al. [20] found similar results when comparing users' performance in following instructions given in Augmented Reality (AR) and physical paper: participants in AR performed worse. On the other hand, Bolder, Grünvogel and Angelescu [2] reported no difference when comparing users' performance in a car infotainment system using Mixed Reality (MR) and the real car.

iii. **How does it affect the usability assessment and usability issues' finding?** It was not possible to identify differences in usability scores on both system versions. Moreover, usability issues were evenly found in both versions of the system. This typifies similar usability on both systems in our context. Bolder, Grünvogel and Angelescu [2] also reported no differences using SUS questionnaire in a MR vs. physical comparison. Werrlich et al. work [20] suggests better usability SUS scores in AR instruction than in paper instructions.

iv. **How does it affect User Experience (UX)?** Attractiveness, pragmatic dimension and hedonic dimension presented no significant contrast when comparing desktop to immersive VR. Even though the users faced some interaction noises further discussed in Sect. 6, they were not enough for significantly decreasing any UX scores. Nevertheless, it's important to mention that all participants of this research have already experienced Virtual Reality and some of them even use VR frequently, so the overall UX might be different for inexperienced people as suggested by Werrlich et al. [20]. The aforementioned authors reported differences on the hedonic dimension (related to novelty and stimulation), but no difference on the pragmatic dimension (related to perspicuity, control and efficiency): since participants were completely inexperienced with AR devices, they seemed to be overstimulated and amazed by Microsoft HoloLens (resulting in higher hedonic scores) and bored with paper-based instructions (resulting in lower scores).

v. **Should the experimenter mind about cybersickness?** We didn't detect significantly worse cybersickness symptoms on the immersive VR simulation than those on the desktop system in the first measurement of each session (i.e., from pre-exposure to post-exposure). We are aware that it could be a particular effect of our participants sample, since some of them experience VR regularly and are used to it. Furthermore, participants remained sat during the entire test, and our immersive VR scene doesn't expose the users to sudden movement, teleportation or other conditions known as potential inducers of cybersickness. This entire scenario might contribute to lower SSQ scores in our case study.

It is also worth mentioning that correlation analysis of cybersickness revealed an interesting behavior. As presented in Sect. 4, "pre-exposure → physical" score differences were moderately correlated with "physical → VR" in the test configuration where users start with the physical prototype scenario and then go to immersive VR scenario. The expectation was that correlation would remain low, because it is natural that cybersickness does not change much when users are exposed to non-immersive VR (the mission reconstruction screen in Fig. 3) and increases when users are exposed to an immersive VR environment (the entire VR control room in Fig. 2 rightmost image). Nevertheless, the users did not report many cybersickness symptoms when exposed to the VR prototype after trying the physical prototype. This suggests that experiencing a non-immersive interface of a system in advance could lead to reduced sickness during user testing on the same system in immersive VR. We speculate that it happens due to factors like reduction of head movements and increased concentration on tasks, since the participant already knows the system features and functionalities.

6   Conclusion

In this paper, we conducted a case study to evaluate the use of immersive VR simulation as an alternative for user testing in expensive and complex functional systems. We collected and compared measures of performance, usability, User Experience and cybersickness of 16 participants by performing user testing in a system prototype used to unclog obstructions in oil pipes. Besides, we also compare observations of usability issues faced by participants during the tests. Results demonstrate that the perceived quality of the immersive VR system is indistinguishable from the physical counterpart regarding User Experience, usability, and cybersickness. Furthermore, we observed that the same usability problems were detected in both systems, promising a consistent approach even for formative evaluation. Nonetheless, the users' performance on immersive VR simulation was significantly slower than on the regular desktop. Also, there is evidence to suggest that training users in a physical system prototype before an immersive VR test session could reduce cybersickness for experienced users.

Limitations of this research include the small and homogeneous sample of participants and a set of technical issues: the occasional inaccuracies on the tracking system that made the virtual fingers of the user flickering (similar problems were faced by Bolder, Grünvogel and Angelescu [2]), the mapping of just three fingers of users in VR potentially reducing the sense of presence, the small differences between virtual and physical control panels, the low resolution of our HMD to present smaller text (logs, tooltips, etc.) on virtual screens, the low resolution home-made trackball on the control panel, and some "hard to push" 3D printed buttons on the physical console. Yet, these noises were not enough for generating a significant difference in any UX dimension.

As future work for this study, we aim to increase the number of participants in order to allow comparison of people experienced and inexperienced in VR, since UX might be quite different. Unfortunately, we are currently unable to perform gaze tracking in immersive VR due to our available apparatus, but the investigation of gaze patterns on both prototypes also might lead to new findings. Furthermore, it seems to be important to compare both the conventional desktop version of the system and the current immersive VR simulation with passive haptics to a new VR simulation that depends on traditional VR controllers.

References

1. Barbosa, S., da Silva, B.: Interação Humano-Computador. Elsevier, Rio de Janeiro (2010)
2. Bolder, A., Grünvogel, S.M., Angelescu, E.: Comparison of the usability of a car infotainment system in a mixed reality environment and in a real car. In: Proceedings of the 24th ACM Symposium on Virtual Reality Software and Technology, pp. 1–10 (2018)
3. Brooke, J.: SUS: a 'quick and dirty' usability scale. In: Usability Evaluation in Industry, pp. 189–194. Taylor Francis, London (1996)
4. Davis, S., Nesbitt, K., Nalivaiko, E.: A systematic review of cybersickness. In: Proceedings of the 2014 Conference on Interactive Entertainment, pp. 1–9 (2014)
5. Higuera-Trujillo, J.L., Maldonado, J.L.T., Millán, C.L.: Psychological and physiological human responses to simulated and real environments: a comparison between photographs, 360° panoramas, and virtual reality. Appl. Ergon. **65**, 398–409 (2017)
6. Hinkle, D.E., Wiersma, W., Jurs, S.G.: Applied Statistics for the Behavioral Sciences, 5th edn. Houghton Mifflin, Boston (2003)
7. Insko, B.E.: Passive haptics significantly enhances virtual environments. Ph.D. thesis, The University of North Carolina, Chapel Hill, NC, USA (2001)
8. ISO 9241–210:2019 - ergonomics of human-system interaction - part 210: Human-centred design for interactive systems. Standard, International Organization for Standardization, Geneva, Switzerland, July 2019
9. Kamide, H., Yasumoto, M., Mae, Y., Takubo, T., Ohara, K., Arai, T.: Comparative evaluation of virtual and real humanoid with robot-oriented psychology scale. In: 2011 IEEE International Conference on Robotics and Automation, pp. 599–604. IEEE (2011)
10. Kennedy, R.S., Lane, N.E., Berbaum, K.S., Lilienthal, M.G.: Simulator sickness questionnaire: an enhanced method for quantifying simulator sickness. Int. J. Aviat. Psychol. **3**(3), 203–220 (1993)
11. Lakatos, E.M., Marconi, M.: Fundamentos de Metodologia Científica, Atlas, São Paulo, SP, Brazil (2017)
12. Laugwitz, B., Held, T., Schrepp, M.: Construction and evaluation of a user experience questionnaire. In: Holzinger, A. (ed.) USAB 2008. LNCS, vol. 5298, pp. 63–76. Springer, Heidelberg (2008). https://doi.org/10.1007/978-3-540-89350-9_6
13. LaViola Jr., J.J.: A discussion of cybersickness in virtual environments. SIGCHI Bull. **32**(1), 47–56 (2000). https://doi.org/10.1145/333329.333344
14. Rubin, J., Chisnell, D.: Handbook of Usability Testing: How to Plan, Design and Conduct Effective Tests, 2nd edn. Wiley, Indianapolis (2008)
15. Satter, K., Butler, A.: Competitive usability analysis of immersive virtual environments in engineering design review. J. Comput. Inf. Sci. Eng. **15**(3) (2015). https://doi.org/10.1115/1.4029750
16. Sauro, J., Lewis, J.: Quantifying the User Experience: Practical Statistics for User Research, 2nd edn. Elsevier, Cambridge (2016)
17. Sharp, H., Rogers, Y., Preece, J.: Interaction Design: Beyond Human-computer Interaction, 2nd edn. John Wiley and Sons Inc., West Sussex (2007)

18. Tullis, T., Albert, B.: Measuring the User Experience: Collecting, Analyzing, and Presenting Usability Metrics. Elsevier, Waltham (2013)
19. Vince, J.: Virtual Reality Systems. Pearson Education, Essex (1995)
20. Werrlich, S., Daniel, A., Ginger, A., Nguyen, P.A., Notni, G.: Comparing HMD-based and paper-based training. In: 2018 IEEE International Symposium on Mixed and Augmented Reality, pp. 134–142. IEEE (2018)
21. Wolfartsberger, J.: Analyzing the potential of virtual reality for engineering design review. Autom. Constr. **104**, 27–37 (2019)

Gaze-Contingent Rendering in Virtual Reality

Fang Zhu[1], Ping Lu[1], Pin Li[2], Bin Sheng[3(✉)], and Lijuan Mao[4(✉)]

[1] ZTE Corporarion, Nanjing, People's Republic of China
[2] The Hong Kong Polytechnic University, Hong Kong, People's Republic of China
[3] Shanghai Jiao Tong University, Shanghai, People's Republic of China
shengbin@sjtu.edu.cn
[4] Shanghai University of Sport, Shanghai, People's Republic of China
maolijuan@sus.edu.cn

Abstract. Virtual reality (VR) is a technology that relies on a computer graphics system and other external display and control interfaces, to create an immersive experience by generating an interactive three-dimensional environment on a computer. Currently, however, most virtual reality scenes are far behind the real world in naturalism. One of the limitations is the insufficient graphics computing performance of the computer. It is difficult for mainstream consumer GPUs to meet the requirements of high picture quality and high fluency at the same time when running VR scenes, resulting in a reduction in the game's visual experience and even human discomfort. In order to balance the quality and fluency of the picture, the areas within and outside the focus range of the user's sight can be rendered hierarchically, so as to efficiently use computing resources. In order to achieve this goal, the following article proposes a model that combines the saliency information of the virtual scene and the head motion information to predict the focus of the field of view in real time. The model can assign different rendering priorities to objects in the field of view according to the prediction results, and give different priorities, use different rendering algorithms to provide a flexible VR scene rendering optimization solution.

Keywords: VR · Viewpoint prediction · Foveated rendering · Picture saliency

1 Introduction

1.1 Significance

In recent years, with the development and progress of virtual reality (VR) technology and the iterative update of VR devices, more and more people choose to use VR games as one of the daily entertainment options. Compared with games displayed on ordinary screens, VR games provide users with a stronger sense of immersion and realism, which greatly improves the amusement of the game.

© Springer Nature Switzerland AG 2020
N. Magnenat-Thalmann et al. (Eds.): CGI 2020, LNCS 12221, pp. 16–23, 2020.
https://doi.org/10.1007/978-3-030-61864-3_2

In addition, VR can also be used in many other fields, such as education and medical treatment. However, the actual expressiveness of VR technology still has a certain gap compared with traditional three-dimensional scenes, and it is far from the "realistic" rendering target.

The reason is that VR technology requires a larger display angle, a higher graphics resolution and a higher number of display frames than traditional flat three-dimensional display. Related research shows that in order to achieve the ideal display effect, the display angle must reach more than 150°, the graphic resolution calculated in real time should reach 4K or even higher, and in order to avoid the dizziness caused by the grainy picture, the display frames needs to reach more than 90 frames per second.

Currently, consumer-grade graphics processors on the market are difficult to meet these two requirements at the same time, which leads to the fact that most of the VR scenes currently put into application have simple structures, rough details, and poor sense of reality.

Compared with non-VR scenes, they have obvious disadvantages. In order to solve the above problems and give full play to the computing performance under the existing hardware to improve the VR display effect, the academic community has proposed a method for tracking the focus of the sight in real time and rendering the areas inside and outside the focus in a hierarchical way.

The basis of this method is that the focus of the visual field where the user's attention is concentrated at any time, as long as the focus area of the visual field is rendered with high precision and the lower precision processing is performed outside the area, it will make efficient use of computing resources, so as to balance the picture quality and fluency. The main difficulty in implementing this solution is the ac-curate prediction of the focus of the field of view (FoV).

The current high-precision prediction method is to use hardware devices, such as eye trackers, to track the eye movement trajectory and calculate the focus of sight in real time. However, this solution has strong hardware dependence, high implementation cost, and small application scope. Another solution is software-level line-of-sight focus prediction.

The specific method is to detect the saliency, depth information, color information, etc. of the scene in combination with the content of the scene, so as to determine the objects in the scene that may become the focus of attention. Based on the head movement information, the line of sight movement trajectory is calculated accordingly.

Based on extensive investigation of existing research results, this article develops a viewpoint prediction system based on head motion and scene information, as well as hierarchical rendering based on the prediction. The structure is simple and easy to use. The main contributions of this system are as follows:

1. The system is completely based on software implementation, and does not rely on eye tracker equipment to achieve better viewpoint prediction, and on this basis, the viewpoint rendering is realized, reducing the rendering overhead.
2. The system structure is streamlined and efficient, and can achieve higher rendering effects under general hardware conditions.

3. By analyzing the experimental results, this article proposes the future development direction of VR rendering.

1.2   Article Structure

The workflow of this article is shown in the Fig. 1 below. First, the motion information of the device sensors including speed, acceleration, etc. is collected through the program, and the saliency information is calculated from the scene screenshots.

Then, the obtained information is input into the Sgaze [6] model, and the predicted view-point position is output, then pass the viewpoint position to the foveated rendering program, and finally realize the foveated rendering of viewpoint tracking.

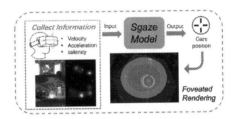

Fig. 1. System structure

2   Related Work

2.1   Image-Based Viewpoint Prediction

Image-based viewpoint prediction has been studied in the field of computer vision, and many saliency models have been proposed in the past thirty years. L. Itti et al. [7] proposed a traditional viewpoint model, which uses multi-scale image features to calculate a saliency map. Oliva et al. [15] noticed the importance of scene content and proposed a saliency model that takes scene content information into account. In short, most existing models use basic information such as color and brightness of the image [2], or specific scenes and objects in the image [10,11]. With the development of deep learning, many models based on CNNs have achieved good performance [5,12,24]. Most of the aforementioned models are applied to a single picture. In addition to these models, researchers also studied the saliency of stereoscopic images [5,9] and videos [18,20], both Sitzmann et al. [16] and Rai et al. [16] studied the saliency of 360° panoramic images. Xu et al. [22] established a model for viewpoint prediction in 360° immersive video. These models usually calculate a density map of the position of the viewpoint rather than directly predict the position of the line of sight in real time. However, in VR applications, functions such as foveated rendering based on view-points and the interaction of eyeball rotation require real-time line-of-sight positions, and calculating positions from density maps is not efficient enough.

2.2 The Relationship Between Eye and Head Movements

The relationship between eye and head movements has been studied in recent years. Yarbus [23] found that when the gaze shifts, the eye and head movements are always coordinated and related to visual cognition. Nakashima and Shioiri [13] further explained that the difference in line-of-sight direction and head direction can interfere with visual processing, that is, humans have the highest visual cognition efficiency when the two directions are the same.

Einhauser et al. [3] discovered the coordination of eyes and heads when people freely observed natural scenes, and some work [1] revealed a delay between eye rotation and head rotation, the former is usually faster than the latter. Many studies have focused on the magnitude of head rotation and eyeball rotation, and have shown that they are closely related [4]. Stahl [19] found that when the eye rotation range is limited to a small range, the head will not rotate, and when the eye rotation range is large, the head rotation range is linearly related to the eye rotation range within a certain range. Nakashima et al. [14] used head rotation information to successfully improve the accuracy of saliency prediction.

2.3 Foveated Rendering

In the field of computer graphics, foveated rendering is a widely studied subject. Based on fixed-point grading or the line-of-sight position obtained by the eye tracker device, VR devices have also begun to implement grading rendering in practical applications.

3 Content and Methods

3.1 Hardware System

This article uses Oculus Rift as the experimental equipment, and the rendering of the scene and the running of the script are implemented through Unity. The system environment of the entire experiment is Windows10 1903, and the CPU and GPU of the platform are Intel® Core i7-9750H @ 2.6 GHz and NVIDIA GeForce 1660Ti 6 GB.

3.2 Viewpoint Prediction

According to the experience and intuition of daily life, there is a strong correlation between the movement of the eyeball and the head, that is to say, when the head turns in a certain direction, the eyeball also has a high probability of moving in the same direction.

It is reflected in the mathematical model that the position of the viewpoint has a certain linear correlation with the speed and acceleration of the head rotation. Many studies [1,21] have shown that there is a delay between head movement and eye movement.

Head movements tend to lag behind eye movements [21], and the magnitude of the delay is different in different speed regions. Therefore, the head motion information used in the prediction model should be the speed and acceleration ahead of the current certain time. In actual situations, the factors that affect human eye movements are complex and diverse, including the current scene, purpose, and delay. Combining various factors, the prediction formula given by the Sgaze model [6] is:

$$\begin{cases} x_{gaze} = a_x \cdot \omega_x(t + \Delta t_{x1}) + b_x \cdot \beta_x(t) + F_x(t + \Delta t_{x2}) + G_x(t) + H_x(t) \\ y_{gaze} = a_y \cdot \omega_y(t + \Delta t_{y1}) + F_y(t + \Delta t_{y2}) + G_y(t) + H_y(t) \end{cases} \quad (1)$$

Picture Saliency and Viewpoint Prediction: The saliency information of the scene picture also has a great influence on human viewpoint prediction; therefore, it is reasonable to introduce the saliency information of the picture image into viewpoint prediction. The model used in this article uses SAM-ResNet saliency predictor [2]. In practical applications, it takes too much resources to calculate the saliency of the image; therefore, it is impossible to achieve real-time prediction. We design to calculate the saliency value of the scene for every 250ms, and only the central part of the picture, to reduce the time spent on prediction. The saliency highlight image in collect information of Fig. 1 is an example of the saliency calculation of the scene in this article.

3.3   Foveated Rendering

MBFR. Mask Based Foveated Rendering (MBFR) is relatively easy to implement foveated rendering, its method is as follows:

1. According to the distance between the pixel and the viewpoint, the image is divided into two areas (or more)
2. During the rendering process: the higher priority area is rendered without any special processing; the lower area discards some pixels without rendering but only reconstruct by calculating the average value from the neighboring pixels.

4   Experiment Results and Analysis

4.1   Test Methods and Evaluation Standards

This article uses the Unity official scene "Corridor Lightning Example" for testing. The scene has more lighting effects. Most of the materials in the scene use the Standard (Specular set-up) shader, which makes the scene have a lot of specular reflection light. There are moving balls and shadows in the scene. During the conversion of the field of view, the model will calculate the position of the viewpoint and use this as the basis to achieve foveated rendering.

When the foveated rendering is turned on and off separately, Unity's own profile performance analyzer will record the GPU time and CPU time required to observe the rendering of a frame and calculate the average. There are more detailed rendering steps in GPU time. Viewpoint prediction results and foveated rendering effects are evaluated by the subjective feelings of participating testers.

4.2   Viewpoint Prediction

Due to the lack of an eye tracker to obtain an accurate gaze position, the reference position of the line of sight is obtained by collecting subjective marks of the participants. Figure 2 shows the effect of line-of-sight prediction, where green dots indicate the line of sight of the participants and red dots indicate the position of the line of sight, and the accuracy of the prediction results is high.

Fig. 2. Viewpoint prediction and ground truth

4.3   Rendering Effect

In the area where the scene is far away from the center of the viewpoint, we per-formed a relatively blurry rendering, but from the perspective of the tester. From the perspective of actual experience, there is no loss of perceived detail, and the expected effect is achieved from a subjective perspective.

4.4   Rendering Efficiency

Table 1 shows the rendering calculation time. It can be seen from the table that the overall rendering time per frame has decreased by about 14% after the foveated rendering is turned on, of which the rendering process time has dropped by about 26%, and the post-processing process has increased by about 4 times. Since the post-processing effect of the test scene is less, pixel reconstruction has become the main part of post-processing. As can be seen from the table, the reduction in rendering time for pixel discarding is greater than the time for pixel reconstruction, so the foveated rendering of this project successfully improves rendering efficiency.

Table 1. System load changes when Hierarchical Rendering On and Off

Foveated rendering	Total time (ms)	Drawing time (ms)	Image effect (ms)
On	1.276	0.893	0.198
Off	1.428	1.208	0.051

5   Conclusion

This article establishes a viewpoint prediction system based on head motion and scene information, implements foveated rendering based on this, afterwards, tests and analyzes this system. The analysis and comparison of viewpoint prediction accuracy, rendering effect and rendering efficiency prove that the system can predict the line-of-sight position more accurately without eye tracker and can improve rendering efficiency without reducing too much image quality and other advantages. Combining viewpoint prediction with foveated rendering are important development directions for VR rendering in the future.

On top of the current results, the following work can be done to further improve the system. Test the project's foveated rendering method in more complex scenarios and collect more data to analyze the actual performance of the method; use an eye tracker to obtain the true position of the line of sight, compare the predicted position of the project method with it, and quantify the error size; try more methods such as deep learning algorithms applied to viewpoint prediction, and compare with the current method, try to improve accuracy; try to use Other technologies such as Variable Rate Shading (VRS) implement foveated rendering and compare with current methods.

Acknowledgement. This work was supported in part by the National Key Research and Development Program of China under Grant 2018YFF0300903, in part by the National Natural Science Foundation of China under Grant 61872241 and Grant 61572316, and in part by the Science and Technology Commission of Shanghai Municipality under Grant 15490503200, Grant 18410750700, Grant 17411952600, and Grant 16DZ0501100.

References

1. Biguer, B., Jeannerod, M., Prablanc, C.: The coordination of eye, head, and arm movements during reaching at a single visual target. Exp. Brain Res. **46**(2), 301–304 (1982)
2. Borji, A., Sihite, D.N., Itti, L.: Probabilistic learning of task-specific visual attention. In: Computer Vision and Pattern Recognition, pp. 470—477 (2012)
3. Einhauser, W., et al.: Human eye-head co-ordination in natural exploration. Netw. Comput. Neural Syst. **18**(3), 267–297 (2007)
4. Fang, Y., Nakashima, R., Matsumiya, K., Kuriki, I., Shioiri, S.: Eye-head coordination for visual cognitive processing. PloS ONE **10**(3), e0121035 (2015)
5. Guo, F., Shen, J., Li, X.: Learning to detect stereo saliency. In: International Conference on Multimedia and Expo (ICME), pp. 1–6 (2014)

6. Hu, Z., Zhang, C., Li, S., Wang, G., Manocha, D.: SGaze: a data-driven eye-head coordination model for realtime gaze prediction. IEEE Trans. Visual Comput. Graphics **25**(5), 2002–2010 (2019)
7. Itti, L., Koch, C., Niebur, E.: A model of saliency-based visual attention for rapid scene analysis. IEEE Trans. Pattern Anal. Mach. Intell. **20**(11), 1254–1259 (1998)
8. Lu, P., Sheng, B., Luo, S., Jia, X., Wu, W.: Image-based non-photorealistic rendering for realtime virtual sculpting. Multimedia Tools Appl. **74**(21), 9697–9714 (2014). https://doi.org/10.1007/s11042-014-2146-4
9. Kamel, A., Sheng, B., Yang, P., Li, P., Shen, R., Feng, D.D.: Deep convolutional neural networks for human action recognition using depth maps and postures. IEEE Trans. Syst. Man Cybern. Syst. **49**(9), 1806–1819 (2019)
10. Karambakhsh, A., Kamel, A., Sheng, B., Li, P., Yang, P., Feng, D.D.: Deep gesture interaction for augmented anatomy learning. Int. J. Inf. Manage. **45**, 328–336 (2019)
11. Kümmerer, M., Wallis, T., Gatys, L., Bethge, M.: Understanding low-and high-level contributions to fixation prediction. In: 19th IEEE International Conference on Computer Vision (ICCV 2017), pp. 4799–4808 (2017)
12. Meng, X., et al.: A video information driven football recommendation system. Comput. Electr. Eng. **85**, 106699 (2020). https://doi.org/10.1016/j.compeleceng.2020.106699
13. Nakashima, R., Shioiri, S.: Why do we move our head to look at an object in our peripheral region? lateral viewing interferes with attentive search. PloS ONE **9**(3), e92284 (2014)
14. Nakashima, R., et al.: Saliency-based gaze prediction based on head direction. Vis. Res. **117**, 59–66 (2015)
15. Oliva, A., Torralba, A., Castelhano, M.S., Henderson, J.M.: Top-down control of visual attention in object detection. In: International Conference on Image Processing, pp. 253–256 (2003)
16. Rai, Y., Gutierrez, J., Callet, P.L.: Dataset of head and eye movements for 360 degree images. In: ACM SIGMM Conference on Multimedia Systems, pp. 205—210 (2017)
17. Sitzmann, V., et al.: Saliency in VR: how do people explore virtual environments? IEEE Trans. Visual Comput. Graphics **24**(4), 1633–1642 (2018)
18. Sheng, B., Li, P., Zhang, Y., Mao, L.: GreenSea: visual soccer analysis using broad learning system. IEEE Trans. Cybern., 1–15 (2020). https://doi.org/10.1109/TCYB.2020.2988792
19. Stahl, J.S.: Amplitude of human head movements associated with horizontal saccades. Exp. Brain Res. **126**(1), 41–54 (1999)
20. Wang, W., Shen, J., Shao, L.: Consistent video saliency using local gradient flow optimization and global refinement. IEEE Trans. Image Process. **24**(11), 4185–4196 (2015)
21. Whittington, D.A., Heppreymond, M.C., Flood, W.: Eye and head movements to auditory targets. Exp. Brain Res. **41**(3–4), 358–363 (1981)
22. Xu, Y., et al.: Gaze prediction in dynamic 360 immersive videos. In: Proceedings of the IEEE Conference on Computer Vision and Pattern Recognition, pp. 5333–5342 (2018)
23. Yarbus, A.: Eye Movements and Vision. New York (1967)
24. Zhang, P., Zheng, L., Jiang, Y., Mao, L., Li, Z., Sheng, B.: Tracking soccer players using spatio-temporal context learning under multiple views. Multimedia Tools Appl. **77**(15), 18935–18955 (2017). https://doi.org/10.1007/s11042-017-5316-3

Hierarchical Rendering System Based on Viewpoint Prediction in Virtual Reality

Ping Lu[1], Fang Zhu[1], Pin Li[2], Jinman Kim[3], Bin Sheng[4(✉)], and Lijuan Mao[5(✉)]

[1] ZTE Corporarion, Nanjing, People's Republic of China
[2] The Hong Kong Polytechnic University, Hong Kong, People's Republic of China
[3] The University of Sydney, Sydney, Australia
[4] Shanghai Jiao Tong University, Shanghai, People's Republic of China
shengbin@sjtu.edu.cn
[5] Shanghai University of Sport, Shanghai, People's Republic of China
maolijuan@sus.edu.cn

Abstract. Virtual reality (VR) systems use multi-modal interfaces to explore three-dimensional virtual worlds. During exploration, the user may look at different objects of interest or in different directions. The field of view of human vision is $135° \times 160°$, but the one requiring the highest resolution is only in $1.5° \times 2°$. It is estimated that in modern VR, only 4% of the pixel resources of the head-mounted display are mapped to the visual center. Therefore, allocating more computing resources to the visual center and allocating fewer viewpoint prediction rendering techniques elsewhere can greatly speed up the rendering of the scene, especially for VR devices equipped with eye trackers. However, eye trackers as additional equipment may be relatively expensive and be harder to use, at the same time, there is considerable work to be done in the development of eye trackers and their integration with commercial head-mounted equipment. Therefore, this article uses an eye-head coordination model combined with the saliencey of the scene to predict the gaze position, and then uses a hybrid method of Level of Detail (LOD) and grid degeneration to reduce rendering time as much as possible without losing the perceived details and required calculations.

Keywords: VR · Hierarchical rendering · LOD · Hand track · Eye-head coordination

1 Introduction

1.1 Significance

With the development of new technologies such as ray tracing, the fidelity and fineness of computer graphics are increasing day by day, but at the same time, the pres-sure of graphics rendering on graphics hardware is also increasing. The

N. Magnenat-Thalmann et al. (Eds.): CGI 2020, LNCS 12221, pp. 24–32, 2020.
https://doi.org/10.1007/978-3-030-61864-3_3

emergence of VR technology has further increased the computing power requirements of graphics rendering, which makes it paramount that we optimize our rendering technologies as much as possible. On this issue, our viewpoint prediction driven hierarchical rendering technology is based on the principal that human vision has a focused range.

Considering the real-time requirements of VR applications [6, 8], the efficiency of the viewpoint position prediction method also needs to be carefully considered. The focus of conventional visual saliency prediction work [1] is mainly on the accuracy of the algorithm, but it does not provide real-time performance guarantee for VR applications. Hardware-based eye tracking is better suited to meet real-time requirements, but this method is limited by the cost of hardware, delay and other factors, in comparison, the model based on eye-head coordination, has fewer limitations and can be better to meet the real-time viewpoint rendering requirements of VR applications.

In terms of hierarchical rendering, this article adopted a hybrid method of LOD and mesh degeneracy: after degenerating the model once, using the retained vertices as the skeleton, the simplified model and the original model are saved separately, and then during the rendering process, the mesh near the viewpoint is merged back with the original model. This method can achieve grid-level precision adjustment. At the same time, no new grid simplification calculation is required during the movement of the viewpoint, which greatly reduces the calculation resource occupation of the GPU part.

1.2   Article Structure

The main operation processes of this method are loading the model and performing simplified model calculations. In this step, one or more simplified models are generated for each object, and the incremental data between the models at various levels is saved, as well as the rendering cycle. The viewpoint prediction algorithm and the model stitching step based on the predicted viewpoint are performed in this step. In the last step, the observer's current visual attention point position is predicted, and the model grid near the viewpoint is restored to a high-precision state.

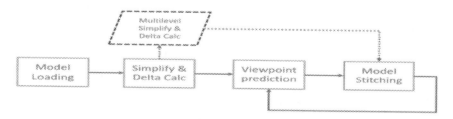

Fig. 1. Software-based predictive viewpoint following rendering framework in VR

2 Related Works

2.1 Visual Saliency Prediction

Visual saliency prediction is a research hotspot in computer vision. Inspired by the neuron structure of the primate visual system, in their paper Laurent Itti, proposed a classic visual attention model [4], which uses multi-scale image features to calculate saliency maps. After that, many models were proposed, such as the use of graph theory, the introduction of Markov absorption chain; layer extraction and training SVM for detection; the image is divided into local, regional, and global, and the center is obtained after multi-scale comparison peripheral histogram. Along with the progress of deep learning, the detection of saliency areas based on convolutional neural networks also appeared [5,10,12]. Sitzmann. [11] discussed the saliency of VR in static images. Xu, Proposed a gaze prediction model in dynamic360° immersion video [13].

2.2 Eye-Head Coordination

The eye tracker can measure eye movement and give the eye fixation position, but the cost of using the eye tracker is too high, plus it also has a certain delay, making it difficult to calculate the real-time eye focus position. Thus, software based real-time prediction is extremely important. Eye-head coordination refers to the coordinated movement between the eyes and head, which has been studied in the fields of cognitive science and Neuroscience. Yarbus [14] found that the eyes and head are in coordinated movement during gaze transfer, and there is a connection between eye-head coordination and visual cognition. In some studies [15], it was found that there is often a delay between eye movement and head movement, and eye movement usu-ally occurs before head movement. Most studies on eye-head coordination have focused on the relationship between the magnitude of head movement and eye movement, and found that the two are closely related. In VR systems, head motion information appears to be extra critical and important, based on a large number of head-eye movement data sets, Hu [3] obtained the correlation between head movement and eye position.

2.3 Model Simplification Algorithm and Hierarchical Rendering Method

Model reduction algorithm. The edge collapse algorithm was proposed by Hugues Hoppe [2] as a progressive mesh implementation in 1996. The basic operation process of edge collapse is to select an edge in the grid and delete it, and merge the vertices at both ends into one point. Each time the edge collapses, two triangles are reduced from the mesh. After this process is repeated, the number of triangles in the grid can be continuously reduced to simplify the model. Low Kok Lim [7] proposed an algorithm that uses clustering algorithm for model simplification in 1997, directly interpolating and merging the set of vertices considered to be close to each other in the grid, means that we can greatly reduce the number of vertices and faces.

Hierarchical rendering method. Face culling algorithms are widely used in modern rendering systems. The most basic method for face culling is back culling, further algorithms are occlusion culling and frustum culling, that is, objects and triangles that are not currently in the view cone are not rendered. In the level of detail (LOD) method, we set several models with different levels of fineness for the same object, or even in some cases not render the object, and the LOD method fits well with viewpoint prediction.

3   Content and Methods

The algorithm in this article is mainly comprised of two parts: the first part is view-point prediction, and the other part is to perform hierarchical rendering optimization based on the results of viewpoint prediction. The following text will explain these two aspects in detail.

Algorithm 1. Gaze Prediction

Input: $angleX, angleY$(set of head rotation degree), $time$(set), $velX, velY$(set of head move speed), $accX, accY$(set of head move acceleration), $meanGazeXStatic$, $HeadVelXThresMin$, $HeadVelXThresMax$
Output: $resultX, resultY$(degree of gaze line)
 1: cal $accMeanX, accMeanY$;
 2: cal $velStdX, velStdY$;
 3: **for** x in $angleX$ **do**
 4:     **if** $velX$ in $StaticRegion$ **then**
 5:         $resultX = meanX$
 6:     **else if** $velX$ in $IntentionalMoveRegion$ **then**
 7:         $resultX = calX()$
 8:     **else if** $velX$ in $SuddenMoveRegion$ **then**
 9:         $resultX = meanX$
10:     **end if**
11: **end for**
12: **for** y in $angleY$ **do**
13:     **if** $velY$ in $StaticRegion$ **then**
14:         $resultY = meanY$
15:     **else if** $velY$ in $IntentionalMoveRegion$ **then**
16:         $resultY = calY()$
17:     **else if** vel in $SuddenMoveRegion$ **then**
18:         $resultY = meanY$
19:     **end if**
20: **end for**

3.1   Viewpoint Prediction

The eye-head coordination model is predicted, mainly based on head movement information. In addition, the gaze behavior in VR is a complicated pattern, which is affected by various factors such as content, task, delay and so on. The eye-head coordination model used in this article can explain the real-time gaze behavior of users when exploring the virtual environment in chronological order. The specific formula [3] is as follows:

$$x_g(t) = \alpha_x \cdot v_{hx}(t + \Delta t_{x1}) + \beta_x \cdot a_{hx(t)} + F_x(t + \Delta t_{x2}) + G_x(t) + H_x(t) \quad (1)$$

$$y_g(x) = \alpha_y \cdot v_{hy}(t + \Delta t_{y1}) + F_y(t + \Delta t_{y2}) + G_y(t) + H_y(t) \quad (2)$$

The model separates horizontal and vertical calculations, and combines the angular velocity and angular acceleration of head movement, delay of eye movement and head movement, content, tasks and other factors. $\alpha_x, \alpha_y, \beta_x$ are the influencing coefficients of various factors, which are solved by further fitting the data. The model is divided into three independent areas of static, intentional movement and sudden movement according to the angular velocity of the head movement. When in the static area or sudden movement area, the user's gaze position is less relevant to the head movement, and is mainly affected by the scene content, the user's psychology, and the influence of factors such as state, emergencies, etc., while in the intentional movement area, the position of the user's gaze on the screen is strongly linearly related to the rotation speed of the head. Algorithm 1 shows the pseudo code of the final prediction algorithm.

3.2   Hierarchical Rendering

In order to cooperate with the viewpoint prediction algorithm, the graded rendering algorithm of this article should meet the following requirements:

1. The rendering fineness can be determined according to the distance of the object from the viewpoint.
2. The rendering fineness of only part of the object can be reduced.
3. Do not add too much computing burden to the CPU.

To this end, the following article designed a multi-precision stitching algorithm, which is based on real-time grid degeneration, and drawing on the idea of LOD. This algorithm will simplify the model mesh to different levels when the model is first loaded, and save the simplified model and the vertices and faces that have changed during the simplification of each level, so that any part of the model mesh can be restored to high precision when necessary. This algorithm consists of simplification and splicing.

The simplification algorithm is similar to the edge collapse algorithm, but vertices are deleted instead of edges. The algorithm first scans all the vertices of the model, if the vertices are on a sharp edge or corner, they are important for maintaining the outline of the model and cannot be deleted, otherwise, check if

---

Algorithm 2. Simplify

Input: V(set of vertices), T(set of triangles),*threshold*
Output: V'(new set), T''(new set), *delta*(dealt data needed by the recovery algorithm)
1: $set\ C=\{\}$; $set\ D=\{\}$; $set\ A=\{\}$;
2: **for** v in V **do**
3:     bool $canCull=true$;
4:     **for** $t1,t2$ in $t \in T\ |$ t contains v **do**
5:         **if** $angle(t1,t2) <threshold$ **then**
6:             $canCull=false$;
7:             *break*;
8:         **end if**
9:     **end for**
10:    **if** $canCull$ **then**
11:        **for** $v2$ in $x \in V\ |$ x and v are connected by an edge **do**
12:            **if** $v2$ in C **then**
13:                $canCull=false$;
14:                *break*;
15:            **end if**
16:        **end for**
17:    **end if**
18:    **if** $canCull$ **then**
19:        C.add(v);
20:    **end if**
21: **end for**

---

any vertex is directly connected to it, if none of them are marked deleted, the vertex is marked as remove-able. After a round of scanning, some vertices will be marked showing that they can be deleted. Traverse this part again and delete all the triangular faces containing these vertices. For each deleted vertex and the surrounding triangular faces, you will get a closed polygon hole. For this hole, choose a vertex, and divide the polygon into a series of triangles through the diagonal line from that point, and add it to the model mesh as a new triangle. The combination of the deleted vertex, the deleted face around the vertex, and the newly added triangular face that fills the hole of the vertex is saved for use in stitching. This simplification algorithm can be run repeatedly to generate multiple levels of simplification, the pseudo code is in Algorithm 2.

Another important part is the stitching algorithm. Compared with the simplified algorithm, the stitching algorithm is relatively simple. After the viewpoint prediction algorithm gives the observer's current viewpoint position, scan the delta set of objects near the viewpoint, find the vertices within a certain distance from the viewpoint, and restore them and the triangles around them to the simplified model according to the stored data.

4   Experiment Results and Analysis

This article implements the model in Unity, in order to compare the rendering performance before and after enabling hierarchical rendering, we recorded the CPU usage, GPU usage, video memory usage and memory usage under two conditions.

As shown in Fig. 2, the model on the screen will be significantly simplified after hierarchical rendering is enabled. Since the line of sight is on the roof of the cabin, there is no obvious change in the details of the roof, but the model of the tower on the left is obviously simplified.

Fig. 2. (a) Without hierarchical rendering, (b)With hierarchical rendering

After separately running the program with hierarchical rendering enabled and following the same route in the scene, we recorded the following data in Table 1 (the system rest load has been removed). It can be seen from the table that the GPU occupancy rate has dropped significantly after the hierarchical rendering is turned on, indicating that our algorithm can indeed further reduce the number of rendered triangles on the existing rendering optimization technology to reduce the GPU load. But it is also worth noting that the CPU usage, memory usage and video memory usage have all increased. After further testing, we found that the CPU-intensive operation is not viewpoint prediction or model stitching, but the process of returning new triangle data to the Unity engine after model stitching is completed. This process involves not only copying an array, but also recalculating normal and texture coordinates. It also takes CPU cycles to transfer vertex data from memory to video memory. It can be seen that frequent and large-scale modification of model data in 3D rendering is very expensive behavior.

The increase in memory usage is because when the simplified algorithm saves incremental data, it must write some auxiliary data, such as indexes, for subsequent correct stitching, which causes the model to occupy more memory. As for the increase in the amount of video memory, after analysis, it may be triggering a certain cache mechanism of the GPU, which saved some of the transition model data to reduce the amount of memory and video memory data transfer, but because of the fact that our model changes are too many, this mechanism fails to effectively reduce our vertex transmission overhead.

Table 1. System load changes when hierarchical rendering On and Off

Data	Off	On	Rate
CPU	17%	28%	+62%
GPU	80%	50%	−37%
Memory	2 GB	3.8 GB	+90%
Video memory	1.1 GB	1.7 GB	+54%

5 Conclusion

The hierarchical rendering method in this article achieves automatic grid-level accuracy adjustment by mixing LOD and model degeneracy methods. At the same time, with the help of the viewpoint detection algorithm, we can use a more aggressive optimization algorithm to further reduce the number of triangles that the GPU needs to render based on the existing optimization algorithm. In the case of highly complex scenes or heavy rendering loads such as VR, GPU performance becomes a bottleneck, the group's hierarchical rendering method can effectively reduce the GPU load at the cost of CPU load, thereby achieving a higher display frame rate and a smoother visual experience.

Acknowledgement. This work was supported in part by the National Key Research and Development Program of China under Grant 2018YFF0300903, in part by the National Natural Science Foundation of China under Grant 61872241 and Grant 61572316, and in part by the Science and Technology Commission of Shanghai Municipality under Grant 15490503200, Grant 18410750700, Grant 17411952600, and Grant 16DZ0501100.

References

1. Borji, A., Itti, L.: State-of-the-art in visual attention modeling. IEEE Trans. Pattern Anal. Mach. Intell. **35**(1), 185–207 (2013)
2. Hoppe, H.: Progressive meshes. In: International Conference on Computer Graphics and Interactive Techniques, pp. 99–108 (1996)
3. Hu, Z., Zhang, C., Li, S., Wang, G., Manocha, D.: SGaze: a data-driven eye-head coordination model for realtime gaze prediction. IEEE Trans. Vis. Comput. Graph. **25**(5), 2002–2010 (2019)
4. Itti, L., Koch, C., Niebur, E.: A model of saliency-based visual attention for rapid scene analysis. IEEE Trans. Pattern Anal. Mach. Intell. **20**(11), 1254–1259 (1998)
5. Kamel, A., Sheng, B., Yang, P., Li, P., Shen, R., Feng, D.D.: Deep convolutional neural networks for human action recognition using depth maps and postures. IEEE Trans. Syst. Man Cybern. Syst. **49**(9), 1806–1819 (2019)
6. Karambakhsh, A., Kamel, A., Sheng, B., Li, P., Yang, P., Feng, D.D.: Deep gesture interaction for augmented anatomy learning. Int. J. Inform. Manag. **45**, 328–336 (2019)
7. Low, K., Tan, T.: Model simplification using vertex-clustering. In: Interactive 3d Graphics and Games, pp. 75–82 (1997)

8. Lu, P., Sheng, B., Luo, S., Jia, X., Wu, W.: Image-based non-photorealistic rendering for realtime virtual sculpting. Multimedia Tools Appl. **74**(21), 9697–9714 (2014). https://doi.org/10.1007/s11042-014-2146-4

9. Meng, X., et al.: A video information driven football recommendation system. Comput. Electr. Eng. **85**, 106699 (2020)

10. Pan, J., Sayrol, E., Giroinieto, X., Mcguinness, K., Oconnor, N.E.: Shallow and deep convolutional networks for saliency prediction. In: Computer Vision and Pattern Recognition, pp. 598–606 (2016)

11. Sitzmann, V., et al.: Saliency in vr: how do people explore virtual environments. IEEE Trans. Vis. Comput. Graph. **24**(4), 1633–1642 (2018)

12. Sheng, B., Li, P., Zhang, Y., Mao, L.: Greensea: visual soccer analysis using broad learning system. IEEE Trans. Cybern., pp. 1–15, May 2020

13. Xu, Y., et al.: Gaze prediction in dynamic 360 immersive videos. In: Computer Vision and Pattern Recognition, pp. 5333–5342 (2018)

14. Yarbus, A.: Eye Movements and Vision. New York (1967)

15. Zangemeister, W.H., Stark, L.: Active head rotations and eye-head coordination. Ann. N.Y. Acad. Sci. **374**(1), 540–559 (1981)

16. Zhang, P., Zheng, L., Jiang, Y., Mao, L., Li, Z., Sheng, B.: Tracking soccer players using spatio-temporal context learning under multiple views. Multimedia Tools Appl. **77**(15), 18935–18955 (2017). https://doi.org/10.1007/s11042-017-5316-3

Reinforcement Learning-Based Redirection Controller for Efficient Redirected Walking in Virtual Maze Environment

Wataru Shibayama and Shinichi Shirakawa$^{(\boxtimes)}$ (iD)

Graduate School of Environment and Information Sciences,
Yokohama National University, Yokohama, Japan
xsssx841@gmail.com, shirakawa-shinichi-bg@ynu.ac.jp

Abstract. Redirected walking (RDW) is a locomotion technique used in virtual reality (VR) that enables users to explore large virtual environments in a limited physical space. Existing RDW techniques mainly work on the obstacle-free physical spaces larger than a square of four-meter sides. To improve usability, RDW techniques that work on comparatively smaller physical spaces with obstacles need to be developed. In RDW, users are restricted to the physical space by redirection techniques (RETs) that control the view of the head-mounted display. Reinforcement learning, a branch of machine learning techniques, is advantageous in designing efficient redirection controllers compared to manual design. In this paper, we propose a reinforcement learning-based redirection controller (RLRC) that aims to realize an efficient RDW in small physical spaces. The controller is trained using the simulator and is expected to select an appropriate redirection technique from the current state and route information of the virtual environment. We evaluate the RLRC with simulator and user tests in a virtual maze in several physical spaces, including a square physical space of four-meter sides with an obstacle, and a square physical space of two-meter sides. The simulator test shows that the proposed RLRC can reduce the number of undesirable redirection techniques performed compared with existing methods. The proposed RLRC is found to be effective in the square physical space of two-meter sides in the user test.

Keywords: Redirected walking · Reinforcement learning · Virtual environment · Virtual reality

1 Introduction

Virtual reality (VR) has become popular with the development of reasonable head-mounted displays (HMDs). Locomotion techniques that enable users to experience a large virtual environment in limited physical spaces have recently

© Springer Nature Switzerland AG 2020
N. Magnenat-Thalmann et al. (Eds.): CGI 2020, LNCS 12221, pp. 33–45, 2020.
https://doi.org/10.1007/978-3-030-61864-3_4

attracted attention. A simple solution is to use a keyboard or a gamepad for long-distance moves, or to allow teleportation in the virtual environment. However, these techniques reduce the immersiveness of the VR experience. Specialized devices such as omnidirectional treadmills have been developed, which enable completely free walking in limited physical spaces, but these devices are expensive and have high installation costs.

Redirected walking (RDW) [12] is a promising technology to realize free walking at low costs without compromising immersion. In RDW, users are guided not to get out of the tracked area and avoid collisions with physical walls and obstacles by controlling the views in the HMDs. The methods to redirect users are called redirection techniques (RETs); various algorithms for controlling RETs have been proposed. A simple algorithm is steer-to-center (S2C), which applies RETs such that users always head to the center of the physical space. Sophisticated algorithms [10,18] can control RETs more effectively than S2C by predicting the user's future path from their current state. However, the computational costs of these algorithms are too expensive for real-time calculations. A few recent works have attempted to construct a control rule for RETs using reinforcement learning algorithms to realize efficient RDWs with reasonable computational costs. The reinforcement learning-based approach trains a redirection controller in the training phase; the trained controller can then be applied to control the RETs at a low computational cost. The steer-to-optimal-target (S2OT) algorithm proposed in [9] is a redirection method using reinforcement learning and shows promising performance. The controller in S2OT selects the target area in the physical space, and the user is guided to move to the selected area using RETs. Obstacles in the physical space are not considered in S2OT. The redirection controllers proposed in [1,15] directly control the parameters of RETs, and the controller is trained by a reinforcement learning algorithm. However, these methods are applied in relatively large physical spaces ($>4 \times 4$ m^2) in relatively simple virtual environments without complicated routes such as mazes; moreover, they are only evaluated using simulators. It is not clear whether the existing reinforcement learning-based approaches for RDWs can handle small physical spaces or physical space with obstacles. Developing advanced reinforcement learning-based redirection controllers and evaluating them in various situations are important to realize efficient RDWs.

In this paper, we propose a reinforcement learning-based redirection controller (RLRC) for RDWs. The policy for controlling the RETs is directly trained in the simulator with a virtual maze environment; this leverages the route information to select the RETs. The efficiency of the proposed RLRC is verified with simulator and user tests comprising several types of physical spaces, including square physical spaces of 4×4 m^2 with an obstacle, and 2×2 m^2 that have not been considered in previous studies. The experimental results of the simulator test shows that the RLRC can reduce the number of undesirable redirection techniques compared with S2C and S2OT. Moreover, the RLRC was observed to be effective in the 2×2 m^2 physical space of the user test. Our results imply that the reinforcement learning-based approach is promising for RDWs in various physical spaces.

2   Algorithms for Redirected Walking

Redirected walking (RDW) [12] was proposed for free walking in virtual environments within limited physical spaces. Applying subtle manipulations, called redirection techniques (RETs), to the view on the HMD, the users unconsciously change the movement directions or speeds. RETs are used to keep users away from physical boundaries such as the border of the tracked area or walls in the physical space. RETs contain rotation, curvature, translation redirections and reset techniques. Rotation and translation redirections control the user's rotation angle and walk speed, respectively. Curvature redirection is applied to turn the user's walking paths to the right or left. It creates a situation where users go straight in virtual environments but walk on curved paths in the physical space. These RETs have detection thresholds to adjust the redirection strength [14]. In addition, if the user is likely to collide with a physical boundary, a reset technique is activated to reorient or transfer the user toward a safe direction or position.

Various redirection algorithms to control RETs have been proposed. Two simple algorithms are the S2C and steer-to-orbit (S2O). The S2C algorithm controls the RETs so that a user always walks toward the center of the tracked area, and the S2O algorithm controls the RETs so that a user goes around in circles in the tracked area. In addition, both algorithms activate the reset technique if the user moves out of a predetermined safe area. These simple algorithms may apply unnecessary RETs and lead to VR sickness. Therefore, more sophisticated algorithms, such as fully optimized redirected walking for constrained environment (FORCE) [18] and model predictive control redirection (MPCRed) [10], have been developed to control RETs more efficiently. These algorithms predict the walking paths from the user's position, direction, and route on the virtual environment, and decide optimal RETs dynamically. Furthermore, Lee et al. [9] pointed out that the computational cost of these dynamic methods is expensive, and proposed the S2OT algorithm using reinforcement learning. In S2OT, the tracked area is divided into a 6×6 grid; grid points are set as the target candidates to redirect users. The policy for selecting the optimal target area is trained using double deep Q-learning [4]. Experimental results in [9] show that S2OT could reduce the frequency of the reset technique. In contrast to S2OT, the method proposed in [15] trains the policy for controlling the parameters of the RETs using reinforcement learning.

The redirection algorithms discussed so far assume square and obstacle-free areas as physical spaces, but obstacles such as furniture and pillars are present in an actual room. Chen et al. [2] proposed the steer-to-farthest (S2F) algorithm to handle such situations. The S2F algorithm applies RETs to redirect a user toward a safe direction minimized by a predefined cost function. Thomas et al. [16] defined the artificial potential function (APF) [7] that represents the degree of walkable area in the physical space and redirects a user to walk along the gradient direction of the APF.

3   Reinforcement Learning-Based Redirection Controller (RLRC)

We train the controller of RETs using reinforcement learning on a simulator. The policy determines the timing and the type of RETs from current observations, e.g., the position and direction of the user in the physical and virtual environments. Reinforcement learning can obtain policies that maximize the expected cumulative reward through trial-and-error by an agent. The state/action spaces and the reward function should be specified to apply a reinforcement learning algorithm. Information on walking paths can help control the RETs efficiently in FORCE [18] and MPCRed [10]. Therefore, we incorporate route information in a virtual environment into the state observation in reinforcement learning.

3.1   Problem Formulation

Here, we describe the design of the state/action spaces and the reward function for reinforcement learning.

State: We use three types of state information: the user's surrounding state in the physical space p, the state in the virtual environment v, and the map state in the virtual environment m. The state variables, p and v, contain distances to the boundaries or obstacles in 36 directions around the user, measured up to 8 m ahead. The distances are normalized within $[0, 1]$, and the dimension of p and v is 36. We note that normalizing the state values would contribute the stable training. We denote state vectors as $p = (p_0, \ldots, p_{35})^{\mathrm{T}}$ and $v = (v_0, \ldots, v_{35})^{\mathrm{T}}$, where p_i and v_i indicate the distances in the ith directions in the physical and virtual environments, respectively. The map state m represents the shape of the route. The route in the virtual environment can be seen as a graph in which the vertices indicate intersections and corners, and the edges indicate the paths and the distances between them. In this work, we assume that the paths in the virtual environment intersect orthogonally. This type of virtual environment is also used in [9,10]. Under this assumption, we then extract the subgraph consisting of vertices within two hops from the vertex in front of the user's position, where the vertices in the backward direction of the user are ignored. The distances between the vertices are used as the state variables of the map state. In addition, we add the distance to the vertex in front of the user's position. Figure 1(left) shows an illustration of the subgraph and the corresponding variables. The map state is given by a 13-dimensional vector as $m = (m_0, \ldots, m_{12})^{\mathrm{T}}$. If the path corresponding to m_i does not exist, the value is set to $m_i = 0$. The distance between the vertices is normalized within $[0, 1]$. Figure 1(right) shows an example of the extracted subgraph. In this case, the map state vector is given by $m = (0, 0, 0, 0, 0, m_5, 0, m_7, 0, 0, m_{10}, m_{11}, m_{12})^{\mathrm{T}}$. Existing redirection controllers using reinforcement learning [1,9,15] only use the user's spatial information and not use map state information. The overall state vector is given by $s = (p^{\mathrm{T}}, v^{\mathrm{T}}, m^{\mathrm{T}})^{\mathrm{T}} \in \mathbb{R}^{85}$.

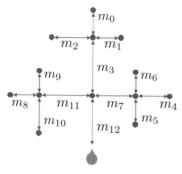

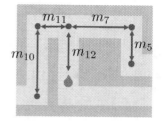

Graphical representation of paths in the virtual environment

Example of a map state

Fig. 1. Map state in the virtual environment

Action: We control the RETs directly as the action in reinforcement learning. The following six actions are used in this work: activating the rotational RET to the right (a_1), activating the rotational RET to the left (a_2), deactivating the rotational RET (a_3), activating the reset technique (a_4), deactivating the reset technique (a_5), and do nothing (a_6). In the experiment, we make action decisions every six steps (frames). If both the rotational RET and the reset technique is activated, the reset technique is applied preferentially. The action "do nothing (a_6)" means that no manipulation is applied at that time steps even if the rotational RET or the reset technique is activated.

The rotational RET and the reset technique used in this work are based on the ones used in MPCRed [10]. The rotational RET consists of the rotation and curvature redirections, and modifies the user's rotation by the following additive angle: $\Delta\hat{\phi} = \max(g_C S_R, (1 - g_R)Y_R)$, where S_R and Y_R are the user's real movement angle and yaw rotation per time step, respectively, and g_C and g_R indicate the curvature and rotation gains, respectively. The gain parameters are decided according to [14]. The sign of g_C determines the direction of the redirection, and we set $|g_C| = 0.13$. Regarding the rotational gain, we set $g_R = 0.67$ if the redirection direction and the user's rotation direction are the same; otherwise $g_R = 1.24$. We use 2:1-turn [17] as the reset technique. When the reset technique is applied, the user turns in the physical space, while the view of the virtual environment rotates by twice the physical amount. It means that the rotational gain of the turn is two. For instance, if the user rotates by 180°, the view of the virtual environment is unchanged since the rotation of the viewpoint becomes 360°.

Reward Function: The reward function employed is the sum of the six elements shown in Table 1. The positive values are added when the user stays away from walls (boundaries) and obstacles in the physical space, or when the rotational RET is not applied. The negative values are added when the direction

Table 1. Elements of the reward function. The symbol $r_{\min}$ indicates the minimum distance to the boundary or obstacles in the physical space, given by $r_{\min} = \min_i r_i$, and t_{reset} is the number of elapsed steps from the start of applying the reset technique.

Description	Condition	Value	Grant frequency
(1) Position in physical space	–	$6 \times 10^{-2} \times r_{\min}^2$	Every step
(2) Rotational RET usage	If no RET is applied	2×10^{-4}	Every step
(3) Rotational RET switch	If the direction of RET is switched	-1×10^{-3}	Every action
(4) Reset technique usage	If the reset technique is activated	-1.6	Every action
(5) Activating time of reset technique	–	$\frac{-1 \times 10^{-2}}{60} \times t_{\text{reset}}$	Every step
(6) Contacting walls or obstacles	If the user collides with walls or obstacles	-0.9	Every step

of the rotational RET is switched, the reset technique is applied, or the user collides with walls and obstacles in the physical space. We strongly penalize the use of the reset technique compared to the rotational RET, because the reset technique is not preferred from the viewpoint of enhancing immersiveness of VR.

3.2   Reinforcement Learning Algorithm

The goal of reinforcement learning is to find a policy that maximizes the expected cumulative reward. We use the proximal policy optimization (PPO) [13] algorithm implemented in the Unity ML-Agents Toolkit (Beta) [5][1]. In the PPO, the policy and value function is represented by a neural network. The neural network used in this work consists of five fully connected hidden layers with 128 units. The activation function of each hidden unit is Swish $f(x) = x \cdot \text{sigmoid}(\beta x)$ [11], which is the default setting of the ML-Agent Toolkit, where $\beta = 1.0$. We use the Adam [8] optimizer to train the neural network. The reinforcement learning algorithm is expected to obtain an optimal policy for RETs that prevents collision with walls or obstacles in the physical space through the training.

3.3   Simulator for Redirected Walking

We implemented a simulator for RDW using Unity[2]. Figure 2 shows the physical space and the virtual environment in the simulator. The virtual environment is

---

[1] https://github.com/Unity-Technologies/ml-agents.
[2] https://unity.com/.

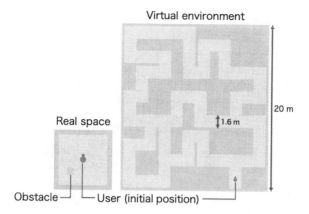

Virtual environment

Real space

20 m

1.6 m

Obstacle ─── └── User (initial position) ───────┘

Fig. 2. Physical space and virtual environment on our simulator

the maze used in [10], and has 1.6 m wide routes in a 20×20 m^2 space. We assume that the shape of the physical space is square. The size of the physical space is $n_p \times n_p$ square meter, and the 0.5×0.5 m^2 obstacle can be located at any position. We note that no obstacle is placed if $n_p \leq 3$ to keep the sufficient walkable area. The redirection controller is trained using this simulator. During the training, the user follows the route as much as possible in the virtual environment. The user will turn along with the route if a corner is reached. At T-junctions, the user turns right or left randomly. The movements of the user are synchronized between the virtual and physical environments. The movement speed of the user is set to 0.34 [m/sec]. The user position is reset to the initial position when 18,000 steps with 60 frames per second (FPS), corresponding to 5 min in real time elapse. In addition, the position of an obstacle and the width $n_p \in \{2, 3, 4, 5, 6\}$ of the physical space are reset randomly.

4   Experimental Evaluation

We evaluate the proposed RLRC with the simulator and user tests. We use the trained redirection controller described in Sect. 3 for both the simulator and the user tests. We apply the redirection controller to four types of square physical spaces, 10×10 m^2, 4×4 m^2, 4×4 m^2 with an obstacle, and 2×2 m^2, and compare the number of reset techniques per minute and the viewpoint rotation angle per second as the performance measures. The viewpoint rotation angle increases by applying the rotational RET. In both performance measures, smaller values indicate better performance.

4.1   Simulator Test

Experimental Setting. We compare the proposed RLRC with S2C and S2OT [9], and follow the experimental setting described in [9] as possible. The

Table 2. Mean and standard deviation of the number of reset techniques per minute [resets/min] in the simulator test. The S2OT results are the values reported in [9].

	10×10 m^2	4×4 m^2	4×4 m^2 + obstacle	2×2 m^2
S2C	0.83 ± 0.14	5.41 ± 0.65	7.61 ± 2.02	14.4 ± 1.60
S2OT [9]	1.15	4.43	–	–
RLRC	$\mathbf{0.56 \pm 0.25}$	$\mathbf{3.77 \pm 0.34}$	$\mathbf{4.44 \pm 0.63}$	$\mathbf{11.9 \pm 0.30}$

Table 3. Mean and standard deviation of the viewpoint rotation angle per second [degrees/sec] in the simulator test. The S2OT results are the values reported in [9].

	10×10 m^2	4×4 m^2	4×4 m^2 + obstacle	2×2 m^2
S2C	6.98 ± 0.15	$\mathbf{5.47 \pm 0.38}$	5.98 ± 0.58	$\mathbf{4.65 \pm 0.35}$
S2OT [9]	9.76	9.52	–	–
RLRC	$\mathbf{5.23 \pm 0.36}$	6.22 ± 0.36	6.11 ± 0.34	5.78 ± 0.19

physical and virtual environments in the simulator are the same as shown in Fig. 2. The user in the simulator acts as explained in Sect. 3.3. For RLRC and S2C, the user moves for 5 min starting from the initial position. When the reset technique is activated, the user rotates by 120 [degree/sec]. We collect the data of 300 trials for each of the four types of physical spaces. The space at least 0.2 m away from the walls or an obstacle in the physical space is considered as the safe area for S2C. In S2C, when the user enters the unsafe area, the reset technique is applied, and the user rotates 180° in the physical space. For S2OT, we refer to the values reported in [9].

Result and Discussion. Tables 2 and 3 summarize the average numbers of reset techniques applied per minute and the average viewpoint rotation angle per second, respectively, for each algorithm in the different physical spaces described. We conducted the Wilcoxon rank sum test between the results of the RLRC and S2C with a significance level $p = 0.01$. If the statistical test shows performance difference, we denote the value of better performance with bold font.

Table 2 shows that the proposed RLRC outperforms S2C and S2OT in all physical space settings. RLRC can reduce the number of reset techniques by 51% and 15% compared with S2OT in the 10×10 m^2 and 4×4 m^2 physical space settings, respectively. This result implies that the design of the state/action spaces, and the reward function of the RLRC are effective; we believe that the map state information we introduced contributes in predicting the middle- or long-term behavior of the user and reducing the number of reset techniques. For instance, consider the situation when the user approaches a corner in the virtual environment and the user is located near the wall in the physical space; it is easy to predict the turn direction within a few seconds, and the controller can decide not to apply the reset technique. Comparing RLRC and S2C, RLRC can better

Fig. 3. Scene of the virtual environment redesigned for the user test

reduce the number of reset techniques in the 4×4 m^2 with an obstacle and 2×2 m^2 physical space settings that have not been considered in existing RDW methods using reinforcement learning [1,9,15]. Therefore, we have shown that reinforcement learning-based approaches have the potential to realize efficient RDWs in small physical spaces.

Regarding the result of the viewpoint rotation angle shown in Table 3, RLRC outperforms S2OT in both the 10×10 m^2 and 4×4 m^2 physical space settings, and reduces the angle by approximately 35–45%. However, RLRC performs better only in the 4×4 m^2 physical space setting compared with S2C. We assume that RLRC concentrates in reducing the number of reset techniques rather than the rotation angle. This is because applying the reset technique generates a strong negative reward, and reinforcement learning tends to avoid the reset technique instead of increasing the rotation angle. We note that reducing the number of reset techniques is more desirable than reducing the viewpoint rotation angle to maintain the immersiveness of VR.

4.2   User Test

Experimental Setting. We evaluated the trained redirection controller with human users; the users employ RDW with the trained controller and experience the VR. We implement the virtual environment shown in Fig. 3, in which the route is the same as the one used in the simulator test. We prepare three conditions of the physical space, 4×4 m^2, 4×4 m^2 with an obstacle, and 2×2 m^2, where the obstacle is located at the relative position $(x, z) = (-0.6, -0.6)$ from the center. We compare RLRC and S2C, resulting in six test patterns (three physical spaces $\times$ two algorithms) being examined. When the reset technique is applied in the user test, a directional arrow is displayed in the HMD, and the user is prompted to rotate in that position. The frame rate is 60 FPS.

We recorded the number of reset techniques and the viewpoint rotation angles for performance comparison. In addition, the participants answered two questionnaires: Kennedy's Simulator Sickness Questionnaire (SSQ) [6] and the NASA Task Load Index (NASA-TLX) [3]. SSQ assesses VR sickness with a 4-point Likert scale (0: None–3: Severe), and the total score is calculated by following [6]. NASA-TLX assesses the task load with a 5-point Likert scale (1: None–5: Severe)

Table 4. Mean and standard deviation of the number of reset techniques per minute [resets/min] in the user test.

	4×4 m^2	4×4 m^2 + obstacle	2×2 m^2
S2C	5.33 ± 1.99	6.58 ± 1.93	12.1 ± 2.32
RLRC	4.30 ± 1.44	8.08 ± 2.34	$\mathbf{8.48 \pm 0.84}$

Table 5. Mean value standard deviation of the viewpoint rotation angle per second [degrees/sec] in the user test.

	4×4 m^2	4×4 m^2 + obstacle	2×2 m^2
S2C	7.67 ± 1.44	6.68 ± 1.03	6.14 ± 0.71
RLRC	6.44 ± 0.88	6.24 ± 1.01	$\mathbf{4.89 \pm 0.37}$

and evaluates the average scores of six evaluation items: (1) mental demand, (2) physical demand, (3) temporal demand, (4) performance for tasks, (5) effort, and (6) frustration level. The procedure of the user test is as follows:

1. **Consent and pre-questionnaire:** After declaring their assent in a consent form, the participants fill out the pre-SSQ to check their condition before performing tasks.
2. **Perform test:** The participants use an HTC VIVE HMD and then walk freely in the virtual environment shown in Fig. 3 for three minutes.
3. **Post-questionnaires and break:** The participants fill out the post-SSQ and NASA-TLX, and then take a break. If a task pattern remains, they continue the test.

Nineteen participants (18 male and 1 female) took part in the user test, with ages between 20 and 25 years. Each participant underwent testing on randomly selected physical space settings. The participants experienced both RLRC and S2C in each selected physical space. The order of the tests was randomized. At least eight data points were collected for each physical space and algorithm. We used a laptop with an Intel Core i7-7820HK CPU, 32 GB RAM, and a GeForce GTX 1070 GPU for the user test, and confirmed that the redirection controllers work on this laptop in real-time.

Result and Discussion. Tables 4 and 5 summarize the number of reset techniques per minute and the viewpoint rotation angle per second in the user test. We conducted the Wilcoxon rank sum test ($p = 0.01$) between the results of RLRC and S2C as well as the simulator test.

It can be seen from Table 4 that RLRC outperforms S2C in the 2×2 m^2 physical space setting in terms of the number of reset techniques. For other physical space settings, there is no statistical significance between RLRC and S2C. The performance improvement of RLRC against S2C is not highlighted as

Table 6. Total SSQ scores calculated by following [6]

	4×4 m²	4×4 m² + obstacle	2×2 m²
pre-SSQ	8.88 ± 6.30	7.90 ± 8.46	5.40 ± 5.95
S2C	36.2 ± 66.1	47.2 ± 53.6	19.5 ± 13.1
RLRC	25.3 ± 26.7	$28.5 \pm 19.4.7$	32.4 ± 31.7

in the simulator test. One reason is the discrepancy of the movements between the simulated user and actual participants. The simulated user always moves mechanically, while human participants naturally make motions like swaying or looking around even when going straight. Since such non-mechanical movements do not appear in the training phase using the simulator, reinforcement learning may not have learned an optimal policy for the user test.

Regarding the viewpoint rotation angle, a similar trend as the number of reset techniques is observed. RLRC outperforms S2C in the 2×2 m² physical space setting. We also observed a tendency of the viewpoint rotation angle to decrease when the number of reset techniques increases. The S2C algorithm applies the rotational RET when the user does not face the center of the physical space. Since human users often change direction even when going straight, the total duration of applying the redirection increases. We assume that RLRC is more robust than S2C in such a situation.

From the user test, we can verify that the trained redirection controller in the simulator is valid for real-life situations, and works well in small physical spaces. Finally, we provide the SSQ results in Table 6. We do not observe any significant differences between RLRC and S2C in the total SSQ score and all six items of the NASA-TLX. The NASA-TLX results have been omitted for conciseness.

5   Conclusions

In this paper, we focused on RDW in virtual maze environments, and developed a reinforcement learning-based redirection controller. The proposed RLRC leverages the map state information and trains the controller using PPO. We conducted simulator and user tests, and compared the performance with existing methods. In the simulator test, four types of square physical spaces were examined, including physical spaces of 4×4 m² with an obstacle, and of 2×2 m². The experimental results of the simulator test suggest that RLRC is superior to S2C, particularly in terms of the number of reset techniques. In addition, we confirmed that the proposed RLRC can realize RDW in the user test, despite using the trained controller on the simulator without additional tuning. In the user test, RLRC can reduce the number of reset techniques and the viewpoint rotation angles in the 2×2 m² physical space better compared to S2C. Our experimental evaluation implies that the reinforcement learning-based approach has the potential to realize an efficient RDW in small physical spaces.

To improve the efficiency of RDW in the user test, a possible future work is to make the behavior of the simulated user in the training phase more realistic, e.g., adding noise to the state and action, and using real paths collected from actual user behavior. Furthermore, it might be possible to construct a universal redirection controller by using various virtual environments during the training.

References

1. Chang, Y., Matsumoto, K., Narumi, T., Tanikawa, T., Hirose, M.: Redirection controller using reinforcement learning. arXiv preprint arXiv:1909.09505 (2019)
2. Chen, H., Chen, S., Rosenberg, E.S.: Redirected walking in irregularly shaped physical environments with dynamic obstacles. In: 2018 IEEE Conference on Virtual Reality and 3D User Interfaces (VR), pp. 523–524 (2018)
3. Hart, S.G., Staveland, L.E.: Development of NASA-TLX (Task Load Index): results of empirical and theoretical research. Adv. Psychol. **52**, 139–183 (1988)
4. Hasselt, H.V., Guez, A., Silver, D.: Deep reinforcement learning with double Q-learning. In: Thirtieth AAAI Conference on Artificial Intelligence (2016)
5. Juliani, A., et al.: Unity: A general platform for intelligent agents. arXiv preprint arXiv:1809.02627 (2018)
6. Kennedy, R.S., Lane, N.E., Berbaum, K.S., Lilienthal, M.G.: Simulator sickness questionnaire: an enhanced method for quantifying simulator sickness. Int. J. Aviat. Psychol. **3**(3), 203–220 (1993)
7. Khatib, O.: Real-time obstacle avoidance for manipulators and mobile robots. In: 1985 IEEE International Conference on Robotics and Automation, vol. 2, pp. 500–505 (1985)
8. Kingma, D.P., Ba, J.: Adam: a method for stochastic optimization. In: International Conference on Learning Representations (ICLR) (2015)
9. Lee, D., Cho, Y., Lee, I.: Real-time optimal planning for redirected walking using deep Q-learning. In: 2019 IEEE Conference on Virtual Reality and 3D User Interfaces (VR), pp. 63–71 (2019)
10. Nescher, T., Huang, Y.Y., Kunz, A.: Planning redirection techniques for optimal free walking experience using model predictive control. In: 2014 IEEE Symposium on 3D User Interfaces (3DUI), pp. 111–118 (2014)
11. Ramachandran, P., Zoph, B., Le, Q.V.: Swish: a self-gated activation function. arXiv preprint arXiv:1710.05941 (2017)
12. Razzaque, S., Kohn, Z., Whitton, M.C.: Redirected walking. In: Eurographics 2001 - Short Presentations. Eurographics Association (2001)
13. Schulman, J., Wolski, F., Dhariwal, P., Radford, A., Klimov, O.: Proximal policy optimization algorithms. arXiv preprint arXiv:1707.06347 (2017)
14. Steinicke, F., Bruder, G., Jerald, J., Frenz, H., Lappe, M.: Estimation of detection thresholds for redirected walking techniques. IEEE Trans. Visual Comput. Graphics **16**(1), 17–27 (2010)
15. Strauss, R.R., Ramanujan, R., Becker, A., Peck, T.C.: A steering algorithm for redirected walking using reinforcement learning. IEEE Trans. Visual Comput. Graphics **26**(5), 1955–1963 (2020)
16. Thomas, J., Rosenberg, E.S.: A general reactive algorithm for redirected walking using artificial potential functions. In: 2019 IEEE Conference on Virtual Reality and 3D User Interfaces (VR), pp. 56–62 (2019)

17. Williams, B., et al.: Exploring large virtual environments with an HMD when physical space is limited. In: 4th Symposium on Applied Perception in Graphics and Visualization (APGV 2007), pp. 41–48 (2007)
18. Zmuda, M.A., Wonser, J.L., Bachmann, E.R., Hodgsons, E.: Optimizing constrained-environment redirected walking instructions using search techniques. IEEE Trans. Visual Comput. Graphics **19**(11), 1872–1884 (2013)

Locality-Aware Skinning Decomposition Using Model-Dependent Mesh Clustering

Fumiya Narita[1(✉)] and Tomohiko Mukai[2]

[1] Waseda University (now at Konami Digital Entertainment Co., Ltd.), Tokyo, Japan
fumiya.narita162@gmail.com
[2] Tokyo Metropolitan University, Tokyo, Japan

Abstract. Skinning decomposition is a popular technique to approximate a vertex animation for memory-efficient playback of complex shape deformation in real-time applications. However, conventional methods have several practical limitations related to computational performance and animation quality. We propose a skinning decomposition method that takes the locality of the skin weight into consideration. Our main idea is to decompose a skin mesh into multiple clusters and estimate the skin weight in each cluster to achieve local weight distribution with compact support. Our framework provides two types of mesh clustering algorithms for enhancing approximation accuracy. We also propose a frame-reduction algorithm for efficient computation. The experimental results indicate that our locality-aware approach produces a highly accurate approximation while significantly reducing the computation time.

Keywords: Skinning decomposition · Locality of skin weight · Linear blend skinning

1 Introduction

A detailed animation synthesis within a limited computational budget is required for real-time computer graphics (CG) applications, such as video games and virtual reality systems. For example, creating a soft body animation requires a per-vertex animation to represent a flexible and complex deformation. Fine-scale animation synthesis is time-consuming; a vertex animation technique (or vertex cache) is used to stream a prerecorded per-vertex animation data efficiently. For example, facial animation is often represented by the vertex animation data and involves precisely reproducing the facial expression of a real actor acquired using a performance capture system. This technology is employed in several commercial CG frameworks because of its straightforward data structure and fast computation. However, vertex animation leaves a large memory footprint and squeezes bandwidth during the streaming playback, which leads to an increase

Electronic supplementary material The online version of this chapter (https://doi.org/10.1007/978-3-030-61864-3_5) contains supplementary material, which is available to authorized users.

N. Magnenat-Thalmann et al. (Eds.): CGI 2020, LNCS 12221, pp. 46–58, 2020.
https://doi.org/10.1007/978-3-030-61864-3_5

in data size in proportion to the number of vertices and frames. Therefore, we use traditional compression techniques, such as quantization and keyframe reduction; however, more efficient data representation is required.

One practical solution is to convert a vertex animation into a skinned animation using a skinning decomposition method [4,5,9,13,19]. These methods approximate the source animation using a linear blend skinning (LBS) model, representing the vertex transformation as a weighted combination of a smaller number of bone transformations [14]. This approach successfully reduces data size. The approximated LBS model is ideal for real-time applications because of its efficient computation. Notably, the smooth skinning decomposition with rigid bones (SSDR) algorithm [9] is highly compatible with general game engines because it assumes the bone transformation to be rigid.

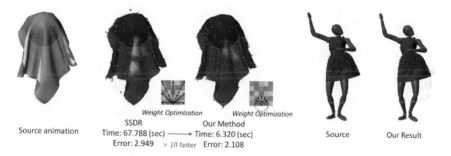

Fig. 1. The proposed method achieves faster skinning decomposition than the previous method by considering the locality of skin weight while reducing the approximation error using improved clustering algorithms (left). Approximation of long garment animation with a large number of bones in practical computation time (right).

However, the SSDR algorithm requires considerable computation time to approximate a long sequence of the high-resolution model with many bones. The computation time increases in proportion to the number of vertices, duration of the animation, and cube of the bones. Furthermore, the SSDR algorithm often results in the skin weights being scattered over the skin mesh, because it handles polygon vertices as a simple point cloud, thereby neglecting the topological information. Ideally, the skin weight should demonstrate a smooth, monomodal, and compact distribution, to allow intuitive post-editing by riggers.

To improve computation performance while preserving the approximation accuracy, we extend the SSDR algorithm by utilizing the locality of the skin weights. Our core idea is to divide the mesh into multiple regions, where skinning decomposition can be independently performed while considering the spatial coherence with surrounding regions. The main improvements to the SSDR algorithm are summarized as follows.

- Model-dependent manual selection of the mesh clustering algorithm for accurate approximation (Sect. 3.1)

- Localized skin-weight optimization through mesh clustering (Sect. 3.2)
- Frame-reduction based on the novel keyshape selection criterion for efficient computation (Sect. 3.3)

The proposed approach significantly improves the computational performance, reduces the numerical error, and generates smooth and intuitive bone transformations as shown in Fig. 1 (left), although the locality-aware algorithm does not theoretically guarantee the global optimality of the animation approximation. We experimentally confirmed that our method is capable of achieving high-precision data compression of production-ready assets with a practical computational cost as detailed in Sect. 4.

2   Background

2.1   Related Work

The concept of skinning decomposition was first proposed by James et al. [5]. It has since evolved into a more efficient method using dimensionality reduction [8], and into skeleton animation estimation methods [4,10]. The SSDR algorithm [9] is one of the most practical methods because of its high compatibility with general production pipelines. However, it has several aforementioned limitations.

In addition, the skinning decomposition has been used for example-based automatic rigging [3,4,10,16,17]. These techniques improve the locality and smoothness of the skin weight to enable manual adjustment of the estimated skin model. The Laplacian normalization term [10] is a typical approach for generating smooth skin weight distribution. However, this method merely minimizes the local dissimilarity in skin weight among adjacent vertices; it cannot prevent multimodal weight distribution over the mesh. Moreover, the conventional methods neglect the mesh topology information. For example, the left-front and right-back paws of a walking quadruped character can be bound to the same bone if these paws exhibit similar movement. Our method is designed for the LBS model [14]. Several skinning models, such as the dual quaternion skinning method [6], delta mush skinning method [12,15], and the optimized center of rotation method [11], have been proposed. Compared to these advanced techniques, animations generated through the LBS are prone to serious quality problems leading to the artifacts with defects, such as the candy-wrapper and elbow-collapse effects. Nevertheless, the LBS is widely deployed to approximate vertex animations because of its efficiency and compatibility with standard graphics frameworks. These advanced skinning models are not suitable for approximating the vertex animations of Elastic models such as clothes, because they are designed for articulated models.

2.2   Preliminaries

The SSDR algorithm solves the inverse problem of the LBS by calculating the skin weights and bone transformations that best approximate a source sequence of shape deformation [9]. This problem is formulated as a nonlinear minimization problem as follows:

$$\min_{w,R,T} \sum_{f=1}^{F} \sum_{i=1}^{V} \left| v_i^f - \sum_{b=1}^{B} w_{ib}(R_b^f p_i + T_b^f) \right|_2^2, \tag{1}$$

where F, V, and B represent the number of frames, mesh vertices, and manually specified bones used for approximation, respectively. p_i and v_i^f are the initial position and position at the f-th frame of the i-th vertex, respectively. R_b^f and T_b^f are the rotation matrix and translation vector of the b-th bone at the f-th frame. w_{ib} is the skin weight indicating the effect of the b-th bone on the i-th vertex. The following four constraints are imposed to satisfy the requirements of the LBS with rigid bones.

- The non-negative skin weight constraint: $\forall i, b, w_{ib} \geq 0$.
- The affinity constraint at each vertex: $\forall i, \sum_{b=1}^{B} w_{ib} = 1$.
- The sparsity constraint that restricts the number of bones affecting each vertex to less than K (typically $K = 4$): $\forall i, |\{w_{ib}|b = \{1, \cdots, B\}\}|_0 \leq K$, where $|\cdot|_\alpha$ denotes L_α norm.
- The bone transformation matrix R is constrained to $SO(3)$ rotation matrix: $\forall f, b, R_b^{f^T} R_b^f = I$, $\det(R_b^f) = 1$.

A threefold process is performed to efficiently solve this highly nonlinear problem. Firstly, the SSDR algorithm decomposes a mesh into B clusters by sorting vertices with similar transformations into the same cluster. Subsequently, the deformation of each cluster is approximated by a rigid transformation. Finally, the skin weight and bone transformation are alternately optimized using the block coordinate descent algorithm. The bone transformation can be efficiently realized using the closed-form analytic solution. On the other hand, the skin weight optimization for each vertex necessitates iterative computation to solve the quadratic programming (QP) problem whose computational order is $O(B^3)$; this is the main bottleneck of the SSDR algorithm. Furthermore, the computation time required to compose the matrices of the QP problem is directly proportional to V and F. To reduce these high computational costs, we utilize the mesh clustering to divide the mesh into multiple clusters in which skin weight optimization is independently performed. This approach decomposes the large QP problem into small-scale subproblems, thereby significantly reducing the overall computation time. We further reduce the computational redundancy by eliminating the repetitive frames in source animation.

3   Algorithm

To enhance the SSDR algorithm, we make three modifications as shown in Fig. 2. Our framework provides two different mesh clustering algorithms, one of which is manually selected depending on the characteristics of the source animation.

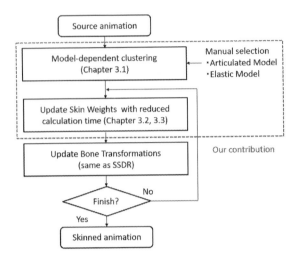

Fig. 2. Overview of our framework

The clustering results are used to identify the bones that bound to each vertex; they are also utilized to extract important frames from the source animation automatically. Finally, the skin weights and bone transformations are optimized using the same iterative procedure in SSDR.

3.1 Model-Dependent Mesh Clustering

The quality of the mesh clustering significantly affects the resultant approximation accuracy. Several clustering methods have been proposed in existing studies [4,5,9,10]; each of them is suitable for different types of source animations. For example, we experimentally validated that motion-driven vertex clustering [10] was reasonably practical for articulated models. The farthest point sampling [7,8], on the other hand, improved the quality of non-articulated and Elastic models, such as clothes and papers. Therefore, our framework facilitates the user with both algorithms for mesh clustering, the optimal one can be selected manually based on the visual observation of the source animation.

Articulated Models. Our system provides a modified version of the motion-driven vertex clustering method [10] for vertex animations indicating skeletal movement. The original algorithm repeatedly splits the cluster and approximates the cluster vertices' movement according to the rigid bone transformation. However, this process is redundant because each cluster is always split into two new clusters, even if the cluster movement can be well approximated with sufficient accuracy. Therefore, in this study, we aim to modify the procedure as detailed below and shown in Fig. 3.

1. Assume the entire model to be a single cluster
2. Estimate the rigid bone transformation that best approximates the movement of the vertices of each cluster
3. Split the cluster into two new clusters, and estimate their bone transformations when its approximation error is in the top $1/n$
4. Repeat processes 2 and 3 until there exist fewer than $n/(n+1)B$ clusters
5. Split the cluster of the worst approximation error into two clusters, and estimate their bone transformations
6. Repeat process 5 until the specified number B is achieved.

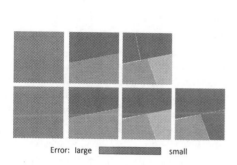

Error: large ▬▬▬▬ small

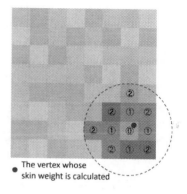

The vertex whose
skin weight is calculated

Fig. 3. Conceptual diagram of mesh clustering. The square model is divided into B clusters based on the original SSDR algorithm (upper) and our method (lower). The original method divides each cluster into two clusters whereas the proposed method focuses on splitting the clusters with large approximation errors.

Fig. 4. Locality constraints of skin weight. For the vertex whose skin weight is calculated, only clusters that are within the second neighbor of the cluster to which the vertex belongs are considered during the calculation of skin weights. In this conceptual diagram, each cluster is displayed in a random color. (Color figure online)

The natural number, n ($2 \leq n \leq B$), determines the error threshold that compels the clusters with relatively large approximation errors to be preferentially split; it was empirically set to 2 or 3 in our experiments. This procedure guarantees that the resulting number of clusters equates to the arbitrary number B. Although additional cost is required for the evaluation of approximation errors, the overhead is more than sufficiently compensated by the other modifications in the skin weight optimization.

Elastic Models. We employ farthest point sampling [7,8], which identifies bone positions as evenly as possible on the surface of the model. Subsequently, the skin weights are optimized according to the positional relationship between the bones and vertices. Finally, each vertex is bound to the bone with the largest skin weight. Note that we calculate the skin weights, which are proportional to the reciprocal of the distance for K-nearest clusters with the minimum Euclidean distance from the vertex. Although this straightforward approach yielded sufficient accuracy in our experiments, it can be improved using a more sophisticated method.

3.2 Locality-Aware Weight Optimization

Our method alternately optimizes the skin weights and bone transformation following the mesh clustering; thus, the bone transformation can be efficiently optimized because it has a closed-form analytic solution [9]. In contrast, skin weight optimization is formulated as a QP problem with nonlinear constraints that requires a higher cost for iterative computation. Moreover, the previous approaches optimize the skin weight of each vertex based on the assumption that all the bones affect each vertex regardless of the distance and mesh topology. Therefore, the same bone is often bound to spatially distant vertices, even when a slight similarity is observed in their movement.

Thiery et al. [19] proposed a skin weight optimization method to minimize as-rigid-as-possible deformation energy. This method makes the optimization problem small and sparse to achieve iterative computation by enforcing the sparsity constraint before the optimization. Similar to this approach, we use the mesh clustering information to limit the area of optimization, followed by achieving local and smooth skin weight distribution. We assume that a skin vertex is bound to the bones of the corresponding mesh cluster and its neighbors only, as illustrated in Fig. 4. The optimization procedure is summarized as follows.

1. For each vertex i, select the cluster b_i which i belongs to and its adjacent clusters $\mathrm{adj}(b_i) = \{b_{i,1}, \cdots, b_{i,B_i}\}$. The choice of $\mathrm{adj}(b_i)$ admits several options. Examples are the second neighbor clusters of bi or the clusters within a given geodesic distance from bi.
2. Optimize the skin weights of each vertex i only for the selected bones $b_i, b_{i,1}, \cdots, b_{i,B_i}$ by solving the QP problem.
3. Re-optimize the weight for K bones with the largest skin weight.

This approach improves the local and compact distribution of weight over the skin mesh. The dimension of the QP problem is reduced from B to B_i. In addition, the computation time is reduced regardless of the total number of bones since B_i is approximately constant and $B > (B_i + 1)$ holds.

3.3 Frame-Reduction

The computational cost of weight optimization is further reduced by utilizing the temporal coherence of the source animation if it includes repetitive or stationary deformation behavior. The existing method uses uniform sampling for eliminating the redundant frames from the source [1]. However, such a naive approach might (1) disregard the rapid deformation, and (2) extract redundant frames from the slow part of the source animation. Our frame reduction method adaptively selects the frames that differ significantly from the previously selected frames in sequential order. We define the frame dissimilarity based on the rigid bone transformation obtained from the mesh clustering, instead of conducting a per-vertex deformation evaluation to minimize the computational overhead. The dissimilarity measure σ is defined as follows:

$$\sigma(f_1, f_2) = \max_b \left| [R_b^{f_1} | T_b^{f_1}] - [R_b^{f_2} | T_b^{f_2}] \right|_2, \tag{2}$$

where $R_b^{f_1}$ and $T_b^{f_1}$ are the rotation matrix and translation vector of the b-th cluster at time f_1, and $R_b^{f_2}$ and $T_b^{f_2}$ are those at time f_2, respectively. The sequential search is commenced by adding the index of the first frame of the source animation to the set of selected frames $\mathcal{T}$. In this iterative process, the frame index f is added to $\mathcal{T}$ if it indicates larger dissimilarity from the selected frames $\mathcal{T}$ than a certain threshold, $\max_{f^* \in \mathcal{T}} \sigma(f, f^*) \geq \bar{\sigma}$. This process is sequentially repeated until the end of the source animation.

The dissimilarity threshold $\bar{\sigma}$ represents the tradeoffs between computational performance and approximation accuracy. The approximation accuracy can be improved using a low threshold value, which does not significantly reduce the number of frames. In contrast, the computational cost can be reduced by degrading the approximation accuracy while using a large threshold.

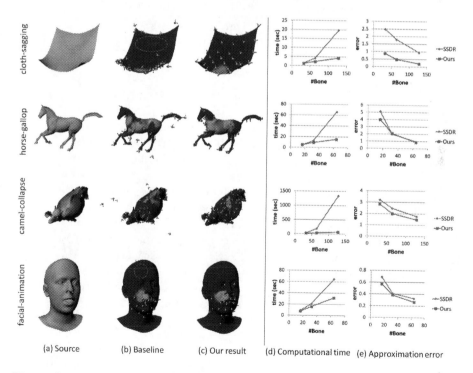

(a) Source   (b) Baseline   (c) Our result   (d) Computational time   (e) Approximation error

Fig. 5. Snapshots of the source animation. The results obtained from the baseline method and our proposed method are shown on the left side. The calculation time and approximation errors are compared on the right side.

4   Results

4.1   Comparison with Baseline Method

We conduct four experiments to evaluate the animation quality, skin weight distribution quality, and computational performance of our method. The original SSDR algorithm [9] with the motion-driven vertex clustering [10] is chosen as the baseline method. The computational time was measured on a 64-bit Windows PC with Intel Core i7-3630 CPU 2.40 GHz. The experimental assets are listed in Table 1. The articulated horse and collapsing camel animations have 48 and 53 frames, respectively [18]. The facial expression data is published as a part of the voice-operated character animation (VOCA) dataset [2].

Table 1. Experimental dataset. The animation category was manually determined based on visual observation.

Dataset	V	F	Category
Cloth-collision	1471	100	Elastic
Cloth-sagging	289	200	Elastic
Horse-gallop	8431	48	Articulated
Camel-collapse	21887	53	Elastic
Facial-animation	5023	204	Articulated
Character-clothing	5293	1000	Elastic

Qualitative Evaluation. The comparative analysis of the source animation and approximation results are presented on the left side of Fig. 5. Please refer to the supplemental video for the animating results. The baseline method generated a scattered weight distribution as shown in the second column, whereas our method achieved local and unimodal distribution as shown in the third column. Our method arranged the bones over the mesh surface more uniformly than the baseline owing to the model-dependent clustering. Moreover, our method generated more stable smooth transformations and compact weight distribution that accurately approximated the local surface deformation around each bone. Conversely, the bone transformation estimation of the baseline method suffers from the slight movement of the distant vertices, which resulted in the jerky and unpredictable bone transformations. The proposed method yielded results that will be more intuitive for riggers and animators. Quantitative comparisons of the bone and weight distribution remain future work.

Quantitative Evaluation. The statistics for the computational performances and approximation accuracies are summarized on the right side of Fig. 5. The left column shows the comparative analysis of the computation time of the proposed and baseline methods. The right column compares the approximation errors,

Fig. 6. Comparison of skin weight distribution. (a) The proposed method with 20 iterations. (b) Laplacian normalization with 20 iterations. (c) Laplacian normalization with 40 iterations.

Fig. 7. Comparison of sagging clothes. The baseline caused wrinkle-like artifacts, whereas the proposed method faithfully reproduced the source animation with smooth bone transformations.

where the approximation error was obtained using the formula proposed in [9]. Our method successfully prevented the computation time from increasing exponentially with the number of bones, because our locality-aware approach reduces the computational order of weight optimization from $O(B^3)$ to $O(B \cdot B_i^3)$, where $B_i < B$ holds (Sect. 3.2). In the case of the galloping horse animation with 16 bones, the increase in the computation time was kept within the acceptable limit through the overhead of the mesh clustering, detection of the neighboring clusters, and frame-reduction. In addition, the proposed method reduced the approximation error for all the animations, excluding that of the horse, which had 32 bones. These results indicate that the model-dependent mesh clustering sufficiently compensated the error caused by the locality-aware weight optimization.

4.2   Validation of Locality-Aware Optimization

The skin weight distribution of the proposed and baseline methods are compared in Fig. 6. The source animation was generated using the nCloth of Autodesk Maya. The baseline method achieved a smooth weight distribution using the iterative optimization with the Laplace normalization term [10].

However, the skin weights were scattered over the mesh, as indicated by the red circle, even after a considerable number of iterations. In contrast, our method achieved both local and compact distribution, because the optimization at each vertex ignored the effect of spatially distant bones. Notably, the proposed method did not always produce smooth distribution, because the weight optimization was performed independently for each vertex. Although it is possible to introduce the Laplacian normalization technique, it significantly increases computation time.

Figure 7 shows the approximation result of cloth deformation. The proposed method produced smooth surface deformation while faithfully reproducing the source animation whereas the baseline method caused wrinkle-like artifacts, and resulted in stiff-looking deformed surfaces. The baseline method minimized the global numerical error by neglecting the detailed high-frequency deformations that are highly visible, even when the numerical error is not significant. In contrast, the proposed method improved visual quality using uniformly assigned bones based on the farthest-point sampling method while decreasing the quantitative accuracy of the other region.

4.3 Validation of Frame-Reduction

We evaluated the effectiveness of the adaptive frame-reduction method by comparing the computation time and approximation error with the uniform sampling method, as shown in Table 2. The experimental asset was created by resampling the horse animation to 1000 frames to highlight the performance differences. We set the frame dissimilarity threshold to $\bar{\sigma} = 0.1$, and the baseline method uniformly sampled at one frame per ten. Our method significantly reduced the computation time without increasing the approximation error because the source data contain many repetitive animations. This result indicates that our method effectively eliminated the redundant frames from the cyclic animation.

Table 2. Performance effect of frame-reduction: (a) without frame-reduction, (b) with the proposed greedy frame-reduction, and (c) with uniform sampling. All experiments used the model-dependent mesh clustering and locality-aware weight optimization

	(a) All	(b) Our method	(c) Uniform
Time (sec)	178.6	123.5	137.4
Error	1.90330	1.90333	1.94166

4.4 Validation Using Practical Asset

The proposed model is validated for complicated shape deformation by using a garment animation included in the Berkeley Garment Library (http://graphics.berkeley.edu/resources/GarmentLibrary), as shown in Fig. 1(right), where $V = 5293$, $F = 1000$, and $B = 200$. The time taken by the proposed method was 472.3 s, and approximation error was 3.32, whereas the baseline method required 1935.7 s, and the error was 3.94. The overall behavior of the garment deformation was successfully approximated in lesser computational time than the previous method. However, the detailed deformations, such as wrinkles, were not precisely reproduced. In addition, the penetration between the garment and body parts occurred as the result of approximation, as demonstrated in the supplemental video. This problem can be resolved using the detail-preservation technique [7].

5 Discussion

We have improved the SSDR algorithm by considering the locality of the skin weight distribution over the skin mesh. Locality-aware weight optimization is achieved by dividing the source model into multiple regions and performing optimization independently in each region. Although this approach does not always guarantee the globally minimum approximation error, it significantly reduces the computation time while preserving the animation quality. We believe that our efficient framework will contribute to practical animation productions by facilitating rapid iterative operation and improving the animation quality.

By adaptively selecting important frames, the proposed method reduces the computation time, which is highly effective for animations including periodic movements. However, the proposed greedy algorithm does not always provide an optimal result, particularly for non-cyclic animation. Moreover, the proposed algorithm neglects the detailed deformation, because frame similarity is evaluated based on the rigid bone transformations of the mesh clustering result. Thus, we are motivated to develop a more effective and efficient frame-reduction algorithm.

Furthermore, in the current prototype, the mesh clustering method is designed to be manually selected based on visual observation. We will automate the selection of the mesh clustering method depending on the source model. The clustering accuracy can be enhanced by using different clustering algorithms for each semantically different region of a complicated model, such as the body, hair, and clothes of a clothed character. It is essential to develop a more efficient algorithm for bone transformation optimization for further improving computational performance.

Acknowledgement. We thank Square Enix Co., Ltd. for giving us the opportunity to conduct this research. In particular, we thank Kazuhisa Chida and Said Michel for their support and useful advice.

References

1. Alexa, M., Müller, W.: Representing animations by principal components. Comput. Graph. Forum **19**(3), 411–418 (2000)
2. Cudeiro, D., Bolkart, T., Laidlaw, C., Ranjan, A., Black, M;: Capture, learning, and synthesis of 3D speaking styles. In: Computer Vision and Pattern Recognition, pp. 10101–10111 (2019). http://voca.is.tue.mpg.de/
3. De Aguiar, E., Theobalt, C., Thrun, S., Seidel, H.P.: Automatic conversion of mesh animations into skeleton-based animations. Comput. Graph. Forum **27**(2), 389–397 (2008)
4. Hasler, N., Thormählen, T., Rosenhahn, B., Seidel, H.P.: Learning skeletons for shape and pose. In: ACM SIGGRAPH Symposium on Interactive 3D Graphics and Games, pp. 23–30 (2010)
5. James, D.L., Twigg, C.D.: Skinning mesh animations. ACM Trans. Graph. **24**(3), 399–407 (2005)
6. Kavan, L., Collins, S., Zara, J., O'Sullivan, C.: Skinning with dual quaternions. In: ACM SIGGRAPH Symposium on Interactive 3D Graphics and Games, pp. 39–46 (2007)
7. Kavan, L., McDonnell, R., Dobbyn, S., Zara, J., O'Sullivan, C.: Skinning arbitrary deformations. In: ACM SIGGRAPH Symposium on Interactive 3D Graphics and Games, pp. 53–60 (2007)
8. Kavan, L., Sloan, P.P., O'Sullivan, C.: Fast and efficient skinning of animated meshes. Comput. Graph. Forum **29**(2), 327–336 (2010)

9. Le, B., Deng, Z.: Smooth skinning decomposition with rigid bones. ACM Trans. Graph. **31**(6), 10 (2012)
10. Le, B.H., Deng, Z.: Robust and accurate skeletal rigging from mesh sequences. ACM Trans. Graph. **33**(4), 84:1–84:10 (2014)
11. Le, B.H., Hodgins, J.K.: Real-time skeletal skinning with optimized centers of rotation. ACM Transactions on Graphics **35**(4), 37:1–37:10 (2016)
12. Le, B.H., Lewis, J.P.: Direct delta mush skinning and variants. ACM Trans. Graph. **38**(4), 113:1–113:13 (2019)
13. Liu, S.L., Liu, Y., Dong, L.F.: RAS: a data-driven rigidity-aware skinning model for 3D facial animation. Comput. Graph. Forum **39**(1), 581–594 (2020)
14. Magnenat-Thalmann, N., Laperrière, R., Thalmann, D.: Joint-dependent local deformations for hand animation and object grasping. In: Graphics Interface 1988, pp. 26–33 (1988)
15. Mancewicz, J., Derksen, M.L., Rijpkema, H., Wilson, C.A.: Delta mush: smoothing deformations while preserving detail. In: Symposium on Digital Production, pp. 7–11 (2014)
16. Mukai, T., Kuriyama, S.: Efficient dynamic skinning with low-rank helper bone controllers. ACM Trans. Graph. **35**(4), 36:1–36:11 (2016)
17. Schaefer, S., Yuksel, C.: Example-based skeleton extraction. In: Eurographics Symposium on Geometry Processing, pp. 153–162 (2007)
18. Sumner, R.W., Popović, J.: Deformation transfer for triangle meshes. ACM Trans. Graph. **23**(3), 399–405 (2004). http://people.csail.mit.edu/sumner/research/deftransfer/data.html
19. Thiery, J., Eisemann, E.: ARAPLBS: robust and efficient elasticity-based optimization of weights and skeleton joints for linear blend skinning with parametrized bones. Comput. Graph. Forum **37**(1), 32–44 (2018)

A New Volume-Based Convexity Measure for 3D Shapes

Xiayan Shi[1]([✉]), Rui Li[1], and Yun Sheng[2]

[1] Shanghai Key Laboratory of Multidimensional Information Processing, East China
Normal University, Shanghai, People's Republic of China
913810856@qq.com, lirui123456@qq.com
[2] The Department of Computer Science, Liverpool John Moores University,
Liverpool L3 3AF, UK
y.sheng@ljmu.ac.uk

Abstract. Convexity, as a global and learning-free shape descriptor, has been widely applied to shape classification, retrieval and decomposition. Unlike its extensively addressed 2D counterpart, 3D shape convexity measurement attracting insufficient attention has yet to be studied. In this paper, we put forward a new volume-based convexity measure for 3D shapes, which builds on a conventional volume-based convexity measure but excels it by resolving its problems. By turning the convexity measurement into a problem of influence evaluation through Distance-weighted Volume Integration, the new convexity measure can resolve the major problems of the existing ones and accelerate the overall computational time.

Keywords: Shape analysis · Convexity measurement · 3D shape retrieval

1 Introduction

Shape analysis has been playing a fundamental role in computer graphics, computer vision and pattern recognition. In shape analysis, research on how to quantify a shape with holistic descriptors such as convexity [5,6,8,19], circularity [15], concavity [17], ellipticity [1], rectilinearity [9], rectangularity [18] and symmetry [4,14] has been booming, because these descriptors can offer a global and efficient way for applications where shape representation is required. Among these holistic descriptors convexity has been most commonly used in shape decomposition [2,10,11], classification [6,12], and retrieval [5,6,8], *etc.*. In general a planar shape $s(s \subset \mathbf{R}^2)$ is regarded as convex if and only if the whole line segment between two arbitrary points in s belongs to s. When it comes to three-dimensional(3D) shapes, this definition can readily be generalised as: A 3D shape $S(S \subset \mathbf{R}^3)$ is said to be convex if and only if all points on the line segment between two arbitrary points in S belong to S. Generally speaking, every convexity measure have to meet four desirable conditions:

© Springer Nature Switzerland AG 2020
N. Magnenat-Thalmann et al. (Eds.): CGI 2020, LNCS 12221, pp. 59–70, 2020.
https://doi.org/10.1007/978-3-030-61864-3_6

1. The value of the convexity measure is a real number between $(0,1]$.
2. The measured convexity value of a given shape equals 1 if and only if this shape is convex.
3. There are shapes whose measured convexity is arbitrary close to 0.
4. The value of the convexity measure should remain invariant under similarity transformation of the shape.

Next, we will review some state-of-the-art convexity measures for 3D shapes and analyse their pros and cons. Note that all the 3D shapes mentioned in this paper are topologically closed.

Definition 1. *For a given 3D shape S with $CH(S)$ denoting its convex hull, its convexity is measured as*

$$C_1(S) = \frac{Volume(S)}{Volume(CH(S))} \tag{1}$$

C_1, a volume-based measure, cannot distinguish two shapes with the same ratio of shape to convex hull volumes, as shown in Fig. 3 (a) and (b).

To resolve the above problem, Lian et al. [8] proposed a projection-based convexity measure for 3D shapes, which was generalised from a 2D projection-based convexity measure reported by Zunic et al. [19].

Definition 2. *For a given 3D shape S, its convexity is measured as*

$$C_2(S) = \min_{\alpha,\beta,\gamma \in [0,2\pi]} \frac{Pview(S,\alpha,\beta,\gamma)}{Pface(S,\alpha,\beta,\gamma)} \tag{2}$$

where $Pface$ is the summed area of surface mesh faces of a 3D shape projected onto the three orthogonal planes, YOZ, ZOX and XOY, with $Pface = Pface_x + Pface_y + Pface_z$, while $Pview$ is the summed area of shape silhouette images projected onto six faces of its bounding box parallel to the orthogonal planes, with $Pview = 2(Pview_x + Pview_y + Pview_z)$. $Pview(S,\alpha,\beta,\gamma)$ and $Pface(S,\alpha,\beta,\gamma)$ are $Pview$ and $Pface$ of S after rotating α, β and γ with respect to x, y and z axes, respectively. Figure 1 illustrates examples of $Pface$ and $Pview$. It is noticeable that there exists an inequality $Pface \geq Pview$ for any 3D shape and that they are equal only if a 3D shape is convex. Therefore, convexity is measured as a minimum value sought by rotating the shape at variant angles.

Since the calculation of C_2 is a nonlinear optimisation problem that traditional methods cannot deal with, a genetic algorithm is used to help seek the minimum value of C_2. However, the genetic algorithm is computationally expensive and requires a plethora of iterations to reach an optimum. To avoid the heavy calculation of C_2, Li et al. proposed a heuristic convexity measure for 3D shape, which is still projection-based but computes the summed area ratio of projected shape silhouette images and surface mesh faces only once, just along principal directions of the shape, followed by a correction process based on shape slicing [5] rather than optimizing the ratio with the genetic algorithm in iterations.

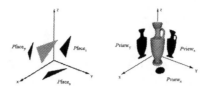

Fig. 1. Projections of a triangular face and a whole shape on the coordinate planes.

Definition 3. *For a given 3D shape S, its convexity is measured as*

$$C_3(S) = Cor\left(\frac{Pview(S \cdot R)}{Pface(S \cdot R)}\right) \tag{3}$$

where R represents the rotation matrix of the initial estimation achieved by principal component analysis (PCA) and $Cor(\cdot)$ indicates the subsequently applied correction process. Compared to C_2, C_3 can accelarate the overall computation by some an order of magnitude.

During the correction process of C_3, Li *et al.* sliced the 3D shape into a sequence of cross sections in equal interval along the principal directions of the shape, then 2D convexity measurement of the cross sections was performed in order to offset the precision loss introduced by the initial estimation of PCA. However, C_3 may introduce some error during the correction process.

In order to resolve the above problems of the existing convexity measures, in this paper we present a new volume-based convexity measure, which builds on the original volume-based C_1 but excels it by resolving its extant problems. The basic idea behind the new convexity is generalised from its 2D counterpart [6].

2 Our Volume-Based Convexity Measure

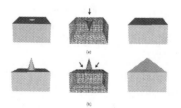

Fig. 2. We can regard both of Shape (a) and (b), with the left and middle columes being their solid and wireframe views, as collapsed from their convex hulls (in the right colume) towards the geometric centres of the convex hulls, with the black arrows implying the collapsing directions.

Our new convexity measure is generalised from a 2D area-based measure [6] and shares the similar philosophy that any nonconvex 3D shape, no matter with protrusions (Fig. 2(b)) or dents (Fig. 2(a)), is formed by its convex hull collapsing towards the geometric centre of the convex hull. We assume that the convexity of an arbitrary 3D shape is associated with the total influence of dents collapsed from the shape convex hull, and consider that dent attributes, such as position and volume with respect to the shape convex hull, directly determine the dent influence.

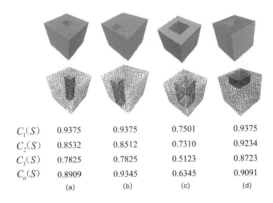

$C_1(S)$	0.9375	0.9375	0.7501	0.9375
$C_2(S)$	0.8532	0.8512	0.7310	0.9234
$C_3(S)$	0.7825	0.7825	0.5123	0.8723
$C_a(S)$	0.8909	0.9345	0.6345	0.9091
	(a)	(b)	(c)	(d)

Fig. 3. The position and volume of dents determine the convexity calculation of 3D shapes. There are four cubes with dents in different positions and volumes. The corresponding convexity values computed by variant measures are listed beneath the shapes.

Some intuitional examples are given in Fig. 3, where four cubes have dents in different positions and volumes. For example, the dents of Shape (a) and (b) are identical in volume but different in position, and Shape (a) is visually more concave than Shape (b) as the dent of Shape (a) is centrally positioned. This distinction cannot be sensed by C_1 and C_3. C_2 considers that Shape (a) is even more convex than Shape (b) which is, however, not the case. Moreover, the dents of both Shape (a) and (c) are centrally positioned but different in volume, while dents of Shape (a) and (d) are the same in volume but different in position. Therefore, the new convexity measure should be able to distinguish all the above differences.

In light of the above analysis the new convexity measure should be defined by taking account of dent position and volume with respect to the shape convex hull. Note that dents here not only mean dents contained in the 3D shape but dents collapsed from the shape convex hull. This semantic nuance can be articulated by Fig. 2, where the former dents can be exemplified by (a) while the latter dents involve both (a) and (b).

To associate our convexity measure with dent position and volume, we consider that the convex hull of a given 3D shape S is made up of infinitely small cubes, and assign each small cube a weight associated with the Euclidean distance from the cube to the geometric centre of the convex hull in order to evaluate the influence of the cube on the convexity measurement. The closer a cube to the geometric centre of the convex hull, the more it influences the calculation of convexity. If the dent volume is symbolised as $D(D \subset \mathbf{R}^3)$, the influence of D on the convexity measurement of S can be calculated by $\iiint_D W(r)dv$, where $W(r)$ represents a weight function. Likewise, the total influence of the convex hull of S can be formulated as $\iiint_{CH(S)} W(r)dv$, and thus the influence of the 3D shape on the convexity measurement can be expressed as

$$\iiint_S W(r)dv = \iiint_{CH(S)} W(r)dv - \iiint_D W(r)dv \qquad (4)$$

Definition 4. *For a given 3D shape S, its convexity is measured as*

$$C_\alpha(S) = \frac{\iiint_S W(r)dv}{\iiint_{CH(S)} W(r)dv} \qquad (5)$$

and

$$W(r) = 1 - \alpha \frac{r}{r_{max}} = \frac{r_{max} - \alpha \cdot r}{r_{max}} \qquad (6)$$

where α, $0 \leq \alpha \leq 1$, represents an influence factor of the weight function; r denotes the Euclidean distance variable between small cubes and the geometric centre of the convex hull of S; r_{max} represents the maximum r.

Equations (5) and (6) define our notion of Distance-weighted Volume Integration. When $r = r_{max}$, $W(r)$ reaches its minimum $1 - \alpha$; when $r = 0$, $W(r)$ has a maximum 1. This distance-weighted strategy emphasises the influence of dents close to the geometric centre of the convex hull and downplays the impact of dents distant from the geometric centre. Moreover, by adjusting α we can control the influence of different attributes. For example, if we want to emphasise the contribution of dent position, we can increase α to lower the influence of distant cubes. If we want to emphasise the contribution of dent volume, we can degrade the weight influence of each cube by decreasing the value of α. When we decrease α to 0, every cube will have an identical weight, and the new measure will degenerate into the traditional volume-based convexity measure C_1, only related to dent volume.

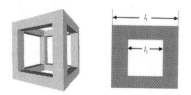

(a) The 3D model (b) Its silhouette

Fig. 4. A hollow cube model. l_1 and l_2 indicate the outer and inner edge lengths of the cube, respectively.

3   Proof of the New Measure

In this section, we verify that the new convexity satisfies the four necessary conditions stated in Sect. 1.

Proof. For a given 3D shape S, assume that it has m dents denoted as $D_1, D_2 \cdots D_m \subset \mathbf{R}^3$. The corresponding influences of dents $D_1, D_2, \cdots, D_m$ can be calculated by $\iiint_{D_1} W(r)dv$, $\iiint_{D_2} W(r)dv, \cdots, \iiint_{D_m} W(r)dv$, respectively. Thus, $C_\alpha(S)$ can be rewritten as

$$C_\alpha(S) = \frac{\iiint_S W(r)dv}{\iiint_S W(r)dv + \sum_{i=1}^{m} \iiint_{D_i} W(r)dv}. \tag{7}$$

It is easy to show that $0 < C_\alpha(S) < 1$. If there is no dent, that is $\sum_{i=1}^{m} \iiint_{D_i} W(r)dv = 0$, then $C_\alpha(S) = 1$. This means that S coincides with its convex hull. To this end, S is convex.

To prove Condition 3 we construct a hollow cube, as shown in Fig. 4. When we keep increasing l_2 making it infinitely close to l_1, we have

$$\lim_{l_2 \to l_1} C_\alpha(S) = 0 \tag{8}$$

Under translation and rotation of a 3D shape, since the relevant distance between each small cube and the geometric centre of the convex hull remains the same, and the volume of the 3D shape and its convex hull also keeps unchanged, the convexity measured by C_α remains the same.

Taking the geometric centre of the convex hull as the origin to establish the coordinate system, we assume that S is scaled by a coefficient k. The convexity of the scaled shape is written as

$$\begin{aligned} C_\alpha(S') &= \frac{\iiint_{S'} (1 - \alpha \cdot r'/r'_{\max})dx'dy'dz'}{\iiint_{CH(S')} (1 - \alpha \cdot r'/r'_{\max})dx'dy'dz'} \\ &= \frac{\iiint_S (1 - \alpha \cdot kr/kr_{\max})k^3 dxdydz}{\iiint_{CH(S)} (1 - \alpha \cdot kr/kr_{\max})k^3 dxdydz} \\ &= C_\alpha(S), \end{aligned} \tag{9}$$

where the prime symbol indicates those corresponding parameters after scaling. Hence Condition 4 of Theorem 1 is proved.

4   Algorithm Implementation

To implement C_α we need a discrete version of Definition 4 for calculation. A straightforward thought similar to its 2D counterpart [6] is to replace the integral symbols by summations and the infinitely small cubes by voxels. Thus we can rewrite C_α into its discrete form as

$$C_\alpha = \frac{N_S - \alpha \dfrac{\sum\limits_{j=1}^{N_S} r_j}{r_{max}}}{N_{CH} - \alpha \dfrac{\sum\limits_{k=1}^{N_{CH}} r_k}{r_{max}}} \tag{10}$$

where N_S and N_{CH} represent the numbers of voxels in S and $CH(S)$, respectively.

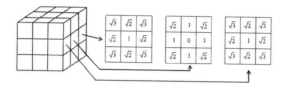

Fig. 5. A $3 * 3 * 3$ illustration of the 3D Distance Dictionary.

Shapes										
Size	Time (sec)	C_a	Time (sec)	C_a	Time (sec)	C_a	Time (sec)	C_a	Time (sec)	C_a
$n_m=80$	0.0045	0.2165	0.0143	0.3225	0.0091	0.4752	0.0161	0.6381	0.0209	0.9934
$n_m=100$	0.0064	0.2118	0.0232	0.3215	0.0203	0.4723	0.0262	0.6401	0.0318	0.9981
$n_m=150$	0.0159	0.2110	0.0447	0.3225	0.0354	0.4741	0.0500	0.6393	0.0659	0.9908
$n_m=250$	0.0536	0.2108	0.1633	0.3223	0.1168	0.4744	0.1651	0.6399	0.2175	0.9942
$n_m=500$	0.2017	0.2113	0.6233	0.3227	0.4577	0.4741	0.6233	0.6396	0.8699	0.9937

Fig. 6. 3D shapes measured in different 3D grid sizes.

Prior to convexity measurement we need to voxelise the measured 3D shape and its convex hull. We first find the minimum bounding box of the shape convex hull with all the faces of the bounding box perpendicular to the x, y and z axes, and tessellate the minimum bounding box into a 3D grid of $n_1 * n_2 * n_3 (n_1, n_2, n_3 \in \mathbf{Z}^+)$ voxels. Then the calculation of shape convexity is carried out in terms of evaluation of the influence of each voxel in the shape convex hull within the $n_1 * n_2 * n_3$ volume grid. We observe that all the 3D shapes can share the same volume grid, and the distances and weights of their voxels will be calculated repeatedly under the same grid during convexity measurement. Hence instead of calculating voxel distances for every 3D shape, we compute them only once by constructing an $N * N * N(N, n_m \in \mathbf{Z}^+$ with $N >= 2n_m$ and $n_m = max(n_1, n_2, n_3))$ Distance Dictionary to pre-store all the Euclidean distances from the voxels to the grid centre of the Distance Dictionary. When computing the convexity of a specific 3D shape, we just need to align the geometric centre of its convex hull to the grid centre of the Distance Dictionary, scale the 3D grid of the shape convex hull to fit the 3D Distance Dictionary in voxel, and then look up Euclidean distances of the corresponding voxels of the 3D shape and its convex hull in the Distance Dictionary.

The 3D Distance Dictionary is an $N * N * N$ tensor, elements of which store values of the Euclidean distances from the voxels of the dictionary to its grid centre. Figure 5 illustrates a $3 * 3 * 3$ example of such a 3D Distance Dictionary. However, the value of the 3D Distance Dictionary N must be larger than two times n_m, and thus the resolution of 3D grid of the minimum bounding box for 3D shapes influenes the convexity measurement. General speaking, the larger the grid resolution, the more accurate the measured convexity, but the more time the computation consumes. In order to choose an appropriate resolution for the 3D minimum bounding box grid, we compare the performances when in turn setting $n_m = 80, 100, 150, 250, 500$. As shown in Fig. 6, convexities measured with different grid resolutions for the same 3D shape are not much different. Therefore, for the sake of computational simplicity, the value of n_m in the rest of this paper is set to 80. Note that in this paper without specification α is set to 1 by default, and the computer configuration is specified in Sect. 5.3. The pseudocode of the new measure is shown in Algorithm 1.

Algorithm 1. $C_\alpha (S)$

Input: A 3D shape S; an influence factor α, and a predefined $N * N * N$ 3D Distance Dictionary;

Output: Convexity value C_α.

1: Compute the convex hull of S, $CH(S)$;
2: find the minimum bounding box of $CH(S)$ with all six faces perpendicular to the x, y, z axes;
3: voxelise the minimum bounding box with an $n_1 * n_2 * n_3$ 3D grid;
4: $N_{CH} \leftarrow$ the number of voxels in $CH(S)$;
5: $N_S \leftarrow$ the number of voxels in S;
6: map both S and $CH(S)$ to the predefined 3D Distance Dictionary with the geometric centre of $CH(S)$ aligned to the grid centre of the 3D Distance Dictionary and the 3D grid of $CH(S)$ scaled to fit the dictionary in voxel;
7: look up Euclidean distances $r[N_{CH}]$ for $CH(S)$ in the 3D Distance Dictionary with the longest one marked as r_{max};
   // Compute the sum of Euclidean distances, ε_S, for S
8: **for** $j = 1$ to N_S **do**
      $\varepsilon_S + = r[j]$;
9: **end for**
   // Compute the sum of Euclidean distances, ε_{CH}, for $CH(S)$
10: **for** $k = 1$ to N_{CH} **do**
       $\varepsilon_{CH} + = r[k]$;
11: **end for**
12: **return** $C_\alpha = \dfrac{N_S - \alpha \frac{\varepsilon_S}{r_{max}}}{N_{CH} - \alpha \frac{\varepsilon_{CH}}{r_{max}}}$.

---

5   Experimental Results

5.1   Quantitative Evaluation

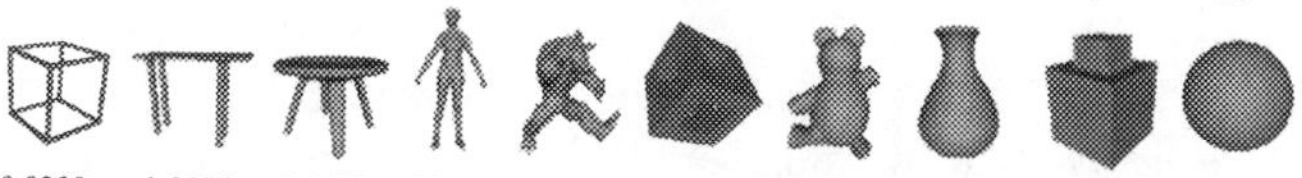

	1	2	3	4	5	6	7	8	9	10
$C_1(S)$	0.0280	0.0776	0.1630	0.2864	0.3019	0.5000	0.6070	0.8042	0.9050	1.0000
$C_2(S)$	0.5108	0.7463	0.7755	0.7720	0.8126	0.5967	0.8848	0.9599	0.9403	0.9999
$C_3(S)$	0.0218	0.2408	0.3101	0.3706	0.4577	0.2995	0.7201	0.8529	0.9528	0.9744
$C_\alpha(S)$	0.0121	0.0583	0.1318	0.2755	0.3225	0.3738	0.6538	0.8412	0.9177	1.0000

Fig. 7. The quantitative convexity measurement of ten 3D shapes.

We carry out the convexity measurement to ten 3D shapes shown in Fig. 7, with eight of them picked from two commonly used 3D shape databases, the McGill Articulated 3D Shape Benchmark [16] and Princeton Benchmark [3], and the other two, the 1st and 6th, being two synthetic 3D shapes. These shapes are ordered in C_α. It can be seen that for those shapes whose dents embrace the geometric centre of the shape convex hull, such as the 1st, 2nd, 3rd and 6th, their convexity values evaluated by C_α are lower than those by C_1. It can also be noticed from the results of Fig. 7 that the convexities measured by C_2 are relatively larger with all the values greater than 0.5, which cannot reflect the reality. As C_3 is a heuristic method that comes with a correction process at the end, C_3 more or less introduces some error into the convexity estimated. For example, the convexity of the sphere measured by C_3 in Fig. 7 is only 0.9744, while the results of C_1, C_2 and C_α on the sphere are either 1 or very close to 1.

5.2   3D Shape Retrieval

Fig. 8. Samples of the 10 categories of watertight shapes for 3D shape retrieval.

Fig. 9. Canonical forms of the shapes. The first row shows the original non-rigid models, while the second row shows their feature-preserved 3D canonical forms.

We also apply C_1, C_2, C_3 and C_α to non-rigid 3D shape retrieval on the McGill articulated 3D shape benchmark [16], which consists of 10 categories of 255 watertight shapes. Some classified samples are shown in Fig. 8. In this dateset shapes in the same categories such as the glasses and hand gestures shown in Fig. 9 may appear in quite different poses but have similar canonical forms. For this reason we apply a method introduced in [7] to construct the feature-preserved canonical forms of the 3D shapes. We compute convexities of the 3D shapes by C_1, C_2, C_3 and C_α and employ the L_1 norm to calculate the dissimilarity between two signatures. The retrieval performance is evaluated by four quantitative measures (NN, 1-Tier, 2-Tier, DCG) [13]. The results in Fig. 10 show that C_3 achieves the best retrieval rates as a solo convexity measure. Note that the smaller the value of α, the higher the retrieval rate. This is because with α increasing, the distribution of the values of C_α for the same category is broadening, making the retrieval less precise. Representing 3D shapes by a solo convexity measure may result in relatively poor retrieval rates. In order to improve the accuracy of retrieval, we employ a shape descriptor, called *CS* (Convexity Statistics) [6], by taking advantage of our new convexity measure by setting α to 0.0, 0.1, 0.2, 0.3, 0.4, 0.5, 0.6, 0.7, 0.8, 0.9, 1.0. We collect the 11 convexities of every 3D shape as a set and calculate the mean, variance, skewness and kurtosis of each set to construct the four-dimensional shape descriptor *CS*. As can be seen from Fig. 10, the *CS* outperforms the competitors in all the retrieval measures.

	$C_{\alpha=0.1}$	$C_{\alpha=0.2}$	$C_{\alpha=0.3}$	$C_{\alpha=0.4}$	$C_{\alpha=0.5}$	$C_{\alpha=0.6}$	$C_{\alpha=0.7}$	$C_{\alpha=0.8}$	$C_{\alpha=0.9}$	$C_{\alpha=1.0}$	$C_1(C_{\alpha=0.0})$	C_2	C_3	*CS*
NN	25.9	24.3	20.0	22.4	21.2	18.0	23.1	21.6	20.4	23.9	25.1	25.9	34.9	**43.1**
1-Tier	25.0	24.5	24.0	23.7	23.4	22.7	22.5	22.3	21.8	22.0	24.9	26.3	26.4	**35.4**
2-Tier	41.5	41.1	40.6	40.1	39.3	38.2	37.3	36.4	35.7	35.8	42.0	45.9	49.8	**56.7**
DCG	58.1	57.8	57.3	56.9	56.6	56.4	56.2	56.0	55.7	55.7	58.4	60.4	61.4	**67.6**

Fig. 10. Retrieval performance of the convexity measures on the McGill dataset.

5.3   Computational Efficiency

In this section we compare computational efficiencies of three convexity measures, as shown in Fig. 11, where some typical shapes are ordered in vertex num-

Shapes						
Vertex No.		673	4463	9261	14872	34817
$C_a(s)$		**0.0285**	**0.0037**	**0.0055**	**0.0070**	**0.0161**
$C_2(s)$		11.34	45.11	86.08	148.4	316.1
$C_3(s)$	One iteration	0.0648	0.0905	0.1400	0.1700	0.3115
	Total	648	905	1400	1700	3115

Fig. 11. Comparison of time consumptions.

ber. C_2 is computationally expensive due to the adopted genetic algorithm with 50 individuals and 200 evolution generations [8], especially when the number of vertices in the shape is large. C_3 also needs to capture silhouette images from the frame buffer and the convexity measurement of 2D slides also takes time. The whole experiment is carried out with a laptop configured with Intel Core i5 CPU and 6G RAM. Note that C_2 and C_3 are computed using Visual Studio 2010 because the codes for calculating silhouette images from the frame buffer were written in C++. Even though C_α is coded and computed using MATLAB, which is normally considered slower than C++, C_α with the Distance Dictionary still accelerates the overall computational time by several orders of magnitude.

6   Limitations

Although C_α can overcome the shortcoming of C_1, C_α shares the same problem with C_1, as it is derived from C_1. If 3D shapes with a long and narrow dent inside or outside, the volume-based convexity measures C_α and C_1 will get unreasonable values. The grid resolution is artificially set, which is decided by n_m. If the dent is infinitesimally small, say smaller than a voxel, it may be missed out.

7   Conclusions

In this paper we proposed a new convexity measure based on Distance-weighted Volume Integration by turning the convexity measurement into a problem of influence evaluation. To facilitate the computation of the new convexity measure for 3D shapes we also introduced the use of a pre-calculated Distance Dictionary so as to avoid the repeated calculation of voxel distances for every 3D shape. The experimental results demonstrated the advantage of the new convexity measure, and the new convexity measure performed several orders of magnitude faster than those competitors. In respect of its application to 3D shape retrieval, we construct a variety of convexity measures by varying the value of α and form a new multi-dimensional shape descriptor with these different convexity measures.

References

1. Aktaş, M.A., Žunić, J.: Sensitivity/robustness flexible ellipticity measures. In: Pinz, A., Pock, T., Bischof, H., Leberl, F. (eds.) DAGM/OAGM 2012. LNCS, vol. 7476, pp. 307–316. Springer, Heidelberg (2012). https://doi.org/10.1007/978-3-642-32717-9_31
2. Attene, M., Mortara, M., Spagnuolo, M., Falcidieno, B.: Hierarchical convex approximation of 3D shapes for fast region selection. Comput. Graph. Forum **27**(5), 1323–1332 (2008)
3. Chen, X., Golovinskiy, A., Funkhouser, T.: A benchmark for 3D mesh segmentation. ACM Trans. Graph. **28**, 1–12 (2009)
4. Leou, J.J., Tsai, W.H.: Automatic Rotational Symmetry Determination For Shape Analysis. Elsevier Science Inc., New York (1987)

5. Li, R., Liu, L., Sheng, Y., Zhang, G.: A heuristic convexity measure for 3D meshes. Vis. Comput. **33**, 903–912 (2017). https://doi.org/10.1007/s00371-017-1385-6
6. Li, R., Shi, X., Sheng, Y., Zhang, G.: A new area-based convexity measure with distance weighted area integration for planar shapes. Comput. Aided Geom. Des. **71**, 176–189 (2019)
7. Lian, Z., Godil, A.: A feature-preserved canonical form for non-rigid 3D meshes. In: International Conference on 3D Imaging, Modeling, Processing, Visualization and Transmission, pp. 116–123 (2011)
8. Lian, Z., Godil, A., Rosin, P.L., Sun, X.: A new convexity measurement for 3D meshes. In: Computer Vision and Pattern Recognition (CVPR), pp. 119–126 (2012)
9. Lian, Z., Rosin, P.L., Sun, X.: Rectilinearity of 3D meshes. Int. J. Comput. Vis. **89**, 130–151 (2010)
10. Mesadi, F., Tasdizen, T.: Convex decomposition and efficient shape representation using deformable convex polytopes. In: Computer Vision and Pattern Recognition (2016)
11. Ren, Z., Yuan, J., Liu, W.: Minimum near-convex shape decomposition. IEEE Trans. Patt. Anal. Mach. Intell. **35**(10), 2546–2552 (2013)
12. Rosin, P.L.: Classification of pathological shapes using convexity measures. Pattern Recogn. Lett. **30**, 570–578 (2009)
13. Shilane, P., Min, P., Kazhdan, M., Funkhouser, T.: The princeton shape benchmark. Shape Model. Appl. IEEE **105**, 167–178 (2004)
14. Sipiran, I., Gregor, R., Schreck, T.: Approximate symmetry detection in partial 3D meshes. Comput. Graph. Forum **33**(7), 131–140 (2014)
15. Wang, G.: Shape circularity measure method based on radial moments. J. Electron. Imaging **22**, 022–033 (2013)
16. Zhang, J., Kaleem, S., Diego, M., Sven, D.: Retrieving articulated 3D models using medial surfaces. Mach. Vis. Appl. **19**, 261–275 (2008)
17. Zimmer, H., Campen, M., Kobbelt, L.: Efficient computation of shortest path-concavity for 3D meshes. In: Computer Vision Pattern Recognition, pp. 2155–2162 (2013)
18. Zunic, D., Zunic, J.: Measuring shape rectangularity. Electron. Lett. **47**, 441–442 (2011)
19. Zunic, J., Rosin, P.L.: A new convexity measure for polygons. IEEE Trans. Pattern Anal. Mach. Intell. **26**, 923–934 (2004)

Deep Inverse Rendering for Practical Object Appearance Scan with Uncalibrated Illumination

Jianzhao Zhang[1,3(✉)], Guojun Chen[2], Yue Dong[2], Jian Shi[4], Bob Zhang[5], and Enhua Wu[1,5]

[1] State Key Laboratory of Computer Science, Institute of Software, Chinese Academy of Sciences, Beijing, China
zhangjz@ios.ac.cn
[2] Microsoft Research Asia, Beijing, China
[3] University of Chinese Academy of Sciences, Beijing, China
[4] Institute of Automation, Chinese Academy of Sciences, Beijing, China
[5] University of Macau, Macao, China

Abstract. In this paper, we propose a practical method to estimate object appearance from an arbitrary number of images. We use a moving flashlight as light source, and encode surface reflectance properties in a pre-learned embedded latent space. Such lighting and appearance model combination enables our method to effectively narrow the solution space. Uncalibrated illumination requirement extremely simplifies our setup and affords it unnecessary to accurately locate light positions in advance. Moreover, our method automatically selects key frames before appearance estimation, which largely reduces calculation cost. Both synthetic and real experiments demonstrate that our method can recover object appearance accurately and conveniently.

Keywords: SVBRDF · Reflectance · Appearance · Flashlight

1 Introduction

Appearance capture is attractive but also challenging in both computer graphics and vision communities. It enables various applications in VR and AR, such as image relighting and virtual object insertion. Specially designed devices are used for accurate appearance capture [2,3,8]. Although these methods can reproduce high-resolution appearance, involved extensive scan effort prevents them from practical applications. In the past decade, consumer digital cameras have evolved a lot and it is quite convenient for non-expert users to capture high-quality images. For reflectance recovery, recent deep learning based methods learn shape, material priors from large-scale datasets, and take fewer images than traditional methods to infer appearance properties. It shows good prospects to design lightweight methods based on mobile phone cameras and deep learning technologies.

© Springer Nature Switzerland AG 2020
N. Magnenat-Thalmann et al. (Eds.): CGI 2020, LNCS 12221, pp. 71–82, 2020.
https://doi.org/10.1007/978-3-030-61864-3_7

In this paper, we aim to capture object appearance from multiple input photographs. We use a neural network as an optimizer to estimate SVBRDF and normal under uncalibrated flashlight illumination. Object reflectance properties are encoded in a pre-learned latent space. Such a well-constructed latent space not only promises a reasonable SVBRDF but also provides an elegant search routine towards the final solution. During optimization, we sum reconstruction loss for each input photograph together as [7,10], and this provides flexibility about the number of input images. Experiments demonstrate that our method can recover SVBRDF from plausible to accurate with the increment of input image number.

For multiple images capture, one concern is how to take photographs efficiently. Since shooting videos of objects under a moving flashlight is quite simple, we select frames from videos as input. Generally there is a trade-off between the image number and recovery accuracy. Given the budget of the input image number, we propose to select the most valuable image collection via classic clustering. Experiments show that our strategy chooses reasonable images collection.

In summary: We propose a practical framework to estimate SVBRDF for objects with only off the shelf devices. Planar material latent space is adopted for object surface via normal decomposition. And we apply key frame selection strategy to promote algorithm efficiency.

2   Related Work

Intensive Measurement. One straightforward approach to capture appearance is brute-force measurement. Researchers design professional devices to control lighting and camera views for such purpose [15,19]. Dana *et al.* [3] used a robot arm to densely sample incident light and view directions for planar material samples. Another kind of common devices are light stages [2], they are mounted with a large number of lights and able to provide incident light from considerable directions. Linear light source reflectometry [8] is also broadly adopted for appearance recovery. Although those methods can recover vivid appearance, their dedicated devices hinder them from consumer applications.

Simplified Acquisition. In order to reduce the operating threshold for average users and simplify the acquisition process, some searchers capture appearance with hand-held commodity devices. Wu *et al.* [20] took Kinect sensors to scan object geometry and acquired illumination via a mirror sphere, then computed object appearance in an inverse rendering framework. With known geometry but unknown natural illumination, Dong *et al.* [6] estimated isotropic surface SVBRDF from a video of a rotating subject. Some methods jointly solve shape and materials with single or several images as input [1,17]. Comparing with these methods, we utilize neural networks to regularize SVBRDF in a reasonable space rather than relying on hand-crafted priors or specified heuristics.

Fig. 1. (a)-(b): Capture setup. During capture, all lights in the room are turned off. Cam_A is fixed to shoot videos of target object. Cam_B serves as a light source. (c): Reconstructed object. (d)-(g): Estimated diffuse, normal, roughness and specular maps.

Deep Inverse Rendering. Li *et al.* [12] proposed a novel self-augment training scheme that effectively expanded training dataset. Deschaintre *et al.* [4] utilized in-network render layers to construct reconstruction loss and estimated reflectance properties from a flash-lit single image. Similar to [4], Li *et al.* [13] benefited from in-network render and added a dense CRF model to refine final results. Taking one image as input, these methods often fail when visible reflectance features are insufficient to distinguish ambiguities. Then novel frameworks [5,7] are proposed to infer SVBRDF from an arbitrary number of images as input. These methods focus on near-planar material sample, in contrast, ours method is able to recover object appearance.

Recently, Li *et al.* [14] proposed a learning-based method to jointly regress shape, SVBRDF and illumination from a single flash-lit image. However it may suffer from insufficient observations. Another related work is [9], they designed an asymmetric deep auto-encoder to model image formation and inverse rendering process. Extended from [9], Kang *et al.* [10] utilized learned lighting patterns to efficiently capture object appearance, and exploited diffuse and normal information from multiple views to reconstruct geometry.

3 Method

3.1 Preliminary

Our goal is to estimate object SVBRDF and normal in a single view. As showed in Fig. 1, a fixed camera is deployed to capture object-center images while a flashlight is moving. The power distribution of the flashlight is roughly concentrated in a solid angle. Therefore, we model the flashlight as a point light source as long as keep it facing the target object during the capture process. We assume that camera inner parameters are fixed, field of view fov is known, and flashlight intensity keeps constant as I_{int}. We adopt the Cook-Torrance microfacet BRDF model with the GGX normal distribution [18] and assign BRDF parameters for each point p: diffuse abledo $k_d(p)$, specular albedo $k_s(p)$ and monocular roughness $\alpha(p)$. Our method solves SVBRDF and normal $n(p)$ for target object in a fix view, with flashlight position l_i unknown for each input photograph I_i.

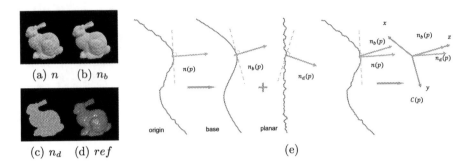

Fig. 2. Decouple shape and surface material. From (a) to (d), we show normal n, base normal n_b and detail normal n_d of ref bunny. In (e): We show 2D slice of object surface. Origin object can be decomposed as base shape and planar material samples.

3.2 Decouple Shape and Surface Material

Demonstrated in [7], a pre-learned latent space can effectively model appearance of planar exemplars and benefits SVBRDF estimation. In our case, we argue that object surface material can be modeled like planar material samples too.

As showed in Fig. 2, object surface can be viewed as warped planar material samples. We decompose normal $n(p)$ as base normal $n_b(p)$ and detail normal $n_d(p)$. Base normal $n_b(p)$ relates with object shape, and detail normal $n_d(p)$ reflects material characteristics. For each point, a local coordinate system $C(p)$ can be constructed: base normal $n_b(p)$ direction is assigned as local z axis $z(p)$ and local y axis $y(p)$ is assigned to be perpendicular to direction $(1, 0, 0)$. In such a local space, detail normal $n_d(p)$ means deviation from base normal $n_b(p)$ and engraves detail variation. Therefore we get:

$$n(p) = n_b(p) \circ n_d(p) \tag{1}$$

Operation $\circ$ means transforming $n_d(p)$ from local space $C(p)$ (constructed according to $n_b(p)$) into global space. It crosses the gap between complex shape and planar material samples.

Once shape and surface material are decoupled, it is easy to convert lighting and viewing directions into the local space of each point $C(p)$. Solving object SVBRDF and detail normal $n_d(p)$ in local space is equal with planar material samples appearance recovery. We adopt local lighting model, object position is needed to calculate light direction and intensity attenuation for each point. But in fact, the distance d_i between the flashlight and object obj is much larger than the scale of object geometry variation. Thus, with known fov, a rough depth map in the camera view is enough to calculate object position.

3.3 Reflectance Recovery Under Uncalibrated Illumination

Object shape, material, and illumination jointly decide how the object looks like. If illumination is under control, SVBRDF estimation would be easier. In

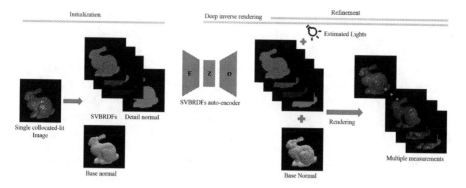

Fig. 3. Overview of the deep inverse rendering framework. We use the method [14] to estimate SVBRDF and base normal from single collocated-lit image as initialization. A specially designed SVBRDF auto-encoder is adopted for deep inverse rendering: we adjust z code to decode SVBRDF and simultaneously update base normal and point light positions. Finally, we directly refine all components in the post-processing step.

this paper, we drop fully-controlled illumination and each input photograph is lit by a flashlight with unknown position l_i. In addition, we assume flashlight intensity I_{int} is constant during the whole capture process.

As showed in Fig. 3, our method consists of three stages: initialization, deep inverse rendering and refinement. The core of our method is deep inverse rendering stage. We constrain object reflectance characteristics in a pre-trained latent space [7] and adjust the latent code z to decode reflectance parameters s:

$$s = D(z),\qquad(2)$$

where $s = (n_d, k_d, \alpha, k_s)$.

We formulate the deep inverse rendering as a minimization that jointly updates the latent code z, base normal n_b and light positions $\{l_i\}$ to minimize the differences between input photograph I_i and corresponding rendering image $R(s, n_b, l_i)$:

$$\underset{z,n_b,\{l_i\}}{\arg\min}\sum_i \mathcal{L}(I_i, R(D(z), n_b, l_i)).\qquad(3)$$

where we use the common loss function [4,7] as:

$$\mathcal{L}(x,y) = ||log(x + 0.01) - log(y + 0.01)||_1.\qquad(4)$$

The whole pipeline of our method is as follows:

1. Use existing methods to initialize base normal, depth and SVBRDF with single collocated-lit image I_{col} as input.
2. Search for initialized light positions for each input photograph I_i.
3. Optimize latent code z, base normal n_b and light positions $\{l_i\}$ in deep inverse rendering stage.
4. Image space refinement for SVBRDF, detail normal n_d, base normal n_b and light positions $\{l_i\}$.

Reflectance Initialization. We capture a special image I_{col} whose correspondent flashlight is collocated with camera lens, as previous methods [13,14,16]. I_{col} can be used [14] to initialize our reflectance properties. The method takes I_{col} as input, and estimates object depth $\hat{d}$, SVBRDF $\hat{s} = (k_d, \alpha, k_s)$ and normal $\hat{n}$ in a cascaded network. We take their estimated normal $\hat{n}$ as base normal n_b, and initialize n_d as a flatten normal map $(n_d(p) = (0,0,1))$. In addition, given camera fov, we project depth map $\hat{d}$ into 3D coordinates as object position map Pos.

Light Initialization. Initialized SVBRDF $\hat{s}$ and normal $\hat{n}$ would help us initialize light position $\hat{l}_i$ for each photograph I_i. We use a try-and-compare strategy to search for light position candidates.

First, we define the metric to evaluate the possibility that a light position candidate lc_i can be used to initialize $\hat{l}_i$. For input image I_i, we use $\hat{s}$, $\hat{n}$ and lc_i to render image R_i, and calculate RMSE for R_i against I_i. Therefore, the goal of light initialization is to quickly find lc_i that has smaller RMSE for R_i.

Then we search for light position candidate lc_i in iterations. 1) At first, we construct a rectangular cuboid centered on the camera. During image capture, the flashlight is moving around the camera. Therefore, we set the cuboid size as $height = w_h * \bar{d}, length = w_l * \bar{d}, depth = w_d * \bar{d}$, where $\bar{d}$ is the average of depth map $\hat{d}$ and w_h, w_l, w_d are scale coefficients. We draw grids with step (w_s, l_s, d_s) in the cuboid and find the current best lc_i from all vertices. 2) Next we construct downsized cuboid centered on lc_i, and draw downsized grids in the new cuboid. Similarly, we find new lc_i from all vertices. We iterate the search process until lc_i is not updated or cuboid size is below the threshold.

Finally, for each photograph I_i, lc_i is used as initialized light position $\hat{l}_i$.

Image Space Refinement. In our optimization network, latent code encodes reflectance properties in the bottle neck of auto-encoder. It usually decodes reflectance properties with details lost. Thus, we add post-process step to refine SVBRDF property maps pixel by pixel [7]. Instead of adjusting the latent code z, we directly update SVBRDF parameters k_d, α, k_s, detail normal n_d and light positions $\{l_i\}$ to minimize the differences between I_i and rendering image $R(s, n_b, l_i)$. We formulate the image space refinement as:

$$\underset{k_d, \alpha, k_s, n_d, n_b, \{l_i\}}{\arg\min} \sum_i \mathcal{L}(I_i, R(s, n_b, l_i)). \tag{5}$$

3.4 Key Frames Selection

We directly select images where the target object shows the distinctive appearance. When photographs look similar, they are possibly lit by flashlights close to each other. Thus, selecting different looking images means choosing different lighting directions. Here we rely on the classic k-means clustering method to divide all captured images into different clusters, and select centroids as picked images. Given recorded videos, our strategy can free users from tedious manual image selection and promotes efficiency.

4   Results

We implement our method in Tensorflow and take built-in layers to construct a differentiable render. For SVBRDF auto-encoder, we inherit trained model from [7]. We choose Adam [11] as optimizer, setting learning rate as 10^{-3} and β_1 as 0.5. In deep inverse rendering stage, we run $6k$ iterations; In refinement stage, we run $1k$ iterations.

At the beginning, we create synthetic datasets to validate proposed method. We randomly compose distorted elementary shapes into synthetic objects like [21] and apply texture from materials dataset [4]. In addition to composed shapes, we also select several models from the Standford 3D Scanning Repository. We render images with pre-defined point lights (used to approximate real flash-lights) in a rectangle area. To demonstrate the effectiveness of the whole method, we gradually relax the restriction from known lighting positions to unknown.

4.1   Known Lighting

For the synthetic experiments, we set camera fov as $60°$, image resolution as 256×256, and the distance between the camera and objects as $2units$. Suppose the camera center is C and the target object is at point O. All point lights are located inside the plane which is perpendicular to the line CO. In the 2×2 $unit^2$ rectangular area, we uniformly place point lights at vertices of the 5×5 grid. These point lights are used to render LDR input images I_i. For testing, we sample point light positions in the 4×4 grid, crossly among 5×5 grid. Given ground truth light positions l_i for each input photograph I_i, we take multiple images as inputs to estimate appearance properties.

To quantitatively evaluate our methods, we adopt metrics as follows: 1) RMSE(root mean square error) for estimated diffuse, specular and roughness albedos against ground truths. $s_{est} = (k_s, k_d, \alpha)$; 2) normal deviation between estimated normal n_{est} and ground truth n_{gt} in degree; 3) RMSE for rendering images $R'(n_{est}, s_{est}, \tilde{l}_i)$ under test lightings $\{\tilde{l}_i\}$. Note that SVBRDF albedos and rendering images are normalized in [0,1] to calculate RMSE.

We test on 21 objects with different materials and show average error in the Table 1. All SVBRDF property errors are smaller than initialization, and normal accuracy has been improved impressively. In general, our results are much closer to the reference than initialization. We show results of bunny in Fig. 4. For simplification, we adopt abbreviations: $diff$ for diffuse, nrm for normal, $spec$ for specular, rou for roughness, $Init$ for initialization, Opt for optimization and Ref for reference. Comparing with initialization, less highlight artifacts show in estimated diffuse albedo, and our estimated normal map contains more details.

4.2   Reflectance Recovery Under Uncalibrated Illumination

Uniformly Sampled Lights. At first, we take 25 images lit by uniformly sampled lights as input, and still test on synthetic objects mentioned in Sect. 4.1 (Without

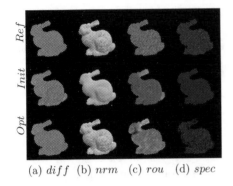
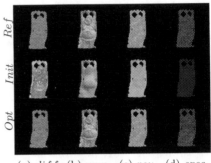

(a) *diff* (b) *nrm* (c) *rou* (d) *spec*   (a) *diff* (b) *nrm* (c) *rou* (d) *spec*

Fig. 4. Results with known lighting.   **Fig. 5.** Result with unknown lighting.

Table 1. Result with 25 images. Opt_1: optimization with uniformly sampled known lighting. Opt_2: optimization with uniformly sampled unknown lighting. Opt_3: optimization with k-means selected unknown lighting.

Error	*diff*	*rou*	*spe*	*nrm*	Render	Light
Init	0.0811	0.1652	0.1096	19.47	0.0976	-
Opt_1	0.0189	0.0729	0.0706	1.2235	0.0548	-
Opt_2	0.0200	0.0716	0.0706	1.3001	0.0549	0.0398
Opt_3	0.0267	0.1048	0.0732	2.1573	0.0545	0.0448

special statement, we take such 21 objects for synthetic experiments by default). Light positions estimation will be measured in distance. We show average error in Table 1. Comparing with initialization, all refectance properties have been improved, and RMSE for rendering images is lower. At the same time, estimated light positions are close to the actual light positions. We show optimization result of buddha in Fig. 5 and light position estimation in Fig. 6. After optimization, light positions converge to ground truth dramatically.

K-means Frames Selection. In synthetic experiments, we render images with 400 uniformly sampled lights from a grid of 20 x 20 in the same rectangular area mentioned in Sect. 4.1. In Fig. 7, we show k-means clustering results for bunny. Each point represents a image lit by a flashlight. Since all lights in synthetic experiments are sampled in a rectangular planar, we take (x, y) from actual light position (x, y, z) as 2D coordinates to draw points in the figure. We observe that k-means clustering results are coincident with flashlight positions. If some flashlights are close, their correspondent images will be clustered in the same group.

Next, we select 25 images and summarize optimization results in Table 1. All SVBRDF properties, rendering images quality, and normal estimation have been improved significantly. As showed in Fig. 9, initialization method [14] cannot distinguish diffuse and specular components clearly. Their method misses normal

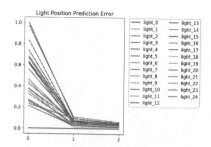

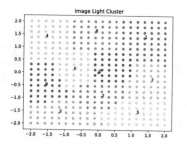

Fig. 6. Vertical: distance between predicted light position and ground truth. Horizontal: initialization, deep inverse rendering and refinement stages.

Fig. 7. Clustering result. 401 images are clustered into 10 groups. Images in groups share the same color and centroids are labeled with cluster id. (Color figure online)

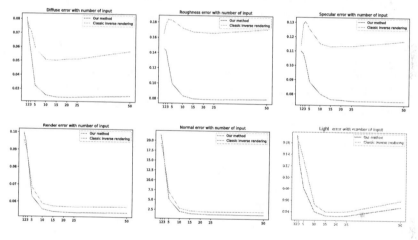

Fig. 8. Optimization result with different number of input.

details, leaving variations in diffuse albedo. In comparison, our method takes multiple images to estimate accurate SVBRDF, and rendering images under novel lighting look almost similar with ground truth.

Number of Input Images. We show how the number of input images affects optimization results. We use k-means strategy to select images with the number k ranging from 1 to 50 and show comparison in Fig. 8. In general, as the increment of input image number k, diffuse, specular and roughness estimation performance improves. Estimated normal becomes dramatically accurate with more input images. When k comes to 10, the rate of improvement slows. Another key point is 25, more images than 25 bring little benefits.

Comparison with Classic Inverse Rendering. We compare our method with classic inverse rendering that directly optimizes SVBRDF and normal in image

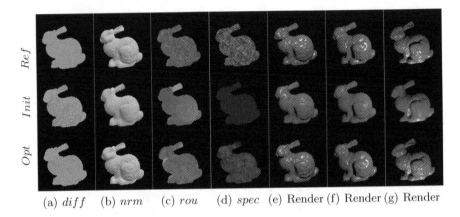

(a) *diff*   (b) *nrm*   (c) *rou*   (d) *spec*   (e) Render (f) Render (g) Render

Fig. 9. Results for bunny with 25 selected images. Each row shows SVBRDF properties, normal map and 3 rendering images under novel lighting.

space. Similar with the post-process step introduced in Sect. 3.3, we take the differentiable render in our network to implement classic inverse rendering. Instead of updating both base normal n_b and detail n_d, classic inverse rendering directly adjusts global normal n. We formulate the classic inverse rendering as:

$$\underset{k_d,\alpha,k_s,n,\{l_i\}}{\arg\min} \sum_i \mathcal{L}(I_i, R(k_s, k_d, \alpha, n, l_i)). \tag{6}$$

We provide the classic inverse rendering with the same initialization and run sufficient number of iterations to make sure convergence. Figure 8 shows that our method recovers more accurate SVBRDF and normal.

4.3   Real Acquisition Results

We use the ProCam app in iPhone 11 to capture all images and videos. We manually adjust ISO, white-balance, aperture and shutter speed parameters. During image capture, all camera configurations are fixed. For each object, we first shot the collocated-lit image, then turn video mode on while moving Cam_B manually around the target.

In Fig. 10, we show an example of real acquisition. Compared with initialized SVBRDF and normal, our method produces accurate diffuse and normal map with more details. Our rendering images are very close to references: highlight appears correctly and image intensity distribution is visually consistent with references. Realistic rendering images illustrate that our method can recover object appearance effectively in real scenarios.

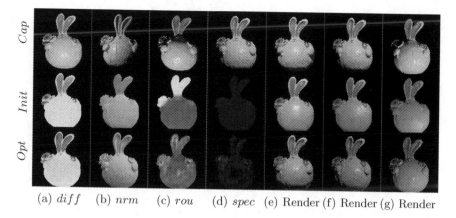

(a) *diff*   (b) *nrm*   (c) *rou*   (d) *spec*   (e) Render (f) Render (g) Render

Fig. 10. Results for real captured object with 25 selected images. First row includes captured images. Left four are part of input, and another three are reference images. In second and third rows: we display SVBRDF properties, normal map and 3 rendering images under novel lighting. Each render image column shares the same novel lighting.

5   Conclusions and Future Work

We propose a lightweight method to recover object reflectance with uncalibrated flash lighting. Modeling object surface material in a pre-learned latent space enables our method to always recover reasonable SVBRDF and constrain optimization routine to reduce ambiguity. Key frames selection strategy reduces both capture and calculation cost. Synthetic and real experiments show that our method can recover accurate SVBRDF and normal efficiently.

One limitation of our method is that we ignore inter-reflection among object components. Thus, we will add multiple bounce reflection estimation modules in the future. Currently, our method may fail if other indoor lights are not switched off. It is interesting to extend our methods under natural illumination.

Acknowledgments. This work is partially supported by the National Natural Science Foundation of China (Nos. 61632003) and is also funded in part by the University of Macau under Grant MYRG2019-00006-FST.

References

1. Barron, J.T., Malik, J.: Shape, illumination, and reflectance from shading. IEEE Trans. Pattern Anal. Mach. Intell. **37**(8), 1670–1687 (2015)
2. Ben-Ezra, M., Wang, J., Wilburn, B., Li, X., Ma, L.: An LED-only BRDF measurement device. In: 26th IEEE Conference on Computer Vision and Pattern Recognition, CVPR (i) (2008)
3. Dana, K.J., Van Ginneken, B., Nayar, S.K., Koenderink, J.J.: Reflectance and texture of real-world surfaces. ACM Trans. Graph. **18**(1), 1–34 (1999)

4. Deschaintre, V., Aittala, M., Durand, F., Drettakis, G., Bousseau, A.: Single-image svbrdf capture with a rendering-aware deep network. ACM Trans. Graph. (SIGGRAPH Conf. Proc.) **37**(128), 1–15 (2018)
5. Deschaintre, V., Aittala, M., Durand, F., Drettakis, G., Bousseau, A.: Flexible svbrdf capture with a multi-image deep network. In: Computer Graphics Forum (Proceedings of the Eurographics Symposium on Rendering), vol. 38, no. 4, July 2019
6. Dong, Y., Chen, G., Peers, P., Zhang, J., Tong, X.: Appearance-from-motion: recovering spatially varying surface reflectance under unknown lighting. ACM Trans. Graph. **33**(6), 1–12 (2014)
7. Gao, D., Li, X., Dong, Y., Peers, P., Xu, K., Tong, X.: Deep inverse rendering for high-resolution svbrdf estimation from an arbitrary number of images. ACM Trans. Graph. **38**(4), 134:1–134:15 (2019)
8. Gardner, A., Tchou, C., Hawkins, T., Debevec, P.: Linear light source reflectometry. ACM Trans. Graph. **22**(3), 749–758 (2003)
9. Kang, K., Chen, Z., Wang, J., Zhou, K., Wu, H.: Efficient reflectance capture using an autoencoder. ACM Trans. Graph. **37**(4), 1–127 (2018)
10. Kang, K., et al.: Learning efficient illumination multiplexing for joint capture of reflectance and shape. ACM Trans. Graph. **38**(6), 1–165 (2019)
11. Kingma, D.P., Ba, J.: Adam: a method for stochastic optimization. In: Bengio, Y., LeCun, Y. (eds.) 3rd International Conference on Learning Representations, ICLR 2015, San Diego, CA, USA, pp. 7–9. Conference Track Proceedings, May 2015
12. Li, X., Dong, Y., Peers, P., Tong, X.: Modeling surface appearance from a single photograph using self-augmented convolutional neural networks. ACM Trans. Graph. **36**(4), 45:1–45:11 (2017)
13. Li, Z., Sunkavalli, K., Chandraker, M.: Materials for masses: svbrdf acquisition with a single mobile phone image. In: Ferrari, V., Hebert, M., Sminchisescu, C., Weiss, Y. (eds.) Computer Vision - ECCV 2018, pp. 74–90. Springer International Publishing, Cham (2018)
14. Li, Z., Xu, Z., Ramamoorthi, R., Sunkavalli, K., Chandraker, M.: Learning to reconstruct shape and spatially-varying reflectance from a single image. ACM Trans. Graph. **37**(6), 1–11 (2018)
15. Matusik, W., Pfister, H., Brand, M., McMillan, L.: Efficient isotropic brdf measurement. In: Proceedings of the 14th Eurographics Workshop on Rendering. EGRW '03, Eurographics Association (2003)
16. Nam, G., Lee, J.H., Gutierrez, D., Kim, M.H.: Practical SVBRDF acquisition of 3D objects with unstructured flash photography. ACM Trans. Graph. **37**(6), 1–12 (2018)
17. Oxholm, G., Nishino, K.: Shape and reflectance estimation in the wild. IEEE Trans. Pattern Anal. Mach. Intell. **38**(2), 376–389 (2016)
18. Walter, B., Marschner, S., Li, H., Torrance, K.: Microfacet models for refraction through rough surfaces. Eurographics, pp. 195–206 (2007)
19. Ward, G.J.: Measuring and modeling anisotropic reflection. In: Proceedings of the 19th Annual Conference on Computer Graphics and Interactive Techniques. SIGGRAPH '92, Association for Computing Machinery (1992)
20. Wu, H., Zhou, K.: Appfusion: interactive appearance acquisition using a kinect sensor. Comput. Graph. Forum **34**(6), 289–298 (2015). https://doi.org/10.1111/cgf.12600
21. Xu, Z., Sunkavalli, K., Hadap, S., Ramamoorthi, R.: Deep image-based relighting from optimal sparse samples. ACM Trans. Graph. **37**(4), 1–13 (2018)

Application of the Transfer Matrix Method to Anti-reflective Coating Rendering

Alexis Benamira[✉] and Sumanta Pattanaik[✉]

University of Central Florida, Orlando, FL, USA
alexis.benamira@knights.ucf.edu, sumant@cs.ucf.edu

Abstract. Thin-film coating is a common practice to modify the appearance of materials. In optics for example, coating is often used on mirrors or lenses to modify their reflectance and transmittance properties. To achieve high transmittance optics or wavelength selective filters for sensors, multilayer coatings are required. Thin-film coating is an active area of research. In this paper we introduce to the rendering community the transfer matrix method to calculate the Fresnel coefficients for multilayer thin-film coating. This method, commonly used in optics, provides an easy way to calculate reflectance and transmittance coefficients for an arbitrary number of thin-film layers. Unlike previous methods [10], which relied on the infinite Airy summation, this method is based on the multiplication of 2×2 matrices which allows handling more general cases. We apply this method to simulate physically based anti-reflective coating where a single layer of thin-film coating is often not enough to obtain a good performance over the full visible spectrum.

Keywords: Reflectance modeling · Thin-film coating · Wave optics

1 Introduction

Thin-film coating is a process that consists in adding on top of a material called substrate, a stack of thin layers of different materials to alter its optical properties. The general principle is as follows: the electromagnetic waves reflected on different layers of the coating will travel different optical lengths. The travelled distance has a direct impact on the phase of the wave, which itself plays an important role when calculating the total intensity of the reflected and transmitted waves. Indeed, when summing the amplitude of the waves, the difference in phase leads to a constructive or destructive summation; this is the phenomenon of interference. The interferences created this way modify the Fresnel coefficients in reflection and in transmission of the substrate. This effect is widely used in industry to design materials with desired reflection or transmission properties. In the visible spectrum, thin-film coating can be applied to obtain perfectly reflecting mirrors over a large waveband. One application that to the best of our

© Springer Nature Switzerland AG 2020
N. Magnenat-Thalmann et al. (Eds.): CGI 2020, LNCS 12221, pp. 83–95, 2020.
https://doi.org/10.1007/978-3-030-61864-3_8

knowledge has received little attention from the Computer Graphics community is anti-reflective coating. Those coatings are critical when simulating the performances of sensors or optical systems since most lenses and semi-conductors sensors receive anti-reflective treatment. Our presented transfer matrix method provides an easy way to account for such coatings inside a ray-tracer. It can be used for simulation in the visible as well as other spectral domains. In this paper we are addressing this property based on wave interference created by multilayer thin-film coating and apply it to global illumination rendering.

At normal incidence, the coefficient of reflection for an air/glass interface is about 4%. To reduce this coefficient, anti-reflective thin-film coatings are applied on top of windows or goggle glasses and their effects can be very notable (see Sect. 5). A useful tool [3] is available to efficiently model the behaviour of one layer thin-film coating. Unfortunately in many applications, one layer coating model has shown severe limitations. It poorly performs over the entire visible spectrum as well as with large angles of incidence. Another way to simulate anti-reflected coating is to multiply the Fresnel term by a coefficient. This method is not physically correct and creates problems for large angles where the Fresnel reflection coefficient is supposed to converge to one but will converge to this multiplying coefficient instead. To achieve high performing anti-reflective coatings, more than one layer is required (see Fig. 1).

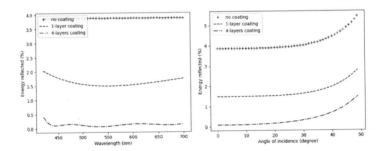

Fig. 1. Energy reflection coefficient variations with light wavelength (left) and light incidence angle (right), at the interface air/BK7 showing no coating (up), one layer (middle) and four layers (bottom) thin-film coating.

In this work, we introduce to the rendering community the matrix transfer method to calculate Fresnel coefficients of a multilayer thin-film coating. Our approach modifies the calculation of Fresnel coefficients and is easy to adapt to the current microfacet models (as illustrated Fig. 2) or smooth interface BRDF (Bidirectional Reflectance Distribution Function). We apply our model and demonstrate its performances on anti-reflective coating. Because multilayered coating design can be a tricky problem [17], we provide, for ease of use, a set of anti-reflective coating examples for several commonly used substrates such as BK7 (high quality optical glass) and polypropylene. We have designed coatings whose behaviour is almost constant over the visible spectrum so that no spectral rendering is required to observe a realistic effect, thus adding little computation time when compared to the computation of non-coated materials. Our method also works perfectly with spectral rendering, enabling coating designers to preview their design.

Our contributions can be summarized as follows:

1. We introduce the matrix transfer method to calculate Fresnel coefficients for multilayer thin-film coating.
2. We provide the code in open source at https://github.com/AlexTintin/Anti-reflective-coating.

2 Previous Work

2.1 Optics

In a pioneering work, Abelès introduced a matrix approach to model multilayer thin-films behaviour [1]. His method differs from ours since he calculates the electric and magnetic fields in each layer whereas we concentrate on the electric field. A vast amount of refining work has followed Abelès', introducing partially coherent, incoherent and anisotropic layers to the methods [5,6,16,18]. Transfer matrix methods can also be applied to flux and not just amplitude of the wave [19]. Design of new coatings is still an active area of research [27].

We have decided to focus on the 2×2 matrix method that model multilayer thin-film coatings following mainly the work of [16,18].

2.2 Computer Graphics

Thin-film Coatings. The issue of multilayer thin-film coatings has been addressed in [10]. Their derivation is based on the Airy summation that results in a recurrence formula. Our method is based on the transfer matrix method and we do not make Stokes reversibility assumption, enabling us to treat non-perfect interfaces (see Sect. 3.4). An extension of their work taking into account anisotropy has been done by [26]. Another work that tries to model the behaviour of multilayer thin-film coatings is [12]. They use the original Abelès' matrix characteristic of a thin-film layer to solve the Kirchhoff diffraction equation and derive a new BRDF model from this diffraction equation. Our work uses the matrix representation to derive a simple 2 dimensional full transfer matrix model, only deriving new Fresnel coefficients making it adaptable to various BRDF formulations. Other thin-film coating models can be found [20,22,23] but they either make approximations in the number of layers or the number of internal reflections. The case of one layer thin-film has been studied recently in [3] to render iridescence. Their model provides a fast and reliable way to perform spectral integration, avoiding spectral aliasing. However, multilayer coatings are required in many settings for high performance coatings.

Anti-reflective coatings. Their usage is common in optics whether it is for solar-panels, windows, sensors or lenses. Their design receives a lot of attention [7,24,

27] and is often a well-kept secret by their manufacturer. In Computer Graphics, it was used as a small application to illustrate the work of [13]. It was used by [11] in order to render lens flare in camera systems. The lack of easy tools to render highly efficient coatings forced them to use a simple one layer coating.

Layered materials and matrix methods. Our approach differs from layered material modeling as investigated by [2,9]. In their work, they focus on geometric optics, leaving out the effect of interference. Our present work embraces the interference phenomenon that cannot be neglected when considering layers, whose thickness are smaller than the coherence length of the light source. In addition, it is noteworthy that we have not tried to derive a full BRDF model. Instead, we are providing a convenient way to calculate Fresnel coefficients. Our approach can thus be added to any layered material model. Matrix methods have been successfully applied [8,15,21,28], especially scattering matrix to account for scattering events in layered material and thus obtaining a new BRDF model. In this work, we calculate new energy coefficients assuming that no scattering happens in the thin-film layers.

3   Theoretical Model

3.1   Hypotheses and Notations

We made several hypotheses to construct our model that we explain in this section. See Fig. 2 for a representation of the situation.

- Let us consider a pile of $N + 1$ locally plane layers separated by N interfaces. The interfaces can be smooth or rough. The layers are parallel to each other and the normal to the parallel surfaces is a local z axis. We consider the problem to be symmetric, so we can place ourselves on a (xz) plane.
- We consider each layer to be isotropic and non-magnetic (i.e. the permeability $\mu = \mu_0$) and each layer is defined by a thickness d_i and a index of refraction n_i. This index of refraction can be complex (it is the case for metals for example), in which case the imaginary part is called the extinction coefficient.
- The first layer and the $(N + 1)^{\text{th}}$ layer are considered infinite. In practice, this approximation is valid because the first layer is the ambient medium and the $(N + 1)^{\text{th}}$ is the substrate that are both much thicker than the thin-film layers.

Let us assume that an incident ray of light is making incident angle θ_i with the z axis. Because we are modeling the interference phenomena happening between the different coating layers, we need to consider light as an electromagnetic field and not just a ray. We define the electric field E as:

$$E(\mathbf{r}, t) = E exp(\mathrm{i}\mathbf{k}_0\mathbf{r} - \mathrm{i}\omega t)$$

with $\mathbf{r} = -\mathbf{w}_i$; $\mathbf{k}_0 = 2\pi n_0(\mathbf{x}\cos\theta_i - \mathbf{z}\sin\theta_i)/\lambda$ and $\omega = c/\lambda$ where λ is the wavelength of the field, $\mathbf{w}_i$ the direction of the incoming wave, c the speed of

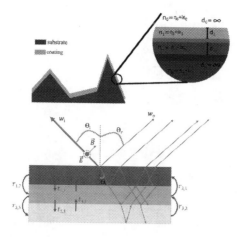

Fig. 2. Multilayered thin-film coating on top of microfacet geometry (left) and propagation of the ray inside the coating (right). (Color figure online)

light in the medium and n_0 the index of refraction of the first medium. The situation is illustrated in Fig. 2. We consider the incoming light to be randomly polarized. To calculate the reflection and transmission coefficients we need to consider the linear polarisation s and p as they form an orthogonal basis of the polarization state. The final coefficients will then be given by $R = (R_s + R_p)/2$ and $T = (T_s + T_p)/2$. Throughout this paper we will use uppercase letters for energy coefficients and lowercase letters for amplitude coefficients. The s polarisation corresponds to the situation where the electric field E is tangential to the incident plane and p polarisation where magnetic field B is tangential to the incident plane.

3.2   Background

When a wave hits an interface between two different mediums, two waves are created, one is transmitted into the second medium, the other one is reflected. The Snell-Descartes laws of refraction gives us that at the interface between a medium m and a medium l, defined by their indices of refraction n_m and n_l, an incoming wave with an incident angle θ_m is reflected in the incident plane with the same angle and is refracted in the medium l with an angle θ_l defined by:

$$n_m \sin \theta_m = n_l \sin \theta_l$$

For a stack of thin-films we have the following equalities:

$$n_0 \sin \theta_0 = n_1 \sin \theta_1 = ... = n_m \sin \theta_m = ... = n_N \sin \theta_N \tag{1}$$

Fresnel Coefficients. From the continuity relations of the electromagnetic field at the interface between two mediums m and l, we can derive the Fresnel coefficients in amplitude for polarisation s and p.

$$r_{m,l}^s = \frac{n_m \cos\theta_m - n_l \cos\theta_l}{n_m \cos\theta_m + n_l \cos\theta_l} \qquad r_{m,l}^p = \frac{n_l \cos\theta_m - n_m \cos\theta_l}{n_m \cos\theta_l + n_l \cos\theta_m} \qquad (2)$$

$$t_{m,l}^s = \frac{2n_m \cos\theta_m}{n_m \cos\theta_m + n_l \cos\theta_l} \qquad t_{m,l}^p = \frac{2n_m \cos\theta_l}{n_m \cos\theta_l + n_l \cos\theta_m} \qquad (3)$$

3.3   One Layer Transfer Matrix

At equilibrium, in each layer a forward electromagnetic wave is propagating toward the $-z$ direction and a backward wave towards the $+z$ direction. We want to express the forward and backward electric field at the layer j as a linear combination of the field at the layer $j+1$. A detailed derivation can be found in [16,18]. We only provide here the matrix equation relating the forward and backward electric field at the layer j noted respectively E_j^- and E_j^+ as a linear combination of the forward and backward field at the layer $j+1$.

$$\begin{bmatrix} E_j^- \\ E_j^+ \end{bmatrix} = P_j D_{j,j+1} \begin{bmatrix} E_{j+1}^- \\ E_{j+1}^+ \end{bmatrix}$$

where the matrix $D_{j,j+1}$ and P_j are defined by:

$$D_{j,j+1} = \frac{1}{t_{j,j+1}} \begin{bmatrix} 1 & -r_{j+1,j} \\ r_{j,j+1} & t_{j,j+1}t_{j+1,j} - r_{j,j+1}r_{j+1,j} \end{bmatrix} \qquad P_j = \begin{bmatrix} e^{-i\delta_j} & 0 \\ 0 & e^{i\delta_j} \end{bmatrix} \qquad (4)$$

with δ_j the phase accumulated by the wave due to the layer j.

$$\delta_j = \frac{2\pi}{\lambda} n_j d_j \cos\theta_j \qquad (5)$$

3.4   Total Transfer Matrix

The efficiency of the transfer matrix method is observable now. Indeed since we have established the transfer matrix for one layer, we can easily express the total transfer matrix that relates E_0^- and E_0^+ to E_N^- and E_N^+ by a product of 2×2 matrices.

$$\begin{bmatrix} E_0^- \\ E_0^+ \end{bmatrix} = D_{0,1} P_1 ... D_{j-1,j} P_j ... P_{N-1} D_{N-1,N} \begin{bmatrix} E_N^- \\ E_N^+ \end{bmatrix}$$

The product of all the matrices makes a new 2 by 2 matrix that we call T.

$$\begin{bmatrix} E_0^- \\ E_0^+ \end{bmatrix} = \begin{bmatrix} T_{11} & T_{12} \\ T_{21} & T_{22} \end{bmatrix} \begin{bmatrix} E_N^- \\ E_N^+ \end{bmatrix}$$

By definition of the amplitude coefficients of reflection and transmission

$$r_{0,N} = \frac{E_0^+}{E_0^-} = \frac{T_{21}}{T_{11}} \qquad t_{0,N} = \frac{E_N^-}{E_0^-} = \frac{1}{T_{11}} \qquad (6)$$

Several comments must be made concerning this final results. First, the final coefficients $r_{0,N}$ and $t_{0,N}$ are defined for $E_N^+ = 0$. We can also define the coefficients $r_{N,0}$ and $t_{N,0}$ by $r_{N,0} = E_N^-/E_N^+ = -T_{12}/T_{11}$ and $t_{N,0} = E_0^+/E_N^+ = Det(T)/T_{11}$ assuming $E_0^- = 0$. $Det(T)$ is the determinant of the matrix T. Considering the case where two incident waves are coming from the two opposite sides of the coating, we can assume they do not interact with one another to create interference inside the coating. We can thus treat each wave separately, using the coefficients defined previously to each wave and add their respective intensity contributions.

For an ideal interface $t_{j,j+1}t_{j+1,j} - r_{j,j+1}r_{j+1,j} = 1$. This is the Stokes reversibility assumption. In the case of rough interface or absorbing media, this difference is not equal to one. In the case of an absorbing medium, the following equality holds true [16] $t_{j,j+1}t_{j+1,j}^* - r_{j,j+1}r_{j+1,j}^* = 1$ where * represent the complex conjugate. Finally the energy coefficients can be computed as follow [6]:

$$R_{s/p} = |r_{s/p}|^2 \qquad T_s = \frac{|t_s|^2 Re(n_N \cos\theta_N)}{n_0 \cos\theta_0} \qquad T_p = \frac{|t_p|^2 Re(n_N^* \cos\theta_N)}{n_0 \cos\theta_0} \qquad (7)$$

4   Results

We implemented our developed matrix transfer method to render anti-reflective coatings on plastic and on thin dielectric materials under global illumination using Mitsuba renderer [14]. More details about anti-reflective coating designs and performances can be found [17]. We provide the designed anti-reflective coatings with our code.

4.1   Single vs Multiple Layers

We first reveal the significant enhancement of multiple layers over a single layer of anti-reflective coating rendering. In a first step we decided to implement a four and a five layers coating because they are the ones which exhibit the best theoretical performances over the full visible spectrum [17]. We want to observe their performances for rendering purposes and chose the most appropriate one for further study. We present the results obtained by rendering a polypropylene material with index of refraction of 1.49. The outcomes are presented in Fig. 3. Similar results can be observed on coatings made for thin dielectrics, which has major real-world applications (see Fig. 4).

As a primary note we confirm the decisive impact of applying anti-reflective thin-film coatings with all our rendering illustrations. The outcomes presented in Fig. 3 show a dramatic rendering enhancement of four layers coating over one layer coating. No noticeable rendering difference can be seen between four and five layers designs. The computing times on the other hand linearly increase with the number of layers as shown Table 1. This is perfectly understandable considering our algorithm whose complexity increases linearly with the number of layers. The algorithm (available in open source) also shows that the number

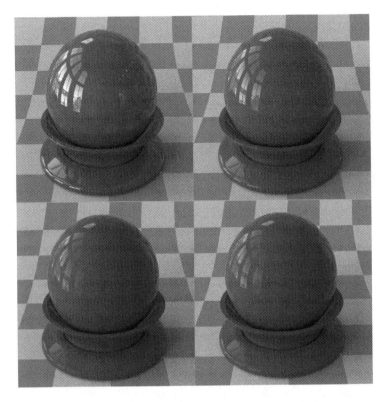

Fig. 3. Comparison between different anti-reflective coating designs on top of blue polypropylene plastic. No coating (top-left corner), one layer (top-right corner), four layers (bottom-left corner) and five layers (bottom right corner) thin-film coatings. (Color figure online)

Fig. 4. Car [4] rendering without (left) and with (right) our four layers anti-reflective coating on the windows and the windshield. (Color figure online)

of wavelengths is a multiplier coefficient for the complexity of the algorithm, explaining the importance of having constant reflective properties to avoid spectral integration. We have not tried to optimize our algorithm, which can be a topic for future work. For computing efficiency we decide to use four layers coating for the rest of our study.

Fig. 5. Teapot [4] rendering without (left) with one layer (middle) and with our four layers (right) anti-reflective coating. (Color figure online)

Table 1. Computation time to render the matpreview scene for different coatings.

Comparative rendering time with pathtracing			
No coating	1 layer	4 layers	5 layers
20.79s	26.43s	38.85s	45.24s

Fig. 6. Spectral rendering with 64 wavelengths between 360 nm and 830 nm (left) and RGB (middle) renderings of the matpreview scene. Pixels with L1 difference value above 5% are represented on the right. (Color figure online)

4.2   Spectral vs RGB

An important point we wanted to demonstrate was to use our model to realistically render real-world coated material without resorting to spectral rendering. While resorting to importance sampling of wavelength have been shown to dramatically improve convergence of spectral rendering [25] and our coatings can certainly benefit from that, the presented multi-layer anti-reflective coatings can be easily supported in a RGB renderer. It is easy to implement and shows good performance to render realistic images quickly. In Fig. 6 we show the comparison of spectral rendering and RGB rendering of an object with polypropylene material with four layers coating. The renderings are very similar. The main differences in the difference image are not due to the coating but the background. Even though the four layers coating reflectance exhibit small undulations of the reflectance value between 400 nm and 700 nm (see Fig. 1), those variations have negligible visual effect.

4.3 Look-Up Table Driven Rendering

Our transfer matrix method lends itself well for look-up table based rendering to achieve higher rendering time performances. Indeed, once the substrate is chosen and the coating is designed with the appropriate number of layers, the two remaining degrees of freedom are the wavelength and the angle of incidence of the light on the surface. Because our four layers anti-reflective coating does not need spectral rendering, we created a table with a sampling step of $1°$ for the incidence angle at three wavelengths: 450 nm, 550 nm, and 580 nm, for the blue, green, and red channels. With a linear interpolation for the incidence angle values, we obtain the renderings shown in Fig. 7 (left image). No noticeable difference can be observed between the renderings with look-up table sampling and with run time matrix evaluation. The rendering overhead with look-up table is insignificant (21.4 seconds with look-up table vs 20.8 seconds for rendering without thin film support) compared to the high overhead in computation time (38.9 seconds) for full calculation of the Fresnel coefficients at runtime.

Fig. 7. Look-up table based rendering (left) compared with the rendering that carries out the full calculation of the Fresnel coefficients at the rendering time (right) for the model with our 4 layers anti-reflection coating. (Color figure online)

Fig. 8. Spaceship [4] rendering without (left) with one layer (middle) and with our four layers (right) anti-reflective coating on windshield. We can observe the sampling issue for both one and four layers coated windshields. (Color figure online)

Fig. 9. Example of iridescence effect with a four layers thin-film that can be obtained with our transfer matrix method. (Color figure online)

5 Conclusion and Future Works

We have introduced the transfer matrix method to render multilayer thin-film coatings, have successfully applied it to render high performing anti-reflective coatings, and have shown that single or multilayer coatings can be efficiently supported in rendering. We have also created coatings, whose behavior over the visible spectrum is constant enough so that they can be directly used in a RGB rendering pipeline to produce antiglare effects without resorting to expensive spectral rendering. Spectral integration works perfectly as well thus offering a tool for coating designers to preview the effect of their work, for which spectral rendering is often required. We have successfully applied our anti-reflective coating on various real-world materials (Figs. 3, 4, 5) and have demonstrated the impressive effect it can provide. Our transfer matrix method can also be applied to render other optical effects introduced by thin-films such as iridescence (Figs. 9). Limits that can be interesting to remove in future works are the symmetry and the isotropic assumptions of the model. Another direction to further refine anti-reflective coating rendering in general would be to address the case of a direct reflection of a light source. Indeed, the sampling of the light source becomes apparent due to the low reflection coefficient, thus requiring more rays to obtain a uniform light (see Figs. 8).

References

1. Abeles, F.: Optical properties of thin absorbing films. JOSA **47**(6), 473–482 (1957)
2. Belcour, L.: Efficient rendering of layered materials using an atomic decomposition with statistical operators. ACM Trans. Graph. **37**(4), 1 (2018)
3. Belcour, L., Barla, P.: A practical extension to microfacet theory for the modeling of varying iridescence. ACM Trans. Graph. **36**(4), 65 (2017)
4. Bitterli, B.: Rendering resources (2016). https://benedikt-bitterli.me/resources/
5. Byrnes, S.J.: Multilayer optical calculations. arXiv preprint arXiv:1603.02720 (2016)

6. Centurioni, E.: Generalized matrix method for calculation of internal light energy flux in mixed coherent and incoherent multilayers. Appl. Opt. **44**(35), 7532–7539 (2005)
7. Cox, J.T., Hass, G., Thelen, A.: Triple-layer antireflection coatings on glass for the visible and near infrared. J. Opt. Soc. Am. **52**(9), 965–969 (1962)
8. Ershov, S., Kolchin, K., Myszkowski, K.: Rendering pearlescent appearance based on paint-composition modelling. In: Computer Graphics Forum, vol. 20, pp. 227–238. Wiley Online Library (2001)
9. Guo, Y., Hašan, M., Zhao, S.: Position-free monte carlo simulation for arbitrary layered bsdfs. ACM Trans. Graph. **37**(6), 1–14 (2018)
10. Hirayama, H., Kaneda, K., Yamashita, H., Monden, Y.: An accurate illumination model for objects coated with multilayer films. Comput. Graph. **25**(3), 391–400 (2001)
11. Hullin, M., Eisemann, E., Seidel, H.P., Lee, S.: Physically-based real-time lens flare rendering. ACM Trans. Graph. **30**(4), 1–10 (2011). https://doi.org/10.1145/2010324.1965003
12. Icart, I., Arquès, D.: A physically-based BRDF model for multilayer systems with uncorrelated rough boundaries. In: Peroche, B., Rushmeier, H.E. (eds.) Proceedings of the Eurographics Workshop on Rendering Techniques 2000, Brno, Czech Republic, 26–28, June 2000, pp. 353–364. Eurographics, Springer (2000). https://doi.org/10.1007/978-3-7091-6303-0_32
13. Imura, M., Oshiro, O., Saeki, M., Manabe, Y., Chihara, K., Yasumuro, Y.: A generic real-time rendering approach for structural colors. In: Proceedings of the 16th ACM Symposium on Virtual Reality Software and Technology, pp. 95–102. Association for Computing Machinery (2009)
14. Jakob, W.: Mitsuba renderer (2010). http://www.mitsuba-renderer.org
15. Jakob, W., D'Eon, E., Jakob, O., Marschner, S.: A comprehensive framework for rendering layered materials. ACM Trans. Graph. (Proc. SIGGRAPH) **33**(4), 118:1–118:14 (2014)
16. Katsidis, C.C., Siapkas, D.I.: General transfer-matrix method for optical multilayer systems with coherent, partially coherent, and incoherent interference. Appl. Opt. **41**(19), 3978–3987 (2002)
17. Macleod, H.A.: Thin-film Optical Filters. CRC Press, Boca Raton (2017)
18. Mitsas, C.L., Siapkas, D.I.: Generalized matrix method for analysis of coherent and incoherent reflectance and transmittance of multilayer structures with rough surfaces, interfaces, and finite substrates. Appl. Opt. **34**(10), 1678–1683 (1995)
19. Simonot, L., Hersch, R.D., Hébert, M., Mazauric, S.: Multilayer four-flux matrix model accounting for directional-diffuse light transfers. Appl. Opt. **55**(1), 27–37 (2016)
20. Smits, B.E., Meyer, G.W.: Newton's colors: simulating interference phenomena in realistic image synthesis. In: Photorealism in Computer Graphics, pp. 185–194. Springer (1992)
21. Stam, J.: An illumination model for a skin layer bounded by rough surfaces. In: Rendering Techniques 2001, pp. 39–52. Springer (2001)
22. Sun, Y.: Rendering biological iridescences with rgb-based renderers. ACM Trans. Graph. **25**(1), 100–129 (2006). https://doi.org/10.1145/1122501.1122506
23. Sun, Y., Wang, Q.: Interference shaders of thin films. Comput. Graph. Forum (2008). https://doi.org/10.1111/j.1467-8659.2007.01110.x
24. Thetford, A.: A method of designing three-layer anti-reflection coatings. Opt. Acta Int. J. Opt. **16**(1), 37–43 (1969)

25. Wilkie, A., Nawaz, S., Droske, M., Weidlich, A., Hanika, J.: Hero wavelength spectral sampling. In: Proceedings of the 25th Eurographics Symposium on Rendering, pp. 123–131. EGSR '14, Eurographics Association, Goslar, DEU (2014)
26. Wu, F.K., Zheng, C.W.: Microfacet-based interference simulation for multilayer films. Graph. Models **78**, 26–35 (2015)
27. Xi, J.Q., et al.: Optical thin-film materials with low refractive index for broadband elimination of fresnel reflection. Nature Photonics **1**(3), 176–179 (2007)
28. Zeltner, T., Jakob, W.: The layer laboratory: a calculus for additive and subtractive composition of anisotropic surface reflectance. Trans. Graph. (Proc. SIGGRAPH) **37**(4), 74:1–74:14 (2018). https://doi.org/10.1145/3197517.3201321

Dynamic Shadow Rendering with Shadow Volume Optimization

Zhibo Fu[1], Han Zhang[2], Ran Wang[3], Zhen Li[3], Po Yang[4], Bin Sheng[5(⊠)], and Lijuan Mao[3(⊠)]

[1] Digital Grid Research Institute China Southern Power Grid,
Guangdong, People's Republic of China
[2] Nanjing University of Aeronautics and Astronautics,
Nanjing, People's Republic of China
[3] Shanghai University of Sport, Shanghai, People's Republic of China
maolijuan@sus.edu.cn
[4] The University of Sheffield, Sheffield, UK
[5] Shanghai Jiao Tong University, Shanghai, People's Republic of China
shengbin@cs.sjtu.edu.cn

Abstract. The shadow volume is utilized extensively for real-time rendering applications which includes updating volumes and calculating silhouette edges. Existing shadow volume methods are CPU intensive and complex occluders result in poor rendering efficiency. In this paper, we propose a hash-culling shadow volume algorithm that uses hash-based acceleration for the silhouette edge determination which is the most time-consuming processing in the traditional shadow volume algorithm. Our proposed method uses a hash table to store silhouette edge index information and thus reduces the time taken for redundant edge detection. The method significantly reduces CPU usage and improves algorithm time efficiency. Furthermore, for low hardware-level systems, especially embedded systems, it is still difficult to render dynamic shadows due to their high demand on the fill-rate capacity of graphics hardware. Our method has low hardware requirements and is easy to implement on PCs and embedded systems with real-time rendering performance with visual-pleasing shadow effects.

Keywords: Shaodow volume · Hash-culling · Dynamic · Artificial intelligence · Explainable AI · Intelligent sensors

1 Introduction

Shadow effects can help viewers to perceive the relative distance and position of objects, as well as the geometry of occluders and occludees [11]. However, rendering realistic shadows is difficult, and doing it in real-time is even more complicated. Offline rendering techniques such as ray tracing can generate shadows automatically; nonetheless, no standard approach to real-time shadow rendering

© Springer Nature Switzerland AG 2020
N. Magnenat-Thalmann et al. (Eds.): CGI 2020, LNCS 12221, pp. 96–106, 2020.
https://doi.org/10.1007/978-3-030-61864-3_9

currently exists. Among numerous shadow rendering methods used in the various applications, shadow volume has been prevalent and is efficient in its ability to generate accurate real-time shadows [17]. When compared with shadow mapping with its aliasing artifacts problem, shadow volume is considered the better choice especially when there is a demand for high-quality shadows. However, the computation complexity of dynamic shadows in the shadow volume algorithm has been a long-standing problem since it is first introduced. The efficiency of the shadow volume algorithm is limited by two main procedures: determination of silhouette edges and shadow volume rendering. Because the number of silhouette edges has a significant impact on the stencil test time and ultimately determines the shadow rendering time, improving silhouette edge determination efficiency is our key objective. Furthermore, in recent years, 3D games and AR application [15] have become prevalent, propelled by concomitant sharp increases in the usage of smartphones and tablets. However, the graphics hardware in smartphones and tablets is resource-constrained, and so efficient implementation of dynamic shadows for 3D games and other 3D applications is crucial. Thus, optimization of the classic shadow volume algorithm for use in such environments is imperative [14,18].

We propose a hash-culling shadow volume algorithm that improves the efficiency of silhouette edge determination. In the proposed algorithm, according to the position of the light source and the mesh, all the faces of the mesh are tested to determine if they are front surfaces. Next, for all front surfaces, silhouette edges are recorded and each silhouette edge is extended away from the light source to infinity to form a shadow volume. We use shadow polygons to refer to polygons that form the bounds of the shadow volume. The efficiency of the search for the silhouette has a significant impact on the overall efficiency of the algorithm because it is the most time-consuming step. Conventionally the per-triangle method makes a high demand on the fill-rate capacity of graphics cards, which can result in process delays. Our proposed hash-culling shadow volume method is based on the per-object shadow volume concept, and therefore significantly reduces the stress on graphics cards without any meaningful increase in CPU usage. In our proposed algorithm, a hash map is used to improve the search performance of silhouette edges. Using this hash map, we can ensure that silhouette edges are distinguished once all front-surface edges are traversed, and our hash function guarantees that all silhouette edges are recorded. The results of timing tests conducted indicate that our method has significant advantages over classic methods. Our contributions include the following:

- Introducing a hash-culling method that greatly improves shadow volume time efficiency by reducing silhouette edge processing time and shadow volume rasterization time.
- Reducing hardware dependency of shadow volume to make it practical for an embedded system to run real-time shadows.
- Gaining the possibility that using the hash-culling method with other shadow volume culling and clamping method to further improve real-time shadow generating efficiency.

2 Related Work

First described by Crow [5], shadow volume defines the shadow region of a specific occluder in space, with a given light source. Subsequent to Crow's work, many methods have been developed to improve the performance of the shadow volume algorithm. Brotman et al. proposed a software-based shadow algorithm with a depth buffer [4]. Hardware support for shadow volume evaluation is also supported in the Pixel Planes method [9]. Bergeron extended the shadow volume algorithm afterwards [3]. He clarified how to deal with open models and non-planar polygons. Further, he showed that close shadow volumes are necessary. Heidmann first implemented the shadow volume algorithm in graphics hardware [12]. They used a stencil test to implement the shadow volume, and front and back surface tests to facilitate practical usage of the algorithm. Stencil buffer implementation of the shadow volume algorithm has subsequently become the most practical and widely-used real-time shadow-generating method [10]. The classic shadow volume algorithm is not very robust. To rectify this drawback, various algorithms have been proposed to help it adapt to various circumstances, such as the Z-fail, ZP+, and ++ZP algorithms [7]. Batagelo et al. presented a shadow volume algorithm that uses Binary Space Partitioning (BSP) trees and stencil buffers [2]. Their algorithm combines the shadow volume technique with BSP trees and improves the efficiency of the shadow volume algorithm with graphics hardware support. Everitt and Kilgard [8] presented several solutions to reduce the fill-rate capacity demand for graphics cards. Kim et al. proposed techniques that extend the shadow volume to non-manifold meshes [16]. Aldridge et al. utilized a per-object shadow volume technique, thereby rectifying the high demand of the fill-rate problem [1]. Culling and clamping of the volumes are used to improve the robustness of this algorithm [20]. Most recently, the per-triangle shadow volume technique was used by Sintorn et al. with Compute Unified Device Architecture (CUDA) implementation [19] and proved to be robust and reduced pre-processing time for shadow volumes.

A shadow volume is, in essence, a volume constructed with a light source and occluders. Several important concepts need to be clarified: Any object that casts a shadow is an occluder. Edges that connect front and back surfaces with consideration to the light source are silhouette edges. Extension of every silhouette edge away from the light source to infinity (usually a very large value in the actual implementation) can result in the formation of shadow polygons. Front and back caps of shadow volumes (faces on the object and their projection at infinity) should be added to form a closed volume. That infinity value should be sufficiently large because even if the light source is very close to the occluder, the shadow should be able to reach the occludee. There are three basic steps in the construction of shadow volumes: (1) Find all silhouette edges, (2) extend all silhouette edges away from the light source to infinity, and (3) add front and back caps to form shadow volumes. After construction of a shadow volume, a stencil buffer is typically used to implement shadows. The two most commonly used techniques are depth-pass and depth-fail also called Z-pass and Z-fail because the depth buffer is often referred to as the Z-buffer [13]. The two most expensive operations in stencil shadow volume implementation are silhouette edge determination and shadow volume rendering [6]. In this paper, our proposed hash-culling technique is presented to address the first problem.

3   Hash-Culling Approach

In the classic shadow volume construction step, after extending silhouette edges away from the light source to infinity, front and back caps should be added to the shadow volume in order to form a closed volume. In the stencil test step, after shadow volume construction, when the light ray that originates from the viewer's eyes to a point in the scene passes through a front surface of a shadow volume, the stencil buffer is incremented by one. Conversely, when it passes through a back surface of a shadow volume, the stencil buffer is decremented by one. Figure 1 demonstrates this Z-pass mechanism which is used to conduct the stencil test. When viewport cuts through the shadow volume, Z-fail is used to obtain the correct result. Because these methods are not the focus of this paper, further details are omitted.

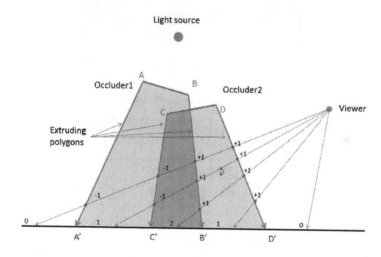

Fig. 1. Basic procedure of Z-Pass algorithm.

The front surfaces of the occluder typically must be projected to infinity. In this scenario, the back cap of the shadow volume is redundant. Since the back cap is at infinity, the receiver should always be covered by the shadow volume. Otherwise, the shadow will never reach the receiver, which is not the target effect. That is, no sight ray will pass through the back cap of the shadow volume before it reaches the occludee. Therefore, the back cap of the shadow volume can be cut. As stated above, the determination of silhouette edges is a very time-consuming process. All edges of the front surfaces with respect to the light sources are added to the edge set used to generate the shadow volume. If we assume that we are using indexed mesh, then the silhouette edges are those edges that are shared by a front surface and a back surface. Figure 2 depicts the silhouette edges of a mesh with a given light source. The following steps are required for determination of silhouette edges: For every triangle of the mesh, if it faces the light source, add the three edges (pairs of vertices) to an edge array; check each of these three edges, respectively, to determine if it (or its reverse) has appeared in the array and, if yes, remove both edges.

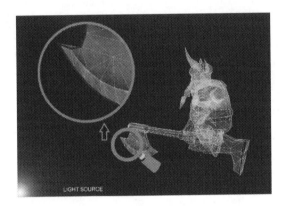

Fig. 2. Silhouette edges depicted with red lines on a mesh with one point light. (Color figure online)

The complexity of S for each edge is $O(n)$. Consequently, the complexity of silhouette edge determination is $O(n^2)$.

$$(1 - p) \times n \times \sum_{i}^{(1-p) \times n} S_i \tag{1}$$

We use a hash table to reduce the time complexity of the silhouette edge determination process and thereby improve the performance. Assume that we use indexed meshes, which means that there is an index array that decides every triangle of the mesh. The index of each vertex means the position for each vertex in vertex array, thus index for each vertex is unique. Every time a new edge is added into an array, we should not go through the whole array to decide whether this edge has appeared or not. Instead, we can use a hash table to provide rapid searching and deleting performance when adding new edges. Each time a new edge is added into the hash table, we check whether it is a duplicate or not. In this way, we ensure that when two edges with the same vertices are added to the hash table, they map to the same position irrespective of the sequence of the vertices. For every hash element, it stores one unsigned integer that is used to store the key-value, two integers that are used to store vertex values, and one Boolean value that is used to store the occupation flag. Assume that

MAX represents the size of the hash table, and V_A and V_B denote indices of two vertices. Then, the equation to calculate the key value is as follows:

$$Key = (V_A^2 + V_B^2) \pmod{MAX}. \tag{2}$$

In this way, we ensure that when edges with identical vertices are added to the hash table, they map to the same position regardless of whether the vertex order is the same or reverse. When adding a new edge, the key value is calculated first, according to vertex indices. Then, the corresponding position in the hash table is checked. If the position is not occupied, the vertex index values are stored and the occupation flag set to *TRUE*. If the position is occupied, the vertex values are checked and, if the values are equal or reverse, which means that a redundant edge is found, the occupation flag is set to *FALSE*. If the vertex values are not equal or the reverse, S is added to the key value and the corresponding position's occupation flag checked again. Here, S can be any number standing for step length.

However, edges are added to the hash table, those edges with a *TRUE* occupation flag are silhouette edges. Finally, we traverse the whole hash table to get all silhouette edges, then use them to render the shadow volume. In an actual implementation, the probability of collision is very low; therefore, the algorithm time efficiency is $O(n)$. Figure 3 demonstrates the rendering pipeline of our method, including loading vertices data, rendering model with ambient lights, searching silhouette edges, rendering shadow volume and doing stencil tests, finally blending shadow color to draw shadows.

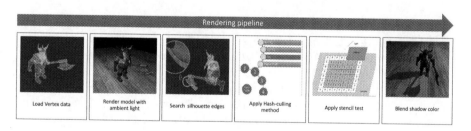

Fig. 3. Rendering pipeline for hash-culling method.

4 Implementation

We implemented our proposed algorithm in C++ with OpenGL and conducted timing tests on a PC with an Intel i5 3210 2.5 GHz CPU, and an Intel 4000 HD graphics card, 8 GB RAM. In our implementation, all scenes were rendered with a resolution of 800 * 600 pixels, 16 bits RGBA color buffers, and 8-bit stencil buffers. For each scene, there was a single-point light source in a distinct place, and the same floor was used to conveniently observe shadows. We also

Algorithm 1. Adding an edge into hash table

```
1: AddEdge(hashtable H, hash-key K, vertex A, vertex B, loop N)
2: //Add edge when not occupied
3: if H[K] is not occupied then
4:     H[K]− > isOccupied = TRUE
5:     H[K]− > Vertex_A = A
6:     H[K]− > Vertex_B = B
7: else
8:     //Remove redundant edge
9:     if Edge(A, B) is in hash table then
10:         H[K]− > isOccupied = FALSE
11:     else
12:         //Map edge to another position
13:         AddEdge(H, K + S, A, B, N + 1)
14:     end if
15: end if
```

implemented our method on several smartphones and tablets, however, timing tests are all conducted on PC.

In the implementation, Z-pass was used to perform the stencil test and, when viewport cuts through shadow volume, Z-fail was used to obtain correct results. The pseudocode for our implemented hash-culling method is shown below.

5   Results and Discussion

In this section, the results of the timing tests conducted on our hash-culling algorithm are presented. For comparison purposes, results for the per-triangle method, which is used in [19] with CUDA, are also presented. It is also a classic shadow volume method that is extensively utilized in various applications. In this timing test, we implemented it with software. In order to obtain convincing and comprehensive results, we used various meshes with a variety of shapes and structures. Transparent meshes are not tested since dealing with this is not the main purpose of our algorithm.

Through the timing tests for both classic per-triangle method and hash-culling method, we have those results and comparisons. Figure 4 helps to demonstrate the time efficiency (in frames per second (FPS)) gained by our hash-culling algorithm. Figure 5 shows the number of shadow volume triangles that needed to be rendered for both two algorithms respectively. Shadow volume can generate pixel-accurate shadow images thus aliasing is not the problem since shadow volume was introduced. The hash-culling method can render shadows whose quality is as good as the results of other shadow volume methods.

The timing test that comparing our method with the per-triangle algorithm, which is commonly used in many games and applications, shows our method tremendously reduces the triangle amount of shadow volume. In most cases, the triangle amount of shadow volume decreases to less than 10% of the amount of

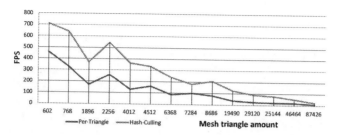

Fig. 4. Performance comparison between the Per-Triangle algorithm and our Hash-culling algorithm.

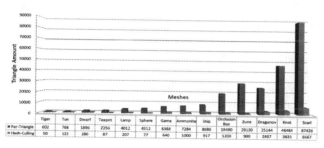

Fig. 5. Shadow volume triangle amount comparison between the Per-Triangle algorithm and our Hash-culling algorithm.

per-triangle's. Generally speaking, the more complex the occluder is, the more triangles will be reduced. Since the majority of shadow rendering time is spent on shadow volume rasterization, decrease of triangle amount leads directly to the decrease of rendering time. With the hash-culling method, traversing all edges of front surfaces is necessary, just as it is in the per-triangle method. However, the hash-culling method records silhouette edges with no gain on time complexity. It has $O(n)$ time complexity and performs quite well in all tests. As a result, FPS for each scene increases over 200%. Good performance makes it possible to run real-time shadows on platforms with minimal hardware, such as embedded systems. Compared with the results for Kim's [1] algorithm, which was implemented on a Pentium 3.0 GHz PC with NVIDIA GeForce 6800, from Table 1 we know that our method performed creditably in terms of FPS improvement with

Table 1. Comparison of performance for Kim's method and our hash-culling method.

Triangles	FPS	Our Triangles	Our FPS
1120	703.4	2256	922
13576	193.1	19490	268
27736	35	29120	225
62724	41.4	87426	55

consideration to hardware difference. The first two columns display the number of triangles and the FPS for Kim's test case, while the last two columns display our test data. Our hash-culling method can achieve very similar performance as Sintorn's [13] method. We have not added support for transparent objects yet, this will require more resource and calculation, but considering the objective of our method that we want to implement dynamic shadow on different platforms and with low-level hardware, our performance is quite convincing and this method is practicable. The Hash-culling method is easy to implement since it doesn't require complex concurrent computation on GPU. Our method's CPU usage is as low as that of the classic per-triangle method. The hash method provides quick and accurate search performance for silhouette edges. We have tested our algorithm on several embedded systems, including Samsung Nexus S with 1 GHz CPU, 512 Mb ram. The embedded systems have relatively low hardware capability, especially the incomplete graphic support, for example, the difference between OpenGL ES and OpenGL. Unlike other algorithms, our algorithm does not require programmable graphic pipeline, and do not use GPU for general concurrency calculation, meanwhile it does not require much CPU calculation. All these features make sure that it can be implemented on embedded systems with low hardware level. On the Nexus S platform, render a shadow for a model with more than 2000 triangles, we can still get more than 60 frames per second.

From the data and the graphs above, the improvement of our algorithm over the classic algorithm is evident. Using the hash-culling algorithm, the triangles that had to be rendered for the shadow volume decreased sharply without any additional burden on the CPU. As a result, the FPS of each scene significantly increased to a new level. Various hardware-dependent shadow volume algorithms have been proposed; however, to the best of our knowledge, none of them can be easily implemented, neither are they used extensively on embedded systems because of poor hardware support. In this scenario, our method can make a big difference when rendering dynamic shadows, which makes it very practical for generating dynamic shadow effects in embedded systems. Figure 6 depicts a number of scenes rendered using our proposed method on smartphones and tablets. Because one of our targets is to efficiently render dynamic shadows on smartphones and tablets, reducing hardware dependency can help the algorithm to become more robust.

Fig. 6. Test scenes on embedded systems with different meshes. From left to right: (1) Dwarf, with 1896 triangles; (2) Car, with 6813 triangles; (3) Gun, with 5630 triangles; (4) Scanner arm, with 6116 triangles.

6   Conclusion

In this paper, we presented a hash-culling shadow volume algorithm that can generate real-time shadows even for relatively complex meshes. Our algorithm is based on shadow volume and a stencil buffer is used in its implementation. As demonstrated by the implementation and test results, our algorithm improves the performance of various kinds of scenes, irrespective of whether the mesh is simple or complex. We improved performance primarily by simplifying silhouette edge determination, resulting in reduced shadow volume rendering time. In the future, graphics hardware may be able to support the two-side stencil test; in which case, only one render pass will be needed to render the shadow volume. This enhancement would advance the shadow volume algorithm to another level.

Acknowledgement. This work was supported in part by the National Key Research and Development Program of China under Grant 2018YFF0300903, in part by the National Natural Science Foundation of China under Grant 61872241 and Grant 61572316, and in part by the Science and Technology Commission of Shanghai Municipality under Grant 15490503200, Grant 18410750700, Grant 17411952600, and Grant 16DZ0501100.

References

1. Aldridge, G., Woods, E.: Robust, geometry-independent shadow volumes. In: Proceedings of the 2nd International Conference on Computer Graphics and Interactive Techniques in Australasia and South East Asia, pp. 250–253 (2004)
2. Batagelo, H.C., Costa, I.: Real-time shadow generation using BSP trees and stencil buffers. In: XII Brazilian Symposium on Computer Graphics and Image Processing (Cat. No. PR00481), pp. 93–102. IEEE (1999)
3. Bergeron, P.: A general version of crow's shadow volumes. IEEE Comput. Graphics Appl. **6**(9), 17–28 (1986)
4. Brotman, L.S., Badler, N.I.: Generating soft shadows with a depth buffer algorithm. IEEE Comput. Graphics Appl. **4**(10), 5–14 (1984)
5. Crow, F.C.: Shadow algorithms for computer graphics. ACM SIGGRAPH Comput. Graph. **11**(2), 242–248 (1977)
6. Dahlbom, M.: Stencil shadow volumes. Rendering of High Quality 3D-Graphics (2002)
7. Eisemann, E., Assarsson, U., Schwarz, M., Valient, M., Wimmer, M.: Efficient real-time shadows. In: ACM SIGGRAPH 2013 Courses, pp. 1–54 (2013)
8. Everitt, C., Kilgard, M.J.: Practical and robust stenciled shadow volumes for hardware-accelerated rendering. arXiv preprint cs/0301002 (2003)
9. Fuchs, H., et al.: Fast spheres, shadows, textures, transparencies, and imgage enhancements in pixel-planes. ACM SIGGRAPH Comput. Graph. **19**(3), 111–120 (1985)
10. Graphics, S.: OpenGL-based real-time shadows (2002)
11. Hasenfratz, J.M., Lapierre, M., Holzschuch, N., Sillion, F., GRAVIR: A survey of real-time soft shadows algorithms. In: Computer Graphics Forum, vol. 22, pp. 753–774. Wiley Online Library (2003)

12. Heidmann, T.: Real shadows, real time. Iris Universe, no. 18, pp. 28–31. Silicon Graphics (1991)
13. Hook III, E.W.: Remembering Thomas Parran, his contributions and missteps going forward: history informs us. Sex. Transm. Dis. **40**(4), 281–282 (2013)
14. Kamel, A., Sheng, B., Yang, P., Li, P., Shen, R., Feng, D.D.: Deep convolutional neural networks for human action recognition using depth maps and postures. IEEE Trans. Syst. Man Cybern. Syst. **49**(9), 1806–1819 (2019)
15. Karambakhsh, A., Kamel, A., Sheng, B., Li, P., Yang, P., Feng, D.D.: Deep gesture interaction for augmented anatomy learning. Int. J. Inf. Manag. **45**, 328–336 (2019). https://doi.org/10.1016/j.ijinfomgt.2018.03.004, http://www.sciencedirect.com/science/article/pii/S0268401217308678
16. Kim, B., Kim, K., Turk, G.: A shadow-volume algorithm for opaque and transparent nonmanifold casters. J. Graph. Tools **13**(3), 1–14 (2008)
17. Lu, P., Sheng, B., Luo, S., Jia, X., Wu, W.: Image-based non-photorealistic rendering for realtime virtual sculpting. Multimedia Tools Appl. **74**(21), 9697–9714 (2014). https://doi.org/10.1007/s11042-014-2146-4
18. Sheng, B., Li, P., Zhang, Y., Mao, L.: GreenSea: visual soccer analysis using broad learning system. IEEE Trans. Cybern., 1–15 (2020). https://doi.org/10.1109/TCYB.2020.2988792
19. Sintorn, E., Olsson, O., Assarsson, U.: An efficient alias-free shadow algorithm for opaque and transparent objects using per-triangle shadow volumes. In: Proceedings of the 2011 SIGGRAPH Asia Conference, pp. 1–10 (2011)
20. Stich, M., Wächter, C., Keller, A.: Efficient and robust shadow volumes using hierarchical occlusion culling and geometry shaders. GPU Gems **3**, 239–256 (2007)

Adaptive Illumination Sampling
for Direct Volume Rendering

Valentin Kraft[(✉)], Florian Link, Andrea Schenk, and Christian Schumann

Fraunhofer MEVIS, Am Fallturm 1, 28359 Bremen, Germany
valentin.kraft@mevis.fraunhofer.de
https://www.mevis.fraunhofer.de/

Abstract. Direct volume rendering is used to visualize data from sources such as tomographic imaging devices. The perception of certain structures depends very much on visual cues such as lighting and shadowing. According illumination techniques have been proposed for both surface rendering and volume rendering. However, in the case of direct volume rendering, some form of precomputation is typically required for real-time rendering. This however limits the application of the visualization. In this work we present *adaptive volumetric illumination sampling*, a ray-casting-based direct volume rendering method that strongly reduces the amount of necessary illumination computations without introducing any noise. By combining it with voxel cone tracing, realistic lighting including ambient occlusion and image-based lighting is facilitated in real-time. The method only requires minimal precomputation and allows for interactive transfer function updates and clipping of the visualized data.

Keywords: Direct volume rendering · Ray casting · Realistic lighting · Ambient occlusion · Voxel cone tracing · Augmented reality

1 Introduction

Modern computer graphics applications pose high requirements on the used hardware and rendering methods with respect to resolution, frame rates and image quality. For most applications, a frame rate of 25 frames per second (fps) poses the absolute minimum, while certain applications such as *augmented reality (AR)* require 60 fps or even more[1]. The used image resolution is often 2K[2] and above. Furthermore, the frame rate or the resolution is inherently doubled for stereo rendering, as utilized in AR. At the same time, expectations regarding image quality and realism are very high, pushed by developments in industries such as movies and gaming. *Global illumination (GI)* is a key technique to generate realistic and compelling images, but is still usually not feasible in real-time and often approximated for example by *ambient occlusion (AO)* [20].

---

[1] https://docs.microsoft.com/en-us/windows/mixed-reality/app-quality-criteria.
[2] 2048 × 1080 pixel.

© Springer Nature Switzerland AG 2020
N. Magnenat-Thalmann et al. (Eds.): CGI 2020, LNCS 12221, pp. 107–118, 2020.
https://doi.org/10.1007/978-3-030-61864-3_10

The competing requirements of high frame rates, high resolution and high quality also concern the field of medical visualization, where *direct volume rendering (DVR)* [3] is used to give insights into the human body based on *computer tomography (CT)* and *magnetic resonance imaging (MRI)*. Several studies showed that a realistic depiction including important visual cues such as realistic lighting and shadows improve spatial understanding and the ability to recognize anatomical structures [11,12,19]. While AO can be computed for surface rendering in real-time using current graphics processing units (GPU), most of the respective methods cannot be directly applied to DVR easily and the computational efforts for DVR are much higher. Therefore, methods for the computation of AO in DVR typically rely on some form of precomputation of illumination values for reuse during interactive rendering [4,5,9,16–18]. However, such approaches typically limit the ability to interactively change clipping planes or the *transfer function (TF)*, a function that maps the value of each voxel to a colour and an opacity. Sophisticated solutions, such as the utilization of progressive path tracing allow for physically correct rendering at the cost of high noise and low update rates.

In this paper, we present *adaptive volumetric illumination sampling (AVIS)*, a GPU-based DVR method that enables realistic lighting in real-time by reducing the number of illumination calculations adaptively during ray casting. *Voxel cone tracing* [2] is adapted to compute AO in combination with *image-based lighting* for the necessary samples. The resulting rendering method allows to compute noise-free images with realistic lighting effects at very high resolutions and frame rates while supporting both interactive transfer function updates and clipping of the visualized data. To ensure practical use, we show its utilization for the visualization of biological and medical data and compare it with two established volume rendering methods.

2 Related Work

A common way to improve upon a pure local illumination model is to approximate indirect illumination by means of AO, which usually uses ray tracing to compute the amount of occlusion over the hemisphere of a surface point [20]. In combination with image-based lighting, which uses environment maps to represent the incoming light [10], very realistic results can be achieved [7]. One solution to enable real-time surface rendering with ambient occlusion is to precompute the AO values and store them in textures [10]. Similarly, AO values can be precomputed and stored in a 3D illumination cache for later usage in interactive DVR. For that, many approaches use filtering operations on the voxel data instead of ray casting [5,18]. These approaches produce plausible results, but are limited with respect to real-time changes of clipping planes or TFs since the cache has to be updated to reflect the changed situation. The need for complete recomputations of the cache during TF changes can be reduced by coding the local voxel neighbourhood with the help of histograms [16] or cube shells [9]. However, these approaches are limited to a small neighbourhood and do not support clipping. Multi-resolution [4,17] and progressively updated caches [5] have been used to overcome some of the described limitations and to enable more effects such as scattering [4] or colour bleeding [17].

The most popular method to compute AO for surface rendering in real-time is *screen space ambient occlusion (SSAO)* [7,15], a 2.5D image space process that can only be applied to DVR in a limited fashion due to the need for distinct depth and normal buffers [9]. Another way to replace ray casting for AO is to use *voxel cone tracing* as proposed by Crassin et al. [2]. Using the GPU, it enables smooth and noise-free results by tracing cones through a precomputed voxelized multi-resolution representation of the scene. The method was recently adapted to DVR to compute a directional occlusion model and shadows for explicit light sources at high frame rates [1]. Occlusion from all directions as well as image-based lighting are not considered, however.

One way to achieve physically correct volume rendering without any caches is the adaption of *path tracing* to DVR [8]. Interactive updates are achieved through progressive rendering, which results in strong noise. Convergence to a noise-free image requires several seconds during which no visualization parameters can be changed. Recently, Martschinke et al. [13] improved the performance of path traced DVR tremendously by using temporal reprojection. Based on a sampling history, samples are reused and only updated when necessary. Even though this greatly improves frame rates, the resulting images are still suffering from noise and blurriness, especially during TF and clipping interactions.

3   Adaptive Volumetric Illumination Sampling

The basic idea of our method is two-fold: The reduction of the number of illumination samples along the primary ray is achieved by using *adaptive volumetric illumination sampling (AVIS)* which subdivides the primary ray into segments based on the opacity of the sampled volumetric data. The complexity of the illumination computation per sample is reduced by means of voxel cone tracing which is used to compute AO in combination with image-based lighting.

3.1   Volumetric Lighting Model

The physical basis for simulating the propagation of light in a volume is given by the emission-absorption model by Max [14]. According to Max [14] and Jönsson [6], the attenuated radiance from a point $\vec{x}_0$ along a ray $\vec{\omega}_0$ reaching a point $\vec{x}$ is given by Eq. (1) (without considering emission):

$$L(\vec{x}, \vec{\omega}_0) = L_0(\vec{x}_0, \vec{\omega}_0) \cdot T(\vec{x}_0, \vec{x}) + \int_{\vec{x}_0}^{\vec{x}} \sigma_s(\vec{x}') \cdot L_{ss}(\vec{x}', \vec{\omega}_0) \cdot T(\vec{x}', \vec{x}) d\vec{x}' \qquad (1)$$

with $\vec{x}'$ representing samples along this ray $\vec{\omega}_0$, L_0 being the background energy entering the volume and the scattering coefficient given as σ_s. The absorption term is defined as:

$$T(\vec{x}_i, \vec{x}_j) = e^{-\int_{\vec{x}_i}^{\vec{x}_j} \sigma_t(\vec{x}') d\vec{x}'} \qquad (2)$$

The term L_{ss} is representing the radiance scattered into direction $\vec{\omega_0}$ from all incoming directions $\vec{\omega_i}$ on the unit sphere for a sample position $\vec{x}'$ on the view ray with s being the material shading function and L_i the incident radiance from all directions $\vec{\omega_i}$:

$$L_{ss}(\vec{x}', \vec{\omega_0}) = \int_{4\pi} s(\vec{x}', \vec{\omega_i}, \vec{\omega_0}) \cdot L_i(\vec{x}', \vec{\omega_i})d\vec{\omega_i} \qquad (3)$$

In order to be efficient enough for real-time rendering in DVR, the integral in Eq. (1) is usually approximated by computing a Riemann sum for the primary ray and compositing these samples using alpha blending, which ends up in the discrete volume rendering equation:

$$C = \sum_{i=1}^{n} C_i \prod_{j=1}^{i-1}(1 - \alpha_j) \qquad (4)$$

Here, the final pixel colour C for a ray travelling through the volume is determined by alpha-blending the opacity values α_j from the preceding samples and multiplying them with the colour values C_i for all samples i along the ray. The lighting is then being calculated for each step along the ray and multiplied with its corresponding sample colour C_i. Usually, the lighting is computed considering only local illumination models since the computation of the global illumination effects and scattering (as represented by the L_{ss} term) is still very costly since it also requires the evaluation of the incoming radiance and occlusion over the whole unit sphere for every step along the ray.

The proposed volumetric lighting model is based on ambient occlusion and image-based lighting. With L_i being the (unscattered) incoming radiance from all directions $\vec{\omega_i}$, L_i can thus be represented by the irradiance environment map E: $L_i(\vec{x}', \vec{\omega_i}) = E(\vec{\omega_i})$. Moreover, only the upper hemisphere of a point $\vec{x}'$ is considered, which is determined by the gradient $\vec{n}$. For L_{ss}, this yields:

$$L_{ss}(\vec{x}') = \frac{1}{\pi} \int_{\Omega^+} V(\vec{x}', \vec{\omega_i}) \cdot E(\vec{\omega_i})d\vec{\omega_i} \qquad (5)$$

with V being the visibility function for $\vec{x}'$ and $\vec{\omega_i}$.

3.2   Adaptive Illumination Sampling

Brute-force approaches that evaluate sophisticated lighting models for every sample along each ray (see Fig. 1, top left) are computationally expensive. To overcome this, our *AVIS* approach splits each primary ray into multiple segments. The volume is still sampled above the Nyquist frequency [3]. Hence, the number of samples fetched from the volume during ray casting is not changed. The segments are only used to group samples that are likely to share a similar illumination (see Fig. 1, left bottom). Each segment contains the alpha-blended accumulated radiance for the corresponding part of the ray so that the final radiance can be determined by adding the segments up. Given that a sufficient number of segments is used, a reasonable lighting approximation can be achieved while the required computations for each primary ray are significantly reduced.

To this end, the segments are determined based on thresholds applied to the accumulated opacity during ray casting. Hence, one segment ends and the next starts as soon as the accumulated opacity reaches the next threshold $t = \frac{s}{s_{max}}$ with s being the current segment number and s_{max} the maximum number of segments. Whenever the next threshold is hit and the next segment is entered, the current accumulated colour C_s (given by Eq. (4)) and a point $\vec{p}_s$ on the ray within the last segment is stored in order to be able to later compute the illumination value and to composite the final pixel value by adding up the attenuated segments (see Eq. (6)). The final pixel colour C (for now, without illumination) for a pixel is thus given by splitting the Riemann sum of the discrete volume rendering Eq. (4) into s partial sums, corresponding to having s segments:

$$ C = \underbrace{\sum_{s=1}^{s_{max}} C_s = \sum_{i=1}^{n_1} C_i \prod_{j=1}^{i-1}(1 - \alpha_j) + \sum_{i=n_1+1}^{n_2} C_i \prod_{j=1}^{i-1}(1 - \alpha_j) + \cdots}_{s \text{ times}} \tag{6} $$

The final illuminated value of a pixel is computed by multiplying each segment colour C_s with its corresponding segment lighting value L_s and summing up all segments. The segment lighting value is calculated for a distinct segment lighting position $\vec{p}_s$ in the segment. The positioning of $\vec{p}_s$ in the segment can be described by the parameter $lightBias$: a value of 0 places $\vec{p}_s$ at the beginning of the segment, a value of 1 at the end. The final compositing equation yielding the pixel colour value with illumination is thus given by Eq. (7), where $L_s(\vec{p}_s)$ is comprised of the ambient occlusion term ao and the incident light L_i:

$$ C_{ill} = \sum_{s=1}^{s_{max}} C_s \cdot L_s(\vec{p}_s) = \sum_{s=1}^{s_{max}} C_s \cdot ao(\vec{p}_s) \cdot L_i(\vec{p}_s) \tag{7} $$

3.3   Voxel Cone Traced Ambient Occlusion

AO is defined as the mean accessibility of a point $\vec{p}$ with $V(\vec{p}, \vec{\omega})$ being the visibility function for a direction $\vec{\omega}$:

$$ ao(\vec{p}) = \frac{1}{\pi} \int_{\Omega} V(\vec{p}, \vec{\omega}) \cdot cos(\omega) d\omega \tag{8} $$

This term is usually approximated by tracing additional secondary rays from $\vec{p}$ over the hemisphere to determine the visibility. In DVR, the visibility is continuous and given by $1 - \alpha_{acc}$ of the secondary ray, which is determined by tracing the secondary rays through the volume and using the emission-absorption model

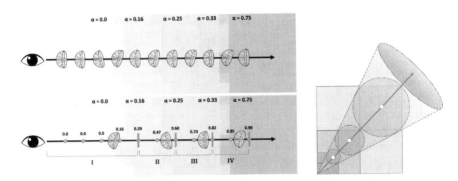

Fig. 1. *left:* Lighting calculations for a primary ray using a naive approach (top) and with our novel AVIS sampling method (bottom). *right:* Schematic depiction of the sampling of the multi-resolution occlusion volume used for cone tracing. The spheres represent the used sample radii.

by Max [14]. The ambient occlusion term for a segment, approximated with K secondary rays over the hemisphere of the point $\vec{p}_s$ can thus be described by:

$$ao(\vec{p}_s) = \frac{1}{K} \sum_{k=1}^{K} (1 - \alpha_{acc}(\vec{\omega}_k)) \cdot cos(\vec{\omega}_k) \qquad (9)$$

Since AO has to be evaluated at multiple locations along each ray, this would quickly result in the tracing of many secondary rays and consequently, in a severe performance penalty. Instead, we propose to adapt voxel cone tracing [2] for DVR to replace the tracing of whole bundles of secondary rays by the sampling of a few cones inside an optimized precomputed data structure. A voxelization of the scene as required by the original approach for surface rendering is not needed as the data is already given as a voxel grid. Hence, the volumetric data is transferred into an additional multi-resolution occlusion volume. Similar to a MIP map, this volume contains the whole scene at various resolution levels including all additional volumes (e.g. for structure highlighting) and corresponding TFs. An octree, as used by the original method is not required, but we still use the rasterization pipeline similar to Crassin et al. [2] for fast creation of the LOD levels. Because we do not compute lighting or shading for the occlusion volume, this additional step is fast and can be performed on the fly when the TF is being changed by the user (see Table 1).

   To compute an occlusion value per cone, the occlusion values from the corresponding LOD levels of the multi-resolution occlusion volume along the cone are summed up. Each level is sampled exactly once. The corresponding step sizes have to be defined such that the extent of a cell of each level fits the local diameter of the cone. Conceptually, this can be thought of as packing spheres into the cone, where for each new sphere the radius doubles, since the size of each cell in the multi-resolution volume doubles from one LOD level to the next (see Fig. 1, right). Hence, the distance d_j of the sphere from the starting point of the cone with the aperture θ for each LOD level j is given as:

$$d_j = \frac{2^j}{\sin\left(\frac{\theta}{2}\right)} \tag{10}$$

This results in an exponential growth of the step length which enables the sampling of a large neighbourhood around each point with very few samples. The determination of sampling points starts at the apex of the cone and stops as soon as a sample would be outside the valid data, also considering clipping planes. The resulting sampling points are used to fetch the opacity from the corresponding LOD level under consideration of tri-linear interpolation. To adapt for the larger step size d', the opacity of each sample i has to be adjusted by a correction term α_i' [2] with d being the standard step size:

$$\alpha_i' = 1 - (1 - \alpha_i)^{\frac{d'}{d}}$$

3.4 Image-Based Lighting

Environment maps can be used in combination with the described voxel-cone traced AO by evaluating the incident light for each cone and by attenuating it with the corresponding occlusion value. To compute the incident light per cone, the environment map has to be integrated over the solid angle of the cone. Instead of using multiple samples to achieve this, we utilize pre-convoluted lighting [7]. Hence, the original environment map is filtered multiple times during a preprocessing step and stored as a MIP map where each level represents the pre-integrated incident light for a certain range of solid angles. The incident light per cone can be approximated by sampling the environment map only once at the MIP map level corresponding to the cone aperture. For a layout with K cones, the illumination for a point $\vec{p}_s$ is thus given by a summation over all cones where the incident light per cone is attenuated with its occlusion. The incident light is defined by $E(\vec{\omega}_k, \gamma_k)$ with $\vec{\omega}_k$ being the secondary ray direction and γ_k being the cone aperture that corresponds to the according MIP map level of the environment map [7]:

$$L_s(\vec{p}_s) = ao(\vec{p}_s) \cdot L_i(\vec{p}_s) = \frac{1}{K} \sum_{k=1}^{K} (1 - \alpha_{acc}(\vec{\omega}_k)) \cdot cos(\vec{\omega}_k) \cdot E(\vec{\omega}_k, \gamma_k) \tag{11}$$

4 Results

The method presented in Sect. 3 has been implemented and tested inside a GLSL-based DVR ray caster. Our cone tracing implementation uses six cones since this allows to have a similar aperture for all cones. We found that using an aperture angle of 67° covers the hemisphere without any gaps. The *lightBias* parameter, which defines the position on each segment at which the illumination is computed, has to be chosen carefully since the computed illumination should represent the whole segment. While for rather homogeneous areas the exact position is less important, it is crucial to evaluate the illumination - in particular ambient occlusion - close to the surface of solid structures, which are characterized by sudden changes of the accumulated opacity. We therefore decided to set *lightBias* to 0.75 which results in the computation of the illumination at the border to the last quarter of each segment (see Fig. 1, left bottom).

Table 1 shows the resulting frame rates for our AVIS method in an AR-friendly stereo resolution (1280 × 720 per eye) with various numbers of segments on a machine that used an Intel i7-9800X, 64 GB RAM and a GeForce RTX 2080 Ti. No changes to the frame rates occur during interactive clipping since only the number of samples evaluated during cone tracing is influenced while the occlusion volume stays unchanged. However, interactive TF definition is less performant due to the needed updates of the occlusion volume. As depicted in Fig. 2, our approach approximates the physically plausible path tracing result very well. Compared to path tracing, however, our method is significantly faster (see Table 1) and introduces no noise. To measure the error that is being introduced when applying our novel adaptive illumination sampling, we compared it to a ground truth version, where the lighting was evaluated on every sample using our proposed lighting model and rendered with DVR (see Fig. 3). It can be seen that the introduced error, measured with the normalized correlation coefficient (NCC), is quite low and visually not recognisable when using 10 or more segments for the Torso dataset. Figure 4 shows a rendering of the Chameleon dataset[3] using our method in combination with image-based lighting.

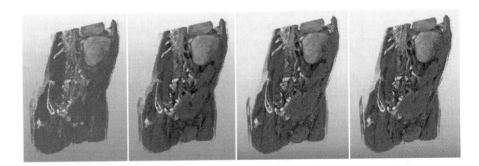

Fig. 2. The clinical "Torso" CT dataset rendered with standard volume rendering (leftmost image), our AVIS method in combination with a white ambient light and AO using 10 segments (middle left), path tracing using 20 iterations (middle right) and the path traced ground truth (rightmost image).

---

[3] https://klacansky.com/open-scivis-datasets/.

Table 1. The resulting frame rates for our method in fps.

Dataset	Chameleon (512 × 512 × 540)		Chameleon (1024 × 1024 × 1080)		Torso (512 × 512 × 317)	
Method	Static TF	TF Change	Static TF	TF Change	Static TF	TF Change
Standard DVR	117		43		103	
AVIS (5 Segments)	116	43	37	16	98	47
AVIS (10 Segments)	115	43	25	13	79	42
AVIS (20 Segments)	87	39	20	12	51	33
Path Tracing (20 iterations)	15	14	10	8	15	13

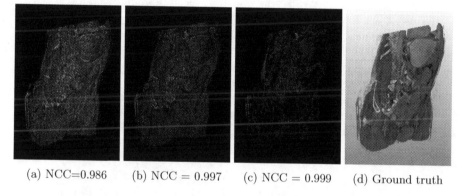

(a) NCC=0.986   (b) NCC = 0.997   (c) NCC = 0.999   (d) Ground truth

Fig. 3. The difference to the ground truth for 5 (a), 10 (b) and 20 (c) segments. Images (a), (b) and (c) are multiplied with a factor of 10 to make the differences recognizable.

Fig. 4. The Chameleon dataset rendered with our method using 10 segments.

5 Discussion

The proposed AVIS method reduces the number of illumination computations by decoupling them from the volume sampling. In combination with voxel cone tracing, this facilitates AO in DVR at high frame rates and allows for the definition of clipping planes and the TF in real-time without any loss of image quality. Although a few similar concepts have already been proposed, some key elements differ significantly from our solution. Hernell et al. [4] employ piecewise integration with segments of a fixed length for the reduction of volume samples on secondary rays during light cache computation. In contrast to that, our approach focuses on the reduction of illumination computations during primary ray traversal in a standard volume ray caster. Many advanced illumination approaches for DVR suffer from lower frame rates and/or artifacts during updates of the TF and clipping planes, although the latter is discussed only in very few works. The reason for this reduced performance are complicated precomputations, that often include the computation of AO values for the whole volume which have to be updated on changes of the TF or clipping planes. The usage of histograms [16] or cube shells [9] might improve performance during TF changes, but does not facilitate interactive clipping and consider only a local neighbourhood. The work by Hernell et al. [5] limits the AO to a small neighbourhood and employs a progressive update scheme that adds more samples to the AO volume over time. This is a sensible solution, which however is also limited to local occlusion and might suffer from noise until the progressive update is finished. Our method however allows for both large-scale and local occlusion effects and does not suffer from noise. The usage of SATs [17] and other proposed multi-resolution approaches is similar to the idea of voxel cone tracing, but the update of the required data structures is more involved. The benefits of voxel cone tracing were recently exploited by Campagnolo et al. [1] for DVR. However, their directional model is still slower than our approach, does not yield results comparable to AO and cannot be combined with image based lighting.

The choice to determine the AVIS-segments based on the accumulated opacity was an empirical one. Other criteria such as the gradient of the opacity along the ray could be used as well, but our experiments showed that a good convergence can be achieved with relatively low numbers of segments. More importantly, in contrast to a gradient-based solution, we are able to limit this number which is beneficial for the performance of the algorithm. Although explicit gradients are not used, this scheme places segment borders at sudden increases of the accumulated opacity and thus successfully represents hard structures. In uniform areas, on the other hand, segment borders are distributed more rarely.

Physically-based GI might be achieved by utilizing path tracing [8] which, however, is computationally expensive and suffers from strong noise during any interaction. The noise might be reduced by the usage of adaptive temporal sampling [13]. Compared to our method, it is still significantly slower and suffers from stronger noise, but offers more illumination effects such as indirect illumination. However, this effect can be very subtle especially in the case of medical visualization where objects are rendered isolated in an empty space. Here, shadows and ambient occlusion and, especially in the case of AR, the light coming from an environment map have a stronger impact.

6   Conclusion and Future Work

In this work, we present a novel technique for computing realistic lighting in direct volume rendering while enabling fully interactive transfer function and clipping plane changes in real-time. At the core of the algorithm, we employ *adaptive volumetric illumination sampling*, a novel method that splits the primary rays into segments, which facilitates the required reduction of the amount of illumination computations along the viewing ray. The illumination itself is computed efficiently using an adaptation of voxel cone tracing. This requires a minimal precomputation and allows for noise-free on-the-fly computation of ambient occlusion in combination with image-based lighting. Typical frame rates for stereo HD-images with usually sized datasets are in the range of 70–100 fps.

The method can be easily integrated into existing volume rendering pipelines that utilize ray casting. We compared our method to Standard Volume Rendering and Path Tracing and demonstrated that our method produces similar good results as path tracing but is significantly faster. For the primary target use case, which is augmented reality, our method represents a suitable compromise as it combines high frame rates with noise-free, realistically illuminated images. It lends itself especially to a combination with image-based lighting, which could facilitate a deeper integration of the rendered image with the real environment. Still, our new illumination sampling scheme is not restricted to these effects. The used lighting term could be extended to include more sophisticated effects or shading models, that cover for instance subsurface scattering or colour bleeding. Also, first and second order scattering might be implemented by evaluating additional cones on a per-light basis. Further improvement of the frame rates during transfer function definition could be achieved by replacing our pragmatic approach for the creation of the multi-resolution volume by a more efficient implementation. In addition to that, we would like to further investigate how to improve the definition of the segment borders and thus the illumination sample positions. This could imply more complex functions that drive the subdivision process, for instance derivatives of the opacity function.

Acknowledgements. We thank our partners, especially Prof. Dr. Weyhe and his team at the Pius hospital Oldenburg in the department of general and visceral surgery, who provided the "Torso" dataset. This research has been funded by the German Federal Ministry of Education and Research (BMBF) in the project VIVATOP (funding code 16SV8078).

References

1. Campagnolo, L.Q., Celes, W.: Interactive directional ambient occlusion and shadow computations for volume ray casting. Comput. Graph. **84**, 66–76 (2019)

2. Crassin, C., Neyret, F., Sainz, M., Green, S., Eisemann, E.: Interactive indirect illumination using voxel cone tracing. Comput. Graph. Forum **30**(7), 1921–1930 (2011)
3. Drebin, R.A., Carpenter, L., Hanrahan, P.: Volume rendering. Comput. Graph. **22**(4), 65–74 (1988)
4. Hernell, F., Ljung, P., Ynnerman, A.: Interactive global light propagation in direct volume rendering using local piecewise integration. In: IEEE/ EG Symposium on Volume and Point-Based Graphics, pp. 105–112 (2008)
5. Hernell, F., Ljung, P., Ynnerman, A.: Local ambient occlusion in direct volume rendering. IEEE Trans. Vis. Comput. Graph. **16**(4), 548–559 (2010)
6. Jönsson, D., Sundén, E., Ynnerman, A., Ropinski, T.: A survey of volumetric illumination techniques for interactive volume rendering. Comput. Graph. Forum **33**(1), 27–51 (2014)
7. Klehm, O., Ritschel, T., Eisemann, E., Seidel, H.P.: Bent normals and cones in screen-space. In: VMV 2011 - Vision, Modeling and Visualization, pp. 177–182 (2011)
8. Kroes, T., Post, F.H., Botha, C.P.: Exposure render: an interactive photo-realistic volume rendering framework. PLoS ONE **7**(7) (2012)
9. Kroes, T., Schut, D., Eisemann, E.: Smooth probabilistic ambient occlusion for volume rendering. In: GPU Pro, vol. 6, pp. 475–485 (2016)
10. Landis, H.: Production-ready global illumination. In: Course notes on RenderMan in Production, p. 15 (2002)
11. Langer, M.S., Bülthoff, H.H.: Depth discrimination from shading under diffuse lighting. Perception **29**(6), 649–660 (2000)
12. Lindemann, F., Ropinski, T.: About the influence of illumination models on image comprehension in direct volume rendering. IEEE Trans. Vis. Comput. Graph. **17**(12), 1922–1931 (2011)
13. Martschinke, J., Hartnagel, S., Keinert, B., Engel, K., Stamminger, M.: Adaptive temporal sampling for volumetric path tracing of medical data. Comput. Graph. Forum **38**(4), 67–76 (2019)
14. Max, N.: Optical models for direct volume rendering. IEEE Trans. Vis. Comput. Graph. **1**(2), 99–108 (1995)
15. Mittring, M.: Finding next gen: CryEngine 2. In: ACM SIGGRAPH 2007 Courses, p. 97 (2007)
16. Ropinski, T., Meyer-Spradow, J., Diepenbrock, S., Mensmann, J., Hinrichs, K.: Interactive volume rendering with dynamic ambient occlusion and color bleeding. Comput. Graph. Forum **27**(2), 567–576 (2008)
17. Schlegel, P., Makhinya, M., Pajarola, R.: Extinction-based shading and illumination in GPU volume ray-casting. IEEE Trans. Vis. Comput. Graph. **17**(12), 1795–1802 (2011)
18. Stewart, A.J.: Vicinity shading for enhanced perception of volumetric data. IEEE Vis. **2003**, 355–362 (2003)
19. Zheng, L., Chaudhari, A.J., Badawi, R.D., Ma, K.L.: Using global illumination in volume visualization of rheumatoid arthritis CT data. IEEE Comput. Graph. Appl. **34**(6), 16–23 (2014)
20. Zhukov, S., Iones, A., Kronin, G.: An ambient light illumination model. In: Rendering Techniques 1998, pp. 45–55 (1998)

Musical Brush: Exploring Creativity Through an AR-Based Tool for Sketching Music and Drawings

Rafael Valer[(✉)], Rodrigo Schramm, and Luciana Nedel

Federal University of Rio Grande do Sul, Porto Alegre, Brazil
{rvaler,nedel}@inf.ufrgs.br, rschramm@ufrgs.br

Abstract. The economic growth and social transformation in the 21st century are hardly based on creativity. To help with the development of this skill, the concept of Creativity Support Tools (CST) was proposed. In this paper, we introduce *Musical Brush* (MB), an artistic mobile application whose main focus is to allow novices to improvise music while creating drawings. We investigated different types of interactions and audio-visual feedbacks in the context of a mobile application that combines music with drawings in a natural way, measuring their impact on creativity support. In this study, we tested different user interactions with real-time sound generation, including 2D drawings, three-dimensional device movements, and visual representations on Augmented Reality (AR). A user study was conducted to explore the support for creativity of each setup. Results showed the suitability of the association of Musical Brush with augmented reality for creating sounds and drawings as a tool that supports the exploration and expressiveness.

Keywords: Augmented reality · Creativity support tools · Mobile application · Music · Drawing

1 Introduction

Digital tools, nowadays, play a crucial role in the most creative practices of our daily life. From young children playing on smartphones to create simple drawings to professional design artists, who depend on advanced graphical interfaces to accomplish their creative works. This growing link between digital instruments and creativity culminated in the emergence of a new subfield of Human-Computer Interaction (HCI), known as Creativity Support Tools (CST) [21].

More specifically, the research on CSTs focuses on the development of interfaces that aim not just the productivity of users but also the enhancement of their innovative potential, with the primary goal to support users on being more creative more often [20]. Among the interests in the study of CSTs, we can highlight the awareness of the benefits that these topics can provide on a global scale [8]. Works like [5,15] also point the importance of creativity on economic growth and social transformation.

© Springer Nature Switzerland AG 2020
N. Magnenat-Thalmann et al. (Eds.): CGI 2020, LNCS 12221, pp. 119–131, 2020.
https://doi.org/10.1007/978-3-030-61864-3_11

In this paper, we introduce *Musical Brush* (MB), an artistic application that allows novices to improvise music while creating drawings in AR. The main idea is to provide people in general with a highly expressive artistic tool that takes advantage of rich stimuli given by immersive environments. With the introduction of 3D drawings, we explore this new way to interact in the field of drawing-based tools. Furthermore, since we are particularly interested in exploring how the different application features may enhance creativity, we propose a practical user study where we explore the impact that the application's distinct features potentially have on the creativity of individuals.

We identify the central contributions of our project as the design and development of a novel immersive drawing-based musical application, along with the evaluation of the tool's main features regarding the enhancement of creativity. While we are aware that the achieved results are particular to our tool, we argue that many of the design choices could easily be extended to other digital tools that combine music and drawing. Moreover, we provide the overall creativity-related application scores, thus encouraging comparison with future works.

2   Related Workd

Since early works, a large number of different interactions and technologies were explored on the conception of new musical interfaces [12,17]. The use of gestural input parameters to control music in real-time is one of the explored approaches [23]. An early example work is the *Iamascope* [4]. The instrument constantly captures the scene image through a camera and uses the input to control and display graphics and sound in real-time. By applying image processing to the input image, users' body movements also directly control the sound and visual outputs. Similarly, in *3DinMotion* [18], real-time motion data from one or more subjects is used to create audiovisual pieces. By tracking the position of hands, it is possible to draw temporary traces in the 3D space.

Many are the possibilities when it comes to techniques and tools used in musical interfaces. One in particular is combining drawings and music. Drawing-based musical tools generally present highly visual elements and thus benefit from the degree of expressiveness that drawing representations offer. *The UPIC System* [11] presents a very early work in this direction. Composed by a drawing board and a pen, the system generates sounds according to the created sketches. On *Hyperscore* [3] the musical performance is composed of a set of several fragments that can be created and edited through drawing in the computer application, characteristics of the strokes such as color represent the timbre of the sound that is being produced. In *MicroJam* [14], users improvise short performances incrementally by creating drawings that represent sounds in a smartphone screen.

Still, most of the research on drawing-based musical interfaces focuses only on 2D interactions. Regarding this issue, immersive technologies have been explored to bring more freedom and expressiveness for musical tools [13]. Due to the capability of creating scenarios not feasible in the real world, new experiences not possible through traditional instruments can be created. Different immersive approaches have been explored for music composition. In Reactable [9], AR is used through physical markers on top of a table, displaying virtual contents and producing sounds based on interactions with the tangibles. Differently, *Virtual Air Guitar* [10] offers a VR guitar that resembles the real instrument through a CAVE-like room.

Different from the above tools, MB was developed as a portable AR experience for mobile devices, lacking any overhead needed for setting up environments, preparing head-mounted displays, or any other external device beforehand for its use. The application itself differs from other tools in several characteristics regarding music and interface. Finally, to produce a fair investigation about its potential capacity on supporting the creativity of individuals, we decided to compare the tool with different variation sets of its features.

3 Design Rational

A list of twelve principles that aim guidance in the development of new CSTs is proposed in [22], they prioritize strong support in hypothesis formation, speedier evaluation of alternatives, improved understanding through visualization, and better dissemination of results. Among the principles, we see relevance in the following: *S2) Low threshold, high ceiling, and wide walls*; *S6) Make it as simple as possible*; and *S12) Evaluate your tools*. *S2* suggests a low entry barrier for novices to use the tool while supporting more sophisticated levels and a range of possible explorations. *S6* reiterates that the tool should be of easy manipulation, and *S12* highlights the importance of evaluating and improving the tools.

Regarding the use of gestures to control music, our tool can be classified as an *'Alternate Controller'*, which design does not follow the behavior of any existing instrument [24]. Among the crucial characteristics for the design of real-time controllers listed in [6], we highlight: *"The human takes control of the situation. The computer is reactive"*; *"Instant responses to the user's movements"*; *"Similar movements produce similar results"*; *"The control mechanism is a physical and multi-parametric device which must be learnt until the actions become automatic"*; and *"Further practice develops increased control intimacy"*;.

Concerning the use of immersive technologies for musical purposes, [19] brings attempts to guide the conception of Virtual Reality (VR) interfaces. Despite focusing exclusively on VR musical instruments, some of the principles can also be addressed in an AR context: *P1) Reduce latency*, concerns the importance of having smooth interactions and highlights that the gap between different feedbacks should be minimized; *P2) Make Use of Existing Skills*, despite providing new experiences not possible in a real-world context, the use of interactions based on real actions can be interesting in the understanding of the tool; and *P3) Consider Both Natural and 'Magical' Interactions*, this principle highlights the importance of having actions that do not respect the real-world constraints and may cause a positive impact on users.

4   Implementation

MB is currently an iOS artistic application, and allows novices to improvise music while creating drawings in AR. The application essential operation consists of mapping different user interactions into sounds and drawings. In a similar concept to a Theremin, the generation of sound and drawings are controlled by 3D movements. When moving the smartphone device and/or performing drag gestures on the screen, the application creates a virtual 3D trace along the path traveled. The drawing strokes will permanently represent the performance melody structure. Both sound and visual outputs are shaped and controlled by several pre-defined interactions.

The app is written in the Swift language and implemented using ARKit. By continuously reading the video frames captured by the device's camera, the SDK detects and extracts feature points that are used for detecting planes and thus, place and anchor contents into the scene. The virtual objects represented as strokes in MB are created using the Metal API, which enables 3D graphics rendering in very high performance.

Fig. 1. Examples of performances composed with Musical Brush.

The main screen consists of two major components (see Fig. 1). The first and more important is the scene image, which is updated in real-time by the phone camera. This layer is also responsible for presenting the virtual drawings during a composition. To create the colored strokes, we continuously collect the position of the device at 60 fps, after that we create a tiny cylinder connecting the current and the last saved positions, thus creating a continuous stroke. The second component is the reproduction control segment, which lays at the bottom of the screen and is responsible for manipulating the performance execution.

4.1   Feature Extraction

To extract features from user input interactions, we are making use of several sensors present in a modern smartphone such as accelerometer, camera, and gyroscope to trigger and control both sound and visual outputs. This design, named *Direct Acquisition* [25], is defined by using one or more sensors to monitor the performer's actions in an independent way. So far, the elements being tracked are related to the device motion, acceleration, and position in a 3D space, as well as the recognition of touch and pressure gestures.

4.2   Mapping

The main concept behind the application is the combination of two distinct art forms: music, and drawing. To achieve this, we explored two distinct feedbacks in our application. The first is the audio, which consists of the real-time generation of sounds. Secondly, we have the visual feedback, which is represented by virtual colored traces, as shown in Fig. 1. Both sound and visual outputs are controlled and shaped based on user interactions and device motion. In this context, the visual strokes act as a way to represent the performance structure.

Several techniques have been considered to achieve our current sound mapping design. By aiming an interface that can be used by people with different degrees of musical experience, we focused on implementing a more naive direct sound mapping approach [27]. In general, simplistic *One-to-One* interfaces tend to be learned easier if compared to more complex mapping strategies, yet, this more straightforward approach can give an impoverished experience to both performers and listeners [6]. For this reason, the tradeoff between simplicity and engagement must be taken into account when designing a mapping strategy. Based on the features extracted from the sensors, the audiovisual characteristics controlled are as follows:

- **Sound/Stroke Generation:** Touching the screen activates the sound and drawing generation.
- **Pitch Control:** The vertical axis controls the sound frequency. The design follows the idea that people relate changes in the vertical axis with variations at the sound frequency [16].
- **Amplitude Control:** The force applied on touch gestures controls the sound amplitude and the thickness of the strokes. The design was based on the guideline that the output sound amplitude should be proportional to the amount of energy from input gestures [7].
- **Timbre Control:** The musical timbre is selected from a list of four pre-fixed waveforms, each responsible for coloring the stroke with a different color.
- **Delay Effect:** the activation of the delay effect is done by moving the phone abruptly. This design was based on the idea that *"there should be some sort of correspondence between the "size" of a control gesture and the acoustic result"* on musical instruments [26]. The effect visual representation causes the virtual strokes to vibrate along the time.

4.3 Sound Synthesis

MB makes use of a *Pure Data* (PD) based engine which allows the mapping of input parameters to a wide range of audio synthesis techniques. Through using Libpd as an embeddable library tool, it is possible to use the audio engine in mobile phone applications. A great benefit of exploring this engine is the high degree of flexibility to the sound generation module, providing an easy and fast way to further extensions of the proposed tool. Aiming to have a better-controlled testing environment, we have developed four different sound timbres using additive synthesis designed with oscillators based on sine, triangular, sawtooth, and square waveforms. The features are extracted in real-time and forwarded to the PD module. There, oscillators create and shape sounds based on the inputs.

4.4 Composition

The composition mechanism in MB is based on an incremental process where the artist creates new tracks (maximum of 6) that together will compose a performance. All the tracks have a duration length of 8 seconds and execute at the same time. The tracks are represented with virtual colored strokes (see Fig. 1), and its path follows the device movement during the composition. After creating a track, users can move the phone around and see the drawings from different perspectives. It is important to note that when played, all the distinct tracks start to be reproduced concurrently. Besides that, while composing a new track, the performer also perceives the audio and visual progress of the other already existent tracks, allowing a better understanding of the music arrangement. A demonstration video of MB is available online.[1]

5 Evaluation

To explore the effectiveness of our prototype concerning the support of creative characteristics, we propose a targeted user study. More specifically, we are interested in the investigation of three main topics: (1) *Is the design of MB successful in supporting creativity?* (2) *What aspects of creativity are impacted most?* (3) *What are the key features that impact substantially on this support?*

Measuring creativity is not trivial since the concept is ill-defined, with its measurement being approached in distinct ways by the community [1]. However, independently of the creativity definition, the Creativity Support Index (CSI) measurement tool [2], a psychometric survey specially designed to measure the capacity of CSTs on supporting individuals engaged on creative works, brings the evaluation of attributes that indirectly express fundamental qualities inherent to the majority of the creative processes, they are: *Results Worth Effort* (RWE), *Exploration, Collaboration, Immersion, Expressiveness*, and *Enjoyment*. In our context, creativity is quantified by the CSI scores measured during the user's interaction with MB when improvising new musical pieces.

---
[1] https://vimeo.com/313557959.

5.1   Compared Versions

In our user study, we compare four different versions of MB (AR, Sound Only (SO), 3D, and 2D) to measure how the different types of interactions and visualizations affect creativity. The three first modes present the same interaction system, where both touch gestures and device motion effects can be used to draw and generate sounds. The main difference is that the AR version presents the user with the camera image as background scene, and the virtual strokes are positioned on the real environment. The 3D version immerses the user in a "virtual" environment, where an infinite checkered floor replaces the camera image. Finally, the SO, does not present any drawing to users, generating only sound as output.

Unlike the above-mentioned versions, the 2D version does not use the motion of the device for the output, being the music composition exclusively affected by touch gestures on the device screen. In this case, the pitch is still controlled by the vertical axis position of the touches, and drawings can be created by sliding the finger over the screen. Figure 2 exemplifies the different compared versions.

Fig. 2. Screenshots of the four compared versions, from left to right: AR, SO, 3D, and 2D.

5.2   Questionnaires

The questionnaires applied in this study are summarized here. The *Intake Questionnaire* (Q1) collects the participants' demographic information and previous experience regarding technology and music. The *CSI Questionnaire* (Q2) asks specific questions regarding the impact of the tool on creativity. Since our application does not offer collaboration, this attribute was not discussed within this work. The *Feedback Questionnaire* (Q3) consists of subjective questions with the objective to explore the participants' points of view on how the different interaction and visualization versions affected the creative process.

5.3 Protocol

The experiment consisted of a user study conducted with a total of 26 subjects. Since the experiment required users to move while performing, we restricted the participation of users that did not present any mobility issues. The experiment was designed as a within-subjects study where each user experienced all the four different application versions. The order of versions to be tested was different for each participant to prevent results to be biased. Each session lasted around 45 min, and was subdivided into four stages.

The ***Introduction*** stage began with an exaplanation of the study objective. Then, after accepting the terms and conditions of the study, Q1 was applied. In the ***Learning*** stage, we explained the features and general tool operation. Volunteers were encouraged to explore the tool and ask questions. In the ***Performing*** stage, participants were asked to create a performance for each different version. The content of the performance was free, and no limit for time was applied. After each session, participants were asked to answer to Q2. Lastly, in the ***Feedback*** stage, the participants were asked to reply to Q3, additionally expressing their thoughts about the full experience.

6 Results

The data from the questionnaires were analyzed by calculating the average (μ) and standard deviations (σ) and are reported here as ($\mu \pm \sigma$). After applying a Shapiro-Wilks test for normality, we observed that our samples deviate from a normal distribution. Consequently, we used the non-parametric Kruskal-Wallis test to identify significant differences between the four groups. Finally, a Dunn's Multiple Comparison post hoc test was applied when necessary for the dependent variables with different distributions. Significance level regarding the statistical tests is indicated in the figures with: (*) for $p < 0.05$.

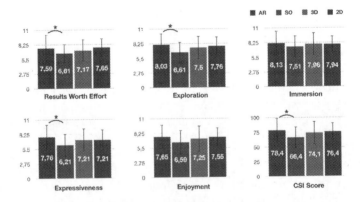

Fig. 3. Results from Q2. Significant differences were found regarding *RWE*, *Exploration*, *Expressiveness*, and the *CSI Score* between the AR and SO.

6.1 Population

The data from Q1 provides us with the necessary demographic information from the participants of the experiment. Among the 26 subjects, the age ranged from 18 to 28 (22.61 ± 2.60). While most of the subjects had at least some previous experience in musical practice (only 38.5% never practiced any instrument before), most of them never had any previous experience with mobile apps for musical creation (69.2%). Regarding AR, only 19.2% had used more than one app that explored this technology on mobile devices.

6.2 Resulting Data

Figure 3 brings the results obtained from Q2. The values of the first five creativity-related attributes (*RWE, Exploration, Immersion, Expressiveness,* and *Enjoyment*) range from 1 to 10 and are the basis for the CSI score calculation, which results in a score that ranges from 0 to 100. As we can notice, the AR version presented higher results in all attributes except for *RWE*. Two very high scores include the sensation of *Immersion* and *Exploration*. Among the results, *RWE, Exploration, Expressiveness*, and the *CSI Score* were significantly different ($p < 0.05$) among the AR and SO versions. The CSI results match the feedback given by users on Q3, where 57.7% of the participants elected the AR as the preferred version, against only 3.8% for the SO mode.

Table 1. Summary of collected usage logs for each of the four compared versions. Bold values indicate the highest average value.

Characteristic	AR	SO	3D	2D
Duration (s)	**184 ± 88.4**	128 ± 43.7	160 ± 72.6	139 ± 64.3
Used Tracks	**4.11 ± 1.1**	3.8 ± 1.1	4.0 ± 1.1	3.92 ± 0.6
Disc. Tracks	**1.15 ± 2.0**	0.80 ± 1.2	0.5 ± 0.9	0.84 ± 1.4
H. Distance (m)	5.34 ± 3.6	4.35 ± 3.5	**6.23 ± 4.8**	–
V. Distance (m)	4.31 ± 3.3	3.99 ± 2.6	**4.32 ± 3.4**	–

Data from user compositions is summarized in Table 1, it includes the time spent in seconds during the task, the number of created and discarded tracks, and total horizontal and vertical device motion distances. Although not finding a significant difference among the conditions, the analysis of this data can reinforce some of our insights from the results. Characteristics such as the performance duration collaborate to the perception of a more enjoyable experience while the number of used and discarded tracks on the performance can be seen as a process of exploring different alternatives.

6.3   Discussion

In general, MB presented high scores for all the individual creativity-related attributes measured by the CSI (see Fig. 3). As final score, in a range from 0 to 100, the tool scored 78.4. The highest scores for individual attributes were 'Immersion' and 'Exploration', presenting scores of 8.13 and 8.03 in a range from 0 to 10, respectively. In the final pair-wise comparison among all the CSI measured attributes, 'Exploration' was considered the most important characteristic, with 28% of the answers relating this as the most essential aspect of the tool.

- 2D vs. 3D Interactions - Surprisingly, the 3D version results were not significantly different from the 2D version. When asked to report the negative points of the 3D version over the 2D, users mentioned difficulties in controlling the tool when performing: *"it is harder to reach the desired note"*, (P19); and *"less precision, since it is hard to control the device rotation and motion"*, (P24). On the other hand, concerning the benefits of the 3D version users highlighted how the third dimension can increase the possibilities of exploration and expressiveness: *"greater space to be creative"*, (P1); and *"you have more freedom and available options to create"*, (P14).

Results from Fig. 3 evidence how the 2D version provides a greater user satisfaction when analyzing the *RWE* aspect. This outcome may be connected to the fact that, differently from all other compared versions, participants were allowed to stay still while performing, once that all interactions were related to touch gestures on the device screen. This lower physical demand may be noted in some comments concerning the 2D version advantages: *"Everything is at one place, no need to move around"*, and (P2); *"I could use while sitting, without much effort..."*, (P10). This ease of use due to reduced operation space can also be seen as an aspect that impacts exploration of ideas: *"with the limited environment it is easily visible the possibilities"*, (P9). Negative comments include being less fun: *"Less playful and interesting experience"*, (P11); and visual pollution due to the overlapping of strokes: *"Limited space for insertion of new points. On longer tracks, dots may overlap and difficult visualization"*, (P6).

- Sound vs. Visual Feedback - When exploring how the visual feedback impacted users' creativity, we were explicitly interested in comparing the AR and SO versions. The results show a significant difference between these two versions concerning *RWE, Exploration, Expressiveness*, and the *CSI Score* (see Fig. 3). The session length was longer on the AR version if compared to the SO, and also presented greater exploration in the number of tracks used (see Table 1). Furthermore, regarding the advantages in the presence of visual strokes the participants mentioned distinct benefits, including:

- Exploration - *"It's more clear on what I am doing, easier to experiment"*, (P3); and *"...they facilitate the creation of sounds, helping to understand if I want to put the sounds close or not"*, (P14);
- Immersion - *"It makes me focus on more than just one sense"*, (P11); and *"...give the feeling that the sounds produced are touchable"*, (P12);

– *Expressiveness* - *"It becomes another art form, in addition to the music it makes"*, (P2); and *"It helped me to come up with more ideas. I was wondering what would be the sound if I drew a happy face, or a star..."*, (P17).

On the other hand, a few users reported how the visual strokes disrupted their focus while composing: *"Attention ends up being dispersed by having visual elements together with the sound"* (P14); and *"When you can't see the strokes it is easier to get focused on using movement as the only input..."*, (P25).

- Real vs Virtual Environment - The comparison between AR and 3D versions was performed within a more exploratory approach, and we acknowledge that comparing a real environment against a virtual one with no visual appeal is unfair. However, although not presenting any appealing objects in its environment, results show that participants moved more in the 3D version. We believe that this may be related to the exploration of a new environment not previously known. On the other hand, the AR version presented higher scores on every CSI attribute (see Fig. 3). User feedback concerning the positive points of interacting with the real environment includes the ability to interact and draw on real objects, and the enhanced sensation of immersion due to the self-perception of being among the virtual strokes: *"It's fun to move around the room and create things everywhere"*, (P5); and *"The real world brings inspiration to try things you wouldn't do normally, it's fun to play with your surroundings"*, (P25).

7   Conclusion and Future Works

In this paper, we presented *Musical Brush*, a drawing-based musical application that allows novices to improvise music while drawing. We conducted a comparative study exploring different features of an interface designed for artistic purposes. More specifically, we were interested in exploring how the tool different features could support distinct attributes related to creativity. Among the key findings, we discovered that the visual drawings are crucial for a significant enhancement of creative-related aspects. By providing visual feedback to the user actions, the drawings were responsible for improving the expressiveness and exploratory capacity. Furthermore, the visual feedback was also highlighted for increasing the immersion of performers due to its surrounding 3D drawings.

Although not presenting significant statistical differences regarding creativity support aspects, the comparison among 2D and 3D versions produced interesting results. It is clear that all types of interactions can be somehow useful for applications that integrate music with drawings. However, the choice of this specific interaction is, in fact, a tradeoff between controllability and expressiveness. Feedback indicated that the 2D was preferred for rapid and efficient control of application parameters, while 3D was preferred for freedom, and exploration of different possibilities.

A limitation of the proposed prototype application, however, was the difficulty of creating some concrete and more pleasant results due to the still non-complex sound generation system. Regarding future steps, we aim to focus on three distinct fronts. Firstly, we would like to explore more AR technology and measure aspects regarding creativity while interacting with outdoor environments. Secondly, we would like to incorporate and evaluate the collaborative aspect. Lastly, we would like to perform further investigations regarding the use of 3D interactions to control real-time audiovisual content, as well as explore more complex sound mappings.

References

1. Carroll, E.A., Latulipe, C.: Triangulating the personal creative experience: self-report, external judgments, and physiology. In: Proceedings of Graphics Interface 2012, GI '12, pp. 53–60. Canadian Information Processing Society (2012)
2. Cherry, E., Latulipe, C.: Quantifying the creativity support of digital tools through the creativity support index. ACM Trans. Comput.-Hum. Interact. **21**(4), 1–25 (2014)
3. Farbood, M., Pasztor, E., Jennings, K.: Hyperscore: a graphical sketchpad for novice composers. IEEE Comput. Graph. Appl. **24**(1), 50–54 (2004)
4. Fels, S., Mase, K.: Iamascope: a graphical musical instrument. Comput. Graph. **23**(2), 277–286 (1999)
5. Florida, R.L.: The flight of the creative class: the new global competition for talent. HarperBusiness (2005)
6. Hunt, A., Kirk, R.: Mapping strategies for musical performance. Trends Gestural Control Music **21**(2000), 231–258 (2000)
7. Hunt, A., Wanderley, M.M.: Mapping performer parameters to synthesis engines. Organised Sound **7**(02), 97 (2002)
8. Ione, A, Mitchell, W.J., Inouye, A.S., Blumenthal, M.S (eds.): Beyond productivity: information technology, innovation, and creativity, illus. Paper, Leonardo, vol. 37, pp. 408–410. The National Academies Press, Washington (2004). ISBN: 0-309-08868-268
9. Jordà, S., Geiger, G., Alonso, M., Kaltenbrunner, M.: The reacTable. In: Proceedings of the 1st International Conference on Tangible and Embedded Interaction - TEI 2007, p. 139. ACM Press (2007)
10. Karjalainen, M., Mäki-patola, T., Kanerva, A., Huovilainen, A.: Virtual air guitar. J. Audio Eng. Soc. **54**(10), 964–980 (2006)
11. Lohner, H.: The UPIC system: a user's report. Comput. Music J. **10**(4), 42 (1986)
12. Lyons, M., Fels, S.: Creating new interfaces for musical expression. In: SIGGRAPH Asia 2013 Courses on - SA '13, pp. 1–164. ACM Press (2013)
13. Mäki-Patola, T., Laitinen, J., Kanerva, A., Takala, T.: Experiments with Virtual Reality Instruments. Technical report (2004)
14. Martin, C.P., Tørresen, J.: MicroJam: an app for sharing tiny touch-screen performances. In: Proceedings of the International Conference on New Interfaces for Musical Expression, pp. 495–496. Aalborg University Copenhagen (2017)
15. Naylor, T.D., Florida, R.: The rise of the creative class: and how it's transforming work, leisure, community and everyday life. Can. Public Policy/Anal. de Politiques **29**(3), 378 (2003)
16. Nymoen, K., Glette, K., St, S., Skogstad, S., Torresen, J., Jensenius, A.R.: Searching for Cross-Individual Relationships between Sound and Movement Features using an SVM Classifier. Technical report (2010)
17. Paradiso, J.: Electronic music: new ways to play. IEEE Spectr. **34**(12), 18–30 (1997)

18. Renaud, A., Charbonnier, C., Chagué, S.: 3DinMotion a mocap based interface for real time visualisation and sonification of multi-user interactions. In: NIME, pp. 495–496 (2014)
19. Serafin, S., Erkut, C., Kojs, J., Nilsson, N.C., Nordahl, R.: Virtual reality musical instruments: state of the art, design principles, and future directions. Comput. Music J. 40(3), 22–40 (2016)
20. Shneiderman, B.: Ben: creativity support tools. Commun. ACM 45(10), 116–120 (2002)
21. Shneiderman, B.: Ben: creativity support tools: accelerating discovery and innovation. Commun. ACM 50(12), 20–32 (2007)
22. Shneiderman, B., et al.: Creativity Support Tools: Report From a U.S. National Science Foundation Sponsored Workshop. Technical Report 2 (2006)
23. Wanderley, M., Battier, M.: Trends in gestural control of music. Ircam (2000)
24. Wanderley, M.M., Orio, N.: Evaluation of input devices for musical expression: Borrowing tools from HCI. Technical Report 3 (2002)
25. Wanderley, M., Depalle, P.: Gestural control of sound synthesis. Proc. IEEE 92(4), 632–644 (2004)
26. Wessel, D., Wright, M.: Problems and prospects for intimate musical control of computers. Comput. Music J. 26(3), 11–22 (2002)
27. Wessel, D.L.: Timbre space as a musical control structure. Comput. Music J. 3(2), 45 (1979)

MR Environments Constructed for a Large Indoor Physical Space

Huan Xing[1,5], Chenglei Yang[1(✉)], Xiyu Bao[1], Sheng Li[2], Wei Gai[1], Meng Qi[3], Juan Liu[1], Yuliang Shi[1], Gerard De Melo[4], Fan Zhang[1], and Xiangxu Meng[1]

[1] School of Software, Shandong University, Jinan, Shandong, China
chl_yang@sdu.edu.cn
[2] Department of Computer Science and Technology,
Peking University, Beijing, China
[3] School of Information Science and Engineering,
Shandong Normal University, Jinan, Shandong, China
[4] Rutgers University, Piscataway, NJ, USA
[5] Taiyuan University of Technology, Taiyuan, Shanxi, China

Abstract. To resolve the problem that existing mixed reality (MR) apparatus are unable to scan and model a large and complex indoor scene at once, we present a powerful toolkit for constructing MR environment easily. Our toolkit establishes and maintains accurate mapping between the virtual and physical space, and sets the occlusion relationships of the walls. Additionally, we design spatial anchor deployment strategy supporting deviation correction between the real and virtual spaces, so that the spatial anchors can maintain a virtual object's location and orientation in the real world. Our experiments and applications show that the toolkit is convenient for constructing MR apps targeting large physical spaces in which users can roam in real time.

Keywords: Mixed reality · Reconstruction · Real-time roaming · Indoor scene

1 Introduction

Popular mixed reality (MR) head mounted display (HMD) enable users to interact with three-dimensional holograms blended with the real world. It is widely used in education, games, surgery and museums [4]. In MR museum deployments, visitors wearing HoloLens can roam in every corridor and room to see different virtual collection items embedded into the real space. When a visitor resides in one room, one cannot see through the physical walls. Evidently, the virtual scene should be rendered in real-time. Given these desiderata, how to

Supported by the National Key Research and Development Program of China under Grant 2018YFC0831003, the National Natural Science Foundation of China under Grant 61972233 and the National Natural Science Foundation of China under Grant 61902225.

ⓒ Springer Nature Switzerland AG 2020
N. Magnenat-Thalmann et al. (Eds.): CGI 2020, LNCS 12221, pp. 132–144, 2020.
https://doi.org/10.1007/978-3-030-61864-3_12

construct the virtual scenes of a large physical space is of principal concern. At present, the virtual models in most MR apps are designed by professionals, making use of specialized tools such as 3D Studio Max, and then deployed on the corresponding MR hardware by software engineers [10]. Additionally, to create a convincing MR experience, end-users need to spatially perceive the real environment. For example, HoloLens provides a spatial mapping module. Prior to using this module, one needs to complete a scan of all parts of the environment that have been observed [10]. For small-scale experience applications, this process is feasible and accurate. However, since the scan distance of a HoloLens is 0.8–3.1 m, it is time-consuming and laborious for a large-scale interior space with complex room structure. Additionally, for a large-scale interior space, as the virtual design content is enriched, the system performance will decline when roaming due to the limited resources provided by the HoloLens [12].

In order to provide users an immersive and real-time MR roaming experience, this paper proposes a toolkit that aids in conveniently and easily constructing MR apps that can provide a real-time experience in large indoor physical spaces via HoloLens. In the preliminary work [15], We have introduced our idea and toolkit briefly. Based on it, an indepth study is made. Overall, our main contributions include:

1) We present a toolkit for conveniently and easily constructing MR apps in large indoor physical spaces. The toolkit establishes and maintains accurate mapping relationships between the virtual and physical spaces.
2) We develop a method to deal with occlusion with respect to walls, and such occlusion information serves as a factor in selecting appropriate virtual models and rendering the virtual objects occluded by translucent walls.
3) We propose a custom data structure called VorPa, based on the Voronoi diagram (VD), to effectively implement path editing, accelerate rendering and collision detection, and correct deviation between the real and virtual spaces.
4) We propose spatial anchor deployment strategy supporting deviation correction between real and virtual spaces when roaming.

2   Related Work

2.1   VR/AR/MR Apps Design

Recently, more and more researchers focus on VR, AR and MR app design. Gai et al. presented a new genre and designed a toolkit for supporting users in easily constructing a VR maze and playing it [6]. However, the physical space is limited by the Kinect's tracking field and the genre is not targeting AR/MR. Hsiao et al. proposed a system in which users can manipulate furniture cards directly in the model house task space, get instantaneous multi-view 3D visual feedback, and re-adjust cards until they are satisfied [7]. Nevertheless, all manipulations of virtual object need additional tools like cards. Wei et al. introduced a conceptual design framework that integrated MR with a multi-touch tabletop interface, which provided an intuitive and efficient interface [14]. Unfortunately, only a conceptual framework was introduced and the experience of MR scenes was not immersive.

2.2   Accelerate Rendering in AR/MR

Acceleration of rendering can improve mobile device's performance. Traditional methods include occlusion culling [3], potentially visible sets (PVS) [9], levels of detail (LOD) [5] etc. Some focus on how to utilize user's visual processing characteristics to accelerate rendering. Kim et al. proposed an accelerated rendering strategy for head-mounted augmented reality display devices and pointed out that during the rotation of the headset, the user's attention to the model in the field of vision will be reduced [8]. Therefore, the rendering performance can be improved by reducing the model quality in user's visual field when the users moves.

Other studies focused on how to optimize the rendering algorithm itself. A set of acceleration strategies such as parallelization of rendering algorithm are invoked to optimize the HoloLens's rendering performance [11]. To avoid rendering delays, the MR 3D GIS deploys HoloLens holographic remote player middleware on a PC to quickly render large virtual scenes, and sends the results to the HoloLens [13]. Despite transferring all calculations from the HoloLens to a higher performance PC, this method could lead to new network latencies.

3   System Design and Implementation

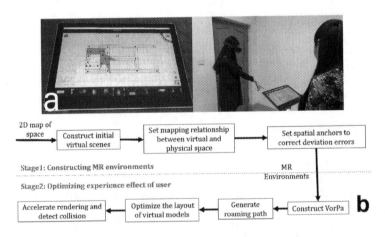

Fig. 1. (a) Overview of our toolkit; (b) Working pipeline of our toolkit.

We developed a toolkit for constructing MR apps with real-time roaming in large indoor physical spaces (see Fig. 1a). The toolkit consists of two parts: one is a 2D interface supporting users designing virtual scenes using multi-touch technology, such that a 2D map of the space can be drawn and the virtual objects can be manipulated easily; the other one is MR experience part, on which the corresponding 3D scenes are automatically generated and displayed on MR devices, like HoloLens.

The overview of methods used in our toolkit is shown in Fig. 1b. Our toolkit has two stages: Stage1: Constructing MR environments. For an indoor physical space, we use 2D map of the space to construct initial virtual scenes and set mapping relationship between virtual and physical space. We set some spatial anchors to correct deviation errors appearing in the process of user roaming; Stage2: Optimizing experience effect of user. Based on a data structure VorPa, we provide some methods to improve user roaming experience and system performance, such as generating roaming path, optimizing virtual model layouts, accelerating rendering and detecting collision.

3.1   Constructing MR Environments

To construct a MR environment for an interior space, especially for a large-scale space, our method includes the following steps:

1. Constructing the initial virtual scenes. We only consider the room structure, mainly walls. The arrangement of virtual objects will be introduced in Sect. 3.2. Using our toolkit, we can obtain a digital 2D map of the real space, which will be displayed on the 2D interface.
2. Setting the mapping between virtual and physical spaces. We set corresponding landmarks in virtual and real spaces, respectively. Through these landmarks, we can calculate the coordinate transformation formula. So for any point in virtual space, we can get its corresponding position in real space. Then, we can construct 3D scene used in HoloLens according to 2D map. The real space is three-dimensional and HoloLens can provide 3D coordinate like (x, y, z). Here, y-dimension can be neglected because the height of wall's location will be set according to ground automatically.
3. Setting transparency of walls. We set transparency value to handle the occlusion relationship of walls with different transparency. For opaque wall in the real space, we set transparency value as 1 and construct a corresponding virtual wall, to which a transparent texture is applied; For transparent or semi-transparent walls such as glass walls, we set the transparency value between 0 and 1. This value will serve as a parameter when rendering the virtual objects.
4. Setting spatial anchors to correct deviation errors. Sometimes, HoloLens is unable to recognize the environment and position of the user so that tracking loss occurs and there is deviation error between virtual models and the real space. We will describe how to solve this problem in Sect. 3.4.

3.2   Optimize the Layouts of MR Environments

As mentioned in Sect. 1, for a large-scale interior space, as the design content is enriched, the system performance will decline while roaming because of the

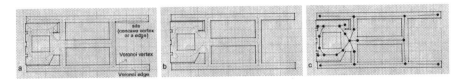

Fig. 2. (a) Voronoi diagram V in polygon P; (b) Initial roaming path R in polygon P; (c) Path editing.

limited computing resources afforded by the HoloLens. Generally, users are easily lost when roaming in complex large scenes. For the designer, predesignating a reasonable roaming path on the design side can effectively help users in better navigating unfamiliar scenes. Therefore, in this section, we propose a custom data structure called VorPa to effectively implement path editing, accelerate rendering, and provide for collision detection.

VorPa is designed based on the Voronoi Diagram (VD) of polygons. The VD is an important geometric structure in computational geometry. A VD records the regions in the proximity of a set of points. We refer to these points as sites. Unlike for a set of points, the regions in the proximity of a set of objects, such as line segments, circular arcs and polygons, also form a VD. VD of a polygon can subdivide the polygon into cells called Voronoi regions based on proximity characteristics [1] (see the grey region in Fig. 2a). In the VD of polygon P, the concave vertex and edge of a polygon are the sites; the common boundary of two adjacent regions is called a Voronoi edge; the points where Voronoi edges meet are called Voronoi vertex. A Voronoi skeleton path is composed of a Voronoi vertex and Voronoi edge.

For a line segment L in polygon P, a point s is weakly visible to L if L has at least one point that is visible to s. The weak visibility polygon (see grey part in Fig. 3a) of L is the set of all points in P that are weakly visible to L [2].

We define the structure of VorPa based on a VD as follows:

Class VorPa {
    List<Edge> P;   //2D design wall list
    List<Path> V;   //Voronoi edge in polygon
    List<Path> R;   //Roaming path in polygon }
Class Path {
    Edge *edge*;   //Current Voronoi edge
    List<Model> *modellist*;   //Virtual models bound to path
    List<Edge> *Vis*; //Weak visibility region of path
    Bool *direction*;   //Direction of edge, route guide for users }

We show the pseudocode of constructing VorPa. The time complexity of constructing VorPa is $O(E)$. The E represents the number of edges in polygon.

Algorithm: Constructing VorPa
Input: 2D Polygon P, Model list M
Output: VorPa Vor
Init VorPa Vor (as shown in Class VorPa)

Copy P to $Vor.P$, Compute the VD V of $Vor.P$ and Copy V to $Vor.V$
For each v_i in $Vor.V$
    If exist p_i in $Vor.P$, and $p_i.Startpoint$ equals $v_i.edge.Startpoint$ or $v_i.edge.Endpoint$
        Continue;
    Else
        Add v_i to list $Vor.R$
For each r_i in $Vor.R$
    Compute weak visibility polygon W of $r_i.edge$ to Polygon $Vor.P$ and Copy W to $r_i.Vis$

Generate Roaming Path. Based on VorPa, we provide a method to automatically generate a roaming path for user, which also can be modified interactively by the designer later.

As shown in the Constructing VorPa Algorithm, we obtain initial roaming path R (see Fig. 2b) by deleting all edges that contain vertices of the polygon in V. Path editing is an interactive operation, and the designer can modify the nodes in the path to optimize the roaming path R, as shown in Fig. 2c. This is an undirected connected graph G, which can be modified, such as by adding vertices, moving vertices, or merging vertices. Designers can also plan a recommended tour path for the users on the experience side by designating a direction. Once designers specify a direction for a path, the presentation of the route guide will be available in the corresponding path in the experience part.

Optimize the Layout of Virtual Models. Given that the system targets general users, VorPa also provides recommendations for the model layout. Designers can click on each sub-path R_i in the roaming path R (see the blue segment in Fig. 3a), and VorPa will calculate the weak visibility region $Visi$ of R_i in polygon P in advance, and then bind it to R_i. This is the grey part in Fig. 3a. Arranging models in $Visi$ helps avoid unreasonable layouts, such as dead corners or large variations in density in different fields of view.

VorPa also pre-processes model data during the layout phase. When the designer places a model, every model is bound to all sub-paths that contain this model in the weak visibility region and sites that contain this model in the Voronoi region. Thus, at the end of the design, each sub-path has multiple models that are within the weak visibility region of the sub-path. Each site also has multiple models, which are located in the Voronoi region corresponding to that site. This pre-processing operation will be used to accelerate rendering and collision detection in the next section.

3.3   Accelerate Rendering Based on the Optimized Deployment

As mentioned in Sect. 1, due to the complexity of the scene and the limited performance of some hardware in AR/MR devices, the over-calculation for rendering or positioning while roaming may lead to latency or even crashes. However, the occlusion culling function in Unity3D cannot solve latency problems due to the high complexity of models in view. Traditional LOD needs extra real-time computing power, which is not desirable for the HoloLens with its limited hardware performance. In addition, we also consider the positioning problem. Traditional method for interaction with virtual objects is through adding collision detection to each object, which not only requires substantial calculations for large-scale scenes, but also has detrimental effects on the user experience. To solve these problems, we introduce some additional strategies based on VorPa.

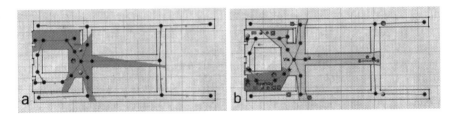

Fig. 3. (a) Laying out models in weak visibility region; (b) The visible region of the current view point. (Color figure online)

Accelerate Rendering. VorPa can locate the user with regard to the appropriate sub-path R_i with the help of the user's location received from the HoloLens and obtain the model list M_i bound to that sub-path. The visible regions of the FOV $RealVisi$ are calculated in real time [16], as shown in Fig. 3b.

First, the HoloLens stops rendering all models that do not belong to M_i. Then, for models in M_i, the HoloLens as well stops rendering the models in $Visi$ but not in $RealVisi$. Finally, we calculate the model complexity F that is in M_i and $RealVisi$. In our tests, we use triangular facets to measure the model complexity. Through experiments, we obtain rough estimates of the upper limit threshold of the recommended rendering effect. According to the distance between the model and the user's location, the accuracy of the model is tuned from far to near so as to guarantee $F < threshold$ and that the average frame rate is at least 15.

For transparent or semi-transparent walls (e.g. glass wall), special handling is introduced. As mentioned in Sect. 3.1, we set a transparency value between 0 and 1 as a parameter to select different levels of detail of the models. When users see through transparent or semi-transparent walls, we reduce the complexity of the models behind the walls according to the distance between models and users' locations and the transparency value of the wall. If the transparency value is 1, the real wall is opaque. For this case, a virtual wall model is needed. The system renders a transparent texture applied to the corresponding virtual wall, so that the virtual objects occluded by the real walls are invisible to users.

Detect Collision. As mentioned above, VorPa can locate users with respect to the corresponding sub-path R_i, which is a Voronoi edge in the VD of the polygon P. Additionally, we bind the model to the site corresponding to its Voronoi region. VorPa only needs to traverse the Voronoi region near R_i within $O(n)$ time complexity and obtain all model lists M in each region within $O(1)$ time. When a user roams in the R_i, we only need to set collision detection on M, which only takes up a small part of the models in the whole scene in real time, thus effectively reducing the calculation cost of location.

3.4   Correct Deviation Using Spatial Anchors

Our approach uses the characteristics of spatial anchors to correct the deviations between the virtual and real space while a user roams around. HoloLens can trace spatial anchors, update their location and coordinates to ensure that the spatial anchor can always mark one point in the real world. Therefore, we place some anchors in the scene and bind the virtual model to the nearest anchor coordinate system. The virtual model constantly updates its position with the anchor. According to the characteristics of spatial anchors, the accurate positioning range of each anchor is 3 m. Moreover, the spatial anchor should be visible at the position of the virtual model. To obtain high efficiency, we should minimize the number of spatial anchors during deployment, and each spatial anchor should cover as many virtual models as possible.

Our spatial anchor layout should meet the following conditions: 1) All virtual models in the scene can be covered by spatial anchors, including virtual wall models and virtual object models placed in the scene; 2) Each spatial anchor is responsible for virtual models within a 3-m radius around the spatial anchor; 3) A spatial anchor is visible at the position of the anchored virtual model; 4) A minimum number of spatial anchors.

Therefore, the input to the spatial anchor deployment algorithm is: the virtual wall set in scene $W = w_1, w_2, w_3, \ldots$, a collection of virtual objects placed in scene $R = r_1, r_2, r_3, \ldots$; the output is: the spatial anchor layout $S = s_1, s_2, s_3, \ldots, s_q$ and the spatial anchor number q.

The wall model is regarded as a special virtual object whose position is the midpoint of the wall. After combining the virtual wall and virtual object sets, we use M to represent the set of all virtual models that need to be covered by spatial anchors in the scene is: $M = W \bigcup R = \{m_1, m_2, m_3, \ldots, m_n\}$

Before using our algorithm, this paper has a pre-processing step based on the data structure VorPa:

1. The value v_i ($i \in n$) is set for each virtual model m_i. Each v_i represents the probability that the virtual model m_i will be seen in the scene. The calculation method is as follows:

$$v_i = \frac{\sum_{path \ in \ VR(m_i)} Length(path)}{\sum Length(p_j)}, \tag{1}$$

where $VR(m_i)$ represents the visible area of m_i in the scene, and p_j represents the roaming sub-path j in the scene. The calculation of v_i is based on the roaming path length, that is, the ratio of the roaming path length falling into the visible area of the relic m_i and the total roaming path length of the scene.

2. Set the value v_{p_j} for each sub-path. In the data structure VorPa, if the virtual model m_i is in the weakly visible region of path p_j, the relic m_i is bound to the modelList of path p_j. The value of all models in the list of p_j models in modelList is the value of path p_j:

$$v_{p_j} = \sum_{m_i \ in \ modelList \ of \ p_j} v_i \qquad (2)$$

We convert this problem into an optimization problem seeking to minimize the number of spatial anchors. Accordingly, we propose an algorithm based on integer linear programming.

1) Get the initial set of spatial anchors. Before constructing the mathematical model, the initial set of l spatial anchors that can cover all the virtual models in the scene is obtained through the following process:
   Create a matrix C that contains the whole scene and is initialized with 0s. Find the intersection area between the circle with $m_i(x_i, y_i)$ as the center and $3m$ as the radius and visibility region $VR(m_i)$ of model m_i. Then add v_i to the value of the corresponding array position in intersection area. Traverse the matrix C, find all the spatial anchors that can cover the different virtual model combinations, and add them to the initial set of spatial anchors without repeating.
2) We build a mathematical model based on the previous problem description:

$$minZ = \sum_{i=1}^{l} s_i, \qquad \begin{cases} s_i = 0 \ or \ 1, \ i = 1, 2, \ldots, l \\ \sum_{i=1}^{l} F_{ij} s_i \geq 1, \ j = 1, 2, \ldots, n \end{cases}$$

where s_i represents the spatial anchor i, assuming that there are initially l spatial anchors that can cover all the virtual models in the scenario, F_{ij} indicates whether the spatial anchor i can cover virtual model j. If it can be covered, the value is 1; if not, the value is 0. We minimize the number of spatial anchors to be placed and satisfy two constraints: 1) the value of spatial anchor s_i is 0 or 1, where 0 means that the spatial anchor i is not placed, and 1 means that it is placed; 2) all models in the scenario can be covered, that is, for any model, the number of spatial anchors that can be covered by this model is greater than or equal to 1. 3) The integer linear programming method is used to solve the model. Specifically, IBM's integer programming solver CPLEX is used to solve the optimized spatial anchor set.

4 Experiments

Fig. 4. (a) Screenshot of 2D design interface; (b) A visitor's view corresponds to position marked with a red dot in (a); (c) Model layout and route design of experiment. (Color figure online)

To test our toolkit and methods, we designed a MR museum (see Fig. 4a and 4b) to conduct a series of experiments. For every exhibition hall in the MR museum, we design different themes, and visitors can choose different halls without interference from other halls. When a visitor is in one hall, the virtual exhibits in another hall will be occluded by the wall via a special texture. In addition, while visitors roam within the MR museum, the system can present the path on the ground as a tour guide while lowering their probability of getting lost. When visitors approach one exhibit, the system automatically plays the introductory audio of the respective exhibit, following the VorPa location algorithm to help visitors better understand the display content.

During roaming, we accelerate rendering based on the design of VorPa. To verify its effectiveness, we design experiments as follows: First, we test the threshold in advance and obtain the result that when the total number of triangles is no more than 10^5, the frame rate is sufficient for a fluid visitor experience; Then, we compare the performance of VorPa with regard to different capacities of scenes. In our experiment, we use the total number of triangles in a scene to quantify its capacity. We rely on frame rates to evaluate the user experience in terms of fluidity. High frame rates entail a low latency and better experience.

We select a room with appropriate lighting as experiment site (to ensure the stable tracking and position effect of HoloLens) and design the model layout and route for experimenter, as shown in Fig. 4c. The red line with arrow is the roaming path, and we place virtual models in region A, B, C, D near the path. Through changing the number of models in region A, B, C, D, we assess four kinds of scene capacities, namely $3.2 * 10^6$, $6.4 * 10^6$, $9.6 * 10^6$, and $12.8 * 10^6$. In each case, we experiment with two conditions, with and without our VorPa algorithm. In the course of the experiment, we request the participant to walk along the recommended path at a constant speed for a specified time and

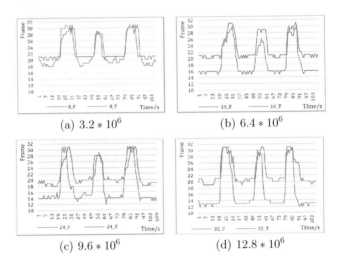

(a) $3.2 * 10^6$ (b) $6.4 * 10^6$

(c) $9.6 * 10^6$ (d) $12.8 * 10^6$

Fig. 5. Results of four scenes capacities. $3.2 * 10^6$ (8_F/8_T denotes result obtained with/without using our algorithm, respectively), $6.4 * 10^6$, $9.6 * 10^6$, $12.8 * 10^6$.

to browse the models placed near the route. To ensure the same experimental conditions, all the experiments were completed by one experimenter in the same time. The system will record the number of frames per second.

We provide the experimental results under each scene capacity condition by means of line charts. By integrating the participant's route, we can explain the peaks and valleys in every line chart. When the participant walks past the areas that feature numerous models, the frame rate declines and reaches the valleys. In circumstances with fewer models, the frame rate is higher. As Fig. 5 shows, the difference in the frame rates between these two conditions (with and without our algorithm) varies in different phases. When the frame rate peaks, the difference is small. In contrast, when the frame rate becomes lower, the difference becomes more apparent. The difference of frame rates between these two conditions is smaller in Fig. 5a than in any other figures, which might stem from the fact that the number of triangles in a participant's view does not exceed the threshold most of the time.

We compare different experimental results in Fig. 6. Overall, the difference in the valley is larger with an increase of capacity. This means that our algorithm effectively improves the rendering effect and keeps it real-time. More specifically, the effect is more obvious as the capacity of the scene increases.

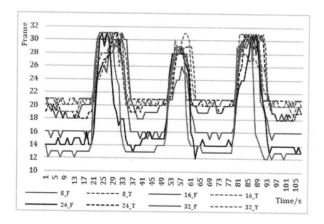

Fig. 6. Frame rate comparison. Solid lines denote results without our algorithm; while dotted lines represent results using our algorithm.

5   Conclusion

This paper presents a toolkit to aid general users in rapidly and conveniently designing MR applications, especially in large indoor spaces. Above all, the MR applications can provide a fluid and immersive roaming experience in real-time. To satisfy this requirement, we introduce VorPa, a data structure based on VD, which is beneficial to the user experience with regard to the strategies of path editing, accelerated rendering, collision detection, and correcting deviations. We apply this toolkit to an application and evaluate it in a set of experiments. Our evaluation shows that such a toolkit effectively improves real-time rendering efficiency of HoloLens.

In the future, we will design an algorithm to automatically calculate the upper limit of the number of rendering polygons for different types of CPU, memory, and other hardware state signals.

References

1. Aurenhammer, F.: Voronoi diagrams—a survey of a fundamental geometric data structure. ACM Comput. Surv. (CSUR) **23**(3), 345–405 (1991)
2. Chen, D.Z., Wang, H.: Weak visibility queries of line segments in simple polygons. Comput. Geom. **48**(6), 443–452 (2015)
3. Coorg, S., Teller, S.: Real-time occlusion culling for models with large occluders. In: Proceedings of the 1997 Symposium on Interactive 3D Graphics, p. 83-ff (1997)
4. Damala, A., Marchal, I., Houlier, P.: Merging augmented reality based features in mobile multimedia museum guides. In: Anticipating the Future of the Cultural Past, CIPA Conference 2007, Athens, Greece, 1–6 October 2007, pp. 259–264 (2007). https://halshs.archives-ouvertes.fr/halshs-00530903
5. Erikson, C.M.: Hierarchical levels of detail to accelerate the rendering of large static and dynamic polygonal environments. Ph.D. thesis. Citeseer (2000)

6. Gai, W., et al.: Supporting easy physical-to-virtual creation of mobile VR maze games: a new genre. In: Proceedings of the 2017 CHI Conference on Human Factors in Computing Systems, pp. 5016–5028 (2017)
7. Hsiao, F.J., Teng, C.J., Lin, C.W., Luo, A.C., Yang, J.C.: Dream home: a multiview stereoscopic interior design system. In: The Engineering Reality of Virtual Reality 2010, vol. 7525, p. 75250J. International Society for Optics and Photonics (2010)
8. Kim, J.B., Choi, J.H., Ahn, S.J., Park, C.M.: Low latency rendering in augmented reality based on head movement. In: International Conference in Central Europe on Computer Graphics (2016)
9. Laakso, M.: Potentially visible set (PVS). Helsinki University of Technology (2003)
10. Liu, Y., Stiles, N.R., Meister, M.: Augmented reality powers a cognitive prosthesis for the blind. bioRxiv, p. 321265 (2018)
11. Morley, C., Choudhry, O., Kelly, S., Phillips, J., Ahmed, F.: Mixed reality visualization of medical imaging data (2017)
12. Shearer, A., Guo, L., Liu, J., Satkowski, M., LiKamWa, R.: Characterizing bottlenecks towards a hybrid integration of holographic, mobile, and screen-based data visualization
13. Wang, W., Wu, X., Chen, G., Chen, Z.: Holo3DGIS: leveraging Microsoft Hololens in 3D geographic information. ISPRS Int. J. Geo-Inf. **7**(2), 60 (2018)
14. Wei, D., Zhou, S.Z., Xie, D.: MTMR: a conceptual interior design framework integrating mixed reality with the multi-touch tabletop interface. In: 2010 IEEE International Symposium on Mixed and Augmented Reality, pp. 279–280. IEEE (2010)
15. Xing, H., et al.: Rotbav: a toolkit for constructing mixed reality apps with real-time roaming in large indoor physical spaces, pp. 1245–1246 (2019)
16. Zhou, K., Pan, Z., Shi, J.: A real-time rendering algorithm based on hybrid multiple level-of-detail methods. J. Softw. **12**(1), 74–82 (2001)

FIOU Tracker: An Improved Algorithm of IOU Tracker in Video with a Lot of Background Inferences

Zhihua Chen[1]([✉]), Guhao Qiu[1], Han Zhang[2], Bin Sheng[3], and Ping Li[4]

[1] Department of Computer Science and Engineering, East China University
of Science and Technology, Shanghai 200237, China
czh@ecust.edu.cn
[2] Nanjing University of Aeronautics and Astronautics, Nanjing 210016, China
[3] Department of Computer Science and Engineering, Shanghai Jiao Tong University,
Shanghai 200240, China
[4] Faculty of Information Technology, Macau University of Science and Technology,
Macau 999078, China

Abstract. Multiple object tracking(MOT) is a fundamental problem in video analysis application. Associating unreliable detection in a complex environment is a challenging task. The accuracy of multiple object tracking algorithms is dependent on the accuracy of the first stage object detection algorithm. In this paper, we propose an improved algorithm of IOU Tracker–FIOU Tracker. Our proposal algorithm can overcome the shortcoming of IOU Tracker with a small amount of computing cost that heavily relies on the precision and recall of object detection accuracy. The algorithm we propose is based on the assumption that the motion of background inference is not obvious. We use the average light flux value of the track and the change rate of the light flux value of the center point of the adjacent object as the conditions to determine whether the trajectory is to be retained. The tracking accuracy is higher than the primary IOU Tracker and another well-known variant VIOU Tracker. Our proposal method can also significantly reduce the ID switch value and fragmentation value which are both important metrics in MOT task.

Keywords: Multiple object tracking · Drone video · FIOU Tracker

1 Introduction

Multiple object tracking (MOT) aims at predicting the trajectory of interesting objects in video sequences. MOT is an important research area in computer vision task. It has a lot of applications, such as automatic driving, traffic monitoring, pedestrian behavior analysis [9] and sport analysis [16,22].

Tracking-by-detection is a widely used paradigm to solve the problem of tracking multiple objects. It includes two parts: 1) detect objects independently in every frame, 2) establish tracks by linking corresponding detection.

© Springer Nature Switzerland AG 2020
N. Magnenat-Thalmann et al. (Eds.): CGI 2020, LNCS 12221, pp. 145–156, 2020.
https://doi.org/10.1007/978-3-030-61864-3_13

Accuracy of object detection is the prerequisite for MOT task. However it is difficult to achieve satisfactory results in some special conditions for example our main research dataset focusing on tracking vehicles on pictures taken by a drone. It is a difficult task mainly because images are collected in various weather conditions and light conditions. Weather conditions are sunny weather, cloudy weather, foggy weather and rainy weather. The images are also collected in both daytime and nighttime. There always exist some small vehicles in video sequences and occlusion in crowded scene.

Linking corresponding object in every frame is also an important part in MOT task. Associating unreliable detected object with recent tracks is a major challenge in this part. The distance calculation is an important part in linking decision. However the calculation of small objects' appearance distance is difficult. It often meets mistake in common linking algorithm.

In this paper, we propose the variant of iou tracker, which is named FIOU Tracker, to solve the multiple object tracking in drone video in batch mode. Inspired by the success of IOU Tracker [4] in Visdrone competition [25] in 2018 and 2019, we use the main idea in iou tracker and make some limitations aiming at removing unreasonable trajectories. The main problem of the object detection algorithm is that similar background objects are mistaken for targets. However the movement of similar background objects is not salient compared with moving vehicle. We use the dense optical flow value to describe every object's moving trends in every trajectory and use some statistical indicators to remove background object trajectories. Our proposal algorithm FIOU Tracker can achieve higher MOTA, smaller ID Switch and smaller Fragmentation compared with IOU Tracker [4] and VIOU Tracker [5].

In sum, our approach has the following contributions:

-Optical flow value as the basis for removing the background inferences In order to solve the problem of many background interference objects predicted by the object detection algorithm, this paper proposes to use the method based on dense optical flow to remove the optical flow formed by objects with insignificant motion and improve the prediction accuracy.

-Specific post-processing algorithm used to process the generated trajectory We propose to use the quantile of the average optical flow value of all the trajectories in the video to remove most of the trajectories caused by background interference that do not meet the statistical rules. At the same time, in order to solve the problem that the trajectories of moving objects will be removed in the later period of temporarily stationary objects, we propose using the optical flow rate of change to extract the trajectories generated by these objects.

-Better performance compared with existing similar MOT algorithms Compared with similar algorithm-IOU Tracker and VIOU Tracker, our proposal algorithm combined with some widely used object detection models can achieve better performance in drone video dataset-UAVDT dataset.

2 Related Work

2.1 Object Detection Models in MOT Models

Faster rcnn+FPN [12] is widely used in MOT task that needs a high accuracy in detection stage. SSD [13] and yolo [14] are used in MOT task that require higher inference speed.

Faster rcnn as the detection stage, KCF as the combined MOT model of the motion estimation module is used in pig detection and tracking task [20]. The general SSD model is used as the detection stage, and the feature map extracted by the SSD is used as the MOT combined model of the motion prediction module of the feature input of the CNN-based correlation filtering is used in vehicle tracking task [24]. Yolov2 and random stern in tracking is used in multiple pedestrian tracking [10].

2.2 Recent MOT Work

Main components in MOT models are the detection stage, feature extraction stage, affinity stage and the data association stage [7]. In this section, we mainly introduce recent work on affinity stage and data association stage.

Affinity Section. In affinity section, appearance difference and motion predictor are needed to calculate the distance or similarity between detected objects between two frames. Sort algorithm only calculates location distance as object difference. Kalman Filter is used as motion predictor [3]. DeepSort algorithm also uses Kalman filter as motion predictor and deep network as feature extraction. Appearance difference is calculated as cosine distance and Location difference is calculated as Mahalanobis distance. The distance between objects are calculated as the weighted sum of appearance distance and location distance [19]. In some recent work, associate embedding calculated by deep network is proposed as the affinity calculation section. JDE combines the object detection models and REID models [18]. It can reduce some inference time compared with the widely used separate use of object detection model and REID model. JDE add a special branch in general faster rcnn which is used as associate embedding.

Data Association Section. Hungarian algorithm is used as data association method in early MOT research including Sort [3] and DeepSort [19]. Recently MOT is often treated as graph problem, which seems each detection as a node and possible link as edges [2]. Then data association can be regarded as shortest path problem. K shortest path algorithm is the main data association section in MOT by K shortest path optimization [1]. The cost is calculated as physical possibility of flow. Explicit occlusion model based on min-cost-flow algorithm is used to handle occlusion in multiple pedestrian tracking algorithm [21]. Affinity matric is calculated among the embedding of detection result and embedding of existing tracks in JDE algorithm [18]. Hungarian algorithm is used in data association section. Motion prediction is also needed to calculate the predicted location of previous frame which is used to reject the assignment results that are far away from the prediction results.

3   Proposal Method

In this section, we briefly introduce the similar algorithm then introduce our proposal algorithm FIOU Tracker. The whole procedure of our proposed algorithm is shown in Fig. 1.

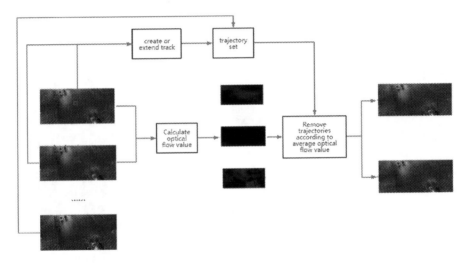

Fig. 1. Flow chart of our proposed FIOU Tracker algorithm

3.1   IOU Tracker

IOU tracker has two important assumptions–high detection accuracy and high video frame rate [4]. The procedure of IOU tracker is very simple. We do not need both feature extraction section and affinity calculation section. The data association section is only to add the detection result of recent frame to the track with the largest IOU in the detection result of the previous frame of the existing track. To further improve the precision of tracker, the length of track is needed to limit the minimum.

IOU tracker is a particular tracker that use no visual information to track. This special feature makes IOU Tracker run in a very high speed-about 100kfps.

3.2   VIOU Tracker

VIOU Tracker is a variant of IOU Tracker which mainly uses single object tracking algorithm to deal with missing detection is frames [5]. The main difference is that IOU Tracker directly uses the unmatched detection frame as the starting point of the new track. VIOU Tracker uses the unmatched detection frame as a single target tracking input to track the object. These modified parts can greatly reduce the ID switch and fragmentation indicators.

3.3   FIOU Tracker

The FIOU Tracker algorithm we proposed aims to solve background interference objects caused by low detection algorithm accuracy. We observe that the error background frame motion detected by the object detection model is significantly weaker than most vehicles that need to be tracked. We consider proposing a new improved IOU Tracker algorithm, keeping the original algorithm as fast as possible, less computational consumption, and reducing ID switch and fragmentation as much as possible.

Considering that the optical flow uses the change of pixels in the time domain and the correlation between adjacent frames to find the corresponding relationship between adjacent frames to describe the instantaneous velocity of the object, we use the average optical flow value to judge whether the track is composed of background inference object. Considering the existence of the temporary stopped tracking object, we propose calculating the optical flow rate of the front and back objects in the above-mentioned filtered trajectory. If there is a certain period of time when the change rate of the optical flow value is greater than a certain threshold, then keep the track, otherwise delete.

The detailed procedure is describe in Algorithm 1 where D_f denotes the detection result in frame f, T_{active} is trajectory record list that can be derived from the detection results after a successful match. T_{del} is the trajectory record list that needs to be judged by the average optical flow value and do not meet the statistical rules.

In the algorithm description, lines 1–22 are basically the same as IOU Tracker, just adding an array to record dense optical flow. It can be seen from the fourth and fifth lines in the algorithm description that the existing trajectory only selects the largest IOU for matching and the largest IOU should be larger than threshold σ_{IOU}. The calculation process is shown in formula 1. In this formula, D_f is the list of object detection prediction boxes, d_s is the selected detection prediction box. In the algorithm, only IOU is used as the basis for the data association section. Generally, there are only a few detection frames that meet this requirement. The Hungarian algorithm commonly used in common MOT algorithms is relatively complicated.

$$d_s = \arg\max_{d_j}   IOU(d_j, t), d_j \in D_f \tag{1}$$

In the new frame, if there is no detection result matching the existing track, the track is terminated, and the maximum IOU and track length in the track are calculated. In order to reduce False Negative, the maximum IOU value of the track needs to be set to a minimum value σ_h, and the length also needs to be set to a minimum value ttl.

After line 22 in Algorithm 1, we describe our proposal method to remove tracks created by background inference objects. We need to calculate average optical flow value for every track. The average value is calculated as formula 2. $flow$ array in this formula refers to the optical flow matrix for the corresponding frame. t_n^{cx}, t_n^{cy} refer to the coordinates of the center point of the predicted position of the nth frame in the trajectory.

$$t_{avg} = \frac{1}{t_{len}} \sum_{n=1}^{t_{len}} flow[t_n^{cx}][t_n^{cy}]) \tag{2}$$

The calculated quantile value is used to remove trajectories that do not conform to statistical rules. The specific number of quantiles needs to be determined according to the prediction accuracy of different target detection models. In our experiment, quantile value in FIOU Tracker with faster rcnn as detection model is set to 25, FIOU Tracker with retinanet and lrfnet is set to 15 and FIOU Tracker with atss is set to 10. In our experiment, it is found that directly removing these trajectories will greatly affect the recall rate. Main reason is that these selected tracks are not all created by background inference objects. The detection prediction box in some frames is a target that does not move temporarily, and will continue to move after a period of time. There are many such targets on the UAVDT dataset. We propose using the rate of change of optical flow to describe the situation where an almost stationary object started to move. The specific calculation is shown in the formula 3. The maximum interval for the rate of change here is set to 10 and the rate of change. The change rate of the sudden movement of the object that is considered to be stationary in the experiment is set to 20%.

$$\Delta^{(n)} fv = |\frac{fvlist_{i+n} - fvlist_i}{fvlist_{i-1}}| \tag{3}$$

4   Experimental Results

4.1   Dataset Introduction

UAVDT dataset is a dataset containing both object detection, single object tracking and multiple object tracking annotations and focusing on tracking task in videos collected by drone [8]. It consists of 100 video sequences, which are selected from over 10 hours of videos taken from UAV platform.

4.2   Implementation Detail

All the object detection models are implemented by pytorch 1.4.0 and mainly use mmdetection [6] framework. The UAVDT data set divides the training set and test set in a 4:1 ratio.

Algorithm 1. FIOU Tracker

Require: Image array list $I = [I_0, \ldots, I_{F-1}]$, Detection result list $D = [[d_0^0, d_1^0, \ldots, d_{N_0}^0], \ldots, [d_0^{F-1}, d_1^{F-1}, \ldots, d_{N_{F-1}}^{F-1}]]$

Ensure: Track list T

1: $T = \varnothing, T_{active} = \varnothing, OF = [], OV = [], T_{del} = []$
2: **for** f=0 to $F - 1$ **do**
3:      calculate dense optical flow matrix $flow$ for image I_{f-1} and I_f
4:      **for** All $i, t \in$ enumerate(T_a) **do**
5:          $d_{best} = argmax_{d_j} IOU(d_j, t), d_j \in D_f$
6:          **if** $IOU(d_{best}, t) > \sigma_{IOU}$ **then**
7:              Calculate optical flow value of detection's center point $flow[cx][cy]$
8:              Add d_{best} to t,Update related track information of t and Remove d_j from D_f
9:              Add $IOU(d_{best}, t)$ to OV list
10:         **else**
11:             **if** $max(OV_i) > \sigma_h$ and $len(t) > ttl$ **then**
12:                 Add t to T
13:             **end if**
14:             Remove t from t_a
15:         **end if**
16:     **end for**
17:     **for** d in D_f **do**
18:         Calculate optical flow value of detection's center point $flow[cx][cy]$
19:         Start new track t_{new},record detection coordinate and optical flow value
20:         Add t_{new} to T_a
21:     **end for**
22: **end for**
23: Calculate average optical flow value AOF for every track in T
24: Calculate the quantile value AOF_q of AOF
25: $T_{del}.add(T_i), if AOF_i < AOF_q$
26: **for** $t in T_{del}$ **do**
27:     Calculate change rate between n interval $\Delta^{(n)} fv = |\frac{fvlist_{i+n} - fvlist_i}{fvlist_{i-1}}|$
28:     **if** $\Delta^{(n)} fv > \Delta_{fv}$ **then**
29:         Remove t from T_{del}
30:     **end if**
31: **end for**
32: $T.del(t), t \in T_{del}$
33: **return** T

All the tracking algorithms are implemented by python. The dense optical flow matrix is calculated by calcOpticalFlowFarneback function in opencv. Some parameter settings are the same as in IOU Tracker. IOU threshold σ_{IOU} for matching the detection frame in the new picture from the last frame of the track is set to 0.3 as suggested in IOU Tracker and VIOU Tracker. The threshold of the maximum IOU value of the track σ_h is set 0.5 as suggested in IOU Tracker.

4.3   Tracking Evaluation Metric

We use multiple metrics to evaluate MOT performance, including identification precision(P) and recall(R), multiple object tracking accuracy(MOTA) and precision(MOTP), number of times when the object ID is mistakenly changed (ID Sw), total number of false negative(FN) and fragmentation(FM).

4.4   Experiment Result

Object Detection Result. We compare the accuracy of some widely used and latest object detection models on the UAVDT dataset. Object detection models include two-stage detector, one-stage detector and anchor-free detector. We also experiment our dataset on lrfnet model mainly due to its high performance in paper [17].

As shown in Table 1, atss achieve the highest performance compared with other models-87.2 mAP. However, the accuracy achieved by atss basically cannot meet the high precision requirements of the IOU Tracker for the detector.

The prediction results in some images are as shown in Fig. 2. It can be seen that there are more background interference objects detected in faster rcnn.

Table 1. Comparison with different detection models in mAP metric in UAVDT dataset

Method	Image size	Backbone	mAP	mAP$_{50}$	mAP$_{75}$
Faster rcnn [15]	1333*800	resnet50	78.6	97.0	93.5
Retinanet [11]	1333*800	resnet50	79.6	98.4	93.0
Lrfnet [17]	512*512	vgg16	81.9	98.8	94.1
atss [23]	1333*800	resnet50	**87.2**	98.9	97.8

MOT Result Compared with Similar Algorithm. We compare FIOU Tracker and IOU Tracker, VIOU Tracker to compare accuracy on UAVDT multi-object tasks on different detection models. In order to compare the effect of the optical flow average limit and the optical flow value change rate limit in the algorithm, we also compare the accuracy of the algorithm using only the optical flow average.

As Table 2 shows, FIOU Tracker, IOU Tracker and VIOU Tracker can achieve higher Precision and MOTA in most detection models, less ID Switch, Fragmentation and FN values with a small amount of Recall loss. The object detection model in FIOU Tracker uses the fastest rcnn with the lowest accuracy to achieve the greatest accuracy improvement,0.23 MOTA improvement. Although the computational complexity is increased compared with FIOU Tracker and IOU Tracker, slightly better overall results are achieved for the UAVDT dataset.

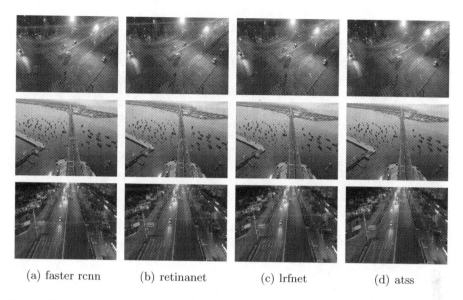

(a) faster rcnn   (b) retinanet   (c) lrfnet   (d) atss

Fig. 2. Some detection results on UAVDT dataset by using faster rcnn, retinanet, lrfnet and atss models. It can be seen from the figure that the prediction results of retinanet, lrfnet and atss are not very different, but faster rcnn often detects background interferences

Table 2. Comparison of the accuracy of IOU Tracker, VIOU Tracker and FIOU Tracker combined with different object detection models on UAVDT multiple object tracking dataset

Detector	Tracker	P($\uparrow$)	R($\uparrow$)	ID Sw($\downarrow$)	FM($\downarrow$)	FN($\downarrow$)	MOTA($\uparrow$)	MOTP($\uparrow$)
Faster rcnn	IOU Tracker	0.403	0.920	5285	7044	63330	−0.452	0.178
	VIOU Tracker	0.365	0.927	5050	5915	108136	−0.694	
	FIOU Tracker (only average limit)	0.439	0.863	3890	5595	57713	−0.244	
	FIOU Tracker	**0.447**	0.868	**3830**	**5511**	**56142**	**−0.221**	
retinanet	IOU Tracker	0.740	0.991	5273	1555	6943	0.636	0.138
	VIOU Tracker	0.717	0.992	9769	1279	6326	0.588	
	FIOU Tracker (only average limit)	0.753	0.952	4884	1679	17758	0.636	
	FIOU Tracker	**0.757**	0.954	**4772**	1592	8692	**0.638**	
lrfnet	IOU Tracker	0.959	0.992	6317	1652	6317	0.948	0.128
	VIOU Tracker	0.956	0.992	1893	1395	6032	0.833	
	FIOU Tracker (only average limit)	0.959	0.992	1652	1516	6317	0.948	
	FIOU Tracker	**0.961**	0.992	**1634**	1491	6142	**0.951**	
atss	IOU Tracker	0.762	0.990	4828	1656	8140	0.674	0.111
	VIOU Tracker	0.840	0.996	2781	544	2785	0.803	
	FIOU Tracker (only average limit)	0.867	0.965	1285	622	2742	0.815	
	FIOU Tracker	**0.871**	0.967	**1247**	608	**2716**	**0.819**	

Comparison Experiment Under Different Parameters. We first study the effect of *ttl* parameters on the performance of IOU Tracker, VIOU Tracker and FIOU Tracker and compare the performance on different object detection models. As shown in Fig. 3, Larger *ttl* value in most algorithms can reduce ID Switch and fragmentation, increase MOTA and precision, but will significantly reduce recall.

A higher ttl value has no significant effect on precision and MOTA in algorithms with higher detection accuracy. The main reason is that the accuracy of the obtained initial trajectory is high, and the improvement effect of the post-processing algorithm is not obvious.

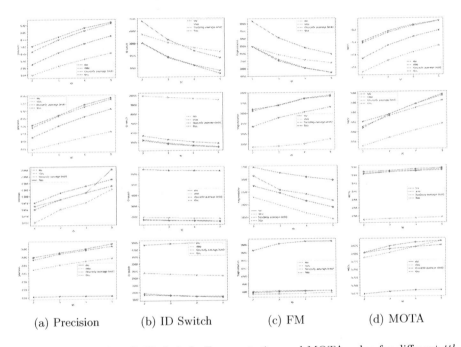

(a) Precision   (b) ID Switch   (c) FM   (d) MOTA

Fig. 3. Precision, Recall, ID Switch, Fragmentation and MOTA value for different *ttl* and IOU Tracker, VIOU Tracker and FIOU Tracker as tracker. The first to third lines are the results of faster rcnn, retinanet, lrfnet and atss as the object detection model

5   Conclusion

In this paper, we showed that simple dense optical flow value can improve the performance of IOU Tracker in multi-object tracking task, especially when the object detector predicts more background interference. In several experiments, we showed that wrong detection result can be compensated by our proposal post-processing algorithm. As a result, the number of ID Switch, fragmentation and false negative is reduced and the quality of tracks improve significantly. In addition, we found that the proposed FIOU Tracker algorithm improves the accuracy of the algorithm with lower object detection accuracy, which can partially solve the problem of the IOU Tracker relying too heavily on the detection algorithm. Our improvement on classic IOU Tracker makes it suitable for many use cases.

References

1. Berclaz, J., Fleuret, F., Turetken, E., Fua, P.: Multiple object tracking using k-shortest paths optimization. IEEE Trans. Pattern Anal. Mach. Intell. **33**, 1806–1819 (2011)
2. Bergmann, P., Meinhardt, T., Leal-Taixé, L.: Tracking without bells and whistles. In: ICCV, pp. 941–951 (2019)
3. Bewley, A., Ge, Z., Ott, L., Ramos, F.T., Upcroft, B.: Simple online and realtime tracking. In: ICIP, pp. 3464–3468 (2016)
4. Bochinski, E., Eiselein, V., Sikora, T.: High-speed tracking-by-detection without using image information. In: AVSS, pp. 1–6 (2017)
5. Bochinski, E., Senst, T., Sikora, T.: Extending IOU based multi-object tracking by visual information. In: AVSS, pp. 1–6 (2018)
6. Chen, K., et al.: Mmdetection: Open mmlab detection toolbox and benchmark (2019). arXiv: Computer Vision and Pattern Recognition
7. Ciaparrone, G., Sánchez, F.L., Tabik, S., Troiano, L., Tagliaferri, R., Herrera, F.: Deep learning in video multi-object tracking: a survey. Neurocomputing **381**, 61–88 (2020)
8. Du, D., et al.: The unmanned aerial vehicle benchmark: object detection and tracking. In: ECCV, pp. 375–391 (2018)
9. Kamel, A., Sheng, B., Yang, P., Li, P., Shen, R., Feng, D.D.: Deep convolutional neural networks for human action recognition using depth maps and postures. IEEE Trans. Syst. Man Cybern. Syst. **49**(9), 1806–1819 (2019)
10. Kim, S.J., Nam, J.Y., Ko, B.C.: Online tracker optimization for multi-pedestrian tracking using a moving vehicle camera. IEEE Access **6**, 48675–48687 (2018)
11. Lin, T., Goyal, P., Girshick, R., He, K., Dollr, P.: Focal loss for dense object detection. In: ICCV, pp. 2999–3007 (2017)
12. Lin, T.Y., Dollár, P., Girshick, R., He, K., Hariharan, B., Belongie, S.: Feature pyramid networks for object detection. In: CVPR, pp. 2117–2125 (2017)
13. Liu, W., et al.: SSD: single shot multibox detector. In: Leibe, B., Matas, J., Sebe, N., Welling, M. (eds.) ECCV 2016. LNCS, vol. 9905, pp. 21–37. Springer, Cham (2016). https://doi.org/10.1007/978-3-319-46448-0_2
14. Redmon, J., Farhadi, A.: Yolov3: An incremental improvement (2018). arXiv: Computer Vision and Pattern Recognition
15. Ren, S., He, K., Girshick, R.B., Sun, J.: Faster r-cnn: Towards real-time object detection with region proposal networks. IEEE Trans. Pattern Anal. Mach. Intell., 1137–1149 (2015)
16. Sheng, B., Li, P., Zhang, Y., Mao, L.: Greensea: visual soccer analysis using broad learning system. IEEE Trans. Cybern., 1–15 (2020)
17. Wang, T., Anwer, R.M., Cholakkal, H., Khan, F.S., Pang, Y., Shao, L.: Learning rich features at high-speed for single-shot object detection. In: ICCV, pp. 1971–1980 (2019)

18. Wang, Z., Zheng, L., Liu, Y., Wang, S.: Towards real-time multi-object tracking. arXiv preprint (2019)
19. Wojke, N., Bewley, A., Paulus, D.: Simple online and realtime tracking with a deep association metric. In: ICIP, pp. 3645–3649 (2017)
20. Zhang, L., Gray, H., Ye, X., Collins, L., Allinson, N.: Automatic individual pig detection and tracking in pig farms. Sensors **19**, 1188 (2019)
21. Zhang, L., Li, Y., Nevatia, R.: Global data association for multi-object tracking using network flows. In: CVPR (2008)
22. Zhang, P., Zheng, L., Jiang, Y., Mao, L., Li, Z., Sheng, B.: Tracking soccer players using spatio-temporal context learning under multiple views. Multimedia Tools Appl. **77**(15), 18935–18955 (2017). https://doi.org/10.1007/s11042-017-5316-3
23. Zhang, S., Chi, C., Yao, Y., Lei, Z., Li, S.Z.: Bridging the gap between anchor-based and anchor-free detection via adaptive training sample selection (2019). arXiv: Computer Vision and Pattern Recognition
24. Zhao, D., Fu, H., Xiao, L., Wu, T., Dai, B.: Multi-object tracking with correlation filter for autonomous vehicle. Sensors **18**, 2004 (2018)
25. Zhu, P., Wen, L., Bian, X., Ling, H., Hu, Q.: Vision meets drones: A challenge. CoRR (2018)

An Approach of Short Advertising Video Generation Using Mobile Phone Assisted by Robotic Arm

Jiefeng Li[1], Yingying She[1(✉)], Lin Lin[2(✉)], Yalan Luo[1], Hao He[1,3],
Weiyue Lin[1], and Shengjing Hou[2]

[1] Informatics School, Xiamen University, Xiamen, China
jiefengli@stu.xmu.edu.cn, yingyingshe@xmu.edu.cn,
{1042181127,501700413}@qq.com, 18960110978@163.com
[2] College of Art, Xiamen University, Xiamen, China
linlinxiamen@xmu.edu.cn, 1403018492@qq.com
[3] Quanzhou Institute of Equipment Manufacturing Haixi Institute,
Chinese Academy of Science, Quanzhou, China

Abstract. Recently, Short Advertising Video has become an increasingly dominant form of advertisement on social media. However, making Short Advertising Video is a challenging task for micro and small businesses, since it requires professional skills and years of experience. In this paper, we present a novel approach of Short Advertising Video generation assisted by robotic arms. We analyzed the professional composition and imaging of advertising videos, and transformed them into an automatic shooting process during the production of Short Advertising Video, assisted by a robotic arm. Practically, we applied our approach in two kinds of robotic arms and the results showed that robotic arm assist solution can highly enhance the efficiency and effect of making Short Advertising Video. In addition, our video generation approach can save time and money for novice users from micro and small business who has very limit resources and budget. And, we believe that our approach might overturn the existing production model of the Short Advertising Video propagated in the online business and social media.

Keywords: Graphical human-computer interaction · Robotics and vision

1 Introduction

With the popularity of smart phones and mobile applications, Short Advertising Video on mobile phones has shown potential. Well-made and professionally-edited Short Advertising Video on social media can assist in product presentation and have high conversion rates, which can greatly increase product sales.

In this paper, we mainly consider short commercial advertising videos for micro and small businesses. Instead of branding, the purpose for them to make

© Springer Nature Switzerland AG 2020
N. Magnenat-Thalmann et al. (Eds.): CGI 2020, LNCS 12221, pp. 157–168, 2020.
https://doi.org/10.1007/978-3-030-61864-3_14

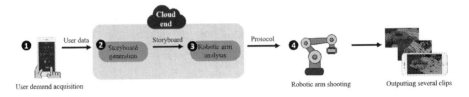

Fig. 1. The Short Advertising Video generation procedure of AD-Designer.

advertising videos is to show the overall appearance and details of the product, which consequently can be able to motivate consumers to buy the product. This kind of Short Advertising Video is usually without actors, and all product shots are filmed in one location. Due to the limit of social media propagation, the length of one video is usually approximately 15 to 30 s.

Though Short Advertising Video on social media has high conversion rates, producing high-quality advertising videos is challenging for novice users from micro and small businesses who can not afford high cost. It not only needs the support of a professional advertising video shooting team, but also requires a long production cycle. Existing mobile applications designed for novice users, such as iMovie and VUE, provide templates that help novices arrange to capture content in a professional and structured way. However, there is no detailed guidance when novice users shoot specific clips. Even though several methods were proposed for post-processing a video to enhance its visual qualities, they are still very inefficient and cannot make up defects of the original video. In addition, several shooting-assisted devices, such as OSMO, solve some problems of manual shooting, but novice users still have to design the motion path of camera by themselves. These problems have created a huge obstacle for novice users to promote their products in online media by Short Advertising Video.

To address the above challenges, we developed AD-Designer, a mobile application coordinated by cloud video processing modules to help novice users make Short Advertising Video. In our work, in order to prevent users' shooting problems mentioned above, we introduced the robotic-arm-based shooting process into our existing script-based interactive advertising video production framework [1]. It is an upgraded version of our previous visual-guided shooting process. Our experiment shows that compared with the manual process, AD-Designer increases the quality of the advertising videos and the cost has been greatly reduced. The whole generation process is shown in Fig. 1.

2   Related Work

2.1   Computational Modeling of Cinematography

Computational modeling has been previously proven effective in a number of situations. Studies have focused on modeling computational cinematography from various aspects. Chen et al. [3] modeled the shooting scene in AR(augmented reality), so that users can plan an aerial video by physically moving their mobile device, as a viewfinder, around a miniature 3D model of the scene. The method presented by Leiva et al. [4] encouraged users' exploration of different contexts for video prototyping by combining video with digital animated sketches. The system proposed by Tien et al. [5] classified shots in basketball game automatically through a GOP-based scene change detection method. Inoue et al. [6,7] proposed a novel concept of actuator-driven, frame-by-frame intermittent tracking for motion-blur-free video shooting of objects which move very fast. Mitarai et al. [8–10] analyzed home-making movies with only one character in the video to assist users. Also, some other studies [11–18] focused on static images, rather than videos, which is different from each other, especially for advertising video.

2.2 Robotics in Video Shooting

Several shooting-assist devices have been used for professional advertising videos. Camera sliders, such as GVM[1], enable users to create smooth sliding image; Camera stabilizers, including the DJI OSMO[2], keep cameras flat no matter how users move the camera. To some extent, these tools can reduce human error such as camera shake. However, novice users still have difficulties in designing path of camera without detailed guidance.

In recent years, the robotic arm has become a widely used tool in various domains. Many studies have shown the stability and flexibility of a robotic arm [19–24]. In order to make the quality of advertising video shooting by novice users close to professional advertising videos and reduce cost and time, we built an automatic shooting system encoding scripting of advertising videos, such as composition and shot type, into the movement of a robotic arm. Therefore, a robotic arm can move automatically to shoot specific shots for novice users, which enhances the quality of Short Advertising Video.

Some robotic arm assisted video capturing devices, such as KIVA[3], have appeared in the market. They can enhance the stabilization of the camera. However, users still have to plan the movement of camera by themselves, which is challenging for novice users. Also, in order to capture one perfect video clip, users may need to adjust the motion of robotic arm over and over again, which is very time-consuming, especially when there are many products needed to be presented.

3 Method

3.1 Overview

The traditional process of making Short Advertising Video can be simplified into three steps. Firstly, the director designs the storyboard, which conveys the overall idea of the advertising video and describes the specifications of every shot.

---

1 https://gvmled.com.
2 https://www.dji.com/osmo.
3 http://motorizedprecision.com.

Secondly, based on the storyboard, the photographer sets the scene and shoots the clip one-by-one. Finally, the editor organizes all the clips from the photographer and renders the output videos. These procedures require professional knowledge and experience and are costly, which makes Short Advertising Video generation almost impossible for novice users from small and micro businesses. Accordingly, our system, AD-Designer, aims to algorithmically encode the technique of making Short Advertising Video by incorporating it into a mobile phone and a robotic arm.

Previously, users could set their advertising video context and use AD-Designer to shoot the clips by themselves at the beginning [1]. However, we found that it was still difficult for novice users to take high-quality videos with simple guidance. Users had difficulty in moving the camera when shooting a specific clip with a complex composition. Users also could not move the camera in a smooth line and its velocity did not remain constant along that line. These mistakes prevented viewers, customers of the product, from understanding the content. Hence, we introduced the robotic arm to take the place of human to shoot the product. The upgraded process is shown in Fig. 1. In this paper, we mainly investigated how robotic arm can take the place of human to take videos automatically.

3.2   Storyboard Design

Storyboard is a representational and textual description of the creative script of an advertising video. It denotes the overall idea of the video, which then determines the basic structure of the output video. In our previous research, with professional advertising video experts, we have collected and analyzed a large number of excellent advertising videos [1]. After users choose the category of their product and the visual style of the video, storyboard is generated on cloud end. In the storyboard, each block represents a video clip and contains all the data of the visual features of this clip. Some of the video clips need to be taken by robotic arm, which are then transfromed into the movements of the robotic arm mentioned in Sect. 3.3.

3.3   Robotic Arm Shooting

The shooting of advertising video relies highly on years of professional training. In our previous research, text prompts and wireframe shooting guidance still could not help novice users shoot high quality videos [1]. Therefore, our system converts the professional shooting skills for advertising video, such as composition and camera movement, into the continuous movement model of a robotic arm. As is shown in Fig. 2, we modeled the abstract visual effects of the camera frame and map that to the camera's movement in the shooting space. After that, inverse kinematic (IK) algorithms are employed to convert the camera's movement into the movement of the robotic arm. During shooting, the mobile phone is fixed on the gripper of the robotic arm, and its movement is driven by the transformation of the robotic arm as well. The input of the shooting module

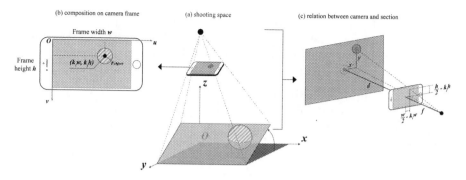

Fig. 2. The modelling of the abstract visual effects of the camera frame and mapping it to the camera's movement in the shooting space.

is the specifications of the camera and storyboard which includes all the visual features of each product clip, while the output is the raw footage captured by the mobile phone carried by the robotic arm. In Sect. 3.3, we describe the process of how abstract visual effects are transformed into movement of the robotic arm.

All the spatial parameters and coordinates shown in Fig. 2 are set to describe the model of the robotic shooting. For any object in the shooting space, assume that its radius is R_{object}. The coordinates of the camera are $C(x, y, z)$. The focal length of camera is f. The distance between the camera and the object is d. Due to the uncertainty of the shape of object, we consider the object as a sphere in this model. The coordinate of the object shown in the video are $O_{x,y}(X_{object}, Y_{object})$ and the radius is r_{object}.

Fig. 3. The Screenshot of Ad-Designer user interface of setting scene guidance.

3.3.1 User Interaction The robotic arm system needs to know where the object is set in the shooting scene. Therefore, an interface for guiding users to set the shooting scene is designed as shown in Fig. 3. The red region with the red dotted line is for the product that users mainly want to represent in the advertising video. The yellow region with yellow dotted line is for the object that serves as the foil in the scene which can create the atmosphere and enhance the quality of the product. The white lines are designed to help users understand the shooting scene and adjust the camera angle. After setting the scene, users can press the button on the right to stimulate the robotic arm to start shooting.

3.3.2 The Composition in the Camera Frame In storyboard generation module, we considered the composition and the shot type of each clip. We set the storyboard as well as the length and width of the camera frame as the input of robotic shooting module. In cinematography, the parameters that affect the composition of an image are: shape and proportion of the object and position/orientation/balance/harmony among the objects. The area of interest, the product, is the most important factor to be considered. Thus, the object's position, size and its relationship with the foil are used to describe the principles of composition within the camera frame. Accordingly, we used the proportion between the object and the camera frame, k_x, k_y and the radius of the object, r_{object}, to characterize the object in the frame. These two features are taken as the initial output of the process. A function F_{2D} is defined to describe the processing:

$$(k_x, k_y, r_{object})_{ij} = F_{2D}(w, h, Q_i)$$
$$i = 1, 2, 3, ..., n; j = start; end. \tag{1}$$

Parameters w and h denotes the width and length of the camera frame. Q represents the paradigms of the clip in the storyboard while i is the serial number of the clip. Because we are dealing with videos instead of static images, the output is the composition of both the start point and the end point. F_{2D} can be divided into three parts as follows:

3.3.2.1 Position. In order to make the object more balanced and harmonious in the video, the position of the object should be aligned according to multiple rules. The rule of thirds, golden section and the horizontal line compositions are commonly used. According to these rules we can specify the proper position of object in the camera frame. The movement of camera and shot type in the storyboard determine which rule is applied in the shot. For example, if a clip is a fixed shot and the shot type is a close shot, the golden section is often applied. The mathematical representation of the position coordinates of an object is usually $(\frac{5w}{8}, \frac{5h}{8})$.

3.3.2.2 Size. Based on the study of massive advertising videos and advice from professional advertisers, we summarized the proportion of the area occupied by objects in the camera frame in different compositions. For example, when a clip is a close-up shot, the proportion of the product in the picture is about one-sixth to one-fourth of the camera frame.

3.3.2.3 Relation Between Product and Foil. During the shooting of the advertising video there is often more than one object in the scene. In order to create the overall atmosphere of the video, it is necessary to place a foil beside the product. When considering the relationship between the object and its foil, there are several rules that we should follow to restrict their positions in the coordinate system. The key rules are: 1) the foil should be placed around the product, 2) the center of the two cannot overlap and the edge line cannot be tangent, 3) the overall arrangement of the objects should be interspersed so that the layering of the image is stronger. We define the 2D coordinates of the foil in the camera frame as (X_{foil}, Y_{foil}) with radius r_{foil}. The position of the object is restricted as follows:

I) The edge lines should not be tangent;

$$\sqrt{(x_{object} - x_{foil})^2 + (y_{object} - y_{foil})^2} > |r_{foil} - r_{object}| \tag{2}$$

II) Objects cannot be completely obscured;

$$\sqrt{(x_{object} - x_{foil})^2 + (y_{object} - y_{foil})^2} > r_{foil} + r_{object} \tag{3}$$

III) The bottom line positions of the objects should not be too close.

$$y_{foil} + r_{foil} \neq y_{object} + r_{object} \tag{4}$$

3.3.3 Movement of the Camera In previous section, the features of the objects appearing in the camera frame have been obtained through F_{2D}. The appearances of objects in the camera frame determine the spatial relation between camera and objects, and vice versa. As shown in Fig. 2(C), this one-to-one mapping allows us to deduce the relation between camera and objects in shooting space according to 2D features of objects in the camera frame. In detail, we can obtain the position of camera $C(x, y, z)$ in shooting space. A function F_{3D} is defined to describe the mapping processing:

$$(C_{x,y,z})_{ij} = F_{3D}\left(f, (k_x, k_y, r_{object})_i, R_{object}\right)$$
$$i = 1, 2, 3, ..., n; j = start; end. \tag{5}$$

R_{object} is the radius of object in shooting scene. F_{3D} can be divided into two parts:

3.3.3.1 Distance Between Camera and Objects. We assume that d is the distance between camera and object. According to the mechanism of 3D perspective projection, the distance between camera and object can be obtained by the ratio between 2D and 3D radius of the object:

$$\frac{f + d}{f} = \frac{R_{object}}{r_{object}} \tag{6}$$

3.3.3.2 Exact Coordinates of Camera. The position of object in the camera frame is corresponding to the X_{camera} and Z_{camera}:

$$k_x w = \frac{w}{2} + \frac{(X_{object} - X_{camera})\,f}{f + d} \tag{7}$$

$$k_y h = \frac{h}{2} + \frac{(Z_{object} - Z_{camera})\,f}{f + d} \tag{8}$$

3.3.4 Movement of the Robotic Arm As mentioned above, the spatial features of the camera from the start to end are obtained in each clip through F_{3D}. Thus, the movement of camera can be an input for the computation of each angle of joints by the inverse kinematics algorithm. The inverse kinematics (IK) algorithm makes use of the kinematic equations to determine the joint parameters that provide a desired position for the end effector of the robotic arm. The IK constraint continually adjusts the rotation on the parent and child bones, so that the tip of the child bone is at the target bone. The direction the parent and child bones bend can be changed based on the IK constraints. A function $F_{Robotics}$ is defined to describe the processing. n is the degree of freedom of the robotic arm:

$$((\theta_1, \theta_2, ..., \theta_n),v)_{ij} = F_{Robotics}\,(C_{x,y,z})_{ij}$$
$$i = 1, 2, 3, ..., n; j = start; end. \tag{9}$$

n is the number of degrees of freedom and θ_i is the joint angle of the i degree of freedom. The velocity of movement of the robotic arm in each clip can be computed by the duration defined in the storyboard and the movement of the camera:

$$v_i = \frac{|C_{end}\,(x, y, z) - C_{start}\,(x, y, z)|}{T_i} \tag{10}$$

T_i is the duration of clip i defined in the storyboard.

However, there exist redundant parts between clips. For example, the end point of clip i might not be the start point of clip $i+1$, the IK module thus needs to compute the path for robotic arm to transition from i to $i + 1$. Accordingly, in order to design a complete continuous motion path, the IK module needs to compute the movement of the robotic arm for not only each clip, but also redundant parts between clips.

4   Experiments

4.1   Implementation

The entire system can be divided into three parts: the mobile front end; the cloud backend and the robotic arm. Users select the style and category of the product on the front-end, which was implemented on iPhoneSE with iOS 10.0.

After users' selecting, the data is sent to storyboard generation module and robotic arm analysis module on the cloud backend. We use Apache Tomcat as the cloud service. Then, the data of motion planning of robotic arm is sent to the control system of robotic arm and robotic arm starts to shoot video clips. Two robotic arms we used in our experiments are shown in Fig. 4(a)(b).

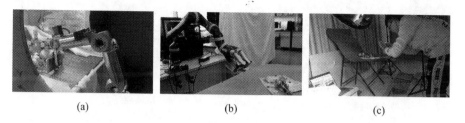

(a)   (b)   (c)

Fig. 4. (a) Shooting with a laboratory self-made robotic arm. (b) Shooting with an industrial robotic arm, KINOVA Ultra Light Weight Robotic Arm 6DOF. (c) A novice user was taking a set of clips under the guidance in the AD-Designer storyboard.

4.2   Procedure

We conducted two sets of controlled experiments for examining the effectiveness of AD-Designer. In the first set of experiments, we selected two types of robotic arms with iPhoneSE as the shooting device to take 6 shots. In the early stage of the experiment, we utilized a self-made robotic arm to carry out the test. After that, we switched to a more professional industrial robotic arm, KINOVA Ultra-light weight robotic arm 6DOF, to conduct a more accurate quantitative experiment. The practical illustrations of the two tested robotic arms are shown in Fig. 4(a)(b). In the second set of experiments, we selected 8 novice users to take a set of clips under the guidance of the AD-Designer storyboard, as shown in Fig. 4(c). For each shot, novice users watched the video demonstration first, then shot clips by themslevels. They repeated the two steps until they finished 3 video clips. Finally, the cost of time and the quality of the final outcome were compared with the results of the automatic shooting by the robotic arm to distinguish the performances of the two sets of experiments.

4.3   Results

Time. In the two sets of experiments, as shown in Fig. 5(b), the time cost on the shooting module of the 2 sets of experiments was significantly different. In the first set of experiments, robotic arms could shoot at least 6 shots consecutively within 1 min. The captured shots could be rendered based on 10 sets of scripts that existed on the cloud, which finally outputted 10 completed advertising videos for users to select. In the second set of experiments, users could only choose one set of the scripts at the shooting stage and followed the guidance

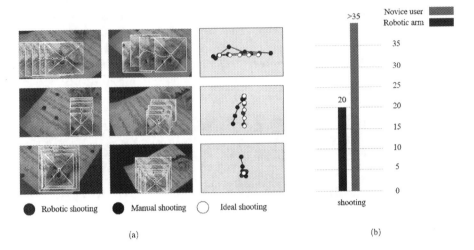

Fig. 5. (a) Comparison of effect of manual shooting and automatic shooting. (b) Comparison of time spent between novice users and robotic arm.

step-by-step. Hence, the robotic shooting assisted system can reduce the time and cost markedly and increase the shooting efficiency significantly.

Quality of Shots. To test whether a robotic arm can perform better than a human, we selected 3 kinds of shots (tracking shots, zoom-in shots, and crane shots) from the output adverting videos of the two sets of experiments. We first extracted keyframes of each shot per 15 frames. After that, we connected the object's center point within the frame to form a sampling curve to compare the final visual results. Figure 5(a) shows the result. From each group of comparisons, we can see that the sampling curve captured by the robotic arm is considerably smoother than that captured by users. The result has proven that our system makes the videos look more stable and enhances the effect of the advertising videos.

4.4 Expert Evaluation

We invited an expert who has many years of professional advertising video production experience to evaluate our system. We showed the working mode of the whole system and then mainly described the process of the automatic robotic arm shooting. The expert approved that the working mode of the whole AD-Designer system conformed with the traditional process of making professional advertising video, and the output videos are also very consistent for the purpose of social media propagation. The effect of the robot arm is similar to the indoor camera dolly, which makes videos look more stable than those taken manually. She proposed that the robot arm can be more flexible when moving along some complex curves. In summary, the expert appreciated the high efficiency and low cost of our approach.

5   Conclusions and Future Work

We proposed a novel appraoch of making Short Advertising Video for novice users from small and micro businesses. In order to minimize human error in the shooting process and enhance the quality of advertising video, we extracted features of professional cinematography and modeled the process of shooting advertising video by a robotic arm. Our testing result confirmed that our automated approach speeds up the process of shooting of Short Advertising Video and removes barriers that novice users shoot videos manually, as well as enhancing the overall quality of Short Advertising Video. As short video becomes an increasingly dominant form of advertisements, Ad-Designer is already used by several small and micro businesses from Internet online sales platform. And, these users really appreciate our approach of Short Advertising Video. It can not only lower the cost in time and money but also increase their product sales on online platform. In summary, our research focuses on exploring new mode of HEC(human-engaged computing), which aims at achieving synergized interactions between human capacities and technological capabilities to help realize progressively developing human potential. In particular, in this paper, we are trying to model the tacit knowledge from experts and apply it into the interactions between novice users, computer and robotic arm, in order to help novice users perform better in creative work.

Notably, even though we used KINOVA in our experiment, it doesn't mean expensive device like that is a necessity. As mentioned in Sect. 2.2, there have been many low-cost devices designed for novice users, like OSMO, which are capable of capturing stable videos flexibly. Our work provides ideas of automated working mode in programmatic creative for making Short Advertising Video, which assists novice users, with no need of professional team, to make professional videos, and reduces human resource cost. In future work, we will expand types of camera movement and composition to improve the flexibility of the system and enhance the quality of the output videos. Furthermore, besides a robotic arm, we believe that our computational model can be applied to other devices such as unmanned aerial vehicles and camera dollies.

References

1. Ji, Y., She, Y., Liu, F., Chen, Y., Shen, Y., He, H.: Ad-designer mode: an interactive approach of guiding non-professional users to make the mobile advertising video. In: Proceedings of the Seventh International Symposium of Chinese CHI (Chinese CHI '19), pp. 79–87 (2019)
2. Chen, Y., She, Y., Yang, L., Wang, D., Ji, Y.: Advertising video automatic visual effects processing for a novel mobile application. In: CSAI, pp. 221–226 (2019)
3. Chen, Y.A., et al.: ARPilot: designing and investigating AR shooting interfaces on mobile devices for drone videography. In: MobileHCI 2018, pp. 42:1–42:8 (2018)
4. Leiva, G., Beaudouin-Lafon, M.: Montage: a video prototyping system to reduce re-shooting and increase re-usability. In: UIST 2018, pp. 675–682 (2018)

5. Tien, M.-C., Chen, H.-T., Chen, Y.-W., Hsiao, M.-H., Lee, S.-Y.: Shot classification of basketball videos and its application in shooting position extraction. In: ICASSP, vol. 1, no. 2007, pp. 1085–1088 (2007)
6. Inoue, M., Qingyi, G., Jiang, M., Takaki, T., Ishii, I., Tajima, K.: Motion-blur-free high-speed video shooting using a resonant mirror. Sensors **17**(11), 2483 (2017)
7. Inoue, M., Qingyi, G., Aoyama, T., Takaki, T., Ishii, I.: An intermittent frame-by-frame tracking camera for motion-blur-free video shooting. In: SII 2015, pp. 241–246 (2015)
8. Mitarai, H., Yoshitaka, A.: Emocap: video shooting support system for non-expert users. IJMDEM **3**(2), 58–75 (2012)
9. Mitarai, H., Yoshitaka, A.: Development of video shooting assistant system for better expression of affective information. In: KICSS 2012, pp. 149–156 (2012)
10. Mitarai, H., Yoshitaka, A.: Shooting assistance by recognizing user's camera manipulation for intelligible video production. In: ISM 2011, pp. 157–164 (2011)
11. Min-Tzu, W., Pan, T.-Y., Tsai, W.-L., Kuo, H.-C., Min-Chun, H.: High-level semantic photographic composition analysis and understanding with deep neural networks. In: ICME Workshops 2017, pp. 279–284 (2017)
12. Lee, J.-T., Kim, H.-U., Lee, C., Kim, C.-S.: Photographic composition classification and dominant geometric element detection for outdoor scenes. J. Vis. Commun. Image Represent. **55**, 91–105 (2018)
13. Ma, S., et al.: SmartEye: assisting instant photo taking via integrating user preference with deep view proposal network. In: CHI 2019, p. 471 (2019)
14. Yan, X., Ratcliff, J., Scovell, J., Speiginer, G., Azuma, R.: Real-time guidance camera interface to enhance photo aesthetic quality. In: CHI 2015, pp. 1183–1186 (2018)
15. Bhattacharya, S., Sukthankar, R., Shah, M.: A framework for photo-quality assessment and enhancement based on visual aesthetics. In: ACM Multimedia 2010, pp. 271–280 (2010)
16. Birklbauer, C., Bimber, O.: Active guidance for light-field photography on smartphones. Comput. Graph. **53**, 127–135 (2015)
17. Rojtberg, P.: User guidance for interactive camera calibration. In: Chen, J.Y.C., Fragomeni, G. (eds.) HCII 2019. LNCS, vol. 11574, pp. 268–276. Springer, Cham (2019). https://doi.org/10.1007/978-3-030-21607-8_21
18. Kim, M., Lee, J.: PicMe: interactive visual guidance for taking requested photo composition. In: CHI 2019, p. 395 (2019)
19. Chen, I.M., Tay, R., Xing, S., Yeo, S.H.: Marionette: from traditional manipulation to robotic manipulation. In: Ceccarelli, M. (ed.) International Symposium on History of Machines and Mechanisms, pp. 119–133. Springer, Dordrecht (2004). https://doi.org/10.1007/1-4020-2204-2_10
20. Zimmermann, S., Poranne, R., Bern, J.M., Coros, S.: PuppetMaster: robotic animation of marionettes. ACM Trans. Graph. **38**(4), 103:1–103:11 (2019)
21. Huang, Y., et al.: Performance evaluation of a foot interface to operate a robot arm. IEEE Rob. Autom. Lett. **4**(4), 3302–3309 (2019)
22. Wang, Y., James, S., Stathopoulou, E.K., Beltrán-González, C., Konishi, Y., Del Bue, A.: Autonomous 3-D reconstruction, mapping, and exploration of indoor environments with a robotic arm. IEEE Rob. Autom. Lett. **4**(4), 3340–3347 (2019)
23. Zhong, F., Wang, Y., Wang, Z., Liu, Y.-H.: Dual-arm robotic needle insertion with active tissue deformation for autonomous suturing. IEEE Rob. Autom. Lett. **4**(3), 2669–2676 (2019)
24. Zhong, M., et al.: Assistive grasping based on laser-point detection with application to wheelchair-mounted robotic arms. Sensors **19**(2), 303 (2019)

"Forget" the Forget Gate: Estimating Anomalies in Videos Using Self-contained Long Short-Term Memory Networks

Habtamu Fanta[1], Zhiwen Shao[2,3](✉), and Lizhuang Ma[1,4](✉)

[1] Department of Computer Science and Engineering,
Shanghai Jiao Tong University, Shanghai, China
habtamu_fanta@sjtu.edu.cn, ma-lz@cs.sjtu.edu.cn
[2] School of Computer Science and Technology, China University of Mining
and Technology, Xuzhou, China
zhiwen_shao@cumt.edu.cn
[3] Engineering Research Center of Mine Digitization, Ministry of Education
of the People's Republic of China, Xuzhou, China
[4] School of Computer Science and Technology, East China Normal University,
Shanghai, China

Abstract. Abnormal event detection is a challenging task that requires effectively handling intricate features of appearance and motion. In this paper, we present an approach of detecting anomalies in videos by learning a novel LSTM based self-contained network on normal dense optical flow. Due to their sigmoid implementations, standard LSTM's forget gate is susceptible to overlooking and dismissing relevant content in long sequence tasks. The forget gate mitigates participation of previous hidden state for computation of cell state prioritizing current input. Besides, the hyperbolic tangent activation of standard LSTMs sacrifices performance when a network gets deeper. To tackle these two limitations, we introduce a bi-gated, light LSTM cell by discarding the forget gate and introducing sigmoid activation. Specifically, the proposed LSTM architecture fully sustains content from previous hidden state thereby enabling the trained model to be robust and make context-independent decision during evaluation. Removing the forget gate results in a simplified and undemanding LSTM cell with improved performance and computational efficiency. Empirical evaluations show that the proposed bi-gated LSTM based network outperforms various LSTM based models for abnormality detection and generalization tasks on CUHK Avenue and UCSD datasets.

Keywords: Abnormal event detection · Long Short-Term Memory · Self-contained LSTM · Abnormality generalization

1 Introduction

Abnormal event detection (AED) is a hot research area that deals with identifying the presence of abnormal behaviour and possibly knowing its details

© Springer Nature Switzerland AG 2020
N. Magnenat-Thalmann et al. (Eds.): CGI 2020, LNCS 12221, pp. 169–181, 2020.
https://doi.org/10.1007/978-3-030-61864-3_15

from images or videos [8]. Developing systems that can execute such abnormality identification tasks is important as the information gained can be used to assess the presence of any threat in an environment [21]. Modelling video data to extract meaningful anomalous features is challenging mainly because of the high dimension of videos and the presence of enormously interacting features across frames [1]. The widespread applicability of AED in industry, academia and surveillance systems has attracted many computer vision researchers [4].

Various abnormality detection methods rely on individually examining moving objects in a particular scene. For this, motion tracking and trajectory extraction techniques are usually employed to model peculiar activities and eventually single out anomalous events from the scene [5,18]. In Wang et al. [23], trajectories having spatial proximity manifesting related motion patterns are classified and used to identify outliers. Such tracking-based methods come short in abnormality detection performance when occlusion occurs amongst objects, which fail to learn intricate features in crowded environments.

Due to the scarcity of large annotated datasets and the context-dependent problem nature [4,20], effectively handling spatio-temporal features and complex long-term interactions between consecutive frames in videos is a challenge [10]. Even though developing generalizing models and employing various motion descriptors have been proposed to tackle these challenges, there is yet a big gap. Recently, deep convolutional neural networks (CNNs) have become a popular tool. However, their ability is limited for learning spatio-temporal sequence data, because of the high dimensionality of videos. Some recent works resort to Recurrent Neural Networks (RNNs) [1] and Long Short-Term Memory (LSTM), which have become popular frameworks for modelling long-term sequences. These methods focus on integrating them with autoencoders and variants of convolutional layers, which limits the full potential of LSTMs. In addition, making LSTMs a primary network component for long-term sequences has not been thoroughly considered.

Considering the gating structures of LSTMs may squash important content in long-term sequences, in this paper we introduce a novel and light long short-term memory cell. We propose an end-to-end network built by stacking layers of the proposed LSTM cells capable of yielding enhanced performance on abnormal event detection benchmarks. During training, our network learns normal motion features from sparse and dense optical flow data independently. The major contributions of this work are summarized below: (i) We propose a novel, light long short-term memory architecture where we discard the forget gate and replace hyperbolic tangent activation with sigmoid function. (ii) We introduce a novel self-contained LSTM network built by stacking layers of the proposed LSTM. (iii) We show that the presented deep-LSTM network is computationally efficient and achieves effective detection performance over standard LSTM networks. (iv) Empirical evaluations show that our method performs better for generalization task over standard LSTMs on AED benchmarks.

2   Related Work

We give an overview of related works on abnormal event detection that focus on convolutional neural network and long short-term memory.

CNN Based Methods. Deep CNNs have shown superior performance for object detection and action recognition tasks. They also yield better results than hand-crafted methods for abnormality detection task. An approach for abnormal event detection is introduced by Hinami et al. [8]. In this work, generic knowledge is used to jointly detect abnormalities and identify their detailed attributes. This work proposes a model that can automatically identify anomalies from a scene without human intervention. A spatio-temporal autoencoder that uses deep neural networks to automatically learn video representation is proposed by Zhao et al. [25]. Three-dimensional convolution layers are used by the deep network to extract spatial and temporal features in a better way. An approach that decouples abnormality detection problem into a feature descriptor extraction appended by a cascade deep autoencoder (CDA) is introduced by Wang et al. [22]. The novel feature descriptor captures motion information from multi-frame optical flow orientations. Feature descriptors of the normal data are then provided as input for training the deep autoencoder based CDA network.

LSTM Based Methods. Recent works have exploited LSTMs for abnormality detection task due to their ability to leverage sequential and temporal features. An unsupervised deep representation algorithm that couples stacked denoising autoencoders (SDAE) and LSTM networks is presented by Feng et al. [4]. Stacked denoising autoencoders are responsible for learning appearance and short-term motion cues while LSTMs keep track of long-term motion features to learn regularities across video frames. A spatiotemporal network for video anomaly detection is presented by Chong et al. [1]. This work introduces a spatial encoder-decoder module populated with convolutional and deconvolutional layers, and a temporal encoder module made of convolutional LSTM layers. The spatial autoencoder handles spatial feature representation while the LSTM module learns sequential and temporal features. Integrating convolutional neural network for appearance representation with convolutional LSTM for storing long-term motion information is introduced by Luo et al. [16]. The developed ConvLSTM-AE architecture is capable of learning regular appearance and motion cues, and encoding variations in appearance and motion of normal scenes. In addition to these CNN and LSTM based works, maintaining temporal coherency between video frames is shown to be effective for video processing tasks like human pose estimation [13,24]. Liu et al. [13] presented structured space learning and halfway temporal evaluation scheme for long-term consistency in videos. Most of the endeavours just couple LSTMs with CNNs and autoencoders for abnormal event detection. In contrast, we investigate the potential of LSTMs without fusing with other networks for learning spatial and temporal features, and propose a novel, effective and efficient LSTM structure.

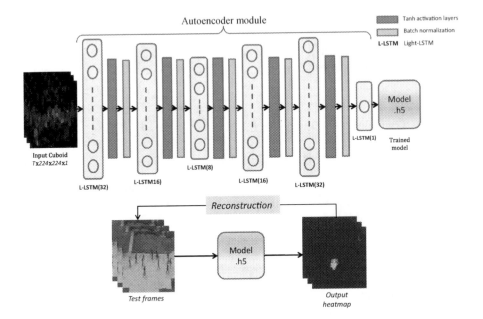

Fig. 1. The architecture of our self-contained sequential network and the subsequent testing process. **Top:** Training Phase - left to right: input layer (cuboid) made up of sequence of dense optical flow frames followed by an autoencoder module. This autoencoder contains five LSTM layers (light-orange shaded) each appended by activation (blue-gray shaded) and batch normalization (light-rose shaded) layers, except the final layer. The vertical dashed lines in the L-LSTM layers indicate recurrent connections among LSTM units. **Bottom:** Testing Phase - left to right: sequence of video frames from test set fed to the trained model; a model file generated from the training phase; an output heatmap sequence produced by the trained model using input test frames. (Color figure online)

3   Method

3.1   Overview

Figure 1 shows the architecture of our proposed LSTM-based model, which learns long-term, spatio-temporal sequential patterns and normal appearance and motion features from dense optical flow data. The network is built from six LSTM layers (each consisting of a varying number of our proposed LSTM unit). We insert batch normalization layers in between these LSTM layers so as to obtain enhanced performance and computationally efficient network models [9].

Input Module. The input module is built by grouping together T (where T is set to 4) consecutive dense optical flow frames in sliding window to generate a temporal cuboid. During preprocessing, we produce sparse and dense optical flows for every training video in CUHK Avenue [14] and UCSD [12] datasets. We convert these optical flow videos into frames and stack them together to form an input cuboid layer.

Autoencoder Module. The autoencoder module emulates the function and structure of conventional autoencoders where we employ LSTM layers instead of convolutional and deconvolutional layers. We use 3 LSTM layers to build the encoding sub-module and 2 LSTM layers to make the decoding sub-module. Each LSTM layer is built based on our proposed LSTM architecture (discussed in Sect. 3.3) with varying number of units. The first and fifth LSTM layers are made from 32 LSTM units. The second and fourth LSTM layers consist of 16 LSTM units, while the third LSTM layer that acts as a bottleneck in the middle contains 8 LSTM units. The final LSTM layer is a single-unit layer that reduces the dimension of the previously learnt sequence back to a size compatible with the input cuboid. During training, a model that is aware of the normal behaviour of a dataset (labelled *"Model.h5"* in Fig. 1) is generated. The model stores motion and appearance information about a normal environment. During testing, the trained model is supplied with test frames mostly consisting of anomalous scenes. The model tries to reconstruct the given frames where it fails on pixels containing anomalies.

3.2 Optical Flow

Sparse Optical Flow. Sparse optical flow selects pixels that can be representative of an image or frame sequence. These representative pixels contain fairly enough content to present an image. Optical flow vectors keep track of these interesting pixels like corners and edges. Extracted features from one frame are sent to the next frame along a sequence to maintain consistency of pixels (features) under consideration. We adopt the Lucas-Kanade motion estimation technique to select and track the movement of interesting pixels in consecutive frames, which generates sparse optical flow vectors for our video data [15]. This technique assumes that pixels in consecutive frames are not considerably far from each other and the time variable does not show noticeable increment between frames. It works by employing partial derivatives on spatial and temporal gradients to calculate the pixel flow at every location in an image.

Dense Optical Flow. Dense optical flow features try to model and track motion information of every available pixel in a given image or frame sequence. Modelling motion cues with dense optical flow yields more precise result than sparse optical flow as the former considers all pixels in an image. Thus, it suits well for applications that require motion learning, video segmentation and semantic segmentation [19]. In this work, we introduce a scheme of modelling normal behaviour by learning a network on dense optical flow vectors of a train set. We deploy the Gunnar Farnebäck [3] method to generate dense optical flow vectors of videos in our train set. This method functions in a two-frame scenario by first employing quadratic polynomials to approximate the neighbourhoods of frames under consideration. It then applies a global displacement technique on these polynomials to build new signals. Finally, the global displacement is computed by using the coefficients yielded from the quadratic polynomials. The quadratic polynomial $f(x)$ is approximated in the local coordinate system using Eq. (1).

$$f(x) \approx x^{\mathrm{T}} A x + b^{\mathrm{T}} x + c, \tag{1}$$

where A is a square matrix; b and c are vector and scalar variables respectively. These coefficients are approximated from the weighted least squares of signals in neighbourhood frames.

Based on the sparse and dense optical flow vectors generated using the Lucas-Kanade and Gunnar Farnebäck methods respectively, we prepare train sets built from these optical flow vectors for each video in train sets. By using a similar setup in the original datasets (i.e., equal number of frames per video) [14,17], we convert these optical flow videos into same number of frames.

3.3   Proposed LSTM Architecture

Even though standard LSTMs are capable of entertaining long-term sequential data and solve the vanishing or exploding gradient problem of RNNs, their gating structures are prone to overlooking important content in a long sequence. Unless they are controlled, such gating structures may lead to ill-learnt models where invaluable contents and long-term dependencies are not well considered during training. We propose a mechanism that mitigates this risk of information loss by proposing a new LSTM architecture which is capable of equally treating important content in long sequences. The modifications we employ on standard LSTM cells are fully removing the forget gate and substituting the hyperbolic tangent activation used for candidate cell state computation with logistic sigmoid activation, as illustrated in Fig. 2(a). These alterations generate an effective and efficient, light-weight model.

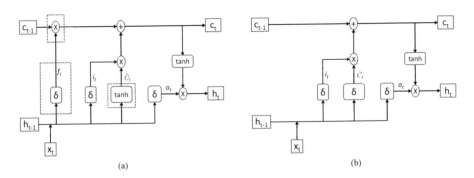

(a)   (b)

Fig. 2. Illustration of our proposed LSTM cell. (a) Alterations made to standard LSTM cell. The forget gate with its associated point-wise multiplication operator in the red-dashed rectangle is eliminated. *tanh(.)* activation in the blue-dashed rectangle is replaced by *sigmoid* activation. (b) The structure of our proposed LSTM cell.

Removing the Forget Gate. The forget gate in LSTMs decides how much of the information from previous hidden states should be removed or kept across a sequence. This enables LSTM-based models to learn which share of previous hidden states are relevant and should be carried to the next hidden state. This behaviour of forget gates is advantageous for scenarios where discontinuations are constantly observed in sequential data or for applications that positively overlook the significance of previous information by prioritizing current content. For these cases, the forget gate tries to nullify the impact of previous memory state while computing candidate memory by giving attention to current input.

For abnormal event detection problems that focus on analyzing appearance and motion patterns, an LSTM-based model should keep information from previous memory for longer duration to effectively compute candidate memory state. Sustaining such information from previous frames and learning their features enables models to reasonably compute the candidate state at every time step. This makes current memory state well informed of previous content and more reliable for performance evaluation. So, we propose removing the forget gate from LSTMs for abnormality detection as we need to keep all information from previous sequences.

Replacing the Hyperbolic Tangent Activation. In addition to removing the forget gate, we also replace the hyperbolic tangent activation of candidate cell state with logistic sigmoid activation:

$$\tilde{C}_t = \delta(W_C \otimes [h_{t-1}, x_t] + b_C). \tag{2}$$

Hyperbolic tangent activation used in conventional LSTMs is not effective when learning feed-forward networks. The performance of such networks decreases significantly whenever the network goes deeper [6].

Compared to standard LSTM, the proposed LSTM architecture where the forget gate is "forgotten" gains performance effectiveness and computational efficiency. The former is attributed to the fact that the model is made to learn long-term sequential data without suppressing previous information. On the other hand, computational efficiency gains are manifested as the proposed LSTM works with lesser number of parametres. The architecture of the new LSTM structure is show in Fig. 2(b), which can formulated as

$$
\begin{aligned}
i_t &= \delta(W_i \otimes [h_{t-1}, x_t] + b_i), \\
\tilde{C}_t &= \delta(W_C \otimes [h_{t-1}, x_t] + b_C), \\
C_t &= C_{t-1} + \tilde{C}_t, \\
o_t &= \delta(W_o \otimes [h_{t-1}, x_t] + b_o), \\
h_t &= o_t \otimes tanh(C_t).
\end{aligned} \tag{3}
$$

4   Experiments

4.1   Datasets and Settings

Datasets. We train and evaluate our model on three popular abnormal event detection datasets; CUHK Avenue [14], UCSD Ped1 and UCSD Ped2 [12].

CUHK Avenue is populated with 16 training and 21 test videos split into 15328 frames for training and 15324 for testing each with a resolution of 640×360 pixels [14]. Avenue's test set contains frame-level masks for ground truth annotations. Fourteen distinct events are classified as abnormal in this dataset like loitering, running, romping, pushing a bike, moving towards camera, and throwing a paper or bag.

UCSD is one of the most challenging datasets for video abnormality detection problem. It consists of video recordings captured from two distinct pedestrian walkways. Videos from the first pedestrian walkway make up Ped1 dataset comprising 34 training and 36 test videos, which are split into frames of 238×158 pixel resolution. On the other hand, Ped2 contains 16 training and 12 test videos whose frames have a resolution of 360×240 pixels [12]. Every video in Ped1 test set is fragmented into 200 frames, whereas each of Ped2's test set videos are split into a varying number of 120, 150 and 180 frames. Both Ped1 and Ped2 datasets contain frame-level annotation for abnormalities. Abnormal events in this dataset include the presence of car, bicycle, wheelchair, skateboard, and walking on grass or moving in wrong direction across a walkway.

Implementation Details. We generate sparse and dense optical flows for every raw video in the training set of Avenue, Ped1 and Ped2 datasets. We then change these video-form optical flows into frames similar to the setup in the original dataset [12,14]. These optical flow vectors of the training set and raw videos from the original test set are converted into frames of size 224×224 pixels. Pixels of the optical flow input frames are then scaled down to a range between 0 and 1 so that the frames are on a same scale. The frames containing optical flow information and image content are then changed to gray-scale and normalized to assume a mean value of zero and a variance of one. The input to the network is a cube built by stacking a sequence of optical flow frames with dynamic number of skipping strides. The input cube has a size of $T \times 224 \times 224 \times 1$ (where T is assigned to 4 in all of our experiments).

We separately train our deep network on sparse and dense optical flow data that we prepare for CUHK Avenue and UCSD datasets for sixty epochs. We also train the network on the original Avenue and UCSD datasets for performance comparison (discussed in Sect. 4.2). We divide the train sets into two sub sets: 1) a set containing eighty five percent of the training data that is used for training the network; and 2) a set that is made of the remaining fifteen percent which is used for validating the model. We use Adam gradient-based optimizer proposed by Kingma and Ba [11] with a learning rate of 10^{-5} for optimizing the network, and a single batch of size 8. Adam is capable of automatically adjusting the learning rate by reviewing previous model weights, and is computationally cheap and efficient. After training for the required number of epochs, we evaluate each model generated after every epoch with test data. We then choose the best AUC by EER evaluation result produced by the most effective model.

Evaluation Metrics. Similar to [2], we evaluate the performance of our developed model using the Area Under Curve (AUC) by Equal Error Rate (EER) metrics, a popular scheme to evaluate the effectiveness of models for such reconstruction based tasks [7,25]. Besides, we use the regularity score that calculates the uniformity of a test data's behaviour.

Table 1. Performance comparison of the proposed method with related methods and Standard LSTM based network on CUHK Avenue and UCSD datasets.

Method	Avenue		Ped1		Ped2	
	AUC	EER	AUC	EER	AUC	EER
Chong et al. [1]	80.3	20.7	89.9	12.5	87.4	12.5
Hasan et al. [7]	70.2	25.1	81.0	27.9	90.0	21.7
Hinami et al. [8]	–	–	69.9	35.9	90.8	17.1
Luo et al. [16]	77.0	–	75.5	–	88.1	–
Wang et al. [22]	–	–	65.2	21.0	–	–
Zhao et al. [25]	80.9	24.4	87.1	18.3	88.6	20.9
Standard LSTM	65.2	36.3	65.2	38.1	75.6	31.4
Ours (bi-gated LSTM)	**67.6**	**36.2**	**69.7**	**32.2**	**87.0**	**18.7**

4.2 Comparison with State-of-the-Art Methods

We compare our method with related works and standard LSTM on video anomaly detection datasets in Table 1. The Standard LSTM method depicts a network built from conventional LSTM cells whose forget gate is not removed. Performance evaluation shows the results we obtain with a model trained on dense optical flow data.

Figure 3 shows AUC-by-EER ROC curves produced by our network trained on dense optical flows. Our proposed LSTM cell and the self-contained network yields enhanced detection performance than standard LSTM based models achieving 11.4% and 12.8% improvement on AUC and EER measures respectively with Ped2 test set, almost 4% improvement on both AUC and EER with Ped1 test set. It also gains 2.5% AUC betterment than standard LSTM based network on Avenue test set. The proposed model shows performance gains when learning on dense optical flow data than learning on videos from the original datasets. Our model that is trained on dense optical flow data achieves 0.9% AUC and 2.0% EER improvement than a model trained on the original dataset for Ped2 test set. Our dense optical flow based model also detects abnormalities better than sparse optical flow based model achieving 0.4% AUC and 1.0% EER

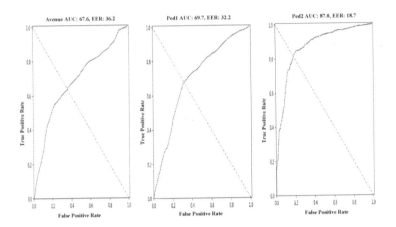

Fig. 3. ROC curves generated by our network trained on dense optical flows of Avenue, Ped1 and Ped2 dataset respectively.

gains for Ped2 test set. Similarly, we notice significant performance improvements on Avenue and Ped1 test sets too. The proposed approach also achieves competent and closer detection performance when compared to other related works on UCSD Ped2 test set. Despite the presence of challenging scenarios in these datasets like camera shakes, illumination variations and low resolution frames, learning our deep LSTM network on dense optical flows results in a robust model capable of effectively discriminating different forms of irregularities.

We also qualitatively evaluate the performance of our trained model on test sets of AED benchmarks. Figure 4(a) shows regularity score of sample test videos from CUHK Avenue, Ped1 and Ped2 datasets respectively. Figure 4(b–e) shows groundtruth abnormalities and the evaluation heatmaps generated using different variants of LSTM based methods. The regions highlighted in dark-yellow and red-yellow show the presence of anomalous events (viz., *throwing a bag* in Avenue, and *car and biking* in both Ped1 and Ped2 datasets) on the specific pixels in the frames.

We can witness that the proposed method can effectively single-out appearance and motion abnormalities in different environments. Whereas the standard LSTM in Fig. 4(c) and LSTM without input gate in Fig. 4(d) are deceived by various normal appearance and motion information such as *person standing*, background colour and *person walking* and treat them as abnormal, our bi-gated LSTM shows robust performance to such challenging scenarios.

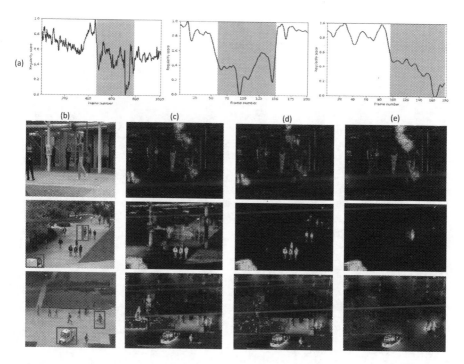

Fig. 4. (a) (Left-to-right) Regularity score of sample videos from Avenue, Ped1 and Ped2 test sets respectively. (b) (Top-to-bottom) groundtruth annotations from Avenue (throwing), Ped1 (car and biking) and Ped2 (car and biking) test sets respectively. (c) (Top-to-bottom) corresponding qualitative results using standard LSTM. (d) (Top-to-bottom) corresponding qualitative results using LSTM (without input gate). (e) (Top-to-bottom) corresponding qualitative results using our LSTM (without forget gate). Regions highlighted in yellow and red-yellow indicate pixels containing anomalous scenes (appears best in colour). (Color figure online)

5   Conclusion

In this work, we introduce a bi-gated LSTM structure for abnormal event detection and generalization task whose forget gate is removed. We present a self-contained, end-to-end network based on this LSTM cell. We show that the proposed LSTM cell gains performance effectiveness and computational efficiency when trained on dense optical flows significantly improving handling of appearance and motion irregularities. Our method also attains performance competitive to the state-of-art methods on UCSD Ped2 dataset. Future works may consider improving performance limitation of the proposed method for Avenue and Ped1 datasets by coupling with other network structures.

Acknowledgments. This work is supported by the National Key R&D Program of China (No. 2019YFC1521104), the National Natural Science Foundation of China

(No. 61972157), and the Start-up Grant, School of Computer Science and Technology, China University of Mining and Technology.

References

1. Chong, Y.S., Tay, Y.H.: Abnormal event detection in videos using spatiotemporal autoencoder. In: Cong, F., Leung, A., Wei, Q. (eds.) ISNN 2017. LNCS, vol. 10262, pp. 189–196. Springer, Cham (2017). https://doi.org/10.1007/978-3-319-59081-3_23
2. Fanta, H., Shao, Z., Ma, L.: SiTGRU: single-tunnelled gated recurrent unit for abnormality detection. Inf. Sci. **524**, 15–32 (2020)
3. Farnebäck, G.: Two-frame motion estimation based on polynomial expansion. In: Bigun, J., Gustavsson, T. (eds.) SCIA 2003. LNCS, vol. 2749, pp. 363–370. Springer, Heidelberg (2003). https://doi.org/10.1007/3-540-45103-X_50
4. Feng, Y., Yuan, Y., Lu, X.: Deep representation for abnormal event detection in crowded scenes. In: ACM International Conference on Multimedia, pp. 591–595. ACM (2016)
5. Fu, Z., Hu, W., Tan, T.: Similarity based vehicle trajectory clustering and anomaly detection. In: IEEE International Conference on Image Processing 2005, vol. 2, pp. II-602. IEEE (2005)
6. Gulcehre, C., Moczulski, M., Denil, M., Bengio, Y.: Noisy activation functions. In: International Conference on Machine Learning, pp. 3059–3068 (2016)
7. Hasan, M., Choi, J., Neumann, J., Roy-Chowdhury, A.K., Davis, L.S.: Learning temporal regularity in video sequences. In: IEEE Conference on Computer Vision and Pattern Recognition, pp. 733–742. IEEE (2016)
8. Hinami, R., Mei, T., Satoh, S.: Joint detection and recounting of abnormal events by learning deep generic knowledge. In: IEEE International Conference on Computer Vision, pp. 3619–3627. IEEE (2017)
9. Ioffe, S., Szegedy, C.: Batch normalization: accelerating deep network training by reducing internal covariate shift. In: International Conference on Machine Learning, pp. 448–456 (2015)
10. Ionescu, R.T., Smeureanu, S., Alexe, B., Popescu, M.: Unmasking the abnormal events in video. In: IEEE International Conference on Computer Vision, pp. 2895–2903. IEEE (2017)
11. Kingma, D.P., Ba, J.: Adam: a method for stochastic optimization. In: International Conference on Learning Representations (2015)
12. Li, W., Mahadevan, V., Vasconcelos, N.: Anomaly detection and localization in crowded scenes. IEEE Trans. Pattern Anal. Mach. Intell. **36**(1), 18–32 (2014)
13. Liu, S., Li, Y., Hua, G.: Human pose estimation in video via structured space learning and halfway temporal evaluation. IEEE Trans. Circuits Syst. Video Technol. **29**(7), 2029–2038 (2018)
14. Lu, C., Shi, J., Jia, J.: Abnormal event detection at 150 FPS in MATLAB. In: IEEE International Conference on Computer Vision, pp. 2720–2727. IEEE (2013)
15. Lucas, B.D., Kanade, T.: An iterative image registration technique with an application to stereo vision. In: International Joint Conference on Artificial Intelligence, pp. 674–679 (1981)
16. Luo, W., Liu, W., Gao, S.: Remembering history with convolutional LSTM for anomaly detection. In: IEEE International Conference on Multimedia and Expo, pp. 439–444. IEEE (2017)

17. Mahadevan, V., Li, W., Bhalodia, V., Vasconcelos, N.: Anomaly detection in crowded scenes. In: IEEE Conference on Computer Vision and Pattern Recognition, pp. 1975–1981. IEEE (2010)
18. Piciarelli, C., Micheloni, C., Foresti, G.L.: Trajectory-based anomalous event detection. IEEE Trans. Circuits Syst. Video Technol. **18**(11), 1544–1554 (2008)
19. Ranjan, A., Black, M.J.: Optical flow estimation using a spatial pyramid network. In: IEEE Conference on Computer Vision and Pattern Recognition, pp. 4161–4170. IEEE (2017)
20. Ravanbakhsh, M., Nabi, M., Sangineto, E., Marcenaro, L., Regazzoni, C., Sebe, N.: Abnormal event detection in videos using generative adversarial nets. In: IEEE International Conference on Image Processing, pp. 1577–1581. IEEE (2017)
21. Sun, J., Shao, J., He, C.: Abnormal event detection for video surveillance using deep one-class learning. Multimed. Tools Appl. **78**(3), 3633–3647 (2017). https://doi.org/10.1007/s11042-017-5244-2
22. Wang, T., Qiao, M., Zhu, A., Shan, G., Snoussi, H.: Abnormal event detection via the analysis of multi-frame optical flow information. Front. Comput. Sci. **14**(2), 304–313 (2019). https://doi.org/10.1007/s11704-018-7407-3
23. Wang, X., Tieu, K., Grimson, E.: Learning semantic scene models by trajectory analysis. In: Leonardis, A., Bischof, H., Pinz, A. (eds.) ECCV 2006. LNCS, vol. 3953, pp. 110–123. Springer, Heidelberg (2006). https://doi.org/10.1007/11744078_9
24. Xiao, Y., Lu, H., Sun, C.: Pose estimation based on pose cluster and candidates recombination. IEEE Trans. Circuits Syst. Video Technol. **25**(6), 935–943 (2014)
25. Zhao, Y., Deng, B., Shen, C., Liu, Y., Lu, H., Hua, X.S.: Spatio-temporal autoencoder for video anomaly detection. In: ACM International Conference on Multimedia, pp. 1933–1941. ACM (2017)

An Improved Image Stitching Method Based on Seed Region Growth and Poisson Fusion

Yewen Pang, Aimin Li[✉], and Jianwen Wang

School of Computer Science and Technology, Qilu University
of Technology (Shandong Academy of Sciences), Jinan 250300, China
lam@qlu.edu.cn

Abstract. In order to address the problem of ghosting and gap in the field of image stitching, we proposed a novel image stitching method based on seed region growth algorithm and Poisson fusion. Firstly, PSO (Particle Swarm Optimization) is used to improve the accuracy of image registration. Then we combine the improved seed region growth algorithm with Poisson fusion to implement image stitching. Experimental results illustrate outstanding performance of our method by comparing with one famous image stitching tool: PTGui and one existing image stitching method. Our method can effectively solve the problem of ghosting and gap in the process of image stitching, and avoid objects distortion.

Keywords: Image stitching · Particle swarm optimization · Seed region growth algorithm · Poisson fusion

1 Introduction

Image stitching is an important research area of computer vision [1–3]. Image stitching has been widely used in virtual reality, medical imaging, intelligent surveillance, military navigation and other fields.

We proposed an image stitching method based on seed region growth algorithm and Poisson fusion, which can generate seamless mosaic images and restore real panoramic images to the greatest extent. The rest of the paper is organized as follows. We first review related work in Sect. 2, and discuss our improved image stitching method in Sect. 3. Section 4 shows the comparison of our experimental results with other methods, and Sect. 5 summarizes our paper.

2 Related Work

2.1 Image Registration

Feature-based image registration has the advantages of stability and accuracy, and has become mainstream registration method for image stitching [4, 5]. SIFT (scale invariant feature transform) algorithm [6] keeps invariance to image translation, rotation, contraction, expansion and so on, but the number of feature points extracted by SIFT algorithm

© Springer Nature Switzerland AG 2020
N. Magnenat-Thalmann et al. (Eds.): CGI 2020, LNCS 12221, pp. 182–192, 2020.
https://doi.org/10.1007/978-3-030-61864-3_16

is too large, which leads to a large amount of computation and low efficiency. On the basis of SIFT algorithm, Bay et al. proposed an accelerated algorithm, SURF (speeded up robust features) [7], which maintains invariance under both scale and affine transformations. The calculating speed of SURF is 3 to 5 times faster than that of SIFT, at the same time, the accuracy has not been reduced. In recent years, researchers have studied and proposed different solutions on feature points detection and matching. Such as an image matching method of improved SIFT algorithm based on PSO [8].

2.2 Image Fusion

The Linear weighted fusion algorithm, such as direct averaging, is often used in image fusion [9]. The direct stitching method [10], the fade-in and the fade-out weighting average method [11] and the multi-resolution blending method [12] are three commonly used image fusion methods. The weighted average incremental gradual fusion method [13] calculates the weight coefficients of the two images respectively. It calculates the relative distance between the boundary of the overlapping region and the current position of the pixel in the overlapping region. Multi-resolution fusion method interprets the image using the structure of an image pyramid [14]. Image pyramid is a kind of original image with decreasing resolution which is arranged into pyramid shape by continuous down sampling with constraints.

3 Our Image Stitching Method

We propose an improved image stitching method to solve the problem of gap and ghost. Particle swarm optimization is introduced to improve the registration accuracy, and then the improved seed region growth algorithm and Poisson fusion are combined to get the final stitching result.

3.1 Image Registration

We conducted the research on the feature point registration method in the previous stage. In order to obtain more accurate feature points registration, ORB feature points image matching method is improved by introducing PSO, which we name it P_ORB [15]. In the following experiment, we take the three pictures of snow mountain scenery in Fig. 1 as the input images.

(a)   (b)   (c)

Fig. 1. Original images of snow mountain: (a) Left image; (b) Middle image; (c) Right image.

184   Y. Pang et al.

From Fig. 2, we can clearly see the comparison between the purified registration images by P_ORB algorithm and the unpurified registration images. By adopting PSO, we can eliminate most mismatching point pairs and get a more accurate matching result.

Fig. 2. Feature points matching: (a) the unpurified result of (a) and (b) in Fig. 1; (b) the purified result using PSO of (a) and (b) in Fig. 1; (c) the unpurified result of (b) and (c) in Fig. 1; (d) the purified result using PSO of (b) and (c) in Fig. 1.

The number of matching points obtained by ORB and P_ORB are shown in Table 1.

Table 1. Correct match rate comparison table.

	ORB	P_ORB
Total matching number	157	123
Correct matching number	93	95
Correct matching rate	59.2%	77.2%

3.2 Poisson Fusion

Poisson fusion [16] was originally used for scene fusion. The basic idea of the fusion method is to use the guide field to perform modular interpolation processing to reconstruct the pixel values in the region. The principle of Poisson fusion is shown in the Fig. 3.

Fig. 3. Poisson fusion schematic.

Where h is the scene in the original image, w is the gradient field of h, S is the image domain after fusion, Ω is the scene covered by S, $\partial\Omega$ is its boundary, g^* is a known scalar function, indicating pixels outside Ω. The value g represents the pixel value within Ω. To achieve a smooth transition without gaps, the gradient values within Ω should be as small as possible to convert the seamless fusion of the image into a gradient field minimization problem. g can be obtained by the following equation:

$$\min_{g} \iint_{\Omega} \|\nabla g\|^2, g|\partial\Omega == g*|\partial\Omega \tag{1}$$

where $\nabla = \left[\frac{\partial}{\partial x}, \frac{\partial}{\partial y}\right]$ is the gradient operator. The minimum of function $G = \|\nabla g\|^2 = g_x^2 + g_y^2$ and G satisfies the Euler-Lagrange equation, therefore its solution can be expressed by the Laplace equation:

$$\Delta g = 0, (x, y) \in \Omega, g|\partial\Omega = g*|\partial\Omega \tag{2}$$

Where, $\Delta = \frac{\partial^2}{\partial x^2}, \frac{\partial^2}{\partial y^2}$ is the Laplace operator.

The Poisson equation cleverly solves the transition smoothing problem by using the gradient field w of h as the guiding field. The purpose of the guiding field is to make the gradient of g as close as possible to the gradient of h, while maintaining the details of the image at the maximum to ensure that the boundary does not show significant transitional traces. After optimization, the following equation is adopted for the calculation:

$$\min_{g} \iint_{\Omega} \|\nabla g - w\|^2 = \min_{g} \iint_{\Omega} \|\nabla g - \nabla h\|^2, g|\partial\Omega = g*|\partial\Omega \tag{3}$$

Bring the Euler-Lagrange equation again, the result is as follows,

$$\Delta g = div(w) = div(\nabla h), g|\partial\Omega = g*|\partial\Omega \tag{4}$$

where $div(w)$ represents the divergence of the gradient field w. This equation is the mathematical basis of Poisson fusion technology. In the image stitching processing of overlapping scenes, the gradient field of the image is used as the guiding field.

According to the edge fusion characteristics of Poisson fusion, we can create a template to eliminate the ghosting and reduce the gap when performing image fusion. How to determine stitching lines is the key to create the template.

3.3 Improved Seed Region Growth Method

In this paper, how to find the optimal stitching lines is taken as a region segmentation problem. We use the gray-scale difference algorithm to optimize the seeded region growth algorithm [17] to get the best stitching line, and then generate the stitching template.

We calculate the Euclidean distance of the intensity difference between the corresponding pixels from high to low between two columns to determine the smallest distance, and furthermore to clarify the overlap. For color images, the color has three channels of RGB, and the average of the intensity distances of the three channels is calculated with Eq. 5. The distance between the *i-th* column in A image ($w \times h$) and the *k-th* column in B image is,

$$d(k, i) = \sum_{j=0}^{h} \frac{1}{3}((R_{kj}^A - R_{kj}^B)^2 + (G_{kj}^A - G_{kj}^B)^2 + (B_{kj}^A - B_{kj}^B)^2) \qquad (5)$$

Where R_{kj}^A represents the R channel value of the pixel in the *j-th* row and the *k-th* column in the A image, and so on. For the *i-th* column in the B image, assuming that the column with the smallest distance from the A image is m, then:

$$d(m, i) = \text{min} d(k, i) \quad k{:}0 \rightarrow w \qquad (6)$$

In this way, for each column in the B image ($0 \le i < w$), the column in the A image with the smallest distance can be found. If the distance is the smallest when i = n, then:

$$d(m, n) = \text{min} d(m, i) \quad i : 0 \rightarrow w \qquad (7)$$

That is, for each column in A image, we find the smallest distance column from B image. The minimum distance determines the two columns with the smallest distance and calculate the overlap area.

According to the overlapping part of the image, the difference in intensity of the overlapping regions is first calculated, and then the image is segmented using seed region growth. Taking (a) and (b) in Fig. 1 as an example, the optimal suture is shown in Fig. 4. The method in this paper selects region 1 as the first seed and region 2 as the second seed. These are restricted seed pixels for region growth, and they represent the region limit to which pixels are selected during region growth.

Fig. 4. The overlapping region's intensity differences between Fig. 1(a) and Fig. 1(b).

After the seed pixels of the region growth are determined, the optimal suture can be calculated combined with the gray-scale difference algorithm by the following steps:

Step 1: Traversing the image and find all foreground pixels (pixel which value is not 0);
Step 2: The pixels are stored in a priority queue, wherein the priority of the elements is the gray value of the images in the luminance difference image;
Step 3: We take the highest priority pixel from the priority queue and check all its neighborhoods. The neighborhood pixels belonging to the background are set to the values of the pixels of the fetched priority queue. Then they are added to the priority queue.

Step 4: When the priority queue is empty, all the pixels in the image have a certain non-zero value, and the boundary between the first seed pixel and the second seed pixel is the preliminary suture.

Step 5: Optimize the final suture using the gray-scale difference algorithm on the preliminary suture.

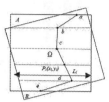

Fig. 5. Initial positioning of the stitching seam.

In Fig. 5, image A represents a reference map, image B represents a registration map, image size is M × N, and Ω represents an overlap portion [18]. $P_i(x_i, y_i)$ is a point in the Ω axis, the length of the i-th row of the overlapping portion is L_i, and for the point $P_i(x_{i+j}, y_i)$ adjacent to $P_i(x_i, y_i)$, the gradation difference Δg_{ij} of the two images is calculated using Eq. 8.

$$\Delta g_{ij} = \sum_{k=-\frac{L_i}{4}}^{\frac{L_i}{4}} |f_A(x_i + j + k, y_i) - f_B(x_i + j + k, y_i)| \qquad (8)$$

After calculating the gray difference of $L_i + 1$ positions, the point $P_i'(x'_i, y'_i)$ of $\min\left\{\Delta g_{ij} \middle| -\frac{L_i}{4} \leq j \leq \frac{L_i}{4}\right\}$ is selected as the final stitching point of the line, and the line of the switching point is the final stitching line [19].

The stitching template image generated according to the above improved method is shown in Fig. 6.

Fig. 6. Initial positioning of the stitching line.

3.4 Poisson Fusion with Improved Seed Region Growth Method

This template is used for subsequent fusion. The method introduced above can be extended to the calculation of stitching seams of multiple images. The result of template of snow mountain is shown in Fig. 7.

Fig. 7. Templates of snow mountain images: (a) Left template; (b) Middle template; (c) Right template.

According to the template, the stitching result obtained by Poisson fusion method of snow mountain images is shown in Fig. 8.

Fig. 8. Snow Mountain Panorama.

4 Experimental Results and Comparative Analysis

In order to evaluate the performance of our method, we compared the results of this paper with the stitching results with PTGui software and the seed region growth method. PTGui is a famous panoramic image stitching software [20]. PTGui can quickly and easily create dazzling panoramic images.

The below figures show the results of image stitching experiments in different scenarios. From Fig. 9(b), the panorama of campus images, we can see that the white vehicle is elongated and the vehicle is deformed. The experimental result in Fig. 10(c) show us obvious distortion in windows and some other places after being stitched by the original seed region growth algorithm. Figure 11(b), the panoramic image stitched by PTGui, shows us that the table boxed with red rectangle is elongated. There are obvious gaps and color changes in Fig. 11(c), the panorama obtained the original seed area growth algorithm. However, the panoramic images obtained by our method have no gaps and shadows, at the same time, maintain the original shape of the object.

Fig. 9. Campus images: (a) Original campus images; (b) Panorama by PTGui; (c) Panorama by seeded region growth method; (d) Panorama by our method.

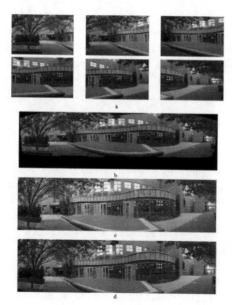

Fig. 10. Building images: (a) Original building images; (b) Panorama by PTGui; (c) Panorama by seeded region growth method; (d) Panorama by our method.

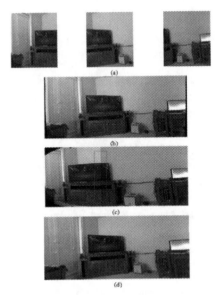

Fig. 11. Indoor images: (a) Original indoor images; (b) Panorama by PTGui; (c) Panorama by seeded region growth method; (d) Panorama by our method. (Color figure online)

The quality of the stitching results obtained by different methods was evaluated by edge spectroscopy DoEM [21] and structural similarity SSIM [22]. The edge difference spectrum DoEM includes three parts: image edge detection score, edge difference spectrum construction score and image difference spectrum information statistical score. The specific calculation formula is,

$$DoEM = e^{-\frac{\varsigma^2}{h^4}}\left(\frac{\beta_e e^{-\frac{\omega_e}{h_1}} + \beta_\omega e^{-\frac{\omega_e}{h_2}}}{\beta_e + \beta_\omega}\right) + \left(1 - e^{-\frac{\varsigma^2}{h^4}}\right)e^{-\frac{\varsigma^2}{h^3}} \tag{9}$$

where β_e represents the mean value of the boundary region of the image edge difference spectrum over region; β_ω and ς^2 respectively represent the overall mean and overall variance of the image edge difference spectrum over region; h_1, h_2, h_3, and h_4 represent four constants, and their values are selected according to the 3 σ criteria. The value of the above formula is between 0 and 1. Greater value indicates less misalignment of the stitching effect diagram, and that the brightness is excessively smoother.

The structural similarity SSIM scoring results are composed of three elements: brightness similarity, contrast similarity and structural similarity of the image lossless mosaic effect map. The specific calculation formula is described as follows,

$$SSIM(x, y) = \frac{(2v_x v_y + h_1)(2\psi_{xy} + h_2)}{(v_x^2 + v_y^2 + h_3)(\psi_x + \psi_y + h_4)} \tag{10}$$

where v_x and v_y respectively represent the average intensity values of two adjacent images. The parameter ψ_x, ψ_y, ψ_{xy} represent the correlation coefficient between two adjacent images, that is, the standard deviation. The SSIM value is closer to 1, and the degree of image distortion is lower.

According to the evaluation indexes introduced above, the objective quality evaluation of the stitching results by different methods is illustrated in Table 2.

Table 2. Objective evaluation comparison result.

Test images	Method of this paper		Seed region growth method		PTGui	
	DoEM	SSIM	DoEM	SSIM	DoEM	SSIM
Building	0.971	0.913	0.821	0.897	0.954	0.905
Campus	0.957	0.938	0.874	0.914	0.933	0.927
Indoor	0.949	0.965	0.883	0.903	0.934	0.942

From Table 2, we can see the image stitching result obtained by the method proposed in this paper is superior to that obtained by PTGui and seed region growth method.

5 Conclusion

This paper proposed an improved image stitching method based on seed region growth algorithm and Poisson fusion to solve the problem of ghost and gap. The key factors of our method are: (1) introducing PSO algorithm to improve the accuracy of feature point matching based on ORB; (2) optimizing the last step of the seed region growth algorithm using the gray difference algorithm; (3) combining the improved seed region growth algorithm with Poisson fusion to get better stitching result. Experimental results show the proposed method achieves robust stitching performance in different scenarios. How to reduce the computation load of our method is our future study.

References

1. Baosen, S., Yongqing, F., Hailiang, S.: New efficient image fusion algorithm for image mosaic. Comput. Sci. **38**(2), 260–263 (2011)
2. Han, X., Tongbin, J.: Multi-source remote sensing image fusion algorithm based on combined wavelet transform and HIS transform. J. Converg. Inf. Technol. **7**(18), 392–400 (2012)
3. Li-Qin, H.U.A.N.G., Cai-Gan, C.H.E.N.: Study on image fusion algorithm of panoramic image stitching. J. Electron. Inf. Technol. **36**(6), 1292–1298 (2014)
4. Brown, M., Szeliski, R., Winder, S.: Multi-image matching using multi-scale oriented patches. In: CVPR, vol. 1, pp. 510–517 (2005)
5. McLauchlan, P.F., Jaenicke, A.: Image mosaicing using sequential bundle adjustment. Image Vis. Comput. **20**(9-10), 751–759 (2002)
6. Lowe, D.: Object recognition from local scale-invariant features. In: Proceedings of the International Conference on Computer Vision, pp. 1150–1157 (1999)
7. Bay, H., Tuytelaars, T., Van Gool, L.: SURF: speeded up robust features. In: Leonardis, A., Bischof, H., Pinz, A. (eds.) ECCV 2006. LNCS, vol. 3951, pp. 404–417. Springer, Heidelberg (2006). https://doi.org/10.1007/11744023_32

8. Wen-hua, C., Ya, Y., Ben-guo, Y.: An image matching method of improved sift algorithm based on particle swarm optimization algorithm. J. Yunnan Norm. Univ. Nat. Sci. Ed. **38**(02), 56–59 (2018). (in Chinese with English abstract)

9. Gupta, R., Awasthi, D.: Wave-packet image fusion technique based on genetic algorithm. In: 2014 5th International Conference-Confluence the Next Generation Information Technology Summit (Confluence). IEEE (2014)

10. Zampoglou, M, Papadopoulos, S., Kompatsiaris, Y.: Detecting image splicing in the wild (web). In: 2015 IEEE International Conference on Multimedia & Expo Workshops (ICMEW), pp. 1–6. IEEE (2015)

11. Li, A., Zhou, S., Wang, R.: An improved method for eliminating ghosting in image stitching. In: 2017 9th International Conference on Intelligent Human-Machine Systems and Cybernetics (IHMSC), vol. 2, pp. 415–418. IEEE (2017)

12. Pan, J., et al.: A multi-resolution blending considering changed regions for Orthoimage mosaicking. Remote Sens. **8**(10), 842 (2016)

13. Hannane, R., et al.: An efficient method for video shot boundary detection and keyframe extraction using SIFT-point distribution histogram. Int. J. Multimed. Inf. Retr. **5**(2), 89–104 (2016). https://doi.org/10.1007/s13735-016-0095-6

14. Du, J., et al.: Union Laplacian pyramid with multiple features for medical image fusion. Neurocomputing **194**, 326–339 (2016)

15. Pang, Y., Li, A.: An improved ORB feature point image matching method based on PSO. In: Tenth International Conference on Graphics and Image Processing (ICGIP 2018), vol. 11069, p.110690S. International Society for Optics and Photonics (2019)

16. Morel, J., Petro, A.B., Sbert, C.: Fourier implementation of Poisson image editing. Pattern Recogn. Lett. **33**(3), 342–348 (2012)

17. Zhao, Y., Xu, D.: Fast image blending using seeded region growing. In: Tan, T., Ruan, Q., Wang, S., Ma, H., Di, K. (eds.) IGTA 2015. CCIS, vol. 525, pp. 408–415. Springer, Heidelberg (2015). https://doi.org/10.1007/978-3-662-47791-5_45

18. Vaughan, N., et al.: A review of virtual reality based training simulators for orthopaedic surgery. Med. Eng. Phys. **38**(2), 59–71 (2016)

19. Luo, G., Zhou, R.-G., Liu, X., Hu, W., Luo, J.: Fuzzy matching based on gray-scale difference for quantum images. Int. J. Theor. Phys. **57**(8), 2447–2460 (2018). https://doi.org/10.1007/s10773-018-3766-7

20. Pingping, Y., Hong, L.: Manufacture methods and application of three-dimensional panoramagram based on PTGui Pro Pano2VR. Urban Geotech. Investig. Surv. **2012**(4), 1–4 (2012)

21. Agostini, G., et al.: XAS/DRIFTS/MS spectroscopy for time-resolved operando investigations at high temperature. J. Synchrotron Radiat. **25**(6), 1745–1752 (2018)

22. Wang, Z., et al.: Image quality assessment: from error visibility to structural similarity. IEEE Trans. Image Process. **13**(4), 600–612 (2004)

Illumination Harmonization with Gray Mean Scale

Shuangbing Song[1], Fan Zhong[1(✉)], Xueying Qin[1], and Changhe Tu[1,2]

[1] Shandong University, Jinan, China
zhongfan@sdu.edu.cn
[2] AICFVE, Beijing Film Academy, Beijing, China

Abstract. Illumination harmonization is an important problem for high-quality image composite. Given the source image and the target background, it aims to transform the foreground appearance that it looks in the same lighting condition as the target background. Because the ground-truth composite image is difficult to get, previous works can use only synthetic datasets, which however, provide with only artificially adjusted and limited inputs. In this paper we contribute to this problem in two aspects: 1) We introduce a semi-automatic approach to capture the ground-truth composite in real scenes, and then create a dataset that enables faithful evaluation of image harmonization methods. 2) We propose a simple yet effective harmonization method, namely the Gray Mean Scale (GMS), which models the foreground appearance transformation as channel-wise scales, and estimates the scales based on gray pixels of the source and the target background images. In experiments we evaluated the proposed method and compared it with previous methods, using both our dataset and previous synthetic datasets. A new benchmark thus is established for illumination harmonization in real environments.

Keywords: Composite image · Harmonization · Illumination estimation · Synthetic dataset

1 Introduction

Image composite is a commonly used technique for image editing. One of the most important case should be background replacement, which needs to cut the interested object (the foreground) from the *source* image and paste it into the new *target* background. Since the source and the target scenes may have very different lighting condition, simply composite images with cut-and-paste may produce unrealistic result.

Generally, to harmonize the foreground appearance, we should first remove the effect of the source illumination, and then add the effect of the target illumination. However, since both the geometry and the lighting condition are unknown, accurate and robust harmonization is very difficult. Previous methods usually work with empirical assumptions, or by learning with image statistics.

© Springer Nature Switzerland AG 2020
N. Magnenat-Thalmann et al. (Eds.): CGI 2020, LNCS 12221, pp. 193–205, 2020.
https://doi.org/10.1007/978-3-030-61864-3_17

    (a) source image   (b) cut-and-paste   (c) harmonized result   (d) groundtruth

Fig. 1. An example of illumination harmonization. (a) The source image and the foreground mask. (b) The target background and the composite without harmonization. (c) The harmonized result. (d) The ground-truth composite.

The pioneer work of Lalonde et al. [7] proposes a learning-based method for the assessment of image realism, the learned model also can be used to harmonize composite image. Xue et al. [20] experimentally identifies some key factors that take effect to the realism of image composite. The power of deep learning can be also exploited for image harmonization (see Sect. 2 for details).

Since the ground-truth appearance of the foreground in the target background is usually unknown and hard to get, previous methods can conduct their evaluations with only user study [20,22] or synthetic datasets [17]. Given a natural image and the foreground mask, a cut-and-paste composite can be produced by artificially adjusting the foreground appearance. The adjusted and unadjusted image then can be used as the input and the ground-truth composite for the harmonization, respectively. In practice this approach presents at least two limitations: First, the source background image is unavailable. As the case in Fig. 1, for usual composite tasks the source background is completely different from the target background, and has consistent lighting condition with the source foreground. The source background provides with important information of the source lighting condition, which however, does not exploited in previous methods due to the limitation of synthetic datasets. Second, the synthetic foreground adjustment maybe different from the appearance changes caused by different lighting conditions, especially for specular and detailed lighting effects, so it maybe inaccurate for high-quality composite.

In this paper we aim to address the above limitations of previous datasets and methods. First, we design a tool to produce image harmonization dataset, which can get the foreground object appearances in different background, and importantly, guarantee accurate spatial registration of the foreground region in different images. Based on this dataset we perform a faithful evaluation to previous methods. Second, we propose a very simple approach that can effectively exploit the source background for improving the realism of composite. Our method is learning-free, and inspired by recent works for color constancy [10]. Instead of using all pixels for harmonization, we find that using only gray pixels [12] can produce significant better results. We propose to compute the foreground appearance transformation as the Gray Mean Scale (GMS), which avoids to estimate the absolute illumination color and intensity, and outperforms previous methods on both our dataset and previous synthetic datasets.

2   Related Work

According to the different properties of input images, image harmonization may be achieved with different techniques, such as color and style transfer [8,13], gradient domain image fusion [11,18], color constancy [5,12], illumination estimation [6,19], etc. Since we focus on only one of the most common cases where the image inconsistency is mostly due to the illumination environments, in the below we just briefly introduce the works closely related with our work, with harmonization methods and datasets being discussed separately.

2.1   Previous Methods

A simple way to harmonize the composite image is to transform the foreground that it has the same mean and variance as the background. This idea was first introduced by Reinhard et al. [13] for color transfer. The Match-Color tool in PhotoShop also adopts this strategy for image harmonization. However, this approach does not distinguish between object color and lighting color, which leads most of the adjusted images disharmonious.

Lalonde et al. [7] provided a measure to judge the realism of a composite image, and recolor unnatural composite images. The method is based on color statistics learned from a collection of natural images. Although this method can be more adaptive to image contents by learning from natural images, it still does not separate the effect of object color and lighting color, and thus suffers from similar problem as [13].

The work of Xue Su et al. [20] experimentally selected some key statistical measures that may determine the naturalness of composite images. Given a composite image, they adjusted the foreground histogram to match the background histogram with respect to the selected key statistical measures, which further excludes the effect of image statistics uncorrelated with image realism.

In recent years the power of deep learning also has been exploited for image harmonization. Zhu [22] trained a CNN model to predict the visual realism of composite images, and adjust the appearance of the foreground area in order to optimize the realism score. Given a large number of composite images and their corresponding ground truth, Tsai [17] trained a deep model to harmonize image in combination with the semantic information of the image.

Although the learning-based methods maybe powerful in capturing the relationship between the foreground and the background, previous methods attempt to learn with all pixels of the foreground and the background, which forms a very large product space dependent on the object and the scene materials as well as their geometry and spatial distribution, making the learning task difficult to capture the true features related with image realism.

2.2 Previous DataSets

In the work of Lalonde et al. [7] for image realism assessment, they semi-automatically created a dataset of composite images based on the segmented image objects from the LabelMe database [14]. The main purpose of this dataset is for assessing image realism. Although it is also adopted for evaluating image harmonization methods [7,20], only qualitative evaluations are supported due to the missing of the groundtruth.

To enable the training of deep network for assessing image realism, Zhu et al. [22] generated a larger dataset with similar approach as Lalonde et al. However, this dataset still does not provide with ground-truth composite.

The image harmonization work of Tsai et al. [17] contributed a synthetic composite dataset with ground truth. The unrealistic composite images are generated by artificially adjusting the foreground appearance of images from COCO [2], MIT-Adobe FiveK [9] and Flicker datasets. With this method it is easy to generate large quantity of images with ground truth. However, as we have analysed in the introduction, this approach can not provide with the source background, and meantime the adjustment to the foreground may be unnatural. In real scenario the source background is almost always available and usually provides more information of the illumination environment, it thus should not be ignored by image harmonization methods.

More recently, Wenyan et al. [4] published a comprehensive synthetic dataset for image harmonization, it contains 4 sub-datasets: HCOCO, HAdobe5k, HFlickr, and Hday2night, each of which contains synthesized composite images, foreground masks of composite images and corresponding real images. However, the synthetic approach of [4] is similar as that in Tsai [17], and thus still suffers from the same limitations.

3 Our DataSet

As mentioned above, firstly we need to create a dataset with ground-truth composite by capturing images in real environments. The main difficulty is that, it is hard to capture images with accurately aligned foreground and completely different background, which requires us to move the foreground object while keeping its relative position and pose with the camera. A potential approach is to fix the object and camera with a rigid frame; however, in practice we found that this way is not easy to be operated since slight movement of the camera or the object may introduce significant registration error to the foreground object.

To address this problem, we propose the computational approach as demonstrated in Fig. 2, which consists of the four steps as follows:

1) *Capture the source image:* Given the selected foreground object (which may have any shape and size), we first capture a reference image, and cutout the foreground object F_s manually with the QuickSelection tool of PhotoShop. The result is as shown in Fig. 2(a). The reference image then will be used as the source image for the composite.

Fig. 2. The proposed approach to get the ground-truth composite in real environments. (a) The source image with the foreground object mask. (b) The captured target image with roughly-aligned foreground. (c) The computed ground-truth composite image with accurately aligned foreground. (d) The target background by image completion.

2) *Capture the roughly-aligned target image:* To get the ground-truth composite of F_s in the target background, we first capture an image of the object in the target background (Fig. 2(b)). Importantly, the target foreground region $\tilde{F}_t$ should be roughly aligned with the reference foreground object F_s. To facilitate this process and guarantee the result precision, we developed an semi-automatic tool which can automatically select the best-aligned view when the camera is moving. Details about this will be covered in Sect. 3.1.

3) *Compute the aligned ground truth:* To guarantee accurate alignment with F_s, the ground truth is finally computed by transforming F_s that the result appearance keep consistent with $\tilde{F}_t$. In order to completely cover the region of $\tilde{F}_t$ in the target image, a spatial transformation A also may be applied to F_s. Figure 2(c) shows an example. Note that the difference of the computed ground truth with the captured target image (Fig. 2(b)) should be very small. Please see Sect. 3.2 for more details.

4) *Compute the target background:* The target background image is finally computed by removing the foreground object. Since the auto-iris camera cannot guarantee that the photos taken continuously are in consistent illumination conditions, it is not appropriate to simply re-take a picture without objects as target background. We adopt the method proposed by Jiahui et al. [21] to complete the target background. The foreground mask is first slightly dilated in order to completely remove the foreground pixels.

With the above approach, we created a dataset of 16 different objects. For each object, one source image and 11 target images in different background scenes and illumination conditions are captured, with image resolution of 1940×1440. The target images have different background scenes (indoor and outdoor) and different illumination conditions. To enrich the illumination conditions, we use PVC transparencies of different colors to mask the lens to simulate different lighting colors. Figure 3 shows some exemplar images from our dataset.

3.1 Capture the Roughly-Aligned Target Image

In order to take target images of the object in different background scenes and roughly-aligned with the reference foreground, we use a laptop computer

Fig. 3. Some examples from our dataset. The first column is the source image and the foreground mask, the remaining columns are the ground-truth composite in different target scenes.

mounted with a HD camera, and developed a tool so that the photographer can easily capture a roughly-aligned target image. Figure 4 demonstrate the interface of our system. The reference foreground is blended with the current frame that the photographer can supervise the alignment and move the camera accordingly. At the same time, the alignment score of the current frame with the reference foreground is computed in realtime, the best-aligned frame together with the registration result and estimated target foreground object boundary are dynamically updated and present to the photographer, who then can move the camera to continuously improve the best-aligned frame, until a satisfactory result has obtained.

The alignment score is computed with a method similar as the BRIEF feature descriptor [3], which is a binary descriptor that is robust to significant illumination changes. Specifically, for the reference image, we first convert it to gray image, and random sample a set of point pairs in the foreground region, with the length of point pairs uniformly distributed in the range of [3, 7]. The point pairs are selected so that the intensity difference of each pair is at least 5, in order to remove point pairs in flat regions. Given the target image, we also convert it to gray image, and then compute a BRIEF-like similarity score based on the selected point pairs.

When the best-aligned frame is updated, we further compute a dense registration with the reference foreground. Since there is no large displacement, we found that using the accurate variational optical flow method of [1] can obtain pretty good registration result. With the flow map, we warp the target image to the reference foreground, and blend them to visualize the registration error, as shown in Fig. 4(c): (a) The current frame blended with the reference foreground; (b) The current best-aligned frame; (c) The blended visualization of registration result by warping the target image to the source foreground using optical flow; (d) The estimated target object boundary. Note that from the blended visualization, the user can easily observe the registration error, so the captured target image would be considered as good enough only if there is no obvious registration error.

Since the reference object boundary is known, the target object boundary can be found easily based on the optical flow registration. To further regularize the flow warp, we estimate a homography transformation from the reference

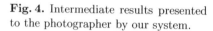

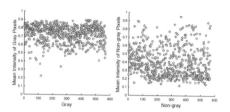

Fig. 4. Intermediate results presented to the photographer by our system.

Fig. 5. The distribution of mean intensity of gray and non-gray pixels for the 568 images of [16].

foreground boundary to the target foreground boundary, based on a set of point pair matches given by the flow map and sampled around the reference foreground boundary. The target object boundary then can be obtained with the homography transformation. Note that although homography can represent only planar object motions, we found that it also works well for the non-planar objects in our dataset. This is mainly because the images are roughly aligned, and the projection difference can be well approximated with a homography. In addition, we need only to fit the motion of the object silhouette, so the non-planar shape of interior regions would not take effect. In fact, the target object mask is used mainly for the background completion, so small errors would not cause any problem.

With the above approach we can easily take aligned target images in different background scenes. The computed flow registration and the target foreground mask are also saved together for further processing.

3.2 Compute the Ground-Truth Composite

Due to the mis-alignment between the reference and the target foreground regions, the captured target image can not be used directly as the ground truth. However, given the flow registration, we can easily transform the reference foreground appearance, so that it is well matched with the target appearance.

If a perfect flow registration can be obtained, the ground truth foreground appearance can be simply computed by warping the target foreground with the flow. However, in practice the computed optical flow would contain some errors more or less. On the other hand, because currently the harmonization methods still not able to model directional and specular lighting effects, it is not necessary to keep all detail effects in the target foreground. Therefore, we choose to compute the ground truth composite simply by uniformly scale the reference foreground intensities: $I_c = k_c T_c$, where $c \in \{R, G, B\}$. The channel-wise scale factor k_c is computed by average the scale factors of the pixel correspondences given by the flow registration.

Note that the above method can be extended easily to involve more spatial-variant lighting effects, by computing the scale factors in overlapped local windows. Obviously, using smaller local windows can better approximate the target object appearance, but may be less robust to registration error.

4   Illumination Harmonization

In this section we will introduce the proposed illumination harmonization method. Not as the previous methods, our method aims to make full use of the cues provided with the whole source images and the corresponding target background images.

4.1   The Reflection Model

According to the Dichromatic Reflection Model [15], pixel values in images can be modeled as:

$$I_i = \gamma_b C_i L_i R_{b,i} + \gamma_s C_i L_i R_{s,i}, \tag{1}$$

where i is the pixel index, L is the global illumination distribution, C_i is the sensor sensitivity. The chromatic terms R_b and R_s account for body and surface reflection, and they are only related to the material of the object. γ_b and γ_s are the weight of the above two reflections.

Based on the global illumination assumption, Eq. 1 can be simplified as:

$$I_i = CL(\gamma_b R_{b,i} + \gamma_s R_{s,i}), \tag{2}$$

where L and C become as constants that only related to the brightness of the incident light and the camera sensor, respectively. Due to the difficulties in estimating the detailed object materials and restoring the 3D illumination environments, we further simplify the reflection model Eq. 2 by ignoring the surface reflection, then we have:

$$I_i = \gamma_b CLR_{b,i}. \tag{3}$$

In fact, given only 2D images it is less likely to model the specular and directional lighting effects.

For two images I^s, I^t of the same object taken in different illumination condition, and possibly with different cameras, the scale factor k_i between corresponding pixel values can be computed as:

$$k_i = \frac{I_i^t}{I_i^s} = \frac{C^t L^t}{C^s L^s}, \tag{4}$$

which means that the scale factor k_i is independent of i, so for illumination harmonization of images, it is reasonable to use a uniform scale factor k for the appearance transformation from the source foreground to the target foreground.

For color images, we use channel-wise scale factors $k_c, c \in \{R, G, B\}$, which we have used for estimating the ground truth composite in Sect. 3.2.

4.2   Gray Mean Scale

For illumination harmonization, Eq. (4) can not be used to compute the foreground appearance scale k_c, because both the sensor sensitivities and the lighting intensities are unknown. In theory, k_c can be estimated with a reference object that appears in both the source and the target background. However, this is still infeasible since the background scenes are usually completely different.

Inspired by recent works for color constancy [12], we find that the pixels with gray reflectance (gray pixels in the below) should be useful for estimating the illumination color and intensity. If I_i is a gray pixel, its reflectance can be denoted as $R_i = (r_i, r_i, r_i)$, so according to Eq. (3), normalized illumination color can be estimated from I_i. However, the illumination intensity can not be obtained because r_i is unknown.

Obviously, if we can find a gray pixel correspondence between the source and the target background that have the same reflectance intensity, k_c can be estimated with Eq. (4). However, this is still difficult without a perfect intrinsic image decomposition. Alternatively, we assume that the distribution of gray pixel reflectance in different background scenes are almost identical, or at least, has much less variations than the non-gray pixels. To verify this, we conducted an experiment with the 568 images from the dataset of Gehler-Shi et al. [16]. For each image, we first remove the lighting effect based on the accompany color cards. In standard illumination condition, the pixel value directly reflects the object reflectivity. Thus, we compute the mean value of color intensity for gray and non-gray pixels, respectively. The gray pixels are classified with the method we will introduce in Sect. 4.2. Figure 5 compares the distribution of mean intensities of gray and non-gray pixels. It can be found that the mean intensity of gray pixels varies much less than that of non-gray pixels. Therefore, we further assume that the mean reflectance of all gray pixels is constant between different images, k_c then can be estimated as:

$$k_c = \frac{g_c^t}{g_c^s},\tag{5}$$

where g^s and g^t are the mean pixel value of gray pixels in the source and the target images, respectively.

To find the gray pixels, we adopt the method proposed in [12], which outputs a grayness index for each pixel of the input image, predicting the likelihood that each pixel is gray pixel. According to gray index, the gray pixels can be selected easily. We select the top 0.1% pixels with highest likelihood as gray pixels, whose mean then is used to compute the channel-wise scales in (5).

5   Experiments

In the experiments part, due to the fact that none of the previous methods using real-captured dataset for quantitative evaluation, we re-evaluate previous outstanding methods and the proposed GMS method among our dataset. In addition, for the sake of fairness, we also exploit previous datasets mentioned above to evaluate all methods. Experimental results show that our method performs state-of-the-art on the above datasets.

5.1   Evaluations with Our Dataset

Based on our dataset, we first evaluated the proposed GMS method together with previous outstanding methods: Reinhard [13], Xue [20], Zhu [22], Tsai [17]. Among them, both Zhu [22] and Tsai [17] are based on CNNs. Due to the limitation of depth network structure, we resized the input images of all methods to be 640 × 480 for fair comparison. Besides Reinhard [13], other methods are implemented with the author-provided source code.

Table 1 shows the Mean Absolute Error (MAE) of different methods. As is shown, our method outperforms previous methods in all ranges of errors. Note that for the *Best 25%* error, previous methods all performs not as good as the cut-and-paste. Actually, when creating the dataset we intentionally added some examples that have no large appearance changes, in order to test the stability of illumination harmonization methods. Table 2 shows the Structural Similarity Index (SSIM) scores of the harmonized image with the groundtruth.

5.2   Comparison with Previous Datasets

In order to get more general evaluations of the proposed method, we also evaluated it with previous datasets.

Table 1 and Table 2 also show the quantitative results of different methods with MIT-Adobe FiveK dataset. For each image it has several versions of different lighting effect produced by professionals using Adobe Lightroom. Different from our dataset, it is still a synthetic dataset, and in addition, the source and the target background are from the same scene (with different lighting effects). We randomly generate 100 composite images including different type of scenes such as landscapes, people and human products. As can be seen, on this dataset our method still constantly outperform previous methods.

We also perform a qualitative comparison of different methods using the color-checker dataset of Gehler-Shi [16]. We generated a test set of 133 composite images. Note that in order for fair comparison, for each test image the color checker is removed from the target background. Due to the lack of the ground truth composite, we are not able to quantitatively evaluate the results of this dataset. However, we analyzed the results of different methods, and found that GMS does perform better than previous methods for most examples. Figure 6 demonstrates some examples from this dataset.

Table 1. Comparisons of methods with MAE scores on our dataset and MIT dataset.

MAE↓	Ours					MIT				
	Mean	Median	Trimean	Best25%	Worst25%	Mean	Median	Trimean	Best25%	Worst25%
cut-and-paste	61.83	52.38	53.23	18.43	121.83	43.29	30.79	33.66	16.14	88.82
Match Color	61.79	54.31	55.59	24.40	111.33	55.92	44.59	46.36	30.10	100.53
Xue (2012)	64.12	51.45	54.77	25.44	121.03	43.28	39.45	38.47	18.58	76.97
Zhu (2015)	57.43	50.72	50.66	24.85	103.16	39.60	29.03	30.13	17.24	79.84
Tsai (2017)	60.44	52.80	54.12	29.10	104.14	36.84	30.52	30.77	17.91	67.22
Ours	**53.02**	**49.06**	**48.90**	**16.46**	**97.57**	**31.61**	**26.78**	**28.28**	**14.14**	**55.58**

Table 2. Comparisons of methods with SSIM scores on our dataset and MIT dataset.

SSIM↑	Ours					MIT				
	Mean	Median	Trimean	Best25%	Worst25%	Mean	Median	Trimean	Best25%	Worst25%
cut-and-paste	0.7648	0.8361	0.8247	**0.9650**	0.4479	0.7717	0.8229	0.8105	0.9178	0.5505
Match Color	0.7431	0.7784	0.7756	0.9391	0.4835	0.6203	0.6865	0.6539	0.7922	0.3827
Xue (2012)	0.6939	0.7575	0.7402	0.9250	0.3729	0.6864	0.6988	0.6994	0.8624	0.4879
Zhu (2015)	0.6862	0.7235	0.7246	0.8755	0.4225	0.7030	0.7596	0.7451	0.8405	0.4856
Tsai (2017)	0.6601	0.6941	0.6879	0.8590	0.4068	0.7311	0.7703	0.7666	0.8703	0.5231
Ours	**0.8066**	**0.8629**	**0.8538**	0.9619	**0.5592**	**0.7822**	**0.8144**	**0.8039**	**0.9185**	**0.6051**

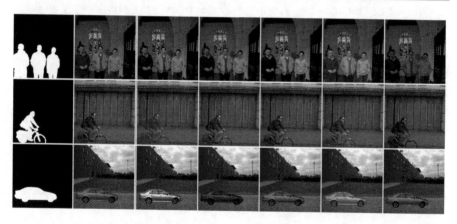

Fig. 6. Comparisons results on Gehler-Shi Dataset. From left to right: foreground mask, Cut-and-Paste, Match Color, Xue [20], Zhu [22], Tsai [17] and ours.

6   Conclusion

In this paper we propose to improve image illumination harmonization. We first developed a method for generating image composite dataset, so that we can easily capture accurately aligned foreground objects in different background scenes. With this tool we create a dataset that provides with the ground truth composite together with the source background. After that, we propose a simple method to estimate the foreground appearance transformation from the source to the target.

Our method is learning-free, and can be better extended to unknown scenes. In experiments we evaluated the proposed methods together with previous methods on our dataset as well as some previous datasets. We therefore established a new benchmark for illumination harmonization, for the first time with complete inputs and ground truth captured in real environments.

Acknowledgements. This work is supported by Industrial Internet Innovation and Development Project in 2019 of China, NSF of China (No. 61772318).

References

1. Brox, T., Bruhn, A., Papenberg, N., Weickert, J.: High accuracy optical flow estimation based on a theory for warping. In: Pajdla, T., Matas, J. (eds.) ECCV 2004. LNCS, vol. 3024, pp. 25–36. Springer, Heidelberg (2004). https://doi.org/10.1007/978-3-540-24673-2_3
2. Bychkovsky, V., Paris, S., Chan, E., Durand, F.: Learning photographic global tonal adjustment with a database of input/output image pairs. In: CVPR, pp. 97–104. IEEE (2011)
3. Calonder, M., Lepetit, V., Strecha, C., Fua, P.: BRIEF: binary robust independent elementary features. In: Daniilidis, K., Maragos, P., Paragios, N. (eds.) ECCV 2010. LNCS, vol. 6314, pp. 778–792. Springer, Heidelberg (2010). https://doi.org/10.1007/978-3-642-15561-1_56
4. Cong, W., et al.: Image harmonization datasets: HCOCO, HAdobe5k, HFlickr, and Hday2night. arXiv preprint arXiv:1908.10526 (2019)
5. Finlayson, G.D., Zakizadeh, R., Gijsenij, A.: The reproduction angular error for evaluating the performance of illuminant estimation algorithms. IEEE TPAMI **39**(7), 1482–1488 (2016)
6. Garon, M., Sunkavalli, K., Hadap, S., Carr, N., Lalonde, J.F.: Fast spatially-varying indoor lighting estimation. In: CVPR, pp. 6908–6917 (2019)
7. Lalonde, J.F., Efros, A.A.: Using color compatibility for assessing image realism. In: ICCV, pp. 1–8. IEEE (2007)
8. Li, Y., Liu, M.-Y., Li, X., Yang, M.-H., Kautz, J.: A closed-form solution to photorealistic image stylization. In: Ferrari, V., Hebert, M., Sminchisescu, C., Weiss, Y. (eds.) ECCV 2018. LNCS, vol. 11207, pp. 468–483. Springer, Cham (2018). https://doi.org/10.1007/978-3-030-01219-9_28
9. Lin, T.-Y., et al.: Microsoft COCO: common objects in context. In: Fleet, D., Pajdla, T., Schiele, B., Tuytelaars, T. (eds.) ECCV 2014. LNCS, vol. 8693, pp. 740–755. Springer, Cham (2014). https://doi.org/10.1007/978-3-319-10602-1_48
10. Maloney, L.T., Wandell, B.A.: Color constancy: a method for recovering surface spectral reflectance. JOSA A **3**(1), 29–33 (1986)
11. P'erez, P., Gangnet, M., Blake, A.: Poisson image editing. In: ACM SIGGRAPH, pp. 313–318 (2003)
12. Qian, Y., Kamarainen, J.K., Nikkanen, J., Matas, J.: On finding gray pixels. In: CVPR, pp. 8062–8070 (2019)
13. Reinhard, E., Adhikhmin, M., Gooch, B., Shirley, P.: Color transfer between images. IEEE Comput. Graphics Appl. **21**(5), 34–41 (2001)
14. Russell, B.C., Torralba, A., Murphy, K.P., Freeman, W.T.: LabelMe: a database and web-based tool for image annotation. Int. J. Comput. Vision **77**(1–3), 157–173 (2008). https://doi.org/10.1007/s11263-007-0090-8

15. Shafer, S.A.: Using color to separate reflection components. Color Res. Appl. **10**(4), 210–218 (1985)
16. Shi, L.: Re-processed version of the gehler color constancy dataset of 568 images (2000). http://www.cs.sfu.ca/color/data/
17. Tsai, Y.H., Shen, X., Lin, Z., Sunkavalli, K., Lu, X., Yang, M.H.: Deep image harmonization. In: CVPR, pp. 3789–3797 (2017)
18. Wu, H., Zheng, S., Zhang, J., Huang, K.: GP-GAN: towards realistic high-resolution image blending. In: ACM International Conference on Multimedia, pp. 2487–2495 (2019)
19. Xing, G., Liu, Y., Ling, H., Granier, X., Zhang, Y.: Automatic spatially varying illumination recovery of indoor scenes based on a single RGB-D image. IEEE TVCG, 1–14 (2018)
20. Xue, S., Agarwala, A., Dorsey, J., Rushmeier, H.: Understanding and improving the realism of image composites. ACM Trans. Graph. (TOG) **31**(4), 84 (2012)
21. Yu, J., Lin, Z., Yang, J., Shen, X., Lu, X., Huang, T.S.: Free-form image inpainting with gated convolution, pp. 4471–4480 (2019)
22. Zhu, J.Y., Krahenbuhl, P., Shechtman, E., Efros, A.A.: Learning a discriminative model for the perception of realism in composite images. In: ICCV, pp. 3943–3951 (2015)

An Unsupervised Approach for 3D Face Reconstruction from a Single Depth Image

Peixin Li[1], Yuru Pei[1(✉)], Yicheng Zhong[1], Yuke Guo[2], Gengyu Ma[3],
Meng Liu[4], Wei Bai[4], Wenhai Wu[4], and Hongbin Zha[1]

[1] Key Laboratory of Machine Perception (MOE), Department of Machine
Intelligence, Peking University, Beijing, China
peiyuru@cis.pku.edu.cn
[2] Luoyang Institute of Science and Technology, Luoyang, China
[3] Usens Inc., San Jose, USA
[4] Huawei Technologies Co. Ltd., Beijing, China

Abstract. In this paper, we propose a convolutional encoder network
to learn a mapping function from a noisy depth image to a 3D expressive facial model. We formulate the task as an embedding problem and
train the network in an unsupervised manner by exploiting the consistent
fitting of the 3D mesh and the depth image. We use the 3DMM-based
representation and embed depth images to code vectors concerning facial
identities, expressions, and poses. Without semantic textural cues from
RGB images, we exploit geometric and contextual constraints in both the
depth image and the 3D surface for reliable mapping. We combine the
multi-level filtered point cloud pyramid and semantic adaptive weighting for fitting. The proposed system enables the 3D expressive face completion and reconstruction in poor illuminations by leveraging a single
noisy depth image. The system realizes a full correspondence between
the depth image and the 3D statistical deformable mesh, facilitating
landmark location and feature segmentation of depth images.

Keywords: 3D face reconstruction · Depth image · Embedding

1 Introduction

To estimate a 3D face from a single depth image is a challenging task considering the device-specific noise and the various facial shapes due to non-planar
deformations, including poses and expressions. Most existing works rely on RGB
[4,9,10,13,33,39] or RGB-D images [2,14,37] to estimate the pose, identity, and
expression parameters of the 3D face, where the facial textures in the color
images provide semantic constraints for facial features, such as mouth, eyes,
and the wrinkle-like facial details. Note that the textures in the color image are
not stable due to the illumination variations. For the outdoor applications with
uncontrolled illuminations, e.g., in-car driving, the deteriorated facial textures

© Springer Nature Switzerland AG 2020
N. Magnenat-Thalmann et al. (Eds.): CGI 2020, LNCS 12221, pp. 206–219, 2020.
https://doi.org/10.1007/978-3-030-61864-3_18

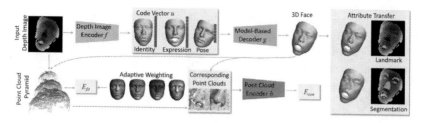

Fig. 1. The overview of the proposed 3D face completion and reconstruction framework from a single depth image. The proposed depth image embedding network (DEN) can be stacked on an existing base such as the ResNet for the inference of the identity, expression, and pose codes. The encoder parameters are learned by the nonrigid alignment of the 3D parametric face resulted from the model-based decoder and the input depth image. The multi-level filtered point cloud pyramid and the semantic adaptive weighting are used for geometric alignment. The resulted dense correspondence enables landmark location and feature segmentation of depth images.

could not act as constraints for the semantic consistency in the 3D face estimation. In contrast, the depth image is invariable to illuminations and provides stable constraints to facial shapes. To identify the semantic correspondence from a single depth image is a cornerstone to fit the 3D face with the depth image. Traditional methods rely on online iterative optimization [37], where the depth images act as a supplement to the RGB-based fitting to provide geometrical constraints. The face estimation using only the depth image is prone to the shape inconsistency because of the lack of textual constraints, especially in the highly deformed region such as a large-opened mouth.

The learning-based method is feasible to exploit the intrinsic data distribution and has been used in the parameter regression for 3D face estimation from images. Regression-based methods are used in depth-based head pose estimation [11,12]. A deep neural network-based Poseidon [6], realizes 3D pose estimation by a face-from-deep model to exploit orientation information in depth images. Whereas, the pose estimation in existing work is restricted to rigid transformation with limited degrees of freedoms. The CNN-based deep regressor [28,34] is feasible to obtain deformable expression and pose parameters from a single RGB image. The parameter regression relieves the online computational cost, though the annotation of training data is tedious. The regressor learned from synthetic data avoids manual labeling, but is prone to the domain shifting [28]. Unsupervised learning is plummy in avoiding the data annotation and domain adaptation between the source and target tasks. The unsupervised auto-encoder-based model [32] produces the 3D face with full-scaled facial details, where the expert-designed decoder is used to derive 2D color image from the 3D face. Instead of relying on RGB channels to infer codes of deformable faces, we present an auto-encoder-based network to realize the semantic fitting of a 3D expressive face with a single depth image.

We propose an end-to-end depth image embedding network (DEN) to esti-mate a 3D face from a single depth image as shown in Fig. 1. We learn the fully convolutional network in an unsupervised manner by utilizing geometric fitting of the nonrigid deformed 3D parametric face and the noisy depth image. We utilize the statistical deformable facial model and realize embedding of the depth image for code vectors regarding the facial pose, identity, and expres-sion, which determine a 3D face uniquely. The proposed system leverages depth images without textural constraints from color images. We present the multi-level filtered point cloud pyramid and the semantic adaptive weighting for the geometric alignment between the 3D expressive face and the depth image. In order to enforce the semantic correspondence, we present the patch-based con-textual constraint to favor the corresponding point pair with similar point cloud encoding of surrounding patches. The system realizes a full correspondence and parametrization of the noisy depth image and the expressive face model, where the 3D face reconstruction is not vulnerable to the poor illumination as the RGB-based face estimation. The dense correspondence enables landmark location and feature segmentation of the depth images.

2   Related Work

The statistical deformable models (SDM), such as the 3D morphable model (3DMM) [5], constitute state-of-the-arts in facial analysis tasks, including 3D face reconstruction, pose estimation, identification, and landmark location. The SDMs are learned from high-quality 3D facial scans and widely used with efficient solvation in a reduced parametric space. The affine parametric model encodes both the geometric and textural information of the available corpus. Traditional 3D face reconstruction approaches rely on online optimization from a collection of photos or internet images [4]. The real-time 3D face tracking based on online optimization is available [33], where the optimization solvation is sensitive to the initialization. The prior landmark detection [18,35] is required to get a coarse and reasonable initialization for 3D face estimation. The direct fitting of the sta-tistical model to the depth image is prone to a mismatch of facial features, such as the wide-opened mouth, without the semantic constraints of facial textures [37].

The learning-based method is feasible to remove the online computational complexity. Richardson et al. [28] generated a large set of random facial images from known 3D geometric face to train the CNN for 3D face inference. They also used the shape-from-shading-like criterion to obtain geometric details [29]. The deep residual network (ResNet) is used to obtain facial geometry and texture for identification [34]. The above supervised learning methods rely on a large set of manual labeling or the generated synthetic data, where the labeling is tedious. The model learned from synthetic data is prone to the domain-shifting problem.

The unsupervised or weak-supervised auto-encoder-based framework has drawn considerable attention recently. Jaderberg et al. [17] proposed the seminal work on the spatial transformers for models invariant to translation, scale, rota-tion, and more generic warping. The 3DMM is used as the spatial transformer in the CNN [3]. Yan et al. [38] formulated the learning procedure of the single-view 3D shape reconstruction as an encoder-decoder network, where the projection transformation was used as regularization. Kundu et al. [19] proposed a differentiable a render-and-compare loss to learn the RCNN-based 3D shape and pose regressor with 2D supervision. Shin et al. [30] predicted multi-view depth images from a single depth image, where the floating scale surface reconstruction (FSSR) method is used for 3D surface reconstruction. The MOFA method [32] combines a CNN-based encoder with an expert-designed decoder. The trainable corrective module was added to the auto-encoder to obtain facial details [31]. The above methods rely on the textural information of the color images for semantic correspondence [31,32] or the postprocessing to estimate 3D surface from resulted multi-view depth and silhouette images [30]. In this paper, the proposed method calculates the 3D face from a single image without textural cues or the intermediate multi-view depth and silhouette images.

3 The Proposed Approach

In this paper, we present a depth image embedding network (DEN) to develop a 3D face completion and reconstruction model. An overview of our DEN-based framework is shown in Fig. 1. The proposed DEN can be stacked on existing bases such as the ResNet for the inference of the identity, expression, and pose codes. The neural network parameters of the encoder are learned by the nonrigid alignment of the parametric expressive 3D face resulted from the model-based decoder and the input depth image. More specifically, the multi-level filtered point cloud pyramid and the semantic adaptive weighting are introduced for geometric alignment. The patch-based contextual constraint favors the corresponding pair with similar point cloud encoding of surrounding patches, facilitating the semantic correspondence and parameterization of depth images and 3D faces.

3.1 Depth Image Embedding

The proposed approach allows the estimation of 3D expressive face $X \in \mathbb{R}^{3N}$ with N vertices from a noisy and incomplete depth image $I \in \mathbb{R}^M$ with M pixels captured by a consumer depth camera. The task is formulated as embedding the input depth image to a low dimensional code vector $u \in \mathbb{R}^k$ that determines the 3D expressive face uniquely. The convolutional residual network-based encoder parameterizes the nonlinear embedding function $f : I \to u$.

We employ the 3DMM-based parametric model [5] and represent the face X as a linear combination of shape and expression basis.

$$X = \bar{X} + \alpha_s B_s + \alpha_e B_e, \tag{1}$$

where $\bar{X} \in \mathbb{R}^{3N}$ denotes the neutral facial shape with N vertices. $B_s \in \mathbb{R}^{k_s \times 3N}$ denotes the first k_s dominant principal components learned from neutral 3D face scans, which are used to span the shape subspaces. $B_e \in \mathbb{R}^{k_e \times 3N}$ denotes the expressive basis. $\alpha_s \in \mathbb{R}^{k_s}$ and $\alpha_e \in \mathbb{R}^{k_e}$ are the identity and expression vectors respectively. We use the Basel Face Model [26] to obtain the facial identity basis. The facial mesh has approx. $36k$ vertices and $70k$ triangles. The expression basis is obtained from the FaceWarehouse [8]. Considering different topologies between the two face datasets, we use the nonrigid ICP algorithm [1] to align the facial meshes of the Basel and the FaceWarehouse for dense correspondence. Our system uses $k_s = 80$ identity basis and $k_e = 64$ expression basis. We also consider the 3D rigid transformation parameters: the rotation $r \in SO(3)$ and the translation $t \in \mathbb{R}^3$. The code vector of the 3D face is defined as $u = (\alpha_s, \alpha_e, r, t)$, and the code vector dimensionality $k = k_s + k_e + 6$.

Given the parametric face model, the encoder performs the code inference. We build the encoder based on the ResNet [16] to augment the multi-level feature fusion and information propagation, where the cascaded convolutional blocks are used for feature extraction. The feature maps are sent to three branches with fully connected layers for code inference regarding the identity, the expression, and the pose.

Given the identity, expression, and pose codes u, the model-based decoder reconstructs the 3D expressive face X from the code vector, and $X = g(u)$. The decoder function g is defined as:

$$g(u) = r(\bar{X} + \alpha_s B_s + \alpha_e B_e) + t, \tag{2}$$

where the function g reconstructs the 3D face using the code vector $u(\alpha_s, \alpha_e, r, t)$.

3.2   Self-supervision

It is not a trivial task to collect paired 3D complete face models and depth images. When given a training dataset $\mathcal{I}$, we leverage an unsupervised framework to find the optimal parameters of the DEN-based model by penalizing the gap between the reconstructed 3D face X and the input depth image $I \in \mathcal{I}$.

Depth Image Fitting. The data term of the depth image fitting penalizes the gap between the input depth image and the estimated 3D face.

$$E_{fit} = \sum_{l=1}^{L} \frac{1}{|\theta_l(I)|} \sum_{p_i \in \theta_l(I)} w_j \| n_i^T \cdot (p_i - \varphi(p_i)) \|^2. \tag{3}$$

The operator θ converts the depth image to a 3D point cloud, and $|\theta|$ returns the point number. Given the DEN-based model, we derive a matching function φ to map a point p in the input depth image I to the reconstructed the 3D face X. For a point p_i, its counterpart $x_j = \varphi(p_i)$ is the nearest neighbor of p_i on X. The loss function is used to minimize the weighted distance between point $p_i \in \theta(I)$ and its counterpart $x_j \in X$. Here we use the point-to-plane distance along the normal n_i.

Instead of using a single-channel depth image for similarity analysis, we build a multi-level hierarchy of the input depth image by denoising and down-sampling of the 3D point clouds. We utilize the Laplacian smoothing and the Poisson

Fig. 2. Depth image denoising and down-sampling. (a) Input depth image. 3D point cloud of (b) $10k$, (c) $3k$, and (d) 500 points. (e) Geometric weighting. Shape variations of (f) the identities and (g) the expressions. (h) Weighting according to the segmentation map of facial features.

disk down-sampling algorithm and build the point cloud pyramid using approximately $10k$, $3k$, and 500 points as shown in Fig. 2. The hierarchy level number L is set to 3. $\theta_l(I)$ denotes the point cloud of level-l obtained by denoising and down-sampling. The more smooth point cloud, the fewer points are used for the similarity analysis between the depth image and the 3D parametric face.

Adaptive Weighing. Instead of using uniform weighting, we present an adaptive weighting scheme according to geometric variations of identities and expressions. The geometric weight $w_{\mathbf{g}}$ is defined by local geometric variations on the neutral 3D face.

$$w_{\mathbf{g}}(x) = \frac{1}{2} \left(1 - \frac{1}{|\mathcal{S}(x)|} \sum_{j \in \mathcal{S}(x)} \langle n_j, n \rangle \right). \tag{4}$$

We measure the normal difference between vertex x and samples in a rectangular region $\mathcal{S}$ centered at x. The smooth region is assigned small $w_{\mathbf{g}}$, while the region with abrupt normal variations, e.g., the lips, the eyes, and the nose, are assigned large weights as shown Fig. 2(e).

We utilize the statistical shape variations of identities and expressions to define vertex weights. The shape variance of 150 neutral scans and 46 expressions of the FaceWarehouse dataset is estimated (see Fig. 2(f, g)), where the lower facial region has large identity and expression variances. We define the shape variation weight $w_{\mathbf{v}}$ by the normalized variance σ_s and σ_e of the identity and the expression respectively. $w_{\mathbf{v}}(x) = \frac{1}{Z_{\mathbf{v}}}(\sigma_s(x) + \sigma_e(x))$. $Z_{\mathbf{v}}$ is set to $\max_x(\sigma_s(x) + \sigma_e(x))$ for normalization.

In order to enforce fitting of facial features, we assign weight $w_{\mathbf{f}}$ to vertices according to their distance from the region of interest $\mathcal{C}$ on the neutral 3D mesh, including the eyebrows, the eyes, the nose, the upper and lower lips (Fig. 2(h)). $w_{\mathbf{f}}(x) = \exp(-\min_{x_i \in \mathcal{C}} \|x - x_i\|^2)$.

In summary, the adaptive vertex weight w in Eq. 3 is defined as a normalized combination of above shape and feature-related weights:

$$w(x) = \sum_{\kappa \in \{\mathbf{g}, \mathbf{v}, \mathbf{f}\}} \mu_\kappa w_\kappa(x). \tag{5}$$

In our experiments, the weight w is set to zero when the distance to $\theta(I)$ is larger than 10% of the maximum span of the 3D neutral face to avoid the effect of data missing in the depth image. μ_g, μ_v, and μ_f are set at 0.3, 0.3, and 0.4, respectively.

Contextual Consistency. We expect to minimize the distance between the 3D face and its semantic counterpart of the depth image. However, the nearest neighbor searching scheme is not guaranteed to find the semantic correspondence. We introduce the contextual consistency constraint to penalize the matching pairs without similar point cloud encoding of surrounding patches. Consider a matching point pair $(p, \varphi(p))$, the contextual consistency loss E_{con} is defined as

$$E_{con} = \frac{1}{|\theta(I)|} \sum_{p_i \in \theta(I)} \|h(S(p_i)) - h(S(\varphi(p_i)))\|^2, \tag{6}$$

where $h(S(p))$ denotes a contextual feature of point p, which is defined by an encoder of 3D point cloud $S(p) \in \mathbb{R}^{3k_p}$ from a patch centered at p. In the experiments, we predefine the sampling pattern $\mathcal{P}$ with k_p points in a $5 \times 5\,\mathrm{cm}^2$ rectangular region to get the point cloud $S(p)$. The point cloud $S(\varphi(p)) \in \mathbb{R}^{3k_p}$ of matching point $\varphi(p)$ on the 3D face is obtained by the nearest neighbor search of $S(p)$ on X. The point cloud S is fed to the point cloud encoder, which results in a feature vector that is enough for reconstruction. The feature vector resulted from the encoder is defined as the contextual feature. The contextual features of facial points on training depth images can be computed in the preprocessing. A two-layer point-wise multi-layer perceptron (MLP) and max-pooling layers are used to model the encoder of point clouds, similar to the PointNet [27]. Three fully-connected (FC) layers are used for the point cloud reconstruction. The neural network parameters of the autoencoder are learned offline from point clouds of both noisy depth images and 3D face meshes. Note that by minimizing E_{con}, we enforce the semantic correspondence and favor the point pairs of the depth image and 3D face with similar contextual point clouds.

Regularization. The shape and expression parameters are regularized for a plausible 3D face. Under the assumption that the model parameters satisfy the zero-mean Gaussian distribution, we use the Tikhonov regularization as:

$$E_{reg} = \|\alpha_s\|^2 + \|\alpha_e\|^2. \tag{7}$$

Note that the extreme case by minimizing the E_{reg} is that we obtain an average 3D face located at the origins of the identity and expression subspaces. In experiments, we relax the regularization term to balance the geometric fitting and a plausible 3D face.

Loss. The overall loss function is defined as follows:

$$E = \gamma_{fit}E_{fit} + \gamma_{con}E_{con} + \gamma_{reg}E_{reg}. \tag{8}$$

The weight γ_{fit}, γ_{con}, and γ_{reg} are set at 50, 500, 2 respectively in experiments to balance the depth image fitting, the context consistency, and the regularization.

Implementation Details. We build the encoder on ResNet34 [16] for the inference of the identity, expression, and pose code vectors. The whole framework is implemented by TensorFlow. The network is optimized using the ADAM algorithm with $\beta_1 = 0.9$ and $\beta_2 = 0.999$. The learning rate is set to $1e-4$ initially and used for the first 50 epochs. Then, the learning rate is divided by 2 after every 10 epochs. The batch size is set to 32. The weight decay is set to $1e-5$. The training of the network is on a PC with a NVIDIA TITAN X GPU, and takes 50 h after 100 epochs. The 3D face estimation in the testing stage takes 0.015 s.

4   Experiments

Dataset and Metrics. We perform experiments on depth images captured by the consumer depth camera Kinect. The dataset consists of $30k$ depth images captured from 10 subjects with a resolution of 640×480. The dataset is split into a training dataset of $25k$ images and the remaining $5k$ for testing. We also use popular depth image datasets captured by Kinect: BIWI [12] and ICT-3DHP [2]. In the preprocessing, we crop the depth images to a resolution of 154×154 with the face centered.

We quantitatively evaluate the proposed method in 3D face reconstruction and attribute transfer scenarios using the mean surface deviation (MSD) metrics. The MSD measures the mean point-to-point distance between the reconstructed 3D face and the input depth image. We evaluate the rigid transformation error using the mean absolute error (MAE) between the estimated Euler angles and the ground truth.

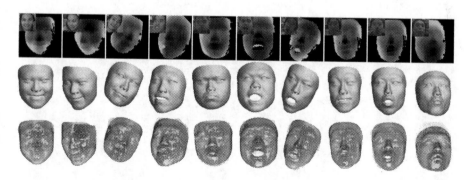

Fig. 3. 3D expressive faces obtained by the proposed method. Top: Input depth images. Middle: 3D faces estimated by the proposed method. Bottom: Overlapping of estimated 3D faces and input point clouds. The RGB images are *NOT* used in our system, which are shown as a reference.

4.1   Results

Figure 3 illustrates the face prediction from the depth images with various poses and expressions. We visualize the overlapping of depth images and estimated 3D faces. The system is capable of fitting the depth images with the asymmetric facial expression and a wide-opened mouth (the 3rd and the 6th cases in Fig. 3). We leverage contextual constraints and adaptive weighting for semantic correspondence between 3D faces and depth images without commonly used textual constraints of facial features.

Table 1. The MSD (mm) of the proposed DEN and the compared state-of-the-art.

	DEN_0	DEN_a	DEN_{ac}	DEN_{acp}	[1]	[36]	[15]	[39]	[13]	[10]	[9]
Whole face	2.11	2.07	2.03	**1.97**	2.11	3.75	2.13	4.31	3.90	3.54	4.00
Brow	1.35	1.33	1.31	**1.23**	1.65	2.73	1.82	3.02	2.86	3.15	2.82
Eye	1.80	1.78	1.79	**1.75**	2.14	2.74	1.91	4.62	4.28	3.59	2.78
Nose	2.74	2.69	2.67	**2.57**	3.92	3.98	2.84	5.67	5.08	4.34	3.48
U-Lip	1.84	1.79	1.75	**1.73**	2.60	2.99	2.39	3.63	2.61	3.32	2.71
L-Lip	2.68	2.63	2.54	**2.50**	4.00	4.03	3.42	2.90	3.48	3.13	3.73

Comparison with State-of-the-Art. We report comparisons of 3D face reconstruction as shown in Fig. 4 and Table 1. The proposed method realizes more accurate 3D face estimation than the compared alignment-based methods, such as the nonrigid ICP (NICP) [1], the 3DN [36], and the 3D-Coded [15] methods.

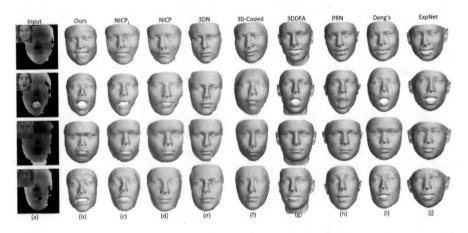

Fig. 4. Comparison of 3D face estimation. (a) Input depth image. (b) Ours. The NICP (c) with and (d) without landmarks. (e) 3DN [36]. (f) 3D-Coded [15]. (g) 3DDFA [39]. (h) PRN [13]. (i) Deng's [10]. (j) ExpNet [9].

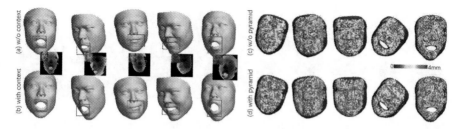

Fig. 5. Comparisons of 3D face estimation from a depth image (a) without and (b) with contextual consistency constraints. Input depth images are plotted at the corner. Comparisons of 3D face estimation errors (c) without and (d) with the point cloud pyramid.

There is no guarantee for the semantic matching in the compared alignment-based methods [1,15,36], where the reconstructed 3D face does not capture the deformable facial expression without the help of predefined landmarks. We compare the proposed method with the RGB-based methods, such as the 3DDFA [39], the PRN [13], Deng's [10], and the ExpNet [9] methods. Compared with the RGB-based methods, the proposed method, as other alignment-based methods, reduces the MSD fitting errors. The poor RGB image quality of the Kinect camera hampers textural constraints in the 3D face estimation. On the other hand, the depth image provides partial 3D geometry, facilitating the estimation of subject-specific facial geometries. Note that the patch-based contextual consistency of our method is capable of capturing the wide-opened mouth (Fig. 4).

Ablation Studies. We perform the ablation experiments to evaluate the adaptive weighting, the point cloud pyramid, and contextual consistency constraints in the proposed DEN-based framework. We compare the variants of the proposed methods, as shown in Table 1. DEN_0 denotes the method without the adaptive weighting, the point cloud pyramid, and contextual consistency constraints. DEN_a denotes the model with only the adaptive weighting. DEN_{ac} denotes the model with both the adaptive weighting and contextual consistency constraints, and DEN_{acp} with an additional point cloud pyramid. The proposed method achieves the MSD of 1.97 mm and outperforms all compared variants. Figure 5(a, b) shows the effect of the contextual consistency constraints for the semantic correspondence. We observe that the lip shape is more accurate by using the patch-based contextual consistency constraints, which favor the corresponding point pair with similar point cloud encoding in the surrounding patches and achieves semantic correspondences. The gap between the estimated 3D face and the depth image reduces when using the adaptive weighting (see Table 1). The point cloud pyramid accommodates facial geometries in different scales, which reduces fitting errors, as shown in Fig. 5(c, d).

Attribute Transfer. The proposed system realizes the dense correspondence between a 3D parametric face and the depth image. The vertex attributes of the parametric facial mesh are transferred to the nearest neighbors on the depth

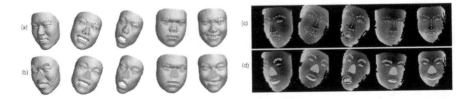

Fig. 6. Attribute transfer. Output 3D face with (a) landmarks and (b) segmentation map overlayed. Transferred (c) landmarks and (d) segmentation maps plotted on depth images (Red-detected landmarks, white-ground truth). (Color figure online)

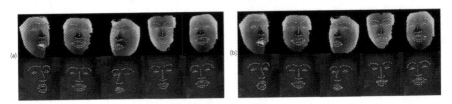

Fig. 7. Comparison of landmark location in bad illuminations using (a) the proposed method and (b) the RGB-based method [7] plotted on both depth (top) and color images (bottom). (Red-detected landmarks, white-ground truth). (Color figure online)

image, as shown in Fig. 6. We visualize the segmentation maps of facial features and 51 landmarks on the depth images. We compare the attribute transfer by our method with state-of-the-art color image-based method [7] (Fig. 7). The proposed method achieves reliable annotations regardless of the bad illuminations.

Pose Estimation. The proposed method is capable of the head pose estimation. We perform the head pose estimation on the BIWI and the ICT-3DHP dataset. We compare with prior arts [6, 12, 20–25] using depth images for 3D head tracking as shown in Table 2. The MAE regarding the Euler angles, including yaw, pitch, and roll, are reported. The proposed method outperforms the compared pose estimation methods on the BIWI and the ICT-3DHP datasets.

Table 2. The MAE ($°$) of 3D pose estimation on the BIWI and the ICT-3DHP datasets.

	BIWI						ICT-3DHP					
	Ours	[12]	[22]	[25]	[23]	[6]	Ours	[12]	[24]	[20]	[21]	[6]
Yaw	**1.2**	8.9	3.6	11.1	2.1	1.7	**2.6**	7.2	6.9	3.3	3.4	4.4
Pitch	**1.5**	8.5	2.5	6.6	2.1	1.6	**2.3**	9.4	7.1	3.1	3.2	4.9
Roll	**1.2**	7.9	2.6	6.7	2.4	1.8	**2.1**	7.5	10.5	2.9	3.3	5.1

5   Conclusion

We have presented a fully convolutional encoder network for 3D face completion and reconstruction from a single depth image, exploiting adaptive weighting and contextual constraints for semantic correspondence. We learn the encoder network in an unsupervised manner and avoid the tedious annotation. The resulting code vector of the facial pose, expression, and identity uniquely determines a 3D face that is consistent with the input depth image. The 3D face estimation technique avoids online iterative optimization and produces stable performances even under poor illuminations. The dense correspondence between the depth image and the 3D deformable model enables the automatic landmark location and feature segmentation on the depth images.

Acknowledgments. This work was supported by NSFC 61876008.

References

1. Amberg, B., Romdhani, S., Vetter, T.: Optimal step nonrigid ICP algorithms for surface registration. In: IEEE CVPR, pp. 1–8 (2007)
2. Baltrušaitis, T., Robinson, P., Morency, L.P.: 3D constrained local model for rigid and non-rigid facial tracking. In: IEEE CVPR, pp. 2610–2617 (2012)
3. Bas, A., Huber, P., Smith, W.A., Awais, M., Kittler, J.: 3D morphable models as spatial transformer networks. In: ICCV Workshop on Geometry Meets Deep Learning, pp. 904–912 (2017)
4. Blanz, V., Basso, C., Poggio, T., Vetter, T.: Reanimating faces in images and video. Comput. Graph. Forum **22**, 641–650 (2003)
5. Blanz, V., Vetter, T.: A morphable model for the synthesis of 3D faces. In: SIGGRAPH 1999, pp. 187–194 (1999)
6. Borghi, G., Venturelli, M., Vezzani, R., Cucchiara, R.: Poseidon: face-from-depth for driver pose estimation. In: IEEE CVPR, pp. 5494–5503 (2017)
7. Bulat, A., Tzimiropoulos, G.: How far are we from solving the 2D 3D face alignment problem? (and a dataset of 230,000 3D facial landmarks). In: IEEE ICCV, pp. 1021–1030 (2017)
8. Cao, C., Weng, Y., Zhou, S., Tong, Y., Zhou, K.: FaceWarehouse: a 3D facial expression database for visual computing. IEEE Trans. VCG **20**(3), 413–425 (2014)
9. Chang, F.J., Tran, A.T., Hassner, T., Masi, I., Nevatia, R., Medioni, G.: ExpNet: landmark-free, deep, 3D facial expressions. In: IEEE FG 2018, pp. 122–129 (2018)
10. Deng, Y., Yang, J., Xu, S., Chen, D., Jia, Y., Tong, X.: Accurate 3D face reconstruction with weakly-supervised learning: from single image to image set. In: IEEE CVPR Workshops (2019)
11. Fanelli, G., Dantone, M., Gall, J., Fossati, A., Van Gool, L.: Random forests for real time 3D face analysis. Int. J. Comput. Vis. **101**(3), 437–458 (2013). https://doi.org/10.1007/s11263-012-0549-0
12. Fanelli, G., Gall, J., Van Gool, L.: Real time head pose estimation with random regression forests. In: CVPR, pp. 617–624 (2011)

13. Feng, Y., Wu, F., Shao, X., Wang, Y., Zhou, X.: Joint 3D face reconstruction and dense alignment with position map regression network. In: Ferrari, V., Hebert, M., Sminchisescu, C., Weiss, Y. (eds.) Computer Vision – ECCV 2018. LNCS, vol. 11218, pp. 557–574. Springer, Cham (2018). https://doi.org/10.1007/978-3-030-01264-9_33

14. Ghiass, R.S., Arandjelović, O., Laurendeau, D.: Highly accurate and fully automatic head pose estimation from a low quality consumer-level RGB-D sensor. In: Proceedings of the 2nd Workshop on Computational Models of Social Interactions: Human-Computer-Media Communication, pp. 25–34 (2015)

15. Groueix, T., Fisher, M., Kim, V.G., Russell, B.C., Aubry, M.: 3D-CODED: 3D correspondences by deep deformation. In: Ferrari, V., Hebert, M., Sminchisescu, C., Weiss, Y. (eds.) ECCV 2018. LNCS, vol. 11206, pp. 235–251. Springer, Cham (2018). https://doi.org/10.1007/978-3-030-01216-8_15

16. He, K., Zhang, X., Ren, S., Sun, J.: Deep residual learning for image recognition. In: IEEE CVPR, pp. 770–778 (2016)

17. Jaderberg, M., Simonyan, K., Zisserman, A., et al.: Spatial transformer networks. In: NIPS, pp. 2017–2025 (2015)

18. Jin, X., Tan, X.: Face alignment in-the-wild: a survey. Comput. Vis. Image Underst. **162**, 1–22 (2017)

19. Kundu, A., Li, Y., Rehg, J.M.: 3D-RCNN: instance-level 3D object reconstruction via render-and-compare. In: IEEE CVPR, pp. 3559–3568 (2018)

20. Li, S., Ngan, K.N., Paramesran, R., Sheng, L.: Real-time head pose tracking with online face template reconstruction. IEEE Trans. PAMI **38**(9), 1922–1928 (2016)

21. Lu, S., Cai, J., Cham, T.J., Pavlovic, V., Ngan, K.N.: A generative model for depth-based robust 3D facial pose tracking. In: IEEE CVPR (2017)

22. Martin, M., Camp, F.V.D., Stiefelhagen, R.: Real time head model creation and head pose estimation on consumer depth cameras. In: 3DV (2015)

23. Meyer, G.P., Gupta, S., Frosio, I., Reddy, D., Kautz, J.: Robust model-based 3D head pose estimation. In: ICCV, pp. 3649–3657 (2015)

24. Morency, L.P.: 3D constrained local model for rigid and non-rigid facial tracking. In: IEEE CVPR (2012)

25. Padeleris, P., Zabulis, X., Argyros, A.A.: Head pose estimation on depth data based on particle swarm optimization. In: IEEE CVPR Workshops, pp. 42–49 (2012)

26. Paysan, P., Knothe, R., Amberg, B., Romdhani, S., Vetter, T.: A 3D face model for pose and illumination invariant face recognition. In: IEEE International Conference on Advanced Video and Signal Based Surveillance, pp. 296–301 (2009)

27. Qi, C.R., Su, H., Mo, K., Guibas, L.J.: PointNet: deep learning on point sets for 3D classification and segmentation. In: IEEE CVPR, pp. 652–660 (2017)

28. Richardson, E., Sela, M., Kimmel, R.: 3D face reconstruction by learning from synthetic data. In: 3DV, pp. 460–469 (2016)

29. Richardson, E., Sela, M., Or-El, R., Kimmel, R.: Learning detailed face reconstruction from a single image. In: IEEE CVPR, pp. 5553–5562 (2017)

30. Shin, D., Fowlkes, C.C., Hoiem, D.: Pixels, voxels, and views: a study of shape representations for single view 3D object shape prediction. In: IEEE CVPR, pp. 3061–3069 (2018)

31. Tewari, A., et al.: Self-supervised multi-level face model learning for monocular reconstruction at over 250 Hz. In: IEEE CVPR, pp. 2549–2559 (2018)

32. Tewari, A., et al.: MoFA: model-based deep convolutional face autoencoder for unsupervised monocular reconstruction. In: IEEE ICCV, vol. 2, p. 5 (2017)

33. Thies, J., Zollhofer, M., Stamminger, M., Theobalt, C., Nießner, M.: Face2Face: real-time face capture and reenactment of RGB videos. In: IEEE CVPR, pp. 2387–2395 (2016)
34. Tran, A.T., Hassner, T., Masi, I., Medioni, G.: Regressing robust and discriminative 3D morphable models with a very deep neural network. In: IEEE CVPR, pp. 1493–1502 (2017)
35. Wang, N., Gao, X., Tao, D., Yang, H., Li, X.: Facial feature point detection: a comprehensive survey. Neurocomputing **275**, 50–65 (2017). https://www.sciencedirect.com/science/article/abs/pii/S0925231217308202
36. Wang, W., Ceylan, D., Mech, R., Neumann, U.: 3DN: 3D deformation network. In: IEEE CVPR, pp. 1038–1046 (2019)
37. Weise, T., Bouaziz, S., Li, H., Pauly, M.: Realtime performance-based facial animation. ACM Trans. Graph. **30**, 77 (2011)
38. Yan, X., Yang, J., Yumer, E., Guo, Y., Lee, H.: Perspective transformer nets: learning single-view 3D object reconstruction without 3D supervision. In: NIPS, pp. 1696–1704 (2016)
39. Zhu, X., Liu, X., Lei, Z., Li, S.Z.: Face alignment in full pose range: a 3D total solution. IEEE Trans. PAMI **41**(1), 78–92 (2017)

Fusing IMU Data into SfM for Image-Based 3D Reconstruction

Hua Yuan[1], Yifan Ma[1(✉)], and Yun Sheng[2]

[1] School of Computer Science and Technology, East China Normal University,
Shanghai, China
{51151201062,51174506077}@stu.ecnu.edu.cn
[2] The Department of Computer Science, Liverpool John Moores University,
Liverpool, UK
y.sheng@ljmu.ac.uk

Abstract. Structure-from-Motion (SfM), one of the most extensively used image-based 3D reconstruction methods in Computer Graphics and Vision, suffers from mismatching of image feature points when input images are sparse, thus leading to miscalculation of camera rotation matrices as well as subsequent reconstruction errors. To address these problems, this paper reports an improved SfM reconstruction system and proposes to suppress the miscalculation of camera rotation matrices during Bundle Adjustment (BA) by forming a rotation constraint with Internal Measurement Unit (IMU) data collected from a smartphone, consequently improving the reconstruction precision and efficiency. More specifically, being refined by the Kalman filter, the IMU data are adopted to estimate the camera rotation matrix of each image captured by the smartphone. As the camera rotation matrix calculated by the IMU data is based on the sensor coordinate system, this paper employs the Lie Algebra theory to transform the reference frame of the rotation matrix from the sensor coordinate system to the camera coordinate system.

Keywords: Image-based 3D Reconstruction · Bundle adjustment · IMU · Structure-from-motion

1 Introduction

Image-based three-dimensional (3D) reconstruction has attracted a considerable amount of attention in recent years due to its strong applicability as well as its ease of use. Among the existing image-based reconstruction approaches, Structure-from-Motion (SfM) has been extensively studied and widely applied to 3D scene reconstruction [1], cultural heritage structure analysis [2], and topographic exploration [3], *etc.* Nevertheless, the early SfM methods, *e.g.* Bundler [4] a systematic implementation of SfM, suffer from computational complexity, calculation speed, and reconstruction completeness and robustness, especially when input images are sparse. To reduce the computational complexity of SfM,

© Springer Nature Switzerland AG 2020
N. Magnenat-Thalmann et al. (Eds.): CGI 2020, LNCS 12221, pp. 220–232, 2020.
https://doi.org/10.1007/978-3-030-61864-3_19

many global SfM algorithms [5–8] activating Bundle Adjustment (BA) only once have been proposed recently. In addition, some hardware-accelerated methods, such as VisualSFM [9] *etc.*, were presented to help speed up the calculation. To improve the reconstruction completeness and robustness of SfM, a variety of methods have been developed, e.g. COLMAP [10], but these methods still have amateur performance if the input images are sparse, that is, camera angles between two adjacent input images are relatively large, leading to difficulties in detecting and matching feature points and miscalculation of camera rotation matrices. In general, sparse input images are much in demand for convenient use, and thus the problem of how to robustly and effectively reconstruct 3D models with sparse input images has yet to be researched.

With the progress of electronic devices, all the smartphones are equipped with built-in sensors, such as Inertial Measurement Unit (IMU), *etc.*, from which approximate camera poses can be readily obtained. Recently, it is demonstrated that SfM in combination with IMU has achieved unprecedented performance in metric scale estimation of 3D models [11,12], Inertial Navigation System (INS) [13], and Robot Operating System (ROS) [14], *etc.* For example, Martinelli [11] utilized IMU data in Visual-inertial structure from motion (Vi-SfM) to estimate the absolute scale of models, absolute roll and pitch angles of the camera, and the speed in the local frame. AliAkbarpour *et al.* [15] directly exploited raw IMU and GPS data to help improve the speed of SfM reconstruction. In this paper, we employ a similar idea by improving the SfM system with auxiliary IMU data of the ubiquitous smartphone. Being elaborately refined, the IMU data, though too noisy to be directly used for 3D reconstruction [5,14], may serve as an informative and valuable prior for 3D reconstruction. Angular velocities read from the gyroscope of the IMU are used to estimate camera rotation matrices, and these estimated rotation matrices are then used to constrain their counterparts in the BA optimization by refining camera extrinsic parameters. Because our approach takes account of rotation matrices computed with the IMU data, it effectively reduces the impact of errors produced during detection and matching of image feature points, and produces robust reconstruction results with fewer input images, lessening the computational complexity.

Before combining the IMU data into SfM for 3D reconstruction, there exist two problems to be overcome beforehand: 1. Values measured by the gyroscope in the IMU are instantaneous angular velocities and cannot be directly used because raw IMU data contain much noise. 2. The camera rotation matrices calculated by the IMU data are based on the sensor coordinate system. However, the SfM reconstruction is conducted on the camera coordinate system. Therefore, two coordinate systems must be normalized prior to any further process. To resolve the first problem, we employ the Kalman filter to smooth out the rotation angles calculated by integrating angular velocities read from the gyroscope over time. To normalize the two coordinate systems, we introduce a method based on the Lie Algebra theory by transforming the reference frame of rotation matrices from the sensor coordinate system to camera coordinate system.

2   Related Work

We brief related work of SfM in this section. SfM algorithms can be divided into two types: Incremental and global SfM.

Incremental SfM: Different from global SfM which activates BA in a global manner, incremental SfM approaches [4,16–18] invoke the BA algorithm repeatedly. A typical representative of incremental SfM is Bundler [4]. Nevertheless, the worst-case time complexities of the image matching part and bundle adjustment part of Bundler are $O(n^2)$ and $O(n^4)$, respectively, which become intractable when the number of input images becomes large. Many remedies were subsequently proposed to tackle this problem. For image matching, graph-based algorithms [19,20] were proposed to improve the efficiency by pruning the original image set. However, the graph construction is time-consuming, and sometimes the completeness of reconstructed scenes cannot be guaranteed. For the bundle adjustment part, parallelism techniques [8,21] were employed to accelerate matrix computation. For example, Wu et al. [9] presented a new inexact Newton type bundle adjustment algorithm by making full use of hardware parallelism for efficient large-scale 3D scene reconstruction. Additionally, reconstruction results of the incremental approaches heavily depend on the estimated fundamental and homography matrices. Since the quality of such estimated entities directly affects that of 3D reconstruction, Moulon et al. [18] proposed to improve their estimation through a contrario methodology. Haner and Heyden [17] presented a new selection and addition rule based on covariance propagation, and pointed out that a well-determined camera should have both small estimated covariance and low reprojection error for the next view planning.

Global SfM: Since incremental SfM that incrementally reconstructs the point cloud and refines the result with BA suffers from computational complexity, global SfM methods [6,7,22–24], that optimize the reconstruction result for all input images only once have attracted much attention in recent years. These methods usually take three steps to solve the SfM problem. The first step is to compute camera rotations by rotation consistency, followed by calculating camera translations; the third step is to refine camera poses and 3D points by performing a final bundle adjustment. Many linear methods [6,22,23] were proposed for resolving global camera orientations and translations in the literatures. For example, Jiang et al. [6] proposed a linear method for global camera pose registration, in which pairwise geometries were required to perform Singular Value Decomposition (SVD) for accurate estimation of camera positions. In order to increase the reconstruction accuracy, many approaches [7,25] resort to the camera triplet. For example, Moulon et al. [7] presented a contrario trifocal tensor estimation method, from which stable translation directions could be extracted. Although these methods can improve the accuracy of reconstructed models, such triplet-based methods may incorrectly remove many useful images from the input image set if the images are out of the minimal connected dominating set. In general, the different optimization strategies adopted by the two types of SfM methods lead to different performances. Global SfM produces lower-fidelity models and is more sensitive to outliers, while incremental SfM is less efficient and more likely to accumulate drift in large-scale scenes. Although global SfM is computationally more efficient, incremental SfM is still our first choice because it can perform more precise and more complete 3D reconstruction and is more suitable for small-scale reconstruction with sparse input images. Thus, this paper focuses on incremental SfM only. The overall process of our method is divided into two stages: Estimation of rotation matrices and IMU-aided reconstruction, as outlined in Fig. 1.

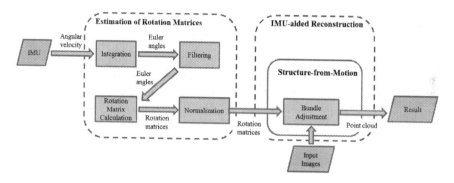

Fig. 1. The overview of our algorithm.

3 Estimation of Rotation Matrices

In estimation of the rotation matrices, the input images and IMU data are simultaneously captured by a smartphone with the Android Operating System (OS). Then the captured IMU data are filtered by the Kalman Filter. Finally, the rotation matrices are calculated from the IMU data and normalized by the Lie Algebra theory so that the reference frame of rotation matrices is in line with the camera coordinate system.

IMU Data Acquisition: Since every smartphone nowadays has an embeded IMU, it is likely to obtain the IMU data with a mobile phone while taking photos. A photographic application is designed to capture the input images and IMU data simultaneously under the Android OS. Since angular velocities of the IMU data measured by the gyroscope are instantaneous, they are integrated with respect to time in order to obtain the rotation angles:

$$\theta_i = \theta_i' + \int \omega_{it}\, dt, \quad i = x, y, z \tag{1}$$

where $\theta_x, \theta_y, \theta_z$ denote the rotation angles around X, Y, Z axes, respectively; $\theta'_x, \theta'_y, \theta'_z$ denote corresponding initial angles; $\omega_{xt}, \omega_{yt}, \omega_{zt}$ are the instantaneous angular velocities around three axes read by the gyroscope. In order to facilitate the implementation, we obtain a sequence of discrete angular velocity values by sampling the IMU readings at a rate of 50 Hz, and then convert the above integration into the following summation with a sampling time interval Δt,

$$\theta_i = \theta'_i + \sum_m \omega_{im} \Delta t, \quad i = x, y, z \tag{2}$$

where $\omega_{xm}, \omega_{ym}, \omega_{zm}$ denote discrete angular velocities with respect to the three axes. The smaller the Δt, the more accurate the result. Here Δt is set to 20 millisecond according to the sampling rate.

IMU Data Filtering: Measurement of the gyroscope suffers from interferences due to various reasons. For example, angular velocities measured by the gyroscope may generate severe run-time drift. In addition, accumulative error is produced in calculating the rotation angles (Eq. 2). To this end, the sequence of rotation angles calculated from the previous step need to be filtered before any further process. In this paper, the Kalman Filter is employed to refine the computed rotation angles and improve the accuracy of computation. When the input of a system is a sequence of observations, the Kalman Filter estimates an optimal value of the current state according to the estimated optimal value of the previous state and the currently observed value. Therefore, Kalman Filtering makes it possible to estimate the optimal value of each observation in an incomplete and noisy sequence.

Rotation Matrix Normalization: Following the Kalman filtering, we can obtain refined rotation angles θ_x, θ_y, θ_z with respect to the three axes of each shooting position. Then the rotation matrix R_{IMU} of each position can be computed through the Euler angles as

$$R_{IMU} = \begin{bmatrix} cos\theta_y cos\theta_z & sin\theta_x sin\theta_y cos\theta_z - cos\theta_x sin\theta_z & cos\theta_x sin\theta_y cos\theta_z + sin\theta_x sin\theta_z \\ cos\theta_y sin\theta_z & sin\theta_x sin\theta_y sin\theta_z + cos\theta_x cos\theta_z & cos\theta_x sin\theta_y sin\theta_z - sin\theta_x cos\theta_z \\ -sin\theta_y & sin\theta_x cos\theta_y & cos\theta_x cos\theta_y \end{bmatrix} \tag{3}$$

The reference coordinate system of this rotation matrix is the internal coordinate system of the gyroscope. Nevertheless, in the image-based 3D reconstruction system, the camera coordinate system is regarded as the reference system because we are not concerned with the actual geographic location of the scene but the relative positions between images. Consequently, the rotation matrix R_{IMU} needs to be normalized, that is, the reference frame of rotation matrix needs to be transformed from the sensor coordinate system to the camera coordinate system. Since the transformation between the sensor coordinate system and camera coordinate system is invariable for every rotation matrix, we can use a sequence of camera positions well estimated from the input images to solve the transformation matrix between two coordinate systems and we only need to calculate it once for each smartphone. Given N input images, a known set of rotation matrices in the camera coordinate system are described as $\{R_c^k | k = 1, 2, ..., N\}$, where R_c^k denotes the rotation matrix of the kth image. A set of rotation matrices in the sensor coordinate system are defined as $\{R_{IMU}^k | k = 1, 2, ..., N\}$. The transformation matrix between the sensor and camera coordinate systems satisfies the following equation:

$$R_c^k R_{trans} = R_{trans} R_{IMU}^k \tag{4}$$

where R_{trans} symbolizes the transformation matrix between the two coordinate systems. Since R_c^k and R_{IMU}^k usually contain noise, Eq. 4 can be converted into an optimization problem under the assumption that there exist multiple pairs of observations, i.e. $\{(R_c^1, R_{IMU}^1), ..., (R_c^N, R_{IMU}^N)\}$, where $N > 2$. Thus, we have

$$min \sum_{k=1}^{N} d\left(R_c^k R_{trans}, R_{trans} R_{IMU}^k\right) \tag{5}$$

where $d(\cdot)$ denotes the Euclidean distance function. To simplify the solution to this minimization problem, we adopt the following least-square method by taking advantage of a logarithm mapping method in the Lie Algebra.

$$min \sum_{k=1}^{N} \|R_{trans}\beta_k - \alpha_k\|^2 \tag{6}$$

where α_k and β_k indicate $logR_c^k$ and $logR_{IMU}^k$, the logarithm mappings of R_c^k and R_{IMU}^k, respectively. In the theory of the Lie Algebra, the logarithm mapping is defined as follows:

$$logA = \frac{\vartheta}{2sin\vartheta}\left(A - A^T\right) \tag{7}$$

where ϑ satisfies the equation $1 + 2cos\vartheta = tr(A)$, where $tr(A)$ denotes the trace of matrix A. The solution to Eq. 6 is

$$R_{trans} = \left(M^T M\right)^{-\frac{1}{2}} M^T, \quad where \quad M = \sum_{k=1}^{N} \beta_k \alpha_k^T \tag{8}$$

Resolving the transformation matrix R_{trans}, we can transform the reference frame of rotation matrices from the sensor coordinate system to the camera coordinate system according to Eq. 4 as

$$R_c = R_{trans} R_{IMU} R_{trans}^{-1} \tag{9}$$

4   IMU-aided Reconstruction

Following the normalization, the rotation matrices considered as a rotation-constraint are combined into the traditional BA optimization in order to enhance reconstruction results when the input images are sparse. The fundamental idea of the BA algorithm is to seek a joint optimal solution of camera poses and 3D points by using a non-linear least square method,

$$\min_{R_i, t_i, X_j} \sum_i \sum_j \tau_{ij} \|q_{ij} - P(R_i, t_i, X_j)\|^2 \qquad (10)$$

where (R_i, t_i) denotes camera extrinsic parameters of the ith image, $i.e.$ the rotation matrix and translation vector; X_j is the jth 3D point in the scene; $P(R_i, t_i, X_j)$ denotes a transformation model which projects a 3D point X_j onto the image plane of camera i using (R_i, t_i); q_{ij} is the corresponding 2D image coordinates of X_j in camera i; τ_{ij} is an indicator, where $\tau_{ij} = 1$ if X_j is actually projected onto the ith image, otherwise $\tau_{ij} = 0$.

If the input images are relatively sparse, the traditional BA algorithm may result in incorrect camera rotation matrices due to mismatch of the feature points. To address this problem, we introduce a rotation constrained term into the traditional BA optimization (Eq. 10) using the rotation matrices normalized previously.

$$\min_{R_i, t_i, X_j} \left(\sum_i \sum_j \tau_{ij} \|q_{ij} - P(R_i, t_i, X_j)\|^2 + \lambda \sum_i \|R_{ci} - R_i\|_F \right) \qquad (11)$$

where $\|\cdot\|_F$ denotes the Frobenius-norm; R_{ci} indicates the rotation matrix of the ith image calculated from the IMU data. The terms in the above energy function are balanced through a regular parameter λ, empirically set to 2.5. We adopt the Levenberg-Marquardt method to resolve this optimization problem.

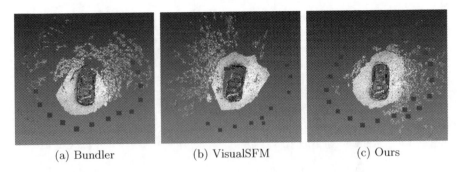

(a) Bundler   (b) VisualSFM   (c) Ours

Fig. 2. A comparison of estimated camera positions on 'Toy car'.

Table 1. Comparison of photo register rate on each image set.

Image set	Photos	Register rate			
		Bundler	VisualSFM	COLMAP	Ours
Toy car	26	57.69%	88.46%	38.46%	**100.00%**
Pencil case	10	**100.00%**	**100.00%**	**100.00%**	**100.00%**
Bear	13	**84.62%**	69.23%	**84.62%**	**84.62%**
Multiple objects	31	96.77%	**100.00%**	41.94%	**100.00%**
Rockery	20	**100.00%**	**100.00%**	95.00%	**100.00%**
Human	22	54.54%	59.09%	50%	**68.18%**

5   Experimental Evaluations

In this section, we carry out experimental evaluations by comparing our method
with some classic incremental SfM systems in 3D reconstruction including
Bundler, VisualSFM, and COLMAP. We compare these algorithms with six self-
captured image sets: 'Toy car', 'Pencil case', 'Bear', 'Multiple objects', 'Rockery',
and 'Human' acquired by a LeX520 smartphone, equipped with an 8-core CPU,
commercial IMU and uncalibrated camera. Each image set, as summarized in
Table 1, consists of images one order of magnitude fewer than those normally
required by conventional SfM algorithms. All experiments are conducted on the
same PC with a NVIDIA GT 750M GPU hosted by the Intel(R) Core(TM)
i5-3230M CPU.

Table 2. Comparison on reconstructed points(pts) and reconstruction time.

	Bundler		VisualSFM		COLMAP		Ours	
	Pts	Time	Pts	Time	Pts	Time	Pts	Time
Toy car	69123	772 s	81981	2063 s	88504	647 s	95131	731 s
Pencil case	39524	519 s	30060	981 s	59703	288 s	39467	336 s
Bear	52806	202 s	53411	1440 s	32532	341 s	70744	417 s
Multiple objects	76223	163 s	97421	2278 s	28599	725 s	71034	506 s
Rockery	84538	462 s	78193	1171 s	89388	387 s	83856	377 s
Human	37361	432 s	42729	897 s	93931	238 s	41188	180 s

On Completeness: We first evaluate the completeness of our improved SfM
algorithm by assessing camera positions estimated. Figure 2 shows the comparison among our method, Bundler, and VisualSFM on the image set 'Toy car',
with the camera positions highlighted in green. It can be seen that neither
Bundler nor VisualSFM can estimate all the camera positions properly, leading to the incomplete reconstruction results. Instead, our method can estimate

all the camera positions located around the object. In addition, all the camera positions estimated by our method are well ordered and visually in line with the initial shooting positions. Note that COLMAP is excluded in this figure because the data structure of camera positions estimated by COLMAP cannot be visualized. Since missing camera positions may cause incomplete reconstruction, we can assess completeness of the four reconstruction algorithms by comparing the number of estimated camera positions. Table 1 shows the numbers of input images and photo register rates, *i.e.* the number of photos with estimated camera positions as a percentage of the total. It can be seen that our method has the highest register rates for all the six datasets.

Next, we carry out a subjective evaluation of the four methods. Generally, in image-based 3D reconstruction systems, apart from targeted foreground, untargeted background of the input images will more or less be reconstructed as a byproduct. If only 3D model of foreground is desired, reconstructed background points will become unnecessary. In addition, there are incorrect points produced during reconstruction. In this paper, we call the unnecessary points background noise and the incorrect points outliers. It can be seen in Fig. 3(b) that many 3D points in the results of Bundler are miscalculated and visualized as outliers hanging around the models, such as the dark points in *'Multiple objects'* and face skin points in *'Human'*. This is due to inaccurate estimation of the camera positions and 3D points coordinates. The reconstruction results of VisualSFM also contain much background noise and many holes, as shown in Fig. 3(c). Moreover, there are a large number of outliers floating around the object for all the six image sets, while the results are incomplete with large missing parts for *'Toy car'* and *'Pencil case'*. It is worth noting that the point cloud of *'Multiple objects'* reconstructed by VisualSFM is slightly more complete than ours, but at the cost of computational complexity, which will be showed in the next section. COLMAP also has amateur performance on these image sets, as shown in Fig. 3(d). COLMAP can produce relatively less background noise and fewer outliers but at the price of necessary details. As shown in *'Toy car'* and *'Multiple objects'*, the point clouds reconstructed by COLMAP have large parts missing. As *'Pencil case'* comes with 10 input images only, the result of COLMAP contains a large number of outliers floating in the air. This is because there are errors during detection and matching of feature points due to the limited number of input images. These errors have a negative impact on the estimation of camera positions. In addition, as shown in Fig. 3(d), the point cloud of *'Rockery'* reconstructed by COLMAP appears unreal. In Fig. 3(e) our method can produce fewer outliers than Bundler and VisualSFM, and retain more details than COLMAP, because the camera rotation matrices calculated from the IMU data are used as *a priori* knowledge to help constrain the estimation of the camera positions.

On Efficiency: In this experiment, we compare the effectiveness of the four reconstruction algorithms by evaluating the number of reconstructed points. As shown in Table 2, our method produces reconstructed points in the same order

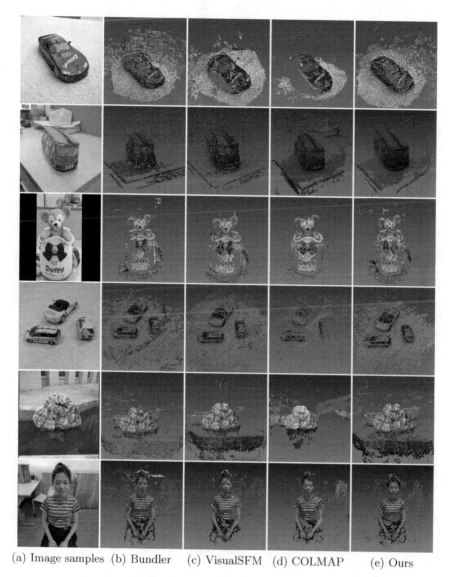

(a) Image samples (b) Bundler   (c) VisualSFM   (d) COLMAP   (e) Ours

Fig. 3. The point clouds reconstructed by different methods. The first column in turn shows samples of the original image sets, 'Toy Car', 'Pencil case', 'Bear', 'Multiple objects', 'Rockery', and 'Human'.

of magnitude as the others. However, the number of reconstructed points alone cannot strictly reflect the effectiveness of an algorithm. For example, for 'Pencil case' the number of points reconstructed by our method is almost equal to that by Bundler, but it is observed in Fig. 3 that the reconstruction result of our method is better off. This is because the points incorrectly reconstructed by

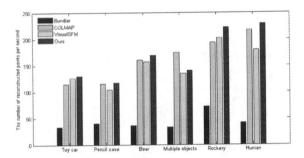

Fig. 4. Comparison of the number of reconstructed points per unit time.

Bundler are also counted as reconstructed points. Therefore, we use runtime of reconstruction to evaluate the computational performance of the algorithms. Table 2 shows the time consumed by the four methods in reconstructing the six image sets. However, the more the reconstructed points, the more time it takes. To this end, we take both the runtime and number of reconstructed points into account by proposing an objective comparison measure, which divides the number of reconstructed points by unit time, as shown in Fig. 3. Our method outperforms the others in five out of six image sets and finishes a runner-up for 'Multiple objects'.

6   Concluding Remarks

This paper proposes to take advantage of the IMU of ubiquitous smartphone by fusing the IMU data into the BA optimization of SfM to enhance the precision and efficiency of reconstruction. Our reconstruction strategy can be implemented with not only smartphone but any apparatus equipped with both the visual sensor and IMU, such as robot and drone, etc. It is worth noting that our reconstruction scheme cannot cope with transparent stuff (refer to the missing windscreen of reconstructed 'Toy car' in Fig. 3) or anything with smooth texture due to failure of the embedded feature matching engine in SfM (refer to the absent parts of reconstructed 'Bear' and the black skirt of reconstructed 'Human' in Fig. 3). However, such problems exist in all the SfM algorithms (refer to Fig. 3). Our strategy differs from the one reported in [2], where the raw IMU data were directly used as the rotation matrices in Eq. 10 to reduce the computational complexity. Our method with the IMU data as a constraint aims to suppress the miscalculation of camera rotation matrices caused by sparse inputs and to reconstruct 3D points more precisely. Moreover, it is worth mentioning many visual-inertial simultaneous localization and mapping (SLAM) systems have adopted IMU [26,27]. However, SLAM systems focusing more on localization serve different purposes from SfM that is mainly used in the context of 3D reconstruction or relevant applications. SLAM system requires a higher frequency of IMU data to achieve real-time performance, which is unnecessary and computationally expensive for those SfM methods. Note that in this paper we only take the gyroscope into account. As uncalibrated accelerators suffer from great noises, fusing the reading of an uncalibrated accelerator will not help improve the reconstruction result.

References

1. Pollefeys, M., et al.: Visual modeling with a hand-held camera. Int. J. Comput. Vision **59**(3), 207–232 (2004)
2. Ducke, B., Score, D., Reevies, J.: Multiview 3D reconstruction of the archaeological site at weymouth from image series. Comput. Graph. **35**(2), 375–382 (2011)
3. Alfredsen, K., Haas, C., Tuhtan, J.A., Zinke, P.: Brief communication: mapping river ice using drones and structure from motion. Cryosphere **12**(2), 627 (2018)
4. Snavely, N., Seitz, S.M., Szeliski, R.: Modeling the world from internet photo collections. Int. J. Comput. Vision **80**(2), 189–210 (2018)
5. Crandall, D.J., Owens, A., Snavely, N., Huttenlochor, D.P.: SfM with MRFs: discrete-continuous optimization for large-scale structure from motion. IEEE Trans. PAMI **35**(12), 2841–2853 (2013)
6. Jiang, N.-J., Cui, Z.-P, Tan, P.: A global linear method for camera pose registration. In: IEEE ICCV, pp. 481-488 (2013)
7. Moulon, P., Monasse, P., Marlet, R.: Global fusion of relative motions for robust, accurate and scalable structure from motion. In: IEEE ICCV, pp. 3248–3255 (2013)
8. Strecha, C., Pylvänäinen, T., Fua, P.: Dynamic and scalable large scale image reconstruction. In: IEEE CVPR, pp. 406–413 (2010)
9. Wu, C.-C., Agarwal, S., Curless, B., Seitz, S.M.: Multicore bundle adjustment. In: IEEE CVPR, pp. 3057–3064 (2011)
10. Schonberger, J.L., Frahm, J.-M.: Structure-from-motion revisited. In: IEEE CVPR, pp. 4104–4113 (2016)
11. Martinelli, A.: Visual-inertial structure from motion: Observability and resolvability. PhD thesis(2013)
12. Mustaniemi, J., Kannala, J., Särkkä, S., Matas, J., Heikkilä, J.: Inertial-based scale estimation for structure from motion on mobile devices. In: IEEE Intelligent Robots and Systems (IROS), pp. 4394–4401 (2017)
13. Tharp, J., Woolley, B.G.: Enhancing inertial navigation with structure from motion trajectory estimates. In: AIAA Guidance, Navigation, and Control Conference (2016)
14. Dewangan, K., Saha, A., Vaiapury, K., Dasgupta, R.: 3D environment reconstruction using mobile robot platform and monocular vision. In: Choudhary, R.K., Mandal, J.K., Auluck, N., Nagarajaram, H.A. (eds.) Advanced Computing and Communication Technologies. AISC, vol. 452, pp. 213–221. Springer, Singapore (2016). https://doi.org/10.1007/978-981-10-1023-1_22
15. AliAkbarpour, H., Palaniappan, K., Seetharaman, G.: Fast structure from motion for sequential and wide area motion imagery. In: IEEE ICCV Workshops, pp. 34–41 (2015)
16. Chatterjee, A., Govindu, V.M.: Efficient and robust large-scale rotation averaging. In: IEEE ICCV, pp. 521–528 (2013)
17. Haner, S., Heyden, A.: Covariance propagation and next best view planning for 3D reconstruction. In: Fitzgibbon, A., Lazebnik, S., Perona, P., Sato, Y., Schmid, C. (eds.) ECCV 2012. LNCS, vol. 7573, pp. 545–556. Springer, Heidelberg (2012). https://doi.org/10.1007/978-3-642-33709-3_39

18. Moulon, P., Monasse, P., Marlet, R.: Adaptive structure from motion with a contrario model estimation. In: Lee, K.M., Matsushita, Y., Rehg, J.M., Hu, Z. (eds.) ACCV 2012. LNCS, vol. 7727, pp. 257–270. Springer, Heidelberg (2013). https://doi.org/10.1007/978-3-642-37447-0_20
19. Lou, Y., Snavely, N., Gehrke, J.: MatchMiner: efficient spanning structure mining in large image collections. In: Fitzgibbon, A., Lazebnik, S., Perona, P., Sato, Y., Schmid, C. (eds.) ECCV 2012. LNCS, vol. 7573, pp. 45–58. Springer, Heidelberg (2012). https://doi.org/10.1007/978-3-642-33709-3_4
20. Snavely, N., Seitz, S.M., Szeliski, R.: Skeletal graphs for efficient structure from motion. In: IEEE CVPR, vol. 1, pp. 1–8 (2008)
21. Choudhary, S., Gupta, S., Narayanan, P.J.: Practical time bundle adjustment for 3D reconstruction on the GPU. In: Kutulakos, K.N. (ed.) ECCV 2010. LNCS, vol. 6554, pp. 423–435. Springer, Heidelberg (2012). https://doi.org/10.1007/978-3-642-35740-4_33
22. Govindu, V.M.: Combining two-view constraints for motion estimation. In: IEEE CVPR, vol. 2, pp. 218–225 (2001)
23. Rother, C.: Linear multi-view reconstruction of points, lines, planes and cameras using a reference plane. In: IEEE ICCV, pp. 1210–1217 (2003)
24. Wilson, K., Snavely, N.: Robust global translations with 1DSfM. In: Fleet, D., Pajdla, T., Schiele, B., Tuytelaars, T. (eds.) ECCV 2014. LNCS, vol. 8691, pp. 61–75. Springer, Cham (2014). https://doi.org/10.1007/978-3-319-10578-9_5
25. Havlena, M., Torii, A., Pajdla, T.: Efficient structure from motion by graph optimization. In: Daniilidis, K., Maragos, P., Paragios, N. (eds.) ECCV 2010. LNCS, vol. 6312, pp. 100–113. Springer, Heidelberg (2010). https://doi.org/10.1007/978-3-642-15552-9_8
26. Liu, H.-M., Chen, M.-Y., Zhang, G.-F., Bao, H.-J., Bao, Y.-Z.: Ice-ba: incremental, consistent and efficient bundle adjustment forvisual-inertial slam. In: IEEE CVPR (2018)
27. Qin, T., Li, P.-L., Shen, S.-J.: Vins-mono: a robust and versatile monocular visual-inertial state estimator. IEEE Trans. Rob. **34**(4), 1004–1020 (2017)

Physics-Guided Sound Synthesis for Rotating Blades

Siqi Xu and Shiguang Liu[✉]

College of Intelligence and Computing, Tianjin University, Tianjin 300350, China
lsg@tju.edu.cn

Abstract. This paper focuses on sound synthesis for rotating blades such as fans, helicopters and wind turbines, which is common in both real world and computer games though has received little attention until now. In this paper, we propose a novel physics-guided sound synthesis method for rotating blades. First, we propose an efficient rotating blade sound solver for Ffowcs Williams-Hawkings (FW-H) equation, which can greatly reduce the computational complexity. Then, inspired by the good expression of Mel-scale Frequency Cepstral Coefficients (MFCC) in speech recognition, we design a new sound parameter A_MFCC to enrich the sound. Specifically, while ensuring the sensitivity of MFCC to formants, we improve MFCC to make it well show the properties of sound timbre and loudness, so that it can be well applied in sound synthesis. Finally, based on the observation that rotating blade sound has similar qualities with noise, we specially devise a method to further enrich the sounding result by combining noise and A_MFCC. Experimental results demonstrated that our method can achieve great sounding results for various rotating blades.

Keywords: Visual-audio · Sound synthesis · Physics-based simulation · Rotating blades

1 Introduction

Air is everywhere. It is invisible, but the sound it makes is all around us such as whirring of an electric fan and the clatter of a helicopter. These sounds are very common in our daily life, computer games and movies. Although we can achieve realistic visual simulation for these scenes, the synthesis of sound incurred by air flow such as the sound of rotating blades, has not been well presented until now. *What causes the sound of rotating blades?* When a rotating blade of a certain thickness causes periodic expansion and contraction of the air on the propeller disc, it generates monopole sound. When the load on the rotating blade exerts a periodic thrust on the gas over the disc, it would also lead to dipole sound. For rotating blades, each area element in motion is its own monopole and dipole

Supported by the Natural Science Foundation of China under grant nos. 61672375 and 61170118.

N. Magnenat-Thalmann et al. (Eds.): CGI 2020, LNCS 12221, pp. 233–244, 2020.
https://doi.org/10.1007/978-3-030-61864-3_20

sound source. As a result, different sizes, angles and even rotation speeds can produce radically different sounds, so that using pre-recorded recordings to play them is quite difficult. Meanwhile, the existing methods cannot synthesize the sound synchronized with it in real time.

Currently, sound synthesis has been developed for more than two decades in computer graphics. However, the most common one is solid sound synthesis [1,12], which is mostly based on modal analysis. In contrast, we focus on sound synthesis for blade rotation, of which the sound source is air rather than solid objects, and therefore the above methods are not applicable. There also have been many studies on fluid sound synthesis. The sounds of flames [14] and water [2] have been extensively studied. Air can be regarded a type of special fluid, but has quite sounding properties compared with the above fluids. However, there are few studies on air sound synthesis. Dobashi et al. [3] proposed a real-time aerodynamic synthesis method based on CFD, which can synthesize the sound of sword brandishing and wind blowing. This method uses CFD to create sound textures and store them, which are then used to synthesize aerodynamic sound in real time according to the motion of the object or the speed of the wind. This method can successfully deal with aerodynamic sound by objects with simple structures such as a sword, that is not applied for our case with more complex structures. Moreover, this method relies on complicated CFD calculation, making real time sound synthesis unpractical. Rod et al. [11] proposed a method to simulate propeller sound by leveraging on the model proposed in [9]. This method is a typical one based on semi-empirical equation, that can synthesize sound according to the flight paths in real time. However, due to the limitations of the empirical/semi-empirical theoretical method itself, only the model of the propeller sound can be calculated, and this method only provides an approximate solution, with relatively rough effect.

In addition, there are also studies on sound in the fields of physics and signal processing. In the field of physics, a subject called aeroacoustics, focuses on the acoustic problems of fluid dynamics. In 1952, Lighthill [6] pioneered the Lighthill equation describing the sound production of air flow, which is of great significance to the solution of aeroacoustics equation. Afterwards, Ffowcs Williams and Hawkings [13] introduced the known Ffowcs Williams-Hawkings (FW-H) equation. Currently, in the aeroacoustics field, sound synthesis calculates near field by using CFD softwares, and solves sound pressure by sound pressure equation for far field. The CFD software calculation is very complicated, which usually consumes a lot of time, and the physics of turbulence phenomenon is also complex to solve. As for signal processing, there are also some methods [10] to synthesize sound. However, the signal processing-based method suffers from lacking automatic analysis strategy to extract the parameters from the animation, that is difficult to generate sounding results highly synchronized with the animation.

In this paper, we propose a physics-guided sound synthesis method for rotating blades. According to the physical properties, we classify rotating blade sound into load noise and thickness noise. We then approximate the solution and extract the parameters, and enrich the sound with the characteristics of rotating blade sound similar to noise. Since our method is guided by physical principles, it thus can synthesize the sound of rotating blades with different sizes and motion states, ensuring the synchronization with animation. In addition, our method does not rely on predictive calculation and occupies less memory space overhead. Moreover, our method is a lightweight operation with high efficiency that can synthesize sound in real time. The contributions of our method can be summarized as follows: 1) A novel, efficient method for rotating blade sound synthesis is presented, which does not need any precomputation. Moreover, our method is efficient without taking much space storage. 2) We propose a new optimization solver for the rotating blade sound model. It is fast and can achieve high-quality sounding results at the same time. 3) We design a rotating blade sound enrichment algorithm, which exploits the noise properties and A_MFCC to produce more realistic results through simple operations.

2   Method Overview

Figure 1 illustrates the whole framework of our method, which is composed of two main components, namely physics-guided sound synthesis (Sect. 3) and sound enrichment (Sect. 4). First, the animation of the rotating blade is simulated as input to system. Then, according to the rotating blade sound characteristics, it is divided into thickness noise and load noise to calculate respectively. In order to solve the problem of low computational efficiency, we design a new optimization solution. Next, we extract A_MFCC from the generated sound in the previous step. The experiment demonstrates that the proposed A_MFCC is effective, that can represent the sound characteristics very well. Finally, we combine A_MFCC and the noise characteristics of rotating blade sound to output the final result.

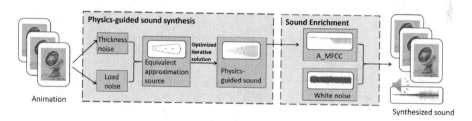

Fig. 1. The framework of our method. Note that there are two main regions in the framework, namely physics-guided sound synthesis and sound enrichment. The orange region shows the process of using physical principles to generate sound synchronized with animation. The green region represents the process of sound enrichment by A_MFCC and white noise. (Color figure online)

3   Physics-Guided Sound Synthesis

The basic theory in aeroacoustics is the Lighthill equation which is proposed by Lighthill in 1952 [6]. To solve the sound caused by moving objects, Ffowcs

Williams and Hawkings [13] extended the Lighthill equation and proposed the Ffowcs Williams-Hawkings (FW-H) equation. Afterwards, Farassat [4] proposed the time domain method for solving FW-H equation. In order to make the solution to the FW-H equation tractable, Farassat divided the sound of rotating blade into *thickness noise* and *load noise* and gave them integral representation, respectively. *Thickness noise* occurs when continuous insertion or removal of a rotating blade of a certain thickness in a fluid. It is equivalent to a monopole sound source. This sound is defined as thickness noise, that can be expressed by Eq. (1),

$$4\pi p_T(x,t) = \int_{f=0} \left[\frac{\rho_0 V_n (r\dot{M}_{ai}\hat{r}_i)}{r^2 (1 - M_{ar})^3}\right]_{ret} ds + \int_{f=0} \left[\frac{c_0 M_{ar} - c_0 M_a^2)}{r^2 (1 - M_{ar})^3}\right]_{ret} ds \quad (1)$$

where c_0 is the speed of sound in a quiescent medium, ρ_0 is the density of air, f is the surface equation of the boundary of a moving object, V_n is the projection of the velocity of object onto the outward normal vector to the surface, r is the distance between the observer and the source, $\hat{r}_i$ is the unit radiation vector, M_a is the local Mach number of the source, M_{ar} is the Mach number of the source in the radiation direction, and $\dot{M}_{ai}$ is the Mach number of the motional element derivative of time. *Load noise* is caused by the object moving in a fluid, that will be subjected to pressure from the surrounding fluid. With the arrival of the blade, the fluid in the plane of the rotating blade will be constantly impacted by the tension and the resistance on the rotating blade. This sound source is a dipole sound source, written as

$$4\pi p_L(x,t) = \frac{1}{c_0} \int_{f=0} \left[\frac{\dot{l}_i \hat{r}_i}{r(1 - M_{ar})^2}\right]_{ret} ds + \int_{f=0} \left[\frac{l_r - l_i M_{ai}}{r^2(1 - M_{ar})^2}\right]_{ret} ds$$
$$+ \frac{1}{c_0} \int_{f=0} \left[\frac{l_r(r\dot{M}_{ai}\hat{r}_i + c_0 M_{ar} - c_0 M_a^2)}{r^2 (1 - M_{ar})^3}\right]_{ret} ds \quad (2)$$

where $\dot{l}_i$ is the derivative of the load with respect to time. We followed the above idea and separately handled thickness noise and load noise. In contrast, we optimized their solution and greatly improved the computational efficiency.

3.1   Optimized Solution

It is obviously complicated to give a direct integral of Eqs. (1) and (2). Instead, we propose an optimization iterative solution. Our method improves the computational efficiency mainly through the following two ways: 1) Equivalent approximation source. 2) Optimized iterative solution.

First, inspired by the idea of physical equivalent substitution, we propose an equivalent approximation source method to set around complex integrals. More specifically, we place four source points on the blade surface as shown in Fig. 2, where c is the chord length of the blade and d is the thickness of the blade. We place S_2 in the middle of the blade, and to better calculate the impact of blade

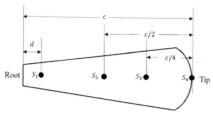

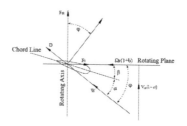

Fig. 2. Equivalent approximation source placement.

Fig. 3. A two-dimensional plane of a blade.

edges, we place S_1 and S_4 at the root and tip, respectively. Since the speed at the root is too small, S_1 is placed at a distance d from the blade root (In our experiment, d is set as the blade thickness). Furthermore, due to the source gain is proportional to v^6 [5] and v of positions near the tip is greater than that of other positions, the sound sources there would have a greater effect on the sound. Accordingly, we place another sound source point S_3 near the tip of the blade. And S_3 is $c/4$ far from the tip. We then solve for each of these sources instead of complex integrals. We also experimented with the results of placing more sound source points. Although the results produced by this step can be more accurate, it would take a lot of time to calculate. But it is worth noting that the information extracted in the next Section (Sect. 4) is not much different. In other words, more sound source points have little effect on the final result of our method. Hence, we place our sound source point as shown in Fig. 2.

Then, we optimize the solution of the Blade Element Momentum (BEM) theory which is widely used in physics to obtain the blade performance parameters by iteratively solving a set of algebraic equations. However, the traditional BEM algorithm suffers from multiple iterations and thus takes a long time to calculate. To this end, we design a new optimized iterative solution to solve BEM. First, as shown in Fig. 3, a blade can been seen as a two-dimensional plane. The inflow angle φ is written as

$$tan\varphi = \frac{V_\infty(1-a)}{r\Omega(1+b)} \tag{3}$$

where V_∞ is the wind speed, r is the radius, Ω is the angular speed, a is the axial induction factor, and b is tangential induction factor. According to the Blade Element theory, the thrust dT generated by each area element can be expressed by $dT = \frac{1}{2}\rho W^2 Bc(C_L cos\varphi + C_D sin\varphi)dr$, meanwhile the torque dM can be expressed by $dM = \frac{1}{2}\rho W^2 Bc(C_L sin\varphi - C_D cos\varphi)rdr$, where W is relative speed of airflow, B is blade number, C_L and C_D are respectively the lift and drag coefficients which are obtained from the NACA standard airfoil. Then, according to the Momentum theory, dT and dM can also be described as $dT = 4\pi\rho V_\infty^2 a(1-a)rdr$, $dM = 4\pi\rho V_\infty(\Omega r)b(1-a)r^2 dr$. Then the above equations can be combined and derived,

$$\frac{a}{1-a} = \frac{Bc}{8\pi r} \frac{C_L sin\varphi + C_D cos\varphi}{sin\varphi cos\varphi} \tag{4}$$

$$\frac{b}{1+b} = \frac{Bc}{8\pi r} \frac{C_L sin\varphi - C_D cos\varphi}{sin\varphi cos\varphi} \tag{5}$$

Next, we use Eqs. (4) and (5) to solve the required physical parameters iteratively. Specifically, we first set the initial values of a_0 and b_0 as the values of the same radius but the previous rotation speed, instead of letting a_0 and b_0 start from 0 each time, which greatly saves the required number of iterations. Then, we use Eq. (3) to calculate φ, and we calculate a, b by Eqs. (4) and (5). After that, we set the initial threshold $error$ to 0.001. Next, we judge whether $abs(a_0 - a) < error$ and $abs(b_0 - b) < error$ are true. If so, the iteration end; if not, a_0 and b_0 are replaced with a and b to calculate iteratively again. To prevent too many iterations, we also set a maximum number of iterations (e.g., 100). When the maximum number of iterations is exceeded, we update $error = error \times 10$. Typically, we end up with fewer than 10 iterations. Afterwards, we can calculate the load on the blade evaluated from this step.

3.2   Delay-Time Algorithm

Due to that sound calculations are performed at all source points on the blade surface, not all sound sources can reach for a certain observation position x at a certain observation time t. Thus we need to compute the time equation,

$$g = t - \frac{r}{c_0} \tag{6}$$

where r is the distance between the observation position x and each source. When $g >= 0$, we solve the sound pressure equation $p = p_T + p_L$. When $g < 0$, we consider that this source point does not contribute to the observation position at this time, and we calculate $p = 0$. We then superimpose each sound source and estimate the result at that time at that position.

4   Sound Enrichment

To make the results sound richer and more pleasing, we need to enrich the sound in the previous step. Considering that the sound of rotating blade has the property of noise, we exploit the white noise and the sound parameters extracted from the previous step for sound enrichment. We design a new parameter, called A_MFCC, for producing more realistic results. Our method is computationally efficient and consumes little memory space.

MFCC is a sound parameter that has achieved great success in speech recognition. However, a naive transfer of MFCC to our case would easily lead to undesired effects, i.e., the undulation of sound result would be weakened. Therefore, we improve MFCC as follows. The fifth dimension c_5 and the sixth dimension c_6 of MFCC are used in our method (By experiments we found that these two dimensions can achieve the best effect). First, we calculate the average of these two dimensional parameters namely cc_{56} ($cc_{56} = \frac{c_5 + c_6}{2}$). Then, to ensure that the parameter values are within a proper range, we handle it by,

$$mfcc' = log(\frac{cc_{56} - min\,cc_{56}}{max\,cc_{56} - min\,cc_{56}}) \tag{7}$$

The $mfcc'$ could not well show the characteristics of sound, therefore we also use the amplitude a. And in order to make this parameter a' insensitive to small differences in sound fluctuations and good sensitivity to large differences, we reformulate it as $a' = e^{\frac{a-\mu}{\sigma}}$ where μ is the mean of amplitude and σ is the standard deviation of amplitude. Next, we define $\tilde{a}$ as,

$$\tilde{a} = \begin{cases} 1, & a'_t < 0.8 \times max\,a' \\ a'_t + \varepsilon \times rand(), & a'_t >= 0.8 \times max\,a' \end{cases} \tag{8}$$

According to the experiments, we discover that when ε is larger, the discrete noise (we explain the discrete noise in Sect. 5.2) is more obvious, and when ε is smaller, the sound result is smoother. We can change ε to get the desired style result (In our experiments, ε is set to 0.5). In order to combine the sound characteristics expressed by MFCC and the amplitude, we finally define A_MFCC as

$$a\_mfcc = mfcc' \times \tilde{a} \tag{9}$$

A_MFCC in the fan scene is shown in Fig. 4. The fan speeds up gradually in this scene. As can be seen from Fig. 4, A_MFCC can well reflect the sound characteristics of this scene. In the first half of the period, the A_MFCC's fluctuation speed is slow and its amplitude is relatively gentle, while in the second half of the period, its fluctuation becomes faster, and its amplitude becomes larger. Finally, we use the idea of signal processing to treat A_MFCC as the excitation signal. We convolve it with the noise to get the final result.

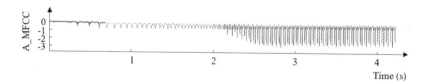

Fig. 4. A_MFCC of the fan scene.

5   Results and Discussions

We tested our method in a variety of rotating blade scenarios. All experiments were conducted in the same environment: Intel Core i7-7700 CPU, Nvidia GeForce GT 730 GPU, and 8 GB RAM.

5.1 Rotating Blade Scenarios

The sounds of various rotating blade scenes were simulated, including fan, helicopter, and wind turbine, to test the applicability of our method. In different
scenes, we changed rotation speeds and relative positions of the observer and
the sound source. We also gradually changed of rotation speed which is the most
common situation in real world to test our method. And our method all achieved
a good result. Moreover, our method runs efficiently. In the fan scene, it costs
6.9 s to synthesize the sound and the length of the video is about 4 s. In the
helicopter scene, it takes 8.1 s to synthesize a video sound of 6 s. And it costs
5.2 s to synthesize the sound of a wind turbine, while the video length is about
4 s. In contrast, traditional physical simulations like CFD would take hours to
calculate the above accompanied sound.

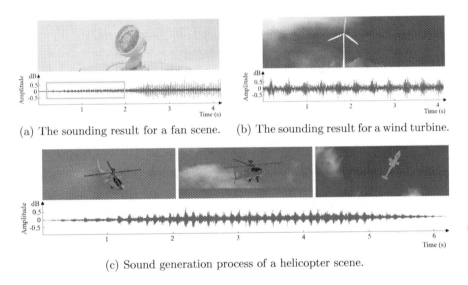

(a) The sounding result for a fan scene.   (b) The sounding result for a wind turbine.

(c) Sound generation process of a helicopter scene.

Fig. 5. The sound results of rotating blade scenarios. (Color figure online)

Fan Sound. We synthesized the sound of a fan. In order to better approximate
the real scene, the fan starts the acceleration process, and we set the fan rotation
speed from 0 rpm to 2400 rpm gradually, then keep the same speed. Our result
is shown in Fig. 5(a). It can be seen that, both the amplitude and the density
of the discrete noise (we explain the discrete noise later in Sect. 5.2) at the
beginning (shown in the green box) are less than those at the second half, which
is consistent with our observation.

Wind Turbine Sound. We also synthesized the sound of a wind turbine scene,
which, unlike the fan and helicopter, has a relatively slow speed. Therefore, there
is a higher requirement for sound synchronization. Figure 5(b) shows the result

of our synthesized wind turbine sound. It demonstrates that our method can also well produce the sound for a scene with an object moving at a low speed.

Helicopter Sound. We simulated a scene of a helicopter taking off and generate the corresponding sound using our method. As shown in Fig. 5(c), from left to right, it is the helicopter propeller gradually accelerating on the ground, the helicopter flying away from the ground, and the helicopter flying into the sky, respectively. Combined with the bottom waveform, it can be seen that our result can maintain great synchronization with the corresponding animation. We suggest the reader to hear the accompanied video for more details.

5.2 Comparison with the State-of-the-Art Method and the Real Recording

Rob et al.'s method [11] is specially designed for the helicopter scene, which can simulate the best helicopter sound as far as we know. Therefore, we compare our helicopter sound result with Rob et al.'s result. Figure 6(a) is our result, (b) is Rod et al.'s result, and (c) is the real recording. It can be seen from the figure that both our method and Rod et al.'s method can present the sound gradient effect about a helicopter flying far, but our result is closer to the real sound than Rod et al.'s. Specifically, the typical helicopter sound has two types, discrete noise and broadband noise. In Fig. 6(c), the green circle is the discrete noise. Obviously, Rod et al.'s result does not perform well in this respect, and in contrast, our method is more approximate to the real sound. As our method is based on the FW-H equation, our result sounds more realistically. As shown in Fig. 6, our result clearly shows the waveform characteristics of discrete noise and broadband noise, which proves that our optimized solution can reproduce correct physical characteristics.

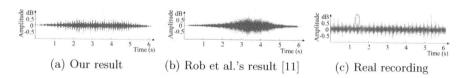

(a) Our result (b) Rob et al.'s result [11] (c) Real recording

Fig. 6. Comparison with the state-of-the-art method. (Color figure online)

Figure 7 shows the comparison of the spectrograms between our result and the real recording of a fan scene. Figure 7(a) is the spectrogram of our result and (b) is the spectrogram of a real recording. As can be seen that our result appears similar to the spectral distribution of real sound, which illustrates the optimized solution and sound enrichment in our method do not affect the spectral distribution of sound. Both of our result and real sound have the higher content of 0-10kHz and the lower content of 10–20 kHz.

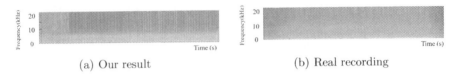

(a) Our result   (b) Real recording

Fig. 7. Comparison between our result and the real recording of a fan scene.

5.3   User Study

To further demonstrate the effectiveness of our method, we designed three user studies to evaluate our method. We tested 50 participants (23 women and 27 men) with a median age of 35, all of whom have normal hearing and vision. The details of the experiment are illustrated as follows.

The first experiment is used to verify the validity of sound enrichment of our method. In this experiment, participants are shown with a series of pages. Each page shows one scene of our demo scenarios (fan, helicopter and wind turbine) and two audio clips which are the result without sound enrichment and the result with sound enrichment of our method. Then, participants are asked to choose which sound is more consistent with the video. Figure 8 shows the selection ratio of the experiment. It can be seen that most participants agree that the result with sound enrichment is better, that can illustrate the effectiveness of our method.

The second experiment is to verify the similarity between the real recording and the sound synthesized by our method. In this experiment, participants can hear a series of audio clips including three real recording rotating blade sounds, two sounds synthesized by Rob et al.'s method [11] and three sounds from our method. Meanwhile, participants only know that these audio clips are sound of rotating blades but they do not know which scene it is. Each participant is asked to tag the sound (1 for real recording and 0 for synthesized sound). Figure 9 shows the sum of the scores for each audio clip. It can be observed from this figure that most of our results are higher than that of Rod et al.'s and slightly lower than the real recording. However, there is a low score of our method (ours-3), which is the sound of wind turbine, due to that our method still has some limitations in sound synthesis for large outdoor scenes. In this scene, the sound is greatly affected by sound reflections or diffraction [7,8], which our method does not involve.

The third experiment is used to evaluate the quality of the sound synthesized by our method. Each participant is shown three test pages (fan, helicopter and wind turbine, respectively), and on each page the participant is presented with a silent animated clip and two or three audio clips to listen. The fan and wind turbine scenes have two audio clips which are separately the result from our method and real recording. Helicopter scene has three audio clips which are result from our method, real recording, and result from Rob et al.'s method [11] which is only applicable to helicopter sound. Participants are asked to score each audio clip from 1 to 10 depending on the matching degree of the animation and audio,

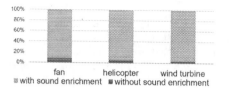
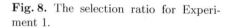

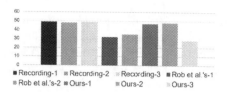

Fig. 8. The selection ratio for Experiment 1.

Fig. 9. The sum of the scores for Experiment 2.

where "Not match" scores 1 and "Very much match" scores 10. Table 1 shows the mean and variance of the scores. Subsequently, we use a paired T-test to check whether there are significant differences on scores in groups. The results of the T-test are also collected in Table 1. Among them, fan, helicopter-1, and wind turbine are the result from our method comparing with the real recording, and the scores are not significantly different ($p > 0.005$). However, it is notable that this is because we chose the real recording that matches the motion of animation as much as possible. In reality, due to the variability of animation, recording collection will become very difficult, it cannot be widely used. Helicopter-2 is a comparison between our method and Rod et al.'s method. It can be observed from Table 1 that we can observe that, the scores are significantly different ($p < 0.005$), due to that Rob et al.'s method relies on semi-empirical model which has a rough sound, leading to a slightly lower score than ours.

Table 1. The user study results for Experiment 3.

Scenario	Mean score of ours	Var. score of ours	Mean score of recording	Var. score of recording	Mean score of Rob et al.'s	Var. score of Rob et al.'s	T value	P value
Fan	7.14	2.37	6.62	1.26	—	—	1.7256	0.0907
Hel.-1	7.46	1.27	7.36	2.11	–	–	0.3769	0.7079
Hel.-2	7.46	1.27	–	–	5.88	2.68	5.9950	0.0000
Wind tur	6.04	2.69	6.38	2.24	–	–	−1.1068	0.2738

6 Conclusion and Future Works

In this paper, we proposed a physics-guided sound synthesis method for rotating blades, guided by the physics theory of the FW-H equation. In order to solve the problem of computational efficiency, we presented an optimization solution. Specifically, we designed an equivalent source approximation method to avoid complex integral problems, and devised a new optimization solution to significantly reduce the number of iterative solutions as well. We then boldly enriched the results by combining noise with the new parameters we propose. Various experiments show that our results are close to the real record and not inferior to the state-of-the-art semi-empirical method.

However, our method is not without limit. For example, the sound of rotating blades is not only pneumatic sound, and the friction of mechanical devices such as gears may also contribute to the sounding result, however, our method does not consider the sound of this part. Another disadvantage of our method is that when the sound source lies in the complex and large outdoor scenes, our result is not convincing, since in these cases the sound propagation would play an vital role that is not involved in our method, and at this time the effects of wide 3D acoustic field localization and the Doppler effect cannot be ignored either. How to add these effects is an important factor to enhance the sense of reality of our sound, which is also a direction of our future research.

References

1. Chadwick, J.N., An, S.S., James, D.L.: Harmonic shells: a practical nonlinear sound model for near-rigid thin shells. ACM Trans. Graph. **28**(5), 119 (2009)
2. Cheng, H., Liu, S.: Haptic force guided sound synthesis in multisensory virtual reality (VR) simulation for rigid-fluid interaction. In: IEEE Conference on Virtual Reality and 3D User Interfaces, VR2019, Osaka, Japan, 23–27 March 2019, pp. 111–119 (2019)
3. Dobashi, Y., Yamamoto, T., Nishita, T.: Real-time rendering of aerodynamic sound using sound textures based on computational fluid dynamics. ACM Trans. Graph. **22**(3), 732–740 (2003)
4. Farassat, F.: Linear acoustic formulas for calculation of rotating blade noise. AIAA J. **19**(9), 1122–1130 (1981)
5. Goldstein, M.E.: Aeroacoustics. McGraw-Hill (1976)
6. Lighthill, M.J.: On sound generated aerodynamically: I. General theory. Proc. Roy. Soc. London **A221**, 564–587 (1952)
7. Liu, J., Liu, S.: Outdoor sound propagation in inhomogeneous atmosphere via precomputation. In: SIGGRAPH Asia 2019 Technical Briefs, SA 2019, Brisbane, QLD, Australia, 17–20 November 2019, pp. 29–32 (2019)
8. Liu, S., Liu, J.: Outdoor sound propagation based on adaptive FDTD-PE. In: IEEE Conference on Virtual Reality and 3D User Interfaces, VR 2020, Atlanta, GA, USA, 22–26 March 2020, pp. 859–867 (2020)
9. Made, J.E., Kurtz, D.W.: A review of aerodynamic noise from propellers, rofors, and liff fans. Jet Propulsion Laboratory, California Institute of Technology (1970)
10. Marelli, D., Aramaki, M., Kronland-Martinet, R., Verron, C.: Time-frequency synthesis of noisy sounds with narrow spectral components. IEEE Trans. Audio Speech Lang. Process. **18**(8), 1929–1940 (2010)
11. Selfridge, R., Moffat, D., Reiss, J.D.: Physically derived sound synthesis model of a propeller. In: Proceedings of the 12th International Audio Mostly Conference on Augmented and Participatory Sound and Music Experiences, London, United Kingdom, 23–26 August 2017, pp. 16:1–16:8 (2017)
12. Wang, J., James, D.L.: KleinPAT: optimal mode conflation for time-domain precomputation of acoustic transfer. ACM Trans. Graph. **38**(4), 122:1–122:12 (2019)
13. Williams, J.E.F., Hawkings, D.L.: Sound generation by turbulence and surfaces in arbitrary motion. Phil. Trans. Roy. Soc. **264**(1151), 321–342 (1969)
14. Yin, Q., Liu, S.: Sounding solid combustibles: non-premixed flame sound synthesis for different solid combustibles. IEEE Trans. Vis. Comput. Graph. **24**(2), 1179–1189 (2018)

Elimination of Incorrect Depth Points for Depth Completion

Chuhua Xian[1]([⊠]), Kun Qian[1], Guoliang Luo[2]([⊠]), Guiqing Li[1], and Jianming Lv[1]

[1] School of Computer Science and Engineering,
South China University of Technology, Guangzhou 510006, China
chhxian@scut.edu.cn, kqian020@gmail.com
[2] Virtual Reality and Interactive Techniques Institute,
East China Jiaotong University, Nanchang 330013, China
luoguoliang@ecjtu.edu.cn

Abstract. Commodity-level scan cameras generally capture RGB-D image with depth missing or incorrect depth points if the surface of the object is transparent, bright, or black. These incorrect depth points are generated randomly and limit the downstream applications of raw RGB-D images. In this paper, we propose a coarse-to-fine method to detect and eliminate the incorrect depth points via RGB semantics. In our flowchart, deep learning-based networks are applied to predict the potential regions with incorrect depth points and the normals of the point cloud. Then we develop a three-step elimination method to remove the incorrect depth points in the regions. Experimental results show that our method leads to great improvements for downstream applications of RGB-D images, especially in depth completion application.

Keywords: Depth value elimination · Point clouds · Depth completion · RGB Semantics

1 Introduction

Depth map are widely utilized in many applications, including human-computer interaction, 3D reconstruction, robotics path planning, and augmented reality. Due to the efficiency and low cost, structure-light or Time-of-Flight (ToF) cameras are commonly available in our daily life. These cameras can capture both color image and depth map in real time. However, because of the limitation of sensing hardware, the captured depth maps usually have missing regions or wrong depth values. For the missing regions, some depth completion methods have been proposed to fill the depth holes [5, 6, 17]. If there are some wrong values in the missing regions, it will generate defective results. To handle these wrong depth values, a straightforward idea is to use the filtering method to remove the noise. However, traditional filtering methods are only the overall filtering of the

© Springer Nature Switzerland AG 2020
N. Magnenat-Thalmann et al. (Eds.): CGI 2020, LNCS 12221, pp. 245–255, 2020.
https://doi.org/10.1007/978-3-030-61864-3_21

depth image. As an example shown in Fig. 1, the depth camera senses the black region with wrong depth values (Fig. 1(a) (b)). If we directly conduct the depth completion method on it, it will induce a bad completion result (Fig. 1(d)). Using the filter method [11] to process it, the completion result is not good neither (Fig. 1(c)). And, we will get a correct completion after conducting our proposed method, see Fig. (Fig. 1(e)).

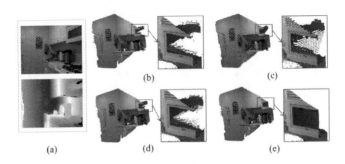

Fig. 1. (a) The captured RGB-D image. (b) The corresponding point cloud. (c) The completion result with the filtering method in [11]. (d) The completion result without any pre-process. (e) The completion result with the pre-process of our proposed method.

To distinguish the missing depth value and the wrong depth value, we call the later as *incorrect depth point* in this paper. In indoor environment, most of the incorrect depth points lay on the regions that are smooth, glossy, bright, black or transparent. Traditional methods are difficult to deal with such problems.

In this paper, we propose a method to eliminate the incorrect depth points by cooperating the RGB semantics. Focusing on the acquired depth map, we use the local 3D geometry property joint with the 2D RGB semantic information. We utilize a segmentation network to recognize a potentially erroneous region in depth map and subsequently conducting the elimination operations on this region. And we extract semantic priors, namely *normal map* from the color map by existed state of the art works [17]. Then we introduce a three-times removal to erase incorrect depth points. In particular, we first remove block error points by using local self-normal similarity and its normal difference between predicted normal and calculated normal. And we use the combined local normal difference and the information of the point removed in the first step to do the second removal. At this time, some outlier points may appear, so we propose the third step in the sensor space to remove.

2   Related Work

In this section, we will briefly introduce previous works on depth errors removal, depth denoising, and depth completion.

2.1 Depth Errors Removal

There are several existing depth errors removal works from the acquisition process perspective earlier work aimed at the acquisition process of Kinect v1. Herrera et al. [1] proposed an optimal calibration by taking color and depth features into account. Lachat et al. [8] investigated the measurement performance and alignment process of Kinect v2 while corrected distance measurement errors on geometric and depth calibration. Plagliari et al. [10] analyzed the collected data of two Kinect versions and adopted a mathematical error model to describes the distance between sensor and object.

2.2 Depth Denoising

The work similar to removing incorrect depth points is depth denoising. Previous researches are inspired by traditional image processing, proposing to utilize local or nonlocal RGB-guided information to denoise depth maps. Joint Bilateral Upsampling(JBU) [7] produced high-quality depth maps by leveraging high-resolution color maps to interpolate depth values. Diebel and Thrun [4] applied the Markov field in enhancing the depth map for the first time. Schall et al. [12] were the first to introduce non-local means into depth map to achieve the effect of denoising. Recently, a considerable literature has grown up around the theme of learning-based denoising methods with RGB-guided [15,16], which shows better results. However, methods mentioned above fail to handle the situation that depths are completely and continuously incorrect.

2.3 Depth Completion

The purpose of depth completion is to fill missing pixels in relatively dense or sparse depth images. Traditional depth completion works overlap with the above-mentioned denoising works, that is, the weighted filtering methods guided by the color map [7]. Recently, due to the popularity of deep learning and the rapid development of computing resources, these data-driven depth completion methods have also aroused widespread concern. Uhrig et al. [14] modified the traditional convolution operations to make it suitable for sparse inputs. Zhang and Funkhouser [17] proposed to use a global optimization with constraints to solve dense depth. These depth completion methods, as mentioned earlier, are valid to a certain extent when the depth prior is error-free. However, their results tend to be biased when there are severe errors in depth.

3 The Proposed Method

In this section, we present a method to eliminate incorrect depth points of acquired depth images. As shown in Fig. 2, he proposed method mainly consists of three components: the potential incorrect depth region localization, normal estimation, and the three elimination steps.

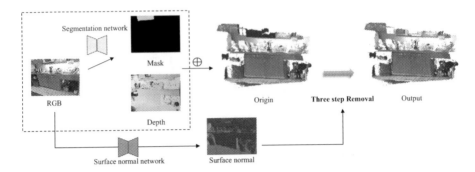

Fig. 2. Overview of our proposed method. Given a RGB-D image, we first locate potential incorrect depth regions through a segmentation network. The blue area in point cloud is the potential error area. Then we use the predicted surface normal to help determine whether the depth is wrong. Last we introduce a three-step removal method to remove the incorrect depth point. (Color figure online)

3.1 Potential Incorrect Depth Region Localization

In this work, we mainly focus on two categories. One category contains the screen, and the other contains opaque objects with reflection. The main reasons are that these two types of objects often appear in indoor scenes, and the incorrect depth points on these objects are often caused by uneven lighting. For this reason, we adopt a state of the art segmentation network [3] to predict these two regions.

To create our dataset for training, we utilize existing public RGB-D images of large indoor environments. For the corresponding RGB images, we label a part of the image containing the target object. Then, we use these labeled data to train a deep network to predict the potential incorrect regions. In order to eliminate the incorrect depth better, we expand the boundary of the predict region to cover more potential areas. We denote the region as L.

3.2 Identification of Incorrect Depth Points

After identifying the potential region L, we continue to distinguish which depth value is incorrect or not. Here we mainly compare the difference between the normal map N^I from the surface estimated network and calculated normal N^D from the depth map. Because the N^I predicted by RGB are more accurate than the N^D in the wrong depth regions. In this work, we utilize the surface normal estimation method in [18] to estimate the N^I. And we convert the corresponding depth D into a 3D space representation, i.e., point cloud $P = \{p_i\}_{i=1}^n \subseteq \mathbb{R}^3$. For each point p_i, we estimate the normal N^D by fitting a local tangent plane [13] as follows:

$$C_i = \frac{1}{|\mathcal{N}_i|} \sum_{p_j \in \mathcal{N}_i} (p_j - p_i) \cdot (p_j - p_i)^T, p_j \in \mathcal{N}_i \tag{1}$$

where $|\mathcal{N}_i|$ is the size of $\mathcal{N}_i$, and p_j is one of neighborhood points of p_i.

The normal vector N_i^D is the corresponding eigenvector of the smallest eigenvalue of the 3×3 covariance matrix C_i. Then we can get the normal N^D of the point cloud by Eq. (1) with automatic radius r. The radius r is used to determine the size of $\mathcal{N}_i$. We compute the naive automatic radius based on Eq. (2):

$$radius = \frac{Dim}{\min(100, \max(size/100))} \tag{2}$$

where $size$ is the number of points in the point cloud and Dim is the maximum dimension among all dimensions of bounding box of point cloud.

3.3   Three-Step Elimination

Due to the ambiguity of the normal and the influence of heavily noises in incorrect regions, we need to take more weighting factors when eliminating the wrong depth values. Here we propose a three-step method to conduct the elimination, which can maintain the correct depth as much as possible when removing the wrong depth values. Let n_i^D be a component of N^D and n_i^I be a part of N^I. Then the normal difference set $\Delta D_i = \{\Delta d_i\}$ of p_i between n_i^D and n_i^I is defined as follows:

$$\Delta d_i = \cos^2(\widehat{n_i^D n_i^I}) \tag{3}$$

where $\widehat{n_i^D n_i^I}$ is the angle between n_i^D and n_i^I. Here the square of the cosine is used to avoid the normal orientation.

Elimination of Block Incorrect Depth Points. Our first step is to eliminate the block-wise incorrect depth points. The characteristics of these points are the significantly large normal difference Δd, and there is heavily noise interfering with the calculation of geometric metrics. In order to reduce the interference of noise points during the elimination process, we use the difference $\tilde{d}_i$ for p_i as follows:

$$\tilde{d}_i = \frac{\sum_{p_j \in \mathcal{N}_i} w\left(\|\mathbf{P}_j - \mathbf{P}_i\|\right) \cdot \Delta d_i}{Z_i} \tag{4}$$

where Z_i is the normalization term, and w is a monotonic decreasing function. Here we use Gaussian function $w(x_i) = e^{-x_i^2/\sigma_i^2}$, w to measure the distance weight of the neighborhood points p_j to the center p_i, where σ_i is the Gaussian distance bandwidth for p_i to adjust the weight of distance x_i. For the bandwidth σ_i, we choose a fixed ratio of the local distance δ_i from the center point to its nearest point to determine it: $\sigma_i = \beta \cdot \delta_i$. The local distance δ_i calculated from the average distance between p_i and its nearest m points(we set $m = 10$ in our implementation).

When the most of the neighborhood points with noise around p_i, the direction of the estimated neighborhood normal vector n_j will be extremely unorganized. Consequently, the value of Δd_i may become large because of the inaccurate local fitting. In this case, Δd_i become less credible. In order to eliminate the incorrect

depth points as many as possible in blocks, we use D_i to measure the difference
weights of neighboring points as:

$$D_i = \frac{\sum_{p_j \in \mathcal{N}_i} w\left(\|\mathbf{p}_j - \mathbf{p}_i\|\right) \cdot \tilde{d_i}}{Z_i}. \tag{5}$$

For any p_i, we then define a threshold function $\varepsilon(D_i)$ to identify the incorrect
depth:

$$\varepsilon(D_i) = \begin{cases} false & \text{if } D_i \geq \delta_1, \\ true & \text{if } D_i < \delta_1. \end{cases} \tag{6}$$

By the definitions of D_i and $\varepsilon(D_i)$, we can distinguish whether a depth
value is effective or not. Figure 3 shows the different results presented by different comparison factors. As shown in Fig. 3(a), one cannot distinguish the
incorrect depth points and correct points if only taking Δd_i into consideration,
because the comparison of the surface normals is ambiguous. In particular, the
PCA-based normal will be severely disturbed by the incorrect depth points,
which makes Δd_i to become less credible. And $\tilde{d_i}$ will eliminate the incorrect
depth points along with some sparse blocks, which cause negative effect for the
subsequent elimination steps (see Fig. 3(e)). On the contrary, further distance
weighting of Δd_i (namely D_i) will reduces residual incorrect depth points, as
illustrated in Figs. 3(c) and 3(f).

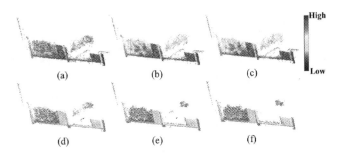

Fig. 3. Each column contains the rendering of different factors (top) and the corresponding wrong depth removal results (bottom). From left to right: Results by Δd_i, $\tilde{d_i}$
and D_i.

Estimation of Sparse Incorrect Depth Points. In the second step, we
focus on the elimination of the sparse incorrect points. These points may have
a small deviation of correct surface normal. Considering this fact, we propose a
method C_i by using weighted comparison of local features to determine whether
each point p_i is incorrect or not:

$$C_i = \rho \cdot \Delta d_i, \tag{7}$$

where ρ is a weighting factor, and Δd_i is the normal difference mentioned above.
Since the first step has eliminated most of the incorrect depth points by the

consistent in the normal direction, we only take into account of Δd_i in the second step. ρ consists of two-term, namely ρ_1 and ρ_2.

ρ_1 assumes such points tend to have a relatively potential relationship with the points eliminated in the first step. Let n_r be the number of points eliminated in the first step within the radius r of point p_i, and n_s be the number of neighborhood points within radius r. Then ρ_1 can be computed as:

$$\rho_1 = 1 - \frac{n_r}{n_s}. \tag{8}$$

In order to explicitly target the sparseness of the incorrect points, we also consider the local density namely ρ_2 within the radius r_n of point p_i. ρ_2 is defined as:

$$\rho_2 = \frac{n+1}{\pi r_n^2}, \tag{9}$$

where n is the number of neighborhood points within the radius r_n of point p_i, and πr^2 is the area of the circle centred at the point p_i. r_n is the farthest distance from the neighborhood point to the point p_i. Here we normalize ρ_2 to [0,1] and we set ρ to the sum of ρ_1 and ρ_2 and then normalize ρ to [0, 1] again for a better weighting. Figure 4 shows an example of the influences of ρ_1, ρ_2 and ρ.

(a)   (b)   (c)

Fig. 4. The influences of different weights to distinguish the incorrect and correct depth points: ρ_1 (a), ρ_2 (b), and ρ (c). These three weights represent a distinct guidance for the second step elimination. The color varies closer to blue, the higher likelihood to be perceived as an error point. (Color figure online)

Meanwhile, considering the weight C_i of nearby points helps us to remove errors without leaving sparse points. Then we define D_i' as follows:

$$D_i' = \frac{\sum_{p_j \in \mathcal{N}_i} w\left(\|\mathbf{p}_j - \mathbf{p}_i\|\right) \cdot C_i}{Z_i}. \tag{10}$$

Subsequently, we use the threshold ε' to determine whether point p_i is an incorrect depth point. If $D_i' > \varepsilon'$, we regard it as correct point. Otherwise if $D_i' < \varepsilon'$, we remove the incorrect point. In this paper, we empirically set ε' as 0.2.

Elimination of Outlier Incorrect Points. The first two-step elimination will result in a few outliers in the point cloud P. Such outliers will also produce biased results for subsequent work. To solve this problem, we use a post-operation to remove these outliers for better visual performance. We first project the processed point cloud P back onto depth image domain D, and we still work in the region L. Let $v_{i,j} \in L$ be the pixel of position (i, j), we define a binary mask M as:

$$M(v_{i,j}) = \begin{cases} 1 & \text{if } v_{i,j} > 0, \\ 0 & \text{if } v_{i,j} = 0. \end{cases} \tag{11}$$

Subsequently, we perform connected component analysis on the mask image M to remove outliers. We first sort the areas S of connected regions in the mask image M in ascending order. To achieve this, we define the total number of the connected areas in the mask image as A, the $i-th$ connected area as S_i. Then we iterate over all the ordered areas. When we find the largest S_{i+1}/S_i, we remove all connected areas less than area S_i. Note that in our implementation, we use the $8-connectivity$ to define the outlier.

4   Results

Fig. 5. 4 examples of incorrect depth point elimination for depth completion. The first row shows: original completion method in [17]. The second row: our proposed method + Zhang et al. method [17].

We have implemented our denoise method on Intel Core i5-4590 3.30 GHz, RAM 16 GB, and NVIDIA Geforce GTX 1060 6 GB.

We select 1192 RGB-D images from the SUNRGB-D datasets as training data, which contains two types of the labeled objects as mentioned in Sect. 3.1. And we use the DeepLabv3+ [3] network because of its competitive performance on image segmentation. Besides, we fine-tune our data with its pre-trained model on the ADE20K [19]. The total mIOU that our test results of the potential regions localization is close to 84%.

Figure 5 shows 4 examples of our experiments. We conduct the completion by the method in [17]. From the visual point cloud, we can see that the completion results with the elimination of incorrect depth points are much better. Four

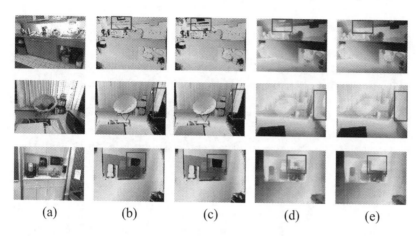

(a)   (b)   (c)   (d)   (e)

Fig. 6. From left to right: the RGB images, the depth maps, the depth maps after conducting our elimination method, the completion depth maps by the method in [17], and the completion depth maps by our proposed method + [17].

example results in pseudo-color in Fig. 6. It can be seen that the completion results are more reasonable with our proposed method.

Comparisons. We compare our method with bilateral filter [11], noise-aware filter [2], and the anisotropic diffusion method. Figure 7 shows 4 results. From this figure, we can obtain the best results by combining our method with Zhang et al.'s method [17]. That is because the traditional filtering method may modify the correct depth value when conducting the denoising operations on the depth map.

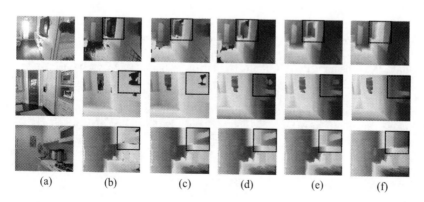

(a)   (b)   (c)   (d)   (e)   (f)

Fig. 7. Comparisons with other denoising methods. (a) the RGB images, (b) the depth maps, (c) the results generated by: [11], (d) the results generated by: [2], (e) the results generated by: [9], and (f) the results generated by: ours + Zhang et al.'s method [17].

4.1 Limitations

There are mainly two limitations of our proposed method.

First, when the predicted normal is not accurate, our method will be biased. One of the solutions is to propose a normal estimation network with strong generalization ability, which can avoid the influence by lights but retain the boundary information of the prediction normal.

Second, when a depth priori is mostly lost, our method may not produce good results. One solution is to integrate the depth estimation network to predict the depth within a certain area, which can predict depth to identify wrong points.

5 Conclusion

In this paper, we propose a method to eliminate the incorrect depth points in RGB-D images in a coarse-to-fine pipeline. We first use the deep learning-based method to predict the potential regions with incorrect depth points, and use the estimated normals of the points to filter the major parts of the incorrect depth points. We then propose a three-step elimination method to remove the sparse incorrect depth points. Our method can retain the correct depth points as many as possible while eliminating incorrect depth points. We test our method on open RGB-D datasets and the experimental results show that our method result in great improvement for the downstream applications of RGB-D images.

Acknowledgement. This work was supported by the Nature Science Fund of Guangdong Province under Grant 2019A1515011793 and NSFC (No.61972160, 51978271, 61962021, 61876065).

References

1. C., D.H., Kannala, J., Heikkila, J.: Joint depth and color camera calibrationwith distortion correction. IEEE Trans. Pattern Anal. Mach. Intell. **34**(10), 2058–2064 (2012).https://doi.org/10.1109/tpami.2012.125
2. Chan, D., Buisman, H., Theobalt, C., Thrun, S.: A noise-aware filter for real-time depth upsampling (2008)
3. Chen, L.-C., Zhu, Y., Papandreou, G., Schroff, F., Adam, H.: Encoder-decoder with atrous separable convolution for semantic image segmentation. In: Ferrari, V., Hebert, M., Sminchisescu, C., Weiss, Y. (eds.) ECCV 2018. LNCS, vol. 11211, pp. 833–851. Springer, Cham (2018). https://doi.org/10.1007/978-3-030-01234-2_49
4. Diebel, J., Thrun, S.: An application of Markov random fields to range sensing. In: Weiss, Y., Schölkopf, B., Platt, J.C. (eds.) Advances in Neural Information Processing Systems, vol. 18, pp. 291–298. MIT Press (2006)
5. Huang, Z., Fan, J., Cheng, S., Yi, S., Wang, X., Li, H.: HMS-net: hierarchical multi-scale sparsity-invariant network for sparse depth completion. IEEE Trans. Image Process. **29**, 3429–3441 (2020). https://doi.org/10.1109/tpami.2012.125
6. Jaritz, M., Charette, R.D., Wirbel, E., Perrotton, X., Nashashibi, F.: Sparse and dense data with CNNs: depth completion and semantic segmentation. In: 2018 International Conference on 3D Vision (3DV). IEEE, September 2018. https://doi.org/10.1109/3dv.2018.00017

7. Kopf, J., Cohen, M.F., Lischinski, D., Uyttendaele, M.: Joint bilateral upsampling. In: ACM SIGGRAPH 2007 Papers on - SIGGRAPH 2007. ACM Press (2007). https://doi.org/10.1145/1275808.1276497

8. Lachat, E., Macher, H., Landes, T., Grussenmeyer, P.: Assessment and calibration of a RGB-d camera (Kinect v2 sensor) towards a potential use for close-range 3D modeling. Remote Sens. **7**(10), 13070–13097 (2015). https://doi.org/10.3390/rs71013070

9. Liu, J., Gong, X.: Guided depth enhancement via anisotropic diffusion. In: Huet, B., Ngo, C.-W., Tang, J., Zhou, Z.-H., Hauptmann, A.G., Yan, S. (eds.) PCM 2013. LNCS, vol. 8294, pp. 408–417. Springer, Cham (2013). https://doi.org/10.1007/978-3-319-03731-8_38

10. Pagliari, D., Pinto, L.: Calibration of Kinect for XBOX one and comparison between the two generations of microsoft sensors. Sensors **15**(11), 27569–27589 (2015). https://doi.org/10.3390/Pagliari_2015

11. Petschnigg, G., Szeliski, R., Agrawala, M., Cohen, M., Hoppe, H., Toyama, K.: Digital photography with flash and no-flash image pairs. In: ACM SIGGRAPH 2004 Papers on - SIGGRAPH 2004. ACM Press (2004). https://doi.org/10.1145/1186562.1015777

12. Schall, O., Belyaev, A., Seidel, H.P.: Feature-preserving non-local denoising of static and time-varying range data. In: Proceedings of the 2007 ACM Symposium on Solid and Physical Modeling - SPM 2007. ACM Press (2007). https://doi.org/10.1145/1236246.1236277

13. Shan, D.R., Ke, Y.L.: Surface reconstruction from unorganized points based on 2D delaunay neighbors. In: Sui, W. (ed.) Second International Conference on Image and Graphics. SPIE, July 2002. https://doi.org/10.1117/12.477093

14. Uhrig, J., Schneider, N., Schneider, L., Franke, U., Brox, T., Geiger, A.: Sparsity invariant CNNs. In: 2017 International Conference on 3D Vision (3DV). IEEE, October 2017. https://doi.org/10.1109/3dv.2017.00012

15. Wang, X., Zhang, P., Zhang, Y., Ma, L., Kwong, S., Jiang, J.: Deep intensity guidance based compression artifacts reduction for depth map. J. Vis. Commun. Image Represent. **57**, 234–242 (2018). https://doi.org/10.1016/j.jvcir.2018.11.008

16. Yan, S., et al.: DDRNet: depth map denoising and refinement for consumer depth cameras using cascaded CNNs. In: Ferrari, V., Hebert, M., Sminchisescu, C., Weiss, Y. (eds.) ECCV 2018. LNCS, vol. 11214, pp. 155–171. Springer, Cham (2018). https://doi.org/10.1007/978-3-030-01249-6_10

17. Zhang, Y., Funkhouser, T.: Deep depth completion of a single RGB-D image. In: 2018 IEEE/CVF Conference on Computer Vision and Pattern Recognition. IEEE, June 2018. https://doi.org/10.1109/cvpr.2018.00026

18. Zhang, Y., et al.: Physically-based rendering for indoor scene understanding using convolutional neural networks. In: 2017 IEEE Conference on Computer Vision and Pattern Recognition (CVPR). IEEE, July 2017. https://doi.org/10.1109/cvpr.2017.537

19. Zhou, B., et al.: Semantic understanding of scenes through the ADE20k dataset. Int. J. Comput. Vis. **127**(3), 302–321, December 2018. https://doi.org/10.1007/s11263-018-1140-0

Pose Transfer of 2D Human Cartoon Characters

Tiezeng Mao[1], Wenbo Dong[1], Aihua Mao[1(✉)], Guiqing Li[1], and Jie Luo[2(✉)]

[1] School of Computer Science and Engineering,
South China University of Technology, Guangzhou, China
ahmao@scut.edu.cn
[2] School of Fine Art and Artistic Design, Guangzhou University,
Guangzhou 510006, China
jieluo@gzhu.edu.cn

Abstract. Pose transfer between two 2D cartoon characters provides a fast way to copy pose without complex deformation operations on the 2D shape. This paper proposes an effective method for transferring the pose of 2D human cartoon characters while preserving the character's geometric features. We compare our method with other similar works and discuss the convergence of the results under geometric constraints. The results show that our method can effectively achieve smooth pose transfer between cartoon characters with good convergence.

Keywords: Human cartoon character · Pose transfer ·
Disentanglement · Space and spectral domain

1 Introduction

Methods in the space domain pay minimal attention to spectral properties and are mainly based on articulated deformation [4,11,15]. Pose transfer in the spectral domain considers geometry holistically during transformation instead of considering each vertex separately [6–8,8,9].

However, most existing methods for pose transfer are mostly aimed at 3D objects [1,11,13], which process subjects holistically in the spectral domain and thus cannot be directly applied to 2D characters. Igarashi et al. [5] presented an interactive system for the users to deform a 2D shape without manually established skeleton. Weng et al. [12] proposed a 2D shape deformation algorithm based on nonlinear least squares optimization, which aims to preserve geometric properties of 2D shapes. Bregler et al. [2] tracked the motion from traditionally animated cartoons and retargeted it onto 3-D models. These works realize the 2D shape deformation with keeping a sense of rigidity of the shape. However, it can be seen that complex user interactions are required to facilitate the 2D shape

Supported by The Science and Technology Planning Project of Guangzhou City (No. 201804010362) and NSF of Guangdong Province (No. 2019A1515010833).

N. Magnenat-Thalmann et al. (Eds.): CGI 2020, LNCS 12221, pp. 256–266, 2020.
https://doi.org/10.1007/978-3-030-61864-3_22

deformation in these methods. That may lead to a bottleneck of efficiency in cartoon character design. We extend the ideas of these works [2, 5, 12] to transfer the pose between 2D characters and efficiently obtain newly posed 2D cartoon characters learning from others and greatly reduce the user interactions.

In this work, we propose an effective method for implementing pose transfer for 2D human cartoon characters. Our framework addresses the issues in implementing 2D cartoon pose transfer, namely, transforming the 2D cartoon character's geometric shape and preserving its somatotype. The proposed method can handle various transfer situations with different poses and effectively preserves the characters details well during pose transfer. Initially, the 2D cartoon character is transformed into a graph, and a uniform Laplace operator is used to disentangle the graph with a two-layer representation. Then, the original cartoon character learns the pose of the target cartoon character through a skeleton skinning-based deformation method. The outline of the cartoon character is relocated following the pose transformation, and the details of the cartoon character which are subjected to conformal transformation are finally fused with the transformed pose to generate the final results. The new contributions of this work are as follows:

- We propose a new effective framework specifically for pose transfer between 2D cartoon characters, which fills in the gap that there is few work for 2D pose transfer.
- Our method is a new attempt to combine the methods in the space and spectral domains, that is, disentangling a cartoon character into a two-layer representation through the spectrum-based method and handling the deformation on each layer through the space-based method, which can preserve the somatotype and details of the original cartoon characters well during pose transfer.

2 Pose Transfer

In the process of pose transfer, the low-resolution layer of the original cartoon character is deformed to learn the pose of the target cartoon character. We use the skeleton comprising a hierarchical set of interconnected bones to facilitate the matching between skeletons. Firstly, the skeletons of the original and target cartoon characters are extracted, then a skeleton mapping algorithm is used to match the two skeletons. The skeleton skinning-based method is further adopted to deform the original cartoon character's pose with the transformation matrix of corresponding skeleton segments. The somatotype of the low-resolution layer can be preserved well during deformation because skeleton skinning is an approximate rigid transformation.

2.1 Two-Layer Representation of the Character

We initially transform a given 2D cartoon character into a graph by formulating connection relations between pixels. The edges of the graph are constructed by resampling the pixels on the characters border and inner points, and is further disentangled into two layers of different resolutions by using the Laplace operator. For a given 2D character, it is first extracted from the image background and then transformed into a graph to achieve the two-layer representation. The Canny edge detector algorithm proposed by [3] is used to identify the character's border (without inner geometric information), which considers the criteria in numerical optimization to derive detectors for arbitrary edges, and the segmentation for the border is assumed in the case of zero-crossings and closed form. The graph then is divided into a two-layer representation via spectral disentanglement using a uniform weight Laplace operator.

$$\delta_i = \frac{1}{d_i} \sum_{j \in N(i)} (v_i - v_j) \tag{1}$$

where, N(i) is the set of adjacent vertices (v_i) in the graph, and $d_i = |N(i)|$ is the degree of a vertex (v_i).The Laplace weight of the vertices $(v_i \ , v_j \ )$ is $\frac{1}{2}$.

The reason of choosing the uniform weight Laplace operator is that it can record the topology information of the graph, so that when projecting the graphs coordinates onto the feature space, the outline and features of the graph are respectively located in the front and back eigenvectors and thus are easy to be differentiated. When regarding the coordinates of the vertices as discrete signals, the eigenbasis and eigenvalues can be interpreted as the vibration mode and frequency of the signals, respectively. Setting the eigenbasis in the order of most to least domain eigenvalues, then the front eigenbasis indicates the smooth part of the graph, which corresponds to the characters outline and has low-frequency, while the back eigenbasis indicates the vibration part of the graph, which corresponds to the characters detail features and has high-frequency signals.

2.2   Skeleton Extraction

The details of the 2D characters significantly affect the skeleton extraction results, such as the fingers and hair. Thus, establishing a two-layer representation in advance benefits the skeleton extraction of 2D characters by eliminating the effect of details on skeletons. With the low-resolution layer, the skeleton is extracted on the basis of the character's border. Although skeleton extraction is sensitive to boundary noise, the character's border exhibits minimal noise after the Laplace operator process during disentanglement, in which the details have been separated into the high-resolution layer. Given the unitary pixel thinness, the skeletons of the original and target characters are extracted by using Zhang's thinning algorithm [14], which can effectively preserve the connectivity of skeletons. The idea is to remove boundary and corner points iteratively and use the remaining points as the skeleton.

Figure 1 compares the results of the skeleton extraction with and without the two-layer representation. The skeleton depicted is clearly smoother in the left than that in the right. It can be seen that the skeleton can reflect the character's pose holistically and without the influence of the details.

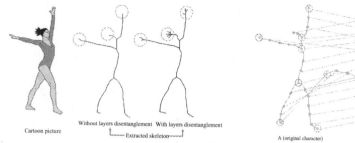

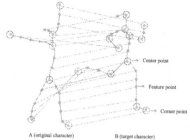

Cartoon picture   Without layers disentanglement   With layers disentanglement

‼------ Extracted skeleton ------‼

Fig. 1. Comparison between extracted skeletons

A (original character)   B (target character)

Fig. 2. Skeleton mapping

2.3 Skeleton Matching

Skeleton matching between skeletons A (original character) and B (target character) is an assistant preparation for skeleton-based shape deformation. The match between two skeletons is obtained under three steps, including Limb matching, torso matching and feature points matching.

Since the human is symmetrical on the limbs parts, it is easy to make confusion for the skeleton match between the limbs of two characters without sematic markup. In order to have a successful match between skeletons A and B, a sematic matching between the cartoon characters A and B is performed preceding to the skeletons match to avoid mismatching. Such as, the skeleton of an arm is matched with that of a leg or even the skeleton a left arm is matched with that of a right arm, these mistakes will lead to a wrong pose transfer result. Therefore, a sematic match between the body parts of characters A and B is helpful. At the beginning of the pose transfer, the user just needs specify a sematic correspondence between six body parts of characters A and B, including head-head, torso-torso, left arm-left arm, right arm-right arm, left leg-left leg and right leg-right leg. The correspondence can be finished by simply selecting an inner point of the character parts, and the sematic match can be established by selecting six pairs of points clicked by the mouse. This approach greatly relieves the user interactions compared to the previous works [5,12], which require heavy user operations for 2D shape deformation. Though it is ideal to have no user interaction involved and achieve a fully automatic pose transfer, manually marking down the sematic identity for each part of the skeleton is not a good alternative solution, we are more efficient to establish the semantic match by quickly mouse clicking for six pairs. Furthermore, for a pair of original and target cartoons, this interaction only happens once at the beginning time, which is quite light user interaction.

With the help of sematic match, it is easy to implement skeleton match under right correspondence. We record the feature points of skeleton B nearest to the center point (shown in Fig. 2) and terminal parts as $p_{b,c}$ and $b_{t,i}$, and record the feature points of skeleton A nearest to the center and terminal parts as $p_{a,c}$ and $a_{t,i}$. The detail feature points are obtained by detecting corner points on the skeleton based on the rules of interval distance between points and skeleton curvature. We used Shi et al.'s method [10] in detecting the corner points and setting up the feature points of the skeleton. The feature points of skeleton B is determined and then accordingly select skeleton A's feature points, because the deformation of skeleton A is learned from the deformation of skeleton B. The feature points having more than two neighboring points are set as branch points, which divide the skeleton into limb and torso pieces. Afterward the limb and torso are firstly matched to develop a rough correspondence and then all the feature points on the whole skeleton are matched in the fine scale.

The skeleton segments of skeletons A and B are also matched when the feature points are matched. Then, we can calculate the transformation matrix between the matched skeleton segment pairs for the next step of deformation. Figure 2 shows a schematics of skeleton mapping through limb and torso and feature points matching. The points with the same color indicate the matched feature points on the two skeletons.

2.4   Skeleton Skinning-Based Deformation

Skeleton skinning is an effective approach for the deformation of the original shape according to the target shape. On the basis of the matched feature points, skeletons A and B have been divided into segments e_i and e_i', respectively. T_i is the transformation matrix from segment e_i to its corresponding segment e_i'. We must map the skeleton to the points of the characters outline, including the border and inner points, to ensure a reliable skinning result. The mapping operations of the border vertices and inner points with the skeleton are considered respectively because the transformation of the inner and the border points differs. Let SS be the set of skeleton segments on the routes from the center point to all terminal points.

Mapping Between the Border and the Skeleton: In the case of border, a vertex of the border v_i is set as being related to three skeleton segments near to it. We define their relation weights as ω_1, ω_2, ω_3 and their relationship as $\omega_1 + \omega_2 + \omega_3 = 1$. The nearest skeleton segment to v_i is considered the first related skeleton segment, and set $\omega_1 = 0.5$. In the same SS_i including the nearest skeleton segment, we select another two segments that are secondary nearest to v_i as the other two related skeleton segments, and set $\omega_2 = 0.25$, $\omega_3 = 0.25$.

Mapping Between the Inner Points and the Skeleton: The movement of the inner points is not as rigid as the movement of the border vertices. Therefore, we relate each inner point to other skeleton segments. We initially determine the t nearest skeleton segments in SS (initially, $t = 5$). Then, the related SS_i has the most skeleton segments in the t segments. If more than one SS have the largest number of skeleton segments, then t is increased by $t = t + 1$, and this process is repeated. The skeleton segments related to an inner point are defined as the nearest t segments in the related SS_i.

We adopt dual quaternions algorithm to perform skinning and achieve the skeleton skinning-based deformation after the mapping between the skeleton and the outline. In this step, a transformed pose represented by the outline could be obtained. The somatotype of the cartoon character can be well preserved because the transformation is conformal, and the transformation of the inner points is rational.

2.5   Geometric Constraints

The geometric properties of the cartoon character may change unexpectedly in the transformation process, although skeleton skinning could obtain a deformed pose. This change will cause errors in the border vertices and inner points. Thus, certain geometric constraints should be imposed to eliminate possible errors. We define the neighbors of border vertices and inner points as follows: The two neighboring points of the inner point are defined as the two nearest points that share the same skeleton section nearest to the inner points, whereas the two neighboring vertices of the border vertex are set as its two adjacent vertices on the border. In this work, we propose two geometric constraints to eliminate errors.

Border Preservation Constraint: The preservation is realized by minimizing the following energy function:

$$E_o = \|\delta' - \delta\|^2 \tag{2}$$

where δ is the original Laplacian coordinate set defined in Eqs. 1, and δ' is the current Laplacian coordinate.

Edge Length Preservation Constraint: The edge is defined as the distance between each vertex and its neighbor vertices. The stretching energy term E_l is minimized to preserve the edge length.

$$E_l = \left\|l' - l\right\|^2 \tag{3}$$

Then, we define an elastic energy as the combination of distortion and stretching energy terms. It can refine the deformation result of the cartoon characters outline by minimizing the elastic energy consisting of energy term E_o and E_l.

$$E = \arg\min(\omega_o E_o + \omega_l E_l) \tag{4}$$

We use the Gauss-Newton method which is effective for little residual problems to solve the energy equation.

3   Graph Reconstruction

The deformed outline of the original cartoon character is achieved by learning from the target one. Then, the details, which are separated in the spectral disentanglement step, will be further combined to generate the final pose-transferred results. Thus, the details should be conformably transformed with the outline deformation. As mentioned previously, the detail features are recorded as vectors from the character's outline to the initial contour. Thus, the conformal transform is realized by the vectors, which are linearly added to the character's outline to reconstruct the final graph with details.

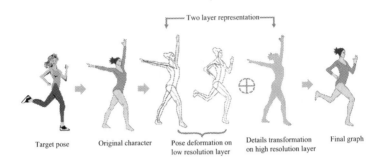

Fig. 3. The pipeline of a cartoon character pose transfer with reconstructed graph.

The vector σ_i of vertex v_i on the outline is formed by its neighbor vertices, namely, $\sigma_i = V_{i+1} - V_{i-1}$ and $\sigma_i = V_{i+1} - V_{i-1}$. In the pose deformation, σ_i is rotated to σ_i' by the rotating matrix R_i. Since the detail features calculated by Eq. 5 are associated with vertex v_i, the details are rotated by the same rotation matrix as $V_{detail}' = R_i V_{detail}$. V_{detail} and V_{detail}' are the detail's offset vectors before and after the step of deforming the pose on the outline. The final graph is reconstructed by adding the detail's offset vector with the deformed vertices of the outline.

$$v_{contour} = R\sigma + RV_{detail} \qquad (5)$$

Figure 3 demonstrates the result of pose transfer by combining the deformed outline and details. The outline and details of the original cartoon character represented by different layers are transformed according to the target pose and then linearly combined to generate the final graph.

Since the Laplace operator disentangles the hight resolution layer through the back eigenbasis indicating the vibration part of the graph, which represents the characters detail features and has high-frequency signals, the texture in the cartoon with smooth pattern can not be extracted and transferred.

4   Implementation

The pose transfer algorithm is implemented via two-layer representation, pose deformation, and graph reconstruction. First, the graph of the cartoon character is disentangled into low- and high-resolution layers. Then, the layers are processed through different deformation methods. For the low-resolution layer, skeleton skinning is utilized to perform the pose deformation of the character's outline according to the target pose. For the high-resolution layer, the deformation is realized by constantly conforming to the outline in the low-resolution layer. The final graph of the pose-transferred cartoon character is reconstructed by combining the transformed high- and low-resolution layers.

5   Results and Comparison

In this section, we compare the results by our method and by other similar methods, and also demonstrate the pose transfer results for different original cartoon characters learning from different target poses. All the experiments are run through a hardware configuration of CPU 2.66 GHz, Intel i5-3230.

5.1   Comparison with Other Works

Currently, there are rare studies have explored pose transfer between 2D cartoon characters. Levy's method [6] is a general algorithm for pose transfer that is based on a Laplacian mesh processing framework [8]. Our method is similar to the techniques that apply Laplacian operators. Thus, we directly compare the results by our method and by Levy's algorithm.

(a)   (b)   (c)   (d)

Fig. 4. Comparison between results by Levy's [6] and our method: (a) original cartoon character; (b) target pose; (c) results by Levy's method [6]; (d) results by our method.

Figure 4 illustrates the comparison of pose-transferred results. In our method, the details of the characters, such as the direction of fingers, hair, and foot, are rotated rationally and the thickness of the waist and leg are well preserved. The limbs of the cartoon characters after pose transfer retain their original somatotype. By contrast, the limbs of the cartoon characters in Levy's method exhibit obvious changes and the details on the head, fingers and feet are distorted or missed. Thanks to the constraint set on the edge length and the Laplacian coordinate of the outline, the final graph of the character is smoother and conveys fewer errors in our method than that of Levy's method.

As reviewed in Sect. 2, though some works are available to generate 2D cartoon picture, they are implemented by shape deformation algorithm through user interactions, and their focus is not on 2D pose transfer, thus it is difficult to compare with them. The literature more similar to our work is Bregler et al.'s work [2], which transfers the pose of 2D drawing onto the 3D model. We attempt to compare the pose-transferred 2D results by our method and the 3D results by [2] based on same input poses. As shown in Fig. 5, the 3D pose-transferred results is generated by Bregler et al.'s work [2], and the 2D pose-transferred results is generated by our work which has better preservation with the input poses than the non-textured 3D pose-transferred results.

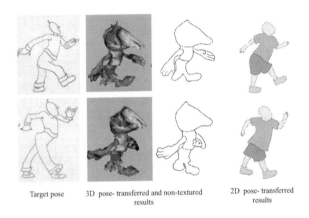

Target pose   3D pose- transferred and non-textured   2D pose- transferred
                              results   results

Fig. 5. Comparison between 3D pose transfer results by Bregler et al.'s [2] and 2D pose transfer results by our work

5.2   More Results

In this section, we demonstrate the results of different cases of 2D cartoon character pose transfer by our method. Three original cartoon characters learn from a group of different target poses, which indicate different application situations, as depicted in Fig. 6–7.

Figure 6 displays the pose transfer results of character 1, which is the famous Japanese cartoon character, Atomu. Character 1 learns the target poses and obtains the transferred results through our pose transfer method. The details of Atomu, including hair, are divided into high-resolution layers, and a conformal transformation with Atomus body is then performed. The hair is maintained rationally in all the results. The character retains its own somatotype well after the pose transfer.

Figure 7 depicts the pose transfer results of character 2, which exhibits rhythmic movements. The results show favorable smoothness, that is, the length of the original character's legs and arms are preserved well, although the length of the target pose's legs and arms vary significantly in different poses. The proposed skeleton skinning method which makes uses of the angle difference between the corresponding parts of the two characters has no influence by the length. The imposed geometric constraints also increase the smoothness of the results by preserving the border and edge length during the outline deformation.

(a) Input target poses

(b) Pose transferred results

Fig. 6. Pose transferred results for cartoon character 1

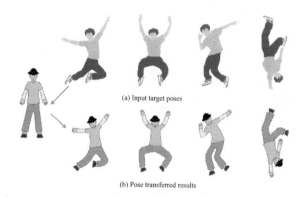

(a) Input target poses

(b) Pose transferred results

Fig. 7. Pose transferred results for cartoon character 2

These cases indicate that our method can easily replace existing cartoon characters with various poses with a simple character without any pose created by artists. The transfer can be implemented for the original character to learn from different target characters. However, our method also has limitation on the cases: 1) the body information is missed, such as self-occlusion or invisible face the details can not be recovered correctly; 2) the body parts has crossed with each other, like the pose of a ballerina artist with crossed hands and legs. Since the adopted Canny edge detection algorithm works for the cases of zero-crossings and closed contour, it fails to extracted right border and skeleton. Though extra heuristic work can facilitate to separate the crossed parts, it has low performance to handle it.

6 Conclusion

In this work, we propose an effective method for implementing pose transfer for 2D human cartoon characters. The proposed method is a new attempt that combines the methods in the space and spectrum domains and is designed specifically for 2D cartoon character pose transfer. The experiment results show the capability of this method in 2D cartoon character pose transfer with different target poses in various situations. Compared with previous works, our method can generate somatotype and details preserved 2D pose-transferred characters. It provides an efficient tool for artists to quickly design and produce digital cartoon drawings by simply creating a simple character template.

References

1. Baran, I., Vlasic, D., Grinspun, E., Popović, J.: Semantic deformation transfer. ACM Trans. Graph. **28**(3), 36:1–36:6 (2009)
2. Bregler, C., Loeb, L., Chuang, E., Deshpande, H.: Turning to the masters: motion capturing cartoons. ACM Trans. Graph. **21**(3), 399–407 (2002)
3. Canny, J.: A computational approach to edge detection. IEEE Trans. Pattern Anal. Mach. Intelli. PAMI **8**(6), 679–698 (1986)
4. Farag, S., Abdelrahman, W., Creighton, D., Nahavandi, S.: Automatic deformation transfer for data-driven haptic rendering. In: 2013 11th IEEE International Conference on Industrial Informatics (INDIN), pp. 264–269 (2013)
5. Igarashi, T., Moscovich, T., Hughes, J.F.: As-rigid-as-possible shape manipulation. ACM Trans. Graph. **24**(3), 1134–1141 (2005)
6. Levy, B.: Laplace-beltrami eigenfunctions towards an algorithm that "understands" geometry. In: IEEE International Conference on Shape Modeling and Applications 2006 (SMI 2006), p. 13, June 2006
7. Ovsjanikov, M., Ben-Chen, M., Solomon, J., Butscher, A., Guibas, L.J.: Functional maps: a flexible representation of maps between shapes. ACM Trans. Graph. **31**, 30:1–30:11 (2012)
8. Reuter, M., Biasotti, S., Giorgi, D., Patanè, G., Spagnuolo, M.: Discrete Laplace-Beltrami operators for shape analysis and segmentation. Comput. Graph. **33**, 381–390 (2009)
9. Petronetto, F., Paiva, A., Helou, E.S., Stewart, D.E., Nonato, L.G.: Mesh-free discrete Laplace-Beltrami operator. Comput. Graph. Forum **32**(6), 214–226 (2013)
10. Shi, J., Tomasi, C.: Good features to track. In: 1994 Proceedings of IEEE Conference on Computer Vision and Pattern Recognition, pp. 593–600, June 1994
11. Sumner, R.W., Popović, J.: Deformation transfer for triangle meshes. ACM Trans. Graph. **23**(3), 399–405 (2004)
12. Weng, Y., Xu, W., Wu, Y., Zhou, K., Guo, B.: 2D shape deformation using nonlinear least squares optimization. Vis. Comput. **22**(9), 653–660 (2006)
13. Yin, M., Li, G., Lu, H., Ouyang, Y., Zhang, Z., Xian, C.: Spectral pose transfer. Comput. Aided Geom. Des. **35**(C), 82–94 (2015)
14. Zhang, T.Y., Suen, C.Y.: A fast parallel algorithm for thinning digital patterns. Commun. ACM **27**, 236–239 (1984)
15. Zhao, Y., Pan, B., Xiao, C., Peng, Q.: Dual-domain deformation transfer for triangular meshes. Comput. Animat. Virtual Worlds **23**(3–4), 447–456 (2012)

Broad-Classifier for Remote Sensing Scene Classification with Spatial and Channel-Wise Attention

Zhihua Chen[1]([✉]), Yunna Liu[1], Han Zhang[1], Bin Sheng[2]([✉]), Ping Li[3], and Guangtao Xue[1]

[1] Department of Computer Science and Engineering,
East China University of Science and Technology, Shanghai 200237, China
czh@ecust.edu.cn

[2] Department of Computer Science and Engineering, Shanghai Jiao Tong University,
Shanghai 200240, China
shengbin@sjtu.edu.cn

[3] Faculty of Information Technology, Macau University of Science and Technology,
Macau 999078, China

Abstract. Remote sensing scene classification is an important technology, which is widely used in military and civil applications. However, it is still a challenging problem due to the complexity of scene images. Recently, the development of remote sensing satellite and sensor devices has greatly improved the spatial resolution and semantic information of remote sensing images. Therefore, we propose a novel remote sensing scene classification approach to enhance the performance of scene classification. First, a spatial and channel-wise attention module is proposed to adequately utilize the spatial and feature information. Compare with other methods, channel-wise module works on the feature maps with diverse levels and pays more attention to semantic-level features. On the other hand, spatial attention module promotes correlation between foreground and classification result. Second, a novel classifier named broad-classifier is designed to enhance the discriminability. It greatly reduces the cost of computing in the meantime by broad learning system. The experimental results have show that our classification method can effectively improve the average accuracies on remote sensing scene classification data sets.

Keywords: Scene classification · Attention mechanism · Remote sensing image · Broad learning system

1 Introduction

The purpose of remote sensing scene classification is to assign a specific semantic category for remote sensing images. It has attracted extensive attention due

This work was supported by the National Natural Science Foundation of China (Grant No. 61672228, 61370174) and Shanghai Automotive Industry Science and Technology Development Foundation (No. 1837).

N. Magnenat-Thalmann et al. (Eds.): CGI 2020, LNCS 12221, pp. 267–275, 2020.
https://doi.org/10.1007/978-3-030-61864-3_23

to the large of applications. The technology of remote sensing scene classification has attracted much attention due to its application potential in new fields, such as urban Monitoring [1], sports broadcast [23–25], environmental detection [2,21,24], geographic structure analysis [3]. The framework for these goals generally composed of two essential networks, feature mapping network and category classification network.

Recently, thanks to the powerful feature learning ability of deep convolutional neural network (CNN), the performance of remote sensing scene classification task has been significantly improved [4–6]. The existing approaches utilized in remote sensing scene classification can be roughly categorized into two structures: the naive CNN approach and the feature mapping approach. The first method directly use the previous CNNs to classify the categories, which only extract the features from the last layer of deep convolutional neural network [7]. The feature mapping methods commonly extract features at first, and then encode these features in some way to enhance the performance of scene classification. Actually, previous remote sensing scene classification methods demonstrates that use the semantic features which extracted from different hierarchical layers will obviously increase the classification accuracy. Furthermore, complex image background information also causes considerable obstacle to the object detection problem which can be improve by the spatial information. However, these methods usually ignore the multilayer structural and spatial area information.

To address these aforementioned problems, an end-to-end classification framework is proposed to integrate the multilayer features and pay attention to the spatial information. In addition, we present a novel classifier named broad-classifier to identify the category label of the remote sensing image. Firstly, a channel-wise attention module is proposed to enhance the relationship between multi-scale feature mappings to solve the problem of error recognition caused by incomplete feature representation. Secondly, to solve the problem of error detection caused by the complex background, we added a spatial-wise mechanism into the original feature map. In the last stage, the broad-classifier is trained with the assistance of the output attention feature maps. Besides, the classifier is composed of a broad learning system (BLS) [8], which can effectively reduce the training time while maintain the performance of classification.

2   Related Work

2.1   Remote Sensing Scene Classification

Recently, deep convolutional neural network has become the main tool for remote sensing scene classification due to its strong feature representation capability. As the remote sensing images cover a wide range and contain complex environment, the scene classification method need represent feature properly. Fan Hu et al. [9] adopted pre-trained CNNs to extract the multilayer CNN features for high-resolution remote sensing scene classification. S. Chaib et al. [19] fully connected the layers of VGG-Net to represent informative features, and DCA is further used to enhance accuracy. Q. Wang et al. [10] proposed a end-to-end framework to make full use of density and distance information simultaneously. Z. Chen et al. [11] presented a recurrent transformer networks to reduce the difference semantic differences between levels. G. Cheng et al. [5] introduced a regularization constraint to the basis of the traditional CNN framework for the problem of object rotation variations. Kamel et al. [20,21] presented Deep CNN for human action recognition.

2.2 Attention Mechanism

Attention mechanism has achieved increasingly use in object detection and classification in the work of the various computer vision tasks. F. Zhu et al. [12] considered both semantic and spatial relations to address the problem of multi-label image classification. Attention mechanism also makes an important contribution to the saliency detection. For the unsupervised feature learning scene classification tasks, F. Zhang et al. [13] extracted a set of patches from region-of-interest, which are robust and efficient. In this paper, we propose a spatial and channel-wise attention mechanism to focus more attention on the feature maps on the different levels.

3   Method

This section describes the proposed method of remote sensing scene classification, including channel-wise attention module, spatial attention mechanism and broad-classifier. The core idea of this approach is to make full use of the relationship between different levels and the spatial information of target object. Hence, the ResNet [14] is used to extract multiscale feature maps. The overview of our proposed architecture is demonstrated in Fig. 1. $\mathbf{X} \in R^{H \times W}$ (where H,W respectively the height and width) denotes the input image, and the residual feature mapping $\mathbf{F} \in R^{H \times W \times C} (R - Conv - 1)$ will be learned from the ResNet. All processes can be summarized as:

$$\mathbf{F}^{'} = \mathbf{F} + sigmoid((\mathbf{W}_s * \mathbf{F}) * (\mathbf{W}_c * \mathbf{F})) \tag{1}$$

where $\mathbf{F}^{'}$ represents the new feature mapping with the spatial and channel-wise mechanism, $\mathbf{W}_s$ and $\mathbf{W}_c$ stands for the spatial attention and channel attention weights respectively, and $*$ denotes the element-wise multiplication.

3.1   Spatial and Channel-Wise Attention Module

The feature map reflects the semantic and structural information of remote sensing image which is significant for the visual classification and recognition tasks. Besides, the feature maps from various levels frequently represent have different characteristics. Hence we proposed a spatial and channel-wise attention module to integrate feature maps from different levels to enhance the discrimination to

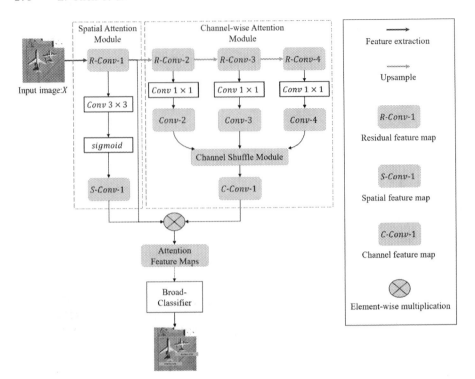

Fig. 1. Overview of our architecture. The architecture consists of two parts, spatial and channel-wise attention mechanism and broad-classifier. R-Conv-1~4 are the last residual blocks of different feature maps from the ResNet [14] backbone.

different scene categories. As shown in Fig. 2, it demonstrates the channel shuffle module. We denote the pyramid feature extract from ResNet as Conv-2~4 and the Conv-3~4 will be upsampled to the same size as Conv-2. Then, the aligned feature maps linked together to form a novel channel map information, which is strengthened among various levels. After that, we split the complementary feature blocks and recover to the original size. In practice, this operation enhances the relationships of these different channel feature representations in actual.

The high-resolution remote sensing image is easy to achieve with the development of remote sensing technology. And the complex background structure makes the classification task more difficult. Therefore it's important to highlight the important parts. Motivated by this, a spatial attention mechanism is added to address this problem. As shown in Fig. 1, the input feature map of spatial attention is $\mathbf{F} \in R^{H \times W \times C}$, and the output is $\mathbf{S} \in R^{H \times W \times C}$. Then the spatial attention mechanism can be denoted as:

$$\mathbf{S} = sigmoid(\mathbf{A}_s F) * \mathbf{F} \tag{2}$$

where *sigmoid* denotes the sigmoid activation function, and $\mathbf{A}_s$ means the convolution kernels of spatial attention network.

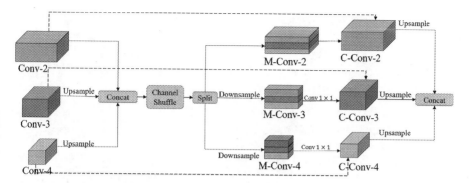

Fig. 2. Channel-wise attention module. The module adopts the multi-channel overlay on the mapped features Conv-2~4 to acquire the intermediary features M-Conv-2~4 with different channels among various levels.

3.2 Broad-Classifier

For the image classification task, it is of vital importance to choose a appropriate way to represent the semantic information of image. We proposed a spatial and channel-wise attention module to address the image representation problem. But image recognition is also important for image classification. Therefore a broad-classifier is proposed to align the categories. A flat network named broad learning system [8] is used to completed the classification task. The whole classification process is divided into two steps: features map and nodes enhance.

Assume that we present the input of broad-classifier as $\mathbf{F}'$, and the ith mapped feature as $\mathbf{M}_i$, therefore the each mapped note can be denoted as:

$$\mathbf{M}_i = \varphi(\mathbf{F}' \mathbf{W}_{si} + \beta_{si}), i = 1, 2, ..., MN \tag{3}$$

where the $\mathbf{W}_{si}$ is the convolution kernel and β_{si} denotes the bias which generate randomly. Hence all mapped features can be denoted as $\mathbf{M}^n = [\mathbf{M}_1, \mathbf{M}_2, ..., \mathbf{M}_n]$, where $n = MN$. After that, the mth group of enhancement modes can be presented as:

$$\mathbf{H}_m = \sigma(\mathbf{M}^n \mathbf{W}_{hm} + \beta_{hm}) \tag{4}$$

Similarly, $\mathbf{W}_{hm}$ and β_{hm} are randomly generated. Hence, the output matrix $\mathbf{Y}$ can be represented as the equation of the form:

$$\mathbf{Y} = [\mathbf{M}_1, ..., \mathbf{M}_n \mid \sigma(\mathbf{M}^n \mathbf{W}_{h1} + \beta_{h1}), ..., \sigma(\mathbf{M}^n \mathbf{W}_{hm} + \beta_{hm})]\mathbf{W}^m \tag{5}$$

where $\mathbf{W}^m$ stands for the connecting weights of mapped nodes and enhancement nodes.

4 Experiments

4.1 Experimental Datasets

To prove the effectiveness of the proposed method, three public datasets is utilized to evaluate the remote sensing scene classification task, including WHU-

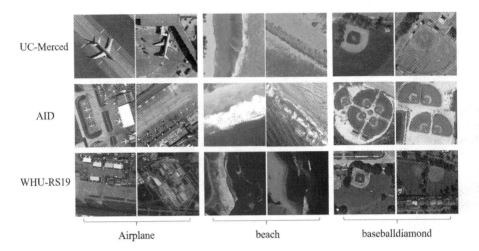

Fig. 3. Samples of the three data sets used in this paper. Airplane, base ball diamond, beach, sparse residential and so on.

RS19 [15], UC-Merced [16] and AID [17]. These datasets are collected from various regions with various remote sense equipments. WHU-RS19 are acquired from the Google Earth Imagery, which has a large size of 600×600 pixels. The data set contains 1013 images. And it divided into 19 classes, each of which consists of 50 images at least. The UC-Merced is got from United States Geological Survey National Map. It contains 21 scene classes and 100 samples of size 256×256 in each class, which a total of 2100 images. It is a challenging datasets due to the complex background among categories. AID is also acquired from Google Earth Imagery, which contains 30 aerial scene categories with a size of 600×600 pixels. There are 10 000 images in total. The categories of these datasets include buildings, airplane, beach, agricultural and so on. We shown some samples in Fig. 3.

Table 1. Performance comparisons with contrasting methods. WHU and UC denote the WHU-RS and UC-Merced dataset respectively.

Method	MSCN [18]			DFF [19]			Ours		
	WHU	*UC*	*AID*	*WHU*	*UC*	*AID*	*WHU*	*UC*	*AID*
Airport red (AP)	98.32%	97.53%	95.45%	98.98%	96.43%	98.91%	99.01%	98.92%	97.89%
Farmland (AP)	93.87%	92.56%	92.78%	94.63%	93.78%	94.44%	95.32%	94.28%	95.89%
Parking lot (AP)	97.45%	97.92%	98.91%	95.72%	96.28%	96.65%	97.43%	97.88%	96.94%
River (AP)	96.33%	95.69%	91.84%	89.94%	93.32%	90.72%	98.37%	97.25%	94.78%
mAP	96.49%	95.92%	94.74%	94.82%	94.95%	95.81%	**97.53%**	**96.46%**	**96.37%**

4.2 Experiment Results and Analysis

The evaluation indicators average precision (AP) and mean average precision (mAP) is used to evaluate the performance of our proposed method. The mAP commonly used in multiple categories problem, and it's a vital indicator in classification tasks.

In order to evaluate the performance of our framework, we implement three groups of experiments for the three datasets. Two contrasting approaches, namely MSCN [18] and Deep Feature Fusion(DFF) [19], is used for a comparison. And some comparative results are shown in Table 1. As we can see, the proposed method gets much better performance than other two approaches. Our method obtains a 97.53%, 96.46% and 96.37% accuracy under the three datasets, respectively. Especially when the background of remote sensing image is very complex, the framework still works well. In addition, these methods achieve a higher accuracy under the WHU-RS19 dataset. This is because the WHU-RS19 is a relatively small remote sensing image data set compared to other datasets.

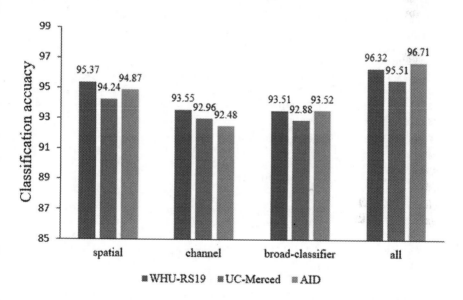

Fig. 4. Evaluation of each component of the proposed method.

In this paper, we proposed three novel components to improve the performance of classification task. There are spatial attention mechanism, channel attention mechanism and broad-classifier. To analyze the impact of each component, we discard one of them to compare the accuracy of the classification task. As we can see in Fig. 4, each component plays a important role for the classification task, but acquires the best performance when all components are connected together.

5   Conclusion

In this paper, we propose a image classification mechanism that includes spatial and channel-wise attention and broad-classifier to deal with the remote sensing scene classification task. We first build a channel-wise attention mechanism to reinforce the correlation among the different levels, which can enhance the information communication effectively. Then, spatial attention is used to highlight the interest region from complex background. Finally, a broad-classifier is designed to make full use of the feature maps and improve the accuracy. Our method obtains the promising results on the public datasets. As for future work, we plan to propose a rotational invariance technique to address the rotation problem in remote sensing scene classification task.

References

1. Zheng, X., Yuan, Y., Lu, X.: Hyperspectral image denoising by fusing the selected related bands. IEEE Trans. Geosci. Remote Sens. **57**(5), 2596–2609 (2019)
2. Yuan, Y., Fang, J., Lu, X., Feng, Y.: Remote sensing image scene classification using rearranged local features. IEEE Trans. Geosci. Remote Sens. **57**(3), 1779–1792 (2019)
3. Cui, S., Datcu, M.: Comparison of approximation methods to Kullback-Leibler divergence between Gaussian mixture models for satellite image retrieval. Remote Sens. Lett. **7**(7), 651–660 (2016)
4. Huo, L.J., Bin, H.E., Zhou, D.B.: A destriping method with multiscale variational model for remote sensing images. Opt. Precis. Eng. **25**, 198–207 (2017)
5. Cheng, G., Zhou, P., Han, J.: Learning rotation-invariant convolutional neural networks for object detection in VHR optical remote sensing images. IEEE Trans. Geosci. Remote Sens. **54**(12), 7405–7415 (2016)
6. Wan, L., Liu, N., Guo, Y., Huo, H., Fang, T.: Local feature representation based on linear filtering with feature pooling and divisive normalization for remote sensing image classification. J. Appl. Remote Sens. **11**(1), 016017 (2017)
7. Liang, Y., Monteiro, S. T, Saber, E. S.: Transfer learning for high resolution aerial image classification, In: Proceedings IEEE Applied Imagery Pattern Recognition Workshop, pp. 1–8 (2016)
8. Chen, C.L.P., Liu, Z.: Broad learning system: an effective and efficient incremental learning system without the need for deep architecture. IEEE Trans. Neural Netw. Learn. Syst. **29**, 10–24 (2018)
9. Hu, F., Xia, G.S., Hu, J., Zhang, L.: Transferring deep convolutional neural networks for the scene classification of high-resolution remote sensing imagery. Remote. Sens. **7**(11), 14680–14707 (2015)
10. Wang, Q., Wan, J., Yuan, Y.: Deep metric learning for crowdedness regression. IEEE Trans. Circ. Syst. Video Technol. **28**(10), 2633–2643 (2018)
11. Chen, Z., Wang, S., Hou, X. Shao, L.: Recurrent transformer network for remote sensing scene categorisation. In: BMVC, pp. 266–278 (2018)
12. Zhu, F., Li, H., Ouyang, W., Yu, N., Wang, X.: Learning spatial regularization with image level supervisions for multi-label image classification. In: IEEE Conference on Computer Vision and Pattern Recognition, pp. 5513–5522 (2017)

13. Zhang, F., Du, B., Zhang, L.: Saliency-guided unsupervised feature learning for scene classification. IEEE Trans. Geosci. Remote. Sens. **53**(4), 2175–2184 (2015)
14. He, K., Zhang, X., Ren, S., Sun, J.: Deep residual learning for image recognition. In: Proceedings of the IEEE Conference on Computer Vision and Pattern Recognition, pp. 770–778 (2016)
15. Xia, G.S., Yang, W., Delon, J., Gousseau, Y., Sun, H., Matre, H.: Structural high-resolution satellite image indexing. In: Proceedings of 7th Symposium ISPRS TC, pp. 298–303 (2010)
16. Yang, Y., Newsam, S.: Bag-of-visual-words and spatial extensions for land-use classification. In: Proceedings of 18th SIGSPATIAL International Conference Advances Geographic Information Systems, San Jose, CA, USA, November 2010, pp. 270–279(2010)
17. Xia, G.S., et al.: AID: a benchmark data set for performance evaluation of aerial scene classification. IEEE Trans. Geosci. Remote Sens. **55**(7), 3965–3981 (2017)
18. Lu, X., Gong, T., Zheng, X.: Multisource compensation network for remote sensing cross-domain scene classification. IEEE Trans. Geosci. Remote. Sens. **58**(4), 2504–2515 (2020)
19. Chaib, S., Liu, H., Gu, Y., Yao, H.: Deep feature fusion for VHR remote sensing scene classification. IEEE Trans. Geosci. Remote Sens. **55**(8), 4775–4784 (2017)
20. Kamel, A., Sheng, B., Yang, P., Li, P., Shen, R., Feng, D.D.: Deep convolutional neural networks for human action recognition using depth maps and postures. IEEE Trans. Syst. Man Cybern. Syst. **49**(9), 1806–1819 (2019)
21. Karambakhsh, A., Kamel, A., Sheng, B., Li, P., Yang, P., Feng, D.D.: Deep gesture interaction for augmented anatomy learning. Int. J. Inf. Manage. **45**, 328–336 (2019)
22. Lu, P., Sheng, B., Luo, S., Jia, X., Wu, W.: Image-based non-photorealistic rendering for realtime virtual sculpting. Multimedia Tools Appl. **74**(21), 9697–9714 (2014). https://doi.org/10.1007/s11042-014-2146-4
23. Meng, X., et al.: A video information driven football recommendation system. Comput. Electr. Eng. **85**, 106699 (2020)
24. Sheng, B., Li, P., Zhang, Y., Mao, L.: Greensea: Visual soccer analysis using broad learning system. IEEE Trans. Cybern. 1–15 (2020)
25. Zhang, P., Zheng, L., Jiang, Y., Mao, L., Li, Z., Sheng, B.: Tracking soccer players using spatio-temporal context learning under multiple views. Multimedia Tools Appl. **77**(15), 18935–18955 (2017). https://doi.org/10.1007/s11042-017-5316-3

GARNet: Graph Attention Residual Networks Based on Adversarial Learning for 3D Human Pose Estimation

Zhihua Chen[1(✉)], Xiaoli Liu[1], Bing Sheng[2], and Ping Li[3]

[1] Department of Computer Science and Engineering,
East China University of Science and Technology, Shanghai 200237, China
czh@ecust.edu.cn
[2] Department of Computer Science and Engineering, Shanghai Jiao Tong University,
Shanghai 200240, China
[3] Faculty of Information Technology, Macau University of Science and Technology,
Macau 999078, China

Abstract. Recent studies have shown that, with the help of complex network architecture, great progress has been made in estimating the pose and shape of a 3D human from a single image. However, existing methods fail to produce accurate and natural results for different environments. In this paper, we proposed a novel adversarial learning approach and studied the problem of learning graph attention network for regression. Graph Attention Residual Networks (GARNet), which processes regression tasks with graphic-structured data, learns to capture semantic information, such as local and global node relationships, through end-to-end training without additional supervision. The adversarial learning module is implemented by a novel multi-source discriminator network to learn the mapping from 2D pose distribution to 3D pose distribution. We conducted a comprehensive study to verify the effectiveness of our method. Experiments show that the performance of our method is superior to that of most existing techniques.

Keywords: Pose estimation · Graph attention networks · Adversarial learning

1 Introduction

Monocular pose estimation has many applications in the field of computer vision, such as action recognition, human-computer interaction and autonomous driving. Among them, 3D human pose estimation is a very active research topic, which refers to estimating the 3D position of body parts on the basis of single or multiple RGB images or 2D human pose coordinates. There are many methods

Supported by the National Natural Science Foundation of China (Grant No. 61672228, 61370174) and Shanghai Automotive Industry Science and Technology Development Foundation (No. 1837).

© Springer Nature Switzerland AG 2020
N. Magnenat-Thalmann et al. (Eds.): CGI 2020, LNCS 12221, pp. 276–287, 2020.
https://doi.org/10.1007/978-3-030-61864-3_24

for 3D human pose estimation. Currently, the popular methods include obtaining the 3D coordinates of human pose directly from a single image [2,3], obtaining the 3D spatial position information from multi-view image [1], and obtaining the 2D pose coordinates first, and then estimating the 3D pose according to the obtained 2D pose coordinates. The most direct method is to predict the 3D pose coordinates directly from a single image, which is to establish the end-to-end mapping from monocular RGB images to 3D coordinates by using the deep learning model. The disadvantage is that the current approach is difficult to meet the performance requirements of learning complex features. Even the most advanced methods so far require additional auxiliary parameters and special network structures. The method of constructing 3D spatial position information through multi-view images, which is take advantage of the information of camera position or camera angle, construct the spatial coordinate system through mathematical operation or machine learning method, and then obtain the final result according to the predicted 2D pose and depth information, which has better performance. However, multi-view images have higher requirements on the number and placement of cameras. For the method of predicting 3D pose through 2D pose coordinates, in order to reduce the learning pressure, 2D pose information is directly used to learn 3D pose through mathematical calculation or lightweight network. However, this method relies on 2D pose input, and the error of 2D pose estimation will be magnified in the process of 3D estimation.

In this work, we proposed a novel graph attention network architecture called Graph Attention Residual Networks (GARNet) for 3D human pose regression. Specifically, we studied the local and global relations of nodes and the influence of GARNet on the 2D to 3D human pose regression task. The goal of 3D human pose estimation is to predict the position of the corresponding 3D joints in a coordinate space for a given 2D human pose. It's intuitive to use GARNet to develop this problem. This method can make 2D and 3D pose be represented by typical skeleton in the forms of 2D or 3D coordinates. GARNet can effectively utilize the spatial relationship between them, which is essential for understanding human behavior. In addition, we propose a novel multi-source discriminator network that, instead of memorizing all the postures from the training set, learns a meaningful variety of feasible human pose. The multi-source discriminator is mainly used to distinguish the predicted 3D pose from the ground truth, which is helpful to enhance the pose estimator to generate the anthropometric pose, especially outdoor sports scene images. The multi-source discriminator consists of three information sources: (1) original input image, (2) kinematic chain space (KCS), (3) 2D location heatmaps and body joint depthmaps. We embed these three information sources and then connect them together to determine whether the input is the ground-truth or estimated pose. As a source of information, the original image can provide rich context information to reduce ambiguity. In order to detect the characteristics of human pose, such as motion chains, symmetry, we included KCS in the discriminator network to improve the quality of the discriminator. As a representation of the original joint position of human body, heatmaps and depthmaps can obtain the complex geometric relationship of human body structure.

Our work makes the following two main contributions: (1) We proposed a Graph Attention Residual Networks (GARNet). The key idea is to learn the channel weight of the edges implied in the Graph and add no-local block to it to capture the local and global relationship between nodes, which greatly improves the performance of 3D human posture regression. (2) We propose a novel multi-source discriminator, which uses the visual information, human pose characteristics and the complex geometry relationships of human body structure as the domain prior knowledge, to improve the generalization ability of the 3D pose estimator.

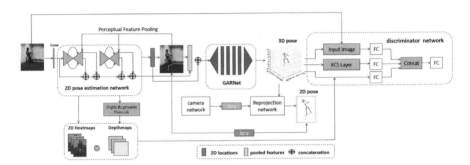

Fig. 1. Framework overview of the proposed 3D human pose estimation approach. We pre-train a 2D pose estimation network to predict 2D joint locations. It also serves as a backbone network where we pool image features. Graph Attention Residual Networks (GARNet) is used for 3D human pose regression tasks. The discriminator distinguishes the ground-truth 3D poses from the predicted ones, so as to further improve the performance of pose estimation.

2   Related Work

2.1   3D Human Pose Estimation

In recent work, many methods have used convolutional neural networks to predict the location of 3D human joints directly from the input images [4–6,30]. Different from the general regression problem, Pavlakos et al. [2] first proposed that 3D keypoints localization problem in the voxel space can be used to handle 3D human pose estimation. Recently, Sun et al. [7] proposed a method to combine volume heat maps with soft-argmax activation, which achieved good performance. An increasing number of studies concentrate on taking advantage of deep neural networks to explore the mapping relation between 2D and 3D joint locations [28,29]. A number of algorithms estimate 3D pose directly from the image [2,3], while others integrate 2D heatmaps with volumetric representation [2], paired distance matrix estimation [8] or image clues [9] for 3D human pose regression. Some recent studies show that 2D pose information is very important for 3D pose estimation. Martinez et al. [10] put forward a simple but resultful method which estimate 3D keypoints merely based on 2D detections. Pavlakos et al. [11] came up with the idea of using the relative depth of the human joints to assist the training of the 3D human pose estimation task. Fang et al. [12] made use of pose grammar networks to ulteriorly extended this approach.

2.2 Graph Attention Networks

It is an important topic in the field of deep learning to extend CNN to input with graphic structure. Recent research on computer vision has achieved advanced performance by using GCN to model relationships between visual objects [14] or time series [13]. GCN is limited by the fact that filters learned on the basis of one domain are not enough to insured behave similarly when put into another base and domain. Compared with GCN, GAT adopted a new method to process the graph neural network, which was to migrate the brilliant attention mechanism in transform to the graph neural network without sharing these limitations. We explored applying GAT to regression tasks. The introduction of the attention mechanism can make the computation efficient, because the calculation of the attention mechanism on all sides can be parallel, and the calculation of the output feature can also be parallel on all nodes. Secondly, the attention mechanism can deal with the problem of input of any size and focus on the most influential input. After the attention mechanism is introduced, it is only related to adjacent nodes, that is, nodes with shared edges, without obtaining the whole graph information.

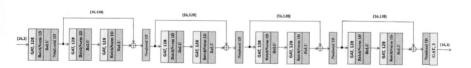

Fig. 2. Example of the proposed Graph Attention Residual Network.

3   Overview

For a color input image, our task is to output the 3D pose information of the human body. The first stage of our network architecture is the 2D pose estimation module. The output is a 2D heatmaps of the joint position of the body, and then the depthmaps is output through the depth regression module. We studied the effect of GARNet on 2D to 3D human pose regression. Given a 2D human pose as input, GARNet is used to predict the position of its corresponding 3D joints in a coordinate space. In the standard generative adversarial network (GAN) training, the generator network learns a mapping from the input distribution to the output distribution, which is evaluated by the discriminant network. Our proposed multi-source discriminator is used to determine whether the input is a ground truth or an estimated pose. Without the knowledge of the camera projection, the 3D pose generated by the network is likely to be an incorrect 3D reconstruction of the input 2D observation. So we introduced a camera estimation network and a reprojection layer. The overall pipeline of our proposed method is given in Fig. 1.

3.1   Graph Attention Residual Networks

In our framework, Graph Attention Residual Network (GARNet) learns the mapping from the distribution of 2D keypoints detected to the distribution of 3D keypoints. From the perspective of generative adversarial network, it can be regarded as generator network, which tries to predict the precise 3D pose to deceive discriminator. We proposed a new network architecture for regression tasks, called Graph Attention Residual Network, where GATNet and non-local layers are interwoven to acquire the semantic relationship between local and non-local layer nodes. A regression function ζ^* that needs to be learned is defined as:

$$\zeta^* = \underset{\zeta}{argmin} \frac{1}{N} \sum_{i=1}^{N} L(\zeta(\mathbf{P_i}), \mathbf{J_i}) \tag{1}$$

where K is the numbers of joints, $P \in \Re^{K \times 2}$ is a series of 2D joints, $J \in \Re^{K \times 3}$ is their corresponding 3D joints in a predefined camera coordinate system.

In this work, as shown in Fig. 2, all blocks are composed of a residual block [18] constructed by two GATNet layers, a total of 128 channels, and then followed by a residual block constitutes a non-local layer. We made this block repeat several times to get a deeper network. At the start of the network, the input is mapped to the potential space, and finally the encoded features are projected back to the output space. Except for the last layer, all layers have been added with batch normalization [19] and ReLU activation [20]. The loss function of our regression task is:

$$L(B, J) = \sum_{i=1}^{M} \|\mathbf{B_i^*} - \mathbf{B_i}\|^2 + \sum_{i=1}^{K} \|\mathbf{J_i^*} - \mathbf{J_i}\|^2 \tag{2}$$

where $\mathbf{B_i}$ and $\mathbf{J_i}$ is ground truth, $J = \{\mathbf{J_i^*}|i = 1, \ldots, K\}$ are predicted 3D joint coordinates, $B = \{\mathbf{B_i^*}|i = 1, \ldots, M\}$ are bones [21] computed from J.

3.2   Discriminator Network

In the standard generative adversarial network, the pose predicted by the generator are often viewed as "fake" examples for training the discriminator. In the adversarial learning stage, the pose estimator was learned, which made it impossible to distinguish the ground-truth of discriminator from the predicted pose. Therefore, the adversarial learning requires that the predicted pose has a similar distribution to ground-truth 3D poses. We use the 3D pose generated by unannotated images as fake examples for learning better discriminators. Accordingly, it can also learn a better pose generator. The quality of the discriminator has an important effect on the performance of the generator, which determines whether the estimated 3D pose is similar to the ground truth. Therefore, we designed a multi-source discriminator network. Selecting the appropriate information source for the discriminator can effectively improve its performance. Considering the description of image pose corresponding and the constraints of human kinematics, our proposed multi-source discriminator consists of three information sources: (1) original input image, (2) kinematic chain space (KCS), (3) 2D location heatmaps and body joint depthmaps.

The first information source is our original input images. Since it provides fund of contextual information, it can be used to model the corresponding pose of the image to reduce the ambiguity in the pose generation process, as shown in Fig. 1. In order to further strengthen the kinematic constraints of body joints, We regard kinematic chain space [15] which is easy to calculate and implement as second source information. Among them, the application of joint length and Angle of descriptor is inspired by [16], as shown in Fig. 1. KCS matrix can be used as an additional feature matrix in discriminator network, which does not need to learn joint length calculation and angle constraint by itself. In fact, in our approach, the KCS matrix plays an important role in achieving acceptable symmetry between the left and right sides of the body. With this constraint, the discriminator network does not memorize all the pose from the training set, but rather learns a meaningful human pose that conforms to the kinesiology. On account of the network can extract the plentiful and complex geometric relationships in the human body structure from the heatmaps, we also study the use of 2D location heatmaps as an part of additional information source, which is resultful for the estimation of 2D adversarial posture [17]. In addition, We also considered incorporating depth information into the representation of the original joints of the body and further linking the heatmaps and depthmaps as third information source.

3.3   Reprojection Layer and Camera Estimation

In order to satisfy the reprojection constraint and be sensitive to overfitting, we learned [18] to add a third neural network to predict camera parameters from the input data, and the inferred camera parameters were used to re-project the estimated 3D pose back to 2D. Reprojection loss function is:

$$L_{rep}(\mathbf{X}, \mathbf{K}) = \|\mathbf{W} - \mathbf{K}\mathbf{X}\|_F \qquad (3)$$

where $\| \cdot \|_F$ denotes the Frobenius norm, $\mathbf{W}$ is the input 2D pose observation matrix, $\mathbf{K}$ is camera matrix, $\mathbf{X}$ is the output pose of the 3D generator network, $\mathbf{K}\mathbf{X}$ denotes the 3D pose is projected back into the 2D coordinate space. Camera loss function is:

$$L_{cam} = \|\frac{2}{trace(\mathbf{KK^T})}\mathbf{KK^T} - \mathbf{I_2}\|_F \qquad (4)$$

where $\mathbf{I_2}$ is the 2×2 identity matrix.

4   Experiment

4.1   Datasets and Evaluation Protocols

Datasets. We evaluate our methods, both quantitative and qualitative, on popular human pose estimation benchmarks: Human3.6M [22] and MPII Human Pose [23]. Human 3.6 m is currently the largest publicly available 3D human pose estimation datasets. This is one of the largest 3D body pose estimates datasets, with 3.6 million images, including 11 actors performing 15 daily activities, such as eating, sitting, walking and taking photos, from 4 camera view. We use this datasets for quantitative evaluation. The MPII human pose datasets is a challenging benchmark for estimating 2D human posture in the wild. According to the previous methods [2,12], this datasets was used for qualitative evaluation of cross-domain generalization.

Table 1. Quantitative comparisons of Mean Per Joint Position Error (mm) between the estimated pose and the ground truth on Human3.6M [22] under Protocol ♯1.

Protocol ♯1	Direct.	Discuss	Eating	Greet	Phone	Photo	Pose	Purch
Du et al. [24]	85.1	112.7	104.9	122.1	139.1	135.9	105.9	166.2
Pavlakos et al. [2]	67.4	71.9	66.7	69.1	72.0	77.0	65.0	68.3
Mehta et al. [5]	52.6	64.1	55.2	62.2	71.6	79.5	52.8	68.6
Zhou et al. [3]	54.8	60.7	58.2	71.4	62.0	65.5	53.8	55.6
Sun et al. [4]	52.8	54.8	54.2	54.3	61.8	53.1	53.6	71.7
Fang et al. [12]	50.1	54.3	57.0	57.1	66.6	73.3	53.4	55.7
Yang et al. [25]	51.5	58.9	50.4	57.0	62.1	65.4	49.8	52.7
Hossain & Little [26]	48.4	50.7	57.2	55.2	63.1	72.6	53.0	51.7
Ours	47.3	55.7	51.4	58.5	61.1	49.9	47.3	64.1

Evaluation Protocols. For human3.6m [22], there are two common evaluation protocols used in the literature to split different training and testing datasets. A standard protocol uses all four camera views in subject S1, S5, S6, S7, and S8 for training, and the same four camera views in subject S9 and S11 for testing. Errors were calculated after the ground truth and prediction were aligned with the root joint. We'll call this protocol ♯1. The other protocol used six subjects S1, S5, S6, S7, S8, and S9 for training and evaluation on frame 64 of S11. It also uses rigid transformations to further align predictions with the ground truth.

Table 2. Quantitative comparisons of Mean Per Joint Position Error (mm) between the estimated pose and the ground truth on Human3.6M [22] under Protocol ♯1.

Protocol ♯1	Sitting	SittingD.	Smoke	Wait	WalkD.	Walk	WalkT	Avg.
Du et al. [24]	117.5	226.9	120.0	117.7	137.4	99.3	106.5	126.5
Pavlakos et al. [2]	83.7	96.5	71.7	65.8	74.9	59.1	63.2	71.9
Mehta et al. [5]	91.8	118.4	65.7	63.5	49.4	76.4	53.5	68.6
Zhou et al. [3]	75.2	111.6	64.1	66.0	51.4	63.2	55.3	64.9
Sun et al. [4]	86.7	61.5	67.2	53.4	47.1	61.6	53.4	59.1
Fang et al. [12]	72.8	88.6	60.3	57.7	62.7	47.5	50.6	60.4
Yang et al. [25]	69.2	85.2	57.4	58.4	43.6	60.1	47.7	58.6
Hossain & Little [26]	66.1	80.9	59.0	57.3	62.4	46.6	49.6	58.3
Ours	86.2	55.0	67.8	61.0	42.1	60.6	45.3	56.9

This protocol is called protocol ♯2. In this work, we used protocol ♯1 in all of our experiments, because it was more challenging and consistent with our method setup. The evaluation metric is the Mean Per Joint Position Error (MPJPE) in millimeter between the ground truth and the predicted 3D coordinates across all cameras and joints after aligning the pre-defined root joints (the pelvis joint). We use this metric in our work to evaluate.

4.2 Configurations and Result

Configurations. According to the standard training process in [3], we first pre-trained the 3D pose estimator on the MPII data set to match the performance reported in [27]. Then, we used the pre-trained 2D module to train the full pose estimator on Human3.6M for 200K iteration. In order to extract the learned 3D pose into the unconstrained data set, we alternately trained the discriminator and the pose estimator for 120 K iteration.

Quantitative Evaluation on Human3.6M. Table 1 and Table 2 reports the comparison with previous methods on Human3.6M. Our method achieves the state-of-the-art results. For Protocol ♯1, our method obtains 56.9 of mm of error, which has 1.4%–8% improvements compared to previous advanced methods [3, 4, 12, 25, 26].

Qualitative Results. In Fig. 3 and Fig. 4, we show the visual results of our approach on the human3.6m and MPII test set. As you can see, our method can accurately predict the 3D pose in the interior and in most in-the-wild images. The experimental results show that our method is able to effectively regress 3D human pose and extend them to some new situations.

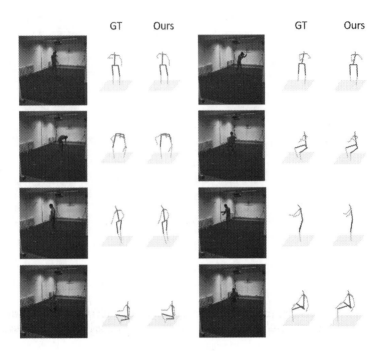

Fig. 3. Predicted 3D poses on the Human3.6M test set. The 3D skeleton on the left is the ground truth (GT), and the results of our method are shown on the right.

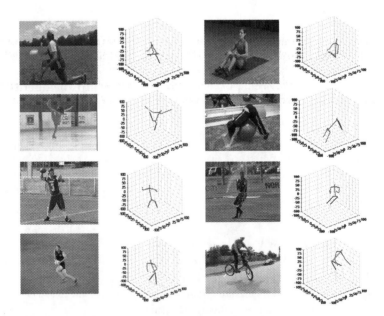

Fig. 4. Example 3D pose estimations from the MPII dataset. Although not perfect, the poses is still reasonable and close to the correct poses.

5   Discussion

In this paper, an adversarial learning framework based on 2D joint detection for 3D human pose estimation neural network is proposed. On this basis, we proposed a new regression model for the 3D human pose regression tasks, which use the graph structure data to learn the local and global node relations to operate the regression tasks. We also proposed a new multi-source discriminator which further improves the performance of 3D human pose estimation. Experimental results demonstrate the effectiveness and flexibility of the proposed framework in 3D human pose estimation tasks. We hope our ideas of 3D regression model and multi-source discriminator can inspire more future work in human pose estimation and other images processing tasks.

References

1. Kocabas, M., Karagoz, S., Akbas, E.: Self-supervised learning of 3D human pose using multi-view geometry. In: IEEE Conference on Computer Vision and Pattern Recognition, pp. 1077–1086 (2019)
2. Pavlakos, G., Zhou, X., Derpanis, K.G., Daniilidis, K.: Coarse-to-fine volumetric prediction for single-image 3D human pose. In: IEEE Conference on Computer Vision and Pattern Recognition, pp. 1263–1272 (2017)
3. Zhou, X., Huang, Q., Sun, X., Xue, X., Wei, Y.: Towards 3D human pose estimation in the wild: a weakly-supervised approach. In: IEEE International Conference on Computer Vision, pp. 398–407 (2017)
4. Liang, S., Sun, X., Wei, Y.: Compositional human pose regression. Comput. Vis. Image Underst. **176–177**, 1–8 (2018)
5. Mehta, D., et al.: Monocular 3D human pose estimation in the wild using improved CNN supervision. In: 2017 International Conference on 3D Vision, pp. 506–516 (2017)
6. Tomè, D., Russell, C., Agapito, L.: Lifting from the deep: convolutional 3D pose estimation from a single image. In: 2017 IEEE Conference on Computer Vision and Pattern Recognition, pp. 5689–5698 (2017)
7. Sun, X., Xiao, B., Wei, F., Liang, S., Wei, Y.: Integral human pose regression. In: Ferrari, V., Hebert, M., Sminchisescu, C., Weiss, Y. (eds.) ECCV 2018. LNCS, vol. 11210, pp. 536–553. Springer, Cham (2018). https://doi.org/10.1007/978-3-030-01231-1_33
8. Morenonoguer, F.: 3D human pose estimation from a single image via distance matrix regression. In: 2017 IEEE Conference on Computer Vision and Pattern Recognition, pp. 1561–1570 (2017)
9. Buades, A., Coll, B., Morel, J.: A non-local algorithm for image denoising. In: 2005 IEEE Conference on Computer Vision and Pattern Recognition, pp. 60–65 (2005)
10. Martinez, J.A., Hossain, R., Romero, J., Little, J.J.: A simple yet effective baseline for 3D human pose estimation. In: IEEE International Conference on Computer Vision, pp. 2659–2668 (2017)
11. Pavlakos, G., Zhou, X., Daniilidis, K.: Ordinal depth supervision for 3D human pose estimation. In: IEEE Conference on Computer Vision and Pattern Recognition, pp. 7307–7316 (2018)

12. Fang, H., Xu, Y., Wang, W., Liu, X., Zhu, S.: Learning pose grammar to encode human body configuration for 3D pose estimation. In: Conference on Artificial Intelligence, pp. 6821–6828 (2018)

13. Yan, S., Xiong, Y., Lin, D.: Spatial tempobral graph convolutional networks for skeleton-based action recognition. In: Conference on Artificial Intelligence, pp. 7444–7452 (2018)

14. Yang, J., Lu, J., Lee, S., Batra, D., Parikh, D.: Graph R-CNN for scene graph generation. In: Ferrari, V., Hebert, M., Sminchisescu, C., Weiss, Y. (eds.) ECCV 2018. LNCS, vol. 11205, pp. 690–706. Springer, Cham (2018). https://doi.org/10.1007/978-3-030-01246-5_41

15. Wandt, B., Ackermann, H., Rosenhahn, B.: A kinematic chain space for monocular motion capture. In: Leal-Taixé, L., Roth, S. (eds.) ECCV 2018. LNCS, vol. 11132, pp. 31–47. Springer, Cham (2019). https://doi.org/10.1007/978-3-030-11018-5_4

16. Wandt, B., Rosenhahn, B.: RepNet: weakly supervised training of an adversarial reprojection network for 3D human pose estimation. In: IEEE Conference on Computer Vision and Pattern Recognition, pp. 7782–7791 (2019)

17. Chen, Y., Shen, C., Wei, X., Liu, L., Yang, J.: Adversarial PoseNet: a structure-aware convolutional network for human pose estimation. In: IEEE International Conference on Computer Vision, pp. 1221–1230 (2017)

18. He, K., Zhang, X., Ren, S., Sun, J.: Deep residual learning for image recognition. In: IEEE Conference on Computer Vision and Pattern Recognition, pp. 770–778 (2016)

19. Ioffe, S., Szegedy, C.: Batch normalization: accelerating deep network training by reducing internal covariate shift. In: Proceedings of the 32nd International Conference on Machine Learning, pp. 448–456 (2015)

20. Nair, V., Hinton, G.E.: Rectified linear units improve restricted Boltzmann machines. In: Proceedings of the 27th International Conference on Machine Learning, pp. 807–814 (2010)

21. Sun, X., Shang, J., Liang, S., Wei, Y.: Compositional human pose regression. In: IEEE International Conference on Computer Vision, pp. 2621–2630 (2017)

22. Ionescu, C., Papava, D., Olaru, V., Sminchisescu, C.: Human3.6m: large scale datasets and predictive methods for 3D human sensing in natural environments. IEEE Trans. Pattern Anal. Mach. Intell. **36**, 1325–1339 (2014)

23. Andriluka, M., Pishchulin, L., Gehler, P V., Schiele, B.: 2D human pose estimation: new benchmark and state of the art analysis. In: 2014 IEEE Conference on Computer Vision and Pattern Recognition, pp. 3686–3693 (2014)

24. Du, Y., et al.: Marker-less 3D human motion capture with monocular image sequence and height-maps. In: Leibe, B., Matas, J., Sebe, N., Welling, M. (eds.) ECCV 2016. LNCS, vol. 9908, pp. 20–36. Springer, Cham (2016). https://doi.org/10.1007/978-3-319-46493-0_2

25. Yang, W., Ouyang, W., Wang, X., Ren, J., Li, H., Wang, X.: 3D human pose estimation in the wild by adversarial learning. In: 2018 IEEE Conference on Computer Vision and Pattern Recognition, pp. 5255–5264 (2018)

26. Hossain, M.R.I., Little, J.J.: Exploiting temporal information for 3D human pose estimation. In: Ferrari, V., Hebert, M., Sminchisescu, C., Weiss, Y. (eds.) ECCV 2018. LNCS, vol. 11214, pp. 69–86. Springer, Cham (2018). https://doi.org/10.1007/978-3-030-01249-6_5

27. Newell, A., Yang, K., Deng, J.: Stacked hourglass networks for human pose estimation. In: Leibe, B., Matas, J., Sebe, N., Welling, M. (eds.) ECCV 2016. LNCS, vol. 9912, pp. 483–499. Springer, Cham (2016). https://doi.org/10.1007/978-3-319-46484-8_29

28. Kamel, A., Sheng, B., Yang, P., Li, P., Shen, R., Feng, D.D.: Deep convolutional neural networks for human action recognition using depth maps and postures. IEEE Trans. Syst. Man Cybern. Syst. **49**(9), 1806–1819 (2019)
29. Karambakhsh, A., Kamel, A., Sheng, B., Li, P., Yang, P., Feng, D.D.: Deep gesture interaction for augmented anatomy learning. Int. J. Inf. Manage. **45**, 328–336 (2019)
30. Sheng, B., Li, P., Zhang, Y., Mao, L.: GreenSea: visual soccer analysis using broad learning system. IEEE Trans. Cybern. 1–15 (2020)

GPU-based Grass Simulation with Accurate Blade Reconstruction

Sheng Wang[1], Saba Ghazanfar Ali[2], Ping Lu[3], Zhen Li[3], Po Yang[4],
Bin Sheng[2(✉)], and Lijuan Mao[5(✉)]

[1] AVIC Shanghai Aviation Electric Co. Ltd., Shanghai, People's Republic of China
[2] Shanghai Jiao Tong University, Shanghai, People's Republic of China
shengbin@sjtu.edu.cn
[3] ZTE Corporarion, Nanjing, People's Republic of China
[4] The University of Sheffield, Sheffield, UK
[5] Shanghai University of Sport, Shanghai, People's Republic of China
maolijuan@sus.edu.cn

Abstract. Grass is a very important element of nature and it could almost be found in every natural scene. Thus grass modeling, rendering as well as simulation becomes an important task for virtual scene creation. Existing manual grass modeling and reconstruction methods have researched on generate or reconstructing plants. However, these methods do not achieve a good result for grass blades for their extremely thin shape and almost invariant surface color. Besides, current simulation and rendering methods for grasses suffer from efficiency and computation complexity problems. This paper introduces a framework that reconstructs the grass blade model from the color-enhanced depth map, simplifies the grass blade model and achieves extremely large scale grassland simulation with individual grass blade response. Our method starts with reconstructing the grass blade model. We use color information to guide the refinement of captured depth maps from cameras based on an autoregressive model. After refinement, a high-quality depth map is used to reconstruct thin blade models, which cannot be well handled by multi-view stereo methods. Then we introduce a blade simplification method according to each vertex's movement similarity. This method takes both geometry and movement characteristics of grass into account when simplifying blade mesh. In addition, we introduce a simulation technique for extremely large grassland that achieve tile management on GPU and allow individual response for each grass blade. Our method excels at reconstructing slender grass blades as well as other similar plants, and realistic dynamic simulation for large scale grassland.

Keywords: Grass · Reconstruction · Simulation · GPU · Intelligent information processing

1 Introduction

Grass is a significant feature of the natural world and it is indispensable in most 3D games and movies. Therefore grass simulation becomes an essential

N. Magnenat-Thalmann et al. (Eds.): CGI 2020, LNCS 12221, pp. 288–300, 2020.
https://doi.org/10.1007/978-3-030-61864-3_25

field of computer graphics and visualization, which includes grass modeling, rendering, and simulation. Individual response from every single grass blade greatly improves viewers' experience for the virtual environment and increase the scene's fidelity. Grass simulation may not be so difficult for a single blade, however, when there is a requirement for simulating a large quantity of grass blades, the vertex amount for a single grass blade is strictly limited to a very small count in order to achieve high simulation performance. Modeling realistic grass blade with vertex amount restriction is challenging, no mater manually creating or recovering grass blade shape from images or videos.

Fig. 1. Large grassland generated with our method, there are over one million grass blades with over 30 million triangles and more than one hundred objects. (Color figure online)

Existing methods usually use manually pre-designed grass blade models [25], these models are created according to the artist's experience and lack variety. Existing works have focused on capturing and recovering macro structures for plants and other man-made objects. Those reconstruction methods use a multi-view stereo to reconstruct the depth map. They rely on color-correlation in different images and calculate depth according to triangulating. However stereo-based methods are not able to handle grass reconstruction well. Extremely thin shape and almost invariant surface color make it difficult to find corresponding point or pixel in reference images when doing triangulating. As for grass dynamic simulation, current works have explored different schemes. Procedural animation is a simple way to simulating grass blades movement, however, it doesn't provide interaction between grass blades and another object. Some methods simulate some grass blades as guide grass, and nearby grass blades would follow the movements of guide grass blades. Those methods relieve the computation burden however suffer from repetition pattern problems. Some previous works use a string-mass system to simulate the movement of grass blades, nevertheless, a balance between blade movement accuracy and simulation performance leads to a very small amount of active grass blades in a very large grassland. Those methods could barely achieve individual responses for each blade in the whole scene.

In this paper, we present a novel and effective framework for simulation of an extremely large amount of grass blades and this framework includes grass blade modeling, rendering, and simulation. Our framework is able to reconstruct a grass blade from images, simplify the grass blade model and render large scale grassland scenes with high quality as well as realistic simulation response to collisions. We use a color-enhanced depth map to reconstruct the thin shape of the grass blade model. Then blade contour is extracted through image-based edge detection. After that, a particle-flow method is used to capture the accurate blade contour of any shape and calculate the blade's skeleton. In order to deal with a large number of grass blades, the vertex amount for a single grass blade is strictly restricted. The blade skeleton may contain hundreds of triangles for a single blade needed for rendering, thus it must be simplified before using. We introduce a blade skeleton simplification algorithm that takes geometry fidelity and vertices movement similarity into account. This iterative algorithm allows us to simplify the blade model to an appropriate level as preset by a user. Finally, We implement the method introduced by Han et al. [9] to simulate our grass blade and extend the method introduced by Fan et al. [6] to do tile management. Our main contributions are listed below:

- **Vertices' movement similarity for blade skeleton simplification**: In order to achieve high simulation performance for an extremely large amount of grass blades, we simplify reconstructed grass blade model according to not only vertices' geometry but also movement similarity in simulation, which lead to more accurate grass blade simplification result.
- **GPU-Based tile management in simulation**: We improve tile management and introduces a more exhaustive GPU-based grass tile management. This scheme allows GPU to calculate all the collisions between objects and tiles, and update the collision tile list automatically, which relieves pressure on CPU and thus improves the overall performance of simulation as well as rendering.

2   Related Work

Grass Rendering and Simulation. The most challenging part of grass modeling, rendering and simulation are caused by extremely large quantities. William Reeves [20] addressed those challenges in 1985. Works about grass mainly discuss the following three topics: grass modeling, rendering, and simulation. For modeling and rendering, Kajiya et al. [10] introduced volumetric textures(texels) for short fur rendering. Texels can use to solve spatial aliasing problems. Neyret extended this work to simulate natural scenes such as realistic grass [15]. Brook et al. [1] improved this method to obtain high rendering performance. The image-based method was used in grass rendering in 2005 [21]. This method used bidirectional texture function for grass. Through length preserving free-form deformation of the 3D skeleton lines of each grass blade and alpha test to implement transparent texture mapping, wang et al. modeled grasses of different shapes with rich details [25]. Boulanger et al. introduced a level-of-detail (LOD) method

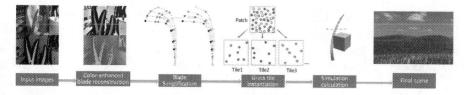

Fig. 2. Overview of system pipeline

for grass rendering with realistic dynamic light and shadow effects [3]. In previous works about grass simulation, grass blades were pushed away when an interaction between grass blades and objects happens [8]. Qiu et al. proposed to propose a method for dynamic simulation of grass field swaying in wind [17]. Spring-mass system was also used to model grass blades and simulate grass-object interaction [5]. We adopt the simulation algorithm introduced by Han et al. [9]. This method treated collision as hard constraint, meanwhile treated length, bending and twisting as soft constraints in the Anastacio 2006 modeling iterative solver for grass-object interaction. Inspire from [11,12], we employ the rendering and simulation framework introduced by [6]. With this framework, we are able to perform collision computation on GPU and do a grass blade instancing on the fly. We implement our capture method on the basis of this framework to obtain more accurate and diverse grass types.

Plant Reconstruction. A number of works for leaf and flora reconstruction have reference value for our method since we want to recover the grass blade model. There are some previous works about using interactive methods to generate or reconstruct leaf shapes and tree shapes [14] and Quan et al. [18] introduced a method to model plant from a dozen of images. This method could recover the plant's shape automatically while relying on the user to provide some hints for segmentation. Tan et al. [24] proposed a method to generate 3D trees from images. They populated tree leaves from segmented source images and used shape patterns of visible branches to predict occluded branches. [13,22] build for realtime virtual realistic based on image. Bradley et al. [4] presented a scaling technique to compute the 3D structure of foliage and extract leaf shapes.

Model Simplification. After capturing, we need to simplify our grass blade model so that it could be applied in real scenes. This is very similar to many Level-of-detail (LOD) methods, which are typical model simplification algorithms. They are used to simplify model geometry complexity and accelerate rendering as well as simulation performance. The framework used to obtain a constant frame rate for visualization of virtual environments was introduced in 1993 [7]. Geometry-based LOD algorithms including quad re-meshing methods were summarized in [2]. Field-guided parameterizations-based methods split quad re-meshing into three steps including cross-field computation, integer-grid parameterizations and quad mesh extraction [19]. Our skeleton simplification method is similar to LOD algorithms, moreover, we take simulation fidelity into account while simplifying the grass blade model. This leads to a more accurate model for rendering and simulation at the same time and we are able to balance the trade-off between performance and quality.

3   Algorithm Details

We introduce a novel and effective framework that is able to reconstruct the grass blade model from the color-enhanced depth map, simplify the model and finally achieve high-quality rendering and realistic individual simulation for each grass blade for very large scale grassland. Figure 1 shows one large grassland generated with our method. This grassland contains over one million grass blades(over 30 million triangles) and more than one hundred objects. The pipeline of our algorithm is shown in Fig. 2. We input a captured depth map and accompanied color image from structured-light based sensing camera. Through the color-enhanced technique, we are able to recover an accurate depth map by filtering noise and complete depth losses. Those depth discontinuities specularly appear near edges of objects. Then blade contour is obtained through image-based edge detection. we design a simplification algorithm to reduce vertex amount while maintaining its geometry as well as simulation features at the same time. We adopt the GPU instancing scheme used in [6] to achieve high-quality rendering and realistic individual simulation.

3.1   Model Simplification

Having reconstructed the grass blade model from the color-enhanced depth map, we design a scheme to simplify this model so that it could possibly be used in large-scale grassland rendering and simulation. Otherwise, any method couldn't afford millions of grass blades each with thousands of vertices. The grass blade model used in our rendering and simulation framework is represented as line segments. We store line segments as degenerated triangles as expand them before rendering. This step will be covered in Sect. 3.2. Thus model simplification is designed to decrease the vertex amount of line segments, which is called a blade skeleton. This skeleton simplification method is similar to some LOD methods, however, most LOD methods are designed for triangle meshes or quad meshes. More importantly, we need to take geometry fidelity as well as vertices' movement similarity into account simultaneously while doing simplification. Therefore we design this scheme that both geometry fidelity and vertices' movement similarities for simulation are important factors in simplification.

In our system, we define any two vertices' movement similarity by the distance between them and their movement trends. Geometrically speaking, for any two vertices, their similarity is determined by the distance between them. And in simulation, for any two vertices, their similarity is determined by the stability of the distance between them. In another word, if two vertices remain the same distance to each other, we consider that they have a unified movement trend, thus they are similar. On the other hand, the distance between tip vertex and root vertex varies significantly during simulation, thus there are less similar obviously. We acquire the position data of all vertices every a few milliseconds, then we are able to calculate distances between any two vertices during a period of time. Variance is usually used to describe data stability. If distance variance is low, it means the distance between two vertices is stable. In another word, this indicates that these two vertices move synchronously. We tend to merge vertices that are both geometrically similar and have high movement similarity. Assume we acquire n frames of position data for each vertex every a few milliseconds, $\vec{v}_m^n$ is mth vertex at nth frame, **Diff** represents difference between any two vertices, **g** denotes geometry difference function, **m** denotes movement difference function, therefore we introduce difference of any two vertices as:

$$\mathbf{Diff}(\vec{v}_1, \vec{v}_2) = \mathbf{g}(\vec{v}_1, \vec{v}_2) \times \mu + \mathbf{m}(\vec{v}_1, \vec{v}_2) \tag{1}$$

$$\mathbf{g}(\vec{v}_1, \vec{v}_2) = \frac{\sum_{i=0}^{n} \| \vec{v}_1^i, \vec{v}_2^i \|}{n} \tag{2}$$

$$\mathbf{m}(\vec{v}_1, \vec{v}_2) = (\frac{\sum_{i=0}^{n} \| \vec{v}_1^i, \vec{v}_2^i \|^2}{n} - \frac{(\sum_{i=0}^{n} \| \vec{v}_1^i, \vec{v}_2^i \|)^2}{n}) \tag{3}$$

where μ is the control parameter for geometry and movement difference wight and it could be set by the user, n is acquired total frame account.

We use an iterative algorithm to complete this skeleton simplification process. After skeleton calculation, we obtain an array of skeleton vertices. We design a greedy algorithm to iteratively merge two adjacent vertices until the target vertex number is achieved. This algorithm based on the assumption that if two vertices are the most similar then they should be adjacent vertices in the array. Because closer vertices are geometrically more similar, meanwhile we find that adjacent vertices get higher movement similarity than non-adjacent vertices.

3.2   Rendering and Simulation

Instanced Rendering. According to our reconstructed grass blade model and simplification result, we pre-generate a list of grass blades with some random scaling. We divide the whole scene into square tiles of the same size. Those blades in the *Patch* are randomly located in a square that has the same size of glass tiles in the scene. Each tile contains a subset of continuous blades in the *Patch*. For each grass tile, its start position to fetch blade data in the *Patch* is calculated by tile's world position coordinate in the scene. With this instancing scheme, we are able to reduce memory use from about 4 GB of 4 M blades to only 24 MB for a *Patch* of 16384 blades with exactly the same high-quality grassland. With this *Patch*, we manage to simulate a grassland with rich variance.

We draw one line segment as two degenerate triangles and expand each knot(two overlapping vertices) of this line segment at run-time according to expansion width, which is stored as grass blade model data. We employ Phong shading along with subsurface scattering effect [23] in our system. In order to avoid a monotone, we use a density map in our system. The density map determines the grass blade amount within each tile. Our density map is generated with Perlin noise [16] and it is continuous among tiles and since each blade is randomly located within each tile, thus density map will not bring in any unnatural-looking caused by strange density.

GPU-Based Tile Management. In our simulation system, we extend the simulation method introduced by Han et al. [9] to simulate grass Blades. We also improve tile management scheme introduced by Fan et al. [6] to GPU-Based tile management. This simulation scheme is compatible with procedural animation. We are able to simulate millions of grass blades with real-time performance.

Compared with CPU-Based tile management, our tile management achieves to perform tile management purely on GPU, which means we accomplish to perform tile-object collision detection on GPU and we do not need to transfer active tile date from CPU to GPU, which relieves the burden for CPU and bandwidth. We set up a thread on GPU to keep track of the collision status of every object and record a possibly-collision tile list for each object. During the data synchronization process, all list of possibly-collision tiles will be merged into one list, this becomes the to-activate tile list used in later steps.

4   Implementation and Results

We implemented our system on a PC with Windows 8.1, Intel i5-4460 CPU running at 3.2 GHz and AMD Radeon HD7970 graphic card. 4-times multi-sampling anti-aliasing is used in all experiments to guarantee satisfactory visual effects.

Instancing rendering is used in our implementation in order to reduce draw call overhead of CPU. Instancing parameters are pre-generated and stored in a structured buffer before rendering. Our rendering scheme is also compatible with different LOD algorithms at far distances.

Timestamps are used in our simulation scheme in order to imitate the energy dissipation process. Tile activation is triggered when objects enter a tile and deactivation starts when all objects leave a tile after a time delay. Since activation and deactivation processes are called so frequently that instant GPU memory allocation would significantly slow down the simulation process and eventually becomes the bottleneck of the whole system, we set up a GPU memory pool and pre-allocate GPU memory before simulation. We assign memory for tiles when the simulation is needed and recycle as soon as tile deactivation starts.

4.1   Reconstructed Model and Simplification Result

Our method could reconstruct the grass blade model from the color-enhanced depth map, simplify the reconstructed blade model for the usage in rendering and simulation. This provides the possibility for the user to capture any appropriate category of grasses or leaves and use them as a blade models for large scale grassland simulation. This is especially useful for virtual-reality or augmented-reality applications where quick reconstruction of grassland with specific grass blade type is needed.

Our grass blade skeleton is essentially represented as line segments, which could be expanded to real grass blade before rendering. Thus simplification quality is determined by the error between the simplified grass blade skeleton and the reconstructed blade skeleton. There is a difference between the simplified blade model and the reconstructed blade model before simplification. This difference is the simplification error, and we intend to measure the "distance" between vertex sets before and after simplification to evaluate the simplification result. Hausdorff distance is usually used to measure how far two subsets of a metric space are from each other [26]. According to Hausdorff distance, simplification error could be defined as:

$$
Error(X, Y) = \max\{ \sup_{\vec{x} \in X} \inf_{\vec{y} \in Y} \| \vec{x} - \vec{y} \|,
$$
$$
\sup_{\vec{y} \in Y} \inf_{\vec{x} \in X} \| \vec{x} - \vec{y} \|\} \tag{4}
$$

where sup represents the supremum of the set and inf represents the infimum. X, Y are two sets while $\vec{x}$, $\vec{y}$ are elements that belong to set X, Y respectively. In our method, Hausdorff distance is used to measure the similarity of a simplified skeleton and the original one before simplification. However, since the skeleton after simplification could be a subset of the original one, Hausdorff distance could become meaningless in that case. Therefore we eliminate the vertices from original skeleton vertex set α if they are also in simplified skeleton vertex set β, let $\alpha' = \alpha - \beta$, then we calculate the Hausdorff distance from α' to β. In this way, we actually measure the distance between the culled vertex set and the remained vertex set after simplification.

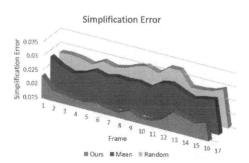

Fig. 3. Skeleton simplification evaluation results: our methods, mean method and random method. (Color figure online)

We record vertex position data every a few milliseconds during the simulation process. Simulation for reconstructed skeleton vertices and simplified skeleton vertices are conducted at the same time with identical collision. Then we calculate Hausdorff distance as simplification result error. For the need of comparison, we implement several other schemes used for skeleton simplification. The random method iteratively deletes vertex randomly from the original vertex set. The mean method selects vertices evenly along with the skeleton from the root to the top according to vertex index. The geometry-based simplification algorithm uses vertices' position as guidance to reduce vertices. It iteratively merges two vertices with the shortest distance. Since the grass blade skeleton is represented as line segments, many LOD methods for meshes eventually degenerate to the geometry-based method used in our comparison. From Fig. 3 we could see that our skeleton simplification algorithm always gets the lowest error among the methods listed above.

4.2   Rendering and Simulation Result

We have evaluated our algorithm in its rendering and simulation performance. In our system, we need only one draw call to rendering the whole scene, which greatly reduces CPU overhead. We are able to render a scene of 15264 tiles in 21 ms, in total there are 976896 blades and over 31 million triangles.

As compared with the multiple-draw call method, the one-draw-call method has an obvious performance advantage. With instanced rendering scheme, all tiles share the same Patch data for blade vertices. Only some parameters should be set up before rendering such as tile world coordinate. Thus we store all the parameters for each tile, and those parameters could be fetched in vertex shader through tile index and vertex index. We pay a small space (less than 1 MB) for about 50%–60% rendering performance improvement.

Table 1 illustrates our rendering performance in FPS (Frame per second) for non-GPU-based tile management method [6] and our GPU-based tile management method. Our GPU-based tile management is designed to improve the simulation efficiency.

Table 1. Rendering performance with and without GPU.

Tile No.	2K	4K	8K	16K	2K	4K	8K	16K
Blade/Tile	GPU-Based method				Non-GPU-Based method			
64	71	66	54	28	73	68	56	31
128	72	56	32	15	74	59	35	18
256	57	30	16	7	60	33	19	9
512	31	16	8	4	33	20	11	6

In Table 2, profiling data for simulation demonstrates the effectiveness of our simulation scheme. Simulation time for a single blade decreases with the increase of simulated tiles as listed in the table. This gives the evidence that our

Table 2. Simulation time data with different activated tiles, objects.

Tiles	Blades	Objects	Sim time (ms)	Sim time/Blade (ns)
6	384	1	0.176	0.458
14	896	2	0.183	0.204
150	9600	20	0.952	0.099
709	45376	128	4.67	0.103

Table 3. GPU time for rendering and simulation with 23 K activated grass blades, 4 million total grass blades and 128 objects. Percentages in the table denote a busy time ratio for a specific stage.

Items	GPU (ms)	VS	PS	CS	Tex
Grass simulation	5.6	0	0	99.9%	99.7%
Grass rendering	5.4	99.9%	75.0%	0	32.1%
Skybox rendering	0.3	0.11%	31.3%	0	92.2%
Terrain rendering	0.3	99.5%	72.7%	0	10.9%

simulation scheme is suitable to solve the high simulation cost problem caused by extremely large grassland.

Table 3 shows GPU time for rendering and simulation in one specific frame with a scene which contains over $23K$ activated grass blades and 128 objects. VS, PS, CS, and Tex represent vertex shader, pixel shader, compute shader and texture operation respectively. The percentage means how busy this stage is during rendering. Due to the parallelism of GPU, the percentages of listed three stages do not sum to one hundred percent. We do not list GPU utilization for simulation because only compute shader is used. We achieved a balance between rendering and simulation since GPU time for them is approximately equal. Vertex shader utilization is up to one hundred percent indicates huge vertex processing in our algorithm, which becomes the bottleneck of the whole system.

Limitations. Restricted by the vertex amount of grass blade, our method has some limitations. First, a small vertex amount is not enough to model jagged blades or leaves. Sharp variation in shape definitely needs more vertices to remain such features. However, vertex amount is severely restricted by performance requirements, we need to balance vertex amount and performance at the same time. Thus simplified results may damage the reconstructed model structure if we have to reduce vertex amount to a small number. Meanwhile, due to the structure of grass blade we use in our system, we are not able to handle horizontally curly blades. Secondly, infrared camera has limitations on its accuracy. This camera could only provide a depth map of low resolution, and it could only detect objects within a one-meter range. If we want to reconstruct a very thin grass blade whose width is even smaller than its infrared dot pattern, we could not recover a good depth map for the grass blade model. Hopefully, this problem would be solved by the development of hardware.

5 Conclusion

In this paper, we present a framework for reconstructing grass blade with color-enhanced depth map, blade extraction, extremely large scale grassland rendering and simulation with GPU-based tile management. We utilize an increasingly popular infrared depth camera and take advantage of depth information provided by a depth camera with our color-enhancement technique to reconstruct the grass blade model. A blade skeleton simplification process according to vertices' movement similarity is introduced to reduce skeleton vertex number so that it can be used in the rendering and simulation system with acceptable performance. As for rendering, we adopt a GPU-instanced scheme to reduce memory usage. An improved GPU-based tile management method is employed to pay simulation costs for those tiles only when needed.

Our proposed method concentrate on reconstructing grass blade shape and simplifying its structure so that it can be used in the rendering and simulation method for large scale grassland. We are able to reconstruct a variety of grass blades. We would also like to extend our method to handle more complex blade shapes or reconstruct another kind of plants. Furthermore, our method does not handle grass fracture and deformation. Skeleton and expansion width calculation may get incorrect results with such cases. We plan to handle grass fracture in future works and add support for structurally different vegetation.

In summary, our work demonstrates how effectively reconstruct the method for this and small plants can be developed and how to use the reconstructed model in rendering and simulation frameworks. This work can be extended to many fields and inspire other reconstruction and modeling methods for plants and other kinds of objects.

Acknowledgement. This work was supported in part by the National Key Research and Development Program of China under Grant 2018YFF0300903, in part by the National Natural Science Foundation of China under Grant 61872241 and Grant 61572316, and in part by the Science and Technology Commission of Shanghai Municipality under Grant 15490503200, Grant 18410750700, Grant 17411952600, and Grant 16DZ0501100.

References

1. Bakay, B., Lalonde, P., Heidrich, W.: Real-time animated grass. In: Eurographics 2002 (2002)
2. Bommes, D., et al.: Quad-mesh generation and processing: a survey, vol. 32(6), pp. 51–76 (2013)
3. Boulanger, K., Pattanaik, S.N., Bouatouch, K.: Rendering grass in real time with dynamic lighting. IEEE Comput. Graphics Appl. **29**(1), 32–41 (2009)

4. Bradley, D., Nowrouzezahrai, D., Beardsley, P.: Image-based reconstruction and synthesis of dense foliage. ACM Trans. Graph. (TOG) **32**(4), 74 (2013)
5. Chen, K., Johan, H.: Real-time continuum grass. In: 2010 IEEE Virtual Reality Conference (VR), pp. 227–234. IEEE (2010)
6. Fan, Z., Li, H., Hillesland, K., Sheng, B.: Simulation and rendering for millions of grass blades. In: Proceedings of the 19th Symposium on Interactive 3D Graphics and Games, pp. 55–60. ACM (2015)
7. Funkhouser, T.A., Séquin, C.H.: Adaptive display algorithm for interactive frame rates during visualization of complex virtual environments. In: Proceedings of the 20th Annual Conference on Computer graphics and Interactive Techniques, pp. 247–254. ACM (1993)
8. Guerraz, S., Perbet, F., Raulo, D., Faure, F., Cani, M.P.: A procedural approach to animate interactive natural sceneries. In: 16th International Conference on Computer Animation and Social Agents, pp. 73–78. IEEE (2003)
9. Han, D., Harada, T.: Real-time hair simulation with efficient hair style preservation. In: Proceedings of the VRIPHYS 2012, pp. 45–51 (2012)
10. Kajiya, J.T., Kay, T.L.: Rendering fur with three dimensional textures. ACM Siggraph Comput. Graph. **23**(3), 271–280 (1989)
11. Kamel, A., Sheng, B., Yang, P., Li, P., Shen, R., Feng, D.D.: Deep convolutional neural networks for human action recognition using depth maps and postures. IEEE Trans. Syst. Man Cybern. Syst. **49**(9), 1806–1819 (2019)
12. Karambakhsh, A., Kamel, A., Sheng, B., Li, P., Yang, P., Feng, D.D.: Deep gesture interaction for augmented anatomy learning. Int. J. Inf. Manage. **45**, 328–336 (2019)
13. Lu, P., Sheng, B., Luo, S., Jia, X., Wu, W.: Image-based non-photorealistic rendering for realtime virtual sculpting. Multimedia Tools Appl. **74**(21), 9697–9714 (2014). https://doi.org/10.1007/s11042-014-2146-4
14. Mündermann, L., MacMurchy, P., Pivovarov, J., Prusinkiewicz, P.: Modeling lobed leaves. In: Proceedings Computer Graphics International 2003, pp. 60–65. IEEE (2003)
15. Neyret, F.: Synthesizing verdant landscapes using volumetric textures. In: Pueyo, X., Schröder, P. (eds.) EGSR 1996. E, pp. 215–224. Springer, Vienna (1996). https://doi.org/10.1007/978-3-7091-7484-5_22
16. Perlin, K.: An image synthesizer. ACM Siggraph Comput. Graph. **19**(3), 287–296 (1985)
17. Qiu, H., Chen, L., Chen, J.X., Liu, Y.: Dynamic simulation of grass field swaying in wind. J. Softw. **7**(2), 431–439 (2012)
18. Quan, L., Tan, P., Zeng, G., Yuan, L., Wang, J., Kang, S.B.: Image-based plant modeling, vol. 25(3), pp. 599–604 (2006)
19. Ray, N., Li, W.C., Lévy, B., Sheffer, A., Alliez, P.: Periodic global parameterization. ACM Trans. Graph. (TOG) **25**(4), 1460–1485 (2006)
20. Reeves, W.T., Blau, R.: Approximate and probabilistic algorithms for shading and rendering structured particle systems. ACM SIGGRAPH Comput. Graph. **19**(3), 313–322 (1985)
21. Shah, M.A., Kontinnen, J., Pattanaik, S.: Real-time rendering of realistic-looking grass. In: Proceedings of the 3rd International Conference on Computer Graphics and Interactive Techniques in Australasia and South East Asia, pp. 77–82. ACM (2005)
22. Sheng, B., Li, P., Zhang, Y., Mao, L.: GreenSea: visual soccer analysis using broad learning system. IEEE Trans. Cybern. 1–15 (2020)

23. Sousa, T.: Vegetation procedural animation and shading in crysis. GPU Gems **3**, 373–385 (2007)
24. Tan, P., Zeng, G., Wang, J., Kang, S.B., Quan, L.: Image-based tree modeling. ACM Trans. Graph. **26**(3), 87 (2007)
25. Wang, C., Wang, Z., Zhou, Q., Song, C., Guan, Y., Peng, Q.: Dynamic modeling and rendering of grass wagging in wind. Comput. Anim. Virtual Worlds **16**(3–4), 377–389 (2005)
26. Wikipedia: Hausdorff distance, Wikipedia, the free encyclopedia (2015). Accessed 16 July 2015

Flow Visualization with Density Control

Shiguang Liu$^{(\boxtimes)}$ and Hange Song

College of Intelligence and Computing, Tianjin University,
Tianjin 300350, People's Republic of China
lsg@tju.edu.cn

Abstract. In flow visualization, it remains challenging to flexibly explore local regions in 3D fields and uniformly display the structures of flow fields while preserving key features. To this end, this paper presents a novel method for streamline generation and selection for 2D and 3D flow fields via density control. Several levels of streamlines are divided by flow density. The lowest level is produced using an entropy-based seeding strategy and a grid-based filling procedure. It can generate uniform streamlines without loss of important structural information. Other levels are then generated by a streamline selection algorithm based on the average distance among streamlines. It could help users understand flow fields in a more flexible manner. For 3D fields, we further provide local density control and density control along any axis for users, which are helpful to explore the fields both globally and locally. Various experimental results validate our method.

Keywords: Flow visualization · Density control · Streamlines · Entropy.

1 Introduction

Fluid simulation is an important research topic in computer graphics. In addition to researches [1–4] of fluid animation, flow visualization also attracts more and more attention, that plays an essential role in analyzing features of flow fields, observing physical phenomena, and verifying physical laws, etc.

Flow visualization can be classified into 2D visualization [6–8] and 3D visualization [13]. For the former, Zhang et al. [9] used grids to control placement of streamlines, that can naturally reflect the topology of flow structures. Wu et al. [18] presented a streamline placement algorithm that produces evenly spaced long streamlines while preserving topological features of a flow field. This method is effective in creating evenly spaced long streamlines and preserving topological features. For highlighting the main features of 2D flow fields, Verma et al. [5] identified critical points and proposed a layout algorithm, by selecting the appropriate template to seed points in the neighborhood of each type of critical

Supported by the Natural Science Foundation of China under grant nos. 61672375 and 61170118.

points. This method may exhibit characteristics near the critical point but it cannot guarantee the criterion of uniformity. Xu et al. [10] proposed an entropy-based flow visualization method to evaluate selected seed points. However, it is computationally intensive. In contrast, we proposed a hybrid method to generate streamlines and used the self-defined parameters to select streamlines, which can satisfy the criteria of consistency, coverage and continuity.

For 3D flow visualization, Ye et al. [11] extended the method in [5] and proposed an algorithm based on topology extraction of the 3D flow structure. Marchesin et al. [12] proposed a view-dependent line selection method by using linear entropy and angular entropy. More recently, Gunther et al. [14] proposed an optimization algorithm, that first randomly generated streamlines and then performed a global optimization process to generate the resulting streamlines. Guo et al. [19] proposed stochastic flow maps (SFMs) for visualizing uncertain transport behaviors of unsteady flows. Rossl and Theisel [15] used Hausdorff distances among streamlines for visualization. In contrast, we select streamlines based on flow density. It is useful for users to understand and explore the structure of flow fieldswith hierarchical levels of visualization results rather than with only one. In addition, the density control along any axis and local density control allow users to explore the field flexibly.

This paper takes special care of the uniformity of flow fields and proposes a novel density-controlling method to hierarchically display flow structures. Our method aims to display the fields by a sequence of images of different densities. Specifically, we first generate streamline sets meeting the above three criteria by a hybrid algorithm. Then, we filter streamline sets based on the average distance between streamlines, generating results with different density levels. In the level that contains fewer streamlines, the structure is clear and the user can manipulate the flow field in real-time to observe the general structure. Moreover, one can explore more features in the level with more streamlines. In 3D fields, our method allows users to flexibly control the density in different directions, which is beneficial for users to explore the field. Besides, the local density control for 3D fields helps to choose several regions of interest to view the flow structures.

2 Multi-level Density Control

The main process of our algorithm includes three modules, namely seeding, grid-based filling, and streamline selection.

2.1 Seeding

In general, flow fields may contain different structural characteristics and the most important features in different fields usually lie around critical points where the velocity is zero. Besides, the distribution of velocity in the local region is also used to define the special structure. The important structure usually has a complex distribution of velocity, that can be referred to [10]. It uses the Shannon entropy [16] to detect the above regions. In a flow field, the direction differences around the critical points are usually larger than others. Therefore, if a flow field contains critical points, they are usually contained in the points with larger entropy, which means that these points are likely critical points or near critical points. We calculate entropy with the algorithm in [10].

2.2   Grid-Based Filling

Due to the blank areas after seeding may not satisfy the criterion of consistency, we perform grid-based filling for 2D and 3D flow fields as follows: (1) Divide the flow field into small cells and mark the cells which streamlines go through or are on the border; (2) Detect the blanks and seed in the center of the blank areas; (3) Repeat Step (1) and Step (2) until the size of the blank fields is below a given threshold.

When detecting the blanks, we regard the unlabelled cells as blank areas in 2D fields. In 3D fields, streamlines cannot divide the space into several unconnected regions, so we change the stop strategy of searching cells as follows: when a labelled cell is found in one searching direction, we will stop searching in this direction; If the blank area is greater than the defined value, we would use the center point of the area as seed to generate streamlines. It is not precise but good enough to fill blanks in a 3D flow field. In practice, the defined value is related to grid resolution and it is usually kept lower than 100.

As for seeding in blanks, we calculate the average value of grid coordinate G_x and G_y in all of the blank grids and set point (G_x, G_y) as a new seed in 2D fields. If the seed does not belong to the blank area, we would first generate two streamlines at that point, which are parallel to horizontal direction and vertical direction. Next, we find two line segments in the blank fields and then compare the length of line segments. Finally, we select the midpoint of the longer segment as a new seed point. In 3D fields, due to the specific methods for detecting blanks, the seed is always located in the blank area. Figures 1(c) and 1(d) show the intermediate result of grid-based filling. In Fig. 1(d), the shaded area means the blank got by the searching algorithm. Figure 3(a) demonstrates the result after grid-based filling, in which the streamlines satisfy the criteria of consistency.

2.3   Streamline Selection

The results of streamlines in 2D fields may be too intensive to satisfy user's demand. Meanwhile, the results of 3D visualization may appear severe occlusions. Therefore, we propose the multi-level density display method that uses streamline property to filter streamlines so as to achieve better visual results.

Streamline Property. We use the streamline length to ensure that there are few short streamlines in the results and exploit the average distance among streamlines to control density. Because the curve is stored as a sequence of points in our method, we calculate length by accumulating the distance between adjacent points. As a result, by controlling the properties with given thresholds,

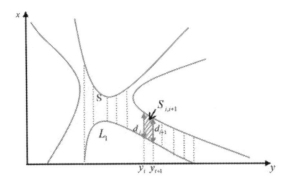

Fig. 1. Illustration of the calculation of the distance among streamlines in the positive direction of the x-axis.

the results will have few short streamlines, that also contributes to the continuity of results.

We use the average distance from a streamline to its neighboring stream-lines to control the density of streamlines. It is difficult to define the uniformity between the streamlines. So we exploited the property D_s to control the density by limiting the distance among streamlines, written as

$$D_s = min\left\{d_{top}, d_{down}, d_{left}, d_{right}\right\} \qquad (1)$$

$$d_p = \frac{\sum \frac{1}{2}(d_i + d_{i+1})\left|y_{i+1} - y_i\right|}{l_{line}}, d_q = \frac{\sum \frac{1}{2}(d_i + d_{i+1})\left|x_{i+1} - x_i\right|}{l_{line}} \qquad (2)$$

where d_{top}, d_{down}, d_{left} and d_{right} represent the distance among streamlines in the positive direction of x-axis, the negative direction of x-axis, the positive direction of y-axis, and the negative direction of y-axis for 2D fields, respectively. The d_i is the distance to the closest streamline point on any other streamline along one axis, l_{line} is the length of the streamline, and p represents top or down, and q is left or right.

Figure 1 describes an example that calculates the distance in the positive direction of the x-axis. We view a streamline as the collection of points. And any dotted line represents the direction of the positive direction of x-axis. Firstly, we calculate d_i for each point of the streamline in this direction. Next, we compute the area $S_{i,i+1}$ between adjacent dotted lines and the streamlines, where we regard the region as the trapezoid for simplicity. Then we will represent the area S with the sum of $S_{i,i+1}$ for every point i. Finally, the area S is divided by the length of the line, i.e., the distance among streamlines in the direction can be evaluated. Similarly, we could get the distance in other directions. The result is the minimum of the all four distances.

Figures 2(a) through 2(e) and Figs. 2(f) through 2(j) show the visualization results with grid resolution 250×250 and 200×200 when the distance threshold δ_t is 0.0, 0.4, 0.8, 1.2 and 1.6, respectively. It can be seen that with different distance thresholds, we can get results with different densities, and all of the results meet the three criteria. Besides, it can be seen that for the images with the same parameter in Fig. 2, the image with larger grid resolution contains more streamlines than that with smaller one.

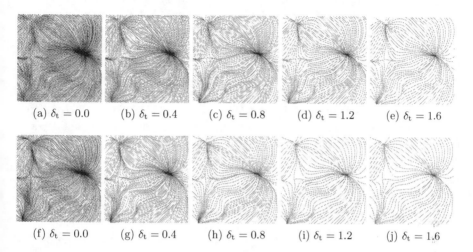

(a) $\delta_t = 0.0$ (b) $\delta_t = 0.4$ (c) $\delta_t = 0.8$ (d) $\delta_t = 1.2$ (e) $\delta_t = 1.6$

(f) $\delta_t = 0.0$ (g) $\delta_t = 0.4$ (h) $\delta_t = 0.8$ (i) $\delta_t = 1.2$ (j) $\delta_t = 1.6$

Fig. 2. The results of 2D flow filed visualization with different grid resolutions and different parameters. (a)–(e) show different results with the grid resolution 250×250, and (f)–(j) show results with the grid resolution 200×200.

Figures 3(a) through 3(d) describe the visualization results for 3D flow fields with different densities. With fewer lines, the structure appears more clear and easier to understand. But the structure will miss some details, especially the structures in higher levels, which will be found in the lower level. The user could understand the main structure in the higher level and then find the missing details in the lower level with suitable viewpoints.

2.4   Parameter Decomposition

The parameter is the average distance among streamlines, and it can work well for 3D fields with the special resolution whose border is a cube, for example $100 \times 100 \times 100$. But, it cannot achieve better results for some resolutions, such as $500 \times 500 \times 100$. Because the density is limited by the shortest direction, the change of the density in other directions could be hardly perceived. In order to achieve more flexible control for understanding, we use three parameters along the x/y/z axes rather than only one parameter in 3D fields as follows:

$$D_x = min\{d_{top}, d_{down}\}, D_y = min\{d_{left}, d_{right}\}, D_z = min\{d_{before}, d_{after}\}$$
(3)

$$d_m = \frac{\sum \frac{1}{2}(d_i + d_{i+1})p_{i,i+1}}{l_{line}}$$
(4)

where D_x, D_y and D_z are control parameters of density; d_{before} and d_{after} represent the distance among streamlines in the positive direction of z-axis, the negative direction of z-axis; m denotes top, down, left, right, before or after; $p_{i,i+1}$ is the distance of two lines which pass through the i_{th} and the $i + 1_{th}$ point in the plane and are perpendicular to the current direction.

The change of the parameters brings more selections for 3D fields. With the three parameters, the user can get more results according to the user's demand that can help understand the flow field more conveniently. The thresholds of the three parameters are δ_x, δ_y and δ_z, respectively. In addition, we could also provide the density control along the axis in any angle. It could be defined by users and could help users to limit the density in this direction. The computation process is similar to Eqs. (3) and (4). The difference is that it takes one direction into consideration. If we set the line from the viewpoint to the object as the direction, the result would have less occlusion and be more clear and understandable.

2.5   Local Density Control

Local density control is another way to explore the flow fields in our method. It means that the size and location of the control box could be changed to show the hidden structure in the local area. Also, more than one control boxes could be employed at the same time. To this end, we need to adjust the size and the

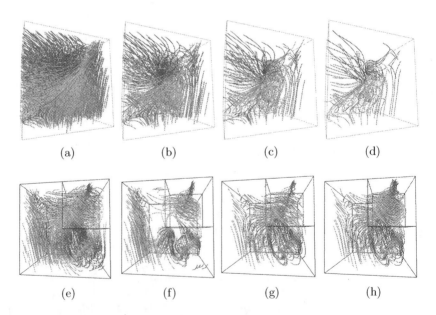

(a)   (b)   (c)   (d)

(e)   (f)   (g)   (h)

Fig. 3. The result with different densities for 3D flow fields, where the parameter δ_l in (a)–(d) is set to 10.0, δ_t is 1.0, 3.0, 5.0, 7.0, respectively; (e)–(h) are the results with local density control, where the small cube is the region of interest. (Color figure online)

location of the control box, which is set as the whole field in the beginning. Then, the condition in Algorithm 1 should be adjusted to suit the case of more controlled boxes. Finally, the results are generated with different densities for each control box.

In our experiment, when more than one control boxes are added, we would compute density and set the condition C_k for the k_{th} controlled box that is usually defined as

$$C_k : D_{x,i} > \delta_x \quad \& \quad D_{y,i} > \delta_y \quad \& D_{z,i} > \delta_z \quad \& \quad l_i > \delta_l \tag{5}$$

where $D_{x,i}$, $D_{y,i}$, and $D_{z,i}$ are the density for the i_{th} streamline in the k_{th} box. l_i means the length of the i_{th} streamline. If one streamline satisfies the condition C_k, it would be added into the field. In Eq. (5), we use the density along the x/y/z axes which could be replaced with the density along other axes or the density without the parameter decomposition. Figures 3(e) through 3(h) describe some results after local density control, where there are two control boxes labelled by the black cube. The small one is the area of interest. Next, we need to deal with the logical relationship between different control boxes. If the logical relation between two control boxes is AND ($C_1 \&\& C_2$), it means that a streamline will be selected for visualization only when the distances of the streamline for every control box are satisfied at the same time. In this way, users could observe the structure in the control box by decreasing the value of the threshold about the density (see Fig. 3(e) and Fig. 3(f)). If the logical relation between two control boxes is OR ($C_1 || C_2$), it means that a streamline will be selected when the distances of the streamline for any control box are satisfied. With this setting, users could show more information in the local area by increasing the density threshold (see Fig. 3(g) and Fig. 3(h)). In addition, the added boxes could be used for colorizing 3D streamlines. The parameter thresholds (δ_x, δ_y, δ_z, δ_l) in Fig. 3(e) and Fig. 3(f) are the same with the big box (2.0, 2.0, 2.0, 5.0) but different with the small box. The one in Fig. 3(e) is (0.0, 0.0, 0.0, 0.0) and the other is (6.0, 6.0, 6.0, 5.0). The hidden information in the small control box is shown in Fig. 3(f). Also, the parameter thresholds of the bigger box in Fig. 3(g) and Fig. 3(h) is (5.0, 5.0, 5.0, 5.0). For the small box, they are (8.0, 8.0, 8.0, 5.0) and (5.0, 5.0, 5.0, 5.0), respectively. More information of local area is shown in Fig. 3(h).

3   Experiments and Results

Our experimental environment is shown as follows: Windows 7.1 64-bit operating systems, Intel(R) Core(TM) i5-4460@ 3.20 GHz, and 8 GB memory.

3.1   Isabel Dataset

The Isabel dataset in our experiment was derived from the IEEE Vis. contest website, whose size is 500×500×100. The set is produced by the Weather Research and Forecast (WRF) model, courtesy of NCAR, and the U.S. National

308   S. Liu and H. Song

Science Foundation (NSF). The dataset includes many types of data but this paper focuses on the wind speed.

Figure 4 demonstrates the results of 3D visualization in the Isabel dataset, including the output of some types of the parameters (the size is $500 \times 500 \times 100$, $\delta_l = 5.0$, and the grid resolution is $100 \times 100 \times 20$). Figures 4(a) and 4(b) show the differences only when the parameter δ_z is different that are respectively 0.5, and 1.5, when (δ_x, δ_y) is (1.0, 1.0). Figures 4(d) and 4(e) show the results only when the parameters (δ_x, δ_z) change which are (0.5, 0.5) and (1.7, 1.7), when δ_y is 1.0. Figures 4(c) and 4(f) display the visualization result by local density control. The small black cuboid represents the controlled area and every line through the area is colored with pink. It could be seen that the main structure of the controlled area with the context is more understandable in Figures 4(c) and 4(f).

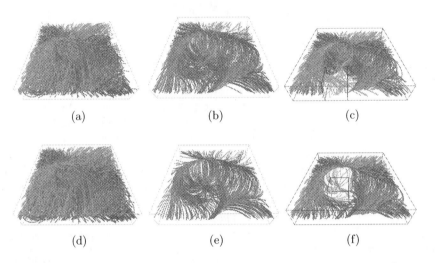

(a)   (b)   (c)

(d)   (e)   (f)

Fig. 4. The results of 3D visualization for the Isabel dataset by parameter control along the x/y/z axes and local density control. (Color figure online)

3.2   Streak Dataset

This is a direct numerical Navier-Stokes simulation by Simone Camarri and Maria-Vittoria Salvetti (University of Pisa), Marcelo Buffoni (Politecnico of Torino), and Angelo Iollo (University of Bordeaux I) [17]. We use a uniformly resampled version provided by Tino Weinkauf. The dataset shows the flow around a square cylinder and its size is $192 \times 64 \times 48$.

Figure 5 shows the results of different densities in Streak dataset ($\delta_l = 5.0$, and the grid resolution is $96 \times 32 \times 24$). The parameters (δ_x, δ_y, δ_z, δ_l) of Fig. 5(a), 5(b), 5(c) and 5(d) are (1.0, 1.0, 1.0, 15.0), (1.0, 4.0, 1.0, 15.0), (1.0, 1.0, 5.0, 15.0) and (4.0, 1.0, 1.0, 15.0), respectively. In this figure, the longer edge of the rectangular represents the x-direction. The z-direction is perpendicular to the projection plane and another edge of the rectangular is the y-direction.

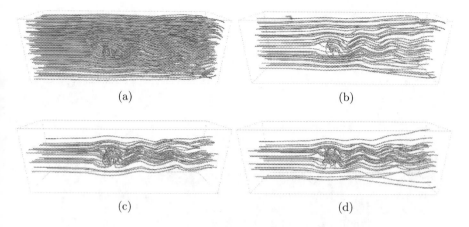

(a)   (b)

(c)   (d)

Fig. 5. 3D visualization result for the Streak dataset.

The time of seeding, filling and selection is 892 s, 189 s and 11 s for the Isabel dataset, and is 18 s, 33 s and 0.6 s for Streak dataset. It can be seen that the time of seeding increases with the size of dataset. Seeding and filling are computed only once for the algorithm which can be accelerated by parallel computing. Compared with other steps, the efficiency of selection is acceptable for users.

3.3   Comparison with State-of-the-art Methods

We compared our method with other state-of-the-art methods in terms of three aspects: coverage, consistency, and continuity.

Figures 5(a), 5(b), and 5(c) show the results of Turk et al.'s method [6], Jobard et al.'s method [7] and Mebarki et al.'s method [8], respectively. Figure 5(d) is our algorithm. In Fig. 5(d), it can be observed that there are fewer short lines in our result. And streamlines satisfy the consistency. Figure 5(e) displays the results by Ye et al.'s method [11] and Fig. 5(f) describes the result by our method where the parameters $(\delta_x, \delta_y, \delta_z, \delta_l)$ is (6.0, 6.0, 6.0, 10.0). Figure 5(g) shows the density results with the threshold 10.0 by our method. It can be seen that our method can greatly reduce the occlusion. Figure 5(h) shows the results with local density control. By comparison, it can be seen that our method can maintain more structures that are obvious in the area marked by yellow circle.

3.4   User Study

To further assess the effectiveness of our method, we designed two experiments to evaluate our method in terms of coverage, consistency, continuity and interactivity. A total of 50 subjects (25 men and 25 women) who are students with the knowledge of the fluid participated in this study.

310   S. Liu and H. Song

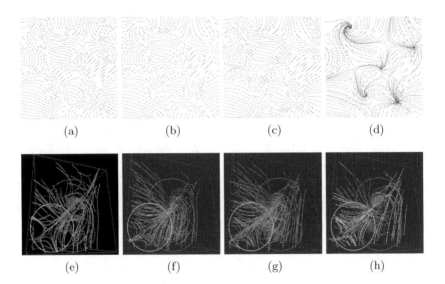

(a)   (b)   (c)   (d)

(e)   (f)   (g)   (h)

Fig. 6. Comparison of the visualization results between our method and other state-of-the-art methods for 2D flow fields (a)–(d) and 3D flow fields (e)–(h). (Color figure online)

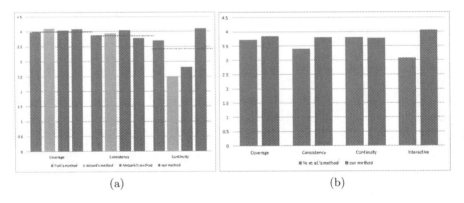

(a)   (b)

Fig. 7. Comparison of the visualization results between our method and other methods for 2D flow fields (a) and 3D flow fields (b). (Color figure online)

The first experiment is about comparison among the results of Turk et al.'s method [6], Jobard et al.'s method [7], Mebarki et al.'s method [8] and our method in the 2D flow fields. We prepared three groups of images, each of which includes the result of different methods with the same 2D field and prepared three questions: (1) "How many critical points you can find?"; (2) "Is the streamline in every result uniform?"; (3) "How many streamlines in current image that is short?". The volunteers are shown one group of images of each method at the same time and they are blind to the method. Then, they need to answer the above questions. About Question 2, they score every method. Each clip has five ranks, from one to five. One means the lowest score and five denotes the highest score. Besides, we compared the answers with the ground truth about questions 1 and 3 and then scored the method from 1 to 5. Figure 6(a) presents the average score of each method in three properties. The red line denotes the average score of three methods. It could be seen that the scores are close with each other about the coverage. However, our method achieves higher score in terms of continuity.

The second experiment focuses on the comparison between the results of Ye et al.'s method [11] and our method for 3D flow fields. We prepared three data sets and four questions: (1) "How many critical points you can find?"; (2) "Is the streamlines of every result uniform?"; (3) "How many streamlines in current image that is short?"; (4) "Is it easy to explore the local information?". The four questions come from the coverage, consistency, continuity and interactivity. In the process, for each dataset, we generated the results for each method with user-defined parameters which include the viewpoint, the number of streamlines, and so on. Also, they are blind to the method and are invited to answer the questions. About Questions 2 and 4, they need to evaluate the methods with the score from one to five. As for Questions 1 and 3, we deal with them like the first experiment. Figure 7(b) shows the average score of each method. It is clear that our method shows advantage in terms of consistency and interactivity. Our method performs better in exploring the local structure which would not lose the information of the critical point as well.

4   Conclusion and Future Work

This paper proposed a new flow visualization method via multi-level density control. The new method includes seeding and grid-based filling, that can make the lowest level of density results not only contain all the important structures, but also maintain the continuity of the streamlines. The multi-level density display mode allows users to better understand the flow. The users can rotate camera in real time at a higher density level to observe the general structure of the flow field characteristics. They can also obtain more information at lower density levels. The local density control can help users to explore the structure in regions of interest. Although our method is effective, there is still room for improving the rendering ways of 3D streamlines. In the future, we will also leverage GPU (Graphics Processing Units) to accelerate our method.

References

1. Zhang, X., Liu, S.: Parallel SPH fluid control with dynamic details. Comput. Animat. Virt. W. **29**(2), e1801 (2018)
2. Feng, G., Liu, S.: Detail-preserving SPH fluid control with deformation constraint. Comput. Animat. Virt. W. **29**(1), e1781 (2018)
3. Zhang, X., Liu, S.: SPH fluid control with self-adaptive turbulent details. Comput. Animat. Virt. W. **26**(3–4), 357–366 (2015)
4. Liu, S., Liu, Q., Peng, Q.: Realistic simulation of mixing fluids. Vis. Comput. **27**(3), 241–248 (2011)

5. Kirby, R., Marmanis, H., Laidlaw, D.H.: Visualizing multivalued data from 2D incompressible flows using concepts from painting. In: Proceeding of IEEE Visualization, pp. 333–340 (1999)
6. Lee, T., Mishchenko, O., Shen, H., Crawfis, R.: View point evaluation and streamline filtering for flow visualization. In: Proceeding of IEEE Pacific Visualization Symposium, pp. 83–90 (2011)
7. Liang, R., et al.: Visual exploration of hardi fibers with probabilistic tracking. Inf. Sci. **330**, 483–494 (2016)
8. Marchesin, S., Chen, C., Ho, C., Ma, K.: View-dependent streamlines for 3D vector fields. IEEE Trans. Vis. Comput. Graph. **16**(6), 1578–1586 (2010)
9. McLoughlin, T., Laramee, R., Peikert, R., Post, F., Chen, M.: Over two decades of integrationbased, geometric flow visualization. Comput. Graph. Forum **29**(6), 1807–1829 (2010)
10. Mebarki, A., Alliez, P., Devillers, O.: Farthest point seeding for efficient placement of streamlines. In: Proceeding of IEEE Visualization, pp. 479–486 (2005)
11. Rossl, C., Theisel, H.: Streamline embedding for 3D vector field exploration. IEEE Trans. Vis. Comput. Graph. **18**(3), 407–420 (2012)
12. Shannon, C.: A mathematical theory of communication. Bell Syst. Tech. J. **27**(4), 379–423 (1948)
13. Song, H., Liu, S.: Dynamic fluid visualization based on multi-level density. In: Proceeding of CASA., pp. 193–196 (2016)
14. Tao, J., Ma, J., Wang, C., Shene, C.: A unified approach to streamline selection and viewpoint selection for 3D flow visualization. IEEE Trans. Vis. Comput. Graph. **19**(3), 393–406 (2013)
15. Theisel, H.: Opacity optimization for 3D line fields. ACM Trans. Graph. **32**(4), 120:1–120:8 (2013)
16. Turk, G., Banks, D.: Image-guided streamline placement. In: Proceeding of ACM SIGGRAPH, pp. 453–460 (1996)
17. Verma, V., Kao, D., Pang, A.: A flow-guided streamline seeding strategy. In: Proceeding of IEEE Visualization, pp. 163–170 (2000)
18. Wu, K., Liu, Z., Zhang, S., Moorhead, R.J.: Topology-aware evenly spaced streamline placement. IEEE Trans. Vis. Comput. Graph. **16**(5), 791–801 (2009)
19. Guo, H., et al.: Extreme-scale stochastic particle tracing for uncertain unsteady flow visualization and analysis. IEEE Trans. Vis. Comput. Graph. **25**(9), 2710–2724 (2019)

DbNet: Double-Ball Model for Processing Point Clouds

Meisheng Shen📵, Yan Gao$^{(\boxtimes)}$, and Jingjun Qiu

East China Normal University, N. Zhongshan Rd, Shanghai 3663, China
51184501041@stu.ecnu.edu.cn,ygao@cs.ecnu.edu.cn

Abstract. Learning and understanding 3D point clouds with convolutional networks is challenging due to the irregular and unordered data format. Reviewing existing network models based on PointNet [13] and PointNet++ [14], they resample in different regions and explore not enough due to the irregularity and sparsity of the geometric structures. In this paper, we proposed a double-ball model embedded in the hierarchical network(DbNet) that directly extracts the features from the point clouds. This method avoids overlapping and better captures the local neighborhood geometry of each point. Double-ball model has two key steps: double-ball query and building features graph. Double-ball query avoids the resampling problem caused by the simple ball query. Building features graph takes angular features and edge features of point clouds into consideration. This method has no requirements for translation and rotation with the object. We apply it to 3D shapes classification and segmentation. And experiments on two benchmarks show that the suggested network outperforms the models based on PointNet/PointNet++ and is able to provide state of the art results.

Keywords: Convolutional network · Double-ball model · Point clouds

1 Introduction

Point clouds, scattered collections of points from 2D or 3D objects, are one of the most straightforward shape representation. 3D sensing technology, such as LiDAR scanners and stereo reconstruction, also outputs this data format. With the development of dramatic 3D point cloud acquisition, recent works on graphs and computer vision often process point clouds directly bypassing expensive mesh reconstruction or denoising considering efficiency or stability of these techniques in the presence of noise. It's a challenge to apply deep learning on point cloud data due to its unorder and irregular. Most critically, the standard deep neural network model consumes input data with regular structure, while the format of point clouds is fundamentally irregular: a point cloud is a discrete representation of an object, and any permutation of their ordering does not change the spatial distribution. One mainstream method to process and analyze point cloud data using deep learning models is to convert the format of point cloud

© Springer Nature Switzerland AG 2020
N. Magnenat-Thalmann et al. (Eds.): CGI 2020, LNCS 12221, pp. 313–325, 2020.
https://doi.org/10.1007/978-3-030-61864-3_27

data into a volumetric representation. However, this approach is constrained by its resolution due to quantization artifacts and excessive memory usage.

In this paper, we mainly consider classification and segmentation tasks in the point clouds processing. To avoid overlapping and better exploit relationships in points, we introduce a double-ball model embedded in the hierarchical neural network, which takes a better strategy to avoid resampling and capture local structure hidden in points' relations and to maintain permutation invariance. The double-ball model takes double-ball query as the searching local points tool and constructs features graphs that describe relations of angle and edge between local points.

2   Related Work

View-Based Methods. View-based techniques use standard CNNs to process images captured from a 3D object in Multi-viewpoint. Notably, CNN exploits each view, and then the outputting features are aggregated to the global feature through a pooling function [5, 18]. View-based methods are also a good choice for application scenarios that the data comes from a 3D sensor and is converted as a range image [23]. This series of methods have achieved dominating performance on 3D shape classification and retrieval tasks [16]. However, it's hard to extend them to 3D semantic segmentation or other tasks such as shape completion and point classification.

Volumetric Methods. One straightforward way is to convert a 3D shape into regular volumetric occupancy grids and then apply standard 3D CNNs to analyze semantic information the data contained [12,24]. Its resolution constrains volumetric representation due to voxelization produces a sparsely-occupied 3D grid. Considered the feasibility of these methods, a lower resolution is adopted when using volume grid. However, in the process of 3D data converted into low-resolution grids, some geometric shape information is lost, especially in analyzing large-scale 3D data. In order to solve these problems, octree-based methods [15, 19–21] have been introduced to make 3D CNNs working on higher resolution grids. PointGrid [8] incorporates a fixed number of points in each grid cell so that can learn more local geometric details. Similarly, Pointwise CNN [4] provides a uniform grid kernel for semantic segmentation and object recognition tasks.

Mesh Based Methods. In addition to the volumetric approaches, several methods have been proposed to develop convolutional networks on a 3D meshes for shape analysis. Geodesic CNN [11] extends CNNs operation from Euclidean to non-Euclidean domains and extracts local patches through a local geodesic system with polar coordinates. Anisotropic CNN [3] is another extension of the Euclidean CNN to the non-Euclidean domain, where the classical convolution is replaced by a projection on a set of oriented anisotropic diffusion kernels. Directionally Convolutional Networks (DCN) [25] applies convolution operations on a three-dimensional triangular mesh to solve partial segmentation problems by combining local and global features. Lastly, Surface Networks [7] recommends upgrading to a graphical neural network to take advantage of the extrinsic differential geometry of the 3D surface to improve its modeling capabilities.

Point Cloud Based Methods. PointNet [13] is the first attempt that applies deep learning on point clouds. PointNet only considers each point and not captures the local correlation structure in the metric space. However, exploiting local structure has proven the key to the success of convolutional networks. PointNet++ [14] is introduced to solve this problem by partitioning the set of points into overlapping local regions induced by the distance metric of the underlying space. By its design, points and features can be resampled at higher levels neurons. Kd-networks [6] is a new deep learning architecture that uses kd-tree structure to construct a computational graph on point sets. KCNet [17] considers the local neighborhood information and defines a set of kernels for local points. PCNN [1] is another way to apply convolutional neural networks to point clouds by defining extension and constraint operators and mapping point cloud functions to volume functions. SO-Net [9] is a permutation-invariant network that exploits the spatial distribution of point clouds by constructing self-organizing maps. PointCNN [10] is a different approach that suggests converting adjacent points to a canonical order and then applying convolution.

3   Approach

In this section, we talk about the main technique components of DbNet on point clouds that include: double-ball query and building feature graph. And in building feature graph, there are two crucial steps: constructing angular feature graph and edge feature graph.

3.1   Double-Ball Query

To learn local structure information of a point cloud, PointNet++ introduces a multi-scale architecture. However, by this design, in the grouping state, the drawback of this method is that may have overlaps in multi-scale regions (i.e., the same neighboring points may be resampling in different scaled regoins), which increased calculations but limits more discriminating features learned from different scale regoins. Figure 1 (a) shows the query method (simple ball query) used in PointNet++ grouping state. To be detail, PointNet++ use a series of simple ball query in different radius to query local points of a point. And in the grouping state, it just concatenates these local points so that some local points must be resampled in a series of simple ball queries.

To solve this problem, we introduce double-ball query (see Fig. 1), which samples local points more wisely to avoid overlaps in multiple scaled regions. Unlike with PointNet++ that directly feed concatenating local points queried by simple ball queries to the network, we apply the double-ball query to sampling local points. Double-ball query is based on two simple ball queries: inner ball query and outer ball query (see Fig. 1 (b)). Cooperation between the inner ball

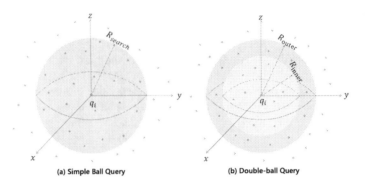

Fig. 1. Simple ball query and double-ball query. (a) depicts the process of simple ball query. Simple ball query searches the local points in a R_{search} ball region. And the red points are the neighbors of point q_i. (b) depicts the process of double-ball query. Double-ball query searches the local points based on two simple ball query: the inner ball query and the outer ball query. And the red points in region of the difference between outer ball and inner ball are the neighbors of point q_i. (Color figure online)

query and the outer ball query to replace the function of the simple ball query to search neighboring points of a point.

We define the radius of inner ball query to be R_{inner}, and the outer ball query is R_{outer}(note that $R_{inner} < R_{outer}$). And in this way, we represent the points set queried from the inner ball as S_{inner} and the outer ball as S_{outer}. The points set S that double-ball query searched can be described using the formula:

$$S = \{S_{outer} - S_{inner}\} \qquad (1)$$

Local points that double-ball queried are the difference between the inner ball query and outer ball query.

3.2   Building Features Graph

PointNet [13] analyzes each point individually, learning a potential feature mapping from 3D space without using local geometric structure. PointNet++ [14] makes some improvements by using mini PointNet in each layer on exploiting local geometry. These two methods do not make good use of the information provided by the 3D point cloud. To solve this problem, we construct features graph to explore the local structure fully. The features graph consists of two parts, the angular feature graph, and edge feature graph (see Fig. 2).

Angular Feature Graph. The angular information is a vital piece in a local structure. To learn relationships between points in a local structure, we need to express the angular information in a suitable way. By our design, we organize local points in a counter wise order to express angular information. And building angular feature graph consists of three main steps: generating normal, projecting and ordering.

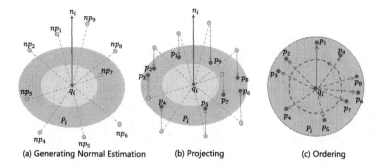

(a) Generating Normal Estimation   (b) Projecting   (c) Ordering

Fig. 2. Building angular feature graph. (a) depicts the process of generating normal estimation. We calculate normal n_i of q_i through its neighboring points np_j. (b) describes the process of projection. We project local points np_j using normals n_i on the normal plane of q_i. (c) illustrates ordering in building angular features graph. After projection, we randomly pick a projected point as the start point and calculate counterwise angles between start point and other projected points. Then, we order neighboring points np_j by the associated angle.

Generating Normal. In 3D shape analysis, normal is an important geometric property. We generate normal on point cloud and use it as a tool for building angular feature graph. Generating the normal n_i at the given point q_i can be described as a least-square plane fitting estimation problem. In order to get the normal n_i, we need to calculate eigenvalues and eigenvectors of the covariance matrix C as:

$$C = \frac{1}{K} \sum_{j=1}^{K} (np_j - q_i) \cdot (np_j - q_i)^T,$$

$$C \cdot v_\gamma = \lambda_\gamma \cdot v_\gamma, \gamma \in \{0, 1, 2\}$$

$$(2)$$

where K is the number of neighboring points np_j select by double-ball query around query point q_i, λ_γ and v_γ are the λth eigenvalue and eigenvector of the covariance matrix C, respectively (Fig. 2 (a) illustrates that use neighboring points to generate normal estimation).

Projecting. After extracting neighboring points np_j for a double-ball query point q_i, we calculate projections p_j of these neighboring points on a tangent plane P_i associated with unit normal n_i. The process of projecting can be depicted by Fig. 2 (b). The projecting points p_j of neighboring points np_j can be calculated with:

$$p_j = np_j - (np_j - q_i) \cdot n_i$$

$$(3)$$

Ordering. Aimed at extracting angular feature from neighboring points, we use angles between a double-ball query point q_i and its neighbors projections p_j to arrange np_j in an ascending order (Fig. 2 (c) depicts the process of ordering).

Firstly, we use dot production to compute the angle between two vectors:

$$cos(\theta_{p_j}) = \frac{c \cdot (p_j - q_i)}{\| c \| \cdot \| p_j - q_i \|} \tag{4}$$

Where c starts from the query point q_i and ends with a randomly starting points(such as p_1), $p_j - q_i$ starts from the query points q_i and ends with other neighboring points p_j.

We know that $cos(\theta_j)$ is in the range $[-1, 1]$, which corresponds to angles between $[0°, 180°]$. To sort the neighboring points around a query point between $[0°, 360°)$, we should consider which semicircle the point p_j belongs to as flows:

$$sign_{p_j} = (c \times (p_j - q_i)) \cdot n_i \tag{5}$$

where $sign_{p_j} \geq 0$ corresponds $\theta_{p_j} \in [0°, 180°]$, and $sign_{p_j} < 0$ corresponds $\theta_{p_j} \in (180°, 360°)$

Then, we can sort the neighboring points np_j through descending the angular value of p_i in the counterwise order as follows the formula:

$$\angle_{p_j} = \begin{cases} -cos(\theta_{p_j}) - 2 & sign_{p_j} < 0 \\ cos(\theta_{p_j}) & sign_{p_j} \geq 0 \end{cases} \tag{6}$$

Finally, we construct the angular feature graph by concatenating each q_i and its neighboring points that sort by projection angles.

Edge Feature Graph. We know that edge in 3D shapes is a fundamental attribute. It is essential to construct edges features between point and point. Based on angular features graph, we focus on exploring edge information in the point cloud. The relations between edges and points can be described by a directed graph $\mathcal{G} = (\mathcal{V}, \mathcal{E})$, where $\mathcal{V} = \{1, 2, \cdots, k\}$ and $\mathcal{E} \in \mathcal{V} \times \mathcal{V}$ are the vertices and edges respectively.

Graph $\mathcal{G}$ contains directed edges of the form $(q_i, np_{i1}), (q_i, np_{i2}), \ldots, (q_i, np_{ik})$ such that points $np_{i1}, np_{i2}, \ldots, np_{ik}$ are the neighbors of q_i. We define edge features as $e_{ij} = h_\Theta(q_i, np_i)$, where $h_\Theta : \mathbb{R}^F \times \mathbb{R}^F \to \mathbb{R}^{F'}$ is some parametric non-leaner function parameterized by the set of learnable parameters Θ. Due to the universal approximation theorem, we use a fully connected layer as an instance of h_Θ. The output of convolutional operation at the i-th vertex can be given by

$$q_i' = h_\Theta(q_i, np_j) \tag{7}$$

The choice of the edge function has a crucial influence on the result of convolutional operation. We use $h_\Theta(q_i, np_j) = h_\Theta(q_i, q_i - np_j)$ to describe the edge features between points which combines both global shape structure (provided by the coordinates of centers q_i) and local neighboring information(provided by $q_i - np_j$). The form of $h_\Theta(q_i, q_i - np_j)$ requires input graph $\mathcal{G}$ that contains both global information and local information. Now, we get angular features graph and edge features graph. And then, we concatenate two graphs and feed it on the deep network.

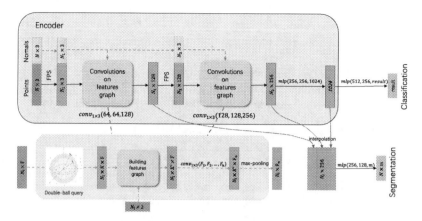

Fig. 3. The architecture of DbNet. Both classification and segmentation networks share encoder part for extracting features. Normals are only used for projection in building angular feature graph to determine the order of local points. N, N_1, N_2 (where $N > N_1 > N_2$) is the number of points as input. *result* is the number of classification classes. m is the number of segmentation classes. "mlp" denotes multi-layer perception. $conv_{1\times3}(F_1, F_2, \ldots, F_n)$ stands for convolutions on information graph with kernel size 1×3 applied sequentially with corresponding feature map sizes F_i, $i \in 1, \ldots, n$.

4 DbNet Architecture

DbNet follows the design that the hierarchical structure is composed of a set of abstract layers. Each layer consists of several operations and produces a subset of input points with newly learned features. Firstly, we use the Farthest Point Sampling(FPS) algorithm to subsample points as the centroids covered by the whole set. Secondly, the double-ball query extracts neighboring points of a centroid for each local region. Thirdly, we construct angular feature graph and edge feature graph through centroids and their neighbors. Finally, we apply sequentially a set of convolutions on the features graph and max pool operation across neighbors to produce new feature vectors, which uniquely describe each local region.

In the following, we discuss more detail about the classification and segmentation network architectures.

4.1 Classification Network

The architecture of the classification network is illustrated at the Fig. 3. This network contains two parts: encoder and classification. The encoder learns features from each features graph independently inside every layer and concatenates them at the end to process further to learn high-level features.

In the encoder part, we construct features graph twice and apply a series of convolutions operation on them. Convolutions applied on the two graphs with the kernel sizes 1×3 and stride 1, followed by a batch normalization (BN) and a rectified linear unit (ReLU). Then, we concatenate aggregated features learned from each feature graph and propagate them to the next layer. The last layer in the encoder uses convolutions with kernel sizes 1×1 followed by BN and ReLU layers. After that aggregated high-level features are fed to the set of fully-connected layers with integrated dropout and ReLU layers to calculate the probability of each class. The output size of the classification network is the number of classes in the dataset.

4.2   Segmentation Network

The segmentation network shares the common encoder with the classification network as illustrated in Fig. 3. To predict each point label in the segmentation task, we need to obtain points features for all original points. Inspired by PU-Net [27], we propagate different levels features from the encoder and concatenate them so that the network can learn the most critical features from different levels.

We know that features at different levels have different sizes due to varying sizes of the kernel. We use an interpolation method [14] to unsample the points in the encoder to the original point cloud size. This method based on the inverse distance weighted average of the k nearest neighbors(in default we use $p = 2, k = 3$) as:

$$f^{(j)}(x) = \frac{\sum_{i=1}^{k} w_i(x) f_i^j}{\sum_{i=1}^{k} w_i(x)} \tag{8}$$

where $w_j(x) = \frac{1}{d(x, np_j)^p}$ is the inverse square Euclidean distance weight.

Then, we concatenate unsampled features and apply 1×1 convolution on them to reduce feature space and learn the relationship between features in different levels. Finally, each point label is predicted.

5   Experiments

In this section, we evaluate our DbNet for two different tasks: classification and segmentation. DbNet is trained on a single NVIDIA GeForce GTX 1080Ti with 11GB DDR5X. The training time of our model is faster than that of PointNet++. In the following, we show more detail on each tasks.

5.1   Classification

We evaluate our classification model on ModelNet40 [24] dataset. ModelNet40 is a largescale 3D CAD model dataset that has 40 categories with $9,843$ models for training and $2,468$ models for testing. We use FPS method to sample 1024 points with normals for the classification experiment (note that normals only be used for building angular features in local structure). For data augmentation, we rotate the object and jitter the position of each points [13].

Table 1. Classification results on ModelNet40. AAC(%) is accuracy average class, OA(%) is overall accuracy.

Method	Input	AAC	OA
AO-CNN [21]	Volume	–	90.5
O-CNN [20]	Volume	–	90.6
MVCNN-MultiRes [18]	Images	91.4	93.8
Kd-Net [6]	2^{15} points	88.5	91.8
PointNet [13]	1024 points	86.2	89.2
PointNet++ [14]	1024 points	–	91.9
PointCNN [10]	1024 points	88.1	92.2
Pointwise CNN [4]	1024 points	81.4	86.1
DGCNN [22]	1024 points	90.2	92.9
DbNet	1024 points	**90.4**	**92.9**

In Table 1, we compare our method with several with several state-of-art methods based on PointNet/PointNet++ in the 3D shape classification results on ModelNet40. DbNet get better results accuracy among point-cloud based methods, such as PointNet [13], PointNet++ [14], PointCNN [10] and Pointwise CNN [4]. And compared with DGCNN [22] our method has better accuracy in AAC. Meanwhile, DbNet performs better than other volumetric approaches, such as AO-CNN [21] and O-CNN [20]. We also have better accuracy compared with Kd-Net [6]. Our model gets a little worse result compared with MVCNN-MultiRes [18]. Because MVCNN-MultiRes takes images in multi-view to represent an object, which can use images networks. However, by this design, MVCNN-MultiRes has no ability in the 3D segmentation task. We also evaluate the robustness of DbNet to point cloud density. And Fig. 4 shows that even half of the points are dropped, our method still achieves reasonable results. However, with the number of points less than 512, performance degenerates dramatically.

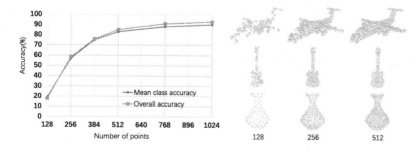

Fig. 4. Left: Results of DbNet tested with random input dropout. The model is trained with 1024 points. **Right:** Point clouds with different number of points. The numbers of points are shown below the bottom row.

PointNet++   DbNet(ours)   Ground truth

Fig. 5. Qualitative results on ShapeNet dataset. We compare our results with Point-Net++ and ground truth.

5.2   Segmentation

We evaluate our model for segmentation task on ShapeNetPart dataset [26]. This dataset contains 16, 881 3D shapes from 16 different categories, annotated with 50 parts in total. The main challenge of the dataset is that the number of different categories is highly imbalanced. We follow the official split scheme as in [26]. To have better generalization, we jitter point locations with point shuffling when in training.

We use Intersection-over-Union(IoU) on points for evaluating our segmentation model and comparing with other benchmarks. We compare our results with some point-based methods, as shown in Table 2. Our model achieves better segmentation results on ShapeNetPart compared with PointNet++ [14], DGCNN [22], KDNet [6] and so on. However, in some categories, our model has slightly worse than 3DmFV-Net [2], PCNN [1] and DGCNN [22].

We also visualize the segmentation result and as is shown in Fig. 5. Compared with PointNet++, our model can better identify various parts of 3D objects.

Table 2. Segmentation on ShapeNetPart, "Mean" is mean IoU (%)

Model	Mean	Air.	Bag	Cap	Car	Chair	Ear.	Guitar	Knife	Laptop
PointNet++ [14]	85.1	82.4	79.0	87.7	77.3	90.8	71.8	91.0	85.9	95.3
DGCNN [22]	85.1	84.2	83.7	84.4	77.1	90.9	78.5	**91.5**	87.3	96.0
Kd-Net [6]	82.3	80.1	74.6	74.3	70.3	88.6	73.5	90.2	87.2	94.9
SO-Net [9]	84.9	82.8	77.8	88.0	77.3	90.6	73.5	90.7	83.9	94.8
KCNet [17]	83.7	82.8	81.5	86.4	77.6	90.3	76.8	91.0	87.2	95.5
PCNN [1]	85.1	82.4	80.1	85.5	**79.5**	90.8	73.2	91.3	86.0	95.7
3DmFV-Net [2]	84.3	82.0	**84.3**	86.0	76.9	89.9	73.9	90.8	85.7	95.2
DbNet(ours)	**86.1**	**85.6**	83.9	**88.4**	79.3	**90.9**	**79.3**	91.3	**87.3**	**96.4**

6   Conclusion

This paper presented a new method to avoid overlapping in quering and explore the local features in point clouds. Our method can capture more detail on the local structure due to the double-ball query and features graph, avoiding overlapping and providing more local information. And our model suggests that local structure features are essential to 3D recognition tasks, even after introducing machinery from deep learning.

Our method can be embedded into existing pipelines for point-cloud based networks. Our model outperforms state-of-art approaches which architecture based on PointNet/PointNet++. The main limitation of our approach compared with point-based CNN is that we use the double-ball query to search neighboring points which needs extra computing power. We will also investigate to apply the model on large-scale outdoor datasets in our future work.

References

1. Atzmon, M., Maron, H., Lipman, Y.: Point convolutional neural networks by extension operators. ACM Trans. Graph. **37**(4), 1–12 (2018)
2. Ben-Shabat, Y., Lindenbaum, M., Fischer, A.: 3DMFV: three-dimensional point cloud classification in real-time using convolutional neural networks. IEEE Rob. Autom. Lett. **3**(4), 3145–3152 (2018)
3. Boscaini, D., Masci, J., Rodolà, E., Bronstein, M.M.: Learning shape correspondence with anisotropic convolutional neural networks (2016)
4. Hua, B.S., Tran, M.K., Yeung, S.K.: Pointwise convolutional neural networks. In: Proceedings of the IEEE Conference on Computer Vision and Pattern Recognition, pp. 984–993 (2018)
5. Huang, H., Kalogerakis, E., Chaudhuri, S., Ceylan, D., Kim, V.G., Yumer, E.: Learning local shape descriptors from part correspondences with multiview convolutional networks. ACM Trans. Graph. (TOG) **37**(1), 6 (2018)
6. Klokov, R., Lempitsky, V.: Escape from cells: Deep KD-networks for the recognition of 3D point cloud models (2017)

7. Kostrikov, I., Bruna, J., Panozzo, D., Zorin, D.: Surface networks (2017)
8. Le, T., Duan, Y.: PointGrid: a deep network for 3D shape understanding. In: Proceedings of the IEEE Conference on Computer Vision and Pattern Recognition, pp. 9204–9214 (2018)
9. Li, J., Chen, B.M., Lee, G.H.: So-net: Self-organizing network for point cloud analysis. In: Computer Vision and Pattern Recognition (CVPR) (2018)
10. Li, Y., Bu, R., Sun, M., Wu, W., Di, X., Chen, B.: PointCNN: convolution on $\mathcal{X}$-transformed points (2018)
11. Masci, J., Boscaini, D., Bronstein, M., Vandergheynst, P.: Geodesic convolutional neural networks on riemannian manifolds. In: Proceedings of the IEEE International Conference on Computer Vision Workshops, pp. 37–45 (2015)
12. Maturana, D., Scherer, S.: VoxNet: a 3D convolutional neural network for real-time object recognition. In: 2015 IEEE/RSJ International Conference on Intelligent Robots and Systems (IROS), pp. 922–928. IEEE (2015)
13. Qi, C.R., Su, H., Mo, K., Guibas, L.J.: PointNet: deep learning on point sets for 3D classification and segmentation. In: Proceedings of the IEEE Conference on Computer Vision and Pattern Recognition, pp. 652–660 (2017)
14. Qi, C.R., Yi, L., Su, H., Guibas, L.J.: PointNet++: deep hierarchical feature learning on point sets in a metric space. In: Advances in Neural Information Processing Systems, pp. 5099–5108 (2017)
15. Riegler, G., Osman Ulusoy, A., Geiger, A.: OctNet: learning deep 3D representations at high resolutions. In: Proceedings of the IEEE Conference on Computer Vision and Pattern Recognition, pp. 3577–3586 (2017)
16. Savva, M., et al.: Shrec16 track: largescale 3D shape retrieval from shapenet core55. In: Proceedings of the Eurographics Workshop on 3D Object Retrieval, pp. 89–98 (2016)
17. Shen, Y., Chen, F., Yang, Y., Dong, T.: Mining point cloud local structures by kernel correlation and graph pooling (2017)
18. Su, H., Maji, S., Kalogerakis, E., Learned-Miller, E.: Multi-view convolutional neural networks for 3D shape recognition. In: Proceedings of the IEEE International Conference on Computer Vision, pp. 945–953 (2015)
19. Tatarchenko, M., Dosovitskiy, A., Brox, T.: Octree generating networks: efficient convolutional architectures for high-resolution 3D outputs. In: Proceedings of the IEEE International Conference on Computer Vision, pp. 2088–2096 (2017)
20. Wang, P.S., Liu, Y., Guo, Y.X., Sun, C.Y., Tong, X.: O-CNN: octree-based convolutional neural networks for 3D shape analysis. ACM Transactions on Graphics (TOG) **36**(4), 72 (2017)
21. Wang, P.S., Sun, C.Y., Liu, Y., Tong, X.: Adaptive O-CNN: a patch-based deep representation of 3D shapes. In: SIGGRAPH Asia 2018 Technical Papers, p. 217. ACM (2018)
22. Wang, Y., Sun, Y., Liu, Z., Sarma, S.E., Bronstein, M.M., Solomon, J.M.: Dynamic graph CNN for learning on point clouds. ACM Trans. Graph. (TOG) **38**(5), 1–12 (2019)
23. Wei, L., Huang, Q., Ceylan, D., Vouga, E., Li, H.: Dense human body correspondences using convolutional networks. In: Proceedings of the IEEE Conference on Computer Vision and Pattern Recognition, pp. 1544–1553 (2016)
24. Wu, Z., et al.: 3D ShapeNets: a deep representation for volumetric shapes. In: Proceedings of the IEEE Conference on Computer Vision and Pattern Recognition, pp. 1912–1920 (2015)

25. Xu, H., Ming, D., Zhong, Z.: Directionally convolutional networks for 3D shape segmentation. In: IEEE International Conference on Computer Vision (2017)
26. Yi, L., et al.: A scalable active framework for region annotation in 3d shape collections. ACM Trans. Graph. (TOG) **35**(6), 210 (2016)
27. Yu, L., Li, X., Fu, C.W., Cohen-Or, D., Heng, P.A.: Pu-net: Point cloud upsampling network (2018)

Evolving L-Systems in a Competitive Environment

Job Talle$^{(\boxtimes)}$ and Jiří Kosinka

Bernoulli Institute, University of Groningen, Groningen, The Netherlands
jobtalle@hotmail.com, j.kosinka@rug.nl

Abstract. Lindenmayer systems (L-systems) have been developed to
model plant growth by repeatedly applying production rules to an initial axiom, and serve as a model for genetically driven growth processes
found in nature. A simulation method is proposed to evolve their pheno-
typic representations through competition in a heterogeneous environment to further expand on this biological analogy. The resulting simulations demonstrate evolution driven by competition, resulting in agents
employing strategies similar to those found in nature.

Keywords: Lindenmayer system · L-system · Competitive
environment · Plant evolution

1 Introduction

In addition to the established biological realism of Lindenmayer systems (L-
systems for short) [15], a model is proposed to evolve systems as agents representing plants in an environment designed to maintain this analogy in several
ways (Fig. 1). Evolutionary algorithms have been deployed to optimize L-systems
before, in two-dimensional environments [17,21] as well as in three-dimensional
environments [3,4,13]. Drawing on these past achievements, the focal points of
the proposed model are:

- using the smallest possible subset of L-system syntax rules to avoid steering
  the algorithm towards a preferred direction,
- simulating competition between realistically modelled agents by simulating
  sunlight occlusion and spatial scarcity,
- modelling an environment with unevenly distributed fertility to simulate natural boundaries and thereby facilitating divergent evolution, and
- allowing the temporary survival of sub-par agents to give them a chance to
  escape local optima.

When these mechanisms reflect their biological counterparts, the simulated
organisms should be able to succeed through strategies employed by real plants.
Our simulation system is thus designed to evoke realistic behaviour by simulating
a realistic environment.

© Springer Nature Switzerland AG 2020
N. Magnenat-Thalmann et al. (Eds.): CGI 2020, LNCS 12221, pp. 326–350, 2020.
https://doi.org/10.1007/978-3-030-61864-3_28

Fig. 1. Two versions of a simulation at generation $g = 20000$ demonstrating the importance of competition: Density factor of 2 (**left**) and 26 (**right**). All other parameters, including the initial state of the environment, are identical.

Elaborate models have been developed to model ecosystems and interactions between them [18]. Our aim is not to model existing ecosystems top down, but rather to make a model that develops properties similar to real world ecosystems based on a minimal number of criteria analogous to the most important constraints that all plants encounter. Our main contribution is to show that even this minimalist and unbiased model gives rise, through competition, to realistic strategies employed in nature.

After discussing related work in Sect. 2, we present and analyse the results of our simulations in Section 3. We discuss our findings in Sect. 4 and conclude the paper in Sect. 5. The interested reader may find details regarding our syntax, method, and implementation in Appendix 1, 2, and 3, respectively.

2   Related Work

In [3], the authors also consider competition in a virtual plant community. They use a very elaborate model for plants and the environment they are put in, and their competition simulation is built directly using pre-defined tree populations (beech and oak). In contrast, our simulations do not predefine any specific plant structure, and rather start from equivalent and very minimal seeds. They also generate the next generation from a set of *elite members*, a fixed size set containing agents with the highest fitness. In contrast, agents in our method only reproduce locally, and define their fitness relative to their immediate neighbours. We show that even with our generic model, the plants develop similar strategies to those observed in [3], such as developing tall trunks to win the 'arms race'.

The suitability of genetic algorithms for simulating plant evolution has been established [9,17,25]; see also [10,24] for overviews. We build on top of these studies by introducing direct competition to the environment. Although we are not the first to consider competition in the setting of evolving plant agents in a realistic environment, existing approaches, including [1,6,7], only estimate sun exposure, and do so without considering individual leaves. In contrast, we simulate occlusion by placing agents with their leaves next to each other in a simulated 3D environment instead of approximating it.

The shapes generated by applied L-systems can be rated using a fitness function, after which selection can be applied to obtain more desirable shapes. Different selection criteria can be defined for two-dimensional shapes created by

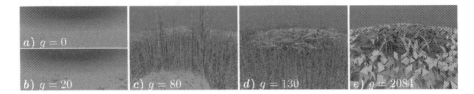

Fig. 2. Five recognizable stages in the evolution process. **a)** The initial state of a simulation at $g = 0$, only producing agents with a single seed. The agents are evenly spaced in this figure, because no iterations have been simulated yet. **b)** The simulation at $g = 20$ after the first agents producing multiple seeds have evolved. Small clusters of these agents emerge and are spreading through the environment. **c)** At $g = 80$, agents develop tall growing structures to disperse their seeds over a large area. This rendering shows the simulation at a stage right before the tall structures overgrow the entire environment. **d)** The first leaves have emerged in the simulation at $g = 130$. These agents are the first ones with a nonzero viability; they are rapidly replacing the existing population. These plants are not very efficient yet. **e)** Leafless agents no longer exist in the simulation at $g = 2084$. More complex plants develop in the fertile central valley, whereas simpler agents live on the edges of the environment. Simulating until $g = 2084$ took approximately 40 min on a standard desktop computer.

turtle graphics [21]. Our method extends these shapes to 3D, again using turtle graphics driven by L-systems (as opposed to other approaches such as Xfrog [16] which relies on predefined building blocks and user modelling). We use this not only for rendering, but also for determining sun exposure, based on grown leaf material. Although more precise models for computing sun exposure [2,5,26] and other features [12,22,23] exist, our rendering-based model strikes a balance between efficiency, and computational and implementation complexity while still giving rise to natural strategies based on competition.

Non-homogeneous environments will cause agents with equal genotypes to develop different phenotypes [19]. If the environment does not permit it, a plant will not grow to its full potential. Plant growth is not hindered during the growth process since this would require significantly more complex L-systems [8], but rather by the environment and the viability score given afterwards. Evolutionary strategies in nature are often tailored to specific environmental conditions; our method aims to simulate this effect in order to encourage the differentiation of evolutionary strategies by which greater biodiversity develops.

3   Simulations and Results

When the simulation environment is initialized with the simplest reproducible agents (Appendix 2), namely agents with only a single seed symbol in the axiom (Appendix 1) and no production rules, the course of the evolutionary process (our implementation is available; see Appendix 3) goes through five distinguishable stages; see Fig. 2.

a) The first very simple agents produce tiny phenotypes. In most agents, no production rules to grow the systems exist yet, and if they exist, the rules usually do not produce growth. Axioms contain one or only a few symbols. During reproduction, some agents lose the ability to produce a single seed, causing the number of agents to drop slightly in the first generations.

b) Some agents develop methods to produce more than one seed, and the number of agents begins to increase. This is the first successful strategy that agents use to compete; they are always more successful than their predecessors regardless of viability as they can rapidly populate all free space in the environment while agents with a single seed can reproduce at most once.

c) Agents start to develop tall structures, enabling them to disperse their seeds over large areas.

d) The first leaves evolve. Their crude initial shapes often yield low viability (they are often too big, intersect each other or are occluded by the branching structures), but nevertheless lift their parents' viability over zero for the first time in the simulation. After all, according to the formula described in Appendix 2, all earlier leafless agents had a viability of zero.

e) The agents start to produce better leaves, and will often develop the ability to produce multiple leaves as well, depending on the configuration of the viability function. The viability scores increase significantly. At this point, agents will start to compete for sunlight with their neighbours. If multiple agents with leaves yield the same utility score without neighbour occlusion, they outcompete their neighbours by growing slightly taller; this lowers viability a little, but dramatically decreases their competitors' viability by occluding their sunlight. When a simulation consist of separated fertile areas, different phenotypes emerge in each of them. Sometimes, agents manage to "escape" their habitat and spread their genotype to a different area. This effect is demonstrated in Fig. 7.

The simulation does not seem to converge once the last phase starts; due to the competitive dynamic, it is never a viable strategy to stop evolving. Agents keep "reacting" to strategies that emerge around them. The genotype keeps changing through mutation in this phase; after a few thousand generations, genotypes that were previously dominant cannot be found or recognized any longer. Agent viability is initially very low, since leaves have not evolved yet. When the first good leaves evolve, an optimum is reached. After this peak, the viability drops slightly again because competition causes agents to develop structures that yield lower viability, but increase their competitive strength.

3.1 Competition

One of the focal points of our method is to simulate competition among agents. The degree of competition that exists in a simulation can be influenced by chancing the density threshold of a simulation; when this number is very low, agents will not reproduce close to each other, preventing them from competing for sunlight. Figure 1 shows the influence of the density threshold on a simulation; the results of the absence of competition are severe.

Without competition, complex structures do not evolve. This can be attributed to the fact that growing larger plants or more leaves always lowers viability. The only reason for evolving complex strategies in this simulation

Fig. 3. An environment resulting from a simulation with a high growth density factor. Competition causes plants to grow leaves wherever sunlight can be caught; no open areas exist. Some agents (top right) try to escape the canopy to avoid occlusion. When density increases, agents employ increasingly complex strategies.

is to compete against other agents. At the less fertile areas around the valleys, agents remain simple as well, because large structures cannot grow there. Plant size and complexity thus increase where a combination of fertile ground and competition takes place. Figure 3 shows an environment with fierce competition. Multiple layers of broad leaves try to catch all available sunlight.

3.2   Leaves

As soon as leaves evolve in a simulation, agents start to compete for sunlight exposure. Figure 4, left, shows plants at an early stage during a simulation; they have recently evolved leaves, and do not yet grow tall in order to compete with their neighbours. They do however produce two seeds instead of one, which causes them to spread through the environment unless a better agent prevents them from reproducing.

The plants in Fig. 4, left, produce a leaf that is divided into segments; this increases viability, since the plant efficiency formula detailed in Appendix 2 penalizes large leaf areas. This strategy of segmenting leaves almost always arises.

Figure 4, right, shows the same simulation at a later stage, when competition between the plants in Fig. 4, left, causes them to compete with one another. This rendering is taken at one of the more fertile locations in the environment, where the agents are able to grow larger and develop competitive strategies.

The same segmented leaves have grown larger where the ground is fertile enough to support larger structures. Since plants need to compete for sunlight because of their proximity, the leaves now start higher on the structures. Their shapes no longer grow vertically, but bend towards the sky as well in order to catch more light. The common ancestor these plants have evolved from would no

Fig. 4. Left: Agents that develop early on in a simulation are often small and vertical. This rendering shows a small colony of low growing plants. At this stage, competition starts to play a role; the plants cast shadows on their neighbours, reducing the amount of sunlight they receive. These plants grow in clusters, since their seeds (brown spheres) are located close to the ground, preventing them from spreading far away. **Right:** Their descendants are taller and more competitive, while remaining structurally similar. (Color figure online)

longer thrive among them, since its descendants would catch most of the light before it reaches the agents closer to the ground.

While the leaves in Fig. 4 evolved from small plants, the first leaves in a simulation can develop on tall plants as well. Figure 5a) shows a rendering of a simulation where the first leaves have evolved on tall inefficient plants; their more successful descendants are smaller and more efficient.

When sunlight only shines directly down (as opposed to multiple light directions that also cast some light from the sides), plants align their leaves horizontally. Figure 6, left, shows an agent taken from such an environment.

3.3 Structural Strategies

Initially, most agents develop as a single branch with one or more leaves connected to it. The tendency to produce phenotypes with many similar leaves or few dissimilar leaves develops at an early stage. Figure 5b) shows a rendering of a simulation during an early stage where the first leaves occur only once on their parent plants. In contrast, Fig. 5c) shows agents developing multiple similar leaves per agent.

In simulation environments where multiple fertile areas exist, different genotypes will be dominant in different areas. They may however share a common

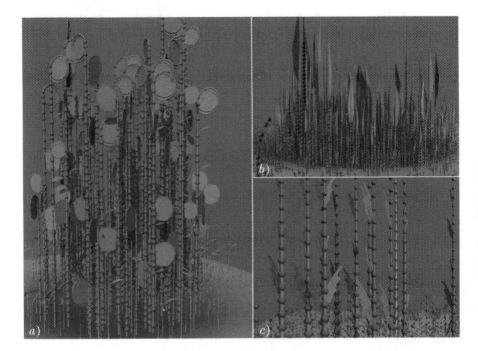

Fig. 5. a) The leaves on these agents have developed early on during a simulation on agents with phenotypes similar to those in Fig. 2c). The leaves are curled up unnecessarily, and the number of seeds produced on the stalk is inefficiently high. **b)** The first leaves have developed in this simulation. They are narrow and segmented, and they do not repeat themselves within the structure. **c)** Similar to b), but instead of developing a single leaf per plant, stalks contain multiple similar leaves instead.

successful ancestor that managed to spread its seeds over the infertile barriers dividing the environment. Figure 7 shows the result of such an event. These four agents share the same growth pattern, but employ it slightly differently to adapt to the different contexts they have evolved in. The second agent from the left has concentrated its leaf mass as high as possible, likely to prevent occlusion. The last agent in the row keeps increasing its leaf sizes as they develop: older leaves have bigger surface area.

Because of the stability criterion described in Appendix 2, agents only grow tall when required, and if they do, their structure will form mostly directly above their center of gravity. Figure 6, right, shows how an agent with a large complex structure managed to keep its eccentricity low.

3.4 Natural Counterparts

Running the simulation for a sufficient number of generations gives rise to agents that employ effective strategies analogous to those found in nature. Figure 8 shows an agent that has developed a similar strategy to the lily of the valley;

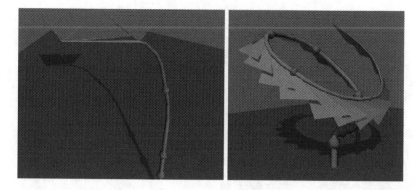

Fig. 6. Left: This agent has evolved in an environment where light only shines directly down. It is taken from a simulation with many competing agents, so the leaf is placed on a high stalk to prevent occlusion. **Right:** An agent with a lot of branch and leaf material. Note that the plant structure is inclined such that the center of gravity is approximately above the root, reducing the eccentricity demonstrated in Fig. 12, right.

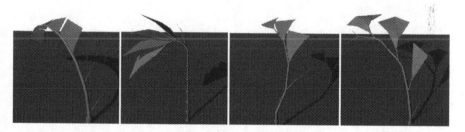

Fig. 7. Four different agents with a common ancestor that existed 1000 generations earlier. All agents share the same structural strategy; new leaves form at the root, starting as a branch and growing into a leaf after multiple iterations. Various specializations have emerged.

a vertical stem contains the reproductive systems (berries), while broad leaves emerging from the same root spiral around the central axis.

Figure 9 shows a group of agents that have developed thin fanning leaves that tend to align on the same plane, a strategy also seen in palm leaves.

Figure 10 shows a close up rendering of evolved leaves compared to real leaves. The leaf efficiency factor described in Appendix 2 causes well nerved leaves to yield higher viability than unsupported large leaf areas, resulting in well structured leaves similar to the ones found in nature.

4   Discussion and Future Work

While the goals (as outlined in Sect. 1) of our method were met, we now discuss several of its features and potential future improvements to our tool [27].

Fig. 8. An illustration of a real "lily of the valley" flower on the right [14] compared to an evolved agent.

The viability function in this simulation method remains constant. While agents adapt to each other and the fertility of the area they grow on, they do not adapt to a climate system, which varies greatly over time in reality. With such a system, agents could be incentivized to produce robust strategies that remain successful when shared conditions change rapidly. An example in our context would be a global drought; terrain fertility could drop globally in a short time, and restore itself afterwards.

The implementation does not model growth over time. Agents develop completely before being compared to each other, which prevents strategies related to growth speed and life span from being relevant.

No *crossover* takes place in our reproductive model; this is a process whereby agents are not merely mutated clones of their parents, but rather a mutated mix of two parents [11]. Crossover could be implemented in this simulation by 'pollinating' each seed before reproduction. This can be simulated by finding a nearby similar agent and mixing these two systems through crossover.

In realistic environments, selective pressure applies to reproductive organs as well. By rating seeds by attractiveness to pollinators (e.g. benefiting seeds surrounded by bright colours), agents will be incentivized to develop flowers and compete on a visual level.

Sunlight exposure can be measured in many different ways [2, 5, 26]; our model treats all leaf surfaces as if they are equal, while in reality leaves differ in opacity, colour, reflectivity and other properties. The lighting model can be extended to allow different leaf types to develop.

Fig. 9. Palm leaves photographed in a greenhouse of the Oxford botanic garden on the right compared to a population of evolved agents on the left.

5   Conclusion

We have demonstrated that the criteria used by the simulation give rise to agents that exhibit strategies similar to those shown by real plants (see Sect. 3.4). Competition plays a critical role in the development of strategies; agent fitness is defined relative to the surrounding agents by calculating leaf occlusion.

The evolutionary process itself displays realistic biological characteristics as well, e.g. divergent evolution (see Fig. 7) and competition (see Sect. 3.2). The heterogeneous environment results in multiple different "species" of agents competing with one another. Each agent species performs optimally within a range of environmental properties.

One of the aims of our method is to allow the temporary survival of subpar agents to allow for different agents to evolve without immediately culling low viability agents. viability plays a role in selection, but reproductive systems, terrain fertility and vegetation density play critical roles as well; Fig. 2 a)–c) shows agents with zero viability competing on other grounds.

On these, the biological analogy of L-systems has been extended by evolving them through the proposed simulation method.

Acknowledgements:. This paper is based on the first author's BSc thesis at the University of Groningen.

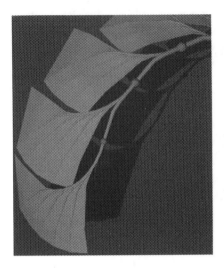

Fig. 10. Clearly nerved leaves photographed in the Oxford botanic garden (**right**) juxtaposed with evolved leaf nerves (**left**). Note that both leaf structures separate their leaf surfaces at regular intervals, and that older leaves have more nerves.

Appendix 1: Syntax

A large number of syntactic variations of L-systems exists; a subset of existing rules was used in our method to allow for effective evolution, but the syntax is chosen to be versatile enough to produce a wide variety of phenotypes.

All production rules take the form $x \to y$, where both x and y are strings of symbols and y can be empty. Rules are applied to axiom a, which is a nonempty string, to produce a'. When performing an iteration on these symbols, the algorithm iterates over a starting at the first symbol. At the iterator position, all matching production rules are gathered and a random one is chosen for application. The index of the iterator is then incremented by the number of symbols in x of the rule, and the symbols matched to x are replaced by y. When no production rules are applicable, the iterator only increments.

To illustrate this process, consider a very simple L-system with axiom $a = A$ and a single production rule $r_1 = A \to ABA$. Iterating over the axiom twice to obtain a' and a'' gives

$$a = A, \quad a' = ABA, \quad a'' = ABABABA.$$

This system is deterministic, since at most one production rule is applicable at a time. It can be made stochastic by introducing the second production rule $r_2 = A \to AB$. In this case, multiple end results are possible.

For every A encountered, both r_1 and r_2 are applicable.

For complex stochastic systems, the number of possible outcomes rises exponentially. A single genotype may lead to a wide variety of phenotypes.

Phenotypic Representation

A specific set of symbols is allowed to arise in the simulation, and different symbols (or combinations thereof) translate into different geometric representations. The string of symbols resulting from a number of iterations is rendered as a branching structure through *turtle graphics*; the "turtle" moves according to the symbols encountered while iterating over all symbols sequentially. The turtle acts like a pen, drawing lines behind it as it moves through space. In our setting, the turtle draws branches, which are modelled as three-dimensional tubes. The radius of the tube is proportional to the amount of structure that rests on it; plant branches get thicker near the roots.

Capital letters are interpreted as forward steps with a constant stride, lower case letters are ignored by the turtle. A seed symbol produces a seed at the turtle location. There are six rotation symbols, which rotate the turtle along each axis in three dimensional space by a fixed amount, either in the positive or negative direction. Branching brackets start or end a branch. Opening a branch does not affect the turtle, but at a closing bracket the turtle jumps back to the position it was at when the corresponding opening bracket was encountered.

A special opening bracket is the *leaf bracket*, which designates that the entire branching structure inside it will be interpreted as a *leaf*. A leaf is modelled by creating leaf material between the branches inside its structure and their child branches recursively. Leaves are not allowed to contain other leaves. By using this method, a leaf can contain more than one piece of leaf surface; if many branches exist in the leaf structure, many different leaf shapes can be modelled.

Figure 11 contains a diagram of a possible leaf shape. The branches $a = \{a_0, a_1, a_2, a_3\}$, $b = \{b_0, b_1, b_2, b_3\}$ and $c = \{c_0, c_1, c_2\}$ exist, where a is the root branch starting at a_0. Branch b is a sub-branch of a, and leaf surface L_{ab} is modelled according to the aforementioned algorithm. Correspondingly, leaf surface L_{bc} is modelled from the point where c branches off b until both branches' end nodes. The result is a leaf structure containing three branches and two surfaces. The shape in Fig. 11 can be constructed from a string using the above algorithm. The sentence producing it is: `<A[++B[++C-C]-B-B]-A-A]` , where

- − rotates the turtle orientation $\frac{\pi}{9}$ radians to the left,
- + rotates $\frac{\pi}{9}$ radians to the right,
- [...] denotes a branch, and
- <...] denotes a leaf.

The initial direction is upwards. At A, B or C, the turtle moves forwards for a fixed distance. In this sentence, the entire shape is surrounded by a leaf branch, and it contains b as a sub-branch, which in turn contains c as a sub-branch.

Alphabet

The experiments performed according to the method in Appendix 2 take place in a three-dimensional environment, but the syntax is almost equal to the one used to model the shape in Fig. 11; the only difference is the use of four more

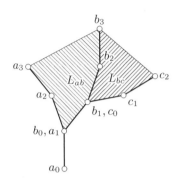

Symbol	Turtle action
A...Z	Move forward
a...z	Ignore
*	Place a seed
[	Open a branch
<	Open a leaf
]	Close leaf/branch
+	Increment pitch
−	Decrement pitch
/	Increment roll
\	Decrement roll
^	Increment yaw
_	Decrement yaw

Fig. 11. Left: Leaf shape modelling. **Right:** The alphabet of possible symbols and related turtle actions.

rotation symbols and a seed symbol. Figure 11, right, shows all symbols that may arise in the simulation together with their effects on the turtle.

The chosen alphabet contains as few symbols as possible to ensure that properties evolve because they are beneficial to agents, and not because we prefer agents to develop in that way (see Sect. 1). To test whether the alphabet is expressive enough, an extension to the alphabet in Fig. 11 is implemented with an extra symbol, which will produce a single triangle shaped leaf. Using this symbol can show whether the simplicity of the standard alphabet prevents leaf features from developing. The results of this extension are detailed at the end of Appendix 2.

Appendix 2: Method

The simulation must be set up before experiments; the parameters that are chosen in this phase influence the course of agent development. The prerequisites of a simulation are categorized in three distinct modules: an environment, which contains the initial agents; a viability function used to rate agents' phenotypes; and a mutator containing the mutation function and its parameters.

Initializing the Simulation Environment

The simulation takes place on a surface where fertility varies locally. Fertility constrains the allowed growth for agents' systems. Higher fertility allows for more iterations of growth, and the number of symbols each iteration may add to a system correlates positively with fertility as well.

An environment is defined as a rectangular terrain which may be sampled for fertility at any point. A terrain $t(x, y)$ yields a fertility factor in the range $[0, 1]$, where a higher value of t denotes higher fertility. More fertile terrain is lowered to visually resemble valleys.

Terrain functions that define infertile barriers separating lush valleys aim to promote divergent evolution of agents; simpler and smaller ancestors of agents may have crossed the low-fertility barriers, but the valleys may give rise to more complex agents that require higher fertility that cannot migrate through scarce regions anymore and thereby speciate. Figure 1 shows a possible environment, where darker highly fertile valleys are surrounded by an infertile plateau.

The formula $n = s + m \cdot i^2$ is used to calculate the number of symbols a system is allowed to have at a certain iteration while being generated; s is the initial number of allowed symbols a system may have (for any system, the axiom must not be larger than s). The parameter i is the iteration for which the maximum number of symbols needs to be sampled, and m is a positive number that may be increased to allow more growth. n relates to iteration i in a way that allows for an exponential increase in plant mass. The parameters s and m are defined such that they correlate positively and linearly with t; if these values are high, agents are able to develop larger structures. The number of iterations a system will be applied for to generate the phenotype also scales linearly with terrain fertility; this is a property of the environment as well.

The environment should be *seeded* with an initial set of agents before the first generation is evaluated. To obtain the results presented in Sect. 3, simulations were at all times seeded with agents containing an L-system without any rules and an axiom containing a single seed symbol. This is indeed the minimal progenitive system that could possibly be used for seeding, since it does not contain any additional information or bias besides the ability to reproduce.

Assigning Viability

An agent's viability determines the chance its offspring will make it to the next generation. The viability function in effect determines the course of the evolutionary process. Because only a limited number of agents may occupy a piece of land, they already compete for real-estate. To realistically model competition, agents are incentivized to compete for sunlight too; small grasses may be efficient at first, but they stand little chance of competing against overshadowing ferns.

The viability of an agent is determined by the following factors: The amount of *sunlight exposure* of an agents' leaves. Well-lit leaves yield a higher score, while occluded leaves or leaves that do not align towards the light source give low scores. The amount of energy a plant receives is derived from the amount of sunlight it receives, and a larger structure requires more sunlight to provide the energy required to build it. A larger agent will therefore require more sunlight exposure in order to get a good viability score.

The *stability*. Stable structures are better. Tall plants will get a lower stability score, and will have to receive benefits in other aspects.

The *efficiency*. A very complex genotype (e.g. a system with many unused or duplicate production rules) requires more energy and lowers viability. Additionally, seeds are very expensive to produce; while growing a very large number of them greatly increases the reproductive chances of an agent, this costs a large amount of energy and is thus not a viable strategy in a competitive scenario.

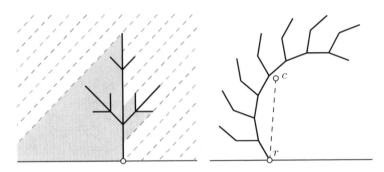

Fig. 12. Left: Sunlight is projected onto an agent from the top right, all lines in this system are treated as leaf surface. The dotted lines represent light rays. A shadow is cast by the plant, occluding its branches on the left side of its vertical axis entirely. **Right:** A two-dimensional agent with root r and center of mass c.

These three components yield three viability scores, which are multiplied together to produce the final viability of an agent.

Rating Sunlight Exposure. The more effectively sunlight is captured, the more efficient a plant is. In the simulation, sunlight is modelled by projecting parallel rays from several different locations representing the sun at different times during the day, and evaluating how many rays of sunlight land on each agents' leaves. Figure 12, left, shows a schematic representation of sunlight projection in a two-dimensional environment.

The origin of light sources in a simulation strongly influences the phenotypes that will evolve; when light shines predominantly straight down (as would be the case in a ravine), flat horizontally aligned leaves will be preferable to other angles. The 2D algorithm illustrated in Fig. 12, left, only registers light exposure to material directly hit by the sun rays. This is not realistic because real leaves are not fully opaque, and because light rays tend to bounce off the surfaces they hit, illuminating things that are initially occluded.

To account for these effects, leaf material has a certain *opacity factor*. This property determines how many rays will hit the surface, and how many will pass through. If the opacity factor is 0.7, 70% of the sun rays hit a leaf they come into contact with, while 30% of them pass through and may hit anything behind it. This allows (partially) occluded leaves to produce energy as well, encouraging plants to develop denser leaf patterns to gather more energy.

Because a higher amount of leaf surface material tends to correlate with a higher sunlight exposure related viability score, plants are incentivized to produce very large leaves; this is not entirely fair. Indeed, the size of an agent is not just determined by the amount of branch material, but also by the amount of leaf material spanned between them (see Fig. 11). The *leaf efficiency factor e* of an agent is therefore defined as:

$$e = \sum_{i=1}^{n_{\mathrm{l}}} \frac{1 - (f_e \cdot a_i)^2}{n_{\mathrm{l}}},$$

where n_{l} is the number of leaves, a_i is the area of the ith leaf on this agent, and f_e is a positive number that can be increased to give a higher penalty to big leaf shapes. This leaf efficiency factor is used to weigh the sunlight exposure viability; this means the viability from light exposure per surface area on a leaf is reduced for larger leaves.

The viability of sunlight exposure of an agent is set as

$$u_{\mathrm{l}} = \frac{h^p}{l} \cdot e.$$

The parameter h stands for the area of lit leaf material; this is the surface area of all leaf material as seen from the perspective of the sun after applying opacity (or the average surface of all sunlight projections if multiple are rendered). l represents the number of symbols a grown agent consists of; dividing by l ensures that plants consisting of many symbols need a high amount of lit leaf material in order to be successful. Finally, p is a power applied to h, with $p \geq 1$. Increasing p increases the number of symbols a system can support per exposed surface area as the total exposed surface area increases. This parameter exists because large plants need bigger support structures, while small plants need very little. The sunlight exposure viability is multiplied by efficiency factor e.

Rating Stability. The stability score is obtained from the *eccentricity* of a structure; this is the amount of deviation of the center of mass from the root of an agent. Figure 12, right, shows an agent phenotype with its center of mass visualized with respect to its root.

Using root r and center of mass c, the agent stability viability is

$$u_{\mathrm{s}} = \frac{1}{1 + f_{\mathrm{x}} \cdot ||c - r||^2},$$

where f_{x} is a positive number; it positively correlates with the viability score penalty given to unstable agents. Since c and r are three-dimensional in the simulation, agents that need to grow tall (along the vertical axis) to catch sunlight will need to reduce their instability along their other two axes with respect to their neighbours to stay competitive. On the other hand, small grasses and undergrowth will have very low or negligible instability penalties, and can thus develop different growth strategies to obtain high viability scores.

Rating Efficiency. Efficiency captures the effectiveness of a genotype and the cost of its reproductive faculties. The effect of this viability score is therefore twofold: it penalizes overly complex L-systems, and it penalizes excessive seed production as well. The following formula captures these functions:

$$u_e = \frac{1}{(f_r \cdot n_r) \cdot (f_s \cdot n_s)}$$

with n_r the number of production rules of the L-system, n_s is the number of seeds that exist in the phenotype. f_r and f_s are positive numbers that may be increased to give higher penalties to high numbers of rules and seeds, respectively.

Negative Viability. The final viability of an agent is $u = u_l \cdot u_s \cdot u_e$. Agents with negative viability cannot be produced by this formula. There are however two exceptions for which the viability is set to -1, namely for agents growing underground, and agents over a certain size without any sunlight exposure.

The first point is obvious: since the simulation does not model roots, growing underground is by definition physically impossible. The second point is implemented to limit nonsensical phenotypes that emerge early in a simulation. The initial best strategy (when no leaves have evolved yet) is to reproduce as often and as far away as possible by growing tall structures with many seeds. Growing such structures is not penalized by a poor sunlight exposure viability as it normally would, because this is zero for all leafless agents. To prevent unrealistic structures that support themselves without any photosynthesis, negative viability is assigned to leafless agents over a certain size.

Reproduction

Agents with a non-negative viability may produce seeds to reproduce themselves in the next generation. When all agents have been rated, their seeds are dispersed in an empty copy of the simulation environment to produce the next generation. Figure 13, left, shows how seeds are dispersed; a seed s at height h describes a cone with its apex at s and an angle α. The seed is placed on a random point on the base of the cone. The angle may vary among simulations, where more windy environments can be modelled by increasing α. Higher values of α also increase the chance of agents spreading their genotype across the natural boundaries.

After seeds have been dispersed and positioned in the environment, they are ranked by their parent agents' viability. Seeds with equal viability are shuffled to eliminate their positional bias; if an agent grows its seeds from top to bottom, the top seeds should not always get the chance to reproduce first.

The seeds produce new agents at their location, starting with the highest ranked seed. Because new agents can only be placed at locations that are not yet (too) occupied (see below), the next generation of agents consists of the best offspring, while poor agents usually (but not always) get no chance to reproduce.

To determine where agents can or cannot grow, a *density map* is maintained while seeds are placed in the environment, similar to the approach of [1]. Figure 13, right, shows how agent density is assigned to the terrain surface. A grid is created for the area for which agent density needs to be known (this is

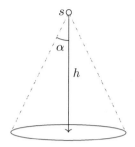

0	0	0	0	0	1	1	1	1	0	0	0
0	0	0	1	1	1	1	1	1	1	1	0
1	0	1	1	1	1	1	1	1	1	1	0
1	1	2	1	1	1	1	1	1	1	1	1
1	1	2	2	1	1	1	1	1	1	1	1
1	1	3	3	2	2	1	1	1	1	1	1
1	2	3	3	2	2	2	1	1	1	1	1
1	2	2	3	2	2	2	1	1	1	1	0
1	2	2	2	2	2	2	1	1	1	1	0
1	2	1	1	1	2	2	1	1	0	1	1
0	0	1	1	1	1	0	0	0	1	1	1
0	0	0	0	0	0	0	0	0	1	1	1

Fig. 13. Left: The seed s may fall anywhere within the base of the cone. **Right:** A part of an agent density map. Four agents increment the cells they overlap.

normally the entire simulation environment), and every cell of this grid contains the number of agents overlapping that cell.

The black dots represent newly placed agents, and the circle around them represents the area they occupy. The radius of the circles is chosen such that the area is equal to the area of the rectangle that the parent plant occupied in the previous generation.

Every simulation has a constant *density threshold*, which is the maximum number of agents that may overlap a grid cell for a seed to sprout when its location lies within that cell. This threshold thus determines how dense vegetation is allowed to grow, and by extension how competitive agents need to be with respect to their neighbours. Simulations with a low density threshold barely experience competition, and thus produce lower growing plants; see Sect. 3.

Mutation

Before the agents in the new generation are "grown", random mutation is applied to their genotypes. Production rules may be created, duplicated or removed. The axiom and the sentences that make up the production rules are mutated as well by inserting and removing symbols, or by creating branches or leaves around existing symbols. When mutating sentences, syntactic correctness is taken into account; every branch or leaf opening symbol has a corresponding closing symbol. Moreover, sentences may never grow larger than a preset limit to prevent overfitting; with no limit, the algorithm could simply evolve entire fixed plant structures in the axiom without creating any production rules.

A sentence is mutated by iterating over each symbol. At each iteration, there is a chance a mutation operation executes, while most symbols do not change. Figure 14 shows all possible mutations on sentences using the syntax outlined in Fig. 11. Mutations are always applied at the position of the iterator. Operations (1), (2), (3) and (5) may be applied when the iterator points to a symbol; operation (4) may only trigger at a branch open symbol and operation (6) may only trigger at a leaf open symbol.

Operation (1) in Fig. 14 creates new symbol x either before or after the symbol the iterator currently points to; there is a 50% chance for both outcomes.

$$\text{Add symbol} = \underline{AB}[C]<D] \; \rightarrow \; AxB[C]<D] \tag{1}$$
$$\rightarrow \; ABx[C]<D]$$
$$\text{Remove symbol} = \underline{AB}[C]<D] \; \rightarrow \; A[C]<D] \tag{2}$$
$$\text{Add branch} = \underline{AB}[C]<D] \; \rightarrow \; A[B][C]<D] \tag{3}$$
$$\text{Remove branch} = AB[\underline{C}]<D] \; \rightarrow \; ABC<D] \tag{4}$$
$$\text{Add leaf} = \underline{AB}[C]<D] \; \rightarrow \; A<B][C]<D] \tag{5}$$
$$\text{Remove leaf} = AB[C]\underline{<D} \; \rightarrow \; AB[C]D \tag{6}$$

Fig. 14. Possible mutation operations on the sentence AB[C]<D]. The underscores in the left hand sides of the operations show the position of the iterator in the sentence; mutation operations are applied at that location.

$$a = B[+A][-A]BA$$
$$r_1 = A \rightarrow B[+A][-A]BA$$
$$r_2 = B \rightarrow BB$$
$$E = [B,B,B,B,B,B,A,A,A,A,A,A,+,+,-,-]$$
$$N = [A...Z] \uplus [a...z] \uplus [*] \uplus R$$

Fig. 15. Multisets E and N of an L-system with axiom a and production rules r_1 and r_2. R is the multiset containing all rotation symbols defined in Fig. 11.

The symbol is randomly chosen from a multiset of possible new symbols. This multiset varies depending on the kind of sentence that is being mutated. Branch or leaf symbols may not occur in this multiset, since mutation rules (3), (4), (5) and (6) already cover branch and leaf mutation.

The symbol x is chosen from multiset E or N. E contains all symbols that may be *produced* by the L-system (the symbols that can exist in the sentence obtained by applying production rules to the axiom for any number of iterations). N contains all possible symbols (that are not branch or leaf symbols) that may exist in a system according to Fig. 11. Figure 15 shows an L-system and its corresponding E and N.

When x is placed in the left hand side of a production rule, it will be chosen from E. This ensures that production rule conditions do not contain symbols that cannot occur in sentences produced by a system, these rules would never be applicable. If it is placed in the axiom or the right hand side of a production rule, it is possible to introduce symbols that do not yet exist in the L-system. In this situation x will be chosen from N or E. The possibility of picking x from E instead of N in this case is introduced to promote reusing existing symbols in the system. This increases the chances of introducing stochastic rules, while also promoting self-similarity by increasing the chance that existing production rules will trigger on newly added symbols.

Fig. 16. Left: A simulation at $g = 40$ using a default leaf symbol to model triangular leaves. **Right:** A simulation at $g = 800$ using the normal leaf modelling syntax from Appendix 1 produces very similar agents to the alternative method, although it takes more generations to evolve them.

The composition of N in Fig. 15 is such that R and $[*]$ are quite rare. In the simulation, these sets are added to N several times to increase their chances of being added when a new symbol is created. The number of repetitions of these sets is a constant setting of the mutator, which may be used to speed up the introduction of seeds and branch rotations as the evolution progresses.

Default Leaf Shapes

The syntax described in Appendix 1 and Fig. 11 uses a relatively complex method to define leaves. The process of modelling "good" leaves is arguably more complex than modelling the supporting structures.

To evaluate whether the complexity of the proposed leaf modelling process does not impair the course of the simulation, a *default leaf symbol* can be introduced (see Appendix 1); when the turtle encounters this symbol, a triangular leaf is created at its position and orientation. The chance to create leaf brackets while mutating is set to zero. Figure 16 shows a rendering of a simulation using this alternative method (left) compared to a simulation using the standard method (right). When default leaf shapes are used, agents with leaves evolve very quickly. Given enough time however, a simulation using the default method produces very similar agents. This shows that agents with multiple similar leaves evolve quicker when default leaf shape symbols are used, but similar results can be achieved without it; the proposed leaf modelling method does not seem to impair the course of the simulation.

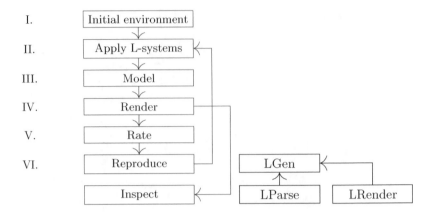

Fig. 17. Left: Stages of a simulation. **Right:** Structure of the *LGen* software.

Appendix 3: Implementation

The *LGen* software [27] built to perform the experiments using the method described in Appendix 2 was implemented in the *C++11* programming language and targets both Windows and Linux platforms. Figure 17 shows the different modules that make up the software. *LGen* performs, stores and loads experiments and configurations. *LParse* parses L-systems according to the syntax set forth in Appendix 1, generating the strings of symbols that are translated into agent phenotypes. *LRender* models and renders populated 3D simulation environments using *OpenGL* according to the algorithm described in Appendix 2, and provides information about these renderings (e.g. sunlight exposure ratios, structure size, and seed locations). *LGen* and *LParse* are both used by *LGen*, but do not require or reference each other.

Stages

The algorithm is divided into several stages per generation. Figure 17 shows the stages, in order of execution, that are required to simulate a generation.

Stage I initializes the environment, including for example its terrain function and seed dispersal angle. In practice, this step is done manually by the user. The initialized simulation can be stored for later use, or to perform different experiments on a set of equal initial conditions.

Subsequently, Stage II creates a string of symbols for each agent by applying their system's production rules to their axioms for a number of iterations that depends on the fertility of the terrain at their respective locations. This process is multithreaded, since no interaction between agents takes place at this stage.

In Stage III, a 3D model of the environment and all its agents is created by applying the modelling rules detailed in Appendix 1. Again, this stage uses multithreading to speed up the modelling process. Summarizing information about agent models (size, center of gravity, etc.) is stored for use in Stage V.

At Stage IV, the GPU is employed to render the scene modelled in Stage III from different angles, where each angle is one of the sunlight directions. Light exposure characteristics for each agent are stored for use in Stage V, which assigns viability to every agent in the simulation. The viability function takes information gathered by Stages III and IV as well as the L-system that gave rise to this agent into account.

Finally, Stage VI creates a list of all seeds produced in the environment, ranks the seeds by the viability assigned to their parents by Stage V, and disperses the seeds. New agents are created from these seeds after mutation. The simulation can now loop back to Stage II and evolve the newly created generation.

The results of the simulation can be queried whenever Stage IV has finished; the software can render the simulation at its current stage, and agents can be inspected by querying their L-systems and viability scores. When presenting a rendered environment to the user, a high-detail scene is modelled; the program uses lower quality agent models while simulating to increase performance.

Randomization

Randomization is used at several points in the simulation: stochastic L-systems may need to choose a random production rule from a list; the initial direction of the turtle when modelling an agent is upwards, but the rotation around the vertical axis is randomized; when dispersing seeds, randomization is used to displace them; mutating L-systems make heavy use of it.

The implementation uses *Mersenne twisters* [20] for randomization. An important feature of the program is that its randomizer can be *seeded*, after which the simulation is completely deterministic; when running the same seeded setup twice, the same results emerge. This feature makes simulation runs reproducible, but it reduces storage space as well. When a simulation of a high number of generations needs to be written to disk completely, it only stores the state every n generations along with the state of its randomizer. Consider a stored simulation of at least 4000 generations. If $n = 1000$ and the 3511th generation needs to be inspected, the system loads the 3000th generation instead (which was saved since $n = 1000$), and simulates for another 511 generations to obtain the state as it was at the 3511th generation.

Leaf Area Projections

To implement the sunlight exposure algorithm, the 3D scene produced in Stage III (see Fig. 17) is rendered using an orthographic projection. Figure 18 shows two renderings; on the left, the modelled scene is rendered for viewing purposes using a perspective projection. On the right, the parallel projection is used to detect sunlight exposure in the same scene. This ensures that the produced pixels can be seen as hits by the parallel rays of sunlight in Fig. 12, left.

In this *exposure projection*, any pixels that contain leaves get a dark color, while the rest of the image stays white. The exposure area of agents can be

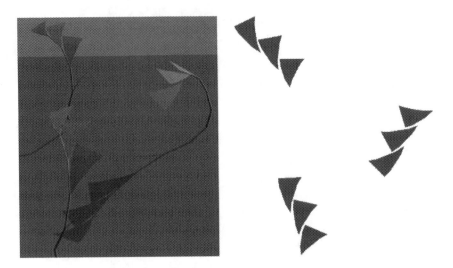

Fig. 18. Left: A 3D rendering of three agents. **Right:** The corresponding exposure projection taken from approximately the same angle. Note that the phenotype has evolved such that the leaves do not occlude each other, while still being compact.

obtained by counting the "hit" pixels in this rendering for each agent. Pixels do not only contain information about whether a leaf was hit there, but they also encode which agent was hit. Additionally, the algorithm uses a depth buffer; the leaves closest to the camera (which represents the sun in this model) receive sunlight while occluded leaves do not. If the opacity factor is smaller than 1 however, every pixel of exposed material has a chance equal to that factor of not being rendered, allowing occluded leaves to receive sunlight as well.

References

1. Alsweis, M., Deussen, O.: Modeling and visualization of symmetric and asymmetric plant competition. In: Proceedings of the First Eurographics Conference on Natural Phenomena, NPH'05, pp. 83–88. Eurographics Association (2005)
2. Beyer, R., Etard, O., Cournède, P.H., Laurent-Gengoux, P.: Modeling spatial competition for light in plant populations with the porous medium equation. J. Math. Biol. **70**, 533–547 (2015)
3. Bornhofen, S., Lattaud, C.: Competition and evolution in virtual plant communities: a new modeling approach. Nat. Comput. 8(2), 349–385 (2009)
4. Burt, T.: Interactive Evolution by Duplication and Diversification of L-systems. Master's thesis, University of Calgary (2013)
5. Chelle, M., Andrieu, B.: Modelling the light environment of virtual crop canopies. In: Functional-Structural Plant Modelling in Crop Production, vol. 22, pp. 75–89. Springer, Heidelberg (2007)
6. Cournède, P., de Reffye, P.: A generalized Poisson model to estimate inter-plant competition for light. In: 2006 2nd International Symposium on Plant Growth Modeling and Applications, pp. 11–15 (2006)

7. Cournède, P.H., Mathieu, A., Houllier, F., Barthélémy, D., de Reffye, P.: Computing competition for light in the GREENLAB model of plant growth: A contribution to the study of the effects of density on resource acquisition and architectural development. Ann. Botany **101**(8), 1207–1219 (2007)
8. Ech, R., Prusinkiewicz, P.: Visual models of plants interacting with their environment. In: Computer Graphics (SIGGRAPH 1996) (1996)
9. Fitch, B.G., Parslow, P., Lundqvist, K.Ø.: Evolving complete L-systems: using genetic algorithms for the generation of realistic plants. In: Lewis, P.R., Headleand, C.J., Battle, S., Ritsos, P.D. (eds.) ALIA 2016. CCIS, vol. 732, pp. 16–23. Springer, Cham (2018). https://doi.org/10.1007/978-3-319-90418-4_2
10. Fourcaud, T., Zhang, X., Stokes, A., Lambers, H., Körner, C.: Plant growth modelling and applications: the increasing importance of plant architecture in growth models. Ann. Botany **101**(8), 1053–1063 (2008)
11. Holland, J.: Adaptation in Natural and Artificial Systems. University of Michigan Press, Ann Arbor (1975)
12. Hua, J., Kang, M.: Functional tree models reacting to the environment. In: ACM SIGGRAPH 2011 Posters, SIGGRAPH '11 (2011)
13. Jacob, C.: Evolving evolution programs: Genetic programming and L-systems. In: Proceedings of the 1st Annual Conf. on Genetic Programming, pp. 107–115. MIT Press, Cambridge (1996)
14. Köhler, F.E.: Lily of the valley illustration. In: Pabst, G. (ed.) Hermann Adolph Köhler's Medicinal Plants (1887)
15. Lindenmayer, A.: Mathematical models for cellular interactions in development II. Simple and branching filaments with two-sided inputs. J. Theor. Biol. **18**(3), 300–315 (1968)
16. Lintermann, B., Deussen, O.: A modelling method and user interface for creating plants. Comput. Graph. Forum **17**(1), 73–82 (1998)
17. MacKenzie, C., Prusinkiewicz, P.: Artificial evolution of plant forms. In: Proceedings of the Fifth Annual Western Computer Graphics Symposium, pp. 1–9 (1993)
18. Makowski, M., Hädrich, T., Scheffczyk, J., Michels, D.L., Pirk, S., Pałubicki, W.: Synthetic silviculture: multi-scale modeling of plant ecosystems. ACM Trans. Graph. **38**(4), 1–14 (2019)
19. Mathieu, A., Cournède, P., Letort, V., Barthélémy, D., de Reffye, P.: A dynamic model of plant growth with interactions between development andfunctional mechanisms to study plant structural plasticity related to trophiccompetition. Ann. Botany **103**, 1173–1186 (2009)
20. Matsumoto, M., Nishimura, T.: Mersenne twister: a 623-dimensionally equidistributed uniform pseudo-random number generator. ACM Trans. Model. Comput. Simul. **8**(1), 3–30 (1998)
21. Ochoa, G.: On genetic algorithms and Lindenmayer systems. In: Eiben, A.E., Bäck, T., Schoenauer, M., Schwefel, H.-P. (eds.) PPSN 1998. LNCS, vol. 1498, pp. 335–344. Springer, Heidelberg (1998). https://doi.org/10.1007/BFb0056876
22. Palubicki, W., et al.: Self-organizing tree models for image synthesis. ACM Trans. Graph. **28**(3), 1–10 (2009)
23. Pirk, S., et al.: Plastic trees: interactive self-adapting botanical tree models. ACM Trans. Graph. **31**(4), 1–10 (2012)
24. Prusinkiewicz, P.: A look at the visual modeling of plants using L-systems. In: Hofestädt, R., Lengauer, T., Löffler, M., Schomburg, D. (eds.) GCB 1996. LNCS, vol. 1278, pp. 11–29. Springer, Heidelberg (1996). https://doi.org/10.1007/BFb0033200

25. Risi, S., Stoy, K., Faíña, A., Veenstra, F.: Generating artificial plant morphologies for function and aesthetics through evolving L-systems. In: The 2019 Conference on Artificial Life, no. 28, pp. 692–699 (2016)
26. Sarlikioti, V., de Visser, P.H.B., Marcelis, L.F.M.: Exploring the spatial distribution of light interception and photosynthesis of canopies by means of a functional-structural plant model. Ann. Botany **107**(5), 875–883 (2011)
27. Talle, J.J.V.: LGen software source code. https://github.com/jobtalle/LGen

ParaGlyder: Probe-driven Interactive Visual Analysis for Multiparametric Medical Imaging Data

Eric Mörth[1,2(✉)] ⓘ, Ingfrid S. Haldorsen[2,3] ⓘ, Stefan Bruckner[1,2] ⓘ,
and Noeska N. Smit[1,2] ⓘ

[1] Department of Informatics, University of Bergen, Bergen, Norway
eric.moerth@uib.no
[2] Mohn Medical Imaging and Visualization Centre, Haukeland University Hospital,
Bergen, Norway
[3] Department of Clinical Medicine, University of Bergen, Bergen, Norway

Abstract. Multiparametric imaging in cancer has been shown to be useful for tumor detection and may also depict functional tumor characteristics relevant for clinical phenotypes. However, when confronted with datasets consisting of multiple values per voxel, traditional reading of the imaging series fails to capture complicated patterns. These patterns of potentially important imaging properties of the parameter space may be critical for the analysis, but standard approaches do not deliver sufficient details. Therefore, in this paper, we present an approach that aims to enable the exploration and analysis of such multiparametric studies using an interactive visual analysis application to remedy the trade-offs between details in the value domain and in spatial resolution. This may aid in the discrimination between healthy and cancerous tissue and potentially highlight metastases that evolved from the primary tumor. We conducted an evaluation with eleven domain experts from different fields of research to confirm the utility of our approach.

Keywords: Medical visualization · Visual analysis · Multiparametric medical imaging data

1 Introduction

Multiparametric medical imaging scans are commonly used in screening procedures and in targeted diagnostics. Basing decisions on the analysis of these datasets is not an easy task and often involves visual inspection of different juxtaposed representations [6]. Multiparametric datasets are generated in medical imaging by, e.g., Magnetic Resonance Imaging (MRI) scanners, by varying acquisition parameters resulting in imaging data with varying contrasts. In the analysis of medical imaging data, the main task is usually to identify discernible patterns to distinguish pathologic from healthy tissue, and identify, e.g., malignant tumors. The identification of metastases, likely to share characteristic imaging properties with the primary tumor, may be difficult to spot only using one

© Springer Nature Switzerland AG 2020
N. Magnenat-Thalmann et al. (Eds.): CGI 2020, LNCS 12221, pp. 351–363, 2020.
https://doi.org/10.1007/978-3-030-61864-3_29

modality, although identifying them at primary diagnostic work-up is essential to develop more tailored and targeted treatment strategies in various cancers. In order to improve the workflow of tumor diagnosis and metastases identification, we have developed a tool for analyzing multiparametric medical imaging data together with gynecological cancer, machine learning and neurological cancer research experts. By employing different views displaying multiparametric data at different levels of detail, we can present imaging data without having to visually compare several modalities in side-by-side views. We enable highlighting of target structures, based on multiparametric similarity, which was not possible before. Medical experts are used to working with 2D slice views. Overlaying multiparametric data on top of these views produces insights which are easy for them to put into a spatial context. Showing multiparametric images in one view reduces the cognitive load and allows the medical experts to see the relevant information at a glance. Our main contributions are the following: (1) We present visualizations that remedy the trade-offs between revealing details in the multiparametric value domain and spatial resolution by introducing a multiparametric star glyph map-based visualization. (2) We present an interactive analysis application primarily targeting cancer imaging, as well as additional workflows in different application areas. (3) We evaluate our system with eleven experts using the System Usability Scale (SUS) [3] and a qualitative evaluation to demonstrate the utility of our approach.

2   Medical Background

Modern imaging techniques are routinely used at many centers in the preoperative diagnostic work-up in endometrial cancer. Imaging markers derived from these advanced MRI techniques have been shown to be linked to endometrial cancer subtype and stage [2,6,9–11]. According to previous findings, low tumor blood flow and a low rate constant for contrast agent intravasation, meaning the backflow of injected contrast into the close vessels, based on dynamic contrast-enhanced (DCE)-MRI, are associated with high-risk histologic subtypes and poor prognosis. Gathering information from parametric maps based on DCE-MRI is usually done using juxtaposed images of the same slice in the different modalities. These maps are derived from a single dynamic acquisition and are therefore co-registered by nature. Examining the images involves comparing the images mentally or by using a manually placed region of interest (ROI). If advanced imaging methods can be utilized to validly predict the aggressiveness of a tumor, this could lead to better risk-stratified treatment algorithms that may be beneficial for the patients. Less invasive treatment regimens may then be given in low-risk patients, and the more invasive treatments can be reserved for high-risk patients in whom the expected survival benefit justifies the increased side effects.

3   Related Work

Lawonn et al. [16] provide an extensive overview of different visualization techniques for multimodal medical imaging datasets. Gleicher et al. [8] introduced

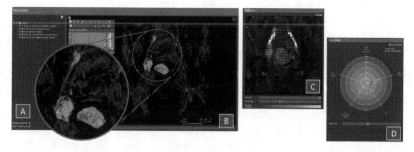

Fig. 1. The ParaGlyder prototype application, featuring a subject overview (A), central view (B), Stixels view (C), and radial boxplot view (D).

a taxonomy of visual comparison approaches and surveyed existing methods according it. Friendly et al. [7] proposed radial boxplots, as a means to visualize data variations. Ropinski et al. [22] provide a thorough overview of different glyph-based visualization techniques in the field of multivariate medical data visualization. Wickham et al. [27] introduced a visualization technique called glyph maps. Opach et al. [20] described that the effectiveness of polyline versus star glyphs is task-dependent. The effective combination of star glyphs presenting non-spatial data and geospatial data has been demonstrated by Friendly et al. [7] and more recently by Jäckle et al. [12]. In contrast to this, we use star glyphs to present an abstract version of multiparametric spatial data on top of spatial data. Smit et al. [24] presented a method to spatially query data by placing a sphere in a 3D view, and interaction techniques to effectively place spheres in volume renderings [25]. Bruckner et al. [4] introduced a probing tool for enabling visual queries. Mlejnek et al. [18] presented interactive glyphs for probing tissue characteristics in medical data. In contrast to these approaches, we provide a probing interaction that acts like a digital biopsy of our multiparametric medical imaging datasets. More closely related to our approach, Stoppel et al. [26] used small multiples to visualize spatio-temporal data in a spatial context. Malik et al. [17] introduced a comparative visualization technique that visualizes up to five modalities together in one view. Jönsson et al. [13] presented a visual environment for hypothesis generation using spatial and abstract data. In contrast to these related publications, our approach enables the exploration and analysis of multiparametric medical imaging datasets of more than five modalities. We provide targeted functionality for the analysis of pathology, which allow for inspection of the multiparametric imaging data in linked spatial and non-spatial data visualizations.

4   Requirement Analysis

Following the nested model for visualization design by Munzner [19], we characterized the problem domain. To meet the requirements and the demands of the target audience, we consulted experts in gynecological cancer imaging, neurological imaging, and machine learning. We identified application related challenges they face in their research practice. Cancer imaging is performed to assess tumors and metastases, in gynecological cancer imaging in the pelvic area and for neurological imaging in the brain. Cancerous tissue is discernible because it differs from its surrounding healthy tissue. Besides analysis of the extent and size of the tumor, analyzing different sub-regions within a tumor may be of interest. Finding abdominal lymph node metastases is a challenging task, as the metastases have variable size, ranging from a few millimeters to sizes exceeding the primary tumor. Metastases often share some of the characteristic imaging features of the primary tumor. Based on our analysis we present the following requirements for our interactive analysis application:

- R1: Visual analysis of multiparametric imaging data in a single view
- R2: Multiparametric inhomogeneity analysis
- R3: Comparing regions within the multiparametric imaging data
- R4: Comparing multiparametric imaging data of multiple subjects
- R5: Multiparametric similarity analysis based on a digital biopsy
- R6: Interactive parameter selection for automatic multiparametric segmentation tasks

When satisfying these requirements, we support gynecological imaging researchers, neurological imaging experts and machine learning experts in their research or clinical routine with the ultimate goal of improving patient care by providing better diagnostic tools that can guide tailored and individual treatment strategies.

5   ParaGlyder

In this section, we present our visualization and interaction design decisions based on the requirement analysis. In Fig. 2, we present the different components of our method and their interplay. Our design combines spatial and non-spatial visualizations, linked by a view combining a non-spatial visualization in spatial context. Our approach consists of several visualization and interaction methods for the interactive analysis of multiparametric data described in the following.

5.1   Data Processing

Our method relies on multidimensional co-registered volumetric data. Our gynecological cancer experts already deliver co-registered volumes due to the nature of the data source. Co-registration is therefore not part of our application but may be performed by using state of the art applications such as Elastix [14]. Standard MRI imaging data cannot be converted to physical units and therefore is highly dependent on the scanner and sequences employed. In order to allow for comparison normalization is required. In our application, we perform two types of normalization. When we use a slice view, we normalize the data of the slice using a min-max normalization of the selected slice. In the 3D volume visualization, we normalize the whole volume by using the min-max value of the volume. This results in the most appropriate normalization based on the tasks the visualizations support.

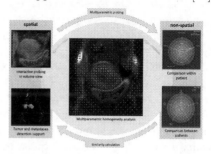

Fig. 2. The ParaGlyder application combines spatial (volumetric view) and non-spatial (radial boxplot) visualization to enable multiparametric analysis and exploration. In between, the Stixels view depicts a combination of both.

5.2   The Stixels View

Based on requirement R1, the goal is to raise the level of detail in the value domain but still keep the details in the spatial resolution. To facilitate this, we employ a glyph map approach, presented in the middle of Fig. 2, which is called the Stixels (**St**ar glyph p**ixels**) view. The glyph map is based on a regular grid which is overlaid on a 2D view of a slice. For every grid cell, we calculate statistics of the multiparametric medical imaging data. The star glyphs are then created by summarizing the statistics within each of the cells. The grid size and the star glyph size can be adapted, depending on the granularity of the structure of

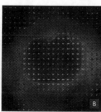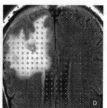

Fig. 3. The Stixels view reveals an inhomogeneous tumor in one subject (a) and a more homogeneous tumor in another subject (b). The outline in red shows the tumor extent for illustration purposes. A tooltip provides details on demand in a radial boxplot (c), The Stixels view reveals oedema in the brain after surgery (d). (Color figure online)

interest. By cropping the slice view to a region of interest, the glyph maps also adapt to the selection and allows for an even more detailed view of the selected structures. We use star glyphs instead of polyline-based glyphs since according to Opach et al. [20] star glyphs are a better choice for finding differences. For the star glyph design, we display the average value of each parameter within the grid cell on the axes. The area described by connecting these points forms a glyph which describes the relation of average parameters within the cell. When designing a star glyph, a homogeneous shape is favorable [15,21]. Therefore, the order in which the parameters are presented is adjustable. While even more information could be encoded on the axes of the star glyph, we opted for a design that is easier to interpret and presents all necessary information at a glance to prevent a steep learning curve. The star glyph map provides an overview which allows the user to identify the tumor since the tissue differs from healthy tissue in the multiparametric dimensions. In addition, the inhomogeneity of the tumor can be analyzed. When spotting interesting parts of the tumor, a closer investigation of the area using the interactive probing can be employed.

5.3   3D Probing Visualization

Requirements R3 and R4 support analyzing different parts of the tumor independently, enabling identification of tumor patterns. Probing spheres deliver detailed information from data within selected regions. Regions of interest can be specified by using multiple probing spheres. This enables a comparison of different regions within the imaging data for a single patient, e.g., healthy tissue and cancerous tissue. All voxels from all parameters within the spheres can be used in the statistical analysis, like the approach used for the star glyph map. For the visual encoding of the probed regions a radial boxplot is used. It shows the user the summary statistics for selected regions of interest at a glance. Comparison is enabled by the superposition of multiple radial boxplots. Radial boxplots are favorable because they align with the use of star glyphs in the Stixels view and represent a more detailed view of selected areas. Differences and similarities over all modalities can be analyzed by placing multiple spheres either within the data of a single patient or multiple patients. To establish visual correspondence between the probing spheres and radial boxplots, both the spheres and boxplot share the same color hue. Interactive probing can be used to define a multiparametric pattern which describes different tumor characteristics based only on imaging data and may also be found in other patients suffering from a similar tumor type.

5.4   Interaction

To support requirements R3 and R4 various interaction methods are provided. The placement of the probing sphere can be performed either in 2D images or in 3D volumes. The size of the sphere can be adapted to fit the scale of the region of interest and the sphere can be placed freely. The quickest option is the free placement where the sphere is placed according to the intersection of

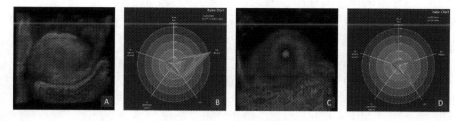

Fig. 4. Volume probing using two different probing spheres (a) results in live updates to the radial boxplot view (b). Probing interaction within another subject (c) results in a radial boxplot comparing data across subjects (d).

a ray going from the screen position, where the mouse is located, towards the volume based on the closest visible point in the volume. In addition to this quick initial placement of the sphere, we introduce a mode where the sphere can only be translated within the current X-Y plane the sphere is located at. Another option only adapts the depth of the sphere along the Z-axis. When using a 2D view, it may occur that the probing sphere is behind the current slice and thus occluded. To remedy this, we provide an option to snap the sphere back to the slice. To support working with brain data, placing a sphere that is automatically mirrored to the other hemisphere is also possible.

5.5   Similarity Visualization

Requirements R5 and R6 state that a similarity analysis and an interactive parameter selection is beneficial in tumor analysis. Analyzing the tumor extent and possible metastases in surrounding tissue is a typical task for radiologists. In addition, segmentation of tumors is an active field of machine learning research, where some algorithms require feature selection. To support these tasks, we employ the multiparametric contents of a probed area in a similarity function. We decided to use the Euclidean distance over all dimensions because they are equally important. When applying this function to each multi-parametric voxel in the volume, we derive a new volume consisting of similarity values between 0 and 1 which can be displayed with an appropriate transfer function. A transfer function that highlights regions of high similarity through color and opacity enables users to identify structures such as tumors and possible metastases and enables a visual clustering with soft boundaries. Metastases which share the same imaging properties as the primary tumor are highlighted using direct volume rendering. Editing the transfer function enables the user to explore the inhomogeneity (R2) and the extent of different parts of the tumor. In addition, this similarity function-based visual encoding is also applied to the star glyph map. The fact that the similarity is based on the user-selected parameters enables the user to perform interactive feature selection (R6).

6 Results

The ParaGlyder application is depicted in Fig. 1 and consists of a center view (Fig. 1B), which provides common spatial visualization features, such as a 3D view, 2D slice-based views, cropping, and transfer function editing, and a probing functionality. Next to the main view, the Stixels view is located (Fig. 1C), which consists of a 2D slice view and an overlaid glyph map consisting of star glyphs. The last view is the probing view, component D in Fig. 1. It consists of a radial boxplot based on probing sphere input. We analyzed different datasets of endometrial cancer patients, provided by one of our co-authors, as well as a brain tumor dataset publicly available and provided by Schmainda and Prah [23] via the Cancer Imaging Archive (TCIA) [5]. The endometrial cancer dataset comprises standard multiparametric MR sequences and derived parameter maps visualizing physical parameters, e.g., blood flow and plasma volume. The data is co-registered due to its origin. For the brain tumor and inflammation data, we have access to the standard parameters acquired in multiparametric MR, such as T1-, T2- and diffusion-weighted images.

6.1 Tumor Detection and Multiparametric Homogeneity Assessment

To detect tumors and assess their multiparametric homogeneity, the Stixels view is used. The user selects the slice and the parameter to show. A detailed view of individual Stixels is presented when the user hovers the mouse over the specific Stixel. A detailed tooltip is shown, visualized in Fig. 3c. In order to support region of interest (ROI) selection, we employ volumetric cropping to select an appropriate Stixel window. The grid of the Stixels adapts accordingly and then probes smaller regions determined by the ROI. When placing a probing sphere, the Stixels are colored by the multiparametric similarity, measured based on Euclidean distance, using the Viridis colormap. The similarity Stixels view, visible in Figs. 3a and 3b, additionally reveals the inhomogeneity of the tumor. The red line marks the outline of the tumor and the color and shape variations of the star glyphs represents the inhomogeneity within the primary tumor. In Fig. 3a, a tumor with a high degree of inhomogeneity is visible, while Fig. 3b reveals a more homogeneous tumor. The inhomogeneity analysis enables the user to spot distinct parts within the tumor, e.g., a necrotic core and allows for further analysis of these specific parts in detail.

6.2 Region Comparison for Tumor Characteristic Assessment

Probing spheres are used to analyze different parts within one patient or across multiple patients. This probing interaction is conceptually similar to a digital biopsy. The result of the probing interaction is a radial boxplot, visible in component D in Fig. 1. Figure 4a showcases placement of two spheres for a single subject, while Fig. 4b shows a sphere placed to compare regions across subjects. The radial boxplot is shown in Fig. 4b and d. On each axis, the median value

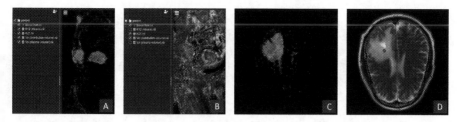

Fig. 5. The similarity view highlighting the uterine primary tumor in the center and two metastatic lymph nodes (a). When an insufficient number of dimensions is selected, the similarity view fails to capture the tumor and metastases (b). The similarity view captures brain inflammation (c), while simple thresholding on one modality would capture the skull as well.

is presented as a dot, and these dots are connected by lines. In addition to the median value, the 25% and the 75% quantile ranges are visible as an overlaid band. This representation allows the user to see the inhomogeneity of the data within the sphere. The maximum values of the axes can be adapted to fit the selected data range. The spheres are used to characterize tumor tissue and to come up with specific signature shapes in the radial boxplot that can be used to classify the imaging data of new patients. The interaction responsiveness is ensured by providing a real-time update of the radar chart with the probed values of the volumetric multiparametric imaging data while the sphere is moved interactively through the volume.

6.3 Similarity Visualization for Metastases Detection and Feature Selection

The similarity view, visible in Fig. 1B and Fig. 5, visualizes the extent of a tumor and potential nearby metastases. Figure 5(a) shows the similarity volume when using all multiparametric images and Fig. 5(b) shows the similarity volume with only three out of five of the multiparametric images. The Figure shows that the three selected images do not contain enough information to segment the tumor and the metastases. The colored Stixels are presented in Fig. 3c. For both approaches the Viridis colormap is chosen as a transfer function, where opacity is mapped to similarity, i.e., the visibility of regions that differ from the current selection is reduced. In component B of Fig. 1, the similarity view of parameter maps of a patient with endometrial cancer is visible. This similarity analysis enables a clear and distinct visualization of the tumor (the lower right structure in the inset), by placing a probing sphere inside the tumor tissue. Due to their multiparametric similarity, metastases in the lymphatic system (structures to the left and above the primary tumor) are also highlighted. When analyzing only one of the multiparametric images at a time the detection of metastases is much more difficult because they are not clearly visible. When probing inflammatory data within the brain, the similarity view provides a quick segmentation of inflamed tissue. The segmentation does not include the bone as a standard thresholding operation based on T2 Flair data only would, visualized in Fig. 5(c) and (d). This demonstrates that the multiparametric similarity function facilitates a rapid multiparametric segmentation, which could be used in diagnosis or treatment planning, as well as feature analysis as input to automatic segmentation methods in a machine learning context.

Table 1. The response of the experts on a 5-point Liker scale. The values range from 1: Strongly disagree to 5: Strongly agree. Statements marked with a star were rephrased to present the positive form in this table, also the scores have been inverted. On the right end of the table the average value over all experts is presented and in the last row the result of the SUS questionnaire is presented.

Statement	N1	N2	N3	Gy1	Gy2	Gy3	Gy4	Gy5	M1	M2	M3	Avg.
G1	The linked interactions between the center view and the radar chart are well established and intuitive	3		4					3			4	4.45
G2	The linked interactions between the analyze view and the Stixel view are well established and intuitive		4	4	5	5		5	4	5	5		4.73
G3	I see myself using the MRI Explorer in the future*	3		3			3					4	4.27
G4	I would like to contribute in the future development of the application	5					4		3	3		4	4.45
G5	I can see the application as a part of my daily work routine*	3		2	4		3		4				3.09
G6	The application is more applicable for research than for daily clinical practice	3	4										3.99
G7	The application should be part of the software used in clinical practice*				3	4	3			4	4		3.64
P1	The navigation in 3D is easy to understand and I can place the sphere where I want*		4	2	2		5						4.27
P2	The resizing operation of the sphere is easy to understand and to carry out*	4	4	2		4					4		4.36
P3	I can place the sphere anywhere on the plane using the provided keyboard interactions	5		3	4		4						4.64
P4	Setting the probing sphere to a specific depth in the volume is intuitive	3		2	3		4	4			4		3.91
P5	Snapping the probing sphere to the current slice selection is useful		4	3				4	3		3		3.45
P6	The probing interaction is responsive*	3											4.73
P7	The automatic update of the Radar chart is beneficial*		5	4	5		5		5	5			4.82
P8	The radar chart helps me to interpret multimodal data										4		4.91
P9	I am confident in interpreting the values that the radar chart presents	3		4			3	4	3			3	3.91
P10	With the probing functionality, I am able to compare different regions within one subject*			3	4	5		5	4		4		4.55
P11	The probing function enables me to compare regions between different subjects	3					4			4			4.36
St1	I understand what the Stixels view shows me and can interpret the star glyphs used.		4	4		3		3		3			4.00
St2	The Stixels view helps me to gather insight of the inhomogeneity of the data*			3						3			4.55
St3	The cropping functionality helps me to focus the Stixel view on the most important region of the subjects data*		2									4	4.27
St4	The different grid sizes help me to first get an overview and add details on demand						4						4.64
St5	The tooltip helps me to see more details in the Stixels view when I need them		4			4				4	4		4.54
S1	I understand the color coding of the Stixels in terms of similarity*	3		4									4.73
S2	The similarity coloring of the Stixels helps me to adapt my probing selection			4		4	4						4.45
S3	The similarity volume visualization shows me interesting parts of the volumetric data	5	4								5	4	4.82
S4	The similarity view is useful to me and I would like to use it in my work routine/research*			5		5	5		5			4	4.55
Gys1	The application can improve the analysis of the inhomogeneity of gynecological cancer												5.00
Gys2	The application can support hypothesis generation for linking parameters with aggressiveness of gynecological cancer				5		5	5	5				5.00
Gys3	I would find this application useful when analyzing patients gynecological cancer MR data*												5.00
Gys4	I would like to use this application to explain pathology and treatment to patients				4		3	3					3.20
Gys5	I would like to use this application to plan a biopsy for analyzing biomarkers of the tumor				X			3					3.50
Gys6	The application is useful for finding metastases*					4	2						4.20
Gys7	The similarity view shows me the structure of the tumor												4.60
Gys8	The similarity view shows me the size and structure of possible metastases					3							4.60
Ns1	The application helps me to visualize lesions in the brain		4										3.33
Ns2	Comparing different regions within the brain using the comparison picker is particularly useful for me*												3.66
Ns3	The similarity view helps me to get a better volumetric view of the lesion*		4										4.67
Ns4	I would like to use this tool to further analyse multiparametric brain imaging data	3		4									4.00
Ns5	The interaction with the comparison tool is suitable for brain images			3									4.33
Ns6	The application helps me see the intensity relations of the different tissue types between modalities*												5.00
Ms1	The application helps me to carry out feature selection prior to applying my machine learning algorithms									4	4	3	3.67
Ms2	I find the similarity view useful to identify which modalities are important for me*									4	4	5	4.33
Ms3	I can imagine using this tool before applying machine learning algorithms*									5	4	4	4.33
Ms4	This application is particularly useful for segmentation based on machine learning									5	4	3	4.67
SUS	System usability scale result	67.5	40	75	85	80	87.5	80	95	92.5	85		81.75

7 Evaluation

We conducted a qualitative evaluation with eleven experts (6 male, 5 female) from the scientific fields of neurological imaging (N1-3), gynecological cancer imaging (Gy1-5) and machine learning research (M1-3). One expert is co-author and provided us with clinical data of gynecological cancer patients and one expert of each domain (N1, Gy2, M2) was included in the interviews during the development of our application. We were especially interested in validating the effectiveness of the various visualization components and identifying opportunities to make our application more suitable for daily research or even clinical practice. The individual evaluation started with a short demonstration of the tool, afterwards experts were encouraged to explore and analyze the multiparametric data themselves. They were invited to comment using a think-aloud protocol. The gynecological cancer and machine learning experts worked with endometrial cancer data and the neurological imaging experts with data provided by Schmainda and Prah [23] via the Cancer Imaging Archive (TCIA) [5]. After this phase, which lasted around 30 min, we conducted a semi-structured interview with the experts. Finally, a questionnaire consisting of 27 generally applicable statements and 4–8 targeted statements for the different expert groups was conducted. The experts were asked to indicate their level of agreement using a five-point Likert scale. In addition to our targeted evaluation form, we asked the experts to fill out the system usability scale (SUS) provided by Brook et al. [3]. The evaluation results of the eleven participants are shown in Table 1.

We conclude from the results presented in Table 1 that the application is overall valuable for the experts. The probing interaction was rated favorably, two participants would appreciate a guided 3D placement of the probe. All study participants think that the Stixels view helps them to see inhomogeneous regions within the Slice view. The similarity view received the most positive feedback and is potentially useful for all involved experts. The targeted statements demonstrate that the application is applicable different scenarios, albeit for different reasons. The gynecological experts envision that the application could improve the assessment of tumor heterogeneity both in primary tumors and metastases. The SUS scores range from 40 to 97,5, where the second lowest score is 75. On average, the SUS score is 81,75. According to Bangor et al. [1], the score can be interpreted to be between good and excellent.

8   Conclusion and Future Work

We present ParaGlyder, a multiparametric image visualization tool. The tool provides different views for tumor detection, inhomogeneity analysis, feature selection, and diagnosis in multiparametric medical images, by a tight coupling of spatial and non-spatial data visualization techniques. Our tool is based on a combination of star glyph maps and radar charts. A built-in similarity visualization of the volumetric data enables the visualization of, e.g., primary tumor and the corresponding metastases. The qualitative evaluation confirmed the utility of our application for diverse application areas. In the future, we plan to extend our approach to analysis of larger patient cohorts in order to assess whether this visualization tool could aid in the detection of metastases. Furthermore, the application has the potential to unravel patient-specific imaging features that may be linked to specific clinical phenotypes and outcomes, thus representing a promising tool to facilitate more personalized treatment strategies.

References

1. Bangor, A., Kortum, P., Miller, J.: Determining what individual SUS scores mean: adding an adjective rating scale. J. Usability Stud. **4**(3), 114–123 (2009)
2. Berg, A., et al.: Tissue and imaging biomarkers for hypoxia predict poor outcome in endometrial cancer. Oncotarget **7**(43), 69844–69856 (2016). https://doi.org/10. 18632/oncotarget.12004
3. Brooke, J.: SUS-a quick and dirty usability scale. In: Jordan, P., Thomas, B., McClelland, I., Weerdmeester, B. (eds.) Usability Evaluation In Industry, pp. 266–290. CRC Press, Boca Raton (2004)
4. Bruckner, S., et al.: BrainGazer - visual queries for neurobiology research. IEEE Trans. Visual. Comput. Graphics **15**, 1497–504 (2009). https://doi.org/10.1109/ TVCG.2009.121
5. Clark, K., et al.: The cancer imaging archive (TCIA): maintaining and operating a public information repository. J. Digit. Imaging **26**(6), 1045–1057 (2013). https:// doi.org/10.1007/s10278-013-9622-7
6. Fasmer, K.E., et al.: Preoperative quantitative dynamic contrast-enhanced MRI and diffusion-weighted imaging predict aggressive disease in endometrial cancer. Acta Radiol. **59**(8), 1010–1017 (2018). https://doi.org/10.1177/0284185117740932
7. Friendly, M.: A.-M. Guerry's Moral Statistics of France: challenges for multivariable spatial analysis. Stat. Sci. **22**(3), 368–399 (2007). https://doi.org/10.1214/07-STS241
8. Gleicher, M., Albers, D., Walker, R., Jusufi, I., Hansen, C.D., Roberts, J.C.: Visual comparison for information visualization. Inf. Vis. **10**(4), 289–309 (2011). https:// doi.org/10.1177/1473871611416549
9. Haldorsen, I.S., et al.: Increased microvascular proliferation is negatively correlated to tumour blood flow and is associated with unfavourable outcome in endometrial carcinomas. Br. J. Cancer **110**(1), 107–114 (2014). https://doi.org/10.1038/bjc. 2013.694
10. Haldorsen, I.S., et al.: Dynamic contrast-enhanced MRI in endometrial carcinoma identifies patients at increased risk of recurrence. Eur. Radiol. **23**(10), 2916–2925 (2013). https://doi.org/10.1007/s00330-013-2901-3
11. Haldorsen, I.S., Salvesen, H.B.: What is the best preoperative imaging for endometrial cancer? Curr. Oncol. Rep. **18**(4), 25 (2016). https://doi.org/10.1007/s11912-016-0506-0
12. Jäckle, D., Fuchs, J., Keim, D.A.: Star glyph insets for overview preservation of multivariate data. In: IS and T International Symposium on Electronic Imaging Science and Technology, pp. 1–9 (2016). https://doi.org/10.2352/issn.2470-1173. 2016.1.vda-506
13. Jönsson, D., et al.: A visual environment for hypothesis formation and reasoning in studies with fMRI and multivariate clinical data. In: Kozlíková, B., Linsen, L., Vázquez, P.P., Lawonn, K., Raidou, R.G. (eds.) Eurographics Workshop on Visual Computing for Biology and Medicine. The Eurographics Association (2019). https://doi.org/10.2312/vcbm.20191232
14. Klein, S., Staring, M., Murphy, K., Viergever, M.A., Pluim, J.P.W.: Elastix: a toolbox for intensity-based medical image registration. IEEE Trans. Med. Imaging **29**(1), 196–205 (2010). https://doi.org/10.1109/TMI.2009.2035616
15. Klippel, A., Hardisty, F., Weaver, C.: Star plots: how shape characteristics influence classification tasks. Cartogr. Geogr. Inf. Sci. **36**(2), 149–163 (2009). https://doi. org/10.1559/152304009788188808

16. Lawonn, K., Smit, N., Bühler, K., Preim, B.: A survey on multimodal medical data visualization. Comput. Graph. Forum **37**(1), 413–438 (2017). https://doi.org/10.1111/cgf.13306
17. Malik, M.M., Heinzl, C., Gröller, M.E.: Comparative visualization for parameter studies of dataset series. IEEE Trans. Visual. Comput. Graphics **16**(5), 829–840 (2010). https://doi.org/10.1109/TVCG.2010.20
18. Mlejnek, M., et al.: Profile flags: a novel metaphor for probing of t2 maps. In: Silva, C.T., Gröller, E., Rushmeier, H. (eds.) Proceedings of IEEE Visualization 2005, pp. 599–606. IEEE CS, October 2005
19. Munzner, T.: A nested model for visualization design and validation. IEEE Trans. Visual Comput. Graphics **15**(6), 921–928 (2009)
20. Opach, T., Popelka, S., Dolezalova, J., Rød, J.K.: Star and polyline glyphs in a grid plot and on a map display: which perform better? Cartogr. Geogr. Inf. Sci. **45**(5), 400–419 (2018). https://doi.org/10.1080/15230406.2017.1364169
21. Peng, W., Ward, M.O., Rundensteiner, E.A.: Clutter reduction in multidimensional data visualization using dimension reordering. In: Proceedings - IEEE Symposium on Information Visualization, INFO VIS, pp. 89–96 (2004). https://doi.org/10.1109/INFVIS.2004.15
22. Ropinski, T., Oeltze, S., Preim, B.: Visual computing in biology and medicine: survey of glyph-based visualization techniques for spatial multivariate medical data. Comput. Graph. **35**(2), 392–401 (2011). https://doi.org/10.1016/j.cag.2011.01.011
23. Schmainda, K., Prah, M.: Data from brain-tumor-progression (2018). https://doi.org/10.7937/K9/TCIA.2018.15quzvnb
24. Smit, N.N., Kraima, A.C., Jansma, D., Ruiter, M.C.d., Botha, C.P.: A unified representation for the model-based visualization of heterogeneous anatomy data. In: Meyer, M., Weinkaufs, T. (eds.) EuroVis - Short Papers. The Eurographics Association (2012). https://doi.org/10.2312/PE/EuroVisShort/EuroVisShort2012/085-089
25. Smit, N.N., Haneveld, B.K., Staring, M., Eisemann, E., Botha, C.P., Vilanova, A.: RegistrationShop: an interactive 3D medical volume registration system. In: Viola, I., Buehler, K., Ropinski, T. (eds.) Eurographics Workshop on Visual Computing for Biology and Medicine. The Eurographics Association (2014). https://doi.org/10.2312/vcbm.20141193
26. Stoppel, S., Hodneland, E., Hauser, H., Bruckner, S.: Graxels: information rich primitives for the visualization of time-dependent spatial data. In: Eurographics Workshop on Visual Computing for Biology and Medicine, pp. 183–192, September 2016. https://doi.org/10.2312/vcbm.20161286
27. Wickham, H., Hofmann, H., Wickham, C., Cook, D.: Glyph-maps for visually exploring temporal patterns in climate data and models. Environmetrics **23**(5), 382–393 (2012). https://doi.org/10.1002/env.2152

3D Geology Scene Exploring Base on Hand-Track Somatic Interaction

Wei Zhang[1], Fang Zhu[2], Ping Lu[2], Pin Li[3], Bin Sheng[1(✉)], and Lijuan Mao[4(✉)]

[1] Shanghai Jiao Tong University, Shanghai, People's Republic of China
shengbin@sjtu.edu.cn
[2] ZTE Corporarion, Nanjing, People's Republic of China
[3] The Hong Kong Polytechnic University, Hong Kong, People's Republic of China
[4] Shanghai University of Sport, Shanghai, People's Republic of China
maolijuan@sus.edu.cn

Abstract. Terrain analysis is the basis of geological research. However, due to factors such as distance and range, it is often difficult to study the terrain environment in the field. Therefore, researchers can observe and study the terrain by making a three-dimensional terrain model. The 3D terrain model can reduce the terrain range, eliminate the limitation on distance, and control the scene through program interface, to achieve human-computer interaction to meet different research needs. The usual human-computer interaction methods are implemented through traditional peripherals such as the mouse and keyboard. With the rapid development of computer network technology and the continuous improvement of intelligent software and hardware, people have greater requirements for interactive manipulation and immersion. This article proposes a method for displaying terrain models based on real-sensing technology by using Intel's RealSense camera to control the scene of the desert model through gestures. The user can observe the model from two different perspectives, and use different gestures to zoom in, zoom out, move, and rotate the scene, as well as choose some options. The traditional method of controlling by mouse is also applicable. The entire project is designed as a game, with a realistic and complete model, an exquisite interface, and strong interactivity.

Keywords: Somatosensory · 3D Scene · Gesture sensing · Unity · Hand track · Depth camera · RealSense

1 Introduction

Motion-sensing technology has become one of the most popular methods for human-computer interaction. Besides mouse and multi-touch, somatosensory interaction may lead to the third revolution of human-computer interaction. With the passage of time, many famous hardware corporations have released their own commercial visually somatic peripheral equipment, including Microsoft's Kinect, Intel's depth camera and so on. Even though there have been

© Springer Nature Switzerland AG 2020
N. Magnenat-Thalmann et al. (Eds.): CGI 2020, LNCS 12221, pp. 364–373, 2020.
https://doi.org/10.1007/978-3-030-61864-3_30

numerous advancements in the field of AR and VR, it is still an emerging field. With all these factors, the loss of suitable interaction method is quite a problem.

In somatic interaction field, we can track eyes, body movements, facial expressions, gestures etc. Eyes tracking is a new technology and so far under experimentation. Body movement based on gyroscope is the first generation of somatic method, which has later been applied in many game industries, for example, Nintendo's somatic game console Wii. However, a gyroscope is not suitable to generate reliable digital data which can be used to model accurate body skeleton information, and then simulate available input data. Visual body movements capture technique based on depth camera is now another method to detect body language. Microsoft's Kinect has been in production with their game console XBOX for years. But the high price keeps it away from mainstream markets. In comparison to this, for movements capture, Kinect's error rate and reaction time has quite a distance from traditional input method like mouse or keyboard. In this paper we applied Intel's new sensor device, the RealSense SR300 depth camera, in our 3D scene exploring platform. Compared with Kinect, SR300's price level is much more reasonable, and makes it more expansible and more developable.

To fulfill gesture interaction, Kinect released a set of official units. For our project, we need to analyze the original image data generated by depth camera, then design recognition algorithms to sort and process them and finally transmit the signal to game controlling input APIs. In addition to this, we also built a 3D game platform to test our techniques using the Unity engine.

Compared with other popular commercial depth cameras such as Kinect, the SR300 is a much cheaper choice, which means that depth camera can be applied in much more fields. And due to Intel's SDKs and development support, SR300 is more open to other developers, and is more friendly to embedded hardware platforms such as Raspberry Pi, etc.

2   Related Work

2.1   Image-Forming Principles of Depth Camera

Depth camera is a kind of camera which applies reflection-based methods to acquire not only color and position of objects in the camera view, but also their distance to the camera. There are three kinds of image-forming principles in the market at present, namely structured-light, stereo vision and time of flight. The RealSense applies the structured-light principle, which casts an encoded line light source to the objects and demodulates their distance from the structural light pattern. Leap Motion applied stereo vision principle, which captures two images of the same scene with two cameras in different relative positions just like what the human eyes do. Then the system will use parallax to calculate the distance of the objects. The RealSense SR300 used in our project applied time of flight principle, which will be discussed in detail in Sect. 3.1.

2.2   Gesture Recognition

The most commonly used human gesture recognition methods are depth-based and skeleton-based [15]. Depth-based methods recognize gestures by filtering out the noise of input and obtaining global features. Existing work mainly differs in how to generate representative global features. For example, HON4D [9] uses a 4D surface normal orientation histogram to describe the depth sequence. The improved HON4D [17] forms a poly-normal, used to characterize local motion and shape information by clustering hyper surface normal vectors in the depth sequence. Skeleton-based methods can be divided into joint-based and body part based. Joint-based methods use a coordinate system to relatively model the position and motion of a couple of joints. One way is to relatively combine the position of different joints to form a coordinate system, like in [6,13]. On the other hand, the human gesture can be recognized by calculating joint orientations against a fixed coordinate system, like in [16]. While in body part based methods, human body parts are represented by some rigid cylinders connected by joints to form an articulated system. Gestures can be distinguished through the 3D geometric relationships between joint cylinders [4,14,18]. After this, the data will go through either handcrafted feature extraction and feature representation or deep learning methods to extract human gesture descriptors. As for Kinect V2 sensor, it evaluates each pixel of the depth image and distinguishes human body parts from the environment background. This process combines a few computer graphics and vision techniques such as edge detection, noise threshold processing and categorization of human body features. Kinect V2 sensor can actively track two players' skeletons and create segmentation masks for each tracked player to reduce calculation. Then the new depth image which has culled background objects is transmitted to Exemplar, a machine learning system that can recognize specific body parts. The last step is to generate a skeleton system according to 25 tracked joints, so that game developers can select and combine preferred components to create unique game experience.

2.3   Natural Interaction Interface

Natural human-computer interaction (HCI) system is an interactive framework that integrates human behavior into technological applications [12]. DesertBox is supposed to be designed as one of such interfaces. Natural interaction systems consist of several modules, such as sensing subsystem and presentation module. The sensing subsystem gathers data from different dimensions in the surroundings with specific sensors, including visual sense, auditory sense, tactile sense, etc. The presentation module is responsible for integrating the signals from sensors and generating output results. There are some rules that should be kept in mind when designing an HCI system. First of all, digital elements in the interface should behave like their counterparts in the real world to give users an intuitive experience. Secondly, the design of the interface should be lightweight and minimalist to help users pay attention to the rich content of the application instead of distracting them with additional operating instructions.

HCI systems have various application scenarios, such interaction with realtime virtual actions [7,8], as multimedia browsing which allows the user to explore multimedia objects intuitively, knowledge building which allows multiple users to accomplish tasks collaboratively [2], interactive exhibition where visitors can enjoy multi-sensory experimental experience [1] and interactive system which stimulates for learning [5,11].

3 Gesture Recognition

3.1 Hardware System

We used Intel's RealSense SR300 to get the original gesture depth image. The RealSense SR300 is a real time sensor camera produced by Intel. Supported by Intel's Realsense SDKs, it can realize gesture sensing with convenient APIs. Combining depth measuring and a 1080p RGB color camera, the application will detect the shape of a moving hand and then model the hand skeleton, realizing Skeleton Tracing.

3.2 Recognition Algorithm

Fig. 1 shows the core algorithm structure of action recognition. We divided the gestures into 2 types of gestures: static and dynamic. The dynamic gestures can also be constituted with several static ones [10].

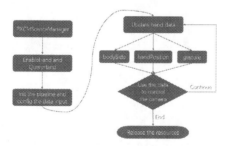

Fig. 1. Core algorithm structure of action recognition

Traditional gesture recognition [19] compares the density of depth data and body movement model to analyze the components of the human body. It then, uses inverse dynamics to reflect this data back to body movement model to realize gesture recognition.

Jamie Shotton [20] proposed a method to measure hand joints through single depth graph without time data. For the pixel x in depth graph I, its eigenvalue is:

$$f_\theta(I, x) = d_I(x + \frac{u}{d_I(x)}) - d_I(x + \frac{v}{d_I(x)}) \qquad (1)$$

In the expression: $d_I(x)$ is the depth of pixel x. When a user enters the recognition area, no matter how far they are from the camera, a coordinate system can always be set on their body. $\theta(u, v)$ is used to confirm the pixel's offset in this system with u and v. Multiply the normalized $d_I(x)$ with these two offsets, then we can get two depth values. Their difference is the eigenvalue f_θ. As for background pixels, their $d_I(x)$ values will be a vastly positive constant. Reaching body structure tags, we can use decision-making tree to sort the pixels in a graph and tag them. Suppose a decision-making forest with size T has a tree t. Every leaf node in this tree contains an eigenvalue f_θ and a threshold τ. In the tree t, there is a known distribution function $P_\tau(C|I, x)$ with the body structure tag C. This function is used to describe the distribution of pixels as:

$$\omega_{ic} = P(C|I, x) \cdot d_I^2(x) \tag{2}$$

In the expression: ω_{ic} is the weight of the pixel, which is used to describe the probability of the tag that fits this pixel. There are several embedded gestures in Intel's RealSense SDK (Fig. 2). Using these embedded gestures, we constructed new gestures to realize game function.

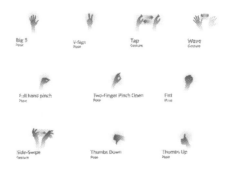

Fig. 2. Samples of intel RealSense SDK embedded gestures

3.3   Shaking Optimization Algorithm

During our recognition progress, due to slight shaking of hands, some operations, especially rotation, will cause an obvious unsteady viewpoint. To solve this, we designed an optimization algorithm 1. This procedure will construct a queue with a size of five, to contain hand skeleton position data. When the depth camera loses the position of hands, it clears the original queue, and fills it with new information, to avoid data from the shaking position, after it re-captures the hands. Every time the position data is requested, the algorithm returns the arithmetic mean value of queue.

Algorithm 1. Shaking Optimization

1: **input**(original single hand position data)
2: **output**(optimized single hand position data)
3: **if** re-capture the hand **then**
4:     clear the queue;
5:     fill the queue with new position untill full;
6: **else**
7:     get position;
8:     new position enqueue;
9:     dequeue;
10: **end if**
11: **if** hand position requested **then**
12:     return average;
13: **end if**

4   Game Platform

4.1   UI Config

Fig. 3 shows us that, from the start panel, we can enter two different scenes. In both situations we can control the character, or exit to the start.

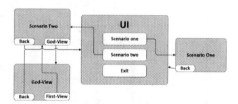

Fig. 3. Game platform structure

4.2   Scene Construction

The .max files created by software 3Dmax are compatible with Unity. So, first, we constructed the scene assets in 3DMax, and then imported them into Unity. To get an acceptable viewing experience, we set up new parameters for main camera, directional lights, shadow, material shaders.

4.3   Hardware Config

Using RealSense SR300 and SDK 2016, we can get depth image schematic information and build a data controlling component.

4.4   Keyboard Event Mapping Design

The controlling system is based on Unity's embedded keyboard input events. To fulfill basic operations in the game scene, we mapped the gesture signal with keyboard events. See Fig. 4.

Function	Keyboard	Gesture	Gesture Sketch	Sense Sketch
Move View Point	ZXCVBN↵	move single hand with v-sign		
Adjust Pitch Angle	UJ↵	two hands up or down		
Scaling	QE	two hands open or close		
Switch View Point	T↵	two hands thumb-up		
Character Movement	WASD or direction keys	move single hand with v-sign		

Fig. 4. Controlling test example

5   Result Analysis

5.1   Effects of Shaking Optimization Algorithm

After applying the shaking optimization algorithm for gesture recognition, an overall smoother experience is obtained during interaction. Moving on to data visualization, as explained by Fig. 5, the red dots mean the original object position, and the blue dots mean optimized position. To obtain these results, we used left hand and kept still during the analysis.

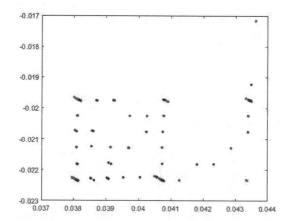

Fig. 5. Hand position differences between frames (Color figure online)

The conclusion that can be drawn from Fig. 6, is that original data had a clear regularity. This is due to maximum resolution of the depth camera. The optimized algorithm reduces the differences in hand positions between each frame, thus making the operation smoother. After designing the algorithm, we set several values for the size of position queue, including 2, 3, 4, and more than 5.

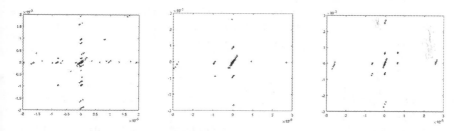

Fig. 6. Relative differences of original and optimized position data with queues sized 2 (left), 3 (mid), 4 (right)

The algorithm was also tested with the size bigger than 5, however, the optimizing effect was no longer discernible. Considering longer queue will cause more computing cost and larger delay, it was decided to finally set the size of queue as 5.

We used the same algorithm to dispose these data points, the result is proved to be good.

The tracking of the hand is much smoother. So, we can get better interaction experience under these conditions.

5.2   Limits of SR300 the Depth Camera

As the SR300 uses active near-infrared light as its structured light source, it runs quite well in dark environments.

However, when faced with bright environments such as outdoor scenes, the light will disturb the camera heavily. It can barely recognize the whole palm at a distance of 20 to 30 cm.

6   Conclusion

During this project, we experimented and analyzed the feasibility of building a gesture-based 3D scene exploring platform with existing camera hardware and game engine. With conclusive evidence we proved that this is a reasonable direction of man-machine interaction. As Internet of things and smart homes become more widespread, gesture controlling will have more numerous applications.

Acknowledgement. This work was supported in part by the National Key Research and Development Program of China under Grant 2018YFF0300903, in part by the National Natural Science Foundation of China under Grant 61872241 and Grant 61572316, and in part by the Science and Technology Commission of Shanghai Municipality under Grant 15490503200, Grant 18410750700, Grant 17411952600, and Grant 16DZ0501100.

References

1. Alisi, T., Bimbo, A.D., Valli, A.: Natural interfaces to enhance visitors' experiences. IEEE Multimed. **12**(3), 80–85 (2005)
2. Baraldi, S., Bimbo, A.D., Landucci, L., Valli, A.: wikiTable: finger driven interaction for collaborative knowledge-building workspaces. In: Proceedings of 2006 IEEE International Conference on Computer Vision and Pattern Recognition Workshop, p. 144 (2006)
3. Kaltenbrunner, M., Jordà, S., Geiger, G., Alonso, M.: The reactable: a collaborative musical instrument. In: Workshop on Tangible Interaction in Collaborative Environments (2006)
4. Kamel, A., Sheng, B., Yang, P., Li, P., Shen, R., Feng, D.D.: Deep convolutional neural networks for human action recognition using depth maps and postures. IEEE Trans. Syst. Man Cybern. Syst. **49**(9), 1806–1819 (2019)
5. Karambakhsh, A., Kamel, A., Sheng, B., Li, P., Yang, P., Feng, D.D.: Deep gesture interaction for augmented anatomy learning. Int. J. Inf. Manage. **45**, 328–336 (2019)
6. Ke, Q., Bennamoun, M., An, S., Sohel, F., Boussaid, F.: A new representation of skeleton sequences for 3D action recognition. In: CVPR, pp. 4570–4579 (2017)
7. Lu, P., Sheng, B., Luo, S., Jia, X., Wu, W.: Image-based non-photorealistic rendering for realtime virtual sculpting. Multim. Tools Appl. **74**(21), 9697–9714 (2015)
8. Meng, X., et al.: A video information driven football recommendation system. Comput. Electr. Eng. **85**, 106699 (2020)
9. Oreifej, O., Liu, Z.: HON4D: Histogram of oriented 4D normals for activity recognition from depth sequences. In: CVPR, pp. 716–723 (2013)

10. Siena, F.L., Byrom, B., Watts, P., Breedon, P.: Utilising the intel RealSense camera for measuring health outcomes in clinical research. J. Med. Syst. **42**(3), 1–10 (2018). https://doi.org/10.1007/s10916-018-0905-x
11. Sheng, B., Li, P., Zhang, Y., Mao, L., Chen, C.L.P.: GreenSea: visual soccer analysis using broad learning system. IEEE Trans. Cybern. 1–15 (2020). https://doi.org/10.1109/TCYB.2020.2988792. https://ieeexplore.ieee.org/document/9098099
12. Stefano, B., Alberto, D., Lea, L., Nicola, T.: Natural interaction. In: Encyclopedia of Database Systems. https://link.springer.com/referenceworkentry/10.1007
13. Vemulapalli, R., Arrate, F., Chellappa, R.: Human action recognition by representing 3D skeletons as points in a lie group. In: CVPR, pp. 588–595 (2014)
14. Vemulapalli, R., Chellappa, R.: Rolling rotations for recognizing human actions from 3D skeletal data. In: CVPR, pp. 4471–4479 (2016)
15. Wang, L., Huynh, D.Q.: Koniusz: a comparative review of recent Kinect-based action recognition algorithms. IEEE Trans. Image Process. **29**, 15–28 (2020)
16. Xia, L., Chen, C., Aggarwal, J. K.: View invariant human action recognition using histograms of 3D joints. In: CVPR, pp. 20–27 (2012)
17. Yang, X., Tian, Y.: Super normal vector for activity recognition using depth sequences. In: CVPR, pp. 804–811 (2014)
18. Zhang, P., et al.: Tracking soccer players using spatio-temporal context learning under multiple views. Multimedia Tools Appl. **77**(15), 18935–18955 (2018)
19. Zhu, Y., Fujimura, K.: Constrained optimization for human pose estimation from depth sequences. In: Asian Conference on Computer Vision [S.l.], pp. 408–418. IEEE Press (2007)
20. Shotton, J., et al.: Real-time human pose recognition in parts from single depth images. In: Computer Vision and Pattern Recognition. [S.l.], pp. 1297–1304. IEEE Press (2011)

GHand: A Graph Convolution Network for 3D Hand Pose Estimation

Pengsheng Wang[1], Guangtao Xue[1], Pin Li[2], Jinman Kim[3], Bin Sheng[1(✉)], and Lijuan Mao[4(✉)]

[1] Shanghai Jiao Tong University, Shanghai, People's Republic of China
shengbin@sjtu.edu.cn
[2] The Hong Kong Polytechnic University, Hong Kong, People's Republic of China
[3] The University of Sydney, Sydney, Australia
[4] Shanghai University of Sport, Shanghai, People's Republic of China
maolijuan@sus.edu.cn

Abstract. Vision-based 3D hand pose estimation plays an important role in the field of human-computer interaction. In recent years, with the development of convolutional neural networks (CNN), the field of 3D hand pose estimation has made a great progress, but there is still a long way to go before the problem is solved. Although recent studies based on CNN networks have greatly improved the recognition accuracy, they usually only pay attention on the regression ability of the network itself, and ignore the structural information of the hands, thus leads to a low accuracy in contrast. In this paper we proposed a new hand pose estimation network, which can fully learn the structural information of hands through an adaptive graph convolutional neural network. The experiment on the public dataset shows the accuracy of our graph convolution network exceeds the SOTA methods in 3D hand pose estimation.

Keywords: 3D hand pose estimation · Adaptive graph convolution · Depth image

1 Introduction

In natural society, hand pose plays an important role when we communicate with each other. It is widely used in the field of AR/VR and human-computer interaction due to its rich expressive ability and comfortable and convenient expression [5,18,25]. With the popularity of depth cameras, depth-image-based hand pose estimation gains more attention and is one of the hottest topic in hand pose estimation [9,22]. Recently, with the development of convolutional neural networks, great progress has been made in this field, but it is still a changeling problem because of the large variations in hand orientations, high flexibility, and severe self-occlusion.

In previous researches, convolution neural network is usually used to regress the 3D coordinates of hand pose joints directly, thus the dependencies between the joints was ignored, which will result in low accuracy and deformed gestures.

© Springer Nature Switzerland AG 2020
N. Magnenat-Thalmann et al. (Eds.): CGI 2020, LNCS 12221, pp. 374–381, 2020.
https://doi.org/10.1007/978-3-030-61864-3_31

CNN has been proved successful in tackling grid-like structure data and RNN in sequence data, but many tasks, e.g. social networks, molecular structures, can only be represented in a form of graph-structure data. To overcome their limitations, recently graph convolution neural networks were introduced to process the graph-structure data due to its effective representations. In this paper we proposed a GCN to regress the 3D co-ordinates of hand joints from a depth image in an end-to-end way. Our main contributions can be summarized as follow:

– We proposed a Graph Convolution Network (GCN) for 3D hand pose estimation, GHand, which can regress the 3D coordinates from a depth image in an end-to-end way.
– For the first time we recommend an adaptive adjacent matrix to learn the structural information of the hands, thus the dependencies between the different joints can be fully exploited.
– Through self-comparison experiment in public dataset, we show that the GCN can significantly improve the accuracy of the network. We also compared our approach with other state-of-the-art models and our approach has a better performance.

2 Related Work

3D hand pose estimation is a hot topic in computer vision, because of its wide use in many scenes. We refer to [3] for an overview of the previous works, and they can be divided into two types of approach. One is based on RGB images and another is based on depth image. With the popularity of depth cameras, depth-image based methods gain more attention. In this paper, we focus on the 3D coordinates regression from a single depth image.

2.1 3D Hand Pose Estimation

Structure information of the hand has proven helpful when predicting the 3D position of the hand joints [22]. In order to utilize the structural properties of hands, many methods have been proposed [10,11]. The main ideas of them can be divided into two types. One way is to treat the structure information as a prior [14,16]. Calculate a prior through the PCA method and directly add it to the convolutional neural network model. [23] designed some handcraft constraints and put them into the loss function. Although these methods can improve the recognition accuracy to a certain extent, handcraft prior of the structure information will also damage the learning ability of the model and thus will reduce the representation ability of the model. Another way is to design a branch network which is similar with the hand structure. [24] designed a three-branch network, where the three branches correspond to the thumb, index finger, and the three other fingers, according to the differences in the functional importance of different fingers. These studies have demonstrated that handling different parts of the hand via a multi-branch CNN can improve the accuracy of 3D hand pose estimation. However, not all dependencies between joints are taken into account. To capture the better structure information of hands, we adopt a GCN to model the hand structure in a learnable way.

2.2   Graph Convolution Method

Graph convolution networks allow learning high-level representations of the relationships between the nodes of graph-based data. [8] used graph convolutional networks for skeleton-based action recognition. [4] designed an adaptive graph convolution network to regress the 3D position of the gesture-object key-points from an RGB image. In this paper we adopt an adaptive convolutional network to model the structural information of hands, and regress the 3D coordinates of the hand joints in an end-to-end way.

The model starts with 4 Residual Blocks as the backbone network to extract the image feature vector and predict the initial 3D coordinates. The coordinates concatenated with the image features vector used as the features of the input graph of a 2-layered graph convolution to exploit the structure information of hands to estimate the better 3D pose.

3   Methodology

3.1   Overall Network Architecture

Figure 1 illustrates the overall architecture of the proposed GCN-based 3D hand pose estimation methods. The proposed network mainly consists of two parts: a backbone convolution neural network to extract the features from an input depth image; a joint regression Graph Convolution Network, which consists two graph convolution layers, to regress the 3D coordinates of the hand pose joints. The input depth image is firstly fed into backbone network for features extraction and initial 3D coordinates regression of the hand pose joints. Then, the GCN take the obtained features and the initial 3D coordinates from the backbone network as an input graph and predict the final 3D coordinates of the hand pose joints.

3.2   Backbone Network

The backbone network of the proposed 3D hand pose estimation method refers to [21], as described in Table 1. Different with [21], our backbone network has only four residual blocks to extract the feature maps from the input depth image. Each of the residual blocks consists of two 3×3 convolutional layer and a 1×1 convolutional layer instead of the identity skip connection when the output dimension of the residual block is increased. Max-pooling layers for down-sampling are appended after each residual block except for the last one block. Following the last block, a global max pooling layer is used to convert the feature maps to a 256D feature vector. Then a fully connection layer regresses the initial 3D coordinates of the hand pose joints. Inspired by the architecture of [12], we concatenate these features with the initial 3D predictions of each joint, yielding a graph with 259 features (256 image features plus initial estimates of x, y and z) for each node in sub-net GCN.

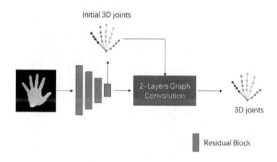

Fig. 1. The overall architecture of the proposed method for 3D hand pose estimation.

Table 1. Detailed architecture of the backbone network for feature vector extraction.

Layers	Kernel size	Channels	Output size
Residual block	3×3	64	96×96
Max pooling	2×2	64	48×48
Residual block	3×3	64	48×48
Max pooling	2×2	64	24×24
Residual block	3×3	128	24×24
Max pooling	2×2	128	12×12
Residual block	3×3	256	12×12
Global average pooling	–	–	256
Fully connection	–	–	42

3.3 GCN Network

Our GCN network consist of two layers graph convolution, which is inspired by [4]: the output features of a graph convolution layer for an input graph with N nodes, k input features, and l output features for each node is computed as,

$$Y = \sigma(\widetilde{A}XW) \qquad (1)$$

where σ is the activation function, $W \in R^{k \times l}$ is the trainable weights matrix, $X \in R^{N \times k}$ is the matrix of input features, and $A \in R^{N \times N}$ is the row-normalized adjacency matrix of the graph,

$$\widetilde{A} = \hat{D}^{-\frac{1}{2}} \hat{A} \hat{D}^{-\frac{1}{2}} \tag{2}$$

where $\hat{A} = A + I$ and $\hat{D}$ is the diagonal node degree matrix. $\hat{A}$ simply defines the extent to which each node uses other nodes' features. So $\hat{A}X$ is the new feature matrix in which each node's features are the averaged features of the node itself and its adjacent nodes.

In order to learn the structure info between each joint, inspired by [4], we also use a learnable adjacency matrix (A) in our graph convolution layer. This approach allows us to fully exploit the dependencies between different joints on different fingers or on same finger.

3.4   Loss Function

Our loss function for training the model has two parts. The first part is the loss for the initial 3D coordinates predicted by Backbone network (L_{init3D}). The other is the loss that calculated from the final 3D coordinates (L_{3D}),

$$L = \alpha L_{init3D} + L_{3D} \tag{3}$$

4   Experiment Results

4.1   Dataset and Evaluate Metrics

We implemented our experiment on the popular public dataset: NYU dataset [20], which was captured with three Microsoft Kinects and contains 72k training and 8k testing images from three different views. The training set was collected from one subject, while the testing set was collected from two subjects. To evaluate the performance of the different 3D hand pose estimation methods, we used two metrics. The first metric is the average 3D distance error between the ground truth and predicted 3D position for each joint. The second one is the percent-age of succeeded frames whose errors for all joints are within a threshold which is the same as [19].

4.2   Self-comparisons

To analyze the function of the GCN, we trained a network without the GCN. The 3D coordinates are directly regressed from the feature vector which extracted by the backbone network from the input of a single depth image. As shown in Fig. 2, the proposal GCN can significantly improve the performance of the network.

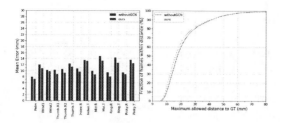

Fig. 2. Self-comparison results. Left: 3D distance errors (mm) per hand joint. Right: percentage of success frames over different error thresholds.

4.3   Comparison with State-of-the-Art Methods

We compared our proposed network on NYU datasets with the most recently proposed methods, including DeepPrior [14], its improved version Deep Prior++ [16], Feed-back [15], REN-9 × 6 × 6 [7], Pose-REN [2], Generalized [17] and DeepModel [23], as well as methods using 3D inputs, includes 3D CNN [6], SHPR-Net [1]. As show in Table 2 and Fig. 3, our results outperform the results of all the state-of-the-art methods no matter whose input is 2D depth map or 3D points cloud.

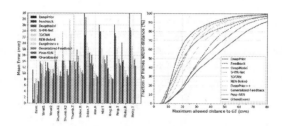

Fig. 3. Compare with other state-of-the-art methods.

Table 2. Comparison with state-of-the-art methods on NYU dataset.

Method	Mean error(mm)	Inputs
DeepPrior [14]	20.75	2D
Deep Prior++ [16]	12.23	2D
Feedback [15]	15.97	2D
REN − 9 × 6 × 6 [7]	12.69	2D
Pose-REN [2]	11.81	2D
Generalized [17]	10.89	2D
DeepModel [16]	17.03	2D
GHand (ours)	**10.33**	**2D**
3D CNN [6]	14.11	3D
SHPR-Net [1]	10.77	3D

5   Conclusion

In this paper, we introduced a Graph Convolution Network for the 3D hand pose estimation from a single depth image. We have experimentally shown that the pro-posed approach outperforms the state-of-the art on the publicly available dataset: NYU hand dataset.

Through experiments on the public dataset, it is shown that Graph Convolution Network works effectively to exploit the structure information of hands and can improve the accuracy of the prediction. For the future work, GCN based classification can be integrated into this network for the classification of the gestures, thus the whole framework can be used for the applications, such as driving control, UAV control.

Acknowledgments. This work was supported in part by the National Key Research and Development Program of China under Grant 2018YFF0300903, in part by the National Natural Science Foundation of China under Grant 61872241 and Grant 61572316, and in part by the Science and Technology Commission of Shanghai Municipality under Grant 15490503200, Grant 18410750700, Grant 17411952600, and Grant 16DZ0501100.

References

1. Chen, X., Wang, G., Zhang, C., Kim, T., Ji, X.: SHPR-Net: deep semantic hand pose regression from point clouds. IEEE Access **6**, 43425–43439 (2018)
2. Chen, X., Wang, G., Guo, H., Zhang, C.: Pose guided structured region ensemble network for cascaded hand pose estimation. Neurocomputing **395**, 138–149 (2020)
3. Doosti, B.: Hand pose estimation: a survey. Computer Vision and Pattern Recognition (2019)
4. Doosti, B., Naha, S., Mirbagheri, M., Crandall, D.: HOPE-Net: a graph-based model for hand-object pose estimation. arxiv.org/abs/2004.00060 (2020)
5. Erol, A., Bebis, G., Nicolescu, M., Boyle, R.D., Twombly, X.: Vision-based hand pose estimation: a review. Comput. Vis. Image Underst. **108**(1), 52–73 (2007)
6. Ge, L., Liang, H., Yuan, J.: 3D Convolutional Neural Networks for Efficient and Robust Hand Pose Estimation from Single Depth Images. Supplementary Material. 1–5 (n.d.)
7. Guo, H., Wang, G., Chen, X., Zhang, C., Qiao, F., Yang, H.: Region ensemble network: improving convolutional network for hand pose estimation. arxiv.org/abs/1702.02447 (2017)
8. Li, M., Chen, S., Chen, X., Zhang, Y., Wang, Y., Tian, Q.: Actional-structural graph convolutional networks for skeleton-based action recognition. In: Computer Vision and Pattern Recognition, pp. 3595–3603 (2019)
9. Lu, P., Sheng, B., Luo, S., Jia, X., Wu, W.: Image-based non-photorealistic rendering for realtime virtual sculpting. Multimedia Tools Appl. **74**(21), 9697–9714 (2014). https://doi.org/10.1007/s11042-014-2146-4
10. Kamel, A., Sheng, B., Yang, P., Li, P., Shen, R., Feng, D.D.: Deep convolutional neural networks for human action recognition using depth maps and postures. IEEE Trans. Syst. Man Cybern. Syst. **49**(9), 1806–1819 (2019)

11. Karambakhsh, A., Kamel, A., Sheng, B., Li, P., Yang, P., Feng, D.D.: Deep gesture interaction for augmented anatomy learning. Int. J. Inf. Manage. **45**, 328–336 (2019)
12. Kolotouros, N., Pavlakos, G., Daniilidis, K.: Convolutional mesh regression for single-image human shape reconstruction. In: Computer Vision and Pattern Recognition, pp. 4496–4505 (2019)
13. Meng, X., et al.: A video information driven football recommendation system. Comput. Electr. Eng. **85**, 106699 (2020)
14. Oberweger, M., Wohlhart, P., Lepetit, V.: Hands deep in deep learning for hand pose estimation. arxiv.org/abs/1502.06807 (2015)
15. Oberweger, M., Wohlhart, P., Lepetit, V.: Training a feedback loop for hand pose estimation. In: International Conference on Computer Vision, pp. 3316–3324 (2015)
16. Oberweger, M., Lepetit, V.: DeepPrior++: improving fast and accurate 3D hand pose estimation. In: International Conference on Computer Vision Workshops (ICCVW), pp. 585–594 (2017)
17. Oberweger, M., Wohlhart, P., Lepetit, V.: Generalized feedback loop for joint hand-object pose estimation. Pattern Anal. Mach. Intell. **45**, 1898–1912 (2020)
18. Sheng, B., Li, P., Zhang, Y., Mao, L.: GreenSea: visual soccer analysis using broad learning system. IEEE Trans. Cybern. 1–15 (2020)
19. Taylor, J., Shotton, J., Sharp, T., Fitzgibbon, A.: The Vitruvian manifold: inferring dense correspondences for one-shot human pose estimation. In: Computer Vision and Pattern Recognition, pp. 103–110 (2012)
20. Tompson, J., Stein, M., Lecun, Y., Perlin, K.: Real-time continuous pose recovery of human hands using convolutional networks. ACM Trans. Graph. (ToG) **33**(5), 169 (2014)
21. Yoo, C., Kim, S., Ji, S., Shin, Y., Ko, S.: Capturing hand articulations using recurrent neural network for 3D hand pose estimation. arxiv.org/abs/1911.07424 (2019)
22. Yuan, S., et al.: Depth-based 3D hand pose estimation: from current achievements to future goals. In: Computer Vision and Pattern Recognition, pp. 2636–2645 (2018)
23. Zhou, X., Wan, Q., Wei, Z., Xue, X., Wei, Y.: Model-based deep hand pose estimation. In: International Joint Conference on Artificial Intelligence, pp. 2421–2427 (2016)
24. Zhou, Y., Lu, J., Du, K., Lin, X., Sun, Y., Ma, X.: HBE: hand branch ensemble network for real-time 3D hand pose estimation. In: Ferrari, V., Hebert, M., Sminchisescu, C., Weiss, Y. (eds.) Computer Vision – ECCV 2018. LNCS, vol. 11218, pp. 521–536. Springer, Cham (2018). https://doi.org/10.1007/978-3-030-01264-9_31
25. Zhang, P., Zheng, L., Jiang, Y., Mao, L., Li, Z., Sheng, B.: Tracking soccer players using spatio-temporal context learning under multiple views. Multimedia Tools Appl. **77**(15), 18935–18955 (2018)

Bézier Curve as a Generalization of the Easing Function in Computer Animation

Łukasz Izdebski[1] ⓘ, Ryszard Kopiecki[2] ⓘ, and Dariusz Sawicki[3]([✉]) ⓘ

[1] JRS Software, Warsaw, Poland
lukasz.izdebski.jrs@gmail.com
[2] Military University of Technology, Warsaw, Poland
ricko@mimuw.edu.pl
[3] Warsaw University of Technology, Warsaw, Poland
Dariusz.Sawicki@ee.pw.edu.pl

Abstract. The description of movement has always been one of the basic problems in traditional and computer animation. A person watching an animated film may accept simplifications in the appearance of the characters, but will not accept unnatural, unexpected motion. The transition problem is an example of movement description which is successfully solved by Penner's easing functions. But, the scope of an easing function is limited to known examples of specific functions proposed by Penner or other developers. However, there is often a need to describe the transition problem by a function resulting from the interpolation of points that approximate the trajectory. A convenient way to describe the shape, in such a situation, would be a Bézier curve. The article is an attempt to generalize the problem of interpolation of transition trajectories using the Bézier curve. By analyzing various cases of the cubic polynomial equations in the context of transition problems in animation, we can limit the solution to several families of the transcendental functions.

Keywords: Easing function · Bézier curve · Keyframe animation · Trajectory of motion

1 Introduction

The description of movement has always been one of the basic problems in traditional and computer animation. A person watching an animated film may accept simplifications in the appearance of the characters, but will not accept unnatural, unexpected motion.

The roots of the keyframe method can be found in traditional freehand animation, which is widely used in virtually all major movie production applications (animated or special effects fragments). In addition, the keyframe method is used in all video games and simulator engines. The keyframe in the keyframe method is an ordered pair of two values (x, y), where the x variable represents the frame number and the y variable the animated parameter selected by the animator. These parameters can include more than just object properties such as position, rotation, and scale, but also other parameters

© Springer Nature Switzerland AG 2020
N. Magnenat-Thalmann et al. (Eds.): CGI 2020, LNCS 12221, pp. 382–393, 2020.
https://doi.org/10.1007/978-3-030-61864-3_32

such as the material properties of the objects (color, transparency, etc.). The intermediate values between the keyframes of the animated parameters are calculated by a computer algorithm. This algorithm is usually an interpolation function (e.g. easing function). Since each successive frame is displayed at a specific point in time, the frame number (x) is in line with the time elapsed from the beginning of the animated movie to the appearance of the frame. Thus, movement (changing the value of the y parameter) is described by an easing function.

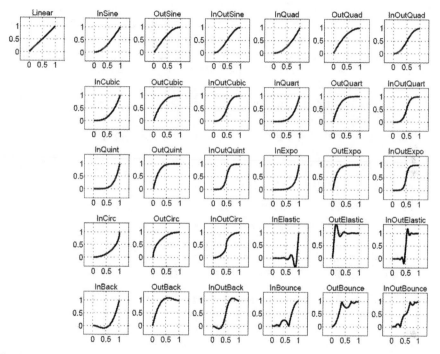

Fig. 1. The set of Penner's easing functions. All functions have been normalized i.e. are realised for $x \in [0, 1]$ and $y \in [0, 1]$

The slope of the easing function curve determines the speed with which parameter value changes between keyframes. A steep slope of the curve means that the value changes quickly, while a slight slope means that the value changes slowly. The easing function allows creating connections between frames [6] also with manipulating frame rates [14]. In the real world, perceived processes in nature rarely change immediately. In computer graphics, this applies primarily to movement, but also changes in luminance or color [15]. The movement of real objects does not begin or end abruptly. Therefore, the set proposed by Robert Penner [11, 13] contains 21 easing functions, shown in Fig. 1. These functions simulate the movement of objects at a variable speed, as expected by the recipients. Easing functions are grouped into types with common features, such as: smooth start (Ease-In), smooth stop (Ease-Out), smooth start and stop (Ease-In-Out). Of course, the set of Penner's functions is not exhaust the topic. Many other features of this type are known. For example, the Qt [12] and Windows Presentation Foundation [17] libraries implement an additional type of easing functions, including rapid start and stop (Ease-Out-In), which was not included in Penner's work.

Known collections of easing functions (e.g. Penner's easing functions) contain examples of specific trajectories. However, in practice, in the work of an animator, there is often a need to describe a trajectory that is defined by a set of points. In such a situation, it would be convenient to interpolate the points to define the expected continuous function.

The problem of "in-between calculation" has been known in computer animation for many years [8, 9]. Today, one of the most popular tools for animation support is Cascading Style Sheets (CSS) [1, 2]. CSS is a specific language, where Bézier curves are used for description of transition.

In this paper, we introduce a new description of the easing function which is identical to the cubic Bézier curve. In a typical application, the description of the Bézier curve is parametric, which uses a system of two at most cubic polynomial equations. This parametric description is not related to the passage of time. Generally, algebraic solving of polynomial equations can be difficult or even impossible. However, we have limited the solution to several families of the curve, by analyzing proper cases of the cubic polynomial equation in the context of time changes in the animation. In addition, new restrictions on the control point coordinates for the cubic Bézier curve have been proposed so that it can define the correct easing function.

2 Bézier Curve as an Easing Function

2.1 Definition of the Problem

Bézier curves and surfaces are widely used in animation (and in all areas of computer graphics) to model 2D and 3D shapes [6, 10]. However, the Bézier curve in its typical application in the keyframe method is the trajectory description [3, 18] and serves as an interpolation function to calculate the values of animated parameters [5, 16] between keyframes. A very practical application is the description of transitions in the movement of rendered objects. The application of Penner's easing function in a form based only on Bézier curves is also known [7].

In our article, only cubic Bézier curves [4] are considered and their parameterization takes the form (1).

$$P(t) = P_0(1-t)^3 + 3P_1 t(1-t)^2 + 3P_2 t^2(1-t) + P_3 t^3 \qquad (1)$$

where $t \in [0, 1]$ and P_0, P_1, P_2, P_3 are control points of the curve.

The vector function $P(t)$ can be also expressed in form (2)

$$P(t) = (x(t), y(t)) \qquad (2)$$

where $x(t)$ and $y(t)$ are at most cubic polynomials (3).

$$x(t) = x_0(1-t)^3 + 3x_1 t(1-t)^2 + 3x_2 t^2(1-t) + x_3 t^3$$
$$y(t) = y_0(1-t)^3 + 3y_1 t(1-t)^2 + 3y_2 t^2(1-t) + y_3 t^3 \qquad (3)$$

where $t \in [0, 1]$.

The formula for parameterization (in the Bernstein basis polynomials) can be represented in the form (4).

$$P(t) = \begin{cases} x(t) = g(t) = \alpha_0 t^3 + \beta_0 t^2 + \gamma_0 t + \delta_0 \\ y(t) = f(t) = \alpha_1 t^3 + \beta_1 t^2 + \gamma_1 t + \delta_1 \end{cases} \tag{4}$$

where $t \in [0, 1]$.

An example of a normalized easing function defined using the cubic Bézier curve is shown in Fig. 2.

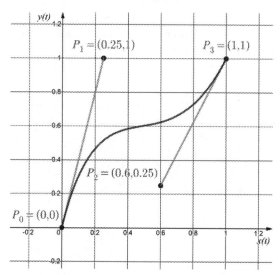

Fig. 2. An example of an easing function defined by Bézier curve. P_0, P_1, P_2, P_3 are control points of the curve.

According to (3) and (4) easing function in this case (Fig. 2) is described parametrically – both x and y are defined as a function of t parameter. This is especially troublesome when the variable x represents time. The expected form of the curve description would be the function graph $y = y(x)$ where x represents simply time without additional parameterization This means that we want to switch from a parametric description to a description of the function of one variable, where a time-dependent function or an easing function is used.

For this purpose, the first equation from (4) should be solved, with respect to the parameter t. Subsequently, the function $t = t(x)$ should be substituted into the second equation of (4). The assembling of $y(x) = y(t(x))$ will be written in a simpler form as (5).

$$C(x) = f\left(g^{-1}(x)\right) \tag{5}$$

Function $C(x)$ is the new parameterization of the Bézier curve, which can be used as an **easing function**. Function g we will call **the internal function**, and the function f **the external function**.

2.2   Problem Conditions

The trajectory described as an easing function is a curve as graph of function. At the same time, it is a description of the location as a function of time, not a certain parameter that is most commonly used in animation. This imposes appropriate requirements in the form of the equation.

There are two related situations, connected to the description of the easing function. Especially using the cubic Bézier curves. Because $y = y(x)$, where the variable x directly represents time, so the situation of "time looping" is not allowed. Such a situation could occur in two types of cases shown in Fig. 3.

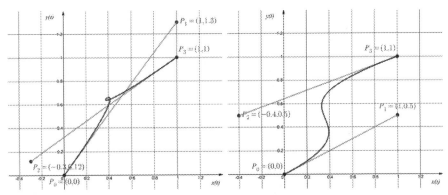

Fig. 3. Example of cubic Bézier curves containing loops or arcs (ambiguous from the point of view of one variable). Not allowed when x represents time.

For the Bézier curve in parameterization (4) which can be used as easing function, not all of its forms are allowed, but only those that meet the condition.

$$g'(x) > 0, \quad x \in [x_0, x_3] \tag{6}$$

This condition (6) guarantees that the internal function will be a strictly increasing function, which means that it will be reversible for x from the range of $[x_0, x_3]$. And also the function $C(x)$ will not have arcs or loops shown in Fig. 3. In addition, a weaker condition is also acceptable (7).

$$g'(x) \geq 0, \quad x \in [x_0, x_3] \tag{7}$$

For $C(x)$ curves that meet the condition (7), it is permissible for one inflection point to be present in $[x_0, x_3]$. In this case, we are not dealing with the local extreme, because the condition of changing the sign of the first derivative of the function in the vicinity of the stationary point, i.e. zero of the function is not fulfilled.

2.3   General Solution

Because the function g is a cubic polynomial, it is defined by its four coefficients a_0, b_0, c_0, d_0, which can be determined based on a formula (8).

$$
\begin{bmatrix} a_0 \\ b_0 \\ c_0 \\ d_0 \end{bmatrix} = \frac{1}{(x_3 - x_0)^3} \begin{bmatrix} -1 & 3 & -3 & 1 \\ 3x_3 & -3x_0 - 6x_3 & 6x_0 + 3x_3 & -3x_0 \\ -3x_3^2 & 6x_0x_3 + 3x_3^2 & -3x_0^2 - 6x_0x_3 & 3x_0^2 \\ x_3^3 & -3x_0x_3^2 & 3x_0^2x_3 & -x_0^3 \end{bmatrix} \cdot \begin{bmatrix} x_0 \\ x_1 \\ x_2 \\ x_3 \end{bmatrix} \tag{8}
$$

Similarly, the function f is a cubic polynomial, so it is determined by the coefficients a_1, b_1, c_1, d_1. As before, these coefficients can be determined based on a formula (9).

$$
\begin{bmatrix} a_1 \\ b_1 \\ c_1 \\ d_1 \end{bmatrix} = \frac{1}{(x_3 - x_0)^3} \begin{bmatrix} -1 & 3 & -3 & 1 \\ 3x_3 & -3x_0 - 6x_3 & 6x_0 + 3x_3 & -3x_0 \\ -3x_3^2 & 6x_0x_3 + 3x_3^2 & -3x_0^2 - 6x_0x_3 & 3x_0^2 \\ x_3^3 & -3x_0x_3^2 & 3x_0^2x_3 & -x_0^3 \end{bmatrix} \cdot \begin{bmatrix} y_0 \\ y_1 \\ y_2 \\ y_3 \end{bmatrix} \tag{9}
$$

For x, the range of variation is the segment $[x_0, x_3]$ determined by the first coordinates of the points, P_0 and P_3 respectively. When deriving the above formulas, the conditions (10) were taken into account.

$$
\begin{cases} C(x_0) = P(0) \\ C(x_3) = P(1) \end{cases} \tag{10}
$$

The transformations determined by the matrices located on the right sides of the formulas (8) and (9) are reversible, so each pair of cubic polynomials (with the coefficients a_0, b_0, c_0, d_0 for the first polynomial and a_1, b_1, c_1, d_1 for the second) in the range $[x_0, x_3]$ can be determined.

2.4   Inverse Function to at Most a Cubic Polynomial

To determine the formula for the $C(x)$ function, defined by the formula (5), it becomes necessary to find the inverse function to at most a cubic polynomial. Let us then consider any at most a cubic polynomial (11).

$$
y = W(x) = ax^3 + bx^2 + cx + d \tag{11}
$$

Equation (11) needs to be resolved with respect to the variable x. It comes down to solving the problem of finding the roots of at most a cubic polynomial. Of course, the problem of finding roots is limited only to the real parameters of the polynomial and the domain of functions in the set of real numbers (such as the use of the equation in computer animation). Additionally, condition (6) must be taken into account that the expectations considered in the article are met.

Several cases are possible depending on the degree of the polynomial. Because zero-degree polynomials are constant functions, i.e. they do not satisfy the condition (6), they will not be considered here.

- $W(x)$ is a linear polynomial of $W(x) = cx + d$. The function of this form satisfies the condition (6) if and only if it occurs (12).

$$c > 0 \tag{12}$$

- $W(x)$ is a quadratic polynomial: $W(x) = bx^2 + cx + d$. Condition (6) means that occurs (13).

$$2bx + c > 0 \Leftrightarrow (b > 0 \wedge x > -\frac{c}{2b}) \vee (b < 0 \wedge x < -\frac{c}{2b}) \tag{13}$$

- $W(x)$ is a cubic polynomial: $W(x) = ax^3 + bx^2 + cx + d$. Function of this form fulfills condition (6) (occurs $3ax^2 + 2bx + c > 0$), if and only if occurs (14).

$$(a > 0 \wedge c > \frac{b^2}{3a}) \vee (a > 0 \wedge c < \frac{b^2}{3a} \wedge x > \frac{\sqrt{b^2 - 3ac} - b}{3a}) \tag{14}$$

2.5 $C(x)$ Function

Having determined formulas for functions $g^{-1}(x)$, it is possible to present the expected parameterization (5) as a function of one variable – as a time-dependent function (easing function). This should be considered in several cases.

- $a_1 = 0 \wedge b_1 = 0$

$$C(x) = ax^3 + \beta x^2 + \gamma x + \delta \tag{15}$$

where $\alpha = a_0 l^2$, $\beta = 3a_0 l^2 k + b_0 l^2$, $\gamma = 3a_0 l k^2 + 2b_0 l k + c_0 l$, and $\delta = a_0 k^3 + b_0 k^2 + c_0 k + d_0$
where $k = -d_1/c_1, l = 1/c_1$.

- $a_1 = 0$

$$C(x) = \alpha \Phi(x)^3 + \beta \Phi(x)^2 + \gamma \Phi(x) + \delta \tag{16}$$

where $\alpha = \text{sgn}(b_0) \cdot a_0$, $\beta = 3a_0 B + b_0$, $\gamma = \text{sgn}(b_0) \cdot (3a_0 B^2 + 2b_0 B + c_0)$, and $\delta = a_0 B^3 + b_0 B^2 + c_0 B + d_0$
where $\Phi(x) = \sqrt{lx + k}, k = c_1^2/4b_1^2 - d_1/b_1, l = 1/b_1, B = -d_1/2b_1$.

- $a_1 \neq 0 \wedge p = 0$

$$C(x) = \alpha \Phi(x)^3 + \beta \Phi(x)^2 + \gamma \Phi(x) + \delta \tag{17}$$

where $\alpha = a_0$, $\beta = 3a_0 B + b_0$, $\gamma = 3a_0 B^2 + 2b_0 B + c_0$, and $\delta = a_0 B^3 + b_0 B^2 + c_0 B + d_0$
where $\Phi(x) = \sqrt[3]{lx + k}, k = (2b_1^3 - 9a_1 b_1 c_1 + 27a_1^2 d_1)/27a_1^3, l = 1/a_1$, and $B = -b/3a_1$.

- $a_1 \neq 0 \wedge p > 0$

$$C(x) = \alpha\Phi(x)^3 + \beta\Phi(x)^2 + \gamma\Phi(x) + \delta \tag{18}$$

where $\alpha = a_0A^3$, $\beta = 3a_0A^2B + b_0A^2$, $\gamma = 3a_0AB^2 + 2b_0AB + c_0A$, and $\delta = a_0B^3 + b_0B^2 + c_0B + d_0$

where $\Phi(x) = \sinh(\operatorname{arcsinh}(lx + k)/3)$, $A = -2\sqrt{p/3}$, $B = -b/3a_1$, and $l = 3/Apa_1$, $k = -3\left(2b_1^3 - 9a_1b_1c_1 + 27a_1^2d_1\right)/\left(27Apa_1^3\right)$.

- $a_1 \neq 0 \wedge p < 0 \wedge 4p3 + 27q2 > 0$

$$C(x) = \alpha\Phi(x)^3 + \beta\Phi(x)^2 + \gamma\Phi(x) + \delta \tag{19}$$

where $\alpha = \operatorname{sgn}(q) \cdot a_0A^3$, $\beta = 3a_0A^2B + b_0A^2$, and $\gamma = \operatorname{sgn}(q) \cdot \left(3a_0AB^2 + 2b_0AB + c_0A\right)$, $\delta = a_0B^3 + b_0B^2 + c_0B + d_0$

where $\Phi(x) = \cosh(\operatorname{arccosh}(|lx + k|)/3)$, $A = -2\sqrt{-p/3}$, $B = -b/3a_1$, and $l = -3/Apa_1$, $k = 3\left(2b_1^3 - 9a_1b_1c_1 + 27a_1^2d_1\right)/\left(27Apa_1^3\right)$.

- $a_1 \neq 0 \wedge p < 0 \wedge 4p3 + 27q2 < 0$

$$C_u(x) = \alpha\Phi_u^3(x) + \beta\Phi_u^2(x) + \gamma\Phi_u(x) + \delta, \quad u \in \{0, 1, 2\} \tag{20}$$

where $\alpha = a_0A^3$, $\beta = 3a_0A^2B + b_0A^2$, $\gamma = 3a_0AB^2 + 2b_0AB + c_0A$, and $\delta = a_0B^3 + b_0B^2 + c_0B + d_0$

where $\Phi_u(x) = \cos(\arccos(lx + k)/3 - 2u\pi/3)$, $A = 2\sqrt{-p/3}$, and $B = -b/3a_1$, $l = -3/Apa_1$, and $k = 3\left(2b_1^3 - 9a_1b_1c_1 + 27a_1^2d_1\right)/\left(27Apa_1^3\right)$.

3 Result

The expected parameterization consists of six function families – formulas (15)–(20). Their form is determined by the values of the coefficients of the internal function $g(x)$. In the general case of the cubic polynomial, there are four coefficients that take values in the set of real numbers. This means that these polynomials form a 4D vector space. This fact partly explains the diversity of the forms of inverse functions to them, and thus the form of the $C(x)$ function.

In case of $a_1 = 0 \hat{\ } b_1 = 0$ (i.e. when internal function g is a linear function) $C(x)$ function is at most a cubic polynomial. In other cases, we receive assembling of polynomial and transcendental functions.

4 Practical Approach – Implementation

The implementation of the Bézier curve as an easing function was made in C++. Proprietary software has been developed for the purposes of carrying out research and tests for this article. The software was created in the IDE Visual Studio 2017/64 bit environment. The performance tests were performed on synthetic data – artificially prepared in such a way as to test the largest number of theoretically possible cases of parameter inter-polation in the keyframe method. All tests were carried out on a PC with the following configuration: Ryzen 7 1700X processor, 32 GB 2400 MHz DDR4 RAM, Windows 10/64 bit operating system.

5 Tests and Discussion

Taking into account different ways of determining the value of the interpolation func-tion, we compared two methods of easing function description using the Bézier curve: traditional (parametric descriptions $y = y(t)$ and $x = x(t)$ and proposed (using $C(x)$). Two types of tests were carried out:

- Subjective tests assessing the ease of use of the animation implementation. These tests assessed the facility of changing the shape of an easing function.
- An attempt to assess how the change of the parameterization affects the easing function.

An example of the application of the proposed solution (using $C(x)$) is shown in Fig. 4. This is the curve corresponding to the curve in Fig. 3. Both curves are identical because $C(x)$ is an algebraic solution of the system of equations describing the Bézier curve in Fig. 3. $C(x)$ for the curve presented in Fig. 4 described Eq. (21).

$$C(x) = 702\Phi(x)^3 + 513\Phi(x)^2 + 126\Phi(x) + 11 \tag{21}$$

where $\Phi(x) = \cos((\arccos(23/27 - 10x/27))/3 - 2\pi/3)$.

However, the implementation of the proposed solution is much simpler because the use of $C(x)$ gives direct control over the description of time – there is no additional parameterization. All the comparative tests of implementation confirmed the ease of realization of the animation in a situation when the description of time is carried out without additional parameterization. So they confirmed the usefulness of the proposed solution.

Synthetic and real tests of interpolating functions showed that the application of the proposed solution accelerates the realization by approx. 15%–20%. This is due to the fact that the implementation of the proposed solution contains fewer branching and jump instructions, which makes the code more predictable and gives the processor more space to efficiently execute more instructions per clock.

Additionally, the proposed solution (using $C(x)$) allowed precisely determining the range of variation of coordinates of the control points P_1 and P_2 for the Bézier curve, which ensures the correctness of the easing function definition. The x coordinates of the control points determine the internal function $g(x)$, thus also the inverse function occurring in the formula $C(x) = f(g^{-1}(x))$. Therefore, for the Bézier curve to be treated as an easing function, restrictions occur only for x coordinates. The y coordinates can be arbitrary. Figure 5 shows the space of the allowed coordinate values x_{P1} (x of the P_1 control point – abscissa axis) and x_{P2} (x of the P_2 control point – ordinate axis) for which

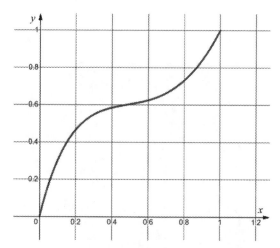

Fig. 4. Easing function from Fig. 3 but described using the proposed solution (using the $C(x)$) function. x in this case represents time directly

the normalized Bézier curve correctly represents the easing function. The boundary of the allowed area is described by the set of Eqs. (22).

$$
\begin{cases}
x_{P1} = 0 & \text{for border part AB} \\
x_{P2} = 1 & \text{for border part BC} \\
x_{P2} = 0.5(x_{P1} + \sqrt{4x_{P1} - 3x_{P1}^2}) & \text{for border part CD} \\
x_{P2} = 0.5(x_{P1} - \sqrt{4x_{P1} - 3x_{P1}^2}) & \text{for border part AD}
\end{cases}
\tag{22}
$$

In many programs for keyframe animation, the Bézier curve is used to describe the easing function. There is often defined a restriction on the coordinates x_{P1} (point P_1) and x_{P2} (point P_2) in the form of the area (square): $x_1, x_2 \in [0, 1]$ (of course for the normalized curves). As can be seen in Fig. 5, the actual area that is allowed to describe the correct easing function is larger. This gives more opportunities in the definition and manipulation of the easing function shape.

The allowed area (Fig. 5) is directly related to formulas (6) and (7). The interior of the area (the gray part in Fig. 2) corresponds to the inequality (6). While, formula (7) covers the entire area: the interior (gray part) and the edge defined by a set of Eqs. (22).

6 Summary

The new description of an easing function in keyframe animation, using the cubic Bézier curve, has been introduced in the paper. In the proposed solution at most cubic polynomial equation has been used.

In considered situations, algebraic transformation to time-dependent equations can be difficult or even impossible. An analysis of various cases of the cubic polynomial equation in the context of time changes in animation was carried out taking into account

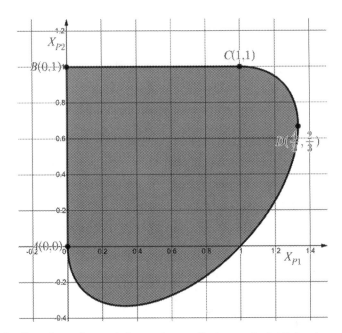

Fig. 5. The allowed area for restriction on the coordinates x_{P1} (point P_1) and x_{P2} (point P_2)

the dependencies related to the passage of time. Trajectories described by time-dependent functions cannot contain loops and other cases, where "turning back time" would take place. As a result of this analysis, we have limited the solution to several families of the transcendental functions. The dependencies of parameters and formulas of function for solving the task were developed.

A set of tests was carried out using the proposed solution. In the paper, we focused on a practical approach to the problem. The implementation of the proposed solution is much simpler because the use of $C(x)$ gives direct control over the description of time – there is no additional parameterization. All comparative tests of implementation with both variants confirmed the ease of animation realization using the proposed solution. We have tested also implementation in various conditions – in synthetic tests and in real animation. The tests have shown that the use of the proposed solution accelerates performance by about 15%–20%.

Additionally we have proposed the new restriction for the area allowed for the implementation of an easing function using the cubic Bézier curves. The proposed solution defines a larger allowed area (than known from animation software) – it gives more opportunities in definition and manipulation of the easing function shape.

In the future, we plan an additional mathematical analysis of the obtained solution in which we will try to simplify the form of families of the transcendental functions.

References

1. Cascading Style Sheets (CSS): The Official Definition, W3C Working Group Note, 13 October 2015. https://www.w3.org/TR/CSS/#css. Accessed 10 July 2020

2. Ceaser CSS Easing Animation Tool. https://matthewlein.com/ceaser/. Accessed 10 July 2020
3. Faraway, J.J., Reed, M.P., Wang, J.: Modelling three-dimensional trajectories by using Bézier curves with application to hand motion. Appl. Statist. **56**(Part 5), 571–585 (2007)
4. Farin, G., Hoschek, J., Kim, M.-S. (eds.): Handbook of Computer Aided Geometric Design. North Holland, Amsterdam (2002)
5. Gordon, W.J., Reisenfeld, R.F.: Bernstein-Bézier methods for the computer-aided design of free-form curves and surfaces. J. ACM **21**(2), 293–310 (1974)
6. Hughes, J.F., et al.: Computer Graphics: Principles and Practice, 3rd edn. Addison Wesley, Boston (2013)
7. Izdebski, Ł., Sawicki, D.: Easing functions in the new form based on Bézier curves. In: Chmielewski, L.J., Datta, A., Kozera, R., Wojciechowski, K. (eds.) ICCVG 2016. LNCS, vol. 9972, pp. 37–48. Springer, Cham (2016). https://doi.org/10.1007/978-3-319-46418-3_4
8. Magnenat-Thalmann, N., Thalmann, D.: Computer Animation: Theory and Practice. Springer, Tokyo (1985). https://doi.org/10.1007/978-4-431-68433-6
9. Owen, M., Willis, P.: Modelling and interpolating cartoon characters. In: Proceedings of the Computer Animation 1994, Geneva, 25–28 May 1994, pp. 148–155. http://ieeexplore.ieee.org/iel2/987/7718/00323996.pdf. Accessed 10 July 2020
10. Parent, R.: Computer Animation, 3rd Revised edn. Morgan Kaufmann, Burlington (2012)
11. Penner, R.: Motion, tweening, and easing. In: Programming Macromedia Flash MX, Chap. 7, pp. 191–240. McGraw-Hill/OsborneMedia (2002). http://robertpenner.com/easing/penner_chapter7_tweening.pdf. Accessed 18 Feb 2020
12. Qt Documentation. Animator QML Type. https://doc.qt.io/qt-5/qml-qtquick-animator.html. Accessed 20 May 2020
13. Robert Penner's Easing Functions. http://robertpenner.com/easing/. Accessed 18 Feb 2020
14. Sakchaicharoenkul, T.: MCFI-based animation tweening algorithm for 2D parametric motion flow/optical flow. Mach. Graph. Vis. Int. J. **15**(1), 29–49 (2006)
15. Sawicki, D., Wolska, A., Wisełka, M., Ordysiński, S.: Easing function as a tool of color correction for display stitching in virtual reality. In: Ricci, E., Rota Bulò, S., Snoek, C., Lanz, O., Messelodi, S., Sebe, N. (eds.) ICIAP 2019. LNCS, vol. 11752, pp. 549–559. Springer, Cham (2019). https://doi.org/10.1007/978-3-030-30645-8_50
16. Van Verth, J.M., Bishop, L.M.: Essential Mathematics for Games and Interactive Applications. A Programmer's Guide, 2nd edn. CRC Press, Boca Raton (2008)
17. Windows Presentation Foundation: Easing Functions. https://docs.microsoft.com/en-us/dotnet/framework/wpf/graphics-multimedia/easing-functions. Accessed 20 May 2020
18. Yao, J., Zhang, H., Zhang, H., Cheng, Q.: Study on Bezier curve applications of pelvis trajectory of virtual human walking. In: Proceedings of 2008 International Conference on Cyberworlds, Hangzhou China, pp. 635–639 (2008)

Generating Orthogonal Voronoi Treemap for Visualization of Hierarchical Data

Yan-Chao Wang◉, Jigang Liu◉, Feng Lin(✉)◉, and Hock-Soon Seah◉

Nanyang Technological University, 50 Nanyang Avenue, Singapore 639798, Singapore
{yanchao.wang,liujg,asflin,ashsseah}@ntu.edu.sg

Abstract. A novel space partitioning strategy is presented for implicit hierarchy visualization. The proposed orthogonal Voronoi treemap (OVT) partitions an empty canvas into nested orthogonal rectangles, thus the generated layout is not only flexible to diversified data value, but also much tidier than the Voronoi treemap with nested polygons. To achieve this, we first introduce a new distance calculation strategy in order to generate axis-aligned segmentation among the sites. To cope with the new segmentation strategy, we then design a sweepline + skyline heuristic algorithm to partition the canvas to generate an orthogonal Voronoi treemap. Comparative analyses on the computational experiment results in terms of aspect ratio is discussed.

Keywords: Orthogonal Voronoi treemap · Hierarchical data visualization · Heuristic algorithm · Sweepline · Skyline

1 Introduction

Hierarchical data structures are common in our daily life, such as the taxonomy of natural species, the organization of computer documents, and data hierarchical clustering used in machine learning [9,13,16]. Hence, visualization of hierarchical data has long been demanded for information visualization to identify potential insight and conduct data analysis [12,14,26]. Some of hierarchical visualization approaches are to explicitly show the hierarchical structure as straight lines, arcs, or curves; while others focus on the value within each node and positionally encode the hierarchy by node overlap or inclusion. Previous research shows the latter can implicitly present the hierarchy in a more space-efficient way [17]. Among these implicit hierarchy visualization methods, treemap [18] and Voronoi treemap [1] are two popular algorithms with nested rectangles and polygons respectively. Treemap divides the empty canvas into rectangular sub-regions so that the area is associated with the relative sizes of the respective sub-hierarchies. Voronoi treemap, in a more general way, partitions the canvas into polygon shapes based on distance to prior specified sites; afterwards, the position and weight of the sites may be iteratively adapted in order to adjust the area of the sub-regions. Unfortunately, both treemap and Voronoi treemap exhibit problems in the flexibility of adjustment for visualization plots. For instance, even when the

© Springer Nature Switzerland AG 2020
N. Magnenat-Thalmann et al. (Eds.): CGI 2020, LNCS 12221, pp. 394–402, 2020.
https://doi.org/10.1007/978-3-030-61864-3_33

hierarchical data changes slightly, the partitioning of empty canvas in treemap need to be regenerated and the new layout may be largely distorted and leads to poor layout stability. Although Voronoi treemap can adjust its layout via slight modification on the status of its sites, its nested polygons are much more untidy and difficult for tracking and comparison compared to the treemap's rectangular divisions. Hence, it is crucial to have the adjustment flexibility while maintaining the orthogonal layout of the plots [11]. In response to all these problems, we propose an orthogonal Voronoi diagram and treemap.

Our orthogonal Voronoi treemap (OVT) partitions the empty canvas into nested orthogonal rectangles based on distance to prior specified sites. Hence, the generated layout is not only flexible to a diversified data value, but also much tidier than the Voronoi treemap with nested polygons. To achieve this, we first introduce a new distance calculation strategy in order to generate axis-aligned segmentation among the sites. In the strategy, a new distance function is defined by considering the relative positions of two sites rather than a single site. Then a horizontal/vertical segmentation line is generated between these two sites. To cope with the new strategy, we design a sweepline + skyline heuristic algorithm to partition the canvas based on the new distance calculation strategy to generate an orthogonal Voronoi diagram. This is inspired by the sweepline algorithm for Voronoi diagram generation [6] and the skyline strategy in handling cutting and packing problems [4]. By iteratively updating the status of the original sites and calling the sweepline + skyline algorithm, the area of the orthogonal rectangular sub-regions will match their corresponding values. An orthogonal Voronoi treemap will be obtained if this process is recursively continued layer by layer until the whole hierarchical structure is traversed.

2   Related Work

Implicit hierarchy visualization methods mainly differ in the canvas subdivision strategies used to generate layouts [17].

Some implicit hierarchy visualization methods that partition the whole space without considering the sites are treated as non-site-based methods, such as the treemap. These methods position the data by following some rules or experiences in order to get expected configurations, which sometimes are also named as heuristic-based algorithms. Starting from the original treemap in 1992 [18], a large number of variants are proposed in the literature [23]. The squarified treemap focuses on the emergence of thin, elongated rectangles in the standard treemaps and presents a new subdivision method such that the resulting rectangles have a lower aspect ratio [3]. The ordered treemap layout is the first type of treemap layout that takes stability into consideration [19]. The split algorithm used in the ordered and quantum treemaps [2] is a modification of the squarified treemaps, following a given one-dimensional ordering. The spiral treemap positions the one-dimensional ordering of the input data along the border following a circular arrangement or an S-shape [22]. Different from previous methods which only consider one dimension, the spatially order treemaps consider two-dimensional consistency by relating node order to Euclidean distance from the parent node's top-left corner [27]. We notice the layout generation problem in treemap which is similar to the two-dimensional (2D) bin packing which is an optimization problem with a wide range of applications in resource management. This is also discussed by Schulz et al. [17]. Since many heuristic algorithms [4,25] have been proposed to solve the bin packing problem, how to utilize them into the layout generation in treemap would be an interesting research direction.

On the other hand, some implicit hierarchy visualization methods partition the space based on a series of pre-defined sites, such as the Voronoi treemap. The Voronoi treemap is originally presented by Balzer et al. [1]. By relaxing the constraint of rectangular shapes, they utilize Voronoi tessellations to generate polygonal subdivisions. Later, the Voronoi treemaps are utilized to visualize dynamic hierarchical data owing to its adjustment ability [8,20]. In 2012, Nocaj and Brandes [15] propose a resolution-independent algorithm by calculating the Voronoi tessellations with power diagrams, such that the new algorithm is faster in both theory and practice. An improvement is then made by setting an initial position for visualizing varying hierarchies [10]. Neighborhood treemap (Nmap) [5], that successively bisects a set of pre-defined sites on the horizontal or vertical directions and then scales the bisections to match the value of each site, is also a site-based method. Circle packing [24] can also be treated as a site-based method since the generation of the layouts is based on the center of each circle, as well as the recently proposed bubble treemaps [7].

3   Methodology

A Voronoi diagram (or Voronoi tessellation) is a partitioning of a plane into sub-regions based on distances to a set of points within the plane. These sub-regions are termed *Voronoi cell* and the points are called *sites* [15]. Formally, given a bounded region $\Omega \subset R^2$ and a set of n sites $S = \{s_1, s_2, ..., s_n\}$, the Voronoi diagram divides Ω into a set of Voronoi cells $v(s_i)$, one for each site s_i. Then the cell $v(s_i)$ can be expressed as

$$v(s_i) = \{p \in \Omega \mid dist(p, s_i) < dist(p, s). \forall s \in S, s \neq s_i\}, \tag{1}$$

where $dist(p, s_i)$ is the weighted power Euclidean distance between point $p = (x_p, y_p)$ and site $s_i = (x_{s_i}, y_{s_i})$. Let $W = \{w_1, w_2, ..., w_n\}$ be a set of positive weights associated with the set of sites S correspondingly. Then the weighted power Euclidean distance is used to control the areas of cells, in order to use the cells to depict data information (e.g. data value). Thus, the Voronoi diagram is defined as the collection of Voronoi cells, $v(S) = \{v(s_1), ..., v(s_n)\}$.

A Voronoi treemap in this study is a recursive partitioning of the 2D bounded region. Starting from the root of a hierarchy, a weighted Voronoi diagram is generated in the region Ω with one cell for each child of the root. An iterative optimization process is taken to adaptively alert the value of weight and the position of the site, such that the areas of the cells meet the requirement. The final layout requires that the area of each cell be in proportion to the associated value. If the area error reaches a threshold, the requirement is met and the

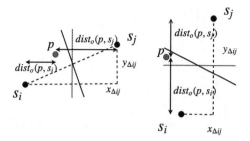

Fig. 1. Two kinds of relative positions for sites s_i and s_j where $x_{\Delta ij} = |x_i - x_j|$ and $y_{\Delta ij} = |y_i - y_j|$.

iterative process converges. Therefore, let $value_{s_i}$ be the associated value of site s_i and $E_{threshold}$ be the threshold of the area error, then the convergent requirement can be expressed as:

$$\frac{\sum_{s_i \in S} \left| A\left(v\left(s_i\right)\right) - A\left(\Omega\right) * \dfrac{value_{s_i}}{value_S} \right|}{A\left(\Omega\right)} < E_{threshold}. \qquad (2)$$

Once the iterative process converges, the above-mentioned processes recurse to subdivide child region until all the leaves of the hierarchy are represented by cells with desired areas.

The proposed OVT is different from the traditional Voronoi treemap with a novel heuristic diagram generation algorithm. An initialization process is first conducted on the hierarchical data to generate the initial positions and weight for each site. Then, an initial weighted centroidal orthogonal Voronoi diagram is generated based on the initial status of sites. After that, an iterative process is taken to update the site status and generate the diagram until meeting the converge requirement as expressed in Eq. 2.

In the following, we focus on the description of the proposed novel heuristic algorithm to generate the diagram. We first introduce a new distance function in Sect. 3.1. Once the partition between two sites is confirmed, how to allocate the partitioned spaces to form a diagram is considered. A sweepline + skyline heuristic algorithm will then be introduced later in Sect. 3.2.

3.1 Distance Function

The new distance function considers the relative positions of two sites rather than only one site in previous distance function. Formally, when calculating the distance of point p and site s_i, we consider the relative positions of site pair s_i and s_j to decide which coordinate should be considered. Since we try to divide the space axis-aligned, we consider two kinds of relative positions between site s_i and s_j based on their x-axis difference $x_{\Delta ij} = |x_i - x_j|$ and y-axis difference $y_{\Delta ij} = |y_i - y_j|$. Then for an arbitrary point p, the distance to site s_i in both cases are depicted in Fig. 1 and defined as:

Y. Wang et al.

Algorithm 1. Compute Orthogonal Voronoi Diagram

$ComputeWOVDiagram$ $(S,\ \Omega,\ W)$

1: Sort S in the order of x_{s_i} ascending ;
2: Initialize $L_{sweepline}$; $L_{skyline}$; $v(S) = [\ ]$;
3: **for** $i = 1 : n$
4:     **for** $j = 1 : i - 1$
5:         **if** site s_j is closed, **then** continue;
6:         **if** site s_j is not the valid neighbor of site s_i, **then** continue;
7:         **if** site s_i and s_j are vertical neighbors, **then**
8:             $L_{s_i s_j} = GenerateWLine(s_i, s_j,\ w_i,\ w_j)$;
9:             Update $L_{skyline}$ with $L_{s_i s_j}$;
10:         **else**
11:             $L_{s_i s_j} = GenerateWLine(s_i, s_j,\ w_i,\ w_j)$;
12:             Mark site s_j as closed;
13:             Generate the bounding polygon $v(s_j)$ for site s_j;
14:             $v(S).push(v(s_j))$;
15:             Update $L_{skyline}$ with $L_{s_i s_j}$;
16:     Update $L_{sweepline}$;
17: **for** $i = 1 : n$
18:     **if** site s_i is closed, **then** continue;
19:     **else**
20:         Generate the bounding polygon $v(s_i)$ for site s_i;
21:         $v(S).push(v(s))$;
22: **return** $v(S)$;

$$dist_o(p, s_i, s_j) = \begin{cases} |x_p - x_{s_i}| - w_i & if\ x_{\Delta ij} > y_{\Delta ij}, \\ |y_p - y_{s_i}| - w_i & if\ x_{\Delta ij} < y_{\Delta ij}. \end{cases} \tag{3}$$

For the case in Fig. 1 (left), since $x_{\Delta ij} > y_{\Delta ij}$, site pair s_i and s_j are horizontal neighbors and a vertical line is needed to separate the site pair. Meanwhile, site pair s_i and s_j in Fig. 1 (right) are vertical neighbors and a horizontal line is needed. Hence, the axis-aligned segmentation line L is defined as:

$$L_{s_i s_j} : \begin{cases} x = \dfrac{1}{2}\left(x_{s_i} + x_{s_j}\right) & if\ x_{\Delta ij} > y_{\Delta ij}, \\ y = \dfrac{1}{2}\left(y_{s_i} + y_{s_j}\right) & if\ x_{\Delta ij} < y_{\Delta ij}. \end{cases} \tag{4}$$

If the two sites have large $y_{\Delta ij}$, they will be separated by a horizontal line. Otherwise, these two sites will be separated by a vertical line. For the case that $x_{\Delta ij} = y_{\Delta ij}$, we break the tie by choosing a horizontal segmentation.

3.2 The Sweepline + Skyline Algorithm

A sweepline + skyline algorithm to automatically partition the canvas is devised here based on the distance function 3. The new idea is inspired by the sweep line algorithm for Voronoi diagram [6] and the skyline strategy in cutting and packing

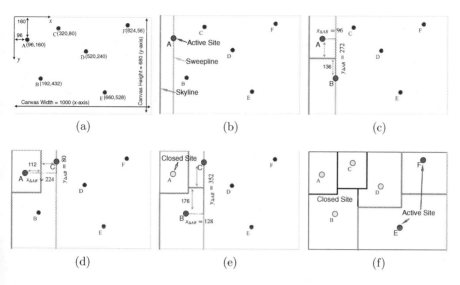

Fig. 2. Overview of the sweepline + skyline algorithm. (a) Initial status. (b) The skyline (in blue) and the sweepline (in pink) are initialized and the first site s_A (left-most) is activated. (c) The sweepline is swept to site s_B. (d) The sweepline is swept to site s_C and a vertical segmentation line is generated between s_A and s_C. Since site s_A is closed, the skyline is updated and site s_A is marked as closed status. (e) A horizontal segmentation line is generated site s_B and s_C and added to the skyline. (f) The process is continued until the last site s_F is considered. (Color figure online)

problem [4]. The sweepline used in our algorithm is a vertical line moving from left to right. When the sweep line hits a new site, the relationship of this new site and all its left-side site pairs are checked to generate vertical or horizontal segmentation lines. Meanwhile, a skyline is defined to record the current segmentation lines for all active sites. When the sweep line hits a new site and new segmentation lines are generated, the skyline will be updated correspondingly.

Figure 2 illustrates an example for this process. For a given rectangular canvas with $width = 1000$ and $height = 680$, six sites are pre-positioned. The first step (Fig. 2b) is to create a vertical sweepline and a vertical skyline. The sweepline is initially located on the left-most site s_A while the skyline is on the left-hand side of the canvas. The length of both lines equal to the height of the canvas. The second step (Fig. 2c) is to sweep the sweepline from left to right to hit the next site s_B. Since $y_{\Delta AB} = 272$ is larger than $x_{\Delta AB} = 96$, a horizontal line $L_{AB} : y = 296$ is built between site s_A and s_B. The skyline is then updated by adding a horizontal line segment. After checking all the left-hand-side site pairs of site s_B, the sweepline moves to the next site s_C (Fig. 2d). Since site s_A is not closed and is the horizontal neighbor of site s_C, then a vertical line $L_{AC} : x = 208$ is built. Once a vertical line is generated, the left site s_A of this horizontal neighbor sites should be closed and the bounding polygon of site s_A is formed based on the current skyline and the new vertical segment (as well as the canvas boundary). After that, the skyline is updated. Since site s_B is not closed and is the vertical neighbor of site s_C, then a horizontal line $L_{BC} : y = 256$ is built and the skyline is updated again (Fig. 2e). This process is repeated until the sweepline reaches the last site s_F (Fig. 2f). The residual sites (s_E and s_F) will then be closed and the bounding polygon for each site is formed by the current skyline and sweepline together. A pseudo-code for the whole process is depicted in Algorithm 1.

4   Experiments and Comparative Analyses

We evaluate the performance of our algorithm in terms of the aspect ratio since it is the most important metric in implicit hierarchy visualization. Our experiments are conducted on the global GDP dataset (two layers with 43 leave nodes), and the Flare class hierarchy (four layers with 220 leave nodes). Our OVT algorithms is implemented in JavaScript with the D3.js package[1] and Voronoi treemap[2].

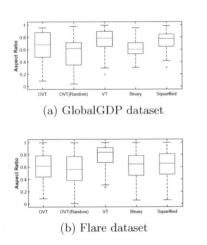

(a) GlobalGDP dataset

(b) Flare dataset

Fig. 3. The boxplots of aspect ratio of different algorithms.

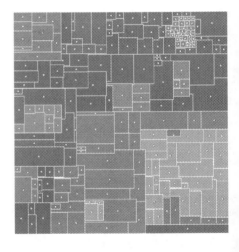

Fig. 4. Our OVT visualization of the Flare class hierarchy (colored by Tree-Colors [21]).

    For our algorithm and the treemaps, the aspect ratio of the axis-aligned minimum bounding box is calculated while for the Voronoi treemap, the aspect ratio of the oriented minimum bounding box is calculated. For our algorithm and the Voronoi treemap, we set the maximum iteration number to 500. The result is illustrated as boxplots shown in Fig. 3.

---

[1] https://d3js.org/.
[2] https://github.com/Kcnarf/.

When considering the mean aspect ratio (the red line) in Fig. 3, our algorithm is better than treemap layouts on the random dataset and has similar results on two real datasets, although the Voronoi treemap has the best aspect ratio in three cases. When comparing the different initial status of our algorithm, we can find that with the designed initialization strategy our algorithm has a better aspect ratio (the closer to one the better) and small distribution range. Figure 4 shows an example of the Flare classes data by our orthogonal Voronoi treemap.

5   Conclusions

To conclude the work, we have described a novel algorithm for the Voronoi treemap with nested orthogonal rectangles. The OVT is flexible to the changes of data value and can still hold the nested orthogonal rectangles to present each cell in a rectangle-like layout. Moreover, as shown in the performance analyses, the OVT algorithm runs in the same time complexity as Voronoi treemap, and holds the similar aspect ratio as the treemap. Actually, our algorithm requires less computation time than the Voronoi treemap and has comparable aspect ratio against the treemap. In future work, we would like to preserve the relative positions of sites during iteration in order to visualize dynamic hierarchical data for which a more stable layout is essential.

Acknowledgment. This work is partially supported by a grant MOE 2017-T1-001-053-04 from Ministry of Education, Singapore.

References

1. Balzer, M., Deussen, O.: Voronoi treemaps. In: Proceedings of the INFOVIS, pp. 49–56. IEEE (2005)
2. Bederson, B.B., Shneiderman, B., Wattenberg, M.: Ordered and quantum treemaps: making effective use of 2D space to display hierarchies. ACM Trans. Graph. **21**(4), 833–854 (2002)
3. Bruls, M., Huizing, K., van Wijk, J.J.: Squarified treemaps. In: de Leeuw, W.C., van Liere, R. (eds.) Data Visualization 2000. EUROGRAPH, pp. 33–42. Springer, Vienna (2000). https://doi.org/10.1007/978-3-7091-6783-0_4
4. Burke, E.K., Kendall, G., Whitwell, G.: A new placement heuristic for the orthogonal stock-cutting problem. Oper. Res. **52**(4), 655–671 (2004)
5. Duarte, F.S., Sikansi, F., Fatore, F.M., Fadel, S.G., Paulovich, F.V.: Nmap: a novel neighborhood preservation space-filling algorithm. IEEE Trans. Visual Comput. Graphics **20**(12), 2063–2071 (2014)
6. Fortune, S.: A sweepline algorithm for Voronoi diagrams. Algorithmica **2**(1–4), 153 (1987). https://doi.org/10.1007/BF01840357
7. Görtler, J., Schulz, C., Weiskopf, D., Deussen, O.: Bubble treemaps for uncertainty visualization. IEEE Trans. Visual Comput. Graphics **24**(1), 719–728 (2018)
8. Gotz, D.: Dynamic Voronoi treemaps: a visualization technique for time-varying hierarchical data. Phys. Rev. A **30**(2), 150–156 (2011)
9. Graham, M., Kennedy, J.: A survey of multiple tree visualisation. Inf. Vis. **9**(4), 235–252 (2010)

10. Hahn, S., Trümper, J., Moritz, D., Döllner, J.: Visualization of varying hierarchies by stable layout of Voronoi treemaps. In: Proceedings of the IVAPP, pp. 50–58. IEEE (2014)

11. Kieffer, S., Dwyer, T., Marriott, K., Wybrow, M.: Hola: human-like orthogonal network layout. IEEE Trans. Visual Comput. Graphics 22(1), 349–358 (2016)

12. Leong, M.C., Prasad, D.K., Lee, Y.T., Lin, F.: Semi-CNN architecture for effective spatio-temporal learning in action recognition. Appl. Sci. 10(2), 557 (2020)

13. Lin, F.: Subspace learning and Hopfield neural networks in biomedical classification. Basic Clin. Pharmacol. Toxicol. 125, 144–145 (2019)

14. Ma, J., Wang, A., Lin, F., Wesarg, S., Erdt, M.: A novel robust kernel principal component analysis for nonlinear statistical shape modeling from erroneous data. Comput. Med. Imaging Graph. 77, 101638 (2019)

15. Nocaj, A., Brandes, U.: Computing Voronoi treemaps: faster, simpler, and resolution-independent. Comput. Graph. Forum 31, 855–864 (2012)

16. Schulz, H.J.: Treevis.net: a tree visualization reference. IEEE Comput. Graphics Appl. 6, 11–15 (2011)

17. Schulz, H.J., Hadlak, S., Schumann, H.: The design space of implicit hierarchy visualization: a survey. IEEE Trans. Visual Comput. Graphics 17(4), 393–411 (2011)

18. Shneiderman, B.: Tree visualization with tree-maps: 2-D space-filling approach. ACM Trans. Graph. 11(1), 92–99 (1992)

19. Shneiderman, B., Wattenberg, M.: Ordered treemap layouts. In: Proceedings of the INFOVIS, pp. 73–78. IEEE (2001)

20. Sud, A., Fisher, D., Lee, H.P.: Fast dynamic Voronoi treemaps. In: Proceedings of the ISVD, pp. 85–94. IEEE (2010)

21. Tennekes, M., de Jonge, E.: Tree colors: color schemes for tree-structured data. IEEE Trans. Visual Comput. Graphics 20(12), 2072–2081 (2014)

22. Tu, Y., Shen, H.W.: Visualizing changes of hierarchical data using treemaps. IEEE Trans. Visual Comput. Graphics 13(6), 1286–1293 (2007)

23. Wang, G., Nakanishi, T., Fukuda, A.: 2-D layout for tree visualization: a survey. In: Proceedings of the MATEC Web of Conferences, vol. 56. EDP Sciences (2016)

24. Wang, W., Wang, H., Dai, G., Wang, H.: Visualization of large hierarchical data by circle packing. In: Proceedings of the CHI, pp. 517–520. ACM (2006)

25. Wang, Y., Chen, L.: Two-dimensional residual-space-maximized packing. Expert Syst. Appl. 42(7), 3297–3305 (2015)

26. Wang, Y., Zhang, Q., Lin, F., Seah, H.S.: EngineQV: investigating external cause of engine failures based on geo-temporal association. In: 2019 IEEE Pacific Visualization Symposium (PacificVis), pp. 184–188. IEEE (2019)

27. Wood, J., Dykes, J.: Spatially ordered treemaps. IEEE Trans. Visual Comput. Graphics 14(6), 1348–1355 (2008)

CGI'20 Short Papers

Preserving Temporal Consistency in Videos Through Adaptive SLIC

Han Zhang[1], Riaz Ali[2], Bin Sheng[2(✉)], Ping Li[3], Jinman Kim[4], and Jihong Wang[5(✉)]

[1] Nanjing University of Aeronautics and Astronautics, Nanjing, People's Republic of China

[2] Shanghai Jiao Tong University, Shanghai, People's Republic of China
shengbin@sjtu.edu.cn

[3] The Hong Kong Polytechnic University, Hong Kong, People's Republic of China

[4] The University of Sydney, Sydney, Australia

[5] Shanghai University of Sport, Shanghai, People's Republic of China
wjh@sus.edu.cn

Abstract. The application of image processing techniques to individual frames of video often results in temporal inconsistency. Conventional approaches used for preserving the temporal consistency in videos have shortcomings as they are used for only particular jobs. Our work presents a multipurpose video temporal consistency preservation method that utilizes an adaptive simple linear iterative clustering (SLIC) algorithm. First, we locate the inter-frame correspondent pixels through the SIFT Flow and use them to find the respective regions. Then, we apply a multiframe matching statistical method to get the spatially or temporally correspondent frames. Besides, we devise a least-squares energy-based flickering-removing objective function by taking into account the inter-frame temporal consistency and inter-region spatial consistency jointly. The obtained results demonstrate the potential of the proposed method.

Keywords: Video processing · Adaptive SLIC · Temporal consistency

1 Introduction

Maintaining the temporal consistency is an essential task in video processing because the temporal consistency is one of the essential video features and has been used in different applications [15,16,18,22]. Temporal inconsistency results in artifacts, like unnatural inter-frame tonal changes or brightness fluctuations, which decrease the video quality significantly [11,23]. Although the flickers may not be easily observed when adjacent video frames are seen individually, they will be apparent when the video is played. Also, these artifacts adversely affect video matching tasks such as motion estimation [8,9]. Thus, preserving the video consistency is a crucial yet laborious problem in video processing.

H. Zhang and R. Ali—Contributed equally to this work.

© Springer Nature Switzerland AG 2020
N. Magnenat-Thalmann et al. (Eds.): CGI 2020, LNCS 12221, pp. 405–410, 2020.
https://doi.org/10.1007/978-3-030-61864-3_34

Some studies, like and [2], solve the temporal consistency problem in the form of energy minimization. Nevertheless, their applications are limited to removing flickers in intrinsic video decomposition. Lang et al. [10] eliminate the flickers through edge-aware filter employed in the temporal domain, but their method only deals with high-frequency perturbations. The technique of [7] removes flickers from video halftoning by using an error diffusion of temporal and spatial terms. The work of Dong et al. [5] uses non-flickering frames to rebuild the flickering frames. However, it is suited to eliminating flickers generated due to directly employing the image enhancement algorithm on a video. In [3], a frame is rebuilt from a neighboring frame to retain the inter-frame temporal consistency. However, it is not feasible because a video may not contain the same object continuously in adjacent frames [17]. Some authors have proposed compensation-based techniques that aim to eliminate the artifacts by aligning the inter-frame brightness or tonal level. In [19], the atmospheric light values are determined with the aid of the adaptive temporal average to eliminate the flickering effects. Farbman et al. [6] and Wang et al. [21] align the video frames by a specified number of designated *key* frames. After interpolating the transformation between the model video and the input video, the authors of [1] enhance the color grade by hand by choosing some key frames that can depict the transformation curve. However, these methods are limited because of requiring to select the key frames first.

In this paper, we propose a multipurpose flickering-removal and spatiotemporal consistency preservation technique. We develop an adaptive SLIC algorithm that creates superpixels from every frame. We also propose a multiframe matching statistical model to capture the frame that is correspondent to other frames temporally or spatially. First, our method matches the inter-frame corresponding pixels through the SIFT Flow [12] algorithm, and then, calculates the corresponding regions using those pixels. Lastly, we use the inter-frame corresponding regions and frame interval to match the corresponding frames. Because several studies have restored temporal coherence in videos with the help of least squares energy [14], we develop the objective function of temporal consistency in the form of least-squares energy comprising temporal and spatial consistencies terms. The former term preserves the inter-frame tonal or illumination variations consistency, and the latter term maintains the consistency in adjacent regions' difference of changes.

2 Methodology

Figure 1 illustrates the overview of our proposed technique. The following sections explain each of the steps.

Adaptive SLIC: The conventional SLIC manually computes the number of superpixels in a repetitive manner, which is a tedious task. We develop an adaptive SLIC algorithm that automatically produces the number of superpixels. We convert the RGB color to HSV color space because, for small color ranges, HSV

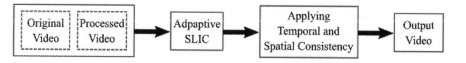

Fig. 1. Overview of the proposed method.

is perceptually uniform. In our experiments, we use the unequal interval to quantize the H, S, V values, and the average occurrence number to decide the number of superpixels.

Applying Temporal Consistency: We reproduce an output frame, denoted as P_x, from its temporally matching frames $f(P_x)$ to preserve the inter-frame coherence. Suppose P_x^k denotes the kth iteration's output frame, then the temporal consistency $F_t(P_x^k)$ can be calculated as Eq. (1):

$$
\begin{aligned}
F_t(P_x^k) = \mu(k) \cdot \sum_{I_m \in f^q(I_x)} \psi_t(I_x, I_m) \left\| P_x^k - \mathrm{warp}(P_m^{\alpha(k)}) \right\|^2 \\
+ \nu(k) \cdot \sum_{I_m \in f^s(I_x)} \psi_t(I_x, I_m) \left\| P_x^k - \mathrm{warp}(P_m^{\beta(k)}) \right\|^2
\end{aligned}
\tag{1}
$$

where I_x, $f(I_x)$, respectively, denote the actual frame and the set of its corresponding frames, I_m is the matching frame of the actual frame, $f^q(I_x)$ and $f^s(I_x)$ represent the sets of previous and subsequent matching frames of I_x, respectively. $\psi_t(I_x, I_m)$ denotes the temporal consistency weight, and the warped output frame from P_m^k is represented as $\mathrm{warp}(P_m^k)$, where $\mathrm{warp}()$ is a function that uses the optical flow [13] to recreate a resultant frame from its matching frame.

Applying Spatial Consistency: We calculate an output frame's spatial consistency in the kth iteration, as shown in Eq. (2):

$$
F_s(P_x^k) = \sum_{a=1}^{A_x} \sum_{\Upsilon_x^b \in \Omega(\Upsilon_x^a)} \psi_s(\Upsilon_x^a, \Upsilon_x^b) \left\| P_x^k - \mathrm{warp}(P_\xi^{\Gamma(x,\xi,k)}) \right\|^2
\tag{2}
$$

where A_x denotes the count of regions inside I_x. Υ_x^a and $\Omega(\Upsilon_x^a)$, respectively, represent a region and a set of its all adjacent regions. To preserve the inter-region spatial consistency, we decrease the change between the output frame and its respective spatially correspondent frame. Υ_x^b is an adjacent region of Υ_x^a, and the regions with the most matching pixels to Υ_x^b is denoted as $\hat{\Upsilon}_x^b$. I_ξ represents the frame containing the $\hat{\Upsilon}_x^b$. We retrieve P_x through warping its spatially matching output frame P_ξ. Therefore, to preserve the spatial consistency, we maintain the consistency in the adjacent regions' variation difference.

Combined Optimization: We optimize the output frame P_x by merging the temporal and spatial consistencies. Equation (3) shows the objective function comprising both the consistency terms

$$\arg\min_{P_x^k} \int [F_g(P_x^k) + \eta_1 F_t(P_x^k) + \eta_2 F_s(P_x^k)] \mathrm{d}u \qquad (3)$$

where u denotes the spatial location in I_x, η_1, and η_2 are, respectively, the weight functions of temporal consistency and spatial consistency.

3   Experimental Results

We have performed experiments on two datasets, SegTrack [20] and Chen and Corso [4]. Figure 2(a)–(c) shows the visual results of flickering removal by our method. The girl's neck and cheek region are darker in the processed video. It is evident that our method satisfactorily removes these effects.

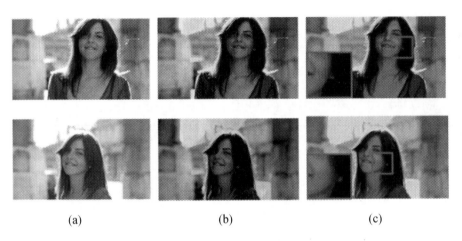

(a)   (b)   (c)

Fig. 2. The flickering removal results on the two frames of the CC video. (a)–(c) actual frame, processed frame, and the result of our approach, respectively.

4   Conclusion

In this paper, we present our proposed method of preserving temporal consistency in videos using adaptive SLIC. We employ the consistency to maintain the tonal shifts or illumination fluctuations constant among the adjacent regions. We find the regions through a new adaptive SLIC segmentation algorithm that uses the color details to automatically calculate the count of superpixels. The proposed temporal consistency solution outperforms previous techniques as our warping procedure comprises both; the spatial and temporal consistencies. The results obtained during the experiments demonstrate that our method provides satisfactory performance in video flickering-removal.

Acknowledgement. This work was supported in part by the National Key Research and Development Program of China under Grant 2018YFF0300903, in part by the National Natural Science Foundation of China under Grant 61872241 and Grant 61572316, and in part by the Science and Technology Commission of Shanghai Municipality under Grant 15490503200, Grant 18410750700, Grant 17411952600, and Grant 16DZ0501100.

References

1. Bonneel, N., Sunkavalli, K., Paris, S., Pfister, H.: Example-based video color grading. ACM Trans. Graph. **32**(4), 39:1–39:12 (2013)
2. Bonneel, N., Sunkavalli, K., Tompkin, J., Sun, D., Paris, S., Pfister, H.: Interactive intrinsic video editing. ACM Trans. Graph. **33**(6), 197:1–197:10 (2014)
3. Bonneel, N., Tompkin, J., Sunkavalli, K., Sun, D., Paris, S., Pfister, H.: Blind video temporal consistency. ACM Trans. Graph. **34**(6), 196:1–196:9 (2015)
4. Chen, A.Y.C., Corso, J.J.: Propagating multi-class pixel labels throughout video frames. In: Western New York Image Processing Workshop, pp. 14–17 (2010)
5. Dong, X., Bonev, B., Zhu, Y., Yuille, A.L.: Region-based temporally consistent video post-processing. In: IEEE Conference on Computer Vision and Pattern Recognition, pp. 714–722 (2015)
6. Farbman, Z., Lischinski, D.: Tonal stabilization of video. ACM Trans. Graph. **30**(4), 89:1–89:10 (2011)
7. Hsu, C.Y., Lu, C.S., Pei, S.C.: Video halftoning preserving temporal consistency. In: 2007 IEEE International Conference on Multimedia and Expo, pp. 1938–1941 (2007)
8. Kamel, A., Sheng, B., Yang, P., Li, P., Shen, R., Feng, D.D.: Deep convolutional neural networks for human action recognition using depth maps and postures. IEEE Trans. Syst. Man Cybern. Syst. **49**(9), 1806–1819 (2019)
9. Karambakhsh, A., Kamel, A., Sheng, B., Li, P., Yang, P., Feng, D.D.: Deep gesture interaction for augmented anatomy learning. Int. J. Inf. Manag. **45**, 328–336 (2019). https://doi.org/10.1016/j.ijinfomgt.2018.03.004. http://www.sciencedirect.com/science/article/pii/S0268401217308678
10. Lang, M., Wang, O., Aydin, T., Smolic, A., Gross, M.: Practical temporal consistency for image-based graphics applications. ACM Trans. Graph. **31**(4), 34:1–34:8 (2012)
11. Li, C., Chen, Z., Sheng, B., Li, P., He, G.: Video flickering removal using temporal reconstruction optimization. Multimedia Tools Appl. **79**, 4661–4679 (2019)
12. Liu, C., Yuen, J., Torralba, A.: SIFT flow: dense correspondence across scenes and its applications. IEEE Trans. Pattern Anal. Mach. Intell. **33**(5), 978–994 (2011)
13. Liu, C.: Beyond pixels: exploring new representations and applications for motion analysis. Ph.D. thesis, Massachusetts Institute of Technology, Cambridge, MA, USA (2009)
14. Mantiuk, R., Daly, S., Kerofsky, L.: Display adaptive tone mapping. ACM Trans. Graph. **27**(3), 1–10 (2008)
15. Meng, X., et al.: A video information driven football recommendation system. Comput. Electr. Eng. **85**, 106699 (2020). https://doi.org/10.1016/j.compeleceng.2020.106699
16. Müller, M., Zilly, F., Riechert, C., Kauff, P.: Spatio-temporal consistent depth maps from multi-view video. In: 2011 3DTV Conference: The True Vision - Capture, Transmission and Display of 3D Video (3DTV-CON), pp. 1–4 (2011)

17. Reso, M., Jachalsky, J., Rosenhahn, B., Ostermann, J.: Occlusion-aware method for temporally consistent superpixels. IEEE Trans. Pattern Anal. Mach. Intell. **41**, 1441–1454 (2019)
18. Sheng, B., Li, P., Zhang, Y., Mao, L.: GreenSea: visual soccer analysis using broad learning system. IEEE Trans. Cybern. 1–15 (2020). https://doi.org/10.1109/TCYB.2020.2988792
19. Shin, D.K., Kim, Y.M., Park, K.T., Lee, D.S., Choi, W., Moon, Y.S.: Video dehazing without flicker artifacts using adaptive temporal average. In: The 18th IEEE International Symposium on Consumer Electronics (ISCE 2014), pp. 1–2 (2014)
20. Tsai, D., Flagg, M., Nakazawa, A., Rehg, J.M.: Motion coherent tracking using multi-label MRF optimization. Int. J. Comput. Vision **100**(2), 190–202 (2012)
21. Wang, C.M., Huang, Y.H., Huang, M.L.: An effective algorithm for image sequence color transfer. Math. Comput. Model. **44**, 608–627 (2006)
22. Wang, Z., Chen, X., Zou, D.: Copy and paste: temporally consistent stereoscopic video blending. IEEE Trans. Circuits Syst. Video Technol. **28**(10), 3053–3065 (2018)
23. Zhang, P., Zheng, L., Jiang, Y., Mao, L., Li, Z., Sheng, B.: Tracking soccer players using spatio-temporal context learning under multiple views. Multimedia Tools Appl. **77**(15), 18935–18955 (2017). https://doi.org/10.1007/s11042-017-5316-3

Efficient Non-fused Winograd on GPUs

Hui Wei[1], Enjie Liu[1], Youbing Zhao[2(✉)], and Hongqing Yu[1]

[1] University of Bedfordshire, Luton, UK
19832599@qq.com
[2] Communication University of Zhejiang, Hangzhou, China

Abstract. This paper presents an optimized implementation for Winograd non-fused convolution. Our optimizations comprise application-independent grouped producer-consumer chains and a set of Winograd-specific software techniques, including specialized interface-kernels data format which enhances memory access efficiency; warp specialization and double buffer prefetching which effectively exploit computational resources and memory bandwidth; utilizing "shuffle" instruction which conserves hardware resources. The paper also provides supplementary explanation of Winograds' tile extraction, which saves memory and computing resources.

The proposed techniques has been evaluated head to head by kernel level in GTX 980 GPU, CUDA 9.2 with a wide range of parameters which meet CNN layers benchmark. Compared with the state-of-the-art Winograd Non-fused convolution in CuDnn 7.6.4 (released in Sept, 2019), our implementation achieves a total speedup of 1.64x.

Keywords: Convolutional neural network · Warp specialization · Producer-consumer

1 Introduction and Related Work

Deep Neural networks (Dnns) have recently attracted considerable attention. Convolutional neural networks (Cnns) are one of the most important Dnns because they have demonstrated state-of-the-art performance in many applications. However, with the trend of large input datasets and more complexity network structure, training Cnns is computationally expensive. Convolution layers are the most time-consuming part which occupies more than 80% of the total computation in many popular neural networks. cuDNN is a library used by most deep learning frameworks for efficient convolution processing on GPUs. It implements many convolution algorithms including the most popular algorithms: GEMM, FFT and Winograd [1]. The Winograd algorithm reduces multiplications by increasing in the number of additions. It is an efficient way to compute the convolution of small kernels with small input sizes. "Although Winograd requires 2.25 times less element-wise multiplications than the direct convolution, the straightforward implementation, in which each processing unit operates in isolation from the others, provides similar performance." [2].

N. Magnenat-Thalmann et al. (Eds.): CGI 2020, LNCS 12221, pp. 411–418, 2020.
https://doi.org/10.1007/978-3-030-61864-3_35

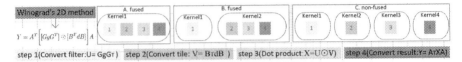

Fig. 1. Winograd's Fused (A and B)/Non-fused (C). The non-fused methods calculate each step in an independent GPU kernel.

The 2D Winograd's fused methods (Fig. 1B) may independently calculate step1 because the filter data is relatively small and is reused by all batches of input. However, it can also be integrated with other three steps in one kernel. Fused methods reduce data transfer significantly but step2 results cannot be used by multiple filters.

With non-fused methods, register pressure is reduced and each step uses tailored block/grid dimension (thread-data mapping). "For configurations with 3×3 filters, the cuDnn Winograd variants are the fastest algorithms in 74.6% of the configurations over other algorithms. For larger batch sizes, Winograd non-fused is clearly the fastest in most cases, where the rest of algorithms are about 50% slower" [3]. There remains a challenge to efficiently implement Winograd convolution on GPUs to deliver the full speedup as promised in theory. We reckon software techniques are required to address challenges, such as the efficiency of data transfers, data reusability issues and managing of the limited resources.

Xygkis et al. implemented fused winograd on edge devices by using data management techniques, Winograd-specific sharing and folding techniques [2]. Xiao et al. effectively implements Winograd on FPGA platform [4] GEMM related works include GEMM-based convolution [5] and fast implementation of DGEMM [6]. Jia et al. proposed a kernel fusion technique which enables better resource balancing and data reuse with minimized dependency overhead [7]. Yan et al. presented an optimized implementation on fused Winograd with their SASS assembler TuringAs that enables turning the performance at the native assembly level [8]. Singe [9] and CudaDMA [10] introduced warp specialization technique. Singe is a compiler that leverages warp specialization achieved up to 3.75x faster than previously optimized data-parallel GPU kernels. CudaDMA, an extensible API, that leveraging efficient inter-warp producer-consumer synchronization mechanisms and other techniques demonstrates speedup. In Sect. 2, the steps used in the proposed method are explained in detail, followed by evaluation and conclusion.

2 Proposed Method

Here we propose a non-fused 2D Winograd method, which improves occupancy and performance significantly compared to cuDnn 7.6.4. In the following subsections, the method is introduced in order of steps mentioned above. The most popular 3×3 filter (tile size $t = 4$) is used for the demonstration purpose.

2.1 Convert Filter (Step 1)

Compared with the input data, the filter data is relatively small in size, though with same number of channels. Despite that this step contributes only a small percentage to the total performance, the storing method and access pattern could make huge influence to the step 3: the dot product step, because each input tile needs to perform a dot product with all filter tiles.

Our observation is that matrix G [1] is small in size and has many zero entries, thus the matrix multiplication can be converted to additions and only 12 multiplications (Fig. 2A). Benefitting from this computational simplification, each thread can calculate one result f[x] independently from other threads without waiting for synchronization. Utilizing this simplification, each thread can be mapped directly to one output, improving efficiency of threads in a warp calculating the same f[x] using the same formula but with different filter inputs. In Fig. 2B "block definition", for example, threads in $warp_0$ are all responsible for calculating element f[0] and the first threads in all 16 warps are all responsible for calculating $filter_0$. In this way, warp threads execute the same instruction set concurrently to avoid thread divergence.

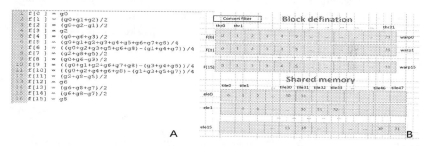

$$
\begin{aligned}
f[0] &= g0 \\
f[1] &= (g0+g1+g2)/2 \\
f[2] &= (g0+g2-g1)/2 \\
f[3] &= g2 \\
f[4] &= (g0+g6+g3)/2 \\
f[5] &= (g0+g1+g2+g3+g4+g5+g6+g7+g8)/4 \\
f[6] &= ((g0+g2+g3+g5+g6+g8)-(g1+g4+g7))/4 \\
f[7] &= (g2+g8+g5)/2 \\
f[8] &= (g0+g6-g3)/2 \\
f[9] &= ((g0+g1+g2+g6+g7+g8)-(g3+g4+g5))/4 \\
f[10] &= ((g0+g2+g4+g6+g8)-(g1+g3+g5+g7))/4 \\
f[11] &= (g2-g8-g5)/2 \\
f[12] &= g6 \\
f[13] &= (g6+g8+g7)/2 \\
f[14] &= (g6+g8-g7)/2 \\
f[15] &= g8
\end{aligned}
$$

Fig. 2. A. Filter formula. B. Thread-data mapping with shared memory access pattern.

Filter data initially comes with layout NCHW (batch **N**, channels **C**, height **H** and width **W**). Threads are reshaped in warps to read global memory coalescing and store data in the shared memory for reuse. When saving the filter data in the shared memory, if we put the same indexed element from different tiles in the same column, threads in the same warp need to access address in the same bank, which may lead to serious bank conflicts. The problem still exists at the calculation stage, elements of the input filter are used multiple times (exp: g0 is used 9 times) during t × t result calculation. As shared memory space in this step is not a limited resource (even if we use 2D [16][32 + 16] shared memory for 16 × 32 threads where 16 is the $tileSize^2$), to solve the problem, the extra 16 columns of shared memory are used for padding to avoid bank conflicts ("shared memory" in Fig. 2B). This pattern assures load/store bank-conflict-free. When the calculation finishes the result is stored in 1D texture memory in a tile united CHWN layout to help loading in step 3 in Fig. 4A.

2.2 Convert Tiles (Step 2)

We noticed that matrix B [1] has the same size as a tile. With a given m output and r filter size, tile size t is computed by (m − r + 1). With Winograd, tile extraction is different from direct convolution with a given stride. The direct convolution slides a filter through each tile on a feature map by the number of stride elements, while the Winograd method slide filter by WT_{stride} elements which is explained below.

Extract Tiles. The [1] method mentioned "Each image channel is divided into tiles of size $(m + r - 1) \times (m + r - 1)$, with $r - 1$ elements of overlap between neighbouring tiles, yielding $P = \lceil H/m \rceil \lceil W/m \rceil$ tiles per channel". This is not true in some cases. For $F(m, r)$ we summarized some direct convolution stride (T_{stride}) and Winograd tile stride (WT_{stride}) pairs in format $F(m, r)$-$[T_{stride}, WT_{stride}]$ as follows: $F(2,3)$- [1, 2], [2], [3]; $F(3,2)$- [1, 3], [2, 4], [3]; $F(4,3)$- [1, 4], [2, 4], [3, 6]. We can see WT_{stride} could be bigger than r. That means less tiles extracted result with less computation and less memory. This is important for improving hardware resources efficiency and performance.

Synchronize Tasks. Each thread is mapped to one output element so that each thread calculates $ai, j = \sum_{t=1}^{T}(U\,i, t \odot Tt, j)$ and then $bi, j = \sum_{t=1}^{T}(a\,i, t \odot Vt, j)$, where U_i is the ith row vector of B^T and V_j is the jth column vector of B. So that each thread only calculates $2 * t$ times multiplication. Assuming the input feature map has size in multiples of 32, we can process 32 column data for each block of the kernel. This facilities memory access to achieve coalescing and avoids bank conflicts. This step can be split into 4 tasks: A. load the original layout (NCHW) input feature map into the first shared memory. B. expand each tile from overlap and calculate $a_{i,j}$ from A and store intermediate results to the second shared memory. C. calculate $b_{i,j}$ from B and store result back to the second shared memory. D. output result to devices from C. These 4 tasks form a producer-consumer chain. The overlapped data in the first shared memory can be reused by the next chain.

We use warp-specialized program to separate memory operations from arithmetic, by assigning individual warps a different task. To ensure these tasks run in parallel with properly synchronized data, 4 producer-consumer chains/iterations are used for the calculation of the 10 row data in the whole block. To prevent the warps' execution from being blocked by too many "synchronization" instructions, grouped producer-consumer chains (Fig. 3A) using "named barriers" in PTX are designed to reduce synchronization and achieve data safety.

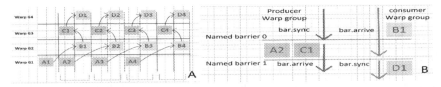

Fig. 3. A. Illustrates data dependent relations between tasks are mapped onto 4 warp groups. B. Illustrates the use of 2 named barriers to synchronize 4 tasks.

In Fig. 3B, 2 named barriers are used in each iteration. Before each iteration starts, task A has already been completed in previous iteration or initialization. Consequently, in the consumer warp groups, the first task executing before named barrier0 by consumers' *bar.arrive* instruction is task B. When calling *bar.sync*, the producer warp groups block and wait at the named barrier0 until the consumer has called *bar.arrive*, which informs all producers that task B is ready and it is safe to write new data in. Task A does not depend on any other tasks and task B in the same iterator does not depend on task A either. The producer starts working on task A and C as soon as the named barrier0 receives the signal from consumer. Then it emits a signal after finishing task A and C by named barrier1 with a *bar.arrive* instruction. Then task D in consumer knows task C has finished and the data is ready for output. At the point task A for the next iteration is also ready. As task D is not followed by the other tasks, the producer and consumer end their relationship and two named barriers are safely recycled for reuse in the next iteration as they are limited resources. The output from step 2 is a tile united 2D array in the order of CHWN (the same as the filter data).

2.3 Dot Product (Step 3)

In this step software prefetching is utilized to hide the latency of moving large chunks of converted tiles in the memory. We also borrowed the idea from blocked GEMM because each input tile is accessed by all filter tiles in the same channel while each filter tile is used by all input tiles in the same channel. Threads in a block collaboratively load data from off-chip global memory to on-chip shared memory and have shared access. As one thread is only responsible for calculating one output, both availability of registers and shared memory for one block become bottlenecks free.

Assuming the total number of channels C is a multiple of "blkChannel" (=32/t), with a 32 × 32 thread block, each block can handle 8 (t = 4) channels of both input and filter data if all threads are fully loaded. We calculate all channels of accumulation by cB = C/blkChannel times iterator (Fig. 4A).

Unlike GEMM, calculation starts after all threads in the block finishes loading. Software prefetching is used to hide the long data transfer latency as calculation in each channel is independent from each other. All threads in a block can start calculating even with only one channel data: 8 tiles of input and 8 tiles of the filter.

Double buffering (Fig. 4B) is used for data transfer to ensure the computing threads always have available data to compute on one of the two buffers. As the global memory latency is about 100 times of that of the shared memory operations, it is important to hide the latency of global memory operations.

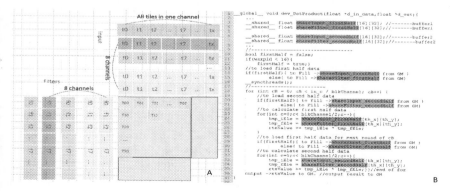

Fig. 4. A. Tile united GEMM (each cube denotes a tile). B. Double buffer prefetching.

As two computation tasks operate on different buffers, the thread scheduler can overlap computing with memory operations. Our prefetching optimization eliminates much of the threads' wait time on the global memory, thus making full utilization of execution resources and prevents threads being stalled on global memory access.

2.4 Convert the Result Tile (Step 4)

One thread is mapped to one tile to generate 4 element outputs. And the calculation is simplified to additions by unfolding multiplication of two matrices because matrix A [1] only contains $(1, 0, -1)$ (Fig. 5A).

However, after each thread has calculated 4 outputs, the outputs directly from registers alone cannot achieve coalescing due to continuous thread access stride address. Big chunk of extra shared memory can be an obstacle that lowers occupancy. Shuffle instruction is a way of exchanging data in a warp, by which any threads can read other threads' registers in the same warp.

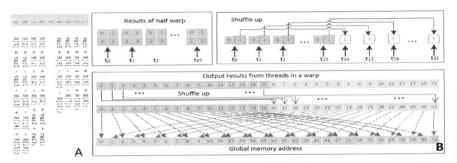

Fig. 5. A. Simplified fomula. B. Shuffle instruction. This figure focus on outputting results calculated by the first half warp threads. They produce 2 × 32 results which need two shuffle up instructions to output these results by leveraging the second half warp threads. This figure only shows one instruction for first line (red) results. Benefits from instruction shuffling include no use of shared memory, reduced index calculation and free from synchronization. (Color figure online)

3 Evaluation

Our kernel level head to head evaluation on optimized Winograd non-fuse convolution is run by wide range of 3 × 3 convolution layer configurations. Kernel running time is collected using nvprof (CUDA profilter) and kernel matrices are collected by nvvp (Nvida visual profiler). We use the most popular 3 × 3 filter with a stride of 1 and use NCHW as the data layout for input/output - the same as CuDnn. Factors not involved in calculation are not shown in each chart, like batch size and input width in chart A, filter number in B and channel number in D. In A, both number of filters and channels show our method outperformed the Cudnn's. Batch and width contribute to show our vantage in B. Width and channels show significant advantage of ours in C. In D, both filter number and width give obvious advantage over Cudnn.

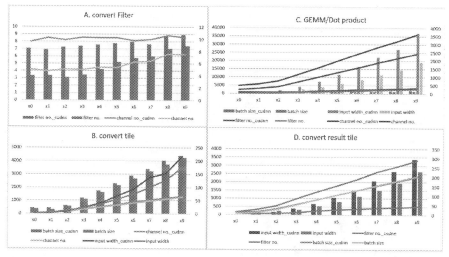

Fig. 6. The evaluation to 4 kernels batch size. The unit of Y axis is in μs (microsecond). Due to the limitation of device memory, parameters in form of "**batch-width-filters-channels**" are values range of "8, 16, 32, 64, 96, 128, 160, 192, 224, 256" for number of filters, channels and batch size. Width (the same as height) is "1, 2, 4, 6, 8, 10, 12, 14, 16, 18" times of 32. These values are commonly used for benchmarking convolution performance. We use "1-1-x-16" for filter attended evaluations, "x-1-8-8" for batch size attended evaluations, "8-x-8-8" for width attended evaluations and "4-2-8-x" for channel attended evaluations where x is a value from the range aforementioned. In this way, we can show performance of each step that affected by multiple factors in one chart by unified variable x in X axis. We use dual y-Axis to show y values to better illustrate tiny difference. Values shown in lines are measured by the right Y axis while those in columns are measured by the left.

4   Conclusion

In the 12 comparisons shown in Fig. 6, our method shows significant improvements over Cudnn winograd non-fuse method in 9 comparisons and only 3 (filter no. in chart C, batch size in D and channel no. in B) show insignificant improvements. In general, our method achieves speedup of 1.64x in total and 1.62x(A), 1.17x(B), 1.77x(C), 1.36x(D) individually. Benefiting from fully coalescing, data reuse, efficient thread-data mapping and suffering no bank conflicts, our method reduces register usage which leads to higher occupancy. To conclude, our major performance improvement has been achieved by the producer-consumer model which enables memory and math operations simultaneously and double buffer prefetching.

References

1. Lavin, A., Gray, S.: Fast algorithms for convolutional neural networks. In: Proceedings of the CVPR 2016, pp. 4013–4021 (2016)
2. Xygkis, A., Soudris, D., Papadopoulos, L., Yous, S., Moloney, D.: Efficient winograd-based convolution kernel implementation on edge devices. In: 55th DAC, pp. 1–6 (2018)

3. Jordà, M., Valero-Lara, P., Peña, A.J.: Performance evaluation of cuDNN convolution algorithms on NVIDIA Volta GPUs. IEEE Access **7**, 70461–70473 (2019)
4. Xiao, Q., Liang, Y., Lu, L., Yan, S., Tai, Y.W.: Exploring heterogeneous algorithms for accelerating deep convolutional neural networks on FPGAs. In: Proceedings of the 54th Annual Design Automation Conference, p. 62. ACM (2017)
5. Abdelfattah, A., Haidar, A., Tomov, S., Dongarra, J.: Performance, design, and autotuning of batched GEMM for GPUs. In: Kunkel, J.M., Balaji, P., Dongarra, J. (eds.) ISC High Performance 2016. LNCS, vol. 9697, pp. 21–38. Springer, Cham (2016). https://doi.org/10.1007/978-3-319-41321-1_2
6. Tan, G., Li, L., Triechle, S., Phillips, E., Bao, Y., Sun, N.: Fast implementation of DGEMM on Fermi GPU. In: HiPC, Networking, Storage and Analysis, pp. 1–11 (2011)
7. Jia, L., Liang, Y., Li, X., Lu, L., Yan, S.: Enabling efficient fast convolution algorithms on GPUs via MegaKernels. IEEE Trans. Comput. **69**(7), 986–997 (2020)
8. Yan, D., Wang, W., Chu, X.: Optimizing batched winograd convolution on GPUs. In: PPoPP, Main Conference (2020)
9. Michael, B., Sean, T., Alex, A.: Singe: leveraging warp specialization for high performance on GPUs. In: ACM SIGPLAN Notices, pp. 119–130 (2014)
10. Bauer, M., et al.: CudaDMA: optimizing GPU memory bandwidth via warp specialization. In: HiPC, Networking Storage and Analysis (2011)

ENGAGE Full Papers

Surface Fitting Using Dual Quaternion Control Points with Applications in Human Respiratory Modelling

Alex Grafton$^{(\boxtimes)}$ [ID] and Joan Lasenby [ID]

Department of Engineering, University of Cambridge, Cambridge CB2 1PZ, UK
{ajg206,jl221}@cam.ac.uk

Abstract. In this paper we present a method for representing surfaces using a set of dual quaternion control points, with the goal of fitting to point clouds. Each control point is defined by a position and radius, which specify the area of the surface it affects, and a dual quaternion defining the transformation it applies. A point is mapped using the surface by a weighted sum of the control points, in a similar method to dual quaternion skinning. A surface is then represented as the transformation of an original surface, such as a unit square plane, using the control points. We demonstrate how we may fit surfaces to point clouds using a modified iterative gradient descent algorithm, adding control points to regions of the surface that are most poorly modelled at the current step. These methods are applied to the problem of representing human breathing by fitting surfaces to a subject's chest as recorded by an RGB-D (image plus depth) camera and parameterizing the breathing using each control point's parameters. Variations in the breathing pattern are shown before and after exercise.

Keywords: Dual quaternions · Clifford algebra · Surface modelling · Respiration

1 Introduction

In this paper we examine how we may fit dual quaternion control point surfaces to point clouds measured from the human chest. Point clouds are recorded for each frame of an RGB-D video recording (image plus depth) before and after exercise, with the goal of characterizing differences in the respiratory pattern.

This paper is structured as follows. Section 2 presents related work on dual quaternions and control point surface fitting from which we build our surface representation, gradient descent processes from which we optimize the parameters of our surface, and existing respiratory pattern measurement. Section 3 discusses the dual quaternions and how our surface is formed. In Sect. 4 we demonstrate how we may fit a surface to a point cloud, by unwrapping a point cloud measurement of a surface into a parameterized plane, then finding the control point locations. In Sect. 5 we fit surfaces to successive point cloud frames from an

© Springer Nature Switzerland AG 2020
N. Magnenat-Thalmann et al. (Eds.): CGI 2020, LNCS 12221, pp. 421–433, 2020.
https://doi.org/10.1007/978-3-030-61864-3_36

RGB-D video recording to interpret the variation in control point parameters over time. In Sect. 6 we show how the behaviour of control point parameters differs in normal and post-exercise breathing.

2   Related Work

Dual Quaternions. Dual quaternions were introduced in [1], and may be used to describe a rigid-body transformation in 3D space. A solution to the skinning problem - the process of deforming a model using a skeleton shape - was proposed using dual quaternions in [2]. Using a weighted sum of dual quaternions produces a high-quality approximation to spherical linear interpolation [3]. [5] uses radial basis functions to deform a shape around a control handle. [4] demonstrates the interpolation path of a *rotor* in Conformal Geometric Algebra.

Gradient Descent. The study of gradient descent optimization has greatly increased in popularity due to the training of deep neural networks. Some of the most popular algorithms are implemented in the Keras library [6], and include: gradient descent with momentum [7], where a momentum parameter helps the optimizer ignore noise in the loss function and escape from local minima; Adagrad [8] uses parameter specific descent rates that adjust to parameters that are rarely updated; Adam [9] computes adaptive learning rates using momentum-like averages of past gradients and gradients-squared. AdaMax is an extension of Adam that uses the infinity-norm of past gradients, rather than the 2-norm. Stochastic gradient descent and Mini-batch gradient descent [10] use subsets of the training data, which may be single samples, and updates on each subset. This leads to fluctuating loss functions but the noise provides the ability to escape local minima. This also helps avoid the inefficient process of training on similar training data, such as nearby points in a point cloud.

Respiratory Analysis. Lung function can be characterized by single measurements such as respiratory rate [11,12], and peak flow [13], measured using equipment such as peak flow meters, electrocardiograms and photoplethysmography. Other measurements include time-domain analysis via flow-volume loops or capnography. Using an RGB-D camera for measurement of anterior chest/abdominal wall movement is an extension of Structured Light Plethysmography, [14] which has been demonstrated to show differences between Healthy and COPD patients [15]. Our RGB-D camera [16] uses a structured light method for producing the depth image, albeit with a much finer grid.

3   Surface Representation

We first briefly describe the dual quaternion algebra. A dual quaternion is the combination of quaternions $\mathbf{q} = w + x\mathbf{i} + y\mathbf{j} + z\mathbf{k}$ and the dual numbers $a + b\epsilon$.

In this paper we denote dual quaternions using tildes, $\tilde{\mathbf{q}} = \mathbf{q}_0 + \epsilon\mathbf{q}_1$ where $\mathbf{q}_0$, $\mathbf{q}_1$ are quaternions, $\epsilon \neq 0$ and $\epsilon^2 = 0$. The representation of various operations in the dual quaternion algebra are given below:

Operation	Representation
Point $\mathbf{p} = x\mathbf{e}_i + y\mathbf{e}_j + z\mathbf{e}_k$ in $\mathbb{R}^3$	$\tilde{\mathbf{q}} = 1 + \epsilon\bar{\mathbf{p}}$ where $\bar{\mathbf{p}} = x\mathbf{i} + y\mathbf{j} + \mathbf{k}$
Rotation by angle θ about axis $\hat{\mathbf{n}}$	$\tilde{\mathbf{q}} = \cos\frac{\theta}{2} + \sin\frac{\theta}{2}\hat{\mathbf{n}} + \epsilon 0$
Translation by $\mathbf{t} \in \mathbb{R}^3$	$\tilde{\mathbf{q}} = 1 + \epsilon\frac{\mathbf{t}}{2}$
Successive transformations $\tilde{\mathbf{q}}_a$, $\tilde{\mathbf{q}}_b$, $\tilde{\mathbf{q}}_c$	$\tilde{\mathbf{q}} = \tilde{\mathbf{q}}_c\tilde{\mathbf{q}}_b\tilde{\mathbf{q}}_a$
Rotation by θ about $\hat{\mathbf{n}}$ and origin $\mathbf{c}$	$(1 + \epsilon\frac{\bar{\mathbf{c}}}{2})(\cos\frac{\theta}{2} + \sin\frac{\theta}{2}\hat{\mathbf{n}})(1 - \epsilon\frac{\bar{\mathbf{c}}}{2})$
Conjugate $\tilde{\mathbf{q}}^*$	$\tilde{\mathbf{q}}^* = \mathbf{q}_0^* - \epsilon\mathbf{q}_1^*$
Application of transformation $\tilde{\mathbf{q}}$	$\tilde{\mathbf{p}}' = \tilde{\mathbf{q}}\tilde{\mathbf{p}}\tilde{\mathbf{q}}^*$

Our surface representation method is formed in a similar method to dual quaternion skinning; we define a set of control points $\{C_i\}$ that represent the surface. Each control point has the following parameters: its position vector, $\mathbf{c}_i$; its 2×2 radius matrix, Σ_i, represented by the three non-zero parameters of the matrix's Cholesky factorization; its dual quaternion transformation $\tilde{\mathbf{q}}_i$. The transformation is formed from five parameters $(r_x, r_y, t_x, t_y, t_z)$ to represent rotations with origin $\mathbf{c}_i$ followed by a translation made of five successive transformations, $\tilde{\mathbf{q}}_{ij}, j = 1 - 5$:

$\tilde{\mathbf{q}}_{i1} = 1 - \frac{1}{2}\epsilon\bar{\mathbf{c}}_i$	Translation by $-\mathbf{c}_i$
$\tilde{\mathbf{q}}_{i2} = \cos\left(\frac{1}{2}r_{ix}\right) + \sin\left(\frac{1}{2}r_{ix}\right)\mathbf{i}$	Rotation by r_{ix} about $\mathbf{e}_i$
$\tilde{\mathbf{q}}_{i3} = \cos\left(\frac{1}{2}r_{iy}\right) + \sin\left(\frac{1}{2}r_{iy}\right)\mathbf{j}$	Rotation by r_{iy} about $\mathbf{e}_j$
$\tilde{\mathbf{q}}_{i4} = 1 + \frac{1}{2}\epsilon\bar{\mathbf{c}}_i$	Translation by $\mathbf{c}_i$
$\tilde{\mathbf{q}}_{i5} = 1 + \frac{1}{2}\epsilon\mathbf{t}_i$	Translation by $\mathbf{t}_i$

We specify a weight function $w(\mathbf{p}_j, \mathbf{c}_i, \Sigma_i)$ as a radial basis function that defines the weight of control point C_i acting on point $\mathbf{p}_j$, which is denoted w_{ij} as shorthand:

$$w(\mathbf{p}_j, \mathbf{c}_i, \Sigma_i) = \exp\left(-\frac{1}{2}(\mathbf{p}_j - \mathbf{c}_i)^T\Sigma_i^{-1}(\mathbf{p}_j - \mathbf{c}_i)\right) = w_{ij} \qquad (1)$$

Each control point has global support. While this is potentially expensive as the number of control points increases, it provides a smooth operation for differentiating, especially if we wish to alter the position of control points without needing to reassign surface points to control points. The transformation dual quaternion for a point $\mathbf{p}_j$ is given by:

$$\tilde{\mathbf{q}}_j = \left(\sum_i w_{ij} \tilde{\mathbf{q}}_i \right) \bigg/ \left(\sum_i w_{ij} \right) \tag{2}$$

The denominator ensures we produce a normalized dual quaternion specifying a rigid body transformation. The normal at a transformed point $\mathbf{p}'_j$ in $\mathbb{R}^3$ is

$$\mathbf{n}_j = \frac{\partial \mathbf{p}'_j}{\partial \mathbf{u}} \times \frac{\partial \mathbf{p}'_j}{\partial \mathbf{v}} \tag{3}$$

The partial derivatives specify the direction $\mathbf{p}'_j$ moves as $\mathbf{p}_j$ moves in each direction $\mathbf{u}$ and $\mathbf{v}$, which are distinct directions lying in the tangent plane to the original surface at point $\mathbf{p}_j$. In the fitting examples that follow, we use the unit square in the $\mathbf{e}_i$-$\mathbf{e}_j$ plane as our original surface, and as such $\mathbf{u} = \mathbf{e}_i$ and $\mathbf{v} = \mathbf{e}_j$.

4   Static Fitting

In this section we demonstrate how we may fit these surfaces to a point cloud. As our surface representation is based on the transformation of an original surface, we require that every point in the cloud has a corresponding point on the original surface. Our application involves data captured using an RGB-D camera where point clouds are reconstructed using inverse projection of the depth image, so we can use $(x, y) = (u, v)$. This is not the case for other point clouds, for multiple reasons. The shape may not be suitable for projection, the projection plane may not be obvious, or the point cloud may be combined from multiple calibrated RGB-D cameras, with their own projection planes. This is a two-part problem: point cloud to local co-ordinates and uv-unwrapping of the local co-ordinates to a 2D plane. We present a simple algorithm for this process here, suitable for open surfaces. A review of related work in this area may be found in [17].

4.1   Unwrapping Point Clouds

For our unwrapping algorithm, we first define notation. Points $\mathbf{p}_i$ are the points in the cloud in $\mathbb{R}^3$. They are mapped to co-ordinates u_i, v_i, in the $\mathbb{R}^2$ parameter space. The derivatives of $\mathbf{p}$ with respect to u and v evaluated at point $\mathbf{p}_i$ are denoted $\mathbf{u}_i$ and $\mathbf{v}_i$ - these are 3D vectors describing the direction taken in $\mathbb{R}^3$ when moving in the parameter space. The energy of the unwrapping is defined as the sum of five sub-energies describing desirable properties of the unwrapping:

$$E = aE_{\text{unit}} + bE_{\text{perp}} + cE_{\text{scale}} + dE_{\text{normal}} + eE_{\text{far}}$$

$$E_{\text{unit}} = \sum_i (|\mathbf{u}_i| - 1)^2 + (|\mathbf{v}_i| - 1)^2$$

$$E_{\text{perp}} = \sum_i (\mathbf{u}_i \cdot \mathbf{v}_i)^2$$

$$E_{\text{scale}} = \sum_{i,j} \lambda_{ij} \left[((\mathbf{p}_i - \mathbf{p}_j) \cdot \mathbf{u}_j - (u_i - u_j))^2 + ((\mathbf{p}_i - \mathbf{p}_j) \cdot \mathbf{v}_j - (v_i - v_j))^2 \right]$$

$$E_{\text{normal}} = \sum_{i,j} \lambda_{ij} \left[(\mathbf{p}_i - \mathbf{p}_j) \cdot (\mathbf{u}_i \times \mathbf{v}_i) \right]^2$$

$$E_{\text{far}} = \sum_{i,j} \mu_{ij} (\mathbf{p}_i - \mathbf{p}_j)^2$$

where a to e are scaling terms, empirically tuned to 0.05, 0.02, 0.002, 0.002, 0.002 respectively in our example. λ_{ij} is a Gaussian radial basis function, scale σ, based on the distance between $\mathbf{p}_i$ and $\mathbf{p}_j$. μ_{ij} the same, but based on the distance between (u_i, v_i) and (u_j, v_j). The σ parameter is dependent on the density of the cloud. As some energies are defined per-point and others per-point-pair, the scales should vary with the number of points in the cloud.

E_{unit} requires that the vectors $\mathbf{u}_i$ and $\mathbf{v}_i$ are unit magnitude; E_{perp} requires that they are perpendicular. E_{scale} ensures that the distance between two points in $u - v$ space is the same as the distance along the directions $\mathbf{u}_i$ and $\mathbf{v}_i$ in $\mathbb{R}^3$. E_{normal} ensures that points $\mathbf{p}_i$ and $\mathbf{p}_j$ are in a plane whose normal is given by $\mathbf{u}_i \times \mathbf{v}_i$. E_{scale} and E_{normal} are only expected to be small when $\mathbf{p}_i$ and $\mathbf{p}_j$ are close to each other, hence the introduction of λ_{ij}. Finally, E_{far} ensures that points that are close together in u-v (specified by μ_{ij}) are close together in $\mathbb{R}^3$. This helps prevent the surface from wrapping around itself in parameter space.

In addition to appropriate selection of σ, the initial conditions of the optimization are important. In the example that follows, we set $\mathbf{u}_i = \mathbf{k}$ and $\mathbf{v}_i = \mathbf{i}$. However, we may also initialise randomly and optimize on a few clustered points in the cloud, expanding gradually. Otherwise it is possible that two parts of the surface optimize differently - e.g. with $\mathbf{u}$ pointing in opposite directions - and find a local minimum. Our example surface is an S-shape which does not support projection.

Figure 1 shows the surface to be unwrapped and the optimized $\mathbf{u}_i$ and $\mathbf{v}_i$ directions. The directions lie in the tangent plane to the surface; this is demonstrated in the lower part of the surface using the view angles chosen. The unwrapped u-v mesh is shown in Fig. 2. The grid is drawn to aid visualization - it should not cross over itself, and after 300 iterations does not - and is not known to the algorithm.

4.2   Fitting Using Gradient Descent

In this section we adapt standard gradient descent methods to fit our surface representation to these points. We consider two types of surface - those generated by randomly selecting control point parameters, and a representation of the human chest. The chest representation is defined over the unit square in x and y, and in metre depth in z. The quality of a fit is measured using mean-square reconstruction error for each point. For each surface, we fit 10 parameters per control point - its position in 2D space (c_x, c_y), its translation (t_x, t_y, t_z), its

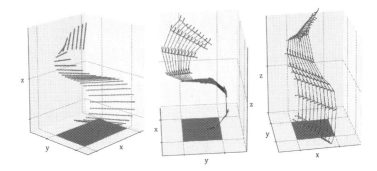

Fig. 1. Left: surface to be unwrapped, with the original unit square shown in grey - the mesh shown is used to check that the unwrapping has been successful, and is not part of the input or output of the algorithm. Middle and Right: $\mathbf{u}_i$ and $\mathbf{v}_i$ at points in the surface, shown from two angles to demonstrate that the resulting directions are in the tangent plane of the surface.

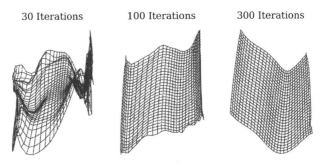

Fig. 2. Unwrapped surface in u-v co-ordinates during optimization. All u_i, v_i are initialized at 0. After 300 iterations, the grid does not cross over itself.

rotation about the x- and y- axes (r_x, r_y) and the three non-zero parameters of its radius matrix's Cholesky factorization $(\sigma_a, \sigma_b, \sigma_c)$.

Using standard gradient descent to optimize the parameters of control points has problems: the converged solution is highly dependent on initial conditions and the result of optimization varies greatly with descent rate as the surface has many local minima. Demonstrations of these issues are shown in Fig. 3. Three descent schemes are considered. Plain gradient descent (GD), gradient descent with momentum (GDM) and adaptive moment gradient descent (ADAM). These algorithms are summarized as follows, where θ_t denotes the parameters at iteration t and g_t denotes the gradient of the parameters with respect to a mean-square-error cost function at iteration t.

Gradient Descent:

$$\theta_{t+1} = \theta_t - \alpha g_t$$

Gradient Descent with Momentum:

$$\hat{g}_t = m\hat{g}_{t-1} + (1-m)g_t \qquad \theta_{t+1} = \theta_t - \alpha\hat{g}_t$$

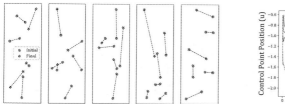 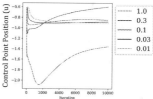

Fig. 3. Demonstration of the dependence of the optimization solution on initialization and parameters. Left: Each box shows a unit square within which the controls points move to different solutions. Right: Movement of control point c_x during optimization when initialization is identical but descent rate, in legend, is varied.

ADAM:

$$m_t = \beta_1 m_{t_1} + (1 - \beta_1)g_t \qquad v_t = \beta_2 v_{t-1} + (1 - \beta_2)g_t^2$$

$$\hat{m}_t = \frac{m_t}{1 - \beta_1^t} \qquad \hat{v}_t = \frac{v_t}{1 - \beta_2^t} \qquad \theta_{t+1} = \theta_t - \frac{\alpha}{\sqrt{\hat{v}_t} + \epsilon}\hat{m}_t$$

where m_t, v_t, $\hat{m}_t$, $\hat{v}_t$ and $\hat{g}_t$ are intermediate values. Each method has a descent rate parameter α; GDM introduces a momentum parameter m; ADAM introduces β_1, β_2 and ϵ which will be left at their defaults of 0.9, 0.999 and 10^{-8} respectively based on the recommendations in [9].

These descent schemes are tested by randomly generating control points over a unit square. Control point transformations and weight radii are controlled to ensure non-self-intersecting surfaces are produced. Noise is added to each of the points; costs are scaled so that a cost of 1.0 represents the mean-square-error of the noisy surface to the original. The median and median absolute deviation (MAD) of the cost over all generated surfaces is shown in Fig. 4. We note that (a) gradient descent has very high MAD, indicating that it often fails to find a good solution; (b) ADAM reaches a good solution much faster than GDM; (c) examining the mean and standard deviation show that the standard deviation (not shown) is much higher than MAD for gradient descent, indicating that gradient descent finds poor solutions much more frequently. While ADAM reaches a low cost quickly, GDM provides a better solution.

It is possible that point clouds have a vast number of points and including every point in the optimization may by computationally prohibitive. The previous experiment is repeated where each point has a probability p of being included in the optimization; the number of iterations is increased by $1/p$ times to compare equivalent computation costs. Mean costs for varying p are shown in Fig. 5. The ADAM optimizer performs worse as p decreases and the solution fluctuates much more. GDM performs much better overall, with $p = 0.2$ producing the best result out of those tested. For lower p, the cost appears noisier. GDM, with $m = 0.8$, $\alpha = 1.0$ and $p = 0.2$ will be used for fitting.

Having found a set of optimization parameters that perform well across multiple surfaces, we now address the issue of multiple local optima. Computing an optimization using these parameters produces the fit shown in Fig. 6. 13 control

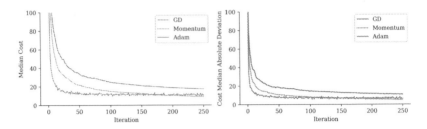

Fig. 4. Median and median absolute deviation of cost, averaged over multiple surface fits.

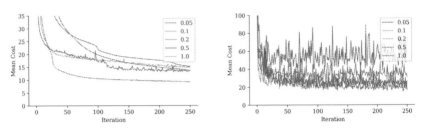

Fig. 5. Optimization using random mini-batches and gradient descent with momentum (left) and ADAM (right), with different mini-batch inclusion probabilities, shown in the legend.

points were used; this number was manually selected by inspecting the resulting surfaces. The fit has failed to capture the creases in the subject's jumper. Instead, we initially fit a surface using four control points, then add further control points one-by-one until we reach the desired number. These control points are added at the position in the u-v space that is modelled worse by the surface. This method is described as follows:

1. Fit an initial surface, using 4 control points and n_1 iterations.
2. Add a control point at the worst-fit location in the surface. Determine the worst fit by using a weighted sum of errors around each point.
3. Fit using the new surface for n_2 iterations.
4. Repeat steps 2 and 3 until all desired control points have been added.
5. Continue to fit for n_3 subsequent iterations or until convergence.

By targeting the worst-fit areas of the surface, we hope to avoid initialization-dependent local minima. The cost during fitting and the reduction in cost from adding additional control points, which provides a measure of how useful each control point is, are shown in Fig. 7, where $n_1 = 1000$, $n_2 = 3000$ and $n_3 = 9000$.

The standard fitter is run for the same total number of iterations, and is surpassed by the targeted fitter once it has a total of 10 control points. The surfaces that result from each step are shown in side view in Fig. 8; this method has successfully modelled the creases.

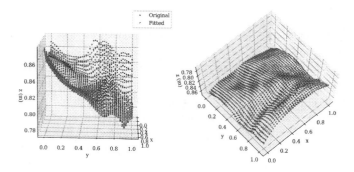

Fig. 6. Fitting of a chest surface using GDM from two angles. The fit is generally good, but does not capture the creases in the subject's jumper, visible at $y = 0.65$ and $y = 0.87$.

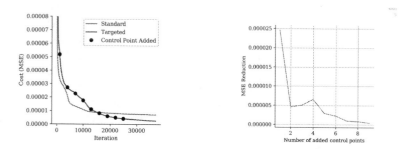

Fig. 7. Left: Comparison of cost at each iteration using standard and targeted fitting. Dots indicate where control points are added. Right: Reduction in cost from adding each control point.

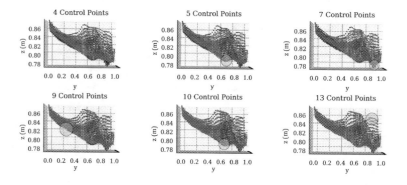

Fig. 8. Fitted surfaces in side view after adding control points. The circles highlight areas that have been better modelled after control points are added.

5 Dynamic Fitting

Our main goal is to fit surfaces to each frame of an RGB-D video recording. While the static fitting process presented works well for single frames, we are unable to usefully compare surfaces between frame sequences because the control points have been placed in different positions in each frame and sequence. Instead we place control points on a grid on the chest surface and fix their positions. Using the solution from frame k as the initialization for frame $k+1$ ensures continuity of parameters and the optimization process requires fewer iterations.

Our data is obtained using an Intel RealSense D315 depth camera [16], captured at 30 frames per second at a distance of around 1 m. The camera produces an RGB-D video - color plus depth. The camera's calibration parameters allow a point cloud to be reconstructed via inverse projection of the depth image and the region containing the subject's chest is tracked between frames.

An initial fit is computed using the GDM scheme with the parameters found previously. We then initialise subsequent frames using the control points from the previous frame and optimize for further iterations. In our experiments, we use 100,000 iterations for the initial fit and 100 for each subsequent fit. The costs should be reviewed to ensure that there is no downward trend - if so, this implies that the initial fit was not sufficient. It is possible that the cost shows oscillation due to the respiratory motion; as the surface's shape changes, the difficulty of modelling it may vary. It could also imply that the subsequent iterations are not enough to properly capture the variation and the modelled surface is remaining constant. We can validate this by checking the resulting t_z from each control point - it should exhibit oscillatory motion at an expected frequency (around 0.2–0.4 Hz) with a few millimetres of motion. Figure 9 shows the validation of an example dynamic fit.

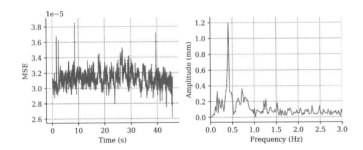

Fig. 9. Validation of a dynamic fit. MSE over time (left) has no trend, and a spectrum (right) has a sharp peak at 0.4 Hz. This is an elevated respiratory rate as this sample is taken after exercise.

6   Respiratory Pattern Analysis

Recordings have been obtained for a seated subject during tidal (normal) breathing and after exercise. Through non-contact imaging, we may observe the breathing pattern after exercise and characterize the difference from normal breathing. To analyze the data obtained from the dynamic fits, we extract three signals from each control point on the 4×4 grid: t_z, r_x and r_y, giving a 48-dimensional observation per frame. These are filtered using a band-pass filter with cut-offs 0.05 Hz 5 Hz. It is expected that the respiratory rate is not below 0.05 Hz; anything below this will be considered a low-frequency trend caused by adjustments in the subject's position, rather than respiration. We require that the subject is predominantly still throughout the recording. Principal component analysis - where t_z, r_x and r_y are variables and each frame is an observation - provides the first component shape (coefficients) and transformed value. We will examine the shape - determining the subject's motion during breathing - and the value waveform, which determines the oscillatory pattern of breathing.

The frequency spectrum of the first component amplitude is shown in Fig. 10. The right-hand view has been scaled in amplitude and shifted in frequency to align the peak at the respiratory rate. Normal breathing has a more constant respiratory rate but variable, and often larger, bandwidth than post-exercise. Exercise results in more variable respiratory rate and a very consistent bandwidth despite these samples being taken on the same healthy subject over multiple days and different clothing. Shown in Fig. 11 are averages of component shapes for normal and post-exercise breathing. Each grid is viewed as though we are looking at the patient; bright regions indicates high movement during respiration. After exercise, we see higher r_x and t_z at the bottom of the torso, indicating greater movement of the stomach, and higher t_z at the top of the chest as the ribs move forward.

Patients who have undergone long periods of assisted breathing, such as mechanical ventilation, may exhibit exercise-like breathing patterns during rehabilitation when tidal breathing does not perform sufficient gas exchange. Measuring using a non-contact device that can be used in a patient's home enables monitoring without requiring a patient to attend a clinic.

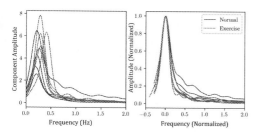
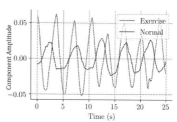

Fig. 10. Frequency spectrum of normal and post-exercise respiration. The center figure has been normalized to have its peak 0 Hz, amplitude 1. The right-hand figure shows examples of the time-domain signals.

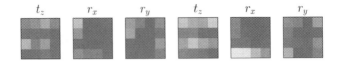

Fig. 11. Component shapes of t_z, r_x and r_y for normal (L) and post-exercise (R).

7   Conclusion

We have presented processes for fitting dual quaternion control point-based surfaces to point clouds. We can fit surfaces either with the goal of best representation of a surface, as in the targeted control point position approach, or comparing surfaces from frames of a recording, across multiple samples. We have demonstrated how using the parameters of these surfaces allows us to observe variation in the human respiratory pattern before and after exercise.

We aim to continue evaluating this approach on multiple subjects and breathing patterns. Optimization parameters have been chosen based on evidence from running many optimization processes; further investigation of why improper configuration can cause instability and how to choose these parameters for differently scaled problems shall also be undertaken.

References

1. Clifford, W.: Mathematical Papers. Macmillan, London (1882)
2. Kavan, L., Collins, S., Žára, J., O'Sullivan, C.: Geometric skinning with approximate dual quaternion blending. ACM Trans. Graph. **27**(4) (2008). https://dl.acm.org/doi/abs/10.1145/1409625.1409627
3. Shoemake, K.: Animating rotation with quaternion curves. In: SIGGRAPH 1985: Proceedings of the 12th Annual Conference on Computer Graphics and Interactive Techniques, pp. 245–254 (1985)
4. Wareham, R., Lasenby, J.: Mesh vertex pose and position interpolation using geometric algebra. In: Perales, F.J., Fisher, R.B. (eds.) AMDO 2008. LNCS, vol. 5098, pp. 122–131. Springer, Heidelberg (2008). https://doi.org/10.1007/978-3-540-70517-8_13
5. Botsch, M., Kobbelt, L.: Real-time shape editing using radial basis functions. Comput. Graph. Forum **24**(3), 611–621 (2005)
6. Chollet, F., et al.: Keras. https://keras.io. Accessed 28 May 2020
7. Qian, N.: On the momentum term in gradient descent learning algorithms. Neural Netw. Off. J. Int. Neural Netw. Soc. **12**(1), 145–151 (1999)
8. Duchi, J., Hazan, E., Singer, Y.: Adaptive subgradient methods of online learning and stochastic optimization. J. Mach. Learn. Res. **12**, 2121–2159 (2011)
9. Kingma, D.P., Ba, J.L.: Adam: a method for stochastic optimization. In: International Conference on Learning Representations (2015)
10. Bengio, Y.: Practical recommendations for gradient descent-based training of deep architectures. arXiv:1206.5533 (2012)
11. Shann, F., Hart, K., Thomas, D.: Acute lower respiratory tract infections in children: possible criteria for selection of patients for antibiotic therapy and hospital admission. Bull. Word Health Organ. **62**(5), p749 (1984)

12. Lim, W.S., et al.: Defining community acquired pneumonia severity on presentation to hospital: an international derivation and validation study. Thorax **58**(5), 377–382 (2003)
13. NHS UK: Peak flow test. https://www.nhs.uk/conditions/peak-flow-test/. Accessed 29 May 2020
14. Weerasuriya, C., et al.: Reproducibility and repeatability of tidal breathing parameters derived from structured light plethysmography when compared to spirometry. Eur. Respir. J. **38**, p2129 (2011)
15. Motamedi-Fakhr, S., Wilson, R.C., Iles, R.: Tidal breathing patterns derived from structured light plethysmography in COPD patients compared with healthy subjects. Med. Devices Evid. Res. **10**, 1 (2016)
16. Intel Corporation: Depth Camera D415. https://www.intelrealsense.com/depth-camera-d415/. Accessed 29 May 2020
17. Berger, M., et al.: State of the art in surface reconstruction from point clouds. In: Eurographics 2014 - State of the Art Reports (2014)

Deform, Cut and Tear a Skinned Model Using Conformal Geometric Algebra

Manos Kamarianakis[1,2]([⊠]) [ID] and George Papagiannakis[1,2] [ID]

[1] University of Crete, Heraklion, Greece
m.kamarianakis@gmail.com,george.papagiannakis@gmail.com
[2] ORamaVR, Heraklion, Greece
http://www.oramavr.com

Abstract. In this work, we present a novel, integrated rigged character simulation framework in Conformal Geometric Algebra (CGA) that
supports, for the first time, real-time cuts and tears, before and/or after
the animation, while maintaining deformation topology. The purpose of
using CGA is to lift several restrictions posed by current state-of-the-art
character animation & deformation methods. Previous implementations
originally required weighted matrices to perform deformations, whereas,
in the current state-of-the-art, dual-quaternions handle both rotations
and translations, but cannot handle dilations. CGA is a suitable extension of dual-quaternion algebra that amends these two major previous
shortcomings: the need to constantly transmute between matrices and
dual-quaternions as well as the inability to properly dilate a model during animation. Our CGA algorithm also provides easy interpolation and
application of all deformations in each intermediate steps, all within the
same geometric framework. Furthermore we also present two novel algorithms that enable cutting and tearing of the input rigged, animated
model, while the output model can be further re-deformed. These interactive, real-time cut and tear operations can enable a new suite of applications, especially under the scope of a medical surgical simulation.

Keywords: Conformal Geometric Algebra (CGA) · Skinning ·
Interpolation · Cutting algorithm · Tearing algorithm · Keyframe
generation

1 Introduction

Skinned model animation has become an increasingly important research area
of Computer Graphics, especially due to the huge technological advancements
in the field of Virtual Reality and computer games. The original animation
techniques, based on matrices [1] for translation, rotation and dilation, are still
applied as the latest GPUs allow for fast parallel matrix operations. The fact
that the interpolation result of two rotation matrices does not result in a rotation matrix, forced the use of quaternions as an intermediate step. The extra
transmutation steps from matrix to quaternions and vice versa, adds some extra

© Springer Nature Switzerland AG 2020
N. Magnenat-Thalmann et al. (Eds.): CGI 2020, LNCS 12221, pp. 434–446, 2020.
https://doi.org/10.1007/978-3-030-61864-3_37

performance burden to the animation but yields better results, solving problems such as the gimbal lock.

Nowadays, the state-of-the-art methods for skinned model animation use dual-quaternions, an algebraic extension of quaternions [13]. Dual quaternions handle both rotation and translation, while the dilation effect is still applied via matrices [12]. It is also noteworthy to mention that quaternions and dual quaternions enable blending techniques that resolve artifacts produced by simple linear blending, while further post-processing can be used to further minimize them [14].

Advances in Virtual Reality technology and the mass production of cheap VR headsets increased the demand of real-time simulation applications for both personal and industrial purposes. The research areas that sprout from these advancements, such as Virtual Surgery Simulation, require more complex model deformation such as cutting, tearing or drilling. Current algorithms [6,20] handle such deformations using tetrahedral mesh representation of the model, which demands a heavy pre-processing to be performed. Since originally introduced, cutting methods have been upgraded and polished to allow real-time results, using mostly finite element methods and clever optimization [4,7,15]. To make the final results even more realistic, physics engines utilizing position-based dynamics are used to simulate soft-tissue cuts at the expense of performance [2,3,5].

Our approach utilizes the Conformal Geometric Algebra (CGA) framework to perform both model animation and cutting. CGA is an algebraic extension of dual-quaternions, where all entities such as vertices, spheres, planes as well as rotations, translations and dilation are uniformly expressed as *multivectors* [8,11,19]. The usage of multivectors allows model animation without the need to constantly transmute between matrices and (dual) quaternions, enabling dilation to be properly applied with translation [17,18]. Furthermore, the interpolation of two multivectors of the same type correctly produce the expected intermediate result [9], which makes creation of keyframes trivial to implement. Finally, usage of the proposed framework demands a single representation type for all data and results, which is the current trend in computer graphics [16].

Our Contribution: The novelty of our work initially involves the complete implementation of rigged model animation in terms of CGA, extending the work of Papaefthymiou et al. [17] with full python-based implementation that enables keyframe generation on-the-fly. The original animation equation involving matrices is translated to its equivalent multivector form (see Sect. 3.1) and all information required to apply the formula (vertices, animation data) is obtained from the model and translated to multivector. This enables us to have future animation models in CGA representation only, which, in combination with an optimized GPU multivector implementation, would produce faster results under a single framework. A novelty of our work is the cutting and tearing algorithm that is being applied on top of the previous framework; given the input animated model, we perform real-time cuts and tears on the skin and then further re-deform the output model. The subpredicates used in these two algorithms utilize the multivector form of their input, so they can be implemented in a CGA-only framework. Their design was made in such a way that little to no pre-processing of the input model is required while allowing a future combination with a physics engine. Furthermore, using our method, we can generate our own keyframes in real-time instead of just interpolating between pre-defined ones. Our all-in-one cpu python implementation is able to process an existing animation model (provided in .dae or .fbx format) and translate the existing animation in the desired CGA form while further tweaks or deformations are available in a simple way to perform. Such an implementation is optimal as far as rapid prototyping, teaching and future connection to deep learning is concerned. It also constitutes the base for interactive cutting and tearing presented in Sect. 3.2.

2   State of the Art

The current state of the art regarding skeletal model animation is based on the representation of bones animation via transformation matrices and quaternions or dual-quaternions. Such an implementation allows for efficient and robust interpolation methods between keyframes; linear interpolation of the quaternions is done in a naive and easy to perceive way. A major drawback of such an implementation is that a dilation method can not be applied as a scaling matrix always refers to the origin and not the parent bone [17].

To be more precise regarding the mechanics of the animation process, in the case of a simple animated model, every bone b_i amounts to an offset matrix O_i and an original transformation matrix t_i. The skin of the model is imported as a list of vertices v and a list of faces f. A bone hierarchy is also provided where $\{t_i\}$ are stored along with information regarding the animation of each joint. This information, usually referred to as *TRS data*, is provided in the form of a quaternion, a translation vector and a scaling vector that represent respectively the rotation, displacement and scaling of the joint with respect to the parent joint for each keyframe (see Sect. 2.1).

In order to determine the position of the skin vertices at any given time k and therefore render the scene by triangulating them using the faces list, we follow the steps described below. Initially, a matrix G is evaluated as the inverse of the transformation matrix that corresponds to the root node. Afterwards, we evaluate the *global transformation matrix* for every bone b_i at time k and denote it as $T_{i,k}$. To evaluate all $T_{i,k}$, we recursively evaluate the matrix product $T_{j,k}t_{i,k}$ where b_j is the parent bone of b_i, given that $T_{r,k}$ is the identity matrix (of size 4), where b_r denotes the root bone. The matrix $t_{i,k}$ is a transformation matrix equal to t_i if there is no animation in the model; in this case, our implementation allows to generate the keyframes ourselves in real-time. Otherwise, $t_{i,k}$ is evaluated as

$$t_{i,k} = TR_{i,k}MR_{i,k}S_{i,k} \tag{1}$$

where $TR_{i,k}, MR_{i,k}, S_{i,k}$ are the interpolated matrices that correspond to the translation, rotation and scaling of the bone b_i at a given time k.

After evaluating the matrices $\{T_{i,k}\}$ for all bones $\{b_i\}$, we can evaluate the global position of all vertices at time k, using the *animation equation*:

$$V_k[m] = \sum_{n \in I_m} w_{m,n} G T_{n,k} O_n v[m] \tag{2}$$

where

- $V_k[m]$ denotes the skin vertex of index m (in homogeneous coordinates) at the animation time k,
- I_m contains up to four indices of bones that affect the vertex $v[m]$,
- $w_{m,n}$ denotes the "weight", i.e., the amount of influence of the bone b_n on the vertex $v[m]$,
- O_n denotes the offset matrix corresponding to bone b_n, with respect to the root bone,
- G denotes the inverse of the transformation matrix that corresponds to the root bone (usually equals the identity matrix) and
- $T_{n,k}$ denotes the deformation of the bone b_n at animation time k, with respect to the root bone.

2.1 State-of-the-Art Representation

The modern way to represent the TRS data of a keyframe is to use matrices for the translation and dilation data as well as quaternions for the rotation data. Let $\{TR_i, R_i, S_i\}$, denote such data at keyframe $i \in \{1, 2\}$, where:

- $TR_i = \begin{bmatrix} 1 & 0 & 0 & x_i \\ 0 & 1 & 0 & y_i \\ 0 & 0 & 1 & z_i \\ 0 & 0 & 0 & 1 \end{bmatrix}$ and $S_i = \begin{bmatrix} sx_i & 0 & 0 & 0 \\ 0 & sy_i & 0 & 0 \\ 0 & 0 & sz_i & 0 \\ 0 & 0 & 0 & 1 \end{bmatrix}$ represent the translation by (x_i, y_i, z_i) and the scale by (sx_i, sy_i, sz_i) respectively and
- R_i is a quaternion representing the rotation.

Before quaternions, euler andgles and the derived rotation matrices were used to represent rotation data. However the usage of such matrices induced a great problem: a weighted average of such matrices does not correspond to a rotation matrix and therefore interpolating between two states would require interpolating the euler angles and re-generate the corresponding matrix. This in turn would sometimes lead to a gimbal lock or to 'candy-wrapper' artifacts such as the ones presented in [12].

The usage of quaternions allowed for easier interpolation techniques while eradicating such problems. Nevertheless, a transformation of the interpolated quaternion to corresponding rotation matrix was introduced since the GPU currently handles only matrix multiplications in a sufficient way for skinning reasons. Therefore, the interpolation between the two keyframes mentioned above follows the following pattern:

1. the matrices $TR_a = (1-a)TR_1 + aTR_2$ and $S_a = (1-a)S_1 + aS_2$ are evaluated for a given $a \in [0, 1]$,

2. the quaternion $R_a = (1 - a)R_1 + aR_2$ is determined and finally,
3. the rotation matrix MR_a that corresponds to R_a is calculated.

The interpolated data TR_a, MR_a and S_a are then imported to the GPU in order to determine the intermediate frame, based on the Eq. (2).

Using the method proposed in this paper, all data are represented in multivector form. A major implication of this change is that the interpolation between two states is done in a more clear and uniform way as presented in Sect. 3. This also makes the need to constantly transform a quaternion to a rotation matrix redundant, although we are now obliged to perform multivector additions and multiplications as well as down project points from $\mathbb{R}_{4,1}$ to $\mathbb{R}_3$ to parse them to the GPU. However, since all our data and intermediate results are in the same multivector form, we could (ideally) program the GPU to implement such operations and therefore greatly improve performance.

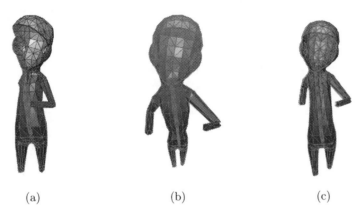

(a)   (b)   (c)

Fig. 1. Skinning via multivectors versus skinning via dual quaternions. The original model is deformed using multivectors and depicted in magenta wireframe, superimposed with the color-graded result (based on the z coordinate of each vertex) of the quaternion method for the same deformation. It is qualitatively verified that linear blending of multivectors produces similar results with the current state-of-the-art method. Evaluating the vector differences of all vertices for the two methods, we have evaluated the approximation error assuming the quaternion method to be the correct, using the infinity (ℓ_∞) norm. (a) Applying rotation on a bone, approximation error 0.3%. (b) Applying dilation on a bone, approximation error 0.00035%. (c) Applying translation, approximation error 1%. The model used contains 1261 vertices and 1118 faces.

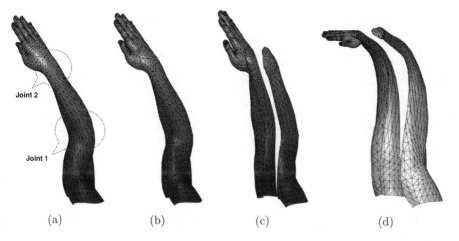

(a)   (b)   (c)   (d)

Fig. 2. Cutting module intermediate steps. (a) The original animated model. (b) The model where the (red) intersection points of the cutting plane and the mesh are calculated and re-triangulated. (c) The model after the cut. (d) The model is deformed by a rotation (axis = $(0, 1, 1)$, 0.7 rad), a translation (vector = $(13, 0, 0)$) and a dilation (factor = 0.5) at joint 1 (elbow), as well as another rotation (axis = $(0, 1, 1)$, 0.3 rad) at joint 2 (wrist). Note that minimal artifacts occur in the final result. The vertices in (d) are colored depending on the influence of joint 1 which is mostly deformed. The vertices in (a)–(c) are colored based on their z coordinate. (Color figure online)

3 Our Algorithms and Results

3.1 Multivector Form of the Animation Equation

The animation Eq. (2), core of the animation algorithm, yields fast results (especially when combined with a GPU implementation) but denies us a robust way to dilate with respect to a bone. Our motivation is to extend and apply the animation equation for multivector input as proposed in [17].

To be more specific regarding our method, we propose the replacement of all matrices appearing in (2) with multivectors for animation purposes. The transformation matrix of t_i of each bone b_i as well as all information regarding translation and rotation for each keyframe can be easily converted to multivectors [8,11]. Consequently, we can evaluate the multivector $M_{i,k}$ which is equivalent to the matrix $T_{i,k}$ by following the same procedure of determining the latter (described in Sect. 2) while substituting all involved matrices with the corresponding multivectors.

Note that various techniques can be used to interpolate between two keyframes to obtain $M_{i,k}$; for existing keyframes logarithmic blending is preferred [9,12], whereas for keyframe generation we use linear blending. In both scenarios, the intermediate results are multivectors of the correct type.

Furthermore, each offset matrix O_n and each skin vertex $v[m]$ is translated to their CGA form B_n and $c[m]$ respectively. Finally, G matrix is normalized to identity and is omitted in the final equation.

Our final task is to translate in CGA terms the matrix product $T_{n,k}O_n v[m]$, where apparently each multiplication sequentially applies a deformation to vertex $v[m]$. To apply the respective deformations, encapsulated by $M_{n,k}$ and B_n, to CGA vertex $c[m]$, we have to evaluate the *sandwich geometric product* $(M_{n,k}B_n)c[m](M_{n,k}B_n)^\star$ where $V^\star$ denotes the *inverse* multivector of V (see [11,13] for details).

Summarizing, if the multivector form of the vertex $V_k[m]$, which corresponds to the final position of the m-th vertex at animation time k, is denoted by $C_k[m]$, then the *multivector animation equation* becomes

$$C_k[m] = \sum_{n \in I_m} w_{m,n}(M_{n,k}B_n)c[m](M_{n,k}B_n)^\star \tag{3}$$

After the evaluation of $C_k[m]$ for all m, we can down-project all these conformal points to the respective euclidean ones in order to represent/visualize them and obtain the final result of the keyframe at time k.

The replacement of matrices with multivectors enables the introduction of dilations in a simple way. The multivector $M_{i,k}$ that represents a rotation and translation with respect to the parent bone of b_i can be replaced with $M_{i,k}D_{i,k}$ where $D_{i,k}$ is the corresponding dilator and the operation between them is the geometric product. The dilator corresponds to a scale factor with respect to the parent bone, information that could not be easily interpreted via matrices. However, since the application of a motor and/or a dilator to a vertex is a sandwich operation, such a dilation becomes possible when using multivectors.

A comparison between the results of our proposed method and the current state-of-the-art is shown in Fig. 1, where we successfully apply dilation to different bones and obtain similar results. Rotations, dilations and translations are obtained in our method using multivectors only, under a single framework with simpler notation/implementation; linear blending is used to interpolate between keyframes.

3.2 Cutting and Tearing Algorithms

A novelty we present in this paper is the cutting and tearing algorithms on skinned triangulated models. As the name suggests, the first module enables the user to make a planar cut of the model whereas the latter is used to perform smaller intersections on the skin. In the following sections, we provide a detailed presentation of the algorithms involved as well as certain implementation details.

Cutting Algorithm. Cutting a skinned model is implemented in current bibliography in many forms [6]. The most common technique is via the usage of tetrahedral meshes which require a heavy preprocessing on the model and currently do not enable further animation of the model. Our work includes an algorithm to planar cut a model (or a part of it) where the final mesh is deformable, as we implemented a function to calculate weights for all additional vertices that did not originally exist (see Fig. 2). Most of the subpredicates used in the cutting algorithm are implemented in terms of conformal geometry and therefore can be used even if the model is provided in multivector form.

Our proposed planar cut implementation is summarized as Algorithm 1. A description of how we tackle the weight evaluation in step 4 is found in Sect. 3.3. Our algorithm does not require tetrahedral meshed models and requires minimum to none preprocessing. It is GA-ready and the low number of operations it demands make it suitable for VR implementations.

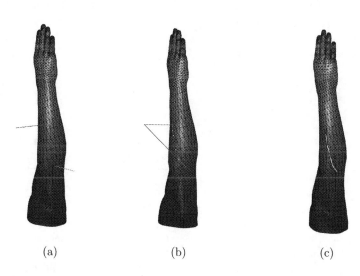

(a)   (b)   (c)

Fig. 3. Tearing module intermediate steps. (a) The original animated model and the scalpel's position at two consecutive time steps. (b) The plane defined by the scalpels (depicted as a red tringle) intersects the skin in the magenta points. (c) The intermediate points are used in the re-triangulation, and are «pushed»away from the cutting plane to form an open tear.

Tearing Algorithm. The purpose of this module is to enable partial cuts on the skinned model, in contrast with the cutting module where the cut is, in a sense, complete. The importance of this module derives from the fact that most

---

Algorithm 1. Cutting Algorithm
***
Input: Triangulated Mesh $M = (v, f)$ (f is the face list), and a plane Π.
Output: Two meshes $M_1 = (v_1, f_1)$ and $M_2 = (v_2, f_2)$, result of M getting cut by Π
  1: Evaluate (using GA) and order the intersection points of Π with each face of M.
  2: Evaluate the weights and bone indices that influence these points.
  3: Re-triangulate the faces that are cut using the intersection points.
  4: Separate faces in f_1 and f_2, depending on which side of the plane they lie.
  5: From f_1 and f_2, construct M_1 and M_2.

of the surgical incisions are partial cuts and therefore they are worth replicating in the context of a virtual surgery. Towards that direction, our work involves an algorithm that both tears a skinned model and also enables animation of the final mesh (see Figs. 3 and 4).

To understand the philosophy behind the design of the tearing algorithm that is described below, one must comprehend the differences between cutting and tearing. In tearing, the movement of a scalpel defines the tear rather than a single plane. To capture such a tear in geometric terms, we have to take into consideration the location of the scalpel in either a continuous way (e.g. record the trail of both endpoints of the scalpel in terms of time) or a discrete way (e.g. know the position of the scalpel at certain times t_i). For VR purposes, the latter way is preferred as it yields results with better fps, since input is hard to be monitored and logged continuously in a naive way. For these reasons, our implementation requires the scalpel position to be known for certain t_i.

The proposed tearing algorithm is summarized in Algorithm 2. A description of how we tackle the weight evaluation in step 4 is found in Sect. 3.3.

Algorithm 2. Tearing Algorithm

Input: Triangulated Mesh $M = (v, f)$, and scalpel position at time steps t_i and t_{i+1}
Require: Scalpel properly intersects M at these time steps
Output: The mesh $M_t = (v_t, f_t)$ resulting from M getting torn by the scalpel
1: Determine the intersection points S_i and S_{i+1} of M with the scalpel at time step t_i and t_{i+1} respectively.
2: Determine the plane Π, containing S_i and the endpoints of scalpel at time t_{i+1}. Small time steps guarantee that Π is well-defined.
3: Evaluate the intersection points Q_j of Π and M, s.t. the points $S_i, Q_0, Q_1, \ldots, Q_m$, S_{i+1} appear in this order on Π when traversing the skin from S_i to S_{i+1}.
4: Assign weights to points S_i, S_{i+1} and all Q_j.
5: Re-triangulate the torn mesh, duplicating Q_j vertices.
6: Move the two copies of Q_j away from each other to create a visible tear (optional).

Our major assumption is that all intermediate intersection points lie on this plane, which is equivalent to the assume that the tearing curve is smooth, given that t_i and t_{i+1} are close enough. In our implementation, during step 6, the intermediate torn points are moved parallel to the direction of the normal of the plane Π and away from it, to replicate the opening of a cut human tissue.

3.3   Implementation Details, Performance and Video Results

The main framework used for skinning and animation with the use of multi-vectors is Python's PyAssimp[1] and Clifford[2] package for the evaluation of the vertices and the Meshplot package for rendering the model. The use of Python

---

[1] PyAssimp Homepage: https://pypi.org/project/pyassimp/.
[2] Clifford Homepage: https://clifford.readthedocs.io/.

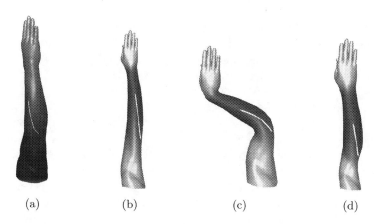

(a)   (b)   (c)   (d)

Fig. 4. Deformation of a torn model. (a) The original model after applying the tear. (b) Two rotations are applied to the torn model, one at elbow joint around y-axis by -1 rad, and another at wrist joint around y-axis by 1 rad. (c) A dilation of scale 1.5 is applied to the torn model, at elbow joint. (d) A translation is applied to the torn model at elbow joint with translation vector $(18, 0, 0)$. In all cases, minor artifacts only arise, despite the great magnitude of the applied deformations. In (b), (c) and (d), vertices are colored depending on the influence of elbow joint which is mostly deformed. In (a), vertices are colored based on their z coordinate.

language was preferred for a more user and presentation-friendly experience; for a more robust and efficient implementation C++ would be advised.

An instance of a class called v_w is used to store for each vertex a list of up to 4 bones that influence it along with the corresponding influence factors. The node tree is then traversed and all information regarding rotation, translation and dilation are translated to multivectors [8,11] and also stored in the instance for convenience. In order to evaluate the final position of the vertices, all that is left is to evaluate the sum in Eq. (3) for all vertices and down project it to $\mathbb{R}^3$, for each vertex. There are two possible ways of achieving this task. The first way is to evaluate the sum and then down project the final result to obtain each vertex in Euclidean form. The second way is to down project each term and then add them to get the final result. Although not obvious, the second method yields faster results since the addition of 4 multivectors (32-dimensional arrays) and one down-projection is slower than down-projecting (up to) 4 multivectors and adding 4 euclidean vectors of dimension 3.

A final implementation detail regards the weight evaluation for newly added vertices in the cutting and tearing modules. In the former module, such vertices necessarily lie on an edge of the original mesh, whose endpoints both lie on different sides of the cutting plane. Another method is the one used in the tearing module where the intersection point can also lie inside a face. Assuming the point X lie somewhere on the face ABC, we can explicitly write $OX = pOA + qOB + rOC$ for some $a, b, c \in [0, 1]$ such that $p + q + r = 1$. The tuple (p, q, r) is called the *barycentric coordinate* of X with respect to the triangle

ABC. Each of the vertices A, B, C are (usually) influenced by up to 4 bones, so let us consider that they are all influenced by a set of $N (\leq 12)$ vertices, where the bones beside the original 4 have weight 0. Let w_A, w_B, w_C, w_X denote the vectors containing the N weights that correspond to vertices A, B, C and X respectively, for the same ordering of the N involved bones. To determine w_X, we first evaluate $w = p w_A + q w_B + r w_C$ and consider two cases. If w contains up to 4 non-zero weights, then $w_X = w$. Otherwise, since each vertex can be influenced by up to 4 bones, we keep the 4 greater values of w, set the others to zero, and normalize the vector so that the sum of the 4 values add to 1; the final result is returned as w_X. We denote this weight as *weight of X via barycentric coordinates*. Variations of this technique can be applied in both modules to prioritize or neglect influences on vertices lying on a specific side of the cutting plane. Different variations of the weight function allows for less artifacts, depending on the model and the deformation subsequent to the cutting/tearing.

Performance: Running the Tearing algorithm in the arm model (5037 faces, 3069 vertices) it took 2437 ms for the final output, for 34 intersection points. Most of this time (2411 ms) were needed just to determine which two faces were intersected by the scalpel. Tearing the cylinders model (758 faces, 634 vertices) took 362 ms for 17 intersection points. Again, most time (331 ms) was spend for the scalpel intersection. For the Cutting Algorithm, it took for the cylinders model a total of 898 ms: 42 ms for vertex separation, 757 ms for re-triangulation of the 92 intersection points, 87 ms to split faces in two meshes and 12 ms to update the weights. To cut the arm model, it took 22805 ms, where most of them (22547 ms) were spent to re-triangulate the 90 intersection points. These running times can be greatly improved as our current unoptimized CPU-based Python implementation has to thoroughly search all faces for cuts/tears. A GPU implementation optimized for multivector operations would allows to the comparison of our proposed method with the current state-of-the-art methods.

Video: A video with our results can be found at https://bit.ly/3fsYkdZ.

4   Conclusions and Future Work

This work describes a way to perform model animation and deformation as well as cutting and tearing under a single geometric framework called Conformal Geometric Algebra. Our results were obtained using python but since our goal is to have a full implementation in real-time virtual reality simulation we will inevitably have to embed in C++ and ultimately Unity/Unreal Engine code. We intend to combine the tearing module in conjunction with a physics engine to obtain a realistic opening effect. A drilling module is in progress that will allow the user to make holes on the skinned model; such a task is useful especially for VR simulations of dental surgeries. Finally, it is our intention to minimize running times to real-time implementation levels via optimization and the use of recently developed acceleration techniques [10].

References

1. Alexa, M.: Linear combination of transformations. ACM Trans. Graph. **21**(3), 380–387 (2002)
2. Bender, J., Müller, M., Otaduy, M.A., Teschner, M., Macklin, M.: A survey on position-based simulation methods in computer graphics. Comput. Graph. Forum **33**(6), 228–251 (2014)
3. Berndt, I.U., Torchelsen, R.P., Maciel, A.: Efficient surgical cutting with position-based dynamics. IEEE Comput. Graphics Appl. **37**(3), 24–31 (2017)
4. Bielser, D., Glardon, P., Teschner, M., Gross, M.: A state machine for real-time cutting of tetrahedral meshes. In: 11th Pacific Conference on Computer Graphics and Applications, pp. 377–386. IEEE Computer Society (2004)
5. Bielser, D., Maiwald, V.A., Gross, M.H.: Interactive cuts through 3-dimensional soft tissue. Comput. Graph. Forum **18**(3), 31–38 (1999)
6. Bruyns, C.D., Senger, S., Menon, A., Montgomery, K., Wildermuth, S., Boyle, R.: A survey of interactive mesh-cutting techniques and a new method for implementing generalized interactive mesh cutting using virtualtools ‡. J. Vis. Comput. Animation **13**(1), 21–42 (2002)
7. Bruyns, C.D., Senger, S.: Interactive cutting of 3D surface meshes. Comput. Graph. **25**(4), 635–642 (2001)
8. Dorst, L., Fontijne, D., Mann, S.: Geometric algebra for computer science - an object-oriented approach to geometry. The Morgan Kaufmann series in computer graphics (2007)
9. Hadfield, H., Lasenby, J.: Direct Linear Interpolation of Geometric Objects in Conformal Geometric Algebra. Advances in Applied Clifford Algebras (2019)
10. Hadfield, H., Hildenbrand, D., Arsenovic, A.: Gajit: symbolic optimisation and JIT compilation of geometric algebra in python with GAALOP and numba. In: Gavrilova, M., Chang, J., Thalmann, N.M., Hitzer, E., Ishikawa, H. (eds.) CGI 2019. LNCS, vol. 11542, pp. 499–510. Springer, Cham (2019). https://doi.org/10.1007/978-3-030-22514-8_50
11. Hildenbrand, D.: Foundations of Geometric Algebra Computing. Springer, Heidelberg (2013). https://doi.org/10.1007/978-3-642-31794-1
12. Kavan, L., Collins, S., Žára, J., O'Sullivan, C.: Geometric skinning with approximate dual quaternion blending. dl.acm.org 27(4) (2008)
13. Kenwright, B.: A beginners guide to dual-quaternions: What they are, how they work, and how to use them for 3D character hierarchies. In: WSCG 2012 - Conference Proceedings, pp. 1–10. Newcastle University, United Kingdom, December 2012
14. Kim, Y.B., Han, J.H.: Bulging-free dual quaternion skinning. In: Computer Animation and Virtual Worlds, pp. 321–329. Korea University, Seoul, South Korea, John Wiley & Sons, Ltd., January 2014
15. Mor, A.B., Kanade, T.: Modifying soft tissue models: progressive cutting with minimal new element creation. In: Delp, S.L., DiGoia, A.M., Jaramaz, B. (eds.) MICCAI 2000. LNCS, vol. 1935, pp. 598–607. Springer, Heidelberg (2000). https://doi.org/10.1007/978-3-540-40899-4_61
16. Müller, M., Chentanez, N., Macklin, M.: Simulating visual geometry. In: Proceedings - Motion in Games 2016: 9th International Conference on Motion in Games, MIG 2016, pp. 31–38 (2016)
17. Papaefthymiou, M., Hildenbrand, D., Papagiannakis, G.: An inclusive Conformal Geometric Algebra GPU animation interpolation and deformation algorithm. Vis. Comput. **32**(6–8), 751–759 (2016)

18. Papagiannakis, G.: Geometric algebra rotors for skinned character animation blending. In: SIGGRAPH Asia 2013 Technical Briefs, SA 2013, December 2013
19. Wareham, R., Cameron, J., Lasenby, J.: Applications of conformal geometric algebra in computer vision and graphics. IWMM/GIAE **3519**(1), 329–349 (2004)
20. Wu, J., Westermann, R., Dick, C.: A survey of physically based simulation of cuts in deformable bodies. Comput. Graph. Forum **34**(6), 161–187 (2015)

The Forward and Inverse Kinematics of a Delta Robot

Hugo Hadfield$^{(\boxtimes)}$ (ID), Lai Wei, and Joan Lasenby (ID)

Department of Engineering, University of Cambridge, Cambridge, UK
hh409@cam.ac.uk, letticewei@gmail.com, jl221@cam.ac.uk

Abstract. The Delta robot is one of the most popular parallel robots in industrial use today. In this paper we analyse the forward and inverse kinematics of the robot from a geometric perspective using Conformal Geometric Algebra. We calculate explicit formulae for all joints in both the forward and inverse kinematic problems as well as explicit forward and inverse Jacobians to allow for velocity and force control. Finally we verify the kinematics in Python and simulate a physical model in the Unity3D game engine to act as a test-bed for future development of control algorithms.

1 Introduction

The Delta robot [1,2] was invented in 1985 by Raymond Clavel at EPFL after being inspired by a visit to a chocolate packing factory [3]. It has since become a particularly popular robot in industrial settings due to its good precision coupled with high speed and acceleration.

The Delta robot is a specific type of robot known as a **parallel manipulator**. Parallel manipulators, also known as parallel robots, are a class of robots that feature end-effectors driven by multiple underactuated parallel kinematic chains [4,5]. Typically a parallel robot is designed such that all actuators remain fixed to the support structure of the robot thereby minimising the mass of the moving parts of the robot and enabling very fast accelerations. Indeed this goal of high speed/fast acceleration has been the primary driving force in the development of parallel robots for industry and today architectures such as the Delta robot are widespread in many high precision, high throughput manufacturing applications. Parallel robots, while practically very useful, are often significantly more difficult to analyse than their serial cousins due to the end-point position being a function of the configuration of multiple kinematic chains.

Conformal Geometric Algebra (CGA) is a specific 5D representation of 3D space that embeds geometric primitives and conformal transformations as elements of the same algebra [6,7]. Our mathematics in this paper will be phrased within CGA. We will use the standard extension of the 3D geometric algebra, where our 5D CGA space is made up of the standard Euclidean basis vectors $\{e_j\}j = 1, 2, 3$, where $e_j^2 = 1$, plus two additional basis vectors, e and $\bar{e}$ with signatures, $e^2 = 1, \bar{e}^2 = -1$. Two *null vectors* can therefore be defined as: $n_\infty = e + \bar{e}$

N. Magnenat-Thalmann et al. (Eds.): CGI 2020, LNCS 12221, pp. 447–458, 2020.
https://doi.org/10.1007/978-3-030-61864-3_38

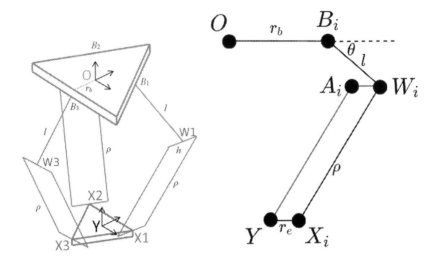

Fig. 1. Left: the 3D geometry of the delta robot. Right: The geometry of a single arm in plane.

and $n_0 = \frac{\bar{e}-e}{2}$. The mapping of a 3D vector x to its conformal representation X is given by $X = F(x) = \frac{1}{2}(x^2 n_\infty + 2x + 2n_0)$.

In this paper we draw inspiration from the established literature of robotic analysis in GA [12–20] as well as the previous literature on Delta robot kinematics [5,8,11] and combine them, leveraging the representational power of CGA to illustrate the geometry of the constraints inherent in the mechanism of the Delta robot.

2   Geometry of a Delta Robot

Since its inception, there have been many variants of the Delta robot [8]. In this paper we will assume the simple robot described in this section and illustrated in Fig. 1. The static part of the robot is a base plate to which three motors are rigidly attached, we will assume a space in which the origin is at the centre of this plate. Each motor shaft is rigidly attached to an 'upper arm' of length l; we will number each upper arm $i \in [1, 2, 3]$. The connection point of the motor and upper arm will be labelled B_i. The arm can only rotate in plane about the motor axis as the motor shaft and upper arm are rigidly connected. We will refer to the other end of this upper arm as the 'elbow point' and will label it W_i. At the elbow point each arm is rigidly attached to a central point of a horizontal rod we will refer to as the 'elbow rod'. At each end of the elbow rod a ball joint connects to a 'forearm' piece. The two forearm pieces for each arm are the same length and, at the other end from the elbow rod, are connected to a rigid plate that we will refer to as the end-effector plate. The point half-way between where the two forearm rods connect to the end-effector plate is labelled X_i. We will label the point at the centre of the end-effector plate Y. Assuming the robot is infinitely stiff, the end plate is constrained, due to this specific arrangement of the forearms, to always remain parallel to the base plate and to have its in-plane orientation fixed as well. The Delta robot is therefore a purely translational mechanism.

The labels have assigned here will also serve as the notation for points in conformal space; for example, the centre of the end-effector plate has 3D position, y with $Y = F(y)$.

3 Inverse Kinematics

The inverse kinematic problem for the Delta robot is summarised as follows: To what angle relative to the base should we move the upper arms given we want the centre of the end-effector plate to be in a specific position in 3D space?

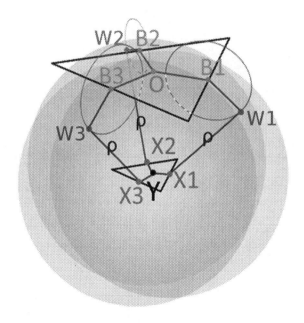

Fig. 2. The geometry of the inverse kinematic problem. There are three spheres, one for each arm of the robot, centred at the conformal points X_i. Each sphere intersects with a circle centred at B_i allowing the extraction of the conformal elbow point W_i.

To solve this problem we need to work backwards from the 3D end-effector plate position y to the motor angles θ_i considering the geometry of the robot as we go. Starting at the end-effector plate the 3D points x_i are translationally offset in plane in the direction s_i giving $x_i = y + r_e s_i$ where r_e is the radius of the end-effector plate. Due to the geometry of the robot the elbow point W_i is constrained to lie on a sphere with radius equal to the length of the forearms

ρ centred at this point x_i. We can represent this sphere as a dual sphere in conformal geometric algebra as follows:

$$\Sigma_i^* = X_i - \frac{1}{2}\rho^2 n_\infty$$

The elbow point is also simultaneously constrained to lie on a circle of radius l centred at the motor shaft to upper-arm joint, B_i. We can represent this circle as the dual circle C_i^* in CGA, where C_i^* is the intersection of a dual sphere of radius l centred at the position B_i, $\left(B_i - \frac{1}{2}l^2 n_\infty\right)$, and the dual plane through the origin, B_i and e_3 which is given by $I_3(s_i \wedge e_3)$. In CGA we calculate the intersection of objects via the 'meet' operator, as both operands are in their dual form however, here we simply need an outer product:

$$C_i^* = \left(B_i - \frac{1}{2}l^2 n_\infty\right) \wedge (I_3(s_i \wedge e_3))$$

where e_3 is the vertical unit vector. So long as y is within the reachable volume of the robot there are two possible solutions for this pair of constraints. These two solutions lie at the intersection points of the sphere and circle and the 'meet' operation of CGA provides us with a direct means to calculate these intersection points. As with the circle, our sphere and circle are in the dual form (i.e. 1 and 2-vectors respectively), and so the point-pair bivector resulting from their meet is calculated as simply their outer product followed by multiplication with the 5D pseudo-scalar, I_5:

$$T_i = (C_i^* \wedge \Sigma_i^*)I_5$$

The individual solutions can be extracted from this point-pair object by projection operators [6]:

$$P_i = \frac{1}{2}\left(1 + \frac{T_i}{\sqrt{T_i^2}}\right)$$

$$W_i = -\tilde{P}_i(T_i \cdot n_\infty)P_i$$

We can then convert from the CGA to the 3D vector point:

$$w_i = -\frac{\sum_{j=1}^{j=3}(W_i \cdot e_j)e_j}{W_i \cdot n_\infty}$$

and so, with a little trigonometry we can extract the motor angles:

$$\theta_i = \text{atan2}(z_i \cdot e_3, z_i \cdot s_i), \qquad z_i = w_i - r_b s_i$$

Figure 2 illustrates the geometry of the inverse kinematic problem graphically.

4   Forward Kinematics

The forward kinematic problem is, in some sense, the opposite of the inverse kinematic one. Our goal here is to calculate the 3D vector position of the end-effector plate y given the motor angles $\theta_i, i \in [1, 2, 3]$.

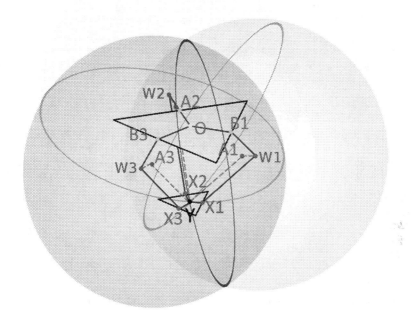

Fig. 3. The geometry of the forward kinematic problem. Each motor connects to an upper arm at position B_i. The upper arms end in the elbow point W_i. Each elbow point has an associated pseudo-elbow point A_i and forearm constraint sphere. All three constraint spheres meet at the centre of the end-point plate, Y.

To solve the forward kinematic problem we will consider the robot one arm at a time. For a given arm motor angle θ_i the 3D position of the elbow point w_i can be calculated as:

$$w_i = (r_b + l\cos(\theta_i))s_i + l\sin(\theta_i)e_3$$

For each arm we will now define a pseudo-elbow point, a_i which is offset horizontally from the true elbow point by the radius of the end effector plate and in the direction of the origin.

$$a_i = (r_b - r_e + l\cos(\theta_i))s_i + l\sin(\theta_i)e_3$$

The equivalent CGA point is then:

$$A_i = \frac{1}{2}a_i^2 n_\infty + a_i + n_0$$

Given the geometry of the robot, these pseudo-elbow points all lie a distance equal to the length of the robot's forearms, ρ, from the centre of the end-point plate Y. Geometrically these fixed distance constraints manifest themselves as spheres, which we will label Σ_i, on which the centre of the end-point plate can lie:

$$\Sigma_i^* = A_i - \frac{1}{2}\rho^2 n_\infty$$

Each arm contributes one constraint sphere and the intersection of the three spheres produces a point-pair, T, that represents the two possible configurations of the end-plate:

$$T = I_5 \bigwedge_{i=1}^{i=3} \Sigma_i^*$$

where the $\bigwedge$ notation implies an outer product of all elements following it.

Practically only one of these possible solutions is feasible, the solution which places Y at a greater position along the e_3 axis. We can once again get the 3D position of this point, y by extracting the point with projectors.

$$P = \frac{1}{2}\left(1 + \frac{T}{\sqrt{T^2}}\right)$$

$$y = \frac{-\sum_{j=1}^{j=3}(Y \cdot e_j)e_j}{Y \cdot n_\infty}, \qquad Y = -\tilde{P}(T \cdot n_\infty)P,$$

Figure 3 illustrates the geometry of the forward kinematic problem.

5   The Inverse Jacobian

Knowing static kinematic solutions is useful but to do more advanced analysis of the Delta robot mechanism we need to look at derivatives. We will start with inverse kinematics and ask ourselves the question, if the end-point plate moves with a specific velocity what speeds must the motors be moving at to be compatible?

First we will write the 3D end-point plate position as a linear combination of basis vectors with coefficients denoted α_j, $j \in 1, 2, 3$:

$$y = \alpha_1 e_1 + \alpha_2 e_2 + \alpha_3 e_3$$

Our goal now becomes to calculate the partial derivative of each motor angle with respect to one each of these α coefficients. Taking partial derivatives of y with respect to one of the α_j coefficients trivially gives:

$$\frac{\partial y}{\partial \alpha_j} = e_j$$

For now we do not need to worry about **which** α parameter we are taking derivatives with respect to, so we will leave the derivative of the end-point written as $\frac{\partial y}{\partial \alpha}$. Using this notation, our ultimate goal in this section is to find an equation for the partial derivative of a given motor angle θ_i with respect to α, i.e. $\frac{\partial \theta_i}{\partial \alpha}$. To find $\frac{\partial \theta_i}{\partial \alpha}$ we select a specific robot arm i and work back through its joints from the end-point.

The first joint position of interest is x_i, we saw in Sect. 3 that:

$$x_i = y + r_e s_i$$

Taking partial derivatives gives:

$$\frac{\partial x_i}{\partial \alpha} = \frac{\partial y}{\partial \alpha}$$

The 3D point x_i can then be represented as the CGA point X_i:

$$X_i = \frac{1}{2}x_i^2 n_\infty + x_i + n_0$$

The derivative of this CGA point is then easily found:

$$\frac{\partial X_i}{\partial \alpha} = \left(\frac{\partial x_i}{\partial \alpha} \cdot x_i \right) n_\infty + \frac{\partial x_i}{\partial \alpha}$$

We then form the dual constraint sphere:

$$\Sigma_i^* = X_i - \frac{1}{2}\rho^2 n_\infty$$

which, as the radius is fixed, has partial derivative:

$$\frac{\partial \Sigma_i^*}{\partial \alpha} = \frac{\partial X_i}{\partial \alpha}$$

As we saw in the previous section, the intersection of this dual constraint sphere Σ_i^* and the dual circle C_i^* centred on the motor shaft produces a point-pair T_i that represents the two possible elbow positions for that arm:

$$C_i^* = \left(B_i - \frac{1}{2}l^2 n_\infty \right) \wedge (I_3(s_i \wedge e_3))$$
$$T_i = (\Sigma_i^* \wedge C_i^*)^*$$

The outer product and taking the dual are both linear, which means that taking derivatives is particularly easy here:

$$\frac{\partial T_i}{\partial \alpha} = \left(\frac{\partial \Sigma_i^*}{\partial \alpha} \wedge C_i^* \right)^*$$

Of course the elbow can only actually be in one position which we can extract via projection operators:

$$P_i = \frac{1}{2}\left(1 + \frac{T_i}{\sqrt{T_i^2}} \right), \qquad \frac{\partial P_i}{\partial \alpha} = \frac{1}{2T_i^2}\left(\sqrt{T_i^2}\frac{\partial T_i}{\partial \alpha} - T_i \frac{\frac{\partial T_i}{\partial \alpha} \cdot T_i}{\sqrt{T_i^2}} \right)$$
$$W_i = -\tilde{P}_i(T_i \cdot n_\infty)P_i$$
$$\frac{\partial W_i}{\partial \alpha} = -\frac{\partial \tilde{P}_i}{\partial \alpha}(T_i \cdot n_\infty)P_i - \tilde{P}_i\left(\frac{\partial T_i}{\partial \alpha} \cdot n_\infty \right)P_i - \tilde{P}_i(T_i \cdot n_\infty)\frac{\partial P_i}{\partial \alpha}$$

454   H. Hadfield et al.

We can then convert from the CGA to the 3D vector point:

$$w_i = -\frac{\sum_{j=1}^{j=3}(W_i \cdot e_j)e_j}{W_i \cdot n_\infty}$$

$$\frac{\partial w_i}{\partial \alpha} = \frac{-\sum_{j=1}^{j=3}\left(\frac{\partial W_i}{\partial \alpha} \cdot e_j\right)e_j(W_i \cdot n_\infty) + \sum_{j=1}^{j=3}(W_i \cdot e_j)e_j\left(\frac{\partial W_i}{\partial \alpha} \cdot n_\infty\right)}{(W_i \cdot n_\infty)^2}$$

and use this to form the derivative of the motor angles with regard to α:

$$z_i = w_i - r_b s_i, \qquad \frac{\partial z_i}{\partial \alpha} = \frac{\partial w_i}{\partial \alpha}$$

$$\theta_i = \text{atan2}(z_i \cdot e_3, z_i \cdot s_i)$$

$$\frac{\partial \theta_i}{\partial \alpha} = \frac{z_i \cdot s_i}{|z_i \cdot s_i|}\frac{(z_i \cdot s_i)\left(\frac{\partial z_i}{\partial \alpha} \cdot e_3\right) - (z_i \cdot e_3)\left(\frac{\partial z_i}{\partial \alpha} \cdot s_i\right)}{z_i^2}$$

This finally gives us an expression for the derivative of the motor angle with respect to the α of the endpoint. Typically in engineering scenarios we would construct a matrix of the partial derivatives with respect to α_j, $j \in 1, 2, 3$, known as the Jacobian matrix:

$$J^* = \begin{bmatrix} \frac{\partial \theta_1}{\partial \alpha_1} & \frac{\partial \theta_1}{\partial \alpha_2} & \frac{\partial \theta_1}{\partial \alpha_3} \\ \frac{\partial \theta_2}{\partial \alpha_1} & \frac{\partial \theta_2}{\partial \alpha_2} & \frac{\partial \theta_2}{\partial \alpha_3} \\ \frac{\partial \theta_3}{\partial \alpha_1} & \frac{\partial \theta_3}{\partial \alpha_2} & \frac{\partial \theta_3}{\partial \alpha_3} \end{bmatrix}$$

This matrix can then be used to convert an end-point velocity vector to a set of motor velocities:

$$\begin{bmatrix} \frac{\partial \theta_1}{\partial t} \\ \frac{\partial \theta_2}{\partial t} \\ \frac{\partial \theta_3}{\partial t} \end{bmatrix} = J^* \begin{bmatrix} \frac{\partial \alpha_1}{\partial t} \\ \frac{\partial \alpha_2}{\partial t} \\ \frac{\partial \alpha_3}{\partial t} \end{bmatrix}$$

As it is the Jacobian matrix for the inverse kinematic problem, this matrix is specifically labelled the inverse Jacobian matrix.

6   The Forward Jacobian

Many problems in robotics require us to take derivatives of the forward kinematic equations. Specifically, we need to know the end-point plate velocity as a function of the motor speeds.

Our forward kinematic solution begins with calculating the position of the elbow point for a given arm i:

$$w_i = (r_b + l\cos(\theta_i))s_i + l\sin(\theta_i)e_3, \qquad \frac{\partial w_i}{\partial \theta_i} = -l\sin(\theta_i)s_i + l\cos(\theta_i)e_3$$

With the elbow point we can then calculate the pseudo-elbow point:

$$a_i = w_i - r_e s_i, \qquad \frac{\partial a_i}{\partial \theta_i} = \frac{\partial w_i}{\partial \theta_i}$$

We then convert the pseudo-elbow to a CGA point:

$$A_i = \frac{1}{2}a_i^2 n_\infty + a_i + n_0, \qquad \frac{\partial A_i}{\partial \theta_i} = \left(\frac{\partial a_i}{\partial \theta_i} \cdot a_i\right) n_\infty + \frac{\partial a_i}{\partial \theta_i}$$

The forearm length dual constraint sphere can then be constructed about the pseudo-elbow point

$$\Sigma_i^* = A_i - \frac{1}{2}\rho^2 n_\infty, \qquad \frac{\partial \Sigma_i^*}{\partial \theta_i} = \frac{\partial A_i}{\partial \theta_i}$$

The intersection of all three constraint spheres, one from each arm, produces the point pair on which the solution lies.

$$T = (\Sigma_1 \vee \Sigma_2 \vee \Sigma_3) \equiv I_5(\Sigma_1^* \wedge \Sigma_2^* \wedge \Sigma_3^*)$$

We can take derivatives of this point-pair with respect to each of the motor angles:

$$\frac{\partial T}{\partial \theta_1} = I_5\left(\frac{\partial \Sigma_1^*}{\partial \theta_1} \wedge \Sigma_2^* \wedge \Sigma_3^*\right), \qquad \frac{\partial T}{\partial \theta_2} = I_5\left(\Sigma_1^* \wedge \frac{\partial \Sigma_2^*}{\partial \theta_2} \wedge \Sigma_3^*\right)$$

$$\frac{\partial T}{\partial \theta_3} = I_5\left(\Sigma_1^* \wedge \Sigma_2^* \wedge \frac{\partial \Sigma_3^*}{\partial \theta_3}\right)$$

We can re-write these derivatives as follows:

$$\frac{\partial T}{\partial \theta_i} = (-1)^{i-1} I_5\left(\frac{\partial \Sigma_i^*}{\partial \theta_i} \wedge C^*\right), \quad \text{where} \quad C^* = \bigwedge_{j \in 1,2,3 \ j \neq i} \Sigma_j^* \tag{1}$$

Practically, when we take partial derivatives with respect to one θ at a time we are effectively freezing two of the motors in position and moving the third. Geometrically, this process forces the end-point plate to move along the surface of the circle formed by the intersection of the two constraint spheres centred at the pseudo-elbow points of the frozen motors.

Figure 4 shows the geometric significance of Eq. 1. To get the end-point plate position we again extract one end of the point-pair T:

$$P = \frac{1}{2}\left(1 + \frac{T}{\sqrt{T^2}}\right), \qquad \frac{\partial P}{\partial \theta_i} = \frac{1}{2T^2}\left(\sqrt{T^2}\frac{\partial T}{\partial \theta_i} - T\frac{\frac{\partial T}{\partial \theta_i} \cdot T}{\sqrt{T^2}}\right)$$

$$Y = -\tilde{P}(T \cdot n_\infty)P, \qquad \frac{\partial Y}{\partial \theta_i} = -\frac{\partial \tilde{P}}{\partial \theta_i}(T \cdot n_\infty)P - \tilde{P}\left(\frac{\partial T}{\partial \theta_i} \cdot n_\infty\right)P - \tilde{P}(T \cdot n_\infty)\frac{\partial P}{\partial \theta_i}$$

Finally we convert our end-point back to a 3D point:

$$y = \frac{-\sum_{j=1}^{j=3}(Y \cdot e_j)e_j}{Y \cdot n_\infty}$$

$$\frac{\partial y}{\partial \theta_i} = \frac{-\sum_{j=1}^{j=3}\left(\frac{\partial Y}{\partial \theta_i} \cdot e_j\right)e_j(Y \cdot n_\infty) + \sum_{j=1}^{j=3}(Y \cdot e_j)e_j(\frac{\partial Y}{\partial \theta_i} \cdot n_\infty)}{(Y \cdot n_\infty)^2}$$

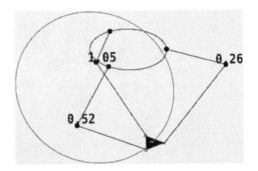

Fig. 4. With two limbs frozen the end-point plate is constrained to move such that its centre always lies on the circle (shown in red) formed from the intersection of the other two limbs' constraint spheres.

We can write the end-point plate position as:

$$y = \alpha_1 e_1 + \alpha_2 e_2 + \alpha_3 e_3, \qquad \frac{\partial y}{\partial \theta_i} = \frac{\partial \alpha_1}{\partial \theta_i} e_1 + \frac{\partial \alpha_2}{\partial \theta_i} e_2 + \frac{\partial \alpha_3}{\partial \theta_i} e_3$$

With $\frac{\partial y}{\partial \theta_i}$ we are therefore in a position to build the forward Jacobian matrix:

$$J = \begin{bmatrix} \frac{\partial y}{\partial \theta_1} \cdot e_1 & \frac{\partial y}{\partial \theta_2} \cdot e_1 & \frac{\partial y}{\partial \theta_3} \cdot e_1 \\ \frac{\partial y}{\partial \theta_1} \cdot e_2 & \frac{\partial y}{\partial \theta_2} \cdot e_2 & \frac{\partial y}{\partial \theta_3} \cdot e_2 \\ \frac{\partial y}{\partial \theta_1} \cdot e_3 & \frac{\partial y}{\partial \theta_2} \cdot e_3 & \frac{\partial y}{\partial \theta_3} \cdot e_3 \end{bmatrix}$$

The inverse Jacobian matrix and the forward Jacobian matrix are, as the names suggest, inverse to each other.

$$JJ^* = I$$

7 Simulation and Verification in Python and Unity3D

To verify our derivatives we implemented the above mathematics in the Clifford Python package [10] and tested it against a central differences approximation.

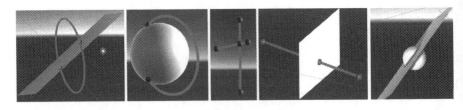

Fig. 5. Intersections of geometric primitives calculated and visualised with the Unity3D CGA library

With the mathematics verified we constructed a CGA Unity3D library based on the C# output of the ganja.js [9] code generator. Figure 5 shows examples of this library being used to intersect circles, lines, spheres and planes in Unity3D. Alongside the CGA library we also constructed a physical delta robot model using Unity3D's built-in joint system and physics system, the right hand side of Fig. 6 shows the model in the Unity3D scene view. The simulated physical model of the robot allows us to design and tune a controller safely and for low cost without requiring us to build or buy a real Delta robot.

The CGA Unity3D library and simulated physical robot together form a test-bed for the design and tuning of control systems. On the left hand side of Fig. 6 is the representation of the robot to a controller constructed using the CGA library and the mathematics described in the previous sections.

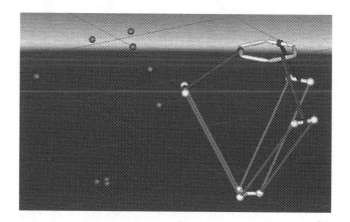

Fig. 6. Left: The internal robot geometry model of the controller. Right: The physically simulated Delta robot in Unity3D.

8 Conclusion

In this paper we have derived, step-by-step, the forward and inverse kinematic solutions for a Delta robot in CGA as well as the forward and inverse Jacobian matrices. We then implemented the mathematics in Python and C# before simulating a physical robot model in Unity3D and using our mathematics to design a basic position and velocity control system to position the end-plate of the robot.

References

1. Clavel, R.: Conception d'un robot parallèle rapide à 4 degrés de liberté. Infoscience (1991). https://doi.org/10.5075/epfl-thesis-925, https://infoscience.epfl.ch/record/31403

2. Clavel, R.: Device for the movement and positioning of an element in space, United States Patent No. 4976582 (1990)
3. Pessina, L.: Reymond Clavel, creator of the Delta Robot, reflects on his career, EPFL website. https://sti.epfl.ch/reymond-clavel-creator-of-the-delta-robot-reflects-on-his-career/
4. Gallardo-Alvarado, J.: Kinematic Analysis of Parallel Manipulators by Algebraic Screw Theory. Springer, Cham (2016). https://doi.org/10.1007/978-3-319-31126-5
5. Merlet, J.-P.: Parallel Robots. Kluwer Academic Publishers, Boston (2006)
6. Lasenby, A., Lasenby, J., Wareham, R.: A covariant approach to geometry using geometric algebra. CUED Technical report CUED/F-INFENG/TR-483. Cambridge University Engineering Department (2004)
7. Dorst, L., Fontijne, D., Mann, S.: Geometric Algebra for Computer Science: An Object-oriented Approach to Geometry, 1st edn. Elsevier, Morgan Kaufmann, Amsterdam (2007)
8. Pierrot, F., Fournier, A., Dauchex, P.: Towards a fully-parallel 6 DOF robot for high-speed applications. In: 1991 IEEE International Conference on Robotics and Automation Proceedings, vol. 2, pp. 1288–1293 (1991)
9. De Keninck, S.: ganja.js (2017). https://github.com/enkimute/ganja.js
10. Arsenovic, A., Hadfield, H., Wieser, E., Kern, R., The Pygae Team: Clifford (Version v1.3.0), 29 May 2020. https://github.com/pygae/clifford. Zenodo. https://doi.org/10.5281/zenodo.3865446
11. Zsombor-Murray, P.J.: Descriptive Geometric Kinematic Analysis of Clavel's "Delta" Robot. Centre for Intelligent Machines, McGill University (2004)
12. Zamora, J., Bayro-Corrochano, E.: Inverse kinematics, fixation and grasping using conformal geometric algebra. In: 2004 IEEE/RSJ International Conference on Intelligent Robots and Systems (IROS) (IEEE Cat. No.04CH37566), vol. 4, pp. 3841–3846 (2004)
13. Hildenbrand, D., Zamora, J., Bayro-Corrochano, E.: Inverse kinematics computation in computer graphics and robotics using conformal geometric algebra. Adv. Appl. Clifford Algebras 18, 699–713 (2008). https://doi.org/10.1007/s00006-008-0096-5
14. Aristidou, A.: Tracking and modelling motion for biomechanical analysis (Doctoral thesis) (2010). https://doi.org/10.17863/CAM.13996
15. Kleppe, A.L., Egeland, O.: Inverse kinematics for industrial robots using conformal geometric algebra. Model. Ident. Control: Norw. Res. Bull. 37, 63–75 (2016)
16. Kim, J.S., Jeong, J.H., Park, J.H.: Inverse kinematics and geometric singularity analysis of a 3-SPS/S redundant motion mechanism using conformal geometric algebra. Mech. Mach. Theory 90, 23–36 (2015)
17. Fu, Z., Yang, W., Yang, Z.: Solution of inverse kinematics for 6R robot manipulators with offset wrist based on geometric algebra. J. Mech. Robot. 5 (2013)
18. Tichý, R.: Inverse kinematics for the industrial robot IRB4400 based on conformal geometric algebra. In: Mazal, J., Fagiolini, A., Vasik, P. (eds.) MESAS 2019. LNCS, vol. 11995, pp. 148–161. Springer, Cham (2020). https://doi.org/10.1007/978-3-030-43890-6_12
19. Hildenbrand, D., Hrdina, J., Návrat, A., Vašík, P.: Local controllability of snake robots based on CRA, theory and practice. Adv. Appl. Clifford Algebras 30(1), 1–21 (2019). https://doi.org/10.1007/s00006-019-1022-8
20. Selig, J.M.: Geometric Fundamentals of Robotics. Springer, Heidelberg (2005). https://doi.org/10.1007/b138859

Constrained Dynamics in Conformal and Projective Geometric Algebra

Hugo Hadfield$^{(\boxtimes)}$ and Joan Lasenby

Department of Engineering, University of Cambridge, Cambridge, UK
{hh409,jl221}@cam.ac.uk

Abstract. In this paper we tackle the problem of constrained rigid body dynamics in the Conformal and Projective Geometric Algebras (CGA, PGA). First we construct a screw-theory based formulation of dynamics in CGA and note the equivalence between this and the PGA dynamics presented by Gunn in [1]. After verifying the formulation via simulation, we move on to the challenge of adding constraints. First we apply the standard mechanical engineering technique of virtual power to the constraint problem in our Geometric Algebra (GA) framework. We then discuss a novel technique for 'pinning' dynamic rigid bodies to geometric primitives, a technique that relies on the invariance of certain multivectors and functions of multivectors to specific rotor transformations.

1 Forces, Moments and Static Equilibrium

For a rigid body to be in static equilibrium certain conditions have to be met. Specifically, there can be no net moment about its centre of mass and no net force acting on it.

1.1 Forces as Dual Lines in CGA

Let us consider how we might go about representing a force as a line in CGA (a detailed description of CGA is beyond the scope of this paper, instead for background the reader is directed towards [7]). First, consider a force represented by the 3D vector f and passing through point a, we could write this as a 6D vector representing the 'force line' F. This 6D representation is known as the Plücker coordinates of the line [2], and is made up of the force vector and moment:

$$ F = \begin{bmatrix} f \\ a \times f \end{bmatrix} $$

We could represent this same force line in CGA as the outer product of two points and infinity. This object has a magnitude equal to the intensity of the force:

$$ F = \mathrm{up}\,(a) \wedge \mathrm{up}\,(a + f) \wedge n_{\infty}, \qquad F^2 = |f|^2 $$

© Springer Nature Switzerland AG 2020
N. Magnenat-Thalmann et al. (Eds.): CGI 2020, LNCS 12221, pp. 459–471, 2020.
https://doi.org/10.1007/978-3-030-61864-3_39

where up (x) denotes the standard embedding of a point x as a 5D conformal point $X = \frac{1}{2}x^2 n_\infty + x + n_0$. Consider the dual form of this CGA line:

$$FI_5 = fI_3 - (a \wedge f)I_3 n_\infty$$

This looks very similar to the 6D Plücker representation and in fact, on inspection, we see that there is a direct mapping between the two. First, look at the first term, fI_3. This is the 3D dual to a 3D vector, giving a bivector, specifically the Euclidean bivector orthogonal to f. Now consider the second term: $-(a \wedge f)I_3 n_\infty$. $-(a \wedge f)I_3$ is the 3D GA equivalent of the cross product, i.e. a vector equal to $a \times f$, just like the lower 3 elements of the 6D plucker representation. As $-(a \wedge f)I_3$ is a Euclidean vector this makes $-(a \wedge f)I_3 n_\infty$ the form of a CGA 'direction bivector'. An important point to note is that under addition the two terms in the formula behave independently, just like in the 6D Plücker representation, i.e.

$$\lambda_1 F_1 I_5 + \lambda_2 F_2 I_5 = (\lambda_1 f_1 + \lambda_2 f_2)I_3 - (\lambda_1 a_1 \wedge f_1 + \lambda_2 a_2 \wedge f_2)I_3 n_\infty$$

Setting $\lambda_1 = \lambda_2$ and $f_1 = f = -f_2$ in the above leaves us with two anti-parallel forces:

$$F_1 I_5 + F_2 I_5 = -(a_1 \wedge f - a_2 \wedge f)I_3 n_\infty$$

which we could re-write as:

$$B = bn_\infty$$

As previously mentioned this is in the form of a CGA 'direction bivector'. These bivectors have the interesting property of being invariant to the action of translation rotors, effectively making them free vectors in the physics sense. Physically two anti-parallel forces create a force couple, a pure moment, and so we will take objects of the form bn_∞ to be representations of moments in our scheme. This seems apt as, physically, a pure moment is often thought of as a free vector.

We can now write down the static equilibrium conditions directly as:

$$\sum_i F_i I_5 + \sum_j B_j = 0$$

where F_i represent external forces acting on a rigid body and B_j represent external moments acting on the body.

1.2   Forces as Lines in PGA

In PGA the canonical way to describe a line is as the intersection of two planes. As by default in PGA we are in a so called 'inner product null space' or IPNS we perform the intersection of these two planes by the outer product. Let's break this down component-wise for the intersection of two planes:

$$P_1 = m_1 + d_1 e_0, \quad P_2 = m_2 + d_2 e_0$$
$$L = P_1 \wedge P_2 = (m_1 + d_1 e_0) \wedge (m_2 + d_2 e_0)$$
$$= m_1 \wedge m_2 + (d_2 m_1 - d_1 m_2) \wedge e_0$$

we can now re-write this in terms that look more familiar:

$$L = m_l I_3 - (a \wedge m_l) I_3 e_0$$

In this form the line looks very similar to the CGA representation of the line. The line squares to a scalar, there is a section that is a euclidean bivector and a section that is a null bivector. In fact the only thing that we have changed is the form of the null element. In CGA we typically use the null element n_∞ constructed from the sum of two orthogonal basis vectors, one squaring to $+1$ and one to -1. Here in PGA the null element e_0 is itself a basis vector. For our 6D force line representation we therefore have exactly the same mapping as we did in CGA:

$$F = f I_3 - (a \wedge f) I_3 e_0$$

and so moments appear as:

$$B = b e_0$$

We note that this is, in fact, the same formulation as is used by Gunn in [1].

2 Time Derivatives of Frame Transformations

Before diving into dynamics, we will lay down some notation. A rotor R takes a multivector U from a frame attached to the rigid body to a multivector V expressed in the world frame:

$$V = R U \tilde{R}, \quad U = \tilde{R} V R$$

We will also take first and second time derivatives as we will need them later:

$$\dot{U} = \dot{\tilde{R}} V R + \tilde{R}(\dot{V} R + V \dot{R})$$
$$\ddot{U} = \ddot{\tilde{R}} V R + 2\dot{\tilde{R}}(\dot{V} R + V \dot{R}) + \tilde{R} \ddot{V} R + 2\tilde{R} \dot{V} \dot{R} + \tilde{R} V \ddot{R} \qquad (1)$$

Standard results [3–5] tell us we can write:

$$\dot{R} = -\frac{1}{2} \dot{B}_w R \qquad (2)$$

where the quantity $\dot{B}_w$ is a generalised instantaneous screw velocity, expressed in the world frame. Geometrically it is a screw and we can transform it just like any other screw between frames. We can therefore write $\dot{B}_w = R \dot{B} \tilde{R}$ and change Eq. (2) to:

$$\dot{R} = -\frac{1}{2} R \dot{B} \tilde{R} R = -\frac{1}{2} R \dot{B} \qquad (3)$$

where $\dot{B}$ is the velocity bivector expressed in the body frame. For reference the reverse of this quantity is:

$$\dot{\tilde{R}} = -\frac{1}{2} \dot{B} \tilde{R}$$

To take further time derivatives we can just use the chain rule:

$$\ddot{R} = -\frac{1}{2} R \ddot{B} - \frac{1}{2} \dot{R} \dot{B}, \quad \ddot{\tilde{R}} = -\frac{1}{2} \ddot{B} \tilde{R} - \frac{1}{2} \dot{B} \dot{\tilde{R}} \qquad (4)$$

3   Momentum and Inertia

3.1   Screw Momentum

In traditional 3D dynamics formulations we specify that resultant force is the rate of change of linear momentum and resultant moment is the rate of change of angular momentum. In a screw formulation we can specify that, for a body under the influence of multiple external forces W_i, the resultant wrench W_r is the rate of change of screw momentum Ω with time:

$$W_r = \sum W_i = \frac{\partial \Omega}{\partial t}$$

We can, of course, write this whether we are working in CGA or PGA.

3.2   The Screw Inertia Tensor

In 3D dynamics we are used to the idea of converting between linear velocity and linear momentum via multiplication or division by the mass of the rigid body:

$$\rho_l = m v_l$$

When it comes to angular velocity and angular momentum however we have a more complicated relationship. In fact, for a body centred reference frame, the two are related by a diagonal matrix known as the inertia tensor that we label here as M:

$$\rho_a = M v_a$$

We can extend the inertia tensor concept to the CGA motor bivectors (by which we mean the bivectors that when exponentiated produce the motors) using their reciprocal frame. An important thing to note here is that this is different to the concept in screw theory [8] of a screw and a twist being reciprocal, which we will come to later when considering virtual work and power.

The reciprocal frame of the motor bivectors in CGA is as follows:

$$-e_1 I_3, \ -e_2 I_3, \ -e_3 I_3, \ e_1 \wedge n_0, \ e_2 \wedge n_0, \ e_3 \wedge n_0$$

Which we can break into the two groups:

$$l_i = e_i I_3, \quad l^i = -e_i I_3$$
$$t_i = e_i \wedge n_\infty, \quad t^i = e_i \wedge n_0$$

and so with these we can construct an inertia tensor:

$$\Omega = M(\dot{B}) = m \sum_{i=1}^{i=3} \left[(\dot{B} \cdot t^i) l_i + \gamma_i (\dot{B} \cdot l^i) t_i \right]$$

we can also construct the inverse inertia tensor:

$$M^{-1}(\Omega) = \dot{B} = \frac{1}{m} \sum_{i=1}^{i=3} \left[\frac{1}{\gamma_i} (\Omega \cdot t^i) l_i + (\Omega \cdot l^i) t_i \right]$$

This inertia tensor performs a 'flip' of the input bivectors, as well as re-scaling component-wise. Effectively our inertia tensor does the following mapping:

$$e_1 I_3 \;\rightarrow\; e_1 \wedge n_\infty, \qquad\qquad e_1 \wedge n_\infty \;\rightarrow\; e_1 I_3$$
$$e_2 I_3 \;\rightarrow\; e_2 \wedge n_\infty, \qquad\qquad e_2 \wedge n_\infty \;\rightarrow\; e_2 I_3$$
$$e_3 I_3 \;\rightarrow\; e_3 \wedge n_\infty, \qquad\qquad e_3 \wedge n_\infty \;\rightarrow\; e_3 I_3$$

This reciprocal frame construction works for many algebras but for degenerate metric algebras such as PGA the fact that we have an element squaring to zero means this setup won't work. Instead we need to do something a little different. The degenerate metric approach to reciprocal frames [6] is to consider some blade which we will label x^i that wedges with a given blade of magnitude b_i i.e. $b_i x_i$ to produce the pseudoscalar with magnitude b_i i.e. $b_i x_i \wedge x^i = b_i I$. Clearly, despite us labelling it x^i, this object is not quite the same as the reciprocal frame although it allows us to perform the same function of coordinate free coefficient selection producing the magnitude b_i as the scalar coefficient of the pseudoscalar. Let's identify this pseudo-reciprocal frame for the PGA bivectors:

$$e_1 \wedge e_2 \;\rightarrow\; -e_3 \wedge e_0, \qquad\qquad e_1 \wedge e_0 \;\rightarrow\; -e_2 \wedge e_3$$
$$e_1 \wedge e_3 \;\rightarrow\; e_2 \wedge e_0, \qquad\qquad e_2 \wedge e_0 \;\rightarrow\; e_1 \wedge e_3$$
$$e_2 \wedge e_3 \;\rightarrow\; -e_1 \wedge e_0, \qquad\qquad e_3 \wedge e_0 \;\rightarrow\; -e_1 \wedge e_2$$

Comparing the PGA pseudo-reciprocal frame mapping with that of our CGA-inertia tensor mapping it is immediately clear that they are equivalent up to a minus sign. Let's define a function to perform this PGA mapping, we will call it J and it will do the following:

$$J(b_i x_i) = \langle b_i x_i \wedge x^i \rangle_{e1230} x^i = b_i x^i$$

where the syntax $\langle A \rangle_{e1230}$ returns the scalar coefficient of $e_1 \wedge e_2 \wedge e_3 \wedge e_0$ in A. We can extend this operation to combinations of basis elements by linearity so that for $X = \sum_i b_i x_i$:

$$X^J = J(X) = J\left(\sum_i b_i x_i\right) = \sum_i J(b_i x_i)$$

As with our CGA reciprocal frame let's now write our PGA pseudo-reciprocal frame in two groups:

$$l_i = e_i I_3, \quad l^i = e_i \wedge e_0$$
$$t_i = e_i \wedge e_0, \quad t^i = e_i I_3$$

This means we can write our PGA inertia tensor and inverse as:

$$\Omega = M(\dot{B}) = -m \sum_{i=1}^{i=3} \left[\langle \dot{B} \wedge l^i \rangle_{e1230} l^i + \gamma_i \langle \dot{B} \wedge t^i \rangle_{e1230} t^i \right] \tag{5}$$

$$M^{-1}(\Omega) = \dot{B} = -\frac{1}{m}\sum_{i=1}^{i=3}\left[\frac{1}{\gamma_i}\langle\Omega\wedge l^i\rangle_{e1230}l^i + \langle\Omega\wedge t^i\rangle_{e1230}t^i\right] \qquad (6)$$

We could also apply the J map first to first 'flip' the input and apply a component-wise scaling A to the result:

$$\Omega = M(\dot{B}) = A[J(\dot{B})]$$

4 Unconstrained Rigid Body Dynamics

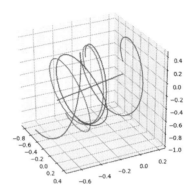

Fig. 1. A cuboid is simulated spinning about its 2nd principal axis of inertia while translating linearly. Due to the intermediate axis theorem small instabilities in the rotation build quickly causing rapid flips in orientation. Despite these rapid flips the linear motion of the centre of mass is unaffected. Blue: the path of the centre of mass, Green, Red, Orange: the path of several vertices on the cuboid as it undergoes a flip in orientation. (Color figure online)

Equipped with forces, moments, momentum, velocities and inertia tensors we are now at a position where we can formulate the equations of motion and simulate them. We will start by considering the dynamics of an unconstrained rigid body moving under the influence of external forces and moments. We can write the state of our rigid body at a time t and its first time derivative as (Fig. 1):

$$Y_t = \begin{bmatrix} R_t \\ \Omega_t \end{bmatrix}, \quad \dot{Y}_t = \begin{bmatrix} \dot{R}_t \\ \dot{\Omega}_t \end{bmatrix} = \begin{bmatrix} -\frac{1}{2}R_t\dot{B}_t \\ R_t W_{bt}\tilde{R}_t \end{bmatrix}$$

where Ω_t is the momentum bivector at time t expressed in the world frame and W_{bt} is the result external wrench acting on the body expressed in the body frame. From this point on we will drop the t subscript and simply state that all variables are functions of time. From our discussion in the previous section we know that we can further expand $\dot{B}$ using the inverse inertia tensor M^{-1}:

$$\dot{B} = M^{-1}[\tilde{R}\Omega R]$$

Re-writing the time derivative of the state with this equation for $\dot{B}$ gives:

$$\dot{Y} = \begin{bmatrix} \dot{R} \\ \dot{\Omega} \end{bmatrix} = \begin{bmatrix} -\frac{1}{2}RM^{-1}[\tilde{R}\Omega R] \\ RW_b\tilde{R} \end{bmatrix}$$

5   Constrained Dynamics via Virtual Power

To impose a constraint on our dynamics model we will use the concept of a **reaction wrench**. The reaction wrench provides a combined external force and moment that acts on the rigid body in addition to the other external wrenches and, in doing so, forces the body to move in a way that respects the constraints. We will write W_b as the sum of external wrenches S plus some reaction wrench F caused by the constraints. As we already know S, all we need to calculate F is the value of W_b required to keep the constraints valid.

In traditional constrained dynamics work the concepts of virtual work and virtual power are widespread. In the virtual work/virtual power literature constraints are enforced by imagining several independent virtual reaction forces and moments at the constraint position and ensuring that any velocity of the body produces zero power against these forces/moments. In the screw framework that we have developed the virtual power P produced by a virtual world frame wrench T when the body moves with a body frame screw velocity $\dot{B}$ is given by:

$$P = \dot{B} \wedge (\tilde{R}TR)$$

and, for CGA, is of the form:

$$P = pI_3 n_\infty$$

where p is a virtual scalar power. Differentiating this gives:

$$\dot{P} = \ddot{B} \wedge (\tilde{R}TR) + \dot{B} \wedge \left(\dot{\tilde{R}}TR + \tilde{R}(\dot{T}R + T\dot{R}) \right)$$

We can now substitute in our dynamics equation for $\ddot{B}$:

$$\ddot{B} = M^{-1}[\dot{\tilde{R}}\Omega R + W_b + \tilde{R}\Omega \dot{R}]$$

$$\dot{P} = M^{-1}[\dot{\tilde{R}}\Omega R + W_b + \tilde{R}\Omega \dot{R}] \wedge (\tilde{R}TR) + \dot{B} \wedge \left(\dot{\tilde{R}}TR + \tilde{R}(\dot{T}R + T\dot{R}) \right)$$

Setting the virtual power and rate of change of virtual power to 0 gives us the virtual power condition for our constraint:

$$0 = \dot{B} \wedge (\tilde{R}TR)$$

Setting the rate of change of virtual power to be zero allows us to write:

$$M^{-1}[\dot{\tilde{R}}\Omega R + W_b + \tilde{R}\Omega \dot{R}] \wedge (\tilde{R}TR) = -\dot{B} \wedge \left(\dot{\tilde{R}}TR + \tilde{R}(\dot{T}R + T\dot{R}) \right)$$

$$M^{-1}[W_b] \wedge (\tilde{R}TR) = -M^{-1}[\dot{\tilde{R}}\Omega R + \tilde{R}\Omega \dot{R}] \wedge (\tilde{R}TR) - \dot{B} \wedge \left(\dot{\tilde{R}}TR + \tilde{R}(\dot{T}R + T\dot{R}) \right)$$

If T is a static constraint we can specify that $\dot{T} = 0$ leaving us with:

$$M^{-1}[W_b] \wedge (\tilde{R}TR) = -M^{-1}[\dot{\tilde{R}}\Omega R + \tilde{R}\Omega\dot{R}] \wedge (\tilde{R}TR) - \dot{B} \wedge \left(\dot{\tilde{R}}TR + \tilde{R}T\dot{R}\right)$$

Which can again be solved for W_b and hence F.

If we specify the way that T varies with time we can add curved surface constraints. Consider a situation in which a rigid body is constrained such that one point A always touches a sphere centred at point V. Given the point is always touching the sphere we know that T must always be parallel to the line joining A and V, we would therefore write:

$$T = A \wedge V \wedge n_\infty$$

taking a time derivative of this we see:

$$\dot{T} = \dot{A} \wedge V \wedge n_\infty$$

As A is driven by the rotor R, we get:

$$A = RA_0\tilde{R}, \quad \dot{A} = \dot{R}A_0\tilde{R} + RA_0\dot{\tilde{R}}$$

and so:

$$\dot{T} = (\dot{R}A_0\tilde{R} + RA_0\dot{\tilde{R}}) \wedge V \wedge n_\infty$$

We can then directly substitute this into:

$$M^{-1}[W_b]\wedge(\tilde{R}TR) = -M^{-1}[\dot{\tilde{R}}\Omega R+\tilde{R}\Omega\dot{R}]\wedge(\tilde{R}TR)-\dot{B}\wedge\left(\dot{\tilde{R}}TR + \tilde{R}(\dot{T}R + T\dot{R})\right)$$

and so calculate W_b. To constrain this same point to a circle we would add an additional planar constraint (or indeed another spherical one), i.e. the point must lie on the plane in which the circle lies and on the sphere of which the circle is the equator.

6   Constrained Dynamics by Pinned Multivectors

As in Sect. 2 consider again a geometric primitive represented by multivector U in the body frame and the same geometric primitive represented by multivector V when expressed in the world frame. As we saw before the two multivectors can be related by the rotor R:

$$V = RU\tilde{R}, \quad U = \tilde{R}VR$$

We also saw previously that we can calculate the first and second time derivatives of this relationship giving us the expressions:

$$\dot{U} = \dot{\tilde{R}}VR + \tilde{R}(\dot{V}R + V\dot{R})$$
$$\ddot{U} = \ddot{\tilde{R}}VR + \dot{\tilde{R}}(\dot{V}R + V\dot{R}) + \dot{\tilde{R}}(\dot{V}R + V\dot{R}) + \tilde{R}(\ddot{V}R + 2\dot{V}\dot{R} + V\ddot{R})$$
$$= \ddot{\tilde{R}}VR + 2\dot{\tilde{R}}(\dot{V}R + V\dot{R}) + \tilde{R}\ddot{V}R + 2\tilde{R}\dot{V}\dot{R} + \tilde{R}V\ddot{R}$$

Let's take a second and think about what these expressions mean physically. Essentially we have two 'views' of the same object, one in body space and one in world space. For example we can imagine the U is a point attached to our rigid body and V is a point in the world that point is also attached to. In a sense we are 'pinning' the rigid body to V by its extremity U (Fig. 2).

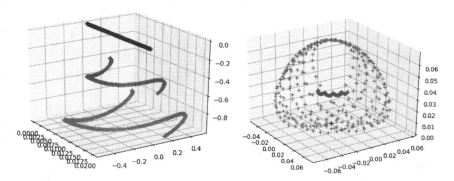

Fig. 2. Left: A physical pendulum moves under the effect of gravity and with a starting linear momentum. It is constrained such that a line, coincident with one end of the pendulum shown in blue, is pinned between the body and world reference frames. The symmetry of the line leads to constrained motion along and about the line. Right: A spinning cone is affected by gravity but is constrained such that its end point, shown in blue, does not move. Precession and nutation are observable in the movement of the centre of mass, shown in green, and a point on the rim of the cone, shown in red. (Color figure online)

Lets consider first the case that both of these 'views' of the object are fixed, i.e. the position and orientation of U cannot change with respect to the coordinate system of the body and the position and orientation of V cannot change with respect to the origin. Mathematically we are stating that $\dot{U}, \ddot{U}, \dot{V}, \ddot{V} = 0$. If we substitute these values into (1) for the time derivatives we end up with the following equation:

$$0 = \ddot{R}VR + \tilde{R}V\ddot{R} + 2\dot{\tilde{R}}V\dot{R} \tag{7}$$

This equation is a constraint on the second time derivative of R that will ensure that U and V do not vary with time. We can go a step further here and substitute our expression for $\ddot{R}$ from Eq. (4), leading to:

$$0 = -\frac{1}{2}\ddot{\tilde{B}}\tilde{R}VR - \frac{1}{2}\dot{\tilde{B}}\dot{\tilde{R}}VR - \frac{1}{2}\tilde{R}VR\ddot{B} - \frac{1}{2}\tilde{R}V\dot{R}\dot{B} + 2\dot{\tilde{R}}V\dot{R}$$

Now if we substitute in $\dot{R} = -\frac{1}{2}R\dot{B}$ and $\dot{\tilde{R}} = -\frac{1}{2}\dot{\tilde{B}}\tilde{R}$:

$$0 = -\frac{1}{2}\ddot{\tilde{B}}\tilde{R}VR + \frac{1}{4}\dot{\tilde{B}}\dot{\tilde{B}}\tilde{R}VR - \frac{1}{2}\tilde{R}VR\ddot{B} + \frac{1}{4}\tilde{R}VR\dot{B}\dot{B} + \frac{1}{2}\dot{\tilde{B}}\tilde{R}VR\dot{B}$$

Simplify and gather, substituting $U = \tilde{R}VR$:

$$0 = -\frac{1}{2}\ddot{B}U - \frac{1}{2}U\ddot{B} + \frac{1}{4}\dot{B}^2 U + \frac{1}{4}U\dot{B}^2 + \frac{1}{2}\dot{B}U\dot{B}$$

Now separate the terms with $\ddot{B}$:

$$\frac{1}{2}\ddot{B}U + \frac{1}{2}U\ddot{B} = \frac{1}{4}\dot{B}^2 U + \frac{1}{4}U\dot{B}^2 + \frac{1}{2}\dot{B}U\dot{B}$$

As $\dot{B}, \ddot{B}$ are bivectors their reverse is just a negation:

$$-\frac{1}{2}\ddot{B}U + \frac{1}{2}U\ddot{B} = \frac{1}{4}\dot{B}^2 U + \frac{1}{4}U\dot{B}^2 - \frac{1}{2}\dot{B}U\dot{B} \tag{8}$$

We have done a lot of algebra but so far appear to be no closer to calculating our reaction wrench. If we calculate an expression for $\ddot{B}$ however we start to make headway towards a solution:

$$\ddot{B} = M^{-1}[\dot{\tilde{R}}\Omega R + \tilde{R}\dot{\Omega}R + \tilde{R}\Omega\dot{R}]$$

using $W_b = \tilde{R}\dot{\Omega}R$ we can also write:

$$\ddot{B} = M^{-1}[\dot{\tilde{R}}\Omega R + \tilde{R}\Omega\dot{R}] + M^{-1}[W_b] \tag{9}$$

and so we can now substitute in on the left hand side of Eq. (8) for $\ddot{B}$:

$$LHS = -\frac{1}{2}\left(M^{-1}[\dot{\tilde{R}}\Omega R + \tilde{R}\Omega\dot{R}] + M^{-1}[W_b]\right)U + \frac{1}{2}U\left(M^{-1}[\dot{\tilde{R}}\Omega R + \tilde{R}\Omega\dot{R}] + M^{-1}[W_b]\right)$$

Now we separate out the terms with W_b

$$= -\frac{1}{2}M^{-1}[W_b]U + \frac{1}{2}UM^{-1}[W_b] + \left(-\frac{1}{2}M^{-1}[\dot{\tilde{R}}\Omega R + \tilde{R}\Omega\dot{R}]U + \frac{1}{2}UM^{-1}[\dot{\tilde{R}}\Omega R + \tilde{R}\Omega\dot{R}]\right)$$

and take all the stuff in brackets onto the right side of the equation. We now have something of the form:

$$-\frac{1}{2}M^{-1}[W_b]U + \frac{1}{2}UM^{-1}[W_b] = \text{Some function of } R, \Omega, U$$

We can rewrite this to use the commutator product:

$$(U \times M^{-1}[W_b]) = \text{Some function of } R, \Omega, U \tag{10}$$

If we now decide to write our total bivector wrench W_b as the sum of external wrenches S plus some reaction wrench F caused by the constraints:

$$(U \times M^{-1}[F]) = -(U \times M^{-1}[S]) + \text{Some function of } R, \Omega, U$$

we now have a constraint expression that fixes the reaction wrench F as a function of the state of the system and the forces applied to it.

For a given R, Ω, U this constraint is linear in F and can be solved for F so long as we provide a correct basis for the constraint wrench. An important point to make here is that this discussion has been entirely algebra agnostic, i.e. this framework works equally well for CGA, PGA or indeed many other geometric algebras, a topic that we will return to later on.

7 Pinning Parametric Multivectors Paths

So far in our construction of multivector pinning constraints we have assumed that the objects that we are pinning are static in both the world and body frame. When working with constrained dynamics in the real world we often want to affix parts of our rigid body to moving things in the real world, such as a manipulator attached to the moving end-point of a robot, or a flywheel fixed in a moving vehicle. Consider once again Eq. (1):

$$\ddot{U} = \ddot{\tilde{R}}VR + 2\dot{\tilde{R}}(\dot{V}R + V\dot{R}) + \tilde{R}\ddot{V}R + 2\tilde{R}\dot{V}\dot{R} + \tilde{R}V\ddot{R}$$

In the previous section we enforced static multivector constraints by setting $\dot{U}, \ddot{U}, \dot{V}, \ddot{V}$ to zero, rearranging to isolate the $\ddot{R}$ terms and solving the resultant linear equation for W_b. Now we will relax the static constraint and consider the cases when U, V are known **time varying** multivector functions, i.e. when $\dot{U}, \ddot{U}, \dot{V}, \ddot{V} \neq 0$.

First note we can still rearrange to separate terms in $\ddot{R}$:

$$\ddot{\tilde{R}}VR + \tilde{R}V\ddot{R} = -2\dot{\tilde{R}}(\dot{V}R + V\dot{R}) - \tilde{R}\ddot{V}R - 2\tilde{R}\dot{V}\dot{R} + \ddot{U}$$

and we can continue as in our previous analysis by breaking up $\ddot{R}$ as a function of $\ddot{B}$ and extracting W_b:

$$\ddot{\tilde{R}}VR + \tilde{R}V\ddot{R} = (-\frac{1}{2}\ddot{\tilde{B}}\tilde{R} - \frac{1}{2}\dot{\tilde{B}}\dot{\tilde{R}})VR + \tilde{R}V(-\frac{1}{2}R\ddot{B} - \frac{1}{2}\dot{R}\dot{B})$$

Continuing to substitute expressions as before we can expand this to the form:

$$(\tilde{R}VR) \times M^{-1}[F] = -\ddot{U} + M^{-1}[S] \times (\tilde{R}VR) + 2\dot{\tilde{R}}(\dot{V}R + V\dot{R}) + \tilde{R}\ddot{V}R + 2\tilde{R}\dot{V}\dot{R}$$
$$+ M^{-1}[\dot{\tilde{R}}\Omega R + \tilde{R}\Omega\dot{R}] \times (\tilde{R}VR) - \frac{1}{2}\dot{\tilde{B}}\dot{\tilde{R}}VR - \frac{1}{2}\tilde{R}V\dot{R}\dot{B}$$

if we substitute $U = \tilde{R}VR$ we have eventually got to a position where:

$$(U \times M^{-1}[F]) = \text{Some function of } R, \Omega, U, \dot{U}, \ddot{U}, V, \dot{V}, \ddot{V}, S$$

Again this is a linear function in F and solvable so long as it is of sufficient rank. What this means practically is that we can set U and V to follow any desired path we like in their respective spaces and extract the reaction forces and moments acting on the body that are required to keep them pinned to each other.

8 Pinning Linear Functions of Parametric Multivector Paths

In the previous two sections we dealt directly with transformations that pin static multivectors or time varying multivector paths directly to each other in space.

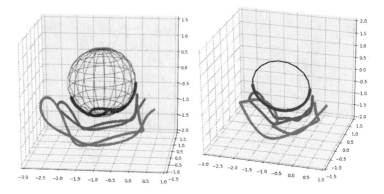

Fig. 3. A physical pendulum moves under gravity is constrained such that one end of it, shown in blue, is always in contact with the surface of an object. The green trace shows the midpoint of the pendulum and the red shows the free end. Left: a sphere. Right: a circle. (Color figure online)

In many practical situations what we would really like to pin is a linear function of one multivector to another. For example we could pin the outer product of a point in the body frame and a plane in the world frame to 0, effectively forcing them to be coincident without specifying anything about their relative orientation (unlike in the transformed plane invariant case). Mathematically we can express our linear function constraint as $A[\,]$ and time derivatives as:

$$U = A\left[\tilde{R}VR\right], \quad \dot{U} = A\left[\dot{\tilde{R}}VR + \tilde{R}(\dot{V}R + V\dot{R})\right]$$
$$\ddot{U} = A\left[\ddot{\tilde{R}}VR + 2\dot{\tilde{R}}(\dot{V}R + V\dot{R}) + \tilde{R}\ddot{V}R + 2\tilde{R}\dot{V}\dot{R} + \tilde{R}V\ddot{R}\right]$$

Once again we can rearrange:

$$A\left[\ddot{\tilde{R}}VR + \tilde{R}V\ddot{R}\right] = A\left[-2\dot{\tilde{R}}(\dot{V}R + V\dot{R}) - \tilde{R}\ddot{V}R - 2\tilde{R}\dot{V}\dot{R}\right] + \ddot{U}$$

leading to an equation of the form:

$$A\left[(\tilde{R}VR) \times M^{-1}[F]\right] = A\left[-((\tilde{R}VR) \times M^{-1}[S]) + \text{Some function of } R, \Omega, U, \dot{U}, \ddot{U}, V, \dot{V}, \ddot{V}\right] - \ddot{U}$$

Again this is linear and solvable as before. Figure 3 shows the simulation with the Clifford Python library [9] of two cases in which the linear function is the outer product with one end of a physical pendulum.

9   Conclusion

In this paper we have looked at forces, moments, free and constrained dynamics in both CGA and PGA. As well as considering how to apply virtual power as a constraint mechanism in our GA formulations we have constructed a novel technique for constrained dynamics in GA via the concept of multivector pinning. While in this paper we have only considered two algebras, CGA and PGA, the techniques are expected to work across the board for algebras with easily representable line elements and motor bivectors. Using other higher dimensional algebras such as Cl(4, 4) [10], Cl(8, 2) [11] or even Cl(9, 6) [12] with this technique in future should allow for easy configurations of exotic constraints such as pinning dynamic objects to the surface of quadrics.

References

1. Gunn, C.: On the homogeneous model of Euclidean geometry. In: Dorst, L., Lasenby, J. (eds.) Guide to Geometric Algebra in Practice, pp. 297–327. Springer, London (2011). https://doi.org/10.1007/978-0-85729-811-9_15

2. Pottmann, H., Wallner, J.: Computational Line Geometry. MATHVISUAL. Springer, Heidelberg (2001). https://doi.org/10.1007/978-3-642-04018-4

3. Lasenby, A., Lasenby, R., Doran, C.: Rigid body dynamics and conformal geometric algebra. In: Dorst, L., Lasenby, J. (eds.) Guide to Geometric Algebra in Practice, pp. 3–24. Springer, London (2011). https://doi.org/10.1007/978-0-85729-811-9_1

4. Candy, L.P.: Kinematics in conformal geometric algebra with applications in strapdown inertial navigation. Ph.D. thesis. University of Cambridge (2012)

5. Boyle, M.: The integration of angular velocity. Adv. Appl. Clifford Algebras **27**(3), 2345–2374 (2017). https://doi.org/10.1007/s00006-017-0793-z

6. Gunn, C.: Non-metric alternatives to reciprocal frames. The bivector.net forums. https://discourse.bivector.net/t/non-metric-alternative-to-reciprocal-frame/105/4. Accessed 12 May 2020

7. Dorst, L., Fontijne, D., Mann, S.: Geometric Algebra for Computer Science: An Object-Oriented Approach to Geometry, 1st edn. Elsevier, Morgan Kaufmann, Amsterdam (2007)

8. Gallardo-Alvarado, J.: Kinematic Analysis of Parallel Manipulators by Algebraic Screw Theory. Springer, Cham (2016). https://doi.org/10.1007/978-3-319-31126-5

9. Arsenovic, A., Hadfield, H., Wieser, E., Kern, R., The Pygae Team: Clifford (Version v1.3.0), 29 May 2020. Zenodo. https://doi.org/10.5281/zenodo.3865446

10. Du, J., Goldman, R., Mann, S.: Modeling 3D geometry in the Clifford algebra $R(4, 4)$. Adv. Appl. Clifford Algebras **27**(4), 3039–3062 (2017). https://doi.org/10.1007/s00006-017-0798-7

11. Easter, R.B., Hitzer, E.: Double conformal geometric algebra. Adv. Appl. Clifford Algebras **27**(3), 2175–2199 (2017). https://doi.org/10.1007/s00006-017-0784-0

12. Breuils, S., Nozick, V., Sugimoto, A., Hitzer, E.: Quadric conformal geometric algebra of $\mathbb{R}^{9,6}$. Adv. Appl. Clifford Algebras **28**(2), 1–16 (2018). https://doi.org/10.1007/s00006-018-0851-1

Application of 2D PGA as an Subalgebra of CRA in Robotics

Radek Tichý[(✉)]

Brno University of Technology, Technická 2896/2, 616 69 Brno, Czech Republic
Radek.Tichy@vutbr.cz

Abstract. We present a concept of 2D Projective Geometric Algebra (PGA) as a subalgebra of Compass Ruler Algebra (CRA) to handle problems in computer graphics and engineering efficiently in terms of an algebra with minimal dimension. In this case, we can benefit from both CRA and PGA simultaneously. When we deal with complex problems, we can use CRA objects such as circles but at the same time we can switch to PGA as a subalgebra of CRA to handle operations with flat-objects more efficiently without the change of structure of any further implementation. We demonstrate this approach on example of inverse kinematics of a planar 3-link manipulator.

Keywords: Projective geometric algebra · Compass ruler algebra · Inverse kinematics

1   Introduction

Compass ruler algebra (CRA) is an algebra for dealing with geometric problems in 2D Euclidean space. It allows a representation of round objects such as circles, moreover conformal transformations and computing intersections are possible, see [4]. An example of application is the inverse kinematics of planar mechanism based on finding intersections between lines and circles, see [1,5]. A problem arises, when we only deal with flat objects (lines). Then it is more efficient to work in projective geometric algebra (PGA) which also allows transformations and representations of flat objects but the dimension of PGA is lower, see [2]. It leads to faster computation. In this paper we would like to present an approach which allows to use both algebras at the same time, since PGA can be found as a subalgebra of CRA. The description of PGA as an subalgebra of conformal geometric algebra for 3D space was originally presented in [7]. We also demonstrate this approach on the planar inverse kinematics problem.

The author was supported by solution grand FV20-31 science Fund of the FME 2020 at Brno University of Technology.

ⓒ Springer Nature Switzerland AG 2020
N. Magnenat-Thalmann et al. (Eds.): CGI 2020, LNCS 12221, pp. 472–481, 2020.
https://doi.org/10.1007/978-3-030-61864-3_40

2   Compass Ruler Algebra - CRA

Algebraically CRA[1] is a Clifford Algebra on $R^{3,1}$ defined by a nondegenerate quadratic form of signature $(3,1,0)$, see Chap. 14 in [6]. Vectors $\{e_0, e_1, e_2, e_\infty\} \in R^{3,1}$ denote a basis of the vector space with inner product given by the quadratic form

$$B_c = \begin{pmatrix} 0 & 0 & -1 \\ 0 & I_{2\times2} & 0 \\ -1 & 0 & 0 \end{pmatrix} \tag{1}$$

thus e_0, e_∞ are null vectors and $e_0 \cdot e_\infty = e_\infty \cdot e_0 = -1$. The duality in CRA of any multivector A is defined as

$$A^* = AI^{-1} = A_c \cdot I^{-1},$$

where $I = e_{012\infty}$ is the CRA pseudoscalar and $I^{-1} = -I$. The signature of CRA allows us to define an embedding of a Euclidean point $P_E = xe_1 + ye_2$ into the algebra as

$$P = P_E + \frac{1}{2}(P_E \cdot P_E)e_\infty + e_0,$$

where $P_E \cdot P_E = x^2 + y^2$. With this embedding we can represent Euclidean objects in two ways. In the first one called OPNS (*outer product null space*) or *direct representation* defined with help of outer[2] (wedge) product, an object is represented by multivector A if and only if the object is formed exactly by points P satisfying

$$P \wedge A = 0.$$

The second representation called IPNS (*inner product null space*) or *dual representation* is dual to OPNS. The same object is now represented by multivector A^* satisfying

$$P \cdot A^* = 0.$$

Both representations of Euclidean elements are listed in Table 1. In IPNS representation, the wedge product has the role of meet operator, i.e. wedge of any two objects represents their intersection. In Table 1 we can see for instance that a point-pair is represented as wedge of two circles. Let us note that points in CRA are actually circles of zero radius, therefore points are considered as round objects. Representation of points as flat objects is also possible, such objects are called flat-points and they are represented as

$$FP = P \wedge e_\infty.$$

---

[1] For full description of CRA we refer to [4].

[2] More about operations and structure of geometric algebras can be found in [8].

Table 1. CRA representation of objects, where r is a radius of a circle, n is a Euclidean normal vector of a line and d is a distance from the origin.

Entity	IPNS	OPNS
Point	$P = xe_1 + ye_2 + \frac{1}{2}(x^2 + y^2)e_\infty + e_0$	
Circle	$C^* = P - \frac{1}{2}r^2 e_\infty$	$C = P_1 \wedge P_2 \wedge P_3$
Line	$L^* = n + de_\infty$	$L = P_1 \wedge P_2 \wedge e_\infty$
Point pair	$Pp^* = C_1 \wedge C_2$	$Pp = P_1 \wedge P_2$

3   Projective Geometric Algebra Inside CRA

2D Projective geometric algebra (PGA) is a Clifford Algebra on $R^{2,0,1}$ generated by a degenerate quadratic form of signature $(2,0,1)$ given by matrix

$$B_p = \begin{pmatrix} 0 & 0 \\ 0 & I_{2\times 2} \end{pmatrix}. \tag{2}$$

The vector basis $\{e_0, e_1, e_2\}$, where e_0 is a null vector, is usually considered, see [2]. From here we will describe PGA as a subalgebra in CRA, for a full description of this approach for general dimension (with focus on dimension 3), see [7] in arXiv database. One can observe that the quadratic form (2) is contained as a block matrix in the quadratic form of CRA given by (1). We can even find two subalgebras of CRA which are both isomorphic to PGA. The first one generated by vectors $\{e_0, e_1, e_2\} \cong R^{2,0,1}$ and the second one generated by $\{e_1, e_2, e_\infty\} \cong R^{2,0,1}$. It is possible to switch between these two subalgebras by bijective linear map $\sharp$ of $R^{3,1}$ onto itself, for $i = 1, 2$ given by

$$\sharp : e_i \mapsto e_i, \; e_\infty \mapsto -e_0, \; e_0 \mapsto -e_\infty.$$

For our application it is more convenient to consider the subalgebra with e_∞ as PGA because, as we will see later, representations of flat objects in PGA and CRA coincide. Since the quadratic form of PGA is degenerate, it is not possible to define a duality with help of an inverse of pseudoscalar. The pseudoscalar in PGA has no inversion. Usually the duality is defined by a table of all coefficients of a multivector. However in [7] a new duality has been defined in terms of CRA. We can take the inverse of pseudoscalar $I_p = e_{12\infty}$ with respect to the inner product. Such an inversion exists in CRA, it is the pseudoscalar of the other copy of PGA, i.e. $I_p^{-1} = -I_p^\sharp = e_{012}$. It is easy to verify that $I_p \cdot (-I_p^\sharp) = 1$. The PGA duality $*_p$ for any multivector $A_p \in PGA$ is then defined by

$$A_p^{*_p} = (A_p \cdot I_p^{-1})^\sharp.$$

Note that such duality satisfies the condition of so called Hodge duality used in traditional PGA $A \wedge A^{*_p} = I_p$ and moreover we can relate it to the standard CRA duality by $A_p^{*_p} = (A_p \wedge e_0)^{*\sharp}$. The duals of the basis blades are given explicitly in Table 2.

Table 2. PGA duality

	1	e_1	e_2	e_∞	e_{12}	$e_{1\infty}$	$e_{2\infty}$	$e_{12\infty}$
A_p	a	b	c	d	e	f	g	h
$A_p^{*_p}$	h	g	-f	e	-d	c	-b	-a

In PGA we can deal with flat objects, in 2D these objects are points and lines. A point $P_E = xe_1 + ye_2$ is represented by bivector

$$P_p = e_{12} - xe_{2\infty} + ye_{1\infty}.$$

The representation of objects in PGA, more precisely lines in 2D PGA, is defined by a regressive product. The regressive product $\vee$ is a dual operation to the outer product, i.e. $(A_p \vee B_p)^{*_p} = A_p^{*_p} \wedge B_p^{*_p}$. Thus a line is represented by a multivector L_p in RPNS (regressive product null space) representation if and only if the line is formed exactly by points P_p satisfying

$$P_p \vee L_p = 0.$$

A line spanned by points P_{p1}, P_{p2} is then represented as

$$L_p = P_{p1} \vee P_{p2}.$$

With this setting there is a correspondence between PGA and CRA flat objects. Particularly for a flat point of a Euclidean point $P_E = xe_1 + ye_2$ in CRA we have

$$FP^* = (P \wedge e_\infty)^* = -e_{12} - ye_{1\infty} + xe_{2\infty} = -P_p. \tag{3}$$

Similarly for a line it can be computed that

$$L^* = -L_p,$$

where L^* is IPNS representation of a line in CRA and L_p is RPNS representation of the same line in PGA. For a proof we refer to [7]. Note that it is possible to compute angle between two lines L_{p1}, L_{p2} by formula

$$\alpha = \arccos \frac{L_{p1} \cdot L_{p2}}{|L_{p1}||L_{p2}|}, \tag{4}$$

where the norm $|L_p| = \sqrt{L_p^2}$. The term $\sqrt{L_p^2}$ is viable since L_p is a vector, thus the square is a positive scalar.

We add one more interesting fact about 2D PGA and CRA. The Euclidean transformations are represented by a sandwich product in both algebras as

$$\bar{O} = VOV^{-1},$$

where V is an invertible element called versor, O is a Euclidean object represented in one of mentioned representations and $\bar{O}$ is the same object after the transformation. For a rotation such a versor is called rotor. In PGA the rotor realizing the rotation around the point P_p by an angle α is

$$R_p = \cos \frac{\alpha}{2} - P_p \sin \frac{\alpha}{2}.$$

In CRA, the same rotation is realized by exactly the same rotor $R = R_p$, however in CRA the bivector P_p has no geometric meaning if we do not consider PGA as its subalgebra.

Now when we have the tool to do computation in CRA and PGA simultaneously and we can easily switch between representations of objects in these algebras, we can demonstrate this approach by solving the inverse kinematics of a planar manipulator.

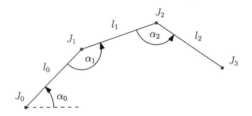

Fig. 1. 2D manipulator

4   Inverse Kinematics of a Planar Manipulator

We consider the planar manipulator displayed in Fig. 1 with 3 links l_0, l_1, l_2 (for simplicity let all links have length 1) connected by revolute joints J_0, J_1, J_2, where J_0 is in the origin, and J_3 is the endpoint. The configuration of the mechanism is given by angles $\alpha_0, \alpha_1, \alpha_2$.

In our problem of inverse kinematics, we are given a position of the end point and the task is to compute angles $\alpha_0, \alpha_1, \alpha_2$ such that the mechanism reaches that position. All points are given by their coordinates (x, y), we can consider them in the form $J = xe_1 + ye_2$. In our experiment, the initial configuration is given by angles $({}^0\alpha_0, {}^0\alpha_1, {}^0\alpha_2) = (45, 155, 150)$ and the input point we want to reach has coordinates $(2, 1.4)$. For the geometric algebra algorithm based on finding intersections of objects, we need to have as many initial inputs as the number of links. In our case we are already given points $\bar{J}_0, \bar{J}_3$ (the bar will denote the points or links in the final configuration). We need to add one additional input, we chose a condition that the last link $\bar{l}_2$ is parallel with the links l_2.

In the first step we represent all points as CRA objects, for $i = 0, \ldots, 3$

$$P_{J_i} = J_i + \frac{1}{2}(J_i \cdot J_i)e_\infty + e_0,$$

$$\bar{P}_{J_3} = \bar{J}_3 + \frac{1}{2}(\bar{J}_3 \cdot \bar{J}_3)e_\infty + e_0.$$

From the inputs we know that $\bar{P}_{J_0} = P_{J_0}$. The links can be represented in geometric algebra as lines passing through them. The last input can be then formulated as finding line $\bar{L}_2$ parallel to the line L_2 (L_2 represents the links l_2) and passing the point $\bar{P}_{J_3}$. For this subproblem it is not efficient to use CRA since we can use a nice formula[3] for a projection of line L_p on point P_p from the algebra of smaller dimension PGA given by

$$(L_p \cdot P_p)P_p. \tag{5}$$

We can use formula 3 to compute PGA representation $P_{p_2}, P_{p_3}, \bar{P}_{p_3}$ of points $P_{J_2}, P_{J_3}, \bar{P}_{J_3}$, respectively. We show an equation for one of these points, the computation of others is the same:

$$P_{p_2} = -(P_{J_2} \wedge e_\infty)^*.$$

A line of the link l_2 in PGA is computed as

$$L_{p_2} = P_{p_2} \vee P_{p_3}$$

and finally the CRA line of link $\bar{l}_2$ in IPNS representation is of the form

$$\bar{L}_2^* = -(L_{p_2} \cdot \bar{P}_{J_3})\bar{P}_{J_3}.$$

Points $\bar{P}_{J_0}, \bar{P}_{J_3}$ and the line $\bar{L}_2^*$ are represented graphically in Fig. 2 by green points and blue line.

Once we have inputs represented we will find points $\bar{P}_{J_1}, \bar{P}_{J_2}$ with help of intersections of objects. For this purpose we will also work with circles. Thus using CRA notation is required. At first we will compute point $\bar{P}_{J_2}$. This point lies on the intersection of the circle with the center $\bar{P}_{J_3}$ and radius of length 1 (it is the length of the link l_2, all links have length equal to 1) represented as

$$C_3^* = \bar{P}_{J_3} - \frac{1}{2}e_\infty$$

and the line $\bar{L}_2^*$. Such the intersection is the point-pair

$$Pp_2^* = C_3^* \wedge \bar{L}_2^*.$$

Two points can be extracted by the formula

$$P_\pm = \frac{Pp_2 \pm \sqrt{Pp_2 \cdot Pp_2}}{-e_\infty \cdot Pp_2}$$

---

[3] The list of many useful PGA formulas can be found in [3].

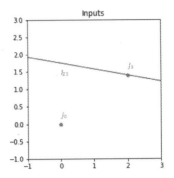

Fig. 2. Inputs of the algorithm (Color figure online)

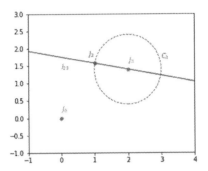

Fig. 3. The point J_2 (Color figure online)

and the point $\bar{P}_{J_2}$ is chosen such that the orientation of the link $\bar{l}_2$ coincide with the orientation of the link l_2, see Fig. 3 the red point.

Only the point $\bar{P}_{J_1}$ remains to be computed. Again we can describe all possible movements of the link l_1 with the fixed point $\bar{P}_{J_0}$ by the circle

$$C_0^* = \bar{P}_{J_0} - \frac{1}{2}e_\infty$$

and similarly we can describe a movement of the link l_1 fixed in the point $\bar{P}_{J_2}$ by the circle

$$C_2^* = \bar{P}_{J_2} - \frac{1}{2}e_\infty.$$

The desired point $\bar{P}_{J_1}$ will lie in the intersection of these circles computed as

$$Pp_1^* = C_0^* \wedge C_2^*.$$

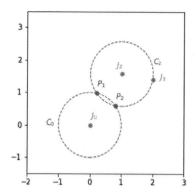

Fig. 4. Two points extracted from the point-pair Pp_1

Two points extracted from the point-pair are obtained as

$$P_1 = \frac{Pp_1 - \sqrt{Pp_1 \cdot Pp_1}}{-e_\infty \cdot Pp_1},$$

$$P_2 = \frac{Pp_1 + \sqrt{Pp_1 \cdot Pp_1}}{-e_\infty \cdot Pp_1},$$

see Fig. 4. The choice of one point is not clear in this case. However a reasonable approach is to choose the point satisfying the condition

$$(\varphi_0)^2 + (\varphi_1)^2 + (\varphi_2)^2 \to \min, \tag{6}$$

where for $i = 0, 1, 2$ $\varphi_i = {}^0\alpha_i - \alpha_i$ denoted the difference between angles of the initial and the final configurations. The most obvious way how to choose the right point is to simply compute angles for both points and compare results. Since this example should primary demonstrate the idea of switching between two algebras, we describe the computation of angles for the point $\bar{P}_{J_1}$ only. Note without proof that this point actually satisfies the condition (6).

For the computation of angles we use Eq. (4). Since there is no need to use circles anymore, we can switch to PGA in order to work in the algebra with lower dimension. At first we switch all computed points to the PGA representation, for $i = 0, 1, 2, 3$ we have

$$\bar{P}_{p_i} = -(\bar{P}_{J_i} \wedge e_\infty)^*.$$

With help of these point we express the lines representing particular links for $i = 0, 1, 2$ as

$$\bar{L}_{p_i} = \bar{P}_{p_i} \vee \bar{P}_{p_{i+1}}$$

and the line representing x axis

$$L_{p_x} = e_{12} \vee (e_{12} - e_{2\infty}).$$

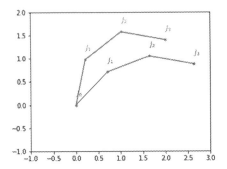

Fig. 5. The initial configuration - red points, the final configuration - green points. (Color figure online)

The angles are then computed as

$$\alpha_0 = \arccos\left(L_{p_0} \cdot L_{p_x}\right),$$
$$\alpha_1 = \arccos\left(L_{p_1} \cdot L_{p_0}\right),$$
$$\alpha_2 = \arccos\left(L_{p_2} \cdot L_{p_1}\right),$$

the values of angles in our experiment are $(\alpha_0, \alpha_1, \alpha_2) \approx (78, 139, 133)$, see Fig. 5.

5   Conclusion

We introduced an approach of considering 2D PGA as an subalgebra of CRA. We showed that the representations of flat objects in CRA and PGA coincide. The PGA duality can be defined in term of algebra operations in CRA. We demonstrated this approach by solving the inverse kinematics of a planar mechanism. This approach allows us to use benefits of both algebras at the same time, i.e. lower dimension of algebra and easy formulas for projections of flat objects in PGA and the representation of round objects (circles) in CRA. With new implementations of geometric algebras based on this approach, it has a great potential especially for applications in 3D Euclidean space, where we can consider 3D PGA as a subalgebra of CGA (conformal geometric algebra). Such implementations (in the meaning that we can handle geometric algebra elements and operations) could improve computational time of geometric algebra algorithms.

References

1. Corrochano, E.B.: Geometric Computing for Perception Action Systems. Springer, New York (2001). https://doi.org/10.1007/978-1-4613-0177-6
2. Gunn, C.G.: Doing Euclidean plane geometry using projective geometric algebra. Adv. Appl. Clifford Algebras **27**(2), 1203–1232 (2016). https://doi.org/10.1007/s00006-016-0731-5

3. Gunn, C.G., De Keninck, S.: 2D Projective Geometric Algebra Cheat Sheet. bivector.net
4. Hildenbrand, D.: Introduction to Geometric Algebra Computing. Taylor & Francis Inc., Milton Park (2018)
5. Hrdina, J., Návrat, A., Vašík, P.: Notes on planar inverse kinematics based on geometric algebra. Adv. Appl. Clifford Algebras **28**(3), 1–14 (2018). https://doi.org/10.1007/s00006-018-0890-7
6. Lounesto, P.: Clifford Algebras and Spinors. Cambridge University Press, Cambridge (2006)
7. Navrat, A., Hrdina, J., Vasik, P., Dorst, L.: Projective Geometric Algebra as a Subalgebra of Conformal Geometric Algebra
8. Perwass, C.: Geometric Algebra with Applications in Engineering. Geometry and Computing, vol. 4. Springer, Heidelberg (2009). https://doi.org/10.1007/978-3-540-89068-3

Outline of Tube Elbow Detection Based on GAC

Roman Byrtus, Anna Derevianko, and Petr Vašík[(⊠)]

Faculty of Mechanical Engineering, Brno University of Technology,
Brno, Czech Republic
171155@vutbr.cz, derev.anna.08.96@gmail.com, vasik@fme.vutbr.cz

Abstract. We outline an algorithm for camera–based tube elbow detection provided that a moving camera is placed in the tube axis together with a light source. We claim that once an elbow is approached, circular contour is replaced by an elliptical one and the displacement of respective circle and ellipse centres is proportional to the elbow angle. We provide Python code for computation in Geometric Algebra for Conics (GAC), parameter extraction and an example of proportionality.

Keywords: Geometric algebra for conics · Conic fitting · Contour detection

1 Introduction

In many applications, e.g. image processing and computer vision, [9,12], a concept of geometric algebra has been successfully used. Standard structure is the Conformal Geometric Algebra (CGA), [1,15], which is a Clifford algebra $Cl(4,1)$ endowed with a quadratic form of signature $(4,1)$ with an embedding of three dimensional Euclidean space such that points are mapped on zero norm vectors (null vectors). More precisely, it is an embedding $\mathbb{R}^3 \to \mathbb{R}^{4,1} \to Cl(4,1)$, where $\mathbb{R}^{4,1}$ is a five dimensional real space with a quadratic form of signature $(4,1)$ meaning that four basis vectors square to 1 and one to -1. Further geometric entities such as spheres of dimension 2 (i.e. sphere surfaces; spheres of other dimensions are point pairs, circles, lines and planes - e.g. the latest as spheres of infinite radii) are mapped on either vectors or 4-vectors (basis elements of degree 4 with respect to number of vectors used in the generating operation, i.e. Clifford product). The sphere representative's degree depends on the type of representation. Moreover, even Euclidean transformations, i.e. translations and rotations, may be viewed as elements of this Clifford algebra, namely they are 2-vectors, [2]. The geometric object manipulation is then performed by conjugation of its representation by the so-called motor. This is the difference from quaternion manipulation where only points may be transformed. Based on these ideas of

The research was supported by a Grant No. FSI–S–20–6187.

© Springer Nature Switzerland AG 2020
N. Magnenat-Thalmann et al. (Eds.): CGI 2020, LNCS 12221, pp. 482–491, 2020.
https://doi.org/10.1007/978-3-030-61864-3_41

David Hestenes many algorithms have been modified in geometrical sense see e.g. [13]. For foundations of computing with geometric algebras see e.g. [3].

Recently, modifications of this construction to more general geometric primitives such as quadrics have been introduced, [6], yet the price is in dimension increase. We consider the model of Geometric Algebra for Conics (GAC), [11], which has all properties of true geometric algebra even with transformations compatibility. GAC is of signature $(5,3)$, which means that there are 8 generators bringing the actual dimension to 2^8. This still may be implemented effectively in Python and therefore may lead to interesting applications, see [7].

In the following, we present a piece of a complex research task called pipe inspecting, leading to an autonomous snake–like robot moving inside a pipe system. We intend to propose a mechanism whose motion, orientation and image processing necessary for detection is mostly based on geometric algebras. Indeed, many subtasks have been already solved, see e.g. [10] for snake control algorithm. We stress that together with algorithm optimizer GAALOP, [4] and a specialised coprocessor GAPPCO, [5], the geometric algebra based mechanism will provide competitive performance. To be more precise about our goal, we propose a path following algorithm for a centralised motion in a pipe. To do so, one has to detect elbows and predict a curve composed of centre–points to be followed. We propose that if a light source and a camera is used, the final curve will be composed of circle centres in the straight parts of pipe and ellipse centres in elbows. To support this idea we show a simulation providing that the elbow angle is proportional to elliptical distortion of detected points.

2   Foundations of Geometric Algebra for Conics (GAC)

By geometric algebra we mean a Clifford algebra with a specific embedding of an Euclidean space (of arbitrary dimension) in such a way that predefined geometric primitives as well as their transformations are viewed as its single elements. Furthermore, geometric operations such as intersections, tangents, distances etc. are described very efficiently. Classically, three dimensional Euclidean space is represented in Clifford algebra $Cl(4,1)$, and the consequent geometric algebra is often denoted as $\mathbb{G}_{3,1}$ with spheres of all types as geometric primitives and Euclidean transformations at hand, see e.g. [1]. For conics, C. Perwass proposed to generalize the concept of (two–dimensional) conformal geometric algebra $\mathbb{G}_{3,1}$, [15]. In the usual basis $\bar{n}, e_1, e_2, n$, embedding of a plane in $\mathbb{G}_{3,1}$ is given by

$$(x,y) \mapsto \bar{n} + x e_1 + y e_2 + \frac{1}{2}(x^2 + y^2)n,$$

where e_1, e_2 form Euclidean basis and $\bar{n}$ and n stand for a specific linear combination of additional basis vectors e_3, e_4 with $e_3^2 = 1$ and $e_4^2 = -1$, giving them the meaning of the coordinate origin and infinity, respectively, [15]. Hence the objects representable by vectors in $\mathbb{G}_{3,1}$ are linear combinations of $1, x, y, x^2 + y^2$, i.e. circles, lines, point pairs and points. If we want to cover also general conics, we need to add two terms: $\frac{1}{2}(x^2 - y^2)$ and xy. It turns out that we need two new infinities for that and also their two corresponding counterparts (Witt pairs), [14]. Thus the resulting dimension of the space generating the appropriate geometric algebra is eight.

Let $\mathbb{R}^{5,3}$ denote the eight–dimensional real coordinate space $\mathbb{R}^8$ equipped with a non–degenerate symmetric bilinear form of signature $(5,3)$. The form defines Clifford algebra $\mathbb{G}_{5,3}$ and this is the Geometric Algebra for Conics in the algebraic sense. To add the geometric meaning we have to describe an embedding of the plane into $\mathbb{R}^{5,3}$. To do so, let us choose a basis of $\mathbb{R}^{5,3}$ such that the corresponding bilinear form is

$$B = \begin{pmatrix} 0 & 0 & -1_{3\times3} \\ 0 & 1_{2\times2} & 0 \\ -1_{3\times3} & 0 & 0 \end{pmatrix}, \tag{1}$$

where $1_{2\times2}$ and $1_{3\times3}$ denote unit matrices of the displayed size. Analogously to CGA and to the notation in [15], we denote the corresponding basis elements as follows

$$\bar{n}_+, \bar{n}_-, \bar{n}_\times, e_1, e_2, n_+, n_-, n_\times.$$

The form of (1) suggests that the basis elements e_1, e_2 will play the usual role of standard basis of the plane while the null vectors $\bar{n}$, n will represent either the origin or the infinity. Note that there are three orthogonal 'origins' $\bar{n}$ and three corresponding orthogonal 'infinities' n. In terms of this basis, a point of the plane $\mathbf{x} \in \mathbb{R}^2$ defined by $\mathbf{x} = xe_1 + ye_2$ is embedded using the operator $C : \mathbb{R}^2 \to \mathcal{C} \subset \mathbb{R}^{5,3}$, which is defined by

$$C(x,y) = \bar{n}_+ + xe_1 + ye_2 + \frac{1}{2}(x^2+y^2)n_+ + \frac{1}{2}(x^2-y^2)n_- + xyn_\times. \tag{2}$$

The image $\mathcal{C}$ of the plane in $\mathbb{R}^{5,3}$ is an analogue of the conformal cone. In fact, it is a two–dimensional real projective variety determined by five homogeneous polynomials of degree one and two.

Definition 1. *Geometric Algebra for Conics (GAC) is the Clifford algebra $\mathbb{G}_{5,3}$ together with the embedding $\mathbb{R}^2 \to \mathbb{R}^{5,3}$ given by (2) in the basis determined by matrix (1).*

To find more details about GAC we refer to [11].

Note that in GAC the pseudoscalar (highest grade element) is given by

$$I = \bar{n}_+\bar{n}_-\bar{n}_\times e_1 e_2 n_+ n_- n_\times.$$

Let us also recall that if a conic is seen as wedge of five different points (which determines a conic uniquely), we call the appropriate 5–vector an outer product null space representation (OPNS) and its dual, indeed a one vector, the inner product null space (IPNS) representation. For instance, the latter representation of a conic in GAC can be written in the form of a vector

$$Q_I = \bar{v}^+\bar{n}_+ + \bar{v}^-\bar{n}_- + \bar{v}^\times\bar{n}_\times + v^1 e_1 + v^2 e_2 + v^+ n_+. \tag{3}$$

More precisely, an ellipse E with the semi–axes a, b centred in $(u, v) \in \mathbb{R}^2$ rotated by angle θ is in the GAC inner representation given by

$$
\begin{aligned}
E_I = \bar{n}_+ &- (\alpha \cos 2\theta) \bar{n}_- - (\alpha \sin 2\theta) \bar{n}_\times \\
&+ (u + u\alpha \cos 2\theta - v\alpha \sin 2\theta) e_1 + (v + v\alpha \cos 2\theta - u\alpha \sin 2\theta) e_2 \\
&+ \tfrac{1}{2} \left(u^2 + v^2 - \beta - (u^2 - v^2)\alpha \cos 2\theta - 2uv\alpha \sin 2\theta \right) n_+ .
\end{aligned}
\tag{4}
$$

It is well known that the type of a given unknown conic can be read off its matrix representation Q, which in our case for a conic given by vector (3) reads

$$
Q = \begin{pmatrix}
-\frac{1}{2}(\bar{v}^+ + \bar{v}^-) & -\frac{1}{2}\bar{v}^\times & \frac{1}{2}v^1 \\
-\frac{1}{2}\bar{v}^\times & -\frac{1}{2}(\bar{v}^+ - \bar{v}^-) & \frac{1}{2}v^2 \\
\frac{1}{2}v^1 & \frac{1}{2}v^2 & -v^+
\end{pmatrix}.
\tag{5}
$$

The entries of (5) can be easily computed by means of the inner product:

$$
\begin{aligned}
q_{11} &= Q_I \cdot \tfrac{1}{2}(n_+ - n_-), \\
q_{22} &= Q_I \cdot \tfrac{1}{2}(n_+ + n_-), \\
q_{33} &= Q_I \cdot \bar{n}_+, \\
q_{12} &= q_{21} = Q_I \cdot \tfrac{1}{2}n_\times, \\
q_{13} &= q_{31} = Q_I \cdot \tfrac{1}{2}e_1, \\
q_{23} &= q_{32} = Q_I \cdot \tfrac{1}{2}e_2.
\end{aligned}
$$

It is also well known how to determine the internal parameters of an unknown conic and its position and the orientation in the plane from the matrix (5). Hence all this can be determined from the GAC vector Q_I by means of the inner product. Ellipse parameters extraction is given by

$$
x_c = (q_{12}q_{23} - 2q_{22}q_{31})/(4q_{11}q_{22} - q_{12}q_{12})
$$

$$
y_c = (q_{31}q_{21} - 2q_{11}q_{32})/(4q_{11}q_{22} - q_{12}q_{12})
$$

$$
\begin{aligned}
a_1 = &(-(2(q_{11}q_{23}q_{23} + q_{22}q_{13}q_{13} - q_{12}q_{13}q_{23} + (q_{12}q_{12} - 4q_{11}q_{22})q_{33})((q_{11} + q_{22}) \\
&+ ((q_{11} - q_{22})(q_{11} - q_{22}) + q_{12}q_{12})))^{\frac{1}{2}})^{\frac{1}{2}}/(q_{12}q_{12} - 4q_{11}q_{22})
\end{aligned}
$$

$$
\begin{aligned}
a_2 = &(-(2(q_{11}q_{23}q_{23} + q_{22}q_{13}q_{13} - q_{12}q_{13}q_{23} + (q_{12}q_{12} - 4q_{11}q_{22})q_{33})((q_{11} + q_{22}) \\
&- ((q_{11} - q_{22})(q_{11} - q_{22}) + q_{12}q_{12})^{\frac{1}{2}}))^{\frac{1}{2}})/(q_{12}q_{12} - 4q_{11}q_{22})
\end{aligned}
$$

where (x_c, y_c) are coordinates of the centre, a_1, a_2 are semiaxes. We encourage the readers to find also transformations' generators in [11].

3   Python Implementation and Parameter Extraction

We present an initial setting of Python to calculate in GAC according to the notation of [11] as well as the procedure for ellipse parameters extraction.

```
nx = e5+e8 #n_x
nxb = 0.5*(-e5+e8) #n_x bar
nm = e4+e7 #n_minus
nmb = 0.5*(-e4+e7)
n = e3+e6 #n_plus
nb = 0.5*(-e3+e6)
def up(x):#creats embedding of
    point into the algebra
a = x[e1]
b = x[e2]
return (nb + a*e1 + b*e2 + 1/2 *
    (a**2 + b**2)*n
+ 1/2 * (a**2 - b**2)*nm + a*b*nx
)


def to_ip_rep(con):#from OPNS to
    IPNS representation
return (con^nmb^nxb)*e12345678


def to_op_rep(con):#from IPNS to
    OPNS representation
return (con^nm^nx)*e12345678


def generate_ipn_func(con):
ipncon = to_ip_rep(con)
def ipn_func(x, y):
return (up(x*e1 + y*e2)|ipncon)
    [0]
return ipn_func


def visualise_conic(xs, ys, con):
ipn_func_con = generate_ipn_func(
    con)
img = np.zeros((len(xs),len(ys)))
for i,x in enumerate(xs):
for j,y in enumerate(ys):
img[j,i] = ipn_func_con(x, y)
return img


def get_Q(ipEllipse):
```

```
q11 =1/2* ipEllipse | (n + nm)
q22 =1/2*ipEllipse | (n -nm)
q33 =ipEllipse | nb
q12 = q21 =ipEllipse |nx
q13 = q31 =ipEllipse | e1
q23 = q32 = ipEllipse | e2
return(q11, q22,q33,q12,q13,q23,
    q21,q31,q32)
```

```
def ellipse(u,v,theta, a,b):#
    ellipse with center in (u,v),
    angle of rotation theta and
    semiaxis a,b
alpha = (a**2 - b**2)/(a**2 + b
    **2)
beta = 2*(a**2)*(b**2)/(a**2 + b
    **2)
ipEllipse = (nb - alpha * np.cos
    (2*theta)*nmb - (alpha * np.
    sin(2*theta))*nxb
+ (u - u*alpha*np.cos(2*theta) -
    v*alpha*np.sin(2*theta))*e1
+ (v +v*alpha*np.cos(2*theta) - u
    *alpha*np.sin(2*theta))*e2
+ 1/2 * (u**2 + v**2 - beta - (u
    **2 - v**2)*alpha*np.cos(2*
    theta)
- 2*u*v*alpha*np.sin(2*theta))*n)
xc,yc,a1,a2,angle=
    extract_ellipse_parameters(
    ipEllipse)
print('center (',xc,';',yc,'),
    semiaxes:',a1,',',a2)
print('angle of rotation: ',angle
    ,'rad;',180*angle/math.pi,'
    degrees')
plt.scatter(xc,yc)
ell = to_op_rep(ipEllipse)
return ell
```

The above code also provides an idea how to work with ellipse representation in Python. Extraction of the parameters provides the following results:

Clearly, to extract inner parameters of the ellipse, one has to solve a system of quadratic and goniometric equations numerically which is time consuming. Plus the polynomial coefficients have to be read off meaning that a data type must be switched. In geometric algebra, this can be done by simple algebra operations and matrix representation of an ellipse. In the sequel, we present a Python code

```
blue ellipse
center ( 1.0 ; 3.0 ), semiaxes: 4.0 , 6.0
angle of rotation:  0.5235987755982993 rad; 30.000000000000025 degrees
orange ellipse
center ( 2.0 ; 1.0 ), semiaxes: 2.0 , 5.0
angle of rotation:  -0.7853981633974482 rad; -44.99999999999999 degrees
green ellipse
center ( 5.0 ; 3.0 ), semiaxes: 3.0 , 4.0
angle of rotation:  0 rad; 0.0 degrees

<matplotlib.contour.QuadContourSet at 0x22206182448>
```

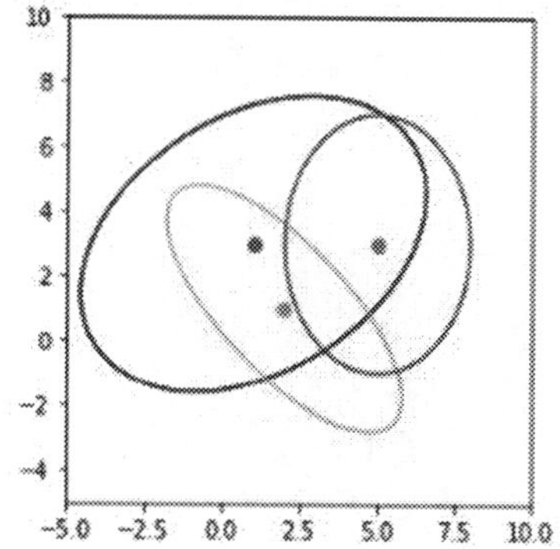

Fig. 1. Ellipse parameters extraction

returning the internal ellipse parameters, see Fig. 1. Note that the operations |
and * are intrinsic geometric algebra operations of inner and geometric product,
respectively, $e_1, e_2, n, nm := n_-, nx = n_\times, ...$, are base vectors and q_{ij} are real
numbers that form the matrix representation of an ellipse, corresponding to
the notation of [11]. By ipEllipse we denote so-called Inner Product Null Space
representation of a conic in GAC, i.e. a 1-vector. Simple code in Fig. 1 proves that
the structure is ready for implementation and visualisation, current calculation
speed is promising. We stress that not all implementation problems are solved,
the question of subalgebras implementation and code optimisation will be subject
to further research. Just as the first observation, all parameters of an ellipse are
obtained by simple operations without a need of changing the data-type to read
off the coefficients of a given conic's polynomial representation. Note that the
code in the above listing requires initialisation of the Python module clifford.gac.

4   Simulation

Let us propose the ellipse centre following algorithm for motion in a tube provided that a camera with the light source moves inside. Indeed, if a directed
light source is used in the centre of a straight pipe, the light cone will determine
a circular edge with greatest contrast gradient and therefore easily detectable
contour, e.g. by Canny edge detection algorithm. Once an elbow is approached,
circular contour is changed to elliptical, Figs. 2 and 3 (2), with the contrast points

488   R. Byrtus et al.

formed on the vanishing surface of the pipe, Figs. 2 and 3 (3) - yellow line. We stress that the dark points are not the edge of the light cone but they indicate an area with no light reflection, i.e. the are where the pipe surface becomes invisible behind the elbow. Indeed, once an elbow is approached, the light cone contour becomes invisible due to a number of reflections.

Once an elliptical set of points is detected, it may be fitted with an ellipse using GAC algorithm, [8], Figs. 2 and 3 (3) - blue line. When compared to actual pipe contour, Figs. 2 and 3 (4) - red line, clearly the ellipse centre follows the elbow direction proportionally. Obviously, there are questions of distance estimate, noise reduction and accuracy to be solved, most of which do not need GAC but some of its subalgebras such as CGA or its projective version, only. Therefore all structures must be compatible and form a system of subalgebras.

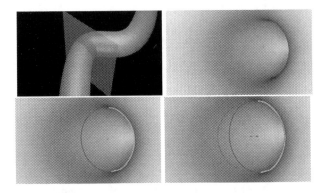

Fig. 2. Simulation of right elbow (Color figure online)

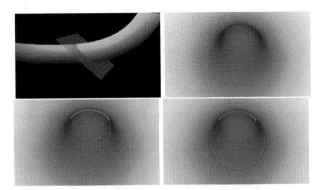

Fig. 3. Simulation of up elbow (Color figure online)

We present an example demonstrating two basic principles of our elbow detection algorithm. The setup is depicted in Fig. 4: there are three tubes of identical circumference, but varying in the overall length and shape. A camera and a directed light source are placed in each to the right of the red plane. The contour detected inside of a tube lies on the red plane (which is orthogonal to a curve of midpoints of the tube) intersecting the tube. We expect the following results (from the front pipe): flat elliptic contour with distorted vertical semiaxis indicating that the elbow goes up (where the shadow points are detected) under great angle (proportional to semiaxis distortion); similarly to previous case, elliptical shape with shorter vertical semiaxis, distorted much less than in the previous case, indicating that the elbow goes up under small angle; last almost straight pipe should provide a circular contour at most little distortion caused by noise.

The results are shown in Fig. 5, starting with the tube with the highest curvature (in the forefront of Fig. 4) and ending with the tube with the lowest curvature (last in Fig. 4) on the right. We recall that the contour of detected points is yellow and the fitted ellipse blue curve, respectively. Ellipse centre is the red point. As we expected, the deformation of the circular shape of the tube into the elliptical shape of the detected contour is more pronounced for the first elbow. Further, due to perspective, the farther ahead we detect the contour, the smaller it is, allowing us to estimate the distance.

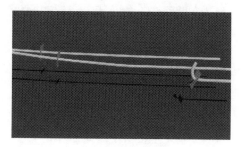

Fig. 4. Overview of the setup (Color figure online)

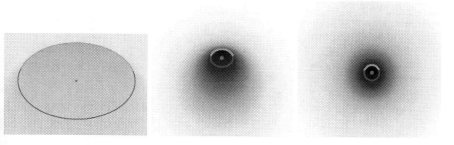

Fig. 5. Simulation of the three tubes (Color figure online)

5 Conclusion

Our simulation supports our hypothesis that the centre displacement of the circular and elliptical contour, respectively, is proportional to the tube elbow angle. By simple direct calculations in the horizontal plane of centre–points, one can determine the elbow angle. Indeed, e.g. in Fig. 2, if the blue elliptical contour is considered a rotated red circle in the elbow direction with common touching point in the middle of yellow points set (in the horizontal plane of centre–points), one can easily determine the spatial horizontal shift of the red circle centre and therefore obtain a consequent point to the path following algorithm.

Yet further questions remain to be solved, e.g. noise reduction. Other can be solved even by tools of geometric algebra such as the distance estimate, [9], although their efficiency may be compromised. Note that even the scale of detected contour may be used for primary distance estimate. We intend to provide the whole solution in terms of geometric algebra and implement it in Python.

References

1. Dorst, L., Fontijne, D., Mann, S.: Geometric Algebra for Computer Science: An Object-Oriented Approach to Geometry, 1st edn. Morgan Kaufmann Publishers Inc., Burlington (2007)
2. Hildenbrand, D.: Foundations of Geometric Algebra Computing, 1st edn. Springer, Heidelberg (2013). https://doi.org/10.1007/978-3-642-31794-1
3. Hildenbrand, D.: Introduction to Geometric Algebra Computing, 1st edn. CRC Press, Taylor & Francis Group, Boca Raton (2019)
4. Hildenbrand, D., Franchini, S., Gentile, A., Vassallo, G., Vitabile, S.: GAPPCO: an easy to configure geometric algebra coprocessor based on GAPP programs. Adv. Appl. Clifford Algebras 27(3), 2115–2132 (2017). https://doi.org/10.1007/s00006-016-0755-x
5. Hildenbrand, D., Pitt, J., Koch, A.: Gaalop–high performance parallel computing based on conformal geometric algebra. In: Bayro-Corrochano, E., Scheuermann, G. (eds.) Geometric Algebra Computing, pp. 477–494. Springer, London (2010). https://doi.org/10.1007/978-1-84996-108-0_22
6. Hitzer, E.: Three-dimensional quadrics in conformal geometric algebras and their versor transformations. Adv. Appl. Clifford Algebras 29(3), 1–16 (2019). https://doi.org/10.1007/s00006-019-0964-1
7. Hrdina, J., Návrat, A., Vašík, P.: GAC application to corner detection based on eccentricity. In: Gavrilova, M., Chang, J., Thalmann, N.M., Hitzer, E., Ishikawa, H. (eds.) CGI 2019. LNCS, vol. 11542, pp. 571–577. Springer, Cham (2019). https://doi.org/10.1007/978-3-030-22514-8_57
8. Hrdina, J., Návrat, A., Vašík, P.: Conic fitting in geometric algebra setting. Adv. Appl. Clifford Algebras 29(4), 1–13 (2019). https://doi.org/10.1007/s00006-019-0989-5
9. Hrdina, J., Návrat, A.: Binocular computer vision based on conformal geometric algebra. Adv. Appl. Clifford Algebras 27(3), 1945–1959 (2017). https://doi.org/10.1007/s00006-017-0764-4

10. Hrdina, J., Návrat, A., Vašík, P., Matoušek, R.: CGA-based robotic snake control. Adv. Appl. Clifford Algebras **27**(1), 621–632 (2016). https://doi.org/10.1007/s00006-016-0695-5
11. Hrdina, J., Návrat, A., Vašík, P.: Geometric algebra for conics. Adv. Appl. Clifford Algebras **28**(3), 1–21 (2018). https://doi.org/10.1007/s00006-018-0879-2
12. Hrdina, J., Matoušek, R., Návrat, A., Vašík, P.: Fisheye correction by CGA nonlinear transformation. Math. Methods Appl. Sci. **41**(11), 4106–4116 (2018)
13. Hrdina, J., Vašík, P., Matoušek, R., Návrat, A.: Geometric algebras for uniform colour spaces. Math. Methods Appl. Sci. **41**(11), 4117–4130 (2018)
14. Lounesto, P.: Clifford Algebra and Spinors, 2nd edn. Cambridge University Press, Cambridge (2006)
15. Perwass, C.: Geometric Algebra with Applications in Engineering, 1st edn. Springer, Heidelberg (2009). https://doi.org/10.1007/978-3-540-89068-3

Optimal Parenthesizing of Geometric Algebra Products

Stéphane Breuils[1]([✉]) [ID], Vincent Nozick[2] [ID], and Akihiro Sugimoto[1] [ID]

[1] National Institute of Informatics, Tokyo, Japan
{breuils,sugimoto}@nii.ac.jp
[2] Université Gustave Eiffel, LIGM,
CNRS - ENPC - ESIEE Paris -UPEM, Paris, France
vincent.nozick@univ-eiffel.fr

Abstract. Manipulating objects using geometric algebra may involve several associative products in a single expression. For example, an object can be constructed by the outer product of multiple points. This number of products can be small for some conformal algebra and high for higher dimensional algebras such as quadric conformal geometric algebras. In these situations, the order of products (i.e. the choice of the parenthesis in the expression) should not change the final result but may change the overall computational cost, according to the grade of the intermediate multivectors. Indeed, the usual left to right way to evaluate the expression may not be most computationally efficient. Studies on the number of arithmetic operations of geometric algebra expressions have been limited to products of only two homogeneous multivectors. This paper shows that there exists an optimal order in the evaluation of an expression involving geometric and outer products, and presents a dynamic programming framework to find it.

Keywords: Geometric algebra · Products · Optimal parenthesis

1 Introduction

1.1 Geometric Algebra Products

Geometric algebra presents intuitive solutions for problems related to geometry. Its theory is more and more investigated in various research fields like physics, mathematics or computational geometry, see [5,9,10] for some examples. In contrast, in the computer science field, the study of computational aspects of the geometric algebra operators is still limited. The pioneering work [7] gave some results about complexity of geometric algebra products in the worst case. The worst case here means that all the elements of a multivector with multiple grades are non-zero. This study was then extended by [2] by investigating the number of arithmetic products required for the geometric product, the outer product, and the inner product of two full homogeneous multivectors, i.e., multivectors with non-zero components only for a single grade. The scope of [2] is well suited

ⓒ Springer Nature Switzerland AG 2020
N. Magnenat-Thalmann et al. (Eds.): CGI 2020, LNCS 12221, pp. 492–500, 2020.
https://doi.org/10.1007/978-3-030-61864-3_42

for expressions involving two full multivectors like intersections of two geometric objects in conformal geometric algebras. However, the representation of geometric objects in quadric conformal geometric algebras [3] includes more than two multivectors in operands, and the arguments of [2] are not valid any more in such a case. The investigation on products of more than two multivectors is desired.

In this paper, we focus on products having the associative property. If the expression consists of only products that have the associative property, we only have to pay our attention to efficiently parenthesize operands in computation. The usual left to right way of computing the expression is not always the most computationally efficient. Moreover, we focus on full homogeneous multivectors since they are the representation of most geometric algebra objects. Note that in many applications, the geometric algebra entity representing any rigid transformations is also often represented as a sum of quasi full homogeneous multivectors.

1.2   Contributions

This paper focuses on products of more than two multivectors where all the products in the expression have the associative property. More specifically, this paper considers only products of more than two multivectors where the products are either outer products or geometric products. We then show that there exists an optimal parenthesising order with respect to computational cost in the evaluation of an expression. Then, we describe a dynamic programming algorithm that yields the optimal product order. We remark that the inner product is not our interest in this paper because it is not associative.

2   Preliminaries

2.1   Notations

As commonly used in the state-of-the-arts ([6] and [11]), lower-case bold letters refer to vectors (vector $\mathbf{a}$) and lower-case non-bold letters to multivector coordinates (coefficient a_i). Multivectors and k-vectors are denoted with upper-case non-bold letters (multivector A). The part of grade k of a multivector A is denoted by $\langle A \rangle_k$. The total number of basis blades is 2^d, where d is the dimension of the vector space, and in this case, the number of basis blades $\mathbf{e}_i$ of grade 1.

By assumption, a multivector A is not necessarily homogeneous but is defined as the sum of homogeneous multivectors. Given the dimension d of the vector space, the set of possible grades for A is $\mathcal{K}_A$ where $\mathcal{K}_A \subseteq \{0, 1, \cdots, d\}$. Then, A can be defined as

$$A = \sum_{k \in \mathcal{K}_A} \langle A \rangle_k. \tag{1}$$

2.2 Product of Two Multivectors

Following the notation of Eq. (1), the product $\odot$ of two multivectors A and B is then

$$A \odot B = \Big(\sum_{k_A \in \mathcal{K}_A} \langle A \rangle_{k_A} \Big) \odot \Big(\sum_{k_B \in \mathcal{K}_B} \langle B \rangle_{k_B} \Big), \tag{2}$$

where $\odot$ can be either the outer product or the geometric product. The linearity of the products of geometric algebra yields

$$A \odot B = \sum_{k_A \in \mathcal{K}_A} \sum_{k_B \in \mathcal{K}_B} \langle A \rangle_{k_A} \odot \langle B \rangle_{k_B}. \tag{3}$$

Theorems 2.1 and 4.1 of [2] give the optimal number of arithmetic operations of the product between two homogeneous multivectors of respective grades k_a and k_b. As for the outer product $\wedge$, this number of arithmetic operations is:

$$p^{\wedge}_{k_a, k_b} = 2 \binom{d}{k_a + k_b} \binom{k_a + k_b}{k_a}, \tag{4}$$

where $\binom{n}{k}$ is the binomial coefficient. On the other hand, the number of arithmetic operations for the geometric product $*$ is:

$$p^{*}_{k_a, k_b} = 2 \sum_{k_c \in \mathcal{I}} \binom{d}{k_c} \left(\frac{k_c}{k_a - k_b + k_c} \right) \left(\frac{d - k_c}{k_a + k_b - k_c} \right), \tag{5}$$

where $\mathcal{I} = \{ |g_a - g_b|, |g_a - g_b| + 2, \ldots, g_a + g_b \}$.

In the more general situation where the two multivectors may not be homogeneous, the product distributivity mentioned in Eq. 3 leads to a double loop over the respective grades of the two multivectors. Thus, the number of required operations is the sum of all per-grade contributions, as described in Algorithm 1.

The resulting multivector usually has a different grade from the two operands used for its computation. For the outer product of homogeneous multivectors $C = A \wedge B$, the grade of C will just be the sum of the grades of A and B. For general multivectors, we again have to follow Eq. 3 to compute the set of resulting grades. The geometric product is a bit more complex and can generate a non-homogeneous multivector even from two homogeneous multivectors. The resulting grades of a product between two general multivectors is summarised in Algorithm 2. For more details about these results, the reader can refer to [2]. Note that $\mathsf{K}^{\wedge}$ or K^{*} can return an empty set of grades (e.g. the wedge of $d + 1$ vectors in a d-dimensional vector space), then the computational cost is 0 since the resulting product is also 0.

3 Optimal Parenthesising of Products

We show that the choice of the order of the product in an expression can affect the complexity of the product. Consider, for example, the following expression $A_1 \wedge A_2 \wedge A_3$ in a 10-dimensional space, where the grade of each multivector is

$$\text{grade}(A_1) = 4, \quad \text{grade}(A_2) = 3, \quad \text{grade}(A_3) = 2.$$

There are in that case two possible parenthesisings, the left to right way as

$$(A_1 \wedge A_2) \wedge A_3, \tag{6}$$

and the right to left way:

$$A_1 \wedge (A_2 \wedge A_3). \tag{7}$$

In the first case, the product $A_1 \wedge A_2$ of Eq. (6) generates a multivector of grade 7, that is finally wedged to A_3. According to Eq. (4), the number of operations for $A_1 \wedge A_2$ is 8400 and then 720 for the second outer product, leading to a total of 9120 arithmetic operations. On the other hand, the first product $A_2 \wedge A_3$ of Eq. (7) generates a multivector of grade 5, that is wedged to A_1. The overall computational cost of this product is 5040 for the first product and 2520 for the second, resulting in 7560 arithmetic operations in total. Thus, in this case, choosing the second way of parenthesising brings a 1.5 times gain in terms of numerical operations. Obviously, the gain can be much higher for longer expressions.

3.1 Expressions

Throughout this paper, we consider an expression as the products of n multivectors:

$$A_1 * A_2 * \cdots * A_n, \qquad n \in \mathbb{N} \tag{8}$$

or

$$A_1 \wedge A_2 \wedge \cdots \wedge A_n, \qquad n \in \mathbb{N}. \tag{9}$$

Algorithm 1: Number of arithmetic operations required for outer product and geometric product of two general multivectors

---

1 **Function** $\mathrm{P}^{\wedge} (\mathcal{K}_A, \mathcal{K}_B)$

    Input: $\mathcal{K}_A$: set of grades for the multivector A

           $\mathcal{K}_B$: set of grades for the multivector B

    Output: total number of arithmetic operations resulting from $A \wedge B$

2   **return** $2 \displaystyle\sum_{k_A \in \mathcal{K}_A} \sum_{k_B \in \mathcal{K}_B} \binom{d}{k_a + k_b} \binom{k_a + k_b}{k_a}$

3 **Function** $\mathrm{P}^{*} (\mathcal{K}_A, \mathcal{K}_B)$

    Input: $\mathcal{K}_A$: set of grades for the multivector A

           $\mathcal{K}_B$: set of grades for the multivector B

    Output: total number of arithmetic operations resulting from $A * B$

4   **return** $2 \displaystyle\sum_{k_A \in \mathcal{K}_A} \sum_{k_B \in \mathcal{K}_B} \sum_{k_c \in \mathcal{I}} \binom{d}{k_c} \binom{k_c}{\frac{k_a - k_b + k_c}{2}} \binom{d - k_c}{\frac{k_a + k_b - k_c}{2}}$

Algorithm 2: Computation of the set of grades resulting to the product of two multivectors.

---

1 **Function** $\text{K}^\wedge\,(\mathcal{K}_A,\,\mathcal{K}_B)$
   Input: $\mathcal{K}_A$: set of grades for the multivector A
   $\mathcal{K}_B$: set of grades for the multivector B
   Output: set of grades $\mathcal{K}_C$ of the result of $A \wedge B$
2   $\mathcal{K}_C = \varnothing$
3   **foreach** $k_a \in \mathcal{K}_A$ **do**
4   **foreach** $k_b \in \mathcal{K}_B$ **do**
5   **if** $k_a + k_b \le d$ **then**
6            $\mathcal{K}_C = \mathcal{K}_C \cup (k_a + k_b)$

7 **Function** $\text{K}^*(\mathcal{K}_A,\,\mathcal{K}_B)$
   Input: $\mathcal{K}_A$: set of grades for the multivector A
   $\mathcal{K}_B$: set of grades for the multivector B
   Output: set of grades $\mathcal{K}_C$ of the result of $A * B$
8   $\mathcal{K}_C = \varnothing$
9   **foreach** $k_a \in \mathcal{K}_A$ **do**
10   **foreach** $k_b \in \mathcal{K}_B$ **do**
11   **foreach** $k_c \in \{|k_a - k_b|, |k_a - k_b| + 2, \cdots, k_a + k_b\}$ **do**
12   **if** $k_c \le d$ **then**
13              $\mathcal{K}_C = \mathcal{K}_C \cup k_c$

Since the outer product and the geometric product are binary operators, i.e. operators between two operands, this overall computation involves the computation of intermediate results. Let $A_{1,n}$ be the chain of multivectors defined by the expression to compute, and $A_{i,j}(0 < i < j \le n)$ a sub-chain resulting from the computation of the product from the multivector A_i to the multivector A_j. The number of arithmetic operations resulting from the product of two successive multivector chains $A_{i,j}$ and $A_{j+1,k}$ is denoted by $\text{P}^\odot_{i,j,k}$. where $\odot$ can be either $\wedge$ or $*$.

3.2 Problem Formulation

Let $C_{i,j}$ be the minimum number of arithmetic operations of the computation (the cost to minimise) of the product between the ith multivector up to the jth multivector. In the final result, we seek for the computation of C_{1n} related to the full expression. For $i < j$, this is equivalent to seek for

$$C_{i,j} = \min_{s \in [i, j-1]} C_{i,s} + C_{s+1,j} + \text{P}^\odot_{i,s,j}. \tag{10}$$

This optimal cost $C_{i,j}$ will be used to define the optimal parenthesising indices 2D table S of size $n \times n$, where $S_{i,j} = s$ $(i < j)$ means that the expression

$A_i \odot A_{i+1} \odot \cdots \odot A_j$ should be parenthesised as

$$(A_i \odot \cdots \odot A_s) \odot (A_{s+1} \odot \cdots \odot A_j). \tag{11}$$

3.3 Minimisation

An easy way to achieve this minimisation is to use a recursive method. However, such an approach will lead to multiple travels over the same recursive sub-trees, resulting in an exponential complexity.

This kind of problems was already addressed for the matrix chain product, for example in [1], by using dynamic programming. The problem is the computation of the same sub-problems for different depth of recursion. The proposed approach to solve it consists in memorising the solution to sub-problems in a bottom-up scheme. Each sub-problem is uniquely identified by the two bounding indices (i, j), in the computation of $C_{i,j}$, $S_{i,j}$ and $\mathcal{K}_{i,j}$ as 2D tables. These tables can be iteratively filled with a bottom up approach.

We achieve our minimisation using the dynamic programming framework. Our proposed method first considers the sub-chains of length one. They correspond to single multivectors and thus take a cost $C_{i,i} = 0$, meaning no optimal parenthesising index. The sub-chains of length two can also be directly computed from Algorithms 1 and 2, where $C_{i,i+1} = \mathrm{P}_{i,i,i+1}^{\odot} = \mathrm{P}^{\odot}\left(\mathcal{K}_{A_i}, \mathcal{K}_{A_{i+1}}\right)$. Obviously, $S_{i,i+1} = i$ and $\mathcal{K}_{i,i+1} = \mathrm{K}^{\odot}(\mathcal{K}_{A_i}, \mathcal{K}_{A_{i+1}})$. Then, the sub-chains of length 3 can be computed from the sub-chains of length 2 using Eq. (10), and so on. The resulting algorithm that computes the optimal parenthesising for each sub-expressions is shown in Algorithm 3.

Once 2D table S is computed, the product can be optimally computed by a recursive travel starting from $S_{1,n}$, as shown in Algorithm 3. In case of a code optimisation, a similar recursive scheme can be adopted to add the optimal parenthesising on the code.

We remark that the complexity of this algorithm is not exponential but polynomial in $\mathcal{O}(n^3)$, see [1]. Note that in the matrix chain product context, there exist some faster methods in $\mathcal{O}(n \times \log n)$, like [8] however, these methods are complex to setup. Moreover, in geometric algebra, n is usually not high enough to see a significant difference.

4   Discussion and Applications

It is not difficult to modify Algorithm 3 so that it computes the worst parenthesis instead of the best, which in turn results in the maximum number of arithmetic operations. We merely have to replace the sign $'<'$ by $'>'$ in line 19 of Algorithm 3 and to change the initialisation of $C_{i,j}$ to 0 in line 16.

From these two algorithms, we can also extract the gain of the optimal parenthesis. The results we have, show that the maximum gain increases as n (the number of multivectors) increases. Moreover, the gain also increases as the dimension increases. For a fixed number of multivectors in the expression, the gain becomes

Algorithm 3: Computation of the optimal parenthesising of a geometric algebra associative product.

---

1 **Function** OptimalParenthesising
  Input: $A_1, \cdots, A_n$: chain of general multivectors.
     $\odot$: the considered associative product.
  Output: $S_{i,j}$: 2D optimal parenthesising index table.
     // define a 2D cost table
2   $C \leftarrow$ 2D table
     // Sub-chain of length 1
3   **for** $i \in [1, n]$ **do**
4     $C_{i,i} = 0$
5     $\mathcal{K}_{i,i} = \mathrm{grades}(A_i)$
     // Sub-chain of length 2
6   **for** $i \in [1, n-1]$ **do**
7     $C_{i,i+1} = \mathrm{P}^{\odot}\big(\mathrm{grades}(A_i), \mathrm{grades}(A_{i+1})\big)$ // from Algo 1
8     $\mathcal{K}_{i,i+1} = \mathrm{K}^{\odot}\big(\mathrm{grades}(A_i), \mathrm{grades}(A_{i+1})\big)$ // from Algo 2
9     $S_{i,i+1} = i$
     // Grade of all sub-chains of length $u > 2$, starting at index i
10   **for** $u \in [3, n]$ **do**
11   **for** $i \in [1, n-u+1]$ **do**
12       $\mathcal{K}_{i,i+u} = \mathrm{K}^{\odot}(\mathcal{K}_{i,i}, \mathcal{K}_{i+1,i+u})$ // grade from any arbitrary cut
     // For all possible length $u > 2$ of sub-chains
13   **for** $u \in [3, n]$ **do**
     // For all sub-chains of length u, starting at i
14   **for** $i \in [1, n-u]$ **do**
15       $j = i + u$ // sub-chain from i to j
16       $C_{i,j} = \infty$
       // For all possible cut of the sub-chain
17   **for** $s \in [i, j-1]$ **do**
         // compute the cost c of this cut with Eq. (10)
18         $c = C_{i,s} + C_{s+1,j} + \mathrm{P}^{\odot}(\mathcal{K}_{i,s}, \mathcal{K}_{s+1,j})$
         // if the cost is better than before, update
19   **if** $c < C_{i,i+u}$ **then**
20           $C_{i,j} = c$
21           $S_{i,j} = s$

22   **return** S
23 First call: $S =$OptimalParenthesising($A_1, \cdots, A_n, \odot$)

---

highest when the sum of the grades of the operands is near the dimension for expressions where the outer product appears.

Furthermore, a practical usage of these kinds of algorithms is in code generators and optimizers. For example, the code developed from the expression of Eq. (6) in the code generator Gaalop [4] results in more arithmetic operations

Algorithm 4: Evaluation of the product $A_1 \odot A_2 \odot \cdots \odot A_n$ using the optimal parenthesising.

```
1 Function ComputeProduct
    Input:  A_1, ..., A_n: chain of general multivectors,
            S: optimal 2D parenthesising index table
            i, j: resp. indices of the start and end of the sub-expression
            ⊙: the considered associative product
    Output: result of the product.
2    if i=j then
3        return A_i
4    s = S_{i,j}
     // left side recursive call
5    A = ComputeProduct(A_1, ..., A_n, S, i, s, ⊙)
     // right side recursive call
6    B = ComputeProduct(A_1, ..., A_n, S, s + 1, j, ⊙)
     // do the product
7    return A ⊙ B
8 First call: Result = ComputeProduct(A_1, ..., A_n, S, 1, n, ⊙)
```

than in the code generated from Eq. (7) arithmetic operations. Note that we consider full multivectors for the three multivectors that appear in the expression.

5 Conclusion

In this paper, we focused on products of more than two multivectors and addressed that there exists an optimal order in the evaluation of an expression. Then, we gave a dynamic programming algorithm that yields the optimal product order in polynomial time. The benefits of this approach arise from the product of three multivectors.

References

1. Aho, A.V., Hopcroft, J.E.: The design and analysis of computer algorithms. Pearson Education India (1974)
2. Breuils, S., Nozick, V., Sugimoto, A.: Computational aspects of geometric algebra products of two homogeneous multivectors (2020). ArXiv abs/2002.11313
3. Breuils, S., Nozick, V., Sugimoto, A., Hitzer, E.: Quadric conformal geometric algebra of $\mathbb{R}^{9,6}$. Adv. Appl. Clifford Algebras **28**(2), 35 (2018). https://doi.org/10.1007/s00006-018-0851-1
4. Charrier, P., Klimek, M., Steinmetz, C., Hildenbrand, D.: Geometric algebra enhanced precompiler for C++, OpenCL and Mathematica's OpenCLLink. Adv. Appl. Clifford Algebras **24**(2), 613–630 (2014)
5. De Keninck, S., Dorst, L.: Geometric algebra levenberg-marquardt. In: Gavrilova, M., Chang, J., Thalmann, N.M., Hitzer, E., Ishikawa, H. (eds.) CGI 2019. LNCS, vol. 11542, pp. 511–522. Springer, Cham (2019). https://doi.org/10.1007/978-3-030-22514-8_51

6. Dorst, L., Fontijne, D., Mann, S.: Geometric Algebra for Computer Science. An Object-Oriented Approach to Geometry. Morgan Kaufmann, Burlington (2007)
7. Fontijne, D.: Efficient Implementation of Geometric Algebra. Ph.D. thesis, University of Amsterdam (2007)
8. Hu, T., Shing, M.: Computation of matrix chain products. Part I. SIAM J. Comput. **11**(2), 362–373 (1982)
9. Kanatani, K.: Understanding Geometric Algebra: Hamilton, Grassmann, and Clifford for Computer Vision and Graphics. A. K. Peters Ltd, Natick (2015)
10. Lasenby, J., Hadfield, H., Lasenby, A.: Calculating the rotor between conformal objects. Adv. Appl. Clifford Algebras **29**(5), 102 (2019). https://doi.org/10.1007/s00006-019-1014-8
11. Perwass, C.: Geometric Algebra with Applications in Engineering, Geometry and Computing, vol. 4. Springer, Heidelberg (2009). https://doi.org/10.1007/978-3-540-89068-3

Geometric Algebra-Based Multilevel Declassification Method for Geographical Field Data

Wen Luo[1,2,3], Dongshuang Li[4,5], Zhaoyuan Yu[1,2,3], Yun Wang[1,2,3], Zhengjun Yan[1,2,3], and Linwang Yuan[1,2,3](✉)

[1] Ministry of Education, Key Laboratory of Virtual Geographic Environment, Nanjing Normal University, Nanjing, China
luow1987@163.com, yuanlinwang@njnu.edu.cn

[2] State Key Laboratory Cultivation Base of Geographical Environment Evolution (Jiangsu Province), Nanjing, China

[3] Jiangsu Center for Collaborative Innovation in Geographical Information Resource Development and Application, Nanjing, China

[4] Jiangsu Key Laboratory of Crop Genetics and Physiology, Jiangsu Key Laboratory of Crop Cultivation and Physiology, Agricultural College of Yangzhou University, Yangzhou, China

[5] Jiangsu Co-Innovation Center for Modern Production Technology of Grain Crops, Yangzhou University, Yangzhou, China

Abstract. The diversity of GIS application patterns leads to the demand for multilevel GIS data declassification. For example, Publicly used data must be declassified to hide confidential spatial information. The reversion process is not a common data permutation like the conventional encryption method does. The reverted data should also keep the general geospatial features. Furthermore, when facing different levels of confidentiality, different levels of reversion were needed. In this paper, A declassification and reversion method with controllable accuracy is realized using geometric algebra (GA). The geographical field is expressed as a GA object and the unified representation of the field is further realized. By introducing the rotor operator and perturbation matrix, the declassification methods are proposed for geographic field data, which can progressively revert the features of the field. A geometric algebraic declassification operator is also constructed to realize the unification operations of field features and spatial coordinate. By exploring the space error and space structure characterization of the results, a quantitative performance evaluation is provided. Experiments have shown that the method can carry out effective precision control and has good randomness and a high degree of freedom characteristics. The experimental data show a correlation coefficient of 0.945, 0.923 and 0.725 for the longitude-oriented field data during the low level, medium level and high level declassification, respectively. The algorithm characteristics meet the application needs of geographic field data in data disclosure, secure transmission, encapsulation storage, and other aspects.

Keywords: Geographic field data · Geometric algebra · Multilevel declassification · Space correlation

© Springer Nature Switzerland AG 2020
N. Magnenat-Thalmann et al. (Eds.): CGI 2020, LNCS 12221, pp. 501–512, 2020.
https://doi.org/10.1007/978-3-030-61864-3_43

1 Introduction

At present, information technology is widely used in the economic and military fields of our country, and there are many kinds of information products. Geographic information technology, in particular, has evolved to unprecedented heights during these two decades. Not only applied to national defense construction but also increasingly serve the people's daily life, is widely used in the fields of land management, urban and rural planning, resources and environment, transportation and logistics, and military operations [1–3]. To protect the geographic information security, the national data declassification policy and regulations on the location accuracy of public maps have put forward clear provisions, which can achieve better confidentiality of the confidential data, but affect the sharing and use of geographic data, causing difficulties between data confidentiality and sharing [4]. Therefore, the multilevel GIS data declassification method, which can generate data with different levels of security are the key method for the geographic information technology application with different application scenarios.

The declassification of GIS data is not a common data permutation like the conventional encryption method used in information science do, the general geospatial features should be kept and only hide the confidential spatial information, which was also known as the declassification technology. Current geographic information declassification mainly includes geometric precision declassification, attributes, and spatial object camouflage. The geometric precision declassification is achieved by random interference of spatial location and linear or nonlinear transformation of geographic coordinates or elements [5], which is not easy to revert the original information, and sensitive information can be avoided.

Among the existing methods for geometric precision declassification, linear declassification is the most mature. E.g. the bilinear interpolation can be used to offset the node coordinates of each element within the grid, and changed the absolute and relative coordinates of each element [6]. Due to the different parameters of each grid offset, geographic information declassification can be achieved. However, linear declassification methods are less secure and do not meet current security needs.

Several scholars have also conducted a series of studies in nonlinear declassification methods, and the concept of encryption space and precision declassification has been introduced [7, 8]. Wu and Bang studied the vector geographic data encryption method based on compound chaotic system, by using the compound chaotic system, the key space of the method was significantly improved [9, 10]. Li proposed a method of information disguise and reduction for GIS vector data. For the illegal user, this method can realize the sensitive information hiding and restrict the use, but for the legitimate user who has key file can restore data without information loss [11]. The nonlinear algorithms usually require more computational resources. For this reason, some scholars selectively encrypt some data in the transform domain, such as the dc component in the DCT domain, so as to reduce the amount of computation and time required for encryption and decryption [12–14]. To solve the problem that nonlinear algorithm is difficult to reversion, Van used line and plane elements in vector map data to encrypt in DWT and DFT fields, which achieved the close-to-zero error during the decryption and reversion process [15]. The security and accuracy of geographic information is ensured. Geographic information data attribute information declassification is primarily a means of bringing geographic information up to public use standards by adding interfering information, deleting critical information, modifying critical information, and replacing critical information, while meeting security requirements. Wang and Neyman introduced the Manhattan distance of adjacent vertices, and constructed the secret information embedding method by difference expansion [16, 17].

In summary, the current research on geographic information data declassification is mostly common vector data declassification and less involved in geographic field data declassification. Some nonlinear declassification models cannot be reverted with the support of the key, which is not conducive to the integration of the declassified data with the original data, and it will also increase the error propagation caused by noise in the network environment. The main reason is that the security of the declassification and the accuracy of the reversion result was the opposite. The declassification method should be hard to reversion by the data attacker but easy to reversion by the users. Moreover, as one of the most important GIS data, the geographical field data was observed or modeled in a decentralized way, geometric coordinates were fixed by gridding and the Geographical objects were implicitly expressed. The traditional methods commonly execute the declassification process through the attribute data, and cannot produce effective results.

Hence the need to find new methods for declassifying geographic field data can be summed up as follows: 1) The declassification and reversion steps should be performed operator; 2) The express of geographical field data should be coordinate independent; 3) the declassification method should be multi-layered and adapted to multi-level applications. Geometric algebra (GA) provides an ideal tool for the expression and computation of geographical objects [18, 19]. Yuan et al. [20] presented a framework for GA-based multidimensional unified computation. The coordinate independent representation and operator-based analysis were one of the important features for GA-based multidimensional unified computation. In the field of spatio-temporal field, Ebling and Yuan proposed the template matching method to extract the structural features of the spatio-temporal field [21, 22]. Yu applied it to the structural filtering of wind field [23]. Geometric algebra plays an increasingly important role in the unified representation, analysis, computation, and application of multidimensional geographic information [24].

This paper proposed a new multilevel declassification method of geographic field data to address the existing declassification problems, using geometric algebraic operation vectorization to construct multidimensional data expression subspaces and declassification algorithms. Based on this, this paper proposes a method for geographic field data declassification based on geometric algebra. An algorithmic implementation of the above methods was also performed, and case studies were validated based on actual geographic field data.

2 Basic Idea

Due to the limitations of the underlying mathematical rules, the traditional data declassification method can only use a rotational matrix to perform declassification operations, such as rotation and projection operations, but not faster and more efficient vectorization operations. Geometric algebra as a unified descriptive language connecting algebra and geometry, mathematics and physics, abstract spacetime, and solid spacetime, is a mathematical language based on dimensional operations. In geometric algebra, the subspace is the basic operation object and the dimensional computation is the basic operation operator, which converts the field data of geographic information in the euclidean space into the field data of geographic information in the subspace of geometric algebra, and then uses the rotating operator and projection operator of geometric algebra to perform declassification operation, since geometric algebra uses dimension as the basis of geometric operation, it is possible to perform coordinate independent geometric computation, which greatly enriches the diversity of declassification keys and meets the declassification needs of geographic information data.

A new mathematical theory system is introduced from the perspective of object properties and spatial coordinates in geographic field data, and a declassification algorithm is built to support geographic field data. The geometric algebraic Rotor and projection operators are used to realize the declassification of geographic field data, which greatly reduces the complexity of declassification of data object properties and spatial coordinates due to the unified operation of object properties and spatial coordinates.

Based on the above analysis, we design the general framework of geometric algebra-based geographic field data declassification method, as shown in Fig. 1 below, which is mainly divided into the following steps: (1) geographic field data vectorization and construction of geometric algebraic subspace; (2) generation of decryption parameters using random numbers which are bound by a certain range decided by the multi-level applications. We also use rotor to regulate the decryption results; (3) reversion of geographic field data using geometric algebraic Rotor operator and projection operator.

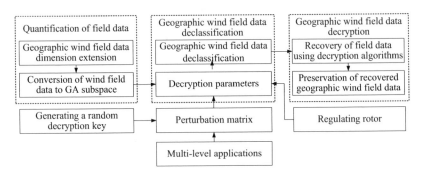

Fig. 1. Framework of geometric algebra-based declassification methods

3   Methodology

3.1   Geometric Algebraic Subspace Construction

The key step in the declassification of geographic field data is the construction of geometric algebraic subspaces. Here, geographic field data is typically organized as property cubes with temporal and spatial dimensions, e.g., global monthly average field data typically have four dimensions (longitude, latitude, elevation, time), and these data dimensions are typically independent of each other and can be encoded as base vectors in geometric algebraic space. For a given n-dimensional geographic information data $Z = R^n$, each dimension can be encoded as $e_i (i = 1, 2, \cdots, n, n + 1)$, which in turn allows the construction of a collection of dimensions as base vectors in a geometric algebraic space. In the base vector, $e_i (i = 1, 2, \cdots, n)$ denotes the field data dimension and $e_{(n+1)}$ denotes the attribute dimension. Thus, the raw n-dimensional scalar field data (F) can be mapped to the geometric algebraic GA $(Cl_{n+1,0})$ space, as follows:

$$GA(Z) = \{GA(F)\} = a_1 e_1 + a_2 e_2 + \cdots + a_n e_n + a_{(n+1)} e_{(n+1)} \qquad (1)$$

where $a_i (i = 1, 2, \cdots, n + 1)$ represents the value of different dimensions. Taking the geographic field data (longitude-latitude - attributes) as an example, the GA mapping is shown in Fig. 2.

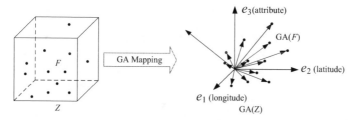

Fig. 2. Vectorization of geographical field data

3.2 Rotation of Geographical Field

Rotor is an operator used to express rotation transformation in geometric algebra. It has the properties of composability, shape preserving and reflexivity, and can realize the multidimensional unified expression of rotation transformation of arbitrary geometry object [25, 26]. The transformation of Geographical field F under the action of rotation operator R can be expressed as: $F \mapsto RFR^{-1}$, where R^{-1} means the inverse of R, RF means the geometric product of R and F. The rotor can also be transformed into an exponential form, which has a more explicit geometric meaning: $R = e^{-\phi l/2}$, where l, ϕ means the axis and angle of rotation.

3.3 Geographic Field Data Declassification and Reversion

In this paper, the rotator is set as a declassification function of the geographic field data, traversing the geographic field data (longitude-latitude-attribute), and setting the longitude-latitude-attribute data to x, y, z, where x represents the longitude in the geographic field data; y represents the latitude in the geographic field data, and z represents the attributes in the geographic field data. At the same time, to eliminate data deformation due to odd coordinate values in the geo-windfarm data, it is necessary to normalize the geo-windfarm coordinates to $[-1, 1]$ using Eq. (2).

$$\begin{cases} nx_i = (x_i - x_{mean})/Length \\ ny_i = (y_i - y_{mean})/Height \end{cases} \tag{2}$$

Where *Length, Height* is the length and width of the geographic field data range to be declassified, and x_{mean}, y_{mean} is the mean value of x_i, y_i in coordinate point x, y of the geographic field data in the declassification process, respectively, and the normalized target coordinate point nx_i, ny_i of the geographic field data is obtained.

At the same time, to reduce the linear correlation of the geographic field data before and after declassification, a perturbation matrix X is added to the horizontal and vertical coordinates of the latitude-oriented and latitude-oriented field data, respectively with the substitution equation:

$$\begin{cases} nrx_i = nx_i + \Delta x_i \\ nry_i = ny_i + \Delta y_i \end{cases} \tag{3}$$

Where $\Delta x_i, \Delta y_i$ is the perturbation matrix. In this paper, we access the Australian National University's Quantum Random Server (https://qrng.anu.edu.au/), whose laboratory generates random numbers in real time by measuring the quantum rise and fall of the vacuum [27, 28], and access its server to obtain four true random numbers RN_1, RN_2, RN_3, RN_4, randomly assign the obtained four true random numbers to the declassification key N_1, N_2, N_3, N_4, and encrypt the $\Delta x_i, \Delta y_i$ and N_1, N_2, N_3, N_4 using the RSA (Rivest-Shamir-Adleman) algorithm and deposit them in the key file Key.txt. And substitute in the declassification function Eq. (4).

$$\begin{cases} X_i = e^{-i\phi/2} nrx_i e^{i\phi/2} \\ Y_i = e^{-i\phi/2} nry_i e^{i\phi/2} \\ Z_i = e^{-i\phi/2} z_i e^{i\phi/2} \\ i = (N_1 e_1 + N_2 e_2) \wedge N_3 e_3 \\ \phi = \mod(N_4, 360) \end{cases} \tag{4}$$

where X_i is the longitude of the declassified geographic field data; Y_i is the latitude of the declassified geographic field data, and Z_i is the property of the declassified geographic field data. From the above equation, it is possible to declassify geographical wind farm data at will. The mean square error (MSE) is also used to control the reversion accuracy. MSE is compared with the declassification index σ; if MSE is greater than the declassification index σ, the perturbation amounts Δx_i and Δy_i of coordinate points of geographic field data in the declassification process need to be adjusted to control the error in declassification; and the perturbation amount of coordinate points of geographic field data in the declassification process is controlled according to Eq. (5), where $\Delta x_{in}, \Delta y_{in}$ is the perturbation amount of the adjusted coordinate points of geographic field data in the declassification process:

$$\begin{cases} \Delta x_{in} = \Delta x_i \cdot \dfrac{MSE - \sigma}{\sigma} \\ \Delta y_{in} = \Delta y_i \cdot \dfrac{MSE - \sigma}{\sigma} \end{cases} \tag{5}$$

The reversion of geographic field data can be regarded as the inverse operation of declassification. The Eq. (2) and (3) are intuitive reversible, furthermore, because of the reversibility of rotor operation, the reversion of Eq. (4) can be realized by Eq. (6). The processing flow of declassification and reversion is shown in Fig. 3.

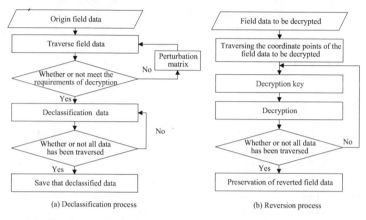

(a) Declassification process   (b) Reversion process

Fig. 3. Geographic field data declassification and reversion process

$$\begin{cases} nrx_i = e^{i\phi/2} X_i e^{-i\phi/2} \\ nry_i = e^{i\phi/2} Y_i e^{-i\phi/2} \\ z_i = e^{i\phi/2} Z_i e^{-i\phi/2} \\ i = (N_1 e_1 + N_2 e_2) \wedge N_3 e_3 \\ \phi = -\bmod(N_4, 360) \end{cases} \tag{6}$$

4 Experimental Procedure

To verify the idea of this paper, the data used in this experiment are the global average monthly wind field data published by the National Oceanic and Atmospheric Administration for the period 1871–2012. The data is organized into temporal and spatial data (longitude-latitude - elevation - time), the data size is $180 \times 91 \times 24 \times 1704$.

4.1 Geographic Wind Field Data Read and Quantified

The wind field data is composed $vwnd \in R^{180 \times 91 \times 24 \times 1704}$ and $uwnd \in R^{180 \times 91 \times 24 \times 1704}$. The data of January 1871 is used first and converted to the geometric algebraic space, as shown in Fig. 4(a). In order to obtain the quantitative description of the declassification results, we use the indicators mean square error (MSE) [29] and peak signal to noise ratio (PSNR) [29] to describe the numerical similarity before and after declassification, the structural similarity index (SSIM) [30] and Pearson Correlation Coefficient (PCC) [30] to describe the structure features before and after declassification.

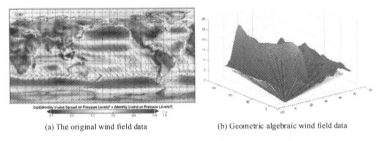

(a) The original wind field data   (b) Geometric algebraic wind field data

Fig. 4. The original data and GA representation

4.2   Generate Multi-layered Key

To simulate different levels of data security, here we used three error ranges to construct the multi-layered key, including the "low declassification level" with the declassification index σ between 5 m and 9 m, the "medium declassification level" with σ between 9 m and 17 m and the "high declassification level" with σ between 18 m and 30 m; the perturbation matrix can be directly generated by the given error range. The rotor parameters were indeterminate, thus, we gave the four preliminary defined rotors in the range of (0, 180), which include 25, 46, 57 and 170. Thus, the multi-layered key was generated: four true random numbers $N_1, N_2, N_3, N_4 = 235, 70, 71, 155$ were obtained using MATLAB access to the Australian National University Quantum Random Server and set as keys, while perturbation matrix $\Delta x_i, \Delta y_i$ was generated using the Rivest-Shamir-Adleman (RSA) algorithm.

4.3   Result

As show in Table 1, all the results satisfied the error requirement of their programmes. At the sametime, the select of the declassification key will directly affect the security of the declassification. Since the key selection is highly random and there is no linear relationship between the four declassification parameters, so the cracking can only be done exhaustively, so the declassification parameters used in this paper have high security. However, we can also found that, the other indicators are different, which means we should also choose propose key parameters to achieve more effective declassification results.

5   Discussion

5.1   Space Error and Space Structure Characterization of the Results

As shown in Table 1, when the higher declassification programme was adopt, the error was much bigger and the correlation expected by PCC was smaller, which indicate that the declassification function was realized. We can also found that the PSNR value was stable, which means the overall structure is similar. This result is also important, because the declassification result should looked-almost-the-same with the original data. Then, the users cannot found the data was declassificated. The SSIM value get larger

Table 1. The declassification result

Programme	Angle	Error	MSE	PSNR	SSIM	PCC_V	PCC_U
Low level declassification (5–9 m)	25	5.528	2.215	44.677	0.941	0.740	0.343
	46	5.095	8.257	38.963	0.770	0.444	0.199
	57	5.042	13.021	36.984	0.624	0.316	0.152
	170	6.475	10.754	37.815	0.737	0.945	0.445
Medium level declassification (9–17 m)	25	10.189	0.247	54.207	0.995	0.676	0.317
	46	9.867	0.248	54.19	0.995	0.378	0.164
	57	9.886	0.55	50.73	0.985	0.266	0.121
	170	11.281	14.413	36.543	0.643	0.923	0.432
High level declassification (18–30 m)	25	25.153	0.247	54.207	0.995	0.372	0.179
	46	24.491	0.247	54.207	0.995	0.181	0.102
	57	24.443	0.247	54.207	0.995	0.121	0.056
	170	26.439	13.267	36.903	0.653	0.725	0.336

when the higher declassificating level was chose, the reason is that the SSIM is almost about the feature scale of the result, and the feature scales were keep stable during the declassification process.

It can be seen from Table 1 that the correlation coefficient of Pearson Correlation Coefficient for longitude direction wind field data before and after declassification is small and has high security. While the correlation coefficient of Pearson Correlation Coefficient for latitude direction wind field data before and after declassification is large, which ensures that the wind field data after declassification still have high similarity. This result also indicated the truth that the wind field changes much more in the zonal direction. The method in this paper guarantees the correctness of the basic geographical law.

5.2 The Best Regulating Angle Selection Based on Space Correlation

According to Sect. 5.1, the SSIM indicator is well maintained and even has better results at high declassification levels, we will discuss that if the declassification scheme can be characterized as SSIM. As shown in Fig. 5, the results are plotted at four angles at the medium declassification level, and compared with the original plot, it is found that although SSIM is similar, it cannot reflect the spatial structural similarity of the image because it reflects the three characteristics of brightness, contrast, and structure.

Assuming the correlation coefficient as the scheme characterization, the one with the largest PCC-V value can be selected as the encryption scheme, then the regulation with angle 170 was choosed. The final declassification results are shown in Fig. 6. As shown in Fig. 6b, 6c, the higher the declassification level, the worse the detail fidelity of the data in the spatial structure, but the overall structure is still fundamentally similar, and it is difficult for the user to notice that the graph is decrypted when he gets it. At the

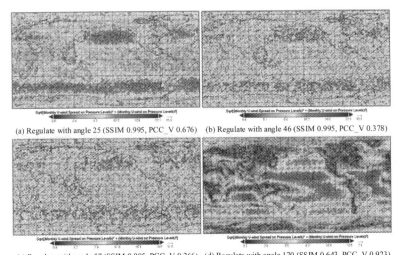

(a) Regulate with angle 25 (SSIM 0.995, PCC_V 0.676)   (b) Regulate with angle 46 (SSIM 0.995, PCC_V 0.378)

(c) Regulate with angle 57 (SSIM 0.985, PCC_V 0.266)   (d) Regulate with angle 170 (SSIM 0.643, PCC_V 0.923)

Fig. 5. The medium level declassification with different regulating angle

maximum declassification level (Fig. 6d), in addition to the detailed structure, the overall structure of the geographic field also shows some degree of deviation, indicating that it is already difficult to guarantee the macrostructure of the geographic field anymore at this error level, and it can also be understood that the macrostructure of the geographic field also needs to be declassified and hidden at this level.

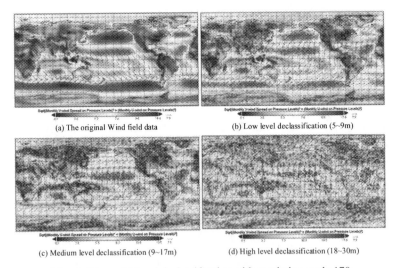

(a) The original Wind field data   (b) Low level declassification (5~9m)

(c) Medium level declassification (9~17m)   (d) High level declassification (18~30m)

Fig. 6. The multi-level declassification with regulating angle 170

6   Conclusions or Summaries

The advantage of this paper is to use geometric algebraic expression in vector field to convert geographic wind field data into geometric algebraic space, and use geometric algebra to construct declassification operator to declassify geographic wind field data to realize object properties and spatial coordinates unified operation, which greatly reduces the complexity of data object properties and spatial coordinates declassification operation, at the same time, the geometric algebraic operator parameterized expression has great freedom to guarantee the multi-level decryption key. The method also solves the problem of balancing the strength and effectiveness of the current traditional declassification algorithm while increasing the declassification strength.

Acknowledgements. This work was financially supported by the National Natural Science Foundation of China [41976186, 42001320].

References

1. Chung, M.S., Choi, Y.B.: A study on policy for national geographic information system. J. Korea Spat. Inf. Syst. Soc. **8**(3), 51–64 (2006)
2. Beconytë, G., Govorov, M., Ningal, T.F., et al.: Geographic information e-training initiatives for national spatial data infrastructures. Technol. Econ. Dev. Econ. **14**(1), 11–28 (2008)
3. Fitch, C.A., Ruggles, S.: Building the national historical geographic information system. Histor. Methods J. Quant. Interdiscip. Histor. **36**(1), 41–51 (2003)
4. Flores, W.R., Antonsen, E., Ekstedt, M.: Information security knowledge sharing in organizations: investigating the effect of behavioral information security governance and national culture. Comput. Secur. **43**, 90–110 (2014)
5. Schoepe, D., Sabelfeld, A.: Understanding and enforcing opacity. In: 2015 IEEE 28th Computer Security Foundations Symposium, pp. 539–553. IEEE (2015)
6. Nian, X.: Research on the security of geospatial data based on the bilinear interpolation model. Geomat. Spat. Inf. Technol. **39**(03), 143–145 (2016). (in Chinese)
7. Liu, S., Guo, C., Sheridan, J.T.: A review of optical image encryption techniques. Opt. Laser Technol. **57**, 327–342 (2014)
8. Hsiao, H., Lee, J.: Color image encryption using chaotic nonlinear adaptive filter. Sig. Process. **117**, 281–309 (2015)
9. Wu, F., Cui, W., Chen, H.: A compound chaos-based encryption algorithm for vector geographic data under network circumstance. In: 2008 Congress on Image and Signal Processing, pp. 27–30 (2008)
10. Bang, N.V., Moon, K.S., Lim, S., et al.: Selective encryption scheme for vector map data using chaotic map. J. Korea Multimed. Soc. **18**(7), 818–826 (2015)
11. Li, A., Li, S., Lv, G.: Disguise and reduction methods of GIS vector data based on difference expansion principle. Procedia Eng. **29**, 1344–1350 (2012)
12. Ngoc, G.P., Lee, S.H., Kwon, K.R.: Selective encryption algorithm for GIS vector map using geometric objects. Int. J. Secur. Appl. **9**(2), 61–71 (2015)
13. Park, J.H., Giao, P.N., Seung, T.Y., et al.: Selective-encrypted GIS vector map with low complexity. In: 2015 International Conference on Information Networking, pp. 98–103 (2015)
14. Pham, N.G., Lee, S.H., Kwon, K.R.: Perceptual encryption based on features of interpolating curve for vector map. IEICE Trans. Fund. Electron. Commun. Comput. Sci. **E100A**(5), 1156–1164 (2017)

15. Van, B.N., Lee, S.H., Kwon, K.R.: Selective encryption algorithm using hybrid transform for GIS vector map. J. Inf. Process. Syst. **13**(1), 68–82 (2017)
16. Wang, X., Shao, C., Xu, X., et al.: Reversible data-hiding scheme for 2-D vector maps based on difference expansion. IEEE Trans. Inf. Forensics Secur. **2**(3), 311–320 (2007)
17. Neyman, S.N., Sitohang, B., Sutisna, S.: Reversible fragile watermarking based on difference expansion using Manhattan distances for 2D vector map. Procedia Technol. **11**, 614–620 (2013)
18. Dorst, L., Fontijne, D., Mann, S.: Why geometric algebra? In: Geometric Algebra for Computer Science, Revised edn. Morgan Kaufmann Publishers, Burlington (2009)
19. Hitzer, E., Nitta, T., Kuroe, Y.: Applications of Clifford's geometric algebra. Adv. Appl. Clifford Algebras **23**(2), 377–404 (2013). https://doi.org/10.1007/s00006-013-0378-4
20. Yuan, L.W., Yu, Z.-Y., Luo, W., et al.: Geometric algebra-based construction and implementation methods for multidimension-unified GIS. Geograph. Res. **32**(05), 974–983 (2013)
21. Ebling, J., Scheuermann, G.: Clifford convolution and pattern matching on vector fields. In: IEEE Visualization 2003, pp. 193–200. IEEE Computer Society, Los Alamitos (2003)
22. Yuan, L., Yu, Z., Luo, W., et al.: Pattern forced geophysical vector field segmentation based on Clifford FFT. Comput. Geosci. **60**, 63–69 (2013)
23. Yu, Z., Luo, W., Yi, L., et al.: Clifford algebra-based structure filtering analysis for geophysical vector fields. Nonlin. Processes Geophys. **20**(4), 563–570 (2013)
24. Yuan, L., Yu, Z., Luo, W., Yi, L., Lü, G.: Geometric algebra for multidimension-unified geographical information system. Adv. Appl. Clifford Algebras **23**(2), 497–518 (2013). https://doi.org/10.1007/s00006-012-0375-z
25. Hestenes, D.: New Foundations for Classical Mechanics. Kluwer, New York (2002)
26. Doran, C., Lasenby, A.: Geometirc Algebra for Computer Science. Morgan Kaufmann, San Mateo (2008)
27. Symul, T., Assad, S.M., Lam, P.K.: Real time demonstration of high bitrate quantum random number generation with coherent laser light. Appl. Phys. Lett. **98**(23), 231103 (2011)
28. Haw, J.Y., Assad, S.M., Lance, A.M., et al.: Maximization of extractable randomness in a quantum random-number generator. Phys. Rev. Appl. **3**(5), 054004 (2015)
29. Minguillon, J., Pujol, J.: JPEG standard uniform quantization error modeling with applications to sequential and progressive operation modes. Electron. Imaging **10**(2), 475–485 (2001)
30. Roy, S., Kumar Jain, A., et al.: A study about color normalization methods for histopathology images. Micron **114**, 42–61 (2018)

Homomorphic Data Concealment Powered by Clifford Geometric Algebra

David W. H. A. da Silva[1]([✉]) [iD], Marcelo A. Xavier[2] [iD], Philip N. Brown[1] [iD],
Edward Chow[1] [iD], and Carlos Paz de Araujo[1] [iD]

[1] University of Colorado at Colorado Springs, Colorado Springs, CO 80918, USA
{dhonorio,pbrown2,cchow,cpazdear}@uccs.edu
[2] Ford Motor Company, Dearborn, MI 48124, USA
maraujox@ford.com
https://www.uccs.edu

Abstract. We propose general-purpose methods for data representation
and data concealment via multivector decompositions and a small subset of functions in the three dimensional Clifford geometric algebra. We
demonstrate mechanisms that can be explored for purposes from plain
data manipulation to homomorphic data processing with multivectors.
The wide variety of algebraic representations in Clifford geometric algebra allow us to explore concepts from integer, complex, vector and matrix
arithmetic within a single, compact, flexible and yet powerful algebraic
structure in order to propose novel homomorphisms. Our constructions
can be incorporated into existing applications as add-ons as well as used
to provide standalone data-centric algorithms. We implement our representation and concealment mechanisms in the Ruby programming language to demonstrate the ideas discussed in this work.

Keywords: Data concealment · Data hiding · Homomorphisms ·
Multivector packing · Clifford geometric algebra

1 Introduction

The digital representation of information creates opportunities as well as challenges given that not everyone should create, access and/or modify data in the
same way to avoid violations of ownership and further forms of tampering [4,5,8].
As a response to this problem, there are several different data protective techniques, including cryptography [16,19,28], steganography, data masking [25],
data obfuscation [2], data encoding [17], data convolution [36], and *Data hiding*
[22]. These technologies have several overlaps, differing however at the application level [5]. With so many different terminologies and set of rules to define
distinct protective data-access techniques, we find important to treat them as

---

Originally with University of Colorado Colorado Springs and is now with Ford Motor
Company.

© Springer Nature Switzerland AG 2020
N. Magnenat-Thalmann et al. (Eds.): CGI 2020, LNCS 12221, pp. 513–525, 2020.
https://doi.org/10.1007/978-3-030-61864-3_44

classes of a general-purpose data protection mechanism, which in this manuscript we refer to as *data concealment*.

Clifford geometric algebra is known by the richness, robustness and flexibility of its algebraic structure, which allows us to take advantage of concepts from several different branches of mathematics such as vector and matrix spaces [20, 32, 33], integer, rational and complex arithmetic [10, 13, 24, 34, 35], all in a single compact system.

1.1   Our Contribution

We demonstrate that through multivector decompositions and a small subset of operations in the Clifford geometric algebra (GA for simplicity from now on) we are able to propose new methods for general-purpose data representation and data concealment with multivectors through processes we refer to as *multivector packing schemes* and *concealment schemes*, respectively. Our methods can be used as part of the necessary reconciliation of data availability and privacy preservation. This is important because once data is concealed, one cannot meaningfully process it, unless the concealment function is *homomorphic* with respect to one or more operations. Therefore, homomorphism is a key concern in our constructions since we are particularly interested in packing and concealment schemes that allow homomorphic computations over concealed data. To the best of our knowledge, this work is first proposition of general purpose methods for both data representation and data concealment based on GA.

1.2   Related Work

Hildebrand [11] highlights the benefits of investing in Clifford geometric algebra as a computing tool, as it can be directly integrated with standard programming languages to achieve compactness of algorithms and implicit use of parallelism, among other advantages, which result in higher run-time performance and robustness [14, 23]. The Clifford Mutivector Toolbox for Matlab, by Sangwine and Hitzer [27], is a practical instance of GA computing, which can also be used to test some of the results that we present in this work. Dorst et al. discusses the object-oriented approach to geometry and the peculiarities of GA from a computer science standpoint in [3, 9, 12], where the use of vectors as a more general modeling tool (and not only a way to represent geometric aspects) and the ability of computing within subspaces of a multivector is approached in detail. This manuscript considers several multivector decompositions, their relationship with complex arithmetic and the evaluation of eigenvalues, in line with the contributions of Josipović [18].

Rockwood et al. [26] propose a method that encodes input data so the structure of objects and their behaviour can be modeled. Carré et al. [6] demonstrated how to apply GA to encode and process color transformations of images. Augello et al. [1] found that Clifford rotors could be used to encode sentences from natural languages through rotations of orthogonal basis of a semantic space which was revealed to be more efficient than natural language representation via vectors in high dimensional spaces. Majumdar [21] also explored GA for data encoding using sub-symbolic codes in order to provide new methods for searching, indexing, clustering, translations and other data transformations. The application of GA as an approach towards fully homomorphic encryption is introduced in [30]. Based on similar ideas, a homomorphic image processing application based on GA is demonstrated in [31]. The experimental homomorphic primitives based on multivector objects enables the construction of additional protocols such as key exchange and key update, as discussed in [29]. To the best of our knowledge, this work is first proposition of general purpose methods for both data representation and data concealment based on GA.

1.3   Preliminaries

Multivectors are denoted by a capital letter with an overbar $(\bar{M})$ in order to provide a quick and easy distinction of a multivector object and any other data structure. The unit basis vectors are denoted as $\bar{e}_i$ as we want the reader to visually and quickly separate the computable coefficients from their bases. In our constructions we use the Clifford signature $\mathcal{Cl}(3,0)$, however, we refer to elements generated in $\mathcal{Cl}(3,0)$ as members of a geometric product space that we denote as $\mathbb{G}^3$. We refer to a datum that we want to represent and conceal as a *message*. We call the multivector that represents a message as a *message multivector*.

2   Basics of Clifford Geometric Algebra $\mathcal{Cl}(3,0)$

Multivectors in $\mathcal{Cl}(3,0)$ are members of the 3-dimensional geometric product space which we denote by $\mathbb{G}^3$. For all $\bar{M} \in \mathbb{G}^3$, a multivector is given by $\bar{M} = m_0\bar{e}_0 + m_1\bar{e}_1 + m_2\bar{e}_2 + m_3\bar{e}_3 + m_{12}\bar{e}_{12} + m_{13}\bar{e}_{13} + m_{23}\bar{e}_{23} + m_{123}\bar{e}_{123}$. Following [7], we refer to the four *grades* of a multivector as the *scalar* part $\langle\bar{M}\rangle_0 := m_0\bar{e}_0$, the *vector* part $\langle\bar{M}\rangle_1 := m_1\bar{e}_1 + m_2\bar{e}_2 + m_3\bar{e}_3$, the *bivector* part $\langle\bar{M}\rangle_2 := m_{12}\bar{e}_{12} + m_{13}\bar{e}_{13} + m_{23}\bar{e}_{23}$ and the *trivector* or *pseudoscalar* part $\langle\bar{M}\rangle_3 := m_{123}\bar{e}_{123}$.

As for the basic operations in $\mathbb{G}^3$, similarly to the operations of a vector space, we can add, subtract, scalar multiply and scalar divide multivectors componentwise. Multiplication of multivectors is achieved with the geometric product, the fundamental operation in $\mathbb{G}^3$ which is given by $\bar{A}\bar{B} = \bar{A}\cdot\bar{B} + \bar{A}\wedge\bar{B}$, where $\bar{A}\cdot\bar{B}$ is the Clifford dot product and $\bar{A}\wedge\bar{B}$ is the Clifford wedge product. We frequently make use of the fact that the subspace spanned by $\{\bar{e}_0, \bar{e}_{123}\}$ is closed under the geometric product, since $(\bar{e}_0)^2 = \bar{e}_0$ and $(\bar{e}_{123})^2 = -\bar{e}_0$. Thus, the trivector part $\langle\bar{M}\rangle_3$ is commonly referred to as a *pseudoscalar* [7,11], since $\bar{e}_{123}$ behaves as the complex number $i = \sqrt{-1}$. Accordingly, when a multivector is comprised only of scalar and trivector parts (i.e., $\bar{M} = m_0\bar{e}_0 + m_{123}\bar{e}_{123}$), we write $\bar{M} \in \mathbb{C}$, treat it as the complex scalar $m_0 + m_{123}i$, and use the geometric product and the scalar product interchangeably.

A multivector *involution* is an operation that changes the signs of specific unit basis vectors of a given multivector [18]. In this manuscript, we make use of the following involutions:

- Clifford conjugation: $\overline{\overline{M}} = \langle \bar{M} \rangle_0 - \langle \bar{M} \rangle_1 - \langle \bar{M} \rangle_2 + \langle \bar{M} \rangle_3$
- Reverse: $\bar{M}^\dagger = \langle \bar{M} \rangle_0 - \langle \bar{M} \rangle_1 + \langle \bar{M} \rangle_2 - \langle \bar{M} \rangle_3$

Note that for all $\bar{M} \in \mathbb{G}^3$, it holds that $\bar{M}\overline{\overline{M}} \in \mathbb{C}$. Furthermore, if $\bar{M} \in \mathbb{C}$, then the Reverse is identical to the complex conjugate: $\bar{M}^\dagger = m_0 \bar{e}_0 - m_{123} \bar{e}_0 123$. Definitions 1–3 are due to [18]:

Definition 1. If $\bar{M}\overline{\overline{M}} \neq 0$, the inverse of $\bar{M}$ is given by $\bar{M}^{-1} = \bar{M} / \left(\bar{M}\overline{\overline{M}} \right)$.

An alternative method of computing the inverse of a multivector relies on a complex numbers technique due to [18], and uses the following definition:

Definition 2. The rationalize of $\bar{M}$, denoted by $R\left(\bar{M} \right)$, is given by $R\left(\bar{M} \right) = \left(\bar{M}\overline{\overline{M}} \right) \left(\bar{M}\overline{\overline{M}} \right)^\dagger$. It always holds that $R\left(\bar{M} \right) \in \mathbb{R}$.

Definition 3. The inverse of $\bar{M} \in \mathbb{G}^3$ in terms of its rationalize is given by $\bar{M}^{-1} = \overline{\overline{M}} \left(\bar{M}\overline{\overline{M}} \right)^\dagger R\left(\bar{M} \right)^{-1}$ such that $\bar{M}\bar{M}^{-1} = 1$.

Another topic of interest in our GA-based framework is eigenvalue computation in Clifford geometric algebra. Multivector $\bar{M}$ is said to have *eigenvalue* $\alpha \in \mathbb{C}$ associated with *eigenelement* $\bar{X} \in \mathbb{G}^3$ if α and $\bar{X}$ satisfy the equation $\bar{M}\bar{X} = \alpha\bar{X}$. Every multivector $\bar{M} \in \mathbb{G}^3$ such that $\bar{M} \neq 0$ has two (not necessarily distinct) eigenvalues.

We summarize the results of computing the eigenvalues of a multivector obtained by Josipović in [18] in Proposition 1 and Theorem 1.

Lemma 1. A multivector $\bar{M} \in \mathbb{G}^3$ can be written in terms of the multivectors $\bar{Z}$ and $\bar{F}$ such that $\bar{M} = \bar{Z} + \bar{F}$ where $\bar{Z} = \frac{1}{2}\left(\bar{M} + \overline{\overline{M}} \right)$ and $\bar{F} = \frac{1}{2}\left(\bar{M} - \overline{\overline{M}} \right)$, for $\bar{Z}$ is a complex scalar in the form of $\bar{Z} = \langle \bar{M} \rangle_0 + \langle \bar{M} \rangle_3$, and $\bar{F} = \langle \bar{M} \rangle_1 + \langle \bar{M} \rangle_2$.

Proof. Given $\bar{M} = \langle \bar{M} \rangle_0 + \langle \bar{M} \rangle_1 + \langle \bar{M} \rangle_2 + \langle \bar{M} \rangle_3$ and $\overline{\overline{M}} = \langle \bar{M} \rangle_0 - \langle \bar{M} \rangle_1 - \langle \bar{M} \rangle_2 + \langle \bar{M} \rangle_3$, then $\bar{M} + \overline{\overline{M}} = 2\left(\langle \bar{M} \rangle_0 + \langle \bar{M} \rangle_3 \right) = 2\bar{Z}$. Therefore we write $\bar{Z} = \frac{1}{2}\left(\bar{M} + \overline{\overline{M}} \right)$. Similarly, $\bar{M} - \overline{\overline{M}} = 2\left(\langle \bar{M} \rangle_1 + \langle \bar{M} \rangle_2 \right) = 2\bar{F}$ and therefore $\bar{F} = \frac{1}{2}\left(\bar{M} - \overline{\overline{M}} \right)$.

Theorem 1. The eigenvalues $\alpha_1, \alpha_1 \in \mathbb{C}$ of a multivector $\bar{M} \in \mathbb{G}^3$ are computed as $\alpha_i = \bar{Z} \pm \sqrt{\bar{Z}^2 - \bar{M}\overline{\overline{M}}} = \bar{Z} \pm \sqrt{\bar{F}^2}$, $i = 1$ for $+$, 2 for $-$.

Proof. We know that $\overline{\overline{M}} = \langle \bar{M} \rangle_0 - \langle \bar{M} \rangle_1 - \langle \bar{M} \rangle_2 + \langle \bar{M} \rangle_3$, which can be rewritten as $\langle \bar{M} \rangle_0 + \langle \bar{M} \rangle_3 - \left(\langle \bar{M} \rangle_1 + \langle \bar{M} \rangle_2 \right)$, and therefore $\overline{\overline{M}} = \bar{Z} - \bar{F}$. Hence, $\bar{M}\overline{\overline{M}} = \left(\bar{Z} + \bar{F} \right)\left(\bar{Z} - \bar{F} \right) = \bar{Z}^2 - \bar{Z}\bar{F} + \bar{F}\bar{Z} - \bar{F}^2$. Since $\bar{Z}$ is a commuting complex scalar, then $\bar{Z}\bar{F}$ and $\bar{F}\bar{Z}$ commutes, so we can write $\bar{M}\overline{\overline{M}} = \bar{Z}^2 - \bar{F}^2$. In order to compute the eigenvalues of a multivector $\bar{M}$, we need to solve for α in the characteristic equation $\bar{M}\bar{X} = \alpha\bar{X}$, $\alpha \in \mathbb{C}$. We write $(\bar{M} - \alpha)\bar{X} = 0$. The determinant of a multivector $\bar{M}$, resulting in a complex scalar, is computed as $\det(\bar{M}) = \bar{M}\overline{\overline{M}}$ [18]. Thus, we write $\det(\bar{M} - \alpha) = 0$ then $\det(\bar{M} - \alpha) = (\bar{M} - \alpha)\overline{(\bar{M} - \alpha)} = 0$. For simplicity, let $\bar{N} = (\bar{M} - \alpha)$, where we want to satisfy $\bar{N}\overline{\overline{N}} = 0$. Let $\bar{Z}_N, \bar{Z}_M, \bar{Z}_\alpha, \bar{F}_N, \bar{F}_M, \bar{F}_\alpha$ be the $\bar{Z}$-type and the $\bar{F}$-type multivectors computed for $\bar{N}, \bar{Z}$ and α, respectively. Then we can write $\bar{N}\overline{\overline{N}} = \bar{Z}_N^2 - \bar{F}_N^2$, which can be expressed as $(\bar{Z}_\alpha + \bar{Z}_M)^2 - (\bar{F}_\alpha + \bar{F}_M)^2 = 0$. Since $\bar{Z}_\alpha$ is the complex-like part of $\alpha \in \mathbb{C}$, then $\bar{Z}_\alpha = \alpha$ and we can write $(\alpha + \bar{Z}_M)^2 - \bar{F}_M^2 = 0$. By expanding the terms, we obtain $\alpha + 2\alpha\bar{Z}_M + \bar{Z}_M^2 - \bar{F}_M^2 = 0$. Since we now only have multivectors in terms of $\bar{M}$, we let $\bar{Z}_M = \bar{Z}$ and $\bar{M}\overline{\overline{M}} = \bar{Z}^2 - \bar{F}^2$ so we can write $\alpha^2 + 2\alpha\bar{Z} + \bar{M}\overline{\overline{M}} = 0$. In order to solve for α, we finally arrive at $\alpha = \bar{Z} \pm \sqrt{\bar{Z}^2 - \bar{M}\overline{\overline{M}}} = \bar{Z} \pm \sqrt{\bar{F}^2}$. $\qquad\square$

2.1 Homomorphisms

Given two messages $a, b \in \mathbb{Z}$, a function f is homomorphic with respect to a given operation $\circ$ if $f(a \circ b) = f(a) \circ f(b)$. When we represent the messages a, b as the multivectors $\bar{A}, \bar{B} \in \mathbb{G}^3$, we say that the function of this representation will be homomorphic with respect to $\circ$ if $f(\bar{A} \circ \bar{B}) = f(\bar{A}) \circ f(\bar{B})$. The two operations of interest is addition and multiplication. Addition of multivectors is achieved element-wise. Multiplication of multivectors is achieved via the geometric product. Thus, when we say that a given function of multivectors is homomorphic with respect to multiplication, in the context of multivector packing and concealment schemes, we mean that the geometric product of multivectors that represent scalars is equivalent to the standard multiplication of the scalars.

Definition 4. *Let $\mathbb{K}$ be an arbitrary space, let $f : \mathbb{K} \to \mathbb{K}$, and let operation $\circ$ be a binary operation $\circ : \mathbb{K} \times \mathbb{K} \to \mathbb{K}$. Function f is said to be homomorphic with respect to $\circ$ if $f(a \circ b) = f(a) \circ f(b)$ for all $a, b \in \mathbb{K}$.*

We are interested in functions that are additive homomorphic, multiplicative homomorphic, or both.

3 Multivector Packing Schemes

Before discussing details of different methods we propose to represent data, we introduce Definition 5 as general definition of what is a *multivector packing*.

Definition 5. *Given a function $f : \mathbb{G}^3 \to \mathbb{R}$, a Multivector Packing Scheme is a probabilistic polynomial-time computable function $g : \mathbb{R} \to \mathbb{G}^3$ such that for all $m \in \mathbb{R}$, $f(g(m)) = m$.*

3.1 Clifford Eigenvalue Packing Scheme

Definition 6 CEP Forward Mapping. $(\bar{M} = \overrightarrow{\text{CEP}}(m))$ *Given a message* $m \in \mathbb{Z}$ *and a random number* r *uniformly selected from* $\{m, \ldots, b-1\}$*, for an arbitrary boundary* b*, where* $r > m$*, and pre-defined auxiliary multivector* $\bar{A} \in \mathbb{G}^3$ *such that* $R(\bar{A}) \neq 0$ *and therefore* $\bar{A}\bar{A}^{-1} = 1$*, a message multivector* $\bar{M} \in \mathbb{G}^3$ *is computed as follows: let* $d_0 = \frac{r+m}{2}$ *and* $d_2 = \frac{r-m}{2}$ *so the multivector* $\bar{D} \in \mathbb{G}^3$ *is defined as* $\bar{D} = d_0\bar{e}_0 + 0\bar{e}_1 + d_2\bar{e}_2 + 0\bar{e}_3 + 0\bar{e}_{12} + 0\bar{e}_{13} + 0\bar{e}_{23} + 0\bar{e}_{123}$*. Therefore,* $\bar{M} = \bar{A}\bar{D}\bar{A}^{-1}$*.*

Remark 1. Since a packing scheme is not meant to hide information, $\bar{A}$ does not need to be secret. $\bar{A}$ can be generated as a system variable and be globally available to the application where the CEP is being implemented and used.

Definition 7 CEP Backward Mapping. $(m = \overleftarrow{\text{CEP}}(\bar{M}))$ *Given a message multivector* $\bar{M} \in \mathbb{G}^3$*, a message* $m \in \mathbb{Z}$ *is computed such that* $m = \bar{Z} - \sqrt{\bar{Z}^2 - \bar{M}\overline{\overline{M}}} = \bar{Z} - \sqrt{\bar{F}^2}$*.*

Theorem 2 Correctness of CEP. *If* $m \in \mathbb{Z}$*, it holds that* $\overleftarrow{\text{CEP}}\left(\overrightarrow{\text{CEP}}(m)\right) = m$*.*

Proof. Given a multivector $\bar{M}$ generated according to Definition 6, we know that $\bar{D}$ does not have a pseudoscalar, thus, $\bar{Z}$ and $\bar{F}^2$ from $\bar{M}$ are integers and thus commute. Since $\bar{F}^2$ is just an integer, the scalar part of $\bar{A}$ is cancelled in $\bar{A}\bar{D}\bar{A}^{-1}$ thus $\bar{F}^2 = d_2^2$. We also know that $\bar{Z} = d_0$. According to Definition 6 we know that we recover m as follows:

$$\bar{Z} - \sqrt{\bar{F}^2} = d_0 - d_2 = m. \tag{1}$$

□

Definition 8 Alternative CEP Backward Mapping. *Since* $\bar{A}$ *is known, an alternative CEP Backward Mapping is computed as follows:*

$$m = d_0 - d_2, \quad \bar{D} = \bar{A}^{-1}\bar{M}\bar{A}. \tag{2}$$

Remark 2. The CEP is a packing scheme that leverages the function that computes the eigenvalue of a multivector. Since this function is both additive and multiplicative homomorphic, the packing scheme is also homomorphic with respect to addition and multiplication, i.e., $\overleftarrow{\text{CEP}}(\bar{A} \circ \bar{B}) = \overleftarrow{\text{CEP}}(\bar{A}) \circ \overleftarrow{\text{CEP}}(\bar{B})$, $\circ \in \{+, \cdot\}$, $\bar{A} = \overrightarrow{\text{CEP}}(a)$, $\bar{B} = \overrightarrow{\text{CEP}}(b)$, $a, b \in \mathbb{Z}$.

3.2 Complex Magnitude Squared Packing Scheme

For this packing scheme, we select two coefficients of $\bar{M}$ to be computed in such a way that $R(\bar{M}) = m$. We take advantage of how the coefficients m_0 and m_1 of the multivector $\bar{M}$ are involved in the computation of $R(\bar{M})$ and, therefore, we define them in terms of a complex number $z = a + bi$, where $|z|^2 = a^2 + b^2$. Due to the lengthy aspect of the final solution, we break it down into auxiliary equations, which are showed in Definition 9. For computing m_0 and m_1, let

$$
\begin{aligned}
\tau &= b^2 - 4bm_2m_{13} + 4bm_3m_{12} + 4m_2^2m_{13}^2 + 4m_2^2m_{23}^2 \\
\mu &= -4m_2^2m_{123}^2 - 8m_2m_3m_{12}m_{13} + 4m_3^2m_{12}^2 + 4m_3^2m_{23}^2 - 4m_3^2m_{123}^2 \\
\upsilon &= -4m_{12}^2m_{23}^2 + 4m_{12}^2m_{123}^2 - 4m_{13}^2m_{23}^2 + 4m_{13}^2m_{123}^2 - 4m_{23}^4 \\
\omega &= 8m_{23}^2m_{123}^2 + 4am_{23}^2 - 4m_{123}^4 - 4am_{123}^2
\end{aligned}
\tag{3}
$$

Definition 9. Auxiliary Equations for m_0 and m_1

Let $x_1 \ldots x_6$ be auxiliary equations for m_0 and $x_7 \ldots x_9$ be auxiliary equations for m_1 such that

$$
\begin{aligned}
x_1 &= \left(b - 2m_2m_{13} + 2m_3m_{12}\right) / \left(2m_{123}\right) \\
x_2 &= m_{23} \\
x_3 &= bm_{23} \\
x_4 &= m_{123} \\
x_5 &= \left(\tau + \mu + \upsilon + \omega\right) \\
x_6 &= \left(-2m_2m_{13}m_{23} + 2m_3m_{12}m_{23}\right) \\
x_7 &= \left(2m_{123}\left(m_{23} + m_{123}\right)\left(m_{23} - m_{123}\right)\right) \\
x_8 &= \left(2\left(m_{23} + m_{123}\right)\left(m_{23} - m_{123}\right)\right)
\end{aligned}
\tag{4}
$$

Definition 10 CMSP Forward Mapping $(\bar{M} = \overrightarrow{\text{CMSP}}\,(m))$. *Given a message $m \in \mathbb{Z}$, $m > 0$, we let m to be expressed as the magnitude squared of a complex number $z = a + bi$ such that $m = |z|^2 = a^2 + b^2$. We first define the coefficients a and b of z as follows: let a be a random number in $\mathbb{Z}$ and $b = \sqrt{m - a^2}$. The message multivector $\bar{M}$ is computed such that $\bar{M}\overline{\overline{M}} = z$. Let the coefficients from m_2 to m_{123} be random numbers in $\mathbb{Z}$ such that $m_{123} \neq 0$ and $m_{123} \neq m_{23}$ in order to avoid division by zero when computing x_1 in (4). We compute m_0 and m_1 such that $m_0 = x_1 - \left(x_2\left(x_3 + x_4\sqrt{x_5} + x_6\right)\right)/x_7$ and $m_1 = -\left(x_3 + x_4\sqrt{x_5} + x_6\right)/x_8$. Notice that given the definition of m_{23} and m_{123}, we guarantee that no division by zero will occur when computing m_0 and m_1.*

Theorem 3. *The operation $\bar{M}\overline{\overline{M}}$ produces a complex scalar. The multiplication of this complex scalar with its own reverse results in the magnitude squared.*

Proof. The Clifford conjugation of a multivector $\bar{M}$ changes the sign of the vector and the bivector part of $\bar{M}$. The geometric product of $\bar{M}$ and its Clifford conjugation $\overline{\overline{M}}$ cancels the vector and bivector parts, i.e., $\left\langle \bar{M}\overline{\overline{M}} \right\rangle_1 = \left\langle \bar{M}\overline{\overline{M}} \right\rangle_2 = 0$, resulting in a multivector consisting of only its scalar and pseudoscalar parts: $\bar{M}\overline{\overline{M}} = \left\langle \bar{M}\overline{\overline{M}} \right\rangle_0 + \left\langle \bar{M}\overline{\overline{M}} \right\rangle_3$. The reverse of a multivector $\bar{M}$ changes the sign of the vector and trivector (pseudoscalar) parts. The reverse of $\bar{M}\overline{\overline{M}}$ will change the sign of $\left\langle \bar{M}\overline{\overline{M}} \right\rangle_3$, which is equivalent to perform the complex conjugation operation on the complex scalar. The product of a complex number and its conjugate results in the magnitude squared of that complex number. From Definition 2 we recall that the rationalize is computed as $R\left(\bar{M}\right) = \left(\bar{M}\overline{\overline{M}}\right)\left(\bar{M}\overline{\overline{M}}\right)^{\dagger}$, where $\left(\bar{M}\overline{\overline{M}}\right)$ results in a complex scalar and $\left(\bar{M}\overline{\overline{M}}\right)^{\dagger}$ is the complex conjugate. The CMSP packs a multivector $\bar{M}$ such that $\bar{M}\overline{\overline{M}} \in \mathbb{C}$, where the rationalize computes the magnitude squared of the complex scalar $\bar{M}\overline{\overline{M}}$. □

Definition 11 CMSP Backward Mapping. $\left(m = \overleftarrow{\text{CMSP}}\left(\bar{M}\right)\right)$ *Given a message multivector $\bar{M} \in \mathbb{G}^3$, a message $m \in \mathbb{C}$ is computed such that $R\left(\bar{M}\right) = m$.*

Theorem 4 Correctness of CMSP. *For all $m \in \mathbb{C}$ and all $\bar{M} \in \mathbb{G}^3$ that are output by $\overrightarrow{\text{CMSP}}\left(m\right)$, the following holds: $\overleftarrow{\text{CMSP}}\left(\overrightarrow{\text{CMSP}}\left(m\right)\right) = m$.*

Remark 3. We omit the full proof for reasons of space, but provide the following proof outline. Given a message m, we compute a complex number $z = a + bi$ by allowing a to be a random integer and $b = \sqrt{m - a^2}$ such that $|z|^2 = m$. We then build a multivector $\bar{M}$ such that $\left\langle \bar{M}\overline{\overline{M}} \right\rangle_0 = a$ and $\left\langle \bar{M}\overline{\overline{M}} \right\rangle_3 = b$. Therefore, it is clear that $R\left(\bar{M}\right) = m$ since the rationalize is the product of the complex scalar $\bar{M}\overline{\overline{M}}$ by its complex conjugate $\left(\bar{M}\overline{\overline{M}}\right)^{\dagger}$, which is the magnitude squared of a complex number. The proof then depends on the correctness of the auxiliary functions in Definition 9. If those equations are correct, then the CMSP is also correct.

Remark 4. The rationalize of a multivector, similarly to the complex magnitude square of a complex number, is multiplicative homomorphic, i.e., $R\left(\bar{A}\bar{B}\right) = R\left(\bar{A}\right)R\left(\bar{B}\right)$. Hence, $\overrightarrow{\text{CMSP}}\left(\bar{A}\bar{B}\right) = \overrightarrow{\text{CMSP}}\left(\bar{A}\right)\overrightarrow{\text{CMSP}}\left(\bar{B}\right)$, $\bar{A} = \overrightarrow{\text{CMSP}}\left(a\right)$, $\bar{B} = \overrightarrow{\text{CMSP}}\left(b\right)$, $a, b \in \mathbb{C}$.

4 Concealment Schemes

We propose methods for concealing arbitrary message multivectors with the support of a secret key. The secret key is a tuple consisting of two secret multivectors $k = \left(\bar{K}_1, \bar{K}_2\right)$, where $\bar{K}_1, \bar{K}_2 \in \mathbb{G}^3$, for which an inverse must exist. We denote the set of invertible secret key multivectors as $K = \left\{ \bar{K} \mid \exists \bar{K}^{-1} \in \mathbb{G}^3 \right\}$.

Definition 12. *A Concealment Scheme is a polynomial-time algorithm that hides a message multivector by computing a concealed multivector with the support of secret key multivectors.*

4.1 Clifford Sylvester's Equation Concealment (CSEC)

The first concealment scheme we propose is based on the well-known Sylvester's equation [15], where we make use of its multivector variant [7].

Definition 13 CSEC Forward Mapping. $(\bar{C} = \overrightarrow{\text{CSEC}}(k, \bar{M}))$ *Given a secret tuple* $k = (\bar{K}_1, \bar{K}_2)$, *where* $\bar{K}_1, \bar{K}_2 \in K$, *and a message multivector* $\bar{M} \in \mathbb{G}^3$, *we can compute a concealed multivector* $\bar{C} \in \mathbb{G}^3$ *such that* $\bar{C} = \overrightarrow{\text{CSEC}}(k, \bar{M}) = \bar{K}_1 \bar{M} + \bar{M} \bar{K}_2$.

Definition 14 CSEC Backward Mapping. $(\bar{M} = \overleftarrow{\text{CSEC}}(k, \bar{C}))$ *Given a secret tuple* $k = (\bar{K}_1, \bar{K}_2)$, *for* $\bar{K}_1, \bar{K}_2 \in \mathbb{G}^3$, *and a concealed multivector* $\bar{C} \in \mathbb{G}^3$, *a message multivector* $\bar{M} \in \mathbb{G}^3$ *is recovered by computing*

$$\bar{M} = \overleftarrow{\text{CSEC}}(k, \bar{C}) = \left(\bar{K}_1 + \overline{\overline{K}}_2 + \bar{K}_1^{-1} \bar{K}_2 \overline{\overline{K}}_2^{-1} + \bar{K}_1 \right)^{-1} \left(\bar{K}_1^{-1} \bar{C} \overline{\overline{K}}_2 + \bar{C} \right) \quad (5)$$

Theorem 5 Correctness of CSEC. *For all* $k \in K$, *where* $R(\bar{K}_1), R(\bar{K}_2) \neq 0$, *and for all* $\bar{M}, \bar{C} \in \mathbb{G}^3$, *the following holds:* $\overleftarrow{\text{CSEC}}\left(k, \overrightarrow{\text{CSEC}}(k, \bar{M})\right) = \bar{M}$.

Proof. Given

$$\bar{C} = \bar{K}_1 \bar{M} + \bar{M} \bar{K}_2 \quad (6)$$

left multiply by $\bar{K}_1^{-1}$ and right multiply by $\overline{\overline{K}}_2$ both sides of (6):

$$\bar{K}_1^{-1} \bar{C} \overline{\overline{K}}_2 = \bar{K}_1^{-1} \bar{K}_1 \bar{M} \overline{\overline{K}}_2 + \bar{K}_1^{-1} \bar{M} \bar{K}_2 \overline{\overline{K}}_2 \quad (7)$$

According to Definition 3, $\bar{K}_1^{-1} \bar{K}_1 = 1$, which allows us to simplify (7) as follows:

$$\bar{K}_1^{-1} \bar{C} \overline{\overline{K}}_2 = \bar{M} \overline{\overline{K}}_2 + \bar{K}_1^{-1} \bar{M} \bar{K}_2 \overline{\overline{K}}_2 \quad (8)$$

If we sum (8) with (6) and combine like terms we obtain the following:

$$\bar{K}_1^{-1} \bar{C} \overline{\overline{K}}_2 = \bar{M} \left(\overline{\overline{K}}_2 + \bar{K}_2 \right) + \bar{K}_1^{-1} \bar{M} \bar{K}_2 \overline{\overline{K}}_2 + \bar{K}_1 \bar{M} \quad (9)$$

Note that $\left(\overline{\overline{K}}_2 + \bar{K}_2 \right)$ and $\bar{K}_2 \overline{\overline{K}}_2$ are commuting complex-like numbers, which allows us to re-write (9) as follows:

$$\bar{K}_1^{-1} \bar{C} \overline{\overline{K}}_2 = \left(\overline{\overline{K}}_2 + \bar{K}_2 + \bar{K}_1^{-1} \bar{K}_2 \overline{\overline{K}}_2 + \bar{K}_1 \right) \bar{M} \quad (10)$$

Assuming that the expression inside the parenthesis that multiplies $\bar{M}$ on the right hand side of the equation above results in a multivector that has an inverse, we can now solve (10) for $\bar{M}$ to obtain:

$$\bar{M} = \left(\overline{\overline{K}}_2 + \bar{K}_2 + \bar{K}_1^{-1} \bar{K}_2 \overline{\overline{K}}_2 + \bar{K}_1 \right)^{-1} \left(\bar{K}_1^{-1} \bar{C} \overline{\overline{K}}_2 + \bar{C} \right). \quad (11)$$

$\square$

Remark 5. The CSEC scheme is homomorphic with respect to addition, since adding $\bar{C}_1 = \bar{K}_1 \bar{M}_1 + \bar{M}_1 \bar{K}_2$ to $\bar{C}_2 = \bar{K}_1 \bar{M}_2 + \bar{M}_2 \bar{K}_2$ results in $\bar{C}_1 + \bar{C}_2 = \bar{K}_1 \left(\bar{M}_1 + \bar{M}_2 \right) + \left(\bar{M}_1 + \bar{M}_2 \right) \bar{K}_2$. However, it is not homomorphic with respect to multiplication.

4.2 Modular Concealment (MC)

Definition 15 MC Forward Mapping. $\left(\bar{C} = \overrightarrow{\mathrm{MC}}\left(k, \bar{M}\right)\right)$ *Given a secret tuple* $k \in K$, *a message multivector* $\bar{M} \in \mathbb{G}^3$, *and a random multivector* $\bar{R} \in \mathbb{G}^3$, *such that the secret key multivectors in* k, $\bar{M}$ *and* $\bar{R}$ *are all packed with* $\overrightarrow{\mathrm{CEP}}$ *(all using the same auxiliary multivector* $\bar{A}$*), we compute a concealed multivector* $\bar{C} \in \mathbb{G}^3$ *such that* $\bar{C} = \overrightarrow{\mathrm{MC}}\left(k, \bar{M}\right) = \bar{R}\bar{K}_1\bar{K}_2 + \bar{M}$.

Definition 16 MC Backward Mapping. $\left(\bar{M} = \overleftarrow{\mathrm{MC}}\left(k, \bar{C}\right)\right)$ *Given a secret tuple* $k = \left(\bar{K}_1, \bar{K}_2\right)$, *for* $\bar{K}_1, \bar{K}_2 \in \mathbb{G}^3$, *and a concealed multivector* $\bar{C} \in \mathbb{G}^3$, *a message multivector* $\bar{M} \in \mathbb{G}^3$ *is recovered as* $\bar{M} = \overleftarrow{\mathrm{MC}}\left(k, \bar{C}\right) = \bar{C} \bmod \left(\bar{K}_1\bar{K}_2\right)$, *where the modulo operation is computed at the eigenvalue level.*

Theorem 6 Correctness of MC. *For all* $k \in K$ *and for all* $\bar{M} \in \mathbb{G}^3$, *the following holds:* $\overleftarrow{\mathrm{MC}}\left(k, \overrightarrow{\mathrm{MC}}\left(k, \bar{M}\right)\right) = \bar{M}$.

Proof. The modulo operation $\bar{A} \bmod \bar{B}$ is computed in terms of the multivector packing that generated the message multivector such that $\bar{M}_1 \bmod \bar{M}_2 \equiv m_1 \bmod m_2$. Let $\bar{R}$, $\bar{K}_1$, $\bar{K}_2$, and $\bar{M}$ be the multivector representation of the integers r, k_1, k_2, and m, respectively, therefore, $\left(\bar{R}\bar{K}_1\bar{K}_2 + \bar{M}\right) \bmod \left(\bar{K}_1\bar{K}_2\right)$, which is equal to $(rk_1k_1 + m) \bmod (k_1k_2) = m$. □

Remark 6. The MC is both additive and multiplicative homomorphic for all message multivectors $\bar{M} < \left(\bar{K}_1\bar{K}_2\right)$, which is equivalent of saying that, given $\bar{C}_1 = \overrightarrow{\mathrm{MC}}\left(k, \bar{M}_1\right)$ and $\bar{C}_2 = \overrightarrow{\mathrm{MC}}\left(k, \bar{M}_2\right)$, then $\overleftarrow{\mathrm{MC}}\left(\bar{C}_1 \circ \bar{C}_2\right) = \left(\bar{C}_1 \circ \bar{C}_2\right) \bmod \left(\bar{K}_1\bar{K}_2\right)$, which is equivalent to $(m_1 \circ m_2) \bmod (k_1k_2)$ for $\circ \in \{+, \cdot\}$.

5 Availability

We implemented our ideas in Ruby language along with numerical examples which is available at https://github.com/davidwilliam/clifford-ga-ruby.git.

6 Conclusions

In this work we demonstrated how multivector involutions, decompositions, and a small set of multivector functions can be combined and explored as the sufficient components to implement protocol-agnostic homomorphic data representation and homomorphic data concealment with Clifford geometric algebra. We introduced two methods for representing numerical data, namely multivector packing schemes, such that a given datum is expressed in terms of the output of the Clifford eigenvalue and the rationalize functions. We introduced also two methods for hiding data represented as multivectors, namely concealment schemes, which consist of operations that compute a concealed multivector with the support of secret key multivectors. The multivector packing and concealment schemes discussed in this work are homomorphic with respect to addition, multiplication or both. These constructions can be used in a wide variety of privacy preserving applications since, due to its homomorphic properties, data can be meaningfully computed while concealed. The homomorphism on both packing and concealment schemes provides a guarantee that applying our methods will not compromise the numerical meaning of the data represented and concealed as multivectors. We made available a Ruby library that implements our constructions, provides numerical examples of each method, illustrates their use on simulations of real-world applications and allows one to test customized ideas. We implemented this library to demonstrate in practice that our ideas work and also to facilitate further experiments by interested researchers so they can not only easily reproduce our results but also quickly implement their own.

References

1. Augello, A., Gentile, M., Pilato, G., Vassallo, G.: Geometric encoding of sentences based on Clifford algebra. In: KDIR, pp. 457–462 (2012)
2. Bakken, D.E., Raramesweraran, R., Blough, D.M., Franz, A.A., Palmer, T.J.: Data obfuscation: anonymity and desensitization of usable data sets. IEEE Secur. Priv. **2**(6), 34–41 (2004)
3. Bayro-Corrochano, E., Scheuermann, G.: Geometric Algebra Computing: In Engineering and Computer Science. Springer, London (2010). https://doi.org/10.1007/978-1-84996-108-0
4. Bellinger, G., Castro, D., Mills, A.: Data, information, knowledge, and wisdom. ufmg.br (2004)
5. Bender, W., Gruhl, D., Morimoto, N., Lu, A.: Techniques for data hiding. IBM Syst. J. **35**(3.4), 313–336 (1996)
6. Carré, P., Berthier, M.: Color representation and processes with Clifford algebra. In: Fernandez-Maloigne, C. (ed.) Advanced Color Image Processing and Analysis, pp. 147–179. Springer, New York (2013). https://doi.org/10.1007/978-1-4419-6190-7_6
7. Chappell, J.M., Iqbal, A., Gunn, L.J., Abbott, D.: Functions of multivector variables. PloS One **10**(3), e0116943 (2015)
8. Cooper, P.: Data, information, knowledge and wisdom. Anaesth. Intensive Care Med. **15**(1), 44–45 (2014)
9. Dorst, L., Fontijne, D., Mann, S.: Geometric Algebra for Computer Science: An Object-Oriented Approach to Geometry. Elsevier, Amsterdam (2010)
10. Gebken, C., Perwass, C., Sommer, G.: Parameter estimation from uncertain data in geometric algebra. Adv. Appl. Clifford Algebras **18**(3–4), 647–664 (2008)
11. Hildenbrand, D.: Foundations of geometric algebra computing. In: AIP Conference Proceedings, vol. 1479, no. 1, pp. 27–30. American Institute of Physics (2012)
12. Hildenbrand, D., Albert, J., Charrier, P., Steinmetz, C.: Geometric algebra computing for heterogeneous systems. Adv. Appl. Clifford Algebras **27**(1), 599–620 (2017). https://doi.org/10.1007/s00006-016-0694-6
13. Hitzer, E.: General steerable two-sided Clifford Fourier transform, convolution and mustard convolution. Adv. Appl. Clifford Algebras **27**(3), 2215–2234 (2017). https://doi.org/10.1007/s00006-016-0687-5

14. Hitzer, E., Nitta, T., Kuroe, Y.: Applications of Clifford's geometric algebra. Adv. Appl. Clifford Algebras **23**(2), 377–404 (2013). https://doi.org/10.1007/s00006-013-0378-4
15. Janovská, D., Opfer, G.: Linear equations in quaternionic variables. Mitt. Math. Ges. Hamburg **27**, 223–234 (2008)
16. Jianhong, Z., Hua, C.: Secuirty storage in the cloud computing: a RSA-based assumption data integrity check without original data. In: 2010 International Conference on Educational and Information Technology, vol. 2, pp. V2–143. IEEE (2010)
17. Johnson, H.J., Chow, S.T., Gu, Y.X.: Tamper resistant software-mass data encoding. US Patent 7,350,085, 25 March 2008
18. Josipović, M.: Geometric Multiplication of Vectors: An Introduction to Geometric Algebra in Physics. CTM. Springer, Cham (2019). https://doi.org/10.1007/978-3-030-01756-9
19. Kwok, Z.S.: Encryption integrity check with CRC encryption in memory using a word count-and address-derived nonce. US Patent 9,697,140, 4 July 2017
20. Kyrchei, I.: Determinantal representations of solutions to systems of quaternion matrix equations. Adv. Appl. Clifford Algebras **28**(1), 23 (2018). https://doi.org/10.1007/s00006-018-0843-1
21. Majumdar, A.: Weighted subsymbolic data encoding. US Patent 10,120,933, 6 November 2018
22. Ni, Z., Shi, Y.Q., Ansari, N., Su, W.: Reversible data hiding. IEEE Trans. Circuits Syst. Video Technol. **16**(3), 354–362 (2006)
23. Perwass, C., Edelsbrunner, H., Kobbelt, L., Polthier, K.: Geometric Algebra with Applications in Engineering. GC, vol. 4. Springer, Heidelberg (2009). https://doi.org/10.1007/978-3-540-89068-3
24. Pozo, J.M., Parra, J.M.: Tensors, spinors and multivectors in the petrov classification. Adv. Appl. Clifford Algebras **17**(4), 663–678 (2007). https://doi.org/10.1007/s00006-007-0049-4
25. Radhakrishnan, R., Kharrazi, M., Memon, N.: Data masking: a new approach for steganography? J. VLSI Sign. Process. Syst. Sign. Image Video Technol. **41**(3), 293–303 (2005). https://doi.org/10.1007/s11265-005-4153-1
26. Rockwood, A., Li, H., Hestenes, D.: System for encoding and manipulating models of objects. US Patent 6,853,964, 8 February 2005
27. Sangwine, S.J., Hitzer, E.: Clifford multivector toolbox (for MATLAB). Adv. Appl. Clifford Algebras **27**(1), 539–558 (2017). https://doi.org/10.1007/s00006-016-0666-x
28. Shen, S.T., Lin, H.Y., Tzeng, W.G.: An effective integrity check scheme for secure erasure code-based storage systems. IEEE Trans. Reliab. **64**(3), 840–851 (2015)
29. da Silva, D.W., de Araujo, C.P., Chow, E.: Fully homomorphic key update and key exchange over exterior product spaces for cloud computing applications. In: 2019 IEEE 24th Pacific Rim International Symposium on Dependable Computing (PRDC), pp. 25–251. IEEE (2019)
30. da Silva, D.W., de Araujo, C.P., Chow, E., Barillas, B.S.: A new approach towards fully homomorphic encryption over geometric algebra. In: 2019 IEEE 10th Annual Ubiquitous Computing, Electronics & Mobile Communication Conference (UEMCON), pp. 0241–0249. IEEE (2019)
31. da Silva, D.W.H.A., de Oliveira, H.B.M., Chow, E., Barillas, B.S., de Araujo, C.P.: Homomorphic image processing over geometric product spaces and finite p-adic arithmetic. In: 2019 IEEE International Conference on Cloud Computing Technology and Science (CloudCom), pp. 27–36. IEEE (2019)

32. Snygg, J.: A New Approach to Differential Geometry Using Clifford's Geometric Algebra. Springer, Boston (2011). https://doi.org/10.1007/978-0-8176-8283-5
33. Song, Y., Lee, D.: Matrix representations of the low order real Clifford algebras. Adv. Appl. Clifford Algebras 23(4), 965–980 (2013). https://doi.org/10.1007/s00006-013-0407-3
34. Tingelstad, L., Egeland, O.: Automatic multivector differentiation and optimization. Adv. Appl. Clifford Algebras 27(1), 707–731 (2016). https://doi.org/10.1007/s00006-016-0722-6
35. Vince, J.: Geometric Algebra for Computer Graphics. Springer, London (2008). https://doi.org/10.1007/978-1-84628-997-2
36. Yule, H.P.: Data convolution and peak location, peak area, and peak energy measurements in scintillation counting. Anal. Chem. 38(1), 103–105 (1966)

An Online Calculator for Qubits Based on Geometric Algebra

D. Hildenbrand[1(✉)], C. Steinmetz[1], R. Alves[2], J. Hrdina[3], and C. Lavor[4]

[1] Technische Universität Darmstadt, 64297 Darmstadt, Germany
dietmar.hildenbrand@gmail.com, christian.steinmetz@arcor.de
[2] Federal University of ABC, Santo André, Brazil
alves.rafael@ufabc.edu.br
[3] Brno University of Technology, Technická 2896/2, 616 69 Brno, Czech Republic
hrdina@fme.vutbr.cz
[4] University of Campinas, Campinas, Brazil
clavor@unicamp.br

Abstract. We use Geometric Algebra for quantum computing motivated by the fact that qubits and gates can be handled as elements of the same algebra. Additionally, Geometric Algebra allows us to describe gate operations very easily, based on the geometrically intuitive description of transformations in Geometric Algebra. As the main contribution of this paper, we make the calculations with the specific QBA (quantum bit algebra) accessible via an online tool based on GAALOPWeb, which can be handled on many computing devices.

Keywords: Geometric algebra · Geometric algebra computing · GAALOP · Quantum computing

1 Introduction

Based on Geometric Algebra, the operations of quantum computing can be understood as algebraic transformations such as reflections or rotations of a so-called state vector. This interplay between the algebraic and geometric representations within Geometric Algebra enables a better grasp of quantum computing. We mainly follow [7] describing Quantum Computing in the sense of Vianna, Trindade, and Fernandes [10], fulfilling a criterion of the core of Geometric Algebra: *In this regard, we share with many authors the idea that operators and operands should be elements of the same space.* The goal is to have a mathematical language making the operations of quantum computing as intuitive as possible, in order to make the understanding of existing algorithms as well as the development of new algorithms as easy as possible. We describe quantum bits and quantum registers based on the specific QBA (quantum bit algebra) in a way mainly addressing the engineering community. As an example for a computing gate we use the NOT operation.

J. Hrdina—Supported by the FSI VUT under the grant no.: FSI-S-14-2290.

N. Magnenat-Thalmann et al. (Eds.): CGI 2020, LNCS 12221, pp. 526–537, 2020.
https://doi.org/10.1007/978-3-030-61864-3_45

As the main contribution of this paper, we extended GAALOP (Geometric Algebra Algorithms Optimizer) to handle QBA and to make all the calculations online via GAALOPWeb. This enables us to make calculations for qubits without the need of installing a specific software. Since GAALOPWeb is webbrowser-based, it can be used on various devices such as PC, tablet or smart phone. We present how the NOT operation can be applied on one as well as on two qubits.

2 Comparing Classic Computers with Quantum Computers

The computers that we use today are deterministic devices with memory and register units composed of unambiguous bits. Each bit can either be entirely in a state of 0 or, oppositely, in a state of 1. They work in the classic domain as each switching operation that changes state 0 to state 1 (or the other way round), still requires an enormous number of charge carriers interacting even with the miniaturisation achieved today.

Thus, stepping up the performance of these classic computers necessitates a reduction in the size of their components. It may, therefore, be expected that soon the threshold to quantum mechanics will be achieved once the components become so small that, rather than by the classic laws, they will behave erratically by the laws of quantum mechanics.

One of the possible solutions to this dilemma consists of implementing the possibilities of quantum computing. The prospects concerning further miniaturisation are bright: So the performance of a quantum computer using a register with 64 qubits, see page 8 of [8], would correspond to the performance of a classic computer with surface covering several thousands of earth globes. Calculating on such a quantum computer thus represents an extremely efficient way of computing. In quantum computing, this is achieved by specifically coding the information. Whereas each bit of a classic computer can assume both states $|0\rangle$ and $|1\rangle$ with the likelihoods of either 100% or 0%, the possible states $|0\rangle$ or $|1\rangle$ of a quantum computer are governed by probabilities lying anywhere between 0% and 100%.

3 Description of Quantum Bits

A quantum computer can simultaneously compute and work with the superposition of all possible classic states. Thus, a myriad of states are modified in a single computing step.

In explaining this fact, the question of what is a state, therefore, plays a key role. As a matter of fact, a quantum mechanics state describes a special property of the particle in question such as the spin of an electron. Now, a spin can be directed either downwards (spin down), which corresponds to the quantum bit state of $|0\rangle$ or upwards (spin up) corresponding to the quantum bit state of $|1\rangle$. Or else, the electron can be in a superposition of

$$|\Psi\rangle = a_0|0\rangle + a_1|1\rangle, \tag{1}$$

where $a_0, a_1 \in \mathbb{C}$. This is the usual representation of a superposition of the two states $|0\rangle$ and $|1\rangle$ in the conventional notation (see, e.g., [6,9]) without using Geometric Algebra. Here the pre-factors or coefficients a_0 and a_1 represent the amplitudes of the wave function and are subject to the normalization condition as complex numbers

$$|a_0|^2 + |a_1|^2 = a_0 a_0^* + a_1 a_1^* = 1. \tag{2}$$

$|a_0|^2$ is the probability that, in a measurement, the quantum bit indicates the state $|0\rangle$ (e.g., spin down), while $|a_1|^2$ is the probability that the quantum bit will be found in the state $|1\rangle$ (e.g., spin up).

If the states $|0\rangle$ and $|1\rangle$ are identified with the spatial basis vectors[1] σ_0 and σ_1 that satisfy the normalization condition

$$\sigma_0^2 = \sigma_1^2 = 1, \tag{3}$$

it is possible to define the wave function (1) in the Complex Geometric Algebra $Cl(2,\mathbb{C})$ as a location vector r in this space:

$$\psi = a_0 \sigma_0 + a_1 \sigma_1. \tag{4}$$

This geometric-algebraic representation of the state of a quantum bit was chosen, for example, by Baylis [2]. According to the Born rule, the probability of the pure state $|0\rangle$ is $|a_0|^2$ and the probability of the pure state $|1\rangle$ is $|a_1|^2$. Finally, the total probability of the system is $\langle\psi|\psi\rangle = 1$, it follows the rule $|a_0|^2 + |a_1|^2 = 1$ and we can write $|\psi\rangle$ in spherical coordinates $(\gamma, \theta, \varphi)$ as an element of the three dimensional Bloch sphere

$$|\psi\rangle = e^{i\gamma} \left(\cos\left(\frac{\theta}{2}\right) |0\rangle + e^{i\varphi} \sin\left(\frac{\theta}{2}\right) |1\rangle \right),$$

which is equivalent to a group of unitary quaternions.

Thus, a quantum bit can be modelled in a complex space with two basis vectors (see Eq. (4)) or else in a real space with four basis vectors (see Eq. (6)). This second alternative can be found, e.g., in Doran and Lasenby (Chapt. 9 of [4]) or Cafaro and Mancini [3].

Our alternative representation of quantum bits can be motivated if one admits temporal vectors in addition to spatial ones, rather than using complex probability amplitudes. Using

$$a_0 = c_0^x + i c_0^t \quad \text{and} \quad a_1 = c_1^x + i c_1^t, \tag{5}$$

the coefficients are transformed into real pre-factors thus doubling the number of basis vectors. In this alternative spatiotemporal notation of Geometric Algebra, the state vector of formula (4) takes the form:

$$\begin{aligned} \psi &= (c_0^x + i c_0^t)\sigma_0 + (c_1^x + i c_1^t)\sigma_1 \\ &= c_0^x \delta_0^x + c_0^t \delta_0^t + c_1^x \delta_1^x + c_1^t \delta_1^t, \end{aligned} \tag{6}$$

---

[1] Concerning the following notations known from physics and their relations to Geometric Algebra please refer to Chapt. 17 of [5].

where we define $\delta_p^x = \sigma_p$ and $\delta_p^t = i\sigma_p$, $p \in \{0, 1\}$. The imaginary units can be taken over by the now temporal basis vectors if the measurements are performed with respect to only one spatial direction as with the quantum bits of a quantum computer. Equations (3) then change to:

$$(\delta_0^x)^2 = (\delta_1^x)^2 = 1;$$
$$(\delta_0^t)^2 = (\delta_1^t)^2 = -1. \tag{7}$$

Remark 1. These four elements cannot form an orthonormal basis of Clifford algebra $Cl(2, 2)$, because of their non-anticommutativity, for example $\delta_0^x \delta_1^x = \sigma_0^x i\sigma_0^x = \delta_1^x \delta_0^x$. It is not even a commutative algebra because of identity $\delta_0^x \delta_0^t = -\sigma_0^t \sigma_0^x = \delta_1^x \delta_0^x$.

We propose to model a qubit by unit elements of a Clifford algebra $Cl(2, 2)$ which is a Clifford algebra over a vector space with an indefinite bilinear form of signature $(+, -, +, -)$. We identify this algebra with the vectors $(\gamma_0^x, \gamma_0^t, \gamma_1^x, \gamma_1^t)$, where

$$(\gamma_0^x)^2 = (\gamma_1^x)^2 = 1;$$
$$(\gamma_0^t)^2 = (\gamma_1^t)^2 = -1, \tag{8}$$

and a qubit can be defined in correspondence with (6) as

$$\psi = c_0^x \gamma_0^x + c_0^t \gamma_0^t + c_1^x \gamma_1^x + c_1^t \gamma_1^t, \tag{9}$$

implying that qubits belong to a 3-dimensional surface defined by the identity

$$(c_0^x)^2 - (c_0^t)^2 + (c_1^x)^2 - (c_1^t)^2 = 1,$$

or to using standard hyperboloid coordinates $(\gamma, \theta, \varphi)$ equivalently,

$$|\psi\rangle = \bar{e}^{i\gamma}\left(\cos\left(\frac{\theta}{2}\right)|0\rangle + \bar{e}^{i\varphi}\sin\left(\frac{\theta}{2}\right)|1\rangle\right),$$

where $\bar{e}^{i\varphi} = \cosh(\varphi) + \sinh(\varphi)i$ and $\bar{e}^{i\gamma} = \cosh(\gamma) + \sinh(\gamma)i$.

4 Quantum Register

A system consisting of several quantum bits is referred to as a quantum register. The simplest case is limited to two quantum bits. Figure 1 illustrates a space in which the corresponding wave function

$$|\Psi\rangle = a_{00}|00\rangle + a_{01}|01\rangle + a_{10}|10\rangle + a_{11}|11\rangle, \tag{10}$$

where $a_{ij} \in \mathbb{C}$ acts mathematically. This is actually an attempt to represent a four-dimensional space, with all four directions of the basic states $|00\rangle, |01\rangle, |10\rangle,$ and $|11\rangle$ are pair-wise perpendicular.

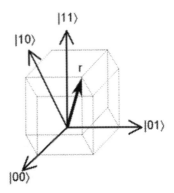

Fig. 1. State vector ψ of a quantum register built from two quantum bits according to [7].

Again, there are two options available of Geometric Algebra representations. We can describe Ψ as an element of complex geometric algebra $\otimes^2 Cl(2, \mathbb{C})$ in the form

$$\Psi = a_{00}\sigma_{00} + a_{01}\sigma_{01} + a_{10}\sigma_{10} + a_{11}\sigma_{11}, \tag{11}$$

where $a_{ij} \in \mathbb{C}$ or as an element of real geometric algebra in the form

$$\begin{aligned}
\Psi = {}& c_{00}^x \gamma_{00}^x + c_{01}^x \gamma_{01}^x + c_{10}^x \gamma_{10}^x + c_{11}^x \gamma_{11}^x \\
& + c_{00}^t \gamma_{00}^t + c_{01}^t \gamma_{01}^t + c_{10}^t \gamma_{10}^t + c_{11}^t \gamma_{11}^t,
\end{aligned} \tag{12}$$

where $\gamma_{jk}^i \in \otimes^2 Cl(2, 2)$ and $a_{ij} \in \mathbb{R}$, so that the probability amplitudes are only real.

5 Computing Steps in Quantum Computing

Each computing step in a quantum computer actually transforms the wave function $|y\rangle$ or the state vector r that represents it. The following examples will show how the algebraic description of the transformation in the image of the wave function $|y\rangle$ can be supplemented by a geometric description that uses Geometric Algebra. The algebraic transformations are represented by reflections or rotations of the state vector r. This interplay between the algebraic and geometric representations within Geometric Algebra, enables a better grasp of quantum computing, which can thus be accessed in two different ways.

6 The NOT-Operation on a Qubit

One of the simplest operations is the simple inversion of the state of a single quantum bit. It is referred to as a NOT-operation. There are three different approaches to describing this operation:

– **Physical approach**
Both states $|0\rangle$ and $|1\rangle$ are mapped on each other:

$$|0\rangle \to |1\rangle \ \text{ and } \ |1\rangle \to |0\rangle; \tag{13}$$

– **Algebraic approach**
The two probability amplitudes are interchanged:

$$a_0 \to a_1 \ \text{ and } \ a_1 \to a_0; \tag{14}$$

– **Geometric approach**
The state vector ψ is reflected about the reflection vector

$$r_{\text{ref}} = \frac{1}{\sqrt{2}}(\sigma_0 + \sigma_1), \tag{15}$$

see Fig. 2 for the geometric meaning of the reflection.

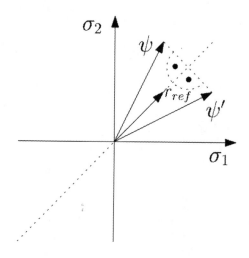

Fig. 2. Reflection about the reflection vector.

The actual physical implementation is achieved by irradiating the quantum bit with a suitable electromagnetic wave. The algebraic transformation is implemented by the transformer

$$U_{\text{NOT}} = |0\rangle\langle 1| + |1\rangle\langle 0| \tag{16}$$

as

$$\begin{aligned}
\psi' &= U_{\text{NOT}}\,\psi \\
&= (|0\rangle\langle 1| + |1\rangle\langle 0|)(a_0|0\rangle + a_1|1\rangle) \\
&= a_1|0\rangle + a_0|1\rangle.
\end{aligned} \tag{17}$$

In Geometric Algebra, using Pauli matrices, this transformation can now be written as the sandwich product

$$
\begin{aligned}
\psi' &= r_{\mathrm{ref}}\,\psi\,r_{\mathrm{ref}} \\
&= \frac{1}{\sqrt{2}}(\sigma_0 + \sigma_1)(a_0\sigma_0 + a_1\sigma_1)\frac{1}{\sqrt{2}}(\sigma_0 + \sigma_1) \\
&= \frac{1}{2}(a_0\sigma_0^2 + a_0\sigma_1\sigma_0 + a_1\sigma_0\sigma_1 + a_1\sigma_1^2)(\sigma_0 + \sigma_1) \\
&= \frac{1}{2}(a_0 + a_0\sigma_1\sigma_0 + a_1\sigma_0\sigma_1 + a_1)(\sigma_0 + \sigma_1) \\
&= \frac{1}{2}(a_0 + a_0\sigma_1\sigma_0 + a_1\sigma_0\sigma_1 + a_1)(\sigma_0 + \sigma_1) \\
&= a_1\sigma_0 + a_0\sigma_1
\end{aligned}
\tag{18}
$$

and, as such, handled as a reflection in the geometric sense.

An analogous geometric interpretation is obtained by using spatiotemporal basis vectors. This, however, requires two reflections. First a reflection is performed about the three-dimensional hyperplane

$$
r_{\mathrm{ref1}} = \frac{1}{\sqrt{2}}(\gamma_0^x + \gamma_1^x)\gamma_0^t\gamma_1^t,
\tag{19}
$$

to reflect the spatial basis vectors. Subsequently, the temporal vectors are reflected at the hyperplane

$$
r_{\mathrm{ref2}} = \frac{1}{\sqrt{2}}(\gamma_0^t + \gamma_1^t)\gamma_0^x\gamma_1^x,
\tag{20}
$$

resulting in

$$
\psi' = r_{\mathrm{ref2}}r_{\mathrm{ref1}}\,\psi\,r_{\mathrm{ref1}}r_{\mathrm{ref2}} = -r_{\mathrm{ref1}}r_{\mathrm{ref2}}\,\psi\,r_{\mathrm{ref1}}r_{\mathrm{ref2}}.
\tag{21}
$$

As the composition of two reflections is a rotation, Eq. (21) can be thought of as a rotation. Let us point that, due to the anticommutative interchanging of different basis vectors:

$$
\begin{aligned}
r_{\mathrm{ref1}}r_{\mathrm{ref2}} &= \frac{1}{\sqrt{2}}(\gamma_0^x + \gamma_1^x)\gamma_0^t\gamma_1^t\frac{1}{\sqrt{2}}(\gamma_0^t + \gamma_1^t)\gamma_0^x\gamma_1^x \\
&= \frac{1}{2}(\gamma_0^x - \gamma_1^x)(\gamma_0^t - \gamma_1^t) \\
&= -r_{\mathrm{ref2}}r_{\mathrm{ref1}}.
\end{aligned}
\tag{22}
$$

So, the element $r_{\mathrm{ref1}}r_{\mathrm{ref2}}$ represents a rotation, by conjugation with sign.

Thus, we have a rotation in the two-dimensional plane represented by the bivector

$$
R = \frac{1}{2}(\gamma_0^x - \gamma_1^x)(\gamma_0^t - \gamma_1^t),
\tag{23}
$$

confirming the complete calculation:

$$
\psi' = R\psi R = c_1^x\gamma_0^x + c_1^t\gamma_0^t + c_0^x\gamma_1^x + c_0^t\gamma_1^t.
\tag{24}
$$

Although this spatiotemporal description seems to demand much more computation power than the version of Geometric Algebra given by Eq. (18) working only with the spatial basis vectors, it is more instructive as the representations of reflections and rotations in spaces of higher dimensions become much clearer both algebraically and geometrically.

7   GAALOPWeb for Qubits

GAALOPWeb[2] is our online tool for optimizing Geometric Algebra algorithms for programming languages like C/C++ and others. We adapted the recent interface in order to support Qubit algebras, see Fig. 3.

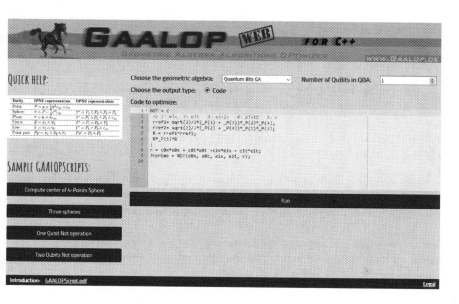

Fig. 3. Screenshot of GAALOPWeb for Qubit algebras.

After the user selected the *Quantum Bits Geometric Algebra* as geometric algebra, a number selection field appears where the user is able to set the number of qubits. Then the user edits the code written in GAALOPScript and pushes the *Run* button. In the background, a new algebra definition is created automatically based on the number of qubits and this is used to compute the resulting C/C++ Code, which is displayed to the user afterwards.

8   Qubit Algebra QBA

The Qubit Algebra is a 4D Geometric Algebra $G_{2,2}$ with one space-like basis vector and one time-like basis vector for each of the two basis states $|0\rangle$ and $|1\rangle$.

---

[2] http://www.gaalop.de/gaalopweb-for-qubits/.

Table 1 shows the 4 basis vectors together with their relation to the qubit states, their signature and their description within GAALOP.

Table 1. The 4 basis vectors of the Qubit Algebra.

	Basis vector	Signature	GAALOPScript
$\lvert 0 \rangle$ (space-like)	γ_0^x	+1	e0x
$\lvert 0 \rangle$ (time-like)	γ_0^t	-1	e0t
$\lvert 1 \rangle$ (space-like)	γ_1^x	+1	e1x
$\lvert 1 \rangle$ (time-like)	γ_1^t	-1	e1t

Listing 1.1 shows the GAALOPScript for the NOT-operation according to Sect. 6.

Listing 1.1. GAALOPScript for the NOT-operation on a qubit

```
1  r = c0x*e0x + c0t*e0t +c1x*e1x + c1t*e1t;
2  rref1= sqrt(2)/2*(e0x + e1x)*e0t*e1t;
3  rref2= sqrt(2)/2*(e0t + e1t)*e0x*e1x;
4  R = rref1*rref2;
5  ?rprime = R*r*R;
```

Line 1 computes the general state vector r as a linear combination of all the basis vectors according to Eq. (6). The line 2 and 3 are responsible for the computation of the hyper planes for the two needed reflections according to the Eqs. (19) and (20). Line 4 computes the combined reflector R for both reflections according to Eq. (22) and finally the transformed state vector is computed as the sandwich product according to Eq. (24).

The result of the generation of C/C++ code is as follows:

Listing 1.2. Result of the NOT-operation

```
1  void calculate(float c0t, float c0x, float c1t, float c1x,
2                 float rprime[16]) {
3
4         rprime[1] = c1x; // e0x
5         rprime[2] = c0x; // e1x
6         rprime[3] = c1t; // e0t
7         rprime[4] = c0t; // e1t
8  }
```

It shows the new coefficients of the basis vectors e0x, e1x, e0t and e1t. Compared to the original state vector r, we realize that both the coefficients of the two space-like basis vectors and of the two time-like basis vectors are now interchanged.

9   The 2-Qubit Algebra QBA2

The following table shows the 8 basis vectors of the 2-Qubit Algebra QBA2 with their signatures and GAALOP notations (Table 2).

Table 2. The 8 basis vectors of the 2-Qubit Algebra QBA2.

		Basis vector	Signature	GAALOPScript
$\|00\rangle$	(space-like)	γ_{00}^{x}	$+1$	e0x
$\|00\rangle$	(time-like)	γ_{00}^{t}	-1	e0t
$\|01\rangle$	(space-like)	γ_{01}^{x}	$+1$	e1x
$\|01\rangle$	(time-like)	γ_{01}^{t}	-1	e1t
$\|10\rangle$	(space-like)	γ_{10}^{x}	$+1$	e2x
$\|10\rangle$	(time-like)	γ_{10}^{t}	-1	e2t
$\|11\rangle$	(space-like)	γ_{11}^{x}	$+1$	e3x
$\|11\rangle$	(time-like)	γ_{11}^{t}	-1	e3t

In order to compute the NOT-operation on the first qubit, we are able to use the same GAALOPScript according to Listing 1.1 as used for QBA. The result as shown in Listing 1.3 is in principle the same as in Listing 1.2 (the only difference is an internal one: the indices of the data structure for the multivector rprime).

Listing 1.3. Result of the NOT-operation on the first qubit.

```
1  void calculate(float c0t, float c0x, float c1t, float c1x,
2                 float rprime[256]) {
3
4       rprime[1] = c1x; // e0x
5       rprime[2] = c0x; // e1x
6       rprime[5] = c1t; // e0t
7       rprime[6] = c0t; // e1t
8  }
```

If we would like to use the NOT-operation for the second qubit, we have to take the corresponding basis vectors according to Listing 1.4.

Listing 1.4. GAALOPScript for the NOT-operation on the second qubit in QBA2.

```
1  r = c2x*e2x + c2t*e2t +c3x*e3x + c3t*e3t;
2  rref1= sqrt(2)/2*(e2x + e3x)*e2t*e3t;
3  rref2= sqrt(2)/2*(e2t + e3t)*e2x*e3x;
4  R = rref1*rref2;
5  ?rprime = R*r*R;
```

We can see in the result of the Listing 1.5 that again both the coefficients of the two space-like basis vectors and of the two time-like basis vectors are now interchanged.

Listing 1.5. Result of the NOT-operation on the second qubit.

```
1
2   void calculate(float c2t, float c2x, float c3t, float c3x,
3                  float rprime[256]) {
4
5           rprime[3] = c3x; // e2x
6           rprime[4] = c2x; // e3x
7           rprime[7] = c3t; // e2t
8           rprime[8] = c2t; // e3t
9   }
```

In order to make code reusable, GAALOPScript offers a macro concept. This allows to write a macro for the NOT-operation which can be used for both qubits as shown in Listing 1.6.

Listing 1.6. NOT-operation on both qubits using a macro.

```
1   NOT = {
2    // 1: eix   2: eit   3: ei+1x   4: ei+1t   5: r
3    rref1= sqrt(2)/2*(_P(1) + _P(3))*_P(2)*_P(4);
4    rref2= sqrt(2)/2*(_P(2) + _P(4))*_P(1)*_P(3);
5    R = rref1*rref2;
6    R*_P(5)*R
7   }
8   r1 = c0x*e0x + c0t*e0t +c1x*e1x + c1t*e1t;
9   ?rprime1 = NOT(e0x, e0t, e1x, e1t, r1);
10
11  r2 = c2x*e2x + c2t*e2t +c3x*e3x + c3t*e3t;
12  ?rprime2 = NOT(e2x, e2t, e3x, e3t, r2);
```

The meaning of the parameters $\_P(1) \ldots \_P(5)$ of the NOT macro is indicated in line 2. The result according to Listing 1.7 is now a summary of the results for each of the qubits.

Listing 1.7. Result of the NOT-operation on both qubits.

```
1   void calculate(float c0t, float c0x, float c1t, float c1x,
2                  float c2t, float c2x, float c3t, float c3x,
3                  float rprime1[256], float rprime2[256]) {
4
5           rprime1[1] = c1x; // e0x
6           rprime1[2] = c0x; // e1x
7           rprime1[5] = c1t; // e0t
8           rprime1[6] = c0t; // e1t
9           rprime2[3] = c3x; // e2x
10          rprime2[4] = c2x; // e3x
11          rprime2[7] = c3t; // e2t
12          rprime2[8] = c2t; // e3t
13  }
```

10   Conclusion

This paper proposes a new formulation for quantum computing with the following advantages:

- one algebra for the description of qubits and operations on them;
- geometrically intuitive description of operations;
- calculations to be easily handled via code snippets of an online application.

In the future, we would like to extend it to other relevant quantum operations, as well as to quantum computing algorithms, such as the Grover's algorithm for searching in unstructured databases [1].

References

1. Alves, R., Lavor, C.: Clifford algebra applied to Grover's algorithm. Adv. Appl. Clifford Algebras **20**, 477–488 (2010). https://doi.org/10.1007/s00006-010-0206-z
2. Baylis, W.: A relativistic algebraic approach to the QC interface: implications for quantum reality. Adv. Appl. Clifford Algebras **18**, 395–415 (2008). https://doi.org/10.1007/s00006-008-0078-7
3. Cafaro, C., Mancini, S.: A geometric algebra perspective on quantum computational gates and universality in quantum computing. Adv. Appl. Clifford Algebras **21**, 493–519 (2011). https://doi.org/10.1007/s00006-010-0269-x
4. Doran, C., Lasenby, A.: Geometric Algebra for Physicists. Cambridge University Press, Cambridge (2003)
5. Hildenbrand, D.: Introduction to Geometric Algebra Computing. Taylor & Francis Group, Boca Raton (2019)
6. Homeister, M.: Quantum Computing verstehen. Grundlagen - Anwendungen - Perspektiven. Friedrich Vieweg & Sohn Verlag (2018)
7. Horn, M.E., Drechsel, P., Hildenbrand, D.: Quanten-computing und geometrische algebra. Proceedings Didaktik der Physik (2012)
8. Johnson, G.: A Shortcut Through Time. The Path to the Quantum Computer. Vintage Books, New York (2004)
9. McMahon, D.: Quantum Computing Explained. Wiley, Hoboken (2008)
10. Vianna, J., Trindade, M., Fernandes, M.: Algebraic criteria for entanglement in multipartite systems. Int. J. Theoret. Phys. **47**, 961–970 (2008). https://doi.org/10.1007/s10773-007-9522-z

ENGAGE Short Papers

On Basis-Free Solution to Sylvester Equation in Geometric Algebra

Dmitry Shirokov[1,2]($\boxtimes$) (iD)

[1] National Research University Higher School of Economics, 101000 Moscow, Russia
dm.shirokov@gmail.com
[2] Institute for Information Transmission Problems of Russian Academy of Sciences,
127051 Moscow, Russia

Abstract. The Sylvester equation and its particular case, the Lyapunov equation, are widely used in image processing, control theory, stability analysis, signal processing, model reduction, and many more. We present the basis-free solution to the Sylvester equation in geometric algebra of arbitrary dimension. The basis-free solutions involve only the operations of geometric product, summation, and the operations of conjugation. The results can be used in symbolic computation.

Keywords: Geometric algebra · Clifford algebra · Sylvester equation · Lyapunov equation · Characteristic polynomial · Basis-free solution

1 Introduction

The Sylvester equation [9] is a linear equation of the form $AX - XB = C$ for the known A, B, C (quaternions, matrices, or multivectors depending on the formalism) and the unknown X. The Sylvester equation and its particular case, the Lyapunov equation (with $B = -A^H$), are widely used in different applications – image processing, control theory, stability analysis, signal processing, model reduction, and many more. In this paper, we study the Sylvester equation in Clifford's geometric algebra $C\ell_{p,q}$ and present the basis-free solution of this equation in the case of arbitrary $n = p + q$.

The Sylvester equation over quaternions corresponds to the Sylvester equation in geometric algebra of a vector space of dimension $n = 2$, because we have the isomorphism $C\ell_{0,2} \cong \mathbb{H}$. Thus the basis-free solution to the Sylvester equation in $C\ell_{p,q}$, $p + q = 2$, is constructed similarly to the basis-free solution to the Sylvester equation over quaternions. The same ideas as in the case $n = 2$ work in the case $n = 3$. The cases $n \leq 3$ are also discussed by Acus and Dargys [1].

In this paper, we present basis-free solutions in the cases $n = 4$ and $n = 5$, which are the most important cases for the applications. The geometric algebra $C\ell_{1,3}$ (the space-time algebra [4]) of a space of dimension 4 is widely used in physics. The conformal geometric algebra $C\ell_{4,1}$ of a space of dimension 5 is

© Springer Nature Switzerland AG 2020
N. Magnenat-Thalmann et al. (Eds.): CGI 2020, LNCS 12221, pp. 541–548, 2020.
https://doi.org/10.1007/978-3-030-61864-3_46

widely used in robotics and computer vision. Also we present the recursive basis-free formulas to the Sylvester equation in $\mathcal{Cl}_{p,q}$ in the case of arbitrary $n = p+q$. They can be used in symbolic computation.

An arbitrary linear quaternion equation with two terms

$$KXL + MXN = P \tag{1}$$

for the known $K, L, M, N \in \mathbb{H}$ and the unknown $X \in \mathbb{H}$ can be reduced to the Sylvester equation. Any nonzero quaternion $Q = a + bi + cj + dk \neq 0$, where $a, b, c, d \in \mathbb{R}$ are real numbers, and i, j, and k are the quaternion units, is invertible and the inverse is equal to

$$Q^{-1} = \frac{\bar{Q}}{Q\bar{Q}},$$

where $\bar{Q} := a - bi - cj - dk$ is the conjugate of Q. Multiplying both sides of (1) on the left by M^{-1} and on the right by L^{-1}, we obtain $M^{-1}KX + XNL^{-1} = M^{-1}PL^{-1}$. Denoting $A := M^{-1}K$, $B := -NL^{-1}$, $C := M^{-1}PL^{-1}$, we get the Sylvester equation

$$AX - XB = C \tag{2}$$

for the known $A, B, C \in \mathbb{H}$ and the unknown $X \in \mathbb{H}$.

Multiplying both sides of (2) on the right by $-\bar{B}$, we get

$$-AX\bar{B} + XB\bar{B} = -C\bar{B}. \tag{3}$$

Multiplying both sides of (2) on the left by A, we get

$$A^2X - AXB = AC. \tag{4}$$

Summing (3) and (4) and using $B + \bar{B} \in \mathbb{R}$, $B\bar{B} \in \mathbb{R}$, we obtain

$$A^2X - (B + \bar{B})AX + B\bar{B}X = AC - C\bar{B}.$$

If $D := A^2 - BA - \bar{B}A + B\bar{B} \neq 0$, then it is invertible and we get the basis-free solution to (2):

$$X = D^{-1}(AC - C\bar{B}) = \frac{\bar{D}(AC - C\bar{B})}{D\bar{D}}.$$

2   The Main Results

Let us consider the Clifford's geometric algebra $\mathcal{Cl}_{p,q}$, $p + q = n$, [2,3,6,7] with the identity element e and the generators e_a, $a = 1, \ldots, n$, satisfying

$$e_a e_b + e_b e_a = 2\eta_{ab}e, \qquad a, b = 1, \ldots, n$$

where $\eta = ||\eta_{ab}|| = \mathrm{diag}(1, \ldots, 1, -1, \ldots, -1)$ is the diagonal matrix with its first p entries equal to 1 and the last q entries equal to -1 on the diagonal. We call the subspace of $Cl_{p,q}$ of geometric algebra elements, which are linear combinations of basis elements with multi-indices of length k, the subspace of grade k and denote it by $Cl_{p,q}^k$, $k = 0, 1, \ldots, n$. We identify elements of the subspace of grade 0 with scalars: $Cl_{p,q}^0 \equiv \mathbb{R}$, $e \equiv 1$. Denote the operation of projection onto the subspace $Cl_{p,q}^k$ by $\langle \ \rangle_k$. The center of $Cl_{p,q}$ is $\mathrm{cen}(Cl_{p,q}) = Cl_{p,q}^0$ in the case of even n and $\mathrm{cen}(Cl_{p,q}) = Cl_{p,q}^0 \oplus Cl_{p,q}^n$ in the case of odd n.

We use the following two standard operations of conjugation in $Cl_{p,q}$: the grade involution $\hat{\ }$ and the reversion (which is an anti-involution) $\tilde{\ }$

$$\hat{U} = \sum_{k=0}^{n} (-1)^k \langle U \rangle_k, \qquad \widehat{UV} = \hat{U}\hat{V}, \qquad \forall U, V \in Cl_{p,q},$$

$$\tilde{U} = \sum_{k=0}^{n} (-1)^{\frac{k(k-1)}{2}} \langle U \rangle_k, \qquad \widetilde{UV} = \tilde{V}\tilde{U}, \qquad \forall U, V \in Cl_{p,q},$$

and one additional operation of conjugation $\triangle$ (see [8])

$$U^\triangle = \sum_{k=0,1,2,3\,\mathrm{mod}\,8} \langle U \rangle_k - \sum_{k=4,5,6,7\,\mathrm{mod}\,8} \langle U \rangle_k, \qquad \forall U \in Cl_{p,q}. \tag{5}$$

In the general case, we have $(UV)^\triangle \neq U^\triangle V^\triangle$ and $(UV)^\triangle \neq V^\triangle U^\triangle$.

Let us consider the Sylvester equation in geometric algebra

$$AX - XB = C \tag{6}$$

for the known $A, B, C \in Cl_{p,q}$ and the unknown $X \in Cl_{p,q}$.

In the case $n = 1$, the geometric algebra $Cl_{p,q}$ is commutative and we get $(A - B)X = C$. Denoting $D := A - B$ and using[1]

$$\mathrm{Adj}(D) = \hat{D}, \qquad \mathrm{Det}(D) = D\hat{D} \in Cl_{p,q}^0 \equiv \mathbb{R}, \qquad D^{-1} = \frac{\mathrm{Adj}(D)}{\mathrm{Det}(D)},$$

we conclude that if

$$Q := D\hat{D} \neq 0, \tag{7}$$

then

$$X = \frac{\hat{D}C}{Q}.$$

In the case $n = 2$, we can do the same as for the Sylvester equation over quaternions. Multiplying both sides of (6) on the right by $-\hat{\tilde{B}}$ and on the left by A, we get

$$-AX\hat{\tilde{B}} + XB\hat{\tilde{B}} = -C\hat{\tilde{B}}, \qquad A^2 X - AXB = AC.$$

---

[1] See on the adjugate, determinant, and inverses in $Cl_{p,q}$ for arbitrary n in [8].

Summing and using $\mathrm{Det}(B) = B\hat{\tilde{B}} \in C\!\ell^0_{p,q} \equiv \mathbb{R}$, $B + \hat{\tilde{B}} \in C\!\ell^0_{p,q} \equiv \mathbb{R}$, we get

$$(A^2 - (B + \hat{\tilde{B}})A + B\hat{\tilde{B}})X = AC - C\hat{\tilde{B}}. \tag{8}$$

Using

$$\mathrm{Adj}(D) = \hat{\tilde{D}}, \qquad \mathrm{Det}(D) = D\hat{\tilde{D}} \in C\!\ell^0_{p,q} \equiv \mathbb{R}, \qquad D^{-1} = \frac{\mathrm{Adj}(D)}{\mathrm{Det}(D)},$$

we conclude that if

$$Q := D\hat{\tilde{D}} \neq 0, \tag{9}$$

then for $D := A^2 - (B + \hat{\tilde{B}})A + B\hat{\tilde{B}}$, we get

$$X = \frac{\hat{\tilde{D}}(AC - C\hat{\tilde{B}})}{Q}.$$

In the case $n = 3$, we have $B\hat{\tilde{B}} \in C\!\ell^0_{p,q} \oplus C\!\ell^3_{p,q} = \mathrm{cen}(C\!\ell_{p,q})$ and $B + \hat{\tilde{B}} \in C\!\ell^0_{p,q} \oplus C\!\ell^3_{p,q} = \mathrm{cen}(C\!\ell_{p,q})$ and obtain again (8). Using

$$\mathrm{Adj}(D) = \hat{D}\tilde{D}\hat{\tilde{D}}, \qquad \mathrm{Det}(D) = D\hat{D}\tilde{D}\hat{\tilde{D}} \in C\!\ell^0_{p,q} \equiv \mathbb{R}, \qquad D^{-1} = \frac{\mathrm{Adj}(D)}{\mathrm{Det}(D)}$$

for $D := A^2 - (B + \hat{\tilde{B}})A + B\hat{\tilde{B}}$, we conclude that if

$$Q := D\hat{D}\tilde{D}\hat{\tilde{D}} \neq 0, \tag{10}$$

then

$$X = \frac{\hat{D}\tilde{D}\hat{\tilde{D}}(AC - C\hat{\tilde{B}})}{Q}. \tag{11}$$

Theorem 1. *Let us consider the Sylvester equation in $C\!\ell_{p,q}$, $p + q = 4$*

$$AX - XB = C, \tag{12}$$

for the known $A, B, C \in C\!\ell_{p,q}$ and the unknown $X \in C\!\ell_{p,q}$. If

$$Q := D\hat{\tilde{D}}(\hat{D}\tilde{D})^\triangle \neq 0, \tag{13}$$

then

$$X = \frac{\hat{\tilde{D}}(\hat{D}\tilde{D})^\triangle F}{Q}, \tag{14}$$

where

$$D := A^4 - A^3(B + \hat{\tilde{B}} + \hat{B}^\Delta + \tilde{B}^\Delta) \tag{15}$$
$$+ A^2(B\hat{\tilde{B}} + B\hat{B}^\Delta + B\tilde{B}^\Delta + \hat{\tilde{B}}\hat{B}^\Delta + \hat{\tilde{B}}\tilde{B}^\Delta + (\hat{B}\tilde{B})^\Delta)$$
$$- A(B\hat{\tilde{B}}\hat{B}^\Delta + B\hat{\tilde{B}}\tilde{B}^\Delta + B(\hat{B}\tilde{B})^\Delta + \hat{\tilde{B}}(\hat{B}\tilde{B})^\Delta) + B\hat{\tilde{B}}(\hat{B}\tilde{B})^\Delta,$$

$$F := A^3 C - A^2 C(\hat{\tilde{B}} + \hat{B}^\Delta + \tilde{B}^\Delta) \tag{16}$$
$$+ AC(\hat{\tilde{B}}\hat{B}^\Delta + \hat{\tilde{B}}\tilde{B}^\Delta + (\hat{B}\tilde{B})^\Delta) - C\hat{\tilde{B}}(\hat{B}\tilde{B})^\Delta.$$

Proof. Multiplying both sides of (12) on the right by $-\hat{\tilde{B}}(\hat{B}\tilde{B})^\Delta$, we get

$$- AX\hat{\tilde{B}}(\hat{B}\tilde{B})^\Delta + XB\hat{\tilde{B}}(\hat{B}\tilde{B})^\Delta = -C\hat{\tilde{B}}(\hat{B}\tilde{B})^\Delta. \tag{17}$$

Multiplying both sides of (12) on the right by $\hat{\tilde{B}}\hat{B}^\Delta + \hat{\tilde{B}}\tilde{B}^\Delta + (\hat{B}\tilde{B})^\Delta$ and on the left by A, we get

$$A^2 X(\hat{\tilde{B}}\hat{B}^\Delta + \hat{\tilde{B}}\tilde{B}^\Delta + (\hat{B}\tilde{B})^\Delta) - AXB(\hat{\tilde{B}}\hat{B}^\Delta + \hat{\tilde{B}}\tilde{B}^\Delta + (\hat{B}\tilde{B})^\Delta)$$
$$= AC(\hat{\tilde{B}}\hat{B}^\Delta + \hat{\tilde{B}}\tilde{B}^\Delta + (\hat{B}\tilde{B})^\Delta). \tag{18}$$

Multiplying both sides of (12) on the right by $-(\hat{\tilde{B}} + \hat{B}^\Delta + \tilde{B}^\Delta)$ and on the left by A^2, we get

$$- A^3 X(\hat{\tilde{B}} + \hat{B}^\Delta + \tilde{B}^\Delta) + A^2 XB(\hat{\tilde{B}} + \hat{B}^\Delta + \tilde{B}^\Delta) = -A^2 C(\hat{\tilde{B}} + \hat{B}^\Delta + \tilde{B}^\Delta). \tag{19}$$

Multiplying both sides of (12) on the left by A^3, we get

$$A^4 X - A^3 XB = A^3 C. \tag{20}$$

Summing (17), (18), (19), and (20), and using the following explicit formulas for the characteristic polynomial coefficients from [8]

$$b_{(1)} := B + \hat{\tilde{B}} + \hat{B}^\Delta + \tilde{B}^\Delta \in C\ell_{p,q}^0,$$
$$b_{(2)} := -(B\hat{\tilde{B}} + B\hat{B}^\Delta + B\tilde{B}^\Delta + \hat{\tilde{B}}\hat{B}^\Delta + \hat{\tilde{B}}\tilde{B}^\Delta + (\hat{B}\tilde{B})^\Delta) \in C\ell_{p,q}^0,$$
$$b_{(3)} := B\hat{\tilde{B}}\hat{B}^\Delta + B\hat{\tilde{B}}\tilde{B}^\Delta + B(\hat{B}\tilde{B})^\Delta + \hat{\tilde{B}}(\hat{B}\tilde{B})^\Delta \in C\ell_{p,q}^0,$$
$$b_{(4)} := -\mathrm{Det}(B) = -B\hat{\tilde{B}}(\hat{B}\tilde{B})^\Delta \in C\ell_{p,q}^0,$$

we get

$$(A^4 - A^3(B + \hat{\tilde{B}} + \hat{B}^\Delta + \tilde{B}^\Delta)$$
$$+ A^2(B\hat{\tilde{B}} + B\hat{B}^\Delta + B\tilde{B}^\Delta + \hat{\tilde{B}}\hat{B}^\Delta + \hat{\tilde{B}}\tilde{B}^\Delta + (\hat{B}\tilde{B})^\Delta)$$
$$- A(B\hat{\tilde{B}}\hat{B}^\Delta + B\hat{\tilde{B}}\tilde{B}^\Delta + B(\hat{B}\tilde{B})^\Delta + \hat{\tilde{B}}(\hat{B}\tilde{B})^\Delta) + B\hat{\tilde{B}}(\hat{B}\tilde{B})^\Delta)X$$
$$= A^3 C - A^2 C(\hat{\tilde{B}} + \hat{B}^\Delta + \tilde{B}^\Delta) + AC(\hat{\tilde{B}}\hat{B}^\Delta + \hat{\tilde{B}}\tilde{B}^\Delta + (\hat{B}\tilde{B})^\Delta) - C\hat{\tilde{B}}(\hat{B}\tilde{B})^\Delta.$$

Denoting (15) and (16), and using the formula for the inverse in $\mathcal{Cl}_{p,q}$ with $n = p + q = 4$

$$\text{Adj}(D) = \hat{\tilde{D}}(\hat{D}\tilde{D})^{\triangle}, \qquad \text{Det}(D) = D\hat{\tilde{D}}(\hat{D}\tilde{D})^{\triangle}, \qquad D^{-1} = \frac{\text{Adj}(D)}{\text{Det}(D)},$$

we obtain (14).

Let us formulate the theorem for the case $n = p + q = 5$.

Theorem 2. *Let us consider the Sylvester equation in* $\mathcal{Cl}_{p,q}$, $p + q = 5$,

$$AX - XB = C \tag{21}$$

for the known $A, B, C \in \mathcal{Cl}_{p,q}$ *and the unknown* $X \in \mathcal{Cl}_{p,q}$*. If*

$$Q := D\tilde{D}(\hat{D}\hat{\tilde{D}})^{\triangle}(D\tilde{D}(\hat{D}\hat{\tilde{D}})^{\triangle})^{\triangle} \neq 0, \tag{22}$$

then

$$X = \frac{\tilde{D}(\hat{D}\hat{\tilde{D}})^{\triangle}(D\tilde{D}(\hat{D}\hat{\tilde{D}})^{\triangle})^{\triangle}F}{Q}, \tag{23}$$

where

$$D := A^4 - A^3(B + \tilde{B} + \hat{B}^{\triangle} + \hat{\tilde{B}}^{\triangle}) \tag{24}$$
$$+ A^2(B\tilde{B} + B\hat{B}^{\triangle} + B\hat{\tilde{B}}^{\triangle} + \tilde{B}\hat{B}^{\triangle} + \tilde{B}\hat{\tilde{B}}^{\triangle} + (\hat{B}\hat{\tilde{B}})^{\triangle})$$
$$- A(B\tilde{B}\hat{B}^{\triangle} + B\tilde{B}\hat{\tilde{B}}^{\triangle} + B(\hat{B}\hat{\tilde{B}})^{\triangle} + \tilde{B}(\hat{B}\hat{\tilde{B}})^{\triangle}) + B\tilde{B}(\hat{B}\hat{\tilde{B}})^{\triangle},$$

$$F := A^3C - A^2C(\tilde{B} + \hat{B}^{\triangle} + \hat{\tilde{B}}^{\triangle}) \tag{25}$$
$$+ AC(\tilde{B}\hat{B}^{\triangle} + \tilde{B}\hat{\tilde{B}}^{\triangle} + (\hat{B}\hat{\tilde{B}})^{\triangle}) - C\tilde{B}(\hat{B}\hat{\tilde{B}})^{\triangle}.$$

In the following theorem, we present recursive formulas for the basis-free solution in the case of arbitrary $n = p + q$.

Theorem 3. *Let us consider the Sylvester equation in* $\mathcal{Cl}_{p,q}$, $p + q = n$, $N := 2^{[\frac{n+1}{2}]}$

$$AX - XB = C \tag{26}$$

for the known $A, B, C \in \mathcal{Cl}_{p,q}$ *and the unknown* $X \in \mathcal{Cl}_{p,q}$*. If*

$$Q := d_{(N)} \neq 0, \tag{27}$$

then

$$X = \frac{(D_{(N-1)} - d_{(N-1)})F}{Q}, \tag{28}$$

where

$$D := - \sum_{j=0}^{N} A^{N-j} b_{(j)}, \qquad F := \sum_{j=1}^{N} A^{N-j} C(B_{(j-1)} - b_{(j-1)}), \qquad (29)$$

and the following expressions are defined recursively[2]:

$$b_{(k)} = \frac{N}{k} \langle B_{(k)} \rangle_0, \quad B_{(k+1)} = B(B_{(k)} - b_{(k)}), \quad B_{(1)} = B,$$

$$d_{(k)} = \frac{N}{k} \langle D_{(k)} \rangle_0, \quad D_{(k+1)} = D(D_{(k)} - d_{(k)}), \quad D_{(1)} = D,$$

$$B_{(0)} = D_{(0)} := 0, \qquad b_{(0)} = d_{(0)} := -1, \qquad k = 1, \dots, N.$$

Note that D (29) is the characteristic polynomial of the element B with the substitution of A. The complete proofs of Theorems 2 and 3 are rather cumbersome and will be given in the extended version of this paper. The simplification of the formulas (29) in the case of odd n will be also discussed.

In this paper, we discuss the most important (nondegenerate) case when the element Q (7), (9), (10), (13), (22), (27) is non-zero and the corresponding Sylvester equation (6) has a unique solution X. The degenerate case $Q = 0$ (with zero divisors) can also be studied. An interesting task is to generalize results of this paper to the case of general linear equations in geometric algebras

$$\sum_{j=1}^{k} A_j X B_j = C, \qquad A_j, B_j, C, X \in C\ell_{p,q} \qquad (30)$$

in the case of arbitrary $n = p + q$. The basis-free solution to the equation (30) in the case of quaternions $\mathbb{H} \cong C\ell_{0,2}$ is given in [5].

Acknowledgment. The author is grateful to the three anonymous reviewers for their helpful comments on how to improve the presentation.

This work is supported by the grant of the President of the Russian Federation (project MK-404.2020.1).

References

1. Dargys, A., Acus, A.: A note on solution of $ax + xb = c$ by Clifford algebras. arXiv:1902.09194 (2019)
2. Doran, C., Lasenby, A.: Geometric Algebra for Physicists. Cambridge University Press, Cambridge (2003)
3. Hestenes, D., Sobczyk, G.: Clifford Algebra to Geometric Calculus. Reidel Publishing Company, Dordrecht Holland (1984)
4. Hestenes D.: Space-Time Algebra. Gordon and Breach, New York (1966)

---

[2] Note that using the recursive formulas $B_{(k+1)} = B(B_{(k)} - b_{(k)})$, the expression (29) can be reduced to the form $\sum_{i,j} b_{ij} A^i C B^j$ with some scalars $b_{ij} \in \mathbb{R}$.

5. Shao, C., Li, H., Huang, L.: Basis-free solution to general linear quaternionic equation. Linear Multilinear Algebra **68**(3), 435–457 (2020)
6. Lounesto, P.: Clifford Algebras and Spinors. Cambridge University Press, Cambridge (1997)
7. Shirokov D.: Clifford algebras and their applications to Lie groups and spinors. In: Proceedings of the 19 International Conference on Geometry, Integrability and Quantization, pp. 11–53. Avangard Prima, Sofia (2018). arXiv:1709.06608
8. Shirokov, D.: On determinant, other characteristic polynomial coefficients, and inverses in Clifford algebras of arbitrary dimension. arXiv:2005.04015 (2020)
9. Sylvester, J.: Sur l'equations en matrices $px = xq$. C.R. Acad. Sci. Paris. **99**(2), 67–71, 115–116 (1884)

Hyperwedge

Steven De Keninck[1]([✉]) and Leo Dorst[2]

[1] Matrix Factory b.v.b.a., Bornem, Belgium
steven@enki.ws
[2] Informatics Institute, University of Amsterdam, Amsterdam, The Netherlands

Abstract. The direct construction of geometric elements in an N dimensional geometric algebra by taking the outer product between $N-1$ primitive points is one of the cornerstone tools. It is used to construct a variety of objects, from spheres in CGA [6], up to quadric [2] and even cubic surfaces [9] in much higher dimensional algebras. Initial implementations of the latter however revealed that this is not without numerical issues. Naively taking the outer product between $N - 1$ vectors in these high dimensional algebras is not practically possible within the limits of IEEE 64 bit floating point. In this paper we show how established techniques from linear algebra can be used to solve this problem and compute a fast *hyperwedge*. We demonstrate superior precision and speed, even for low dimensional algebras like 3D CGA.

Keywords: Geometric algebra · Outer product · Wedge product · Linear algebra · Numerical precision

1   Introduction

In recent years, a series of novel geometric algebras [2,9] has enabled the direct manipulation of quadric and cubic surfaces. These high-dimensional algebras (e.g. $\mathbb{R}^{9,6}$) allow easy calculation of intersections of these surfaces, as well as the direct construction of quadric and cubic surfaces by wedging together a given set of primitive points.

Initial implementations in GARAMON [1] and Ganja.js [3] however revealed substantial numerical issues - up to the point where it renders the direct construction of these surfaces impossible when IEEE 64 bit floating point numbers are used. Both the high dimensionality and the presence of high powers in the point parametrisation place a substantial strain on the numerical requirements. Initial attempts to simplify these calculations using GAALOP [8] offered only small improvements.

Without a practical solution for the direct construction, the usefulness of these new algebras is substantially crippled. In this short technical paper we present a remarkably simple solution to this problem using only basic techniques from linear algebra. The resulting method is not only numerically stable, it is also substantially faster and directly applicable to improving both the precision and speed even in lower dimensional algebras like 5-dimensional CGA (the conformal algebra of 3D space).

© Springer Nature Switzerland AG 2020
N. Magnenat-Thalmann et al. (Eds.): CGI 2020, LNCS 12221, pp. 549–554, 2020.
https://doi.org/10.1007/978-3-030-61864-3_47

2   The Outer Product as Matrix Solver

In a previous paper [4] , we demonstrated how a system of n linear equations in n variables can be solved by casting it into an $n + 1$ dimensional algebra (of arbitrary metric), and viewing it as an incidence problem – which is then easily solved using the outer product.

For the specific example of 2 equations in 2D:

$$a_1 x + a_2 y + a_3 = 0$$
$$b_1 x + b_2 y + b_3 = 0, \tag{1}$$

we write the coefficients as vectors in a 3D geometric algebra of arbitrary metric:

$$\mathbf{a} = a_1 \mathbf{e}_1 + a_2 \mathbf{e}_2 + a_3 \mathbf{e}_3$$
$$\mathbf{b} = b_1 \mathbf{e}_1 + b_2 \mathbf{e}_2 + b_3 \mathbf{e}_3, \tag{2}$$

and find the homogeneous solution $\mathbf{s}$ to the original matrix equation using just the outer product, by computing the element:

$$\mathbf{s} = \mathbf{a} \wedge \mathbf{b}, \tag{3}$$

and then extracting the coefficients of the solution vector $(x, y)^\top$ via a homogeneous divide:

$$(x, y) = \left(\frac{\mathbf{s}_{\mathbf{e}_{23}}}{\mathbf{s}_{\mathbf{e}_{12}}}, \frac{\mathbf{s}_{\mathbf{e}_{31}}}{\mathbf{s}_{\mathbf{e}_{12}}} \right) \tag{4}$$

The subscript basis-blades denote metric-independent coordinate extraction. Note that the choice of ordering of basis elements needs some care, since it may introduce extra minus signs (e.g. if we had picked $\mathbf{e}_{13}$ instead of $\mathbf{e}_{31}$, an extra minus sign for the y coefficient would be needed).

The use of a homogeneous 3-dimensional algebra thus explicitly reveals the correspondence between the geometrically motivated outer product and solving linear equations, which in turn is equivalent to solving a 2×2 matrix equation $A\boldsymbol{x} = \boldsymbol{b}$. We generalize this relationship, and then exploit it.

3   The n-blades and n Equations

In n dimensions, the construction is essentially the same as above, when we have n equations. By introducing an extra basis vector $\mathbf{e}_{n+1}$ (and thus extending the space), the n equations

$$\sum_{j=1}^{n} a_{ij} x_j = -a_{i,n+1} \tag{5}$$

can each be expressed in terms of a zero dot product of a vector

$$\mathbf{x} = \sum_{i=1}^{n} x_i \, \mathbf{e}_i + \mathbf{e}_{n+1}, \tag{6}$$

with vectors we will denote as

$$\mathbf{a}_i = \sum_{j=1}^{n} a_{ij} \, \mathbf{e}_j + a_{i,n+1} \, \mathbf{e}_{n+1}, \tag{7}$$

so as:

$$\begin{aligned}
\mathbf{x} \cdot \mathbf{a}_1 &= 0 \\
\mathbf{x} \cdot \mathbf{a}_2 &= 0 \\
&\vdots \\
\mathbf{x} \cdot \mathbf{a}_n &= 0
\end{aligned} \tag{8}$$

If the vectors $\mathbf{a}_i$ are linearly independent, the familiar inner product properties of the outer product can be used to convert this into the equivalent statement:

$$\mathbf{x} \cdot (\mathbf{a}_1 \wedge \mathbf{a}_2 \wedge \cdots \wedge \mathbf{a}_n) = 0. \tag{9}$$

This may be rephrased by duality as:

$$\mathbf{x} \wedge (\mathbf{a}_1 \wedge \mathbf{a}_2 \wedge \cdots \wedge \mathbf{a}_n)^* = \mathbf{x} \wedge \mathbf{A}_n^* = 0, \tag{10}$$

defining the n-blade $\mathbf{A}_n$. This equation shows that the solution $\mathbf{x}$ is proportional to the vector $\mathbf{A}_n^*$.

$$\alpha \mathbf{x} = \mathbf{A}_n^*.$$

One can normalize $\mathbf{x}$ to make the coefficient of $\mathbf{e}_{n+1}$ equal to 1, as desired.

Although this representation method is independent of the actual metric, we find it natural to think of this $n + 1$ dimensional homogeneous embedding as an instance of PGA, the algebra in which vectors represent hyperplanes in n dimensional space [5,7], and where the outer product of n vectors computes the intersection point as an n-blade. But for the present paper, we avoid the complications of a degenerate metric, and consider the $n + 1$ dimensional space as Euclidean.

4   Hyperwedge: The Matrix Solver as Outer Product

We therefore establish that the linear equations and the outer product are closely related. It is exactly this correspondence that we can use for the numerical stable calculation of outer products of n factors in an $n + 1$ dimensional algebra. Now turning things around, we propose to use existing and proven methods from linear algebra (LU, QR, SVD, ...) to perform a fast *hyperwedge* construction of these practically important blades of codimension 1.

Suppose we are in an algebra of dimension N and desire to compute the hyperwedge, i.e. the outer product of $N-1$ vectors in that algebra. Let these vectors be $\mathbf{a}_i$ with $i = 1, N-1$. They have N components. We arbitrarily (or in a numerically informed way, e.g., by pivoting) choose one of the components as the artificial homogeneous dimension; to be specific, let us pick the last dimension N for this role. Then, working towards the mapping on a set of $n = N-1$ equations, $\mathbf{a}_i$ can be split as an $(N-1)$-dimensional part, plus a bit of the dimension chosen as the homogeneous coordinate. With our choice of $\mathbf{e}_N$, we rewrite

$$\mathbf{a}_i = \boldsymbol{a}_i + a_{iN}\,\mathbf{e}_N \tag{11}$$

We now compose a matrix A of which the columns are $\boldsymbol{a}_i$, and a vector $\boldsymbol{b}$ consisting of the values a_{iN} used as coefficients on the basis $\{\mathbf{e}_1, \cdots, \mathbf{e}_{N-1} = \mathbf{e}_N\}$:

$$A = \begin{bmatrix} \boldsymbol{a}_1^\top \\ \boldsymbol{a}_2^\top \\ \vdots \\ \boldsymbol{a}_n^\top \end{bmatrix}, \quad \boldsymbol{b} = \begin{bmatrix} a_{1N} \\ a_{2N} \\ \vdots \\ a_{nN} \end{bmatrix}. \tag{12}$$

Then by the previous section, the matrix equation

$$A\,\boldsymbol{x} = \boldsymbol{b}. \tag{13}$$

yields precisely the system of linear equations associated with the desired hyperwedge

$$\mathbf{A}_{N-1} = \mathbf{a}_1 \wedge \mathbf{a}_2 \wedge \cdots \wedge \mathbf{a}_{N-1}, \tag{14}$$

in the sense that

$$\mathbf{A}_{N-1} = \alpha\,(\boldsymbol{x} + \mathbf{e}_N)^*, \tag{15}$$

where $\boldsymbol{x} = A^{-1}\boldsymbol{b}$ is the solution to the matrix equation. The dualization here is relative to the pseudoscalar of the N-dimensional space. Let us relate that to the pseudoscalar I_n in the n-dimensional space of our equations by $I_N = \mathbf{e}_N\,I_n$.

Unless you are working in a homogeneous representation (where scale factors are of less interest), the constant α should be determined. Since it is the factor of $\mathbf{e}_N$, it must be related to the only purely n-space term on the left hand side. We choose a Euclidean metric for the N-dimensional space (and we can, since the outer product is non-metric anyway) so that $\mathbf{e}_N^2 = 1$. Then computing the only term not involving $\mathbf{e}_N$ we obtain

$$\alpha\,I_n = \alpha\,\mathbf{e}_N^* = \boldsymbol{a}_1 \wedge \cdots \wedge \boldsymbol{a}_n, \tag{16}$$

so we find that $\alpha = (\boldsymbol{a}_1 \wedge \cdots \wedge \boldsymbol{a}_n)I_n^{-1} = \det(A)$. Therefore we obtain as our final hyperwedge:

$$\mathbf{A}_n = \det(A)\left(A^{-1}\boldsymbol{b} + \mathbf{e}_N\right)^*. \tag{17}$$

In a coordinate based representation, the dualization boils down to reading the vector coordinates of the vector on the right from the vector basis, and placing them in the appropriate slots of the dual basis for n-blades. (This employs the linearity of dualization: $(\sum_i x_i \mathbf{e}_i)^* = \sum_i x_i \mathbf{e}_i^*$.)

An implementational note: in (17) we see that the chosen $\mathbf{e}_N$ always ends up with a non-zero coefficient. Since at least one of the vectors must do so (if the resulting hyperwedge is non-zero), this does not lose generality. But it does mean that one could have made an unfortunate choice in picking $\mathbf{e}_N$ as the homogeneous dimension at the start of this procedure, which would have prevented a solution. We currently have no better proposal than: pick another component for the role of $\mathbf{e}_N$ and try again.

5 An Example of the Gain in 3D CGA

In 3D CGA we would represent a sphere through four points as the outer product of the corresponding four conformal points. This clearly geometrical construction permits a good test of speed and accuracy of the hyperwedge computation. Following the method we outlined, the outer product requires inverting a 4×4 matrix, for which we used 'LU with pivoting'. The resulting vector should be immediately interpretable as a weighted dual sphere (or we could undualize the outcome to the 4-blade representing the sphere).

Table 1. Comparison of the numerical precision, for 10,000 trials in 3D CGA.

Method	Average error	Run time
Outer product	0.0000554	42.4 ms
Hyperwedge	0.00000281	19.6 ms

To evaluate the precision, we generate four random points on a random known normalized sphere and reconstruct the sphere using the standard outer product, as well as the hyperwedge. The errors (MSE of the coefficients of the reconstructed sphere relative to the original) after 10,000 runs are shown in Table 1 and clearly demonstrate the numerical superiority of the hyperwedge, even in the low dimensional CGA algebra. The ganja.js implementation used also reveals the hyperwedge to be more than twice as fast.

6 Future Work

This paper demonstrated an advantage of the use of well-honed techniques from numerical linear algebra for the accurate and fast computation of a specific product in geometric algebras. This principle may well generalize to other products and techniques.

The efficacy of this way of thinking for the hyperwedge of $N - 1$ blades in N-dimensional algebras already suggests various extensions to other wedge products. For m-blades in N-dimensional space, with $m < N - 1$, one might connect to fast numerical software that deals properly with null spaces, and use that to generate the correct blades. At least as interesting for practical applications are overdetermined sets of equations: computing an m-blade using $k > m$ vectors. We could then base computation of such a 'pseudowedge' on least squares methods; it will be interesting to study how one would choose the metric aspects of such an optimal non-metric product.

References

1. Breuils, S., Nozick, V., Fuchs, L.: Garamon: a geometric algebra library generator. Adv. Appl. Clifford Algebras **29**(4), 69 (2019). https://doi.org/10.1007/s00006-019-0987-7, http://link.springer.com/10.1007/s00006-019-0987-7
2. Breuils, S., Nozick, V., Sugimoto, A., Hitzer, E.: Quadric conformal geometric algebra of $R_{9,6}$. Adv. Appl. Clifford Algebras **28**(2), 35 (2018). https://doi.org/10.1007/S00006-018-0851-1, http://link.springer.com/10.1007/s00006-018-0851-1
3. De Keninck, S.: ganja.js (2020). https://doi.org/10.5281/ZENODO.3635774, https://github.com/enkimute/ganja.js
4. De Keninck, S., Dorst, L.: Geometric algebra levenberg-marquardt. In: Gavrilova, M., Chang, J., Thalmann, N.M., Hitzer, E., Ishikawa, H. (eds.) Advances in Computer Graphics, vol. 11542, pp. 511–522. Springer, Cham (2019). https://doi.org/10.1007/978-3-030-22514-8_51, http://link.springer.com/10.1007/978-3-030-22514-8_51
5. Dorst, L.: A guided tour to the plane-based geometric algebra PGA (version 1.15) (2020). https://bivector.net/PGA4CS.html
6. Dorst, L., Fontijne, D., Mann, S.: Geometric Algebra for Computer Science: An Object-Oriented Approach to Geometry. Morgan Kaufmann, San Francisco (2009). oCLC: 851078633
7. Gunn, C.G., De Keninck, S.: Geometric algebra and computer graphics. In: ACM SIGGRAPH 2019 Courses on - SIGGRAPH '19, pp. 1–140. ACM Press, Los Angeles (2019). https://doi.org/10.1145/3305366.3328099, http://dl.acm.org/citation.cfm?doid=3305366.3328099
8. Hildenbrand, D., Pitt, J., Koch, A.: Gaalop-high performance parallel computing based on conformal geometric algebra. In: Bayro-Corrochano, E., Scheuermann, G. (eds.) Geometric Algebra Computing, pp. 477–494. Springer, London (2010). https://doi.org/10.1007/978-1-84996-108-0_22, http://link.springer.com/10.1007/978-1-84996-108-0_22
9. Hitzer, E., Hildenbrand, D.: Cubic curves and cubic surfaces from contact points in conformal geometric algebra. In: Gavrilova, M., Chang, J., Thalmann, N.M., Hitzer, E., Ishikawa, H. (eds.) Advances in Computer Graphics, vol. 11542, pp. 535–545. Springer, Cham (2019). https://doi.org/10.1007/978-3-030-22514-8_53, http://link.springer.com/10.1007/978-3-030-22514-8_53

Author Index

Ali, Riaz 405
Ali, Saba Ghazanfar 288
Alves, R. 526

Bai, Wei 206
Bao, Xiyu 132
Barone, Dante A. C. 3
Benamira, Alexis 83
Breuils, Stéphane 492
Brown, Philip N. 513
Bruckner, Stefan 351
Byrtus, Roman 482

Cheiran, Jean F. P. 3
Chen, Guojun 71
Chen, Zhihua 145, 267, 276
Chow, Edward 513

da Silva, Antonio A. S. 3
da Silva, David W. H. A. 513
de Araujo, Carlos Paz 513
De Keninck, Steven 549
De Melo, Gerard 132
de Souza, Gabrielle A. 3
Derevianko, Anna 482
Dong, Wenbo 256
Dong, Yue 71
Dorst, Leo 549

Fanta, Habtamu 169
Fu, Zhibo 96

Gai, Wei 132
Gao, Yan 313
Grafton, Alex 421
Guo, Yuke 206

Hadfield, Hugo 447, 459
Haldorsen, Ingfrid S. 351
He, Hao 157
Hildenbrand, D. 526
Hou, Shengjing 157
Hrdina, J. 526

Izdebski, Łukasz 382

Kamarianakis, Manos 434
Kim, Jinman 24, 374, 405
Kopiecki, Ryszard 382
Kosinka, Jiří 326
Kraft, Valentin 107

Lasenby, Joan 421, 447, 459
Lavor, C. 526
Li, Aimin 182
Li, Dongshuang 501
Li, Guiqing 245, 256
Li, Jiefeng 157
Li, Peixin 206
Li, Pin 16, 24, 364, 374
Li, Ping 145, 267, 276, 405
Li, Rui 59
Li, Sheng 132
Li, Zhen 96, 288
Lin, Feng 394
Lin, Lin 157
Lin, Weiyue 157
Link, Florian 107
Liu, Enjie 411
Liu, Jigang 394
Liu, Juan 132
Liu, Meng 206
Liu, Shiguang 233, 301
Liu, Xiaoli 276
Liu, Yunna 267
Lu, Ping 16, 24, 288, 364
Luo, Guoliang 245
Luo, Jie 256
Luo, Wen 501
Luo, Yalan 157
Lv, Jianming 245

Ma, Gengyu 206
Ma, Lizhuang 169
Ma, Yifan 220
Maciel, Anderson 3
Mao, Aihua 256

Mao, Lijuan   16, 24, 96, 288, 364, 374
Mao, Tiezeng   256
Meng, Xiangxu   132
Mörth, Eric   351
Mukai, Tomohiko   46

Narita, Fumiya   46
Nedel, Luciana   119
Nedel, Luciana P.   3
Nozick, Vincent   492

Pang, Yewen   182
Papagiannakis, George   434
Pattanaik, Sumanta   83
Pei, Yuru   206

Qi, Meng   132
Qian, Kun   245
Qin, Xueying   193
Qiu, Guhao   145
Qiu, Jingjun   313

Sawicki, Dariusz   382
Schenk, Andrea   107
Schramm, Rodrigo   119
Schumann, Christian   107
Seah, Hock-Soon   394
Shao, Zhiwen   169
She, Yingying   157
Shen, Meisheng   313
Sheng, Bin   16, 24, 96, 145, 267, 288, 364,
    374, 405
Sheng, Bing   276
Sheng, Yun   59, 220
Shi, Jian   71
Shi, Xiayan   59
Shi, Yuliang   132
Shibayama, Wataru   33
Shirakawa, Shinichi   33
Shirokov, Dmitry   541
Smit, Noeska N.   351
Song, Hange   301
Song, Shuangbing   193
Steinmetz, C.   526
Sugimoto, Akihiro   492

Talle, Job   326
Tichý, Radek   472
Torres, Laura A.   3
Tu, Changhe   193

Valer, Rafael   119
Vašík, Petr   482

Wang, Jianwen   182
Wang, Jihong   405
Wang, Pengsheng   374
Wang, Ran   96
Wang, Sheng   288
Wang, Yan-Chao   394
Wang, Yun   501
Wei, Hui   411
Wei, Lai   447
Wu, Enhua   71
Wu, Wenhai   206

Xavier, Marcelo A.   513
Xian, Chuhua   245
Xing, Huan   132
Xu, Siqi   233
Xue, Guangtao   267, 374

Yan, Zhengjun   501
Yang, Chenglei   132
Yang, Po   96, 288
Yu, Hongqing   411
Yu, Zhaoyuan   501
Yuan, Hua   220
Yuan, Linwang   501

Zha, Hongbin   206
Zhang, Bob   71
Zhang, Fan   132
Zhang, Han   96, 145, 267, 405
Zhang, Jianzhao   71
Zhang, Wei   364
Zhao, Youbing   411
Zhong, Fan   193
Zhong, Yicheng   206
Zhu, Fang   16, 24, 364

Printed in the United States
By Bookmasters